THE **ESSENTIAL HISTORY** OF
ASTON VILLA

FOREWORD BY DENNIS MORTIMER

ADAM WARD AND **JEREMY GRIFFIN**

First published in 2002
by Headline Book Publishing
for WHSmith, Greenbridge Road, Swindon SN3 3LD

10 9 8 7 6 5 4 3 2 1

ISBN 0 7553 1140 X

Design by designsection, Frome, Somerset

The authors would like to thank Tony Matthews for providing the statistics and the memorabilia used throughout the book.

The authors found the following publications extremely useful during their research:

Aston Villa, Peter Morris, William Heinemann Ltd, 1962
The Aston Villa Story, Ian Johnson, Arthur Baker, 1981
Docherty, Brian Clarke, Kingswood Press, 1991
Football with a Smile, Joe Mercer – The Authorised Biography, Gary James, ACL and Polar Publishing, 1993
The Great Years of Aston Villa, David Goodyear, David Goodyear, 1982
Hamlyn Illustrated History of Aston Villa, Graham McColl, Hamlyn, 1998
Ron Saunders' Aston Villa Scrapbook, Ron Saunders, Souvenir Press Ltd, 1981
Triumphs of the Football Field, narrated by Archie Hunter, the Famous Villa Captain, first published by the *Birmingham Weekly Mercury* [1890], re-published by Sports Projects Ltd, 1997
The Villans – Day-to-Day Life at Villa Park, Graham Betts, Mainstream Publishing, 1998
The Birmingham Daily Gazette, *The Birmingham Daily Mail*, *The Birmingham Daily Post*, *The Birmingham Pictorial & Dart*, *The Birmingham Mail*, *The Birmingham Post*, *The Grasshopper*, *The Owl*, *The Sports Argus*

Printed and bound in Great Britain by Clays Ltd, St Ives PLC, Bungay, Suffolk

HEADLINE BOOK PUBLISHING
A division of Hodder Headline
338 Euston Road
London NW1 3BH

www.headline.co.uk
www.hodderheadline.com

Contents

Foreword
by Dennis Mortimer

When the local press announced my arrival at Aston Villa on Boxing Day 1975 as a 'present to the fans', little did we know that this would mark the beginning of a seven-year journey that would culminate in winning the European Cup. Ron Saunders' astute management laid the foundations for the first great Villa team I was a member of. That team included players of the calibre of Andy Gray, Brian Little, John Gidman, Chris Nichol and a young Gordon Cowans. We played exciting, enterprising football, but had little silverware to show for it. Winning the League Cup that season should have provided the momentum for further success, but injuries and the need to sell key players upset Ron's plans.

Dennis Mortimer, Aston Villa captain during their 1982 European Cup win.

The following season, the arrival of Allan Evans, Kenny Swain, Des Bremner and Ken McNaught brought much needed defensive stability to the team, and the young talents of Gary Williams, Colin Gibson and Gary Shaw gave it longevity. However, it was the signing of Peter Withe that brought the Villa attack the cutting edge necessary to guarantee success. And sure enough, that season saw the League Championship come to Villa Park for the first time in 70 years and with it an opportunity to emulate the achievements of Manchester United, Liverpool and Nottingham Forest. Even the sudden departure of Ron Saunders midway through our European Cup campaign did not serve to disrupt the momentum the team had attained. The appointment of Tony Barton merely galvanized the players and ensured the continuity necessary to succeed. On 26 May 1982 a goal by Peter Withe in a close, tense match against Bayern Munich enabled Villa and their loyal fans to reach the pinnacle of the club's achievements.

It was a privilege to have played a part in that achievement. Like many ex-Villa players and fans my one regret is that winning the European Cup did not serve as a springboard for further success. However, after the low of relegation in 1986-87, the club has maintained its First and now Premier Division status and therefore the potential for future success remains with Villa's patient yet expectant fan base.

Dennis Mortimer

Chapter One: 1874-87
Humble Beginnings to Cup Winners

In 1874 there was no Football League, no Wembley Stadium and no such thing as professional football. Names like Manchester United and Chelsea would remain unspoken for another quarter of a century and the rules of the game had only recently been changed to ban carrying the ball and hacking. Away from football, William Gladstone was prime minister and income tax was set at 2d in the pound, while the controversy over Charles Darwin's book *The Origin of Species* still raged. Against such a backdrop of Victorian values and sporting change, Aston Villa Football Club was born.

Football may have been in its infancy, but the game's leading figures were already engaged in stormy debates about rules and competitions. The issue of professionalism would soon divide the game still further, leaving the 'gentlemen players' of the South somewhat isolated. But, in 1874, such concerns were of little consequence to Aston Villa's members who, initially at least, were only concerned with finding a sporting pursuit to occupy themselves during the long months of the cricket close season.

Aston Villa FC had been formed by members of the Villa Cross Wesleyan Chapel who, according to legend, gathered beneath a flickering street light to discuss the possibility of playing football after witnessing an impromptu game on a meadow off Heathfield Road. The erstwhile cricketers can have had no inkling of where their innocent desire for an energetic winter pursuit would lead. Thirteen years on, their fledgling club had won English football's premier trophy, the FA Cup, and had provided the motivating force behind the development of the Football League. However, Aston Villa's meteoric rise did not end there, and by the close of the 19th century the club had become the pre-eminent force in English football, winning trophy after trophy and shifting football's balance of power from the Northwest to the Midlands.

The Wrong-Shaped Ball

Back in 1874, the newly formed Aston Villa had few thoughts of glory and were desperate for a game of any kind, never mind a cup final. W.H. Price, the club's newly appointed captain, found it extremely difficult to find opponents for his team, since football was not yet a popular sport in the Birmingham area. There were some established clubs, most notably

Calthorpe FC, on the other side of the city, and Wednesbury Old Athletic, but Villa were not yet ready to take on such experienced opponents.

Aston Villa's debut, in fact, came against a rugby club. Aston Brook St Mary's provided the opposition for the match in March 1874. The first half of the game was played under rugby rules with the second played under the Association code. Thirty players were used during the match and, of course, two balls. Villa managed to keep the game scoreless until half-time and using a radical 3-4-7 formation, they won the game 1-0 with a goal from Jack Hughes. It proved to be Villa's only fixture of their debut season.

Throughout the club's formative years, Aston Villa, like most successful football teams, enjoyed its fair share of good fortune, as borne out by two events that took place in 1876. First, and most significantly, the club secured the services of George Ramsay, a footballer of rare talent and ambition, and then, shortly afterwards, with Ramsay himself playing a key role, the club established its first proper home at Perry Barr.

Ramsay's role in the Villa story is pivotal, but the Scotsman, who had already played first-class football north of the border, only joined the club by chance. He had come to Birmingham for work as a 21-year-old and stumbled across a Villa practice session while out walking in Aston Park. The skills of the Villa men were, to say the least, rudimentary and Ramsay later described their approach to the game as 'a dash at the man and a big kick at the ball'. However, the Scot had clearly seen some potential because he joined in the game and after bewitching his new acquaintances with a display of mesmerizing dribbling and control, the like of which they had never seen before, he was persuaded to join the club.

Ramsay immediately took charge of training his new team-mates and brought about a sharp improvement in their performances. Inevitably, word of the talented Scot got around, and Ramsay soon received invitations to join several more established clubs. He refused and remained a Villa man for 59 years, during which time he captained the club to their first trophy (the Birmingham Senior Cup in 1880), was club secretary and a vice-president until his death in October 1935. As Archie Hunter later observed: 'Mr Hunter was practically the founder of the Aston Villa Football Club.'

Ramsay is also credited with securing the lease on Perry Barr in 1876. Aston Villa had until then been somewhat nomadic, often playing their home games on the Aston Lower Grounds, which would later become the site of the present Villa Park but was then a Victorian leisure park. Ramsay was acutely aware of the need for the club to establish a headquarters and Perry Barr was taken on a three-year lease at a rent of £7 10s for the first year, rising to £15 and then £20 in the following years. The most significant factor in the lease, however, was not the price but the fact that it made no restriction on Villa charging spectators for admission. By contrast, Calthorpe, who were one of Birmingham's leading clubs in the Victorian era, floundered after an ill-advised move to a rented private ground owned by Lord Calthorpe where they were not allowed to charge gate money.

Archie Hunter Joins the Perry Barr Pets

Calthorpe's plight was not helped when the club failed to secure the services of a promising young Scotsman called Archie Hunter. The 19-year-old Scot had planned to join the Calthorpe club after moving down from Ayr, but when he could not find the club's ground he joined Aston Villa on the recommendation of a work-mate. Hunter would go on to become Aston Villa's captain and Birmingham's first great player. However, in 1878, he and fellow Scots, Ramsay and John Lindsay, were providing the driving force behind a new tactical approach to the game that saw Villa adopt the passing game popular in Scotland as opposed to the dribbling game that was common south of the border.

By the late 1870s, Villa were becoming a dominant local side. Hunter would recall a particularly one-sided game against Small Heath that ended in a 22-0 victory and which saw a joker from the crowd bring out a chair for the underworked Villa keeper, Copley, to sit upon: '… he had nothing at all to do and was getting tired of standing and never having a chance of a kick,' remarked Hunter.

Aston Villa's growing status and confidence was reflected in their decision to enter the FA Cup for the first time in the 1879-80 season. It was a bold move for a club that was barely five years old, but Villa made it past Wolverhampton side Stafford Road Railway Works after a replay at Perry Barr, and then drew Oxford University in the second round. However, for some inexplicable reason, the club withdrew from the competition and handed the students a bye to the third round. It was a disappointing end to a promising campaign, but Villa's time would come soon enough.

Despite Aston Villa's rapid progress, football was not yet capturing the interest of the Birmingham media. To illustrate this point, Villa's victory over Nottingham Forest in the Birmingham Challenge Cup received no more coverage in the *Birmingham Daily Post* than a lecture on the history and literature of chess which had been delivered to the Birmingham Chess Club three days later. Villa were, however, developing an impressive following for their games at Perry Barr, and another clash with Forest in 1880, this time in the FA Cup, attracted a crowd of 4,000.

The move to Perry Barr was an immediate success, although the ground itself left much to be desired. 'Perry Barr ... was covered pretty thickly with trees and the players had to run "round about and in and out" of them, in order to get at the ball,' explained Archie Hunter. 'It was very amusing, but it didn't always conduce to scientific play. When we first played there, there were two trees on each side of the ground which served as goalposts and there were trees on the touchline.'

Both sets of players changed in a blacksmith's shed opposite the ground and a horse and van was moved in on match days to offer half-time refreshment to spectators. Villa were by now wearing 'cardinal red and blue striped shirts' and had been nicknamed 'The Perry Barr Pets'. The first game at Perry Barr, which was against Wednesbury Town, had brought in gate receipts of 5s 3d, but by the end of the decade the club's support had grown significantly and,

50 Greatest Players

GEORGE RAMSAY   Forward

Born: Glasgow, 1 March 1855

Joined Aston Villa: 1876   **From:** unknown

Left Aston Villa: 1882 (retired)

George Ramsay is a central figure in the Villa story. The Scotsman was a man whose ambition was matched only by his resourcefulness, and it was his foresight that inspired Villa's rapid progress in the early days of the 1870s and 1880s. Ramsay was behind the move to Perry Barr, he was the man who improved the club's playing staff and his progressive tactics were the key to a host of famous victories. However, it should not be forgotten that Ramsay was also a gifted footballer in his own right. He had played first-class football in Scotland as a young man and when he stumbled across an early Aston Villa practice game in 1876, he bewitched his future team-mates with a display that, according to Archie Hunter, left them amazed. According to sources, 'When all was over they surrounded the player who had footed the ball and asked him a hundred questions.' The most important question asked was, 'Will you join us?' The answer was affirmative. It was a decision for which Aston Villa Football Club would be eternally grateful.

with receipts occasionally rising to as much as £10, the club had sufficient money to finance clearing the trees from around the ground.

Villa were pulling up trees in every sense, and, according to Hunter, by the early 1880s the Perry Barr outfit 'was beginning to more than maintain its own as a first-class club'. The 1880-81 season saw them win 21 of their 25 games and lift the Staffordshire Cup into the bargain. However, it was the club's FA Cup progress that hinted most strongly at the illustrious path that lay ahead for Aston Villa FC. In both 1883 and 1884 the club reached the quarter-finals of the competition.

The Long Arm of Harry Cursham

In 1883, Villa took on Notts County in a match that did much to raise the club's profile. The Midlanders took 8,000 fans to Nottingham to take on County, but the match ended in controversial defeat for the visitors and pandemonium on the terraces, with several temporary stands broken down and mayhem on the pitch. With the score at 4-3 to the home side, Villa claimed to have forced the ball over the line, only to see it punched clear. The visitors protested that the intervening hand did not belong to the Notts keeper but to the long arm of Harry Cursham. Villa appealed to the FA and went to London, taking with them the accounts of 'independent witnesses' who claimed to have seen Cursham's intervention. The authorities were unimpressed and the result stood.

A year later, Villa again made it to the last eight of the FA Cup, but this time their defeat was more emphatic than controversial. Scottish side Queen's Park proved Villa's nemesis, crushing the Midlanders 6-1 in Glasgow. However, defeat to the Scots was no disgrace since Queen's Park were among Britain's leading clubs at the time. Nicknamed the Spiders, they had won the Scottish Cup seven times and had also reached the final of the FA Cup. The Spiders were regular entrants in the FA Cup at the time – though they would boycott the competition soon after when professionalism began to creep into the English game – and Villa learned much from playing against such accomplished opponents. Most notably, George Ramsay attempted to adapt his team's defensive strategy by copying Queen's Park's system, built around two full backs rather than one. After some initial teething troubles, the system began to pay dividends.

At the start of the following season, 1884-85, Queen's Park travelled to Perry Barr for a friendly match. The game was a great occasion, as reflected in the recollections of Archie Hunter: 'Queen's Park were always favourites with the Birmingham public and as they bowled along in their brake to the field they were cordially cheered ... no sooner had we begun to take up our positions [for the match] than pigeons could be seen flying from all parts bearing away the news that the battle had begun.'

The match turned out to be far more competitive than the previous season's FA Cup encounter, and when Villa bundled the ball over the line for a 2-1 victory with a late goal, it was the cue for hearty celebrations. 'At night people went about singing a ballad, with a refrain, "The Villa have licked Queen's Park,"' said Hunter, 'and I was followed home by a multitude roaring as if I had won the Battle of Waterloo.'

Villa were by now the dominant force in Birmingham football, so it was a huge disappointment to the club that their 1884-85 FA Cup campaign floundered unexpectedly at West Bromwich Albion's Four Acres ground in the third round. Villa had underestimated their opponents, fielding a weakened team, and had paid the price. Fortunately, it was a defeat that Villa would avenge when the two teams met next in the competition.

Villa Target Cup Glory

With the Football League not yet formed and local cup competitions offering no great glory, the FA Cup had become Aston Villa's number one priority. Club secretary Mr Samuel Richardson noted in his annual report of 1884 that: 'Though your committee have again to record defeat in the competition for the National Trophy, they can point you to this season's victories over some of the most renowned teams in the kingdom, notably: Blackburn Rovers (English Cup holders, 1884), Blackburn Olympic (English Cup holders, 1883), Notts County, Oxford University, Dumbarton, Edinburgh University, Darwen &c. and further would remind you that on only two occasions, when opposed by the Queen's Park, has Aston Villa been beaten while playing the full strength of the FA Cup team.'

Aston Villa's progress had also been noted by England's international selection committee, and, in 1883, Arthur Brown and Howard Vaughton became the club's first senior internationals, winning their caps against Scotland. Both players would also play their part in Villa's glorious FA Cup run of 1887.

More than 130 teams entered the FA Cup in 1886-87 and, with no league programme to consider and no effective system of seeding, teams began playing cup-ties in the autumn. Several leading Scottish sides were among the entrants, but it was the English trio of Preston North End and the previous season's finalists, Blackburn Rovers and West Bromwich Albion, who were the favourites to lift the cup at The Oval in Queen Victoria's Jubilee year.

Villa for their part made light work of their opening-round ties, waltzing past Wednesbury Old Athletic 13-0, before disposing of Derby Midland 6-1. With their forward line bolstered by the arrival of moustachioed winger Dennis Hodgetts from St George's FC, and their defensive system based around reliable full backs Frank Coulton and Joey Simmonds, Villa were in confident mood when they took on Wolves in the third round. However, there would be no breezing past their Midland rivals and it took four matches and seven-and-a-half hours of football before the tie reached a decisive conclusion.

The first match was played at Perry Barr on 11 December and ended in a 2-2 draw after a fierce struggle that had seen Villa have two goals disallowed and their unfancied opponents belie their underdog status. After several postponements a replay was eventually played out on a frozen pitch at Wolves' Dudley Road ground on 15 January. In preparation for the match, hundreds of tons of snow were cleared from the pitch and ashes were spread all over the playing surface. However, a layer of ice remained and both teams protested about the conditions. The match went ahead nevertheless and ended in a 1-1 draw, but the FA failed to recognize the result and ordered a re-match at Dudley Road. Somewhat predictably, this match ended in a draw as well, albeit a more entertaining encounter in which the teams shared six goals.

On 29 January, some seven weeks after the original tie, Wolves and Villa returned to Perry Barr to conclude their epic encounter. A crowd of 12,000 – then a record for a Villa home match – packed into the ground, while others found vantage points on top of nearby trees and buildings. Archie Hunter recalled that: 'Vehicles of all kinds from the coach of the local MP ... to the humble one-horse shay, surrounded the meadow; and all round the ropes the surging multitude stood, swaying backwards and forwards in their intense anxiety to obtain a glimpse of the play.' An early goal from Dawson settled the nerves of the watching Villa fans, before Hunter himself struck to put the tie beyond the Wanderers.

A bye and a comfortable 5-0 victory against modest opponents Horncastle took Villa into the quarter-finals of the FA Cup, but they were still not yet among the competition's fancied teams – West Bromwich Albion and Preston North End continued to enjoy the status of favourites. However, Hunter confessed that he had a 'lurking suspicion that we might well do the trick ourselves', although he added, 'but that might have been vanity'. Vanity or not, Villa's impressive work ethic and inventive attacking play made for a formidable combination.

Darwen, a team who had themselves already played in two FA Cup semi-finals, put up stern resistance in the quarter-finals. Villa began the game well enough, and at half-time held a seemingly unassailable 3-0 lead. However, Darwen scored twice after the interval to leave the Midlanders clinging gratefully to the slenderest of winning margins at the final whistle. According to legend, Villa's poor second-half performance was down to the fact that they were plied with alcohol at half-time after the president of the Moseley Football Club filled his team's newly won Rugby Cup with champagne and offered it to the visiting team.

Having reached the semi-final of the English Cup for the first time, Hunter and co now faced Scottish opponents, in the formidable shape of Glasgow Rangers. Villa's task was made all the more difficult by the fact that Rangers had drafted in players from all the leading Scottish teams, including both Hibernian and Queen's Park, for the tie at Crewe's Nantwich Road ground. To reach the final, Villa would have to overcome a team comprised entirely of Scottish internationals.

Fortunately for the Midlanders, the most talented Scotsman on the Nantwich pitch that day was in Villa's colours, and despite the efforts of Rangers' team of assembled talents, it was the uncapped Archie Hunter who played the decisive role in a match played out before a crowd of 10,000. The Villa forward struck once in each half, either side of an Albert Brown goal, to earn a 3-1 victory and a place in the final. It was later suggested that Rangers' somewhat sluggish display owed something to over-indulgence after former team-mate Hugh McIntyre took his erstwhile comrades out for a hearty meal prior to the game. Rangers' excuses were of little interest to Villa, who would now take on West Bromwich Albion in the final at The Oval. The Throstles had overcome favourites Preston in the other semi-final to set up a mouth-watering Midlands derby.

West Midlands Derby at The Oval

Villa had scored 32 goals in six ties en route to the final and had conceded just four. However, they remained slight underdogs against an Albion team that had been FA Cup runners-up the previous season. Villa prepared for the final with a stay at Holt Fleet near Droitwich where it was reported that they 'engaged a field to practice in, and have indulged in salt baths'. But while the players were quietly going about their preparations in the countryside, back in Birmingham anticipation was growing for The Oval showdown between the two great West Midlands rivals. The Great Western Railway put on special excursions to the capital and many thousands of fans from both clubs took advantage of this initiative.

Both teams were at full strength for the final, which was played in bright sunshine on 2 April. However, with the wind at their backs and on a muddy pitch that prevented Villa from employing their trademark passing game, Albion controlled play throughout the first half. The score remained 0-0 at half-time, but Villa were greatly indebted to the efforts of their keeper, Jimmy Warner, who had produced several important saves and had shown commendable stoicism in resisting the Albion players as they attempted to barge him across the line with the ball in his hands.

With the wind and the slope of the pitch now in their favour, Villa produced an improved display in the second half and, after several near misses, soon took the lead. Right winger Rich Davis broke forward down his flank and crossed towards Dennis Hodgetts, who sidefooted the ball past the static figure of Albion keeper Bob Roberts. Roberts, believing that Hodgetts was in an offside position, made no attempt to make a save, and he immediately protested to referee Major Marindin. However, the official was unmoved and the goal stood. Albion were distraught, and their misery was complete when Archie Hunter stabbed the ball over the line to make it 2-0 in the last minute. The cheers of the Villa fans in the crowd were still audible when Major Marindin blew his whistle for full-time.

'As soon as the whistle blew I was surrounded by the enthusiastic crowd and, for a few minutes, I thought I should be torn to pieces,' remembered Archie Hunter. 'They nearly wrung my hand off and those who could not get near enough put all the heart they could into shouting "Bravo, Archie" and "Well done, Villa".'

News of Aston Villa's FA Cup final triumph was greeted with no less gusto back in Birmingham, where shops had been posting regular updates from the game based on telegrams sent from The Oval. Once the final score was known, the crowds took to the streets before moving on to New Street station to welcome their returning heroes home at around 3am on the Sunday morning.

The *Birmingham Daily Post* commented that after their FA Cup final performance, Villa could 'hold against all comers their proud title of champion team of the United Kingdom'. By contrast, the Lancashire-published newspaper *The Football Field*, still smarting from Preston's semi-final defeat against West Bromwich Albion in Nottingham, commented that: 'For a match of this kind, the play, on the whole, was very disappointing, and we feel sure that, but for the unlucky disaster at Nottingham, the North End would simply have romped in.'

Great Matches

FA CUP FINAL   The Oval, 2 April 1887

Aston Villa 2   **West Bromwich Albion 0**   Attendance: 15,334

Hodgetts
Hunter

Aston Villa's victory over West Bromwich Albion in the 1887 FA Cup final may not have been a great match in terms of the entertainment sampled by the 15,000 fans at The Oval, but its significance to the future of Aston Villa Football Club was nonetheless immense. Success in English football's premier competition automatically promoted Villa to the ranks of the game's elite, and with football on the brink of great change, their success could not have been better timed.

Soon after the final, Villa director William McGregor provided the driving force behind the formation of the new Football League. Victory at The Oval meant that he now spoke for the 'English champions' who would, of course, be ensured membership of the new league.

Back in April 1887, however, the players and supporters of Aston Villa cared little for talk of new competitions and league structures. Villa had reached the FA Cup final for the first time in their 13-year history and the match against local rivals West Bromwich Albion captured the imagination of the West Midlands public.

The Throstles from West Brom were favourites to lift the cup, having reached the final the previous year, but Villa started the game strongly and, despite playing into the wind and against the slope in the first half, the game remained scoreless at the interval. The cup was there for Villa to win and the Birmingham side did not disappoint their travelling fans. Winger Dennis Hodgetts opened the scoring, stealing in to slot the ball home while Roberts in the Albion goal appealed for offside. Archie Hunter added the *coup de grâce* in the dying minutes of the game with a typically predatory finish to make the final score 2-0 and ensure the Throstles wouldn't be singing this year.

The victorious Aston Villa team from the 1887 FA Cup final against West Brom. Front row (l to r): Brown, Yates; second row (l to r): Simmonds, Archie Hunter, Vaughton, Hodgetts; third row (l to r, in kit): Burton, Davis, Warner, Dawson, Coulton.

'The victory of the Villa was very popular,' declared the *Football Field*'s correspondent. 'They fully deserved to win, and the Albion have no grounds for endeavouring to explain away their defeat.'

Aston Villa: Warner, Coulton, Simmonds, Yates, Dawson, Burton, Davis, Brown, Hunter, Vaughton, Hodgetts.

West Bromwich Albion: Roberts, H. Green, Aldridge, Horton, Perry, Timmins, Woodhall, T. Green, Bayliss, Paddock, Pearson.

Referee: Major Marindin.

50 Greatest Players

ARCHIE HUNTER   Forward

Born: Joppa, Ayr, 23 September 1859

Joined Aston Villa: 1878   **From:** Ayr Thistle

Appearances: 73   **Goals:** 42

Left Aston Villa: 1890 (retired)

Archie Hunter was a Victorian sporting celebrity. He was Aston Villa's first truly great footballer and was the idol of the Perry Barr supporters for more than a decade. Archie was a forward who played the game with a rare blend of power and skill, and his strength was a particularly useful quality at a time when barging and kicking were often considered legitimate defensive tactics. Like George Ramsay, his fellow Scot, Archie's Villa career began by chance, but soon blossomed into a lifelong association. He had previously played with Third Lanark and Ayr Thistle north of the border, but it was as a Villa man that he enjoyed his greatest moment when he captained the club to victory in its first FA Cup final appearance in 1887. His popularity transcended club loyalties and his dashing style and deep-seated sense of sportsmanship made him a favourite with all fair-minded football fans. However, on 4 January 1890, his career came to a tragic and premature end when he suffered a suspected stroke during a game against Everton at Anfield. Although he made a partial recovery, he died four years later at the age of just 35 in a room in the Royal Exchange Hotel at Six Ways, Aston.

Soon enough both Preston North End and Aston Villa would have the chance to test their credentials against one another in a new competition, but, for the time being, the North Enders would have to wait their turn as Villa revelled in the glory of their first major trophy. Fourteen years after the club's formation, Aston Villa FC had established itself as a major force in English football.

Chapter Two: 1887-1900
Villa Reign Supreme

English football was on the verge of sporting revolution in 1887. A growing tide of professionalism was sweeping the game, bringing with it an almost intolerable financial burden on the many clubs who were left struggling to meet increased wage bills with only a limited and unpredictable income from friendlies and FA Cup ties. Change was clearly needed and most clubs favoured the establishment of a regular programme of competitive fixtures. However, chairman and administrators, initially at least, struggled to reach agreement on how best to proceed.

Set against such a climate of change, Aston Villa's FA Cup triumph over West Bromwich Albion at The Oval could not have been better timed. As champions of England, the Villa had now ensured their membership in the country's footballing elite and, as such, they were sure to be among the leading players in any new competition.

For the 1887-88 season, however, the FA Cup remained England's premier trophy and as holders, Villa were now the team to beat. With a ruthless efficiency, the Midlanders lived up to their exalted status, scoring 17 goals without reply to dispose of Oldbury Town, Small Heath and Shankhouse en route to the competition's fifth round. After three away ties Villa were finally drawn at home, but their opponents would be the mighty Preston North End. It was the match that all neutrals wanted to see. The FA Cup holders against the ruthlessly ambitious Lancashire men who had blazed the trail of professionalism by luring many of Scotland's best players south of the border. North End were a team with a big reputation, but they had not yet won the FA Cup, and they were desperate to put the record straight.

Soldiers Restore Order at Perry Barr

English football's summit meeting of 1887-88 captured the imagination of the supporters, and 27,000 turned up at Perry Barr, despite the competing attraction of Buffalo Bill's travelling rodeo show at the Aston Lower Grounds on the same day. By midday the roads around Perry Barr were swamped with fans and as the kickoff at 2.15pm approached, it became apparent that the 50 policemen on duty would be wholly insufficient to control the record crowd. Many spectators were unable to see the pitch and as the inevitable jostling got more forceful, the crowd encroached onto the playing area. The kickoff was delayed as the police attempted to get the fans back over the touchline. The game eventually got under way, but order had only been restored temporarily. Twice the crowd broke onto the pitch and eventually mounted police were called for to help clear the playing area. However, the rescue party was made up not only of mounted police but also of Hussars from the nearby Great Brook Street Barracks.

An uneasy peace was eventually restored, but the chaos had taken its toll on the Perry Barr pitch, which had been trampled into a quagmire by the combined efforts of the supporters, the police and the army. With chaotic scenes all around them, the Preston and Villa captains agreed halfway through the match that the game would be played as a friendly and would not be considered a cup-tie. Preston went on to win 3-1, but the Villa players had clearly been subdued throughout the remainder of the game. Archie Hunter recalled: 'It was a welcome relief to us all when the whistle sounded, for the crowd had again grown unruly and the mounted police arrived too late to be of any use.'

However, much to Villa's consternation, when the referee's report arrived at the FA's headquarters the following week, it became clear that Preston were claiming victory in a cup-tie and not a friendly. Villa appealed and it was put to the vote whether the game should be replayed. The FA's committee was divided equally and the casting vote was left to the president, Major Marindin, who declared that Preston should be awarded the game because Villa had failed in their duty to control the crowd. The club countered that it was the police who were culpable, having underestimated the manpower required to control a record crowd at Perry Barr, but their protestations fell on deaf ears. Villa were out of the FA Cup.

McGregor Inspires Birth of Football League

Preston would go on to meet West Bromwich Albion in the final, where a 2-1 victory for the Throstles kept the trophy in the West Midlands for another year. Events at The Oval, however, would soon seem insignificant when set against the historic meeting that took place at a London hotel on the eve of the Cup final. With the need for regular, competitive football growing ever more urgent, directors of Aston Villa, Blackburn Rovers, Bolton Wanderers, Preston North End and West Bromwich Albion met in Anderton's Hotel to discuss the possibility of establishing a league competition. The man behind this meeting was none other than Villa's own William McGregor. The Scot, having grown tired of the lack of progress being made

Aston Villa director, William McGregor (back row, far left), pictured here with an England XI, was the driving force behind the creation of the Football League.

on this key issue, had written to his counterparts at other leading clubs on 2 March requesting a meeting.

McGregor was concerned by falling attendances, which he believed had been caused in part by confusion over the dates and times of matches. Cup-ties were often hastily rearranged, while friendlies were frequently cancelled with little notice.

The meeting at Anderton's Hotel resulted in an agreement on both the name – the Football League – and structure of the new competition. At a second meeting, which was held in Manchester because no London team had expressed an interest in joining the new league, the 12 founder members of the Football League were chosen. Aston Villa, who through McGregor's efforts had been the architects of the new competition, were, of course, among the 12.

League Debut at Wolves

On 8 September 1888 Aston Villa made their Football League debut before 3,000 fans at Wolverhampton Wanderers' Dudley Road ground. The match ended in a 1-1 draw with inside forward Tom Green scoring the goal that earned the Villans a point. A week later, Perry Barr played host to its first league fixture, with Stoke the visitors for a match played out before a crowd of 4,000. Villa's league campaign quickly gathered momentum, and after a run of five victories in the next seven games, including a 9-1 triumph over Notts County, the Midlanders sat second in the table just three points behind their next opponents, Preston North End. The top two met at Deepdale on 10 November and the Villans played with great spirit to recover from the setback of conceding a goal after just two minutes. With the final whistle approaching, Green struck another important goal after good work from Archie Goodall. It proved to be the only point collected by any away team at Deepdale all season, while Green's goal was one of only 15 conceded by the North Enders during the inaugural Football League campaign.

The impressive performance at Deepdale, however, was followed by a 5-1 reverse against Blackburn Rovers and, although Villa won four of their next five games, they were eight points behind North End with six games to play as they took on Burnley at Turf Moor. It proved to be a disappointing day for the Villans, who had to play the game with ten men after Archie Hunter was detained at work and failed to arrive at the ground. Burnley won 4-0 and with Preston winning at Notts County, the Lancashire side now had an unassailable 11-point lead at the top of the table. Preston would go on to clinch the Double and would remain unbeaten throughout the whole season. It was a record that earned them the nickname the 'Invincibles'.

Villa, meanwhile, managed to cling on to second place, despite a disappointing end to the season that saw them close their league campaign with a 5-2 defeat at Derby. The club had enjoyed no better fortune in the FA Cup during the spring of 1888 and were eliminated in the third round after a humiliating 8-1 reverse against Blackburn Rovers.

Testing Times at Perry Barr

Aston Villa may have finished their debut league season as runners-up, but the club had profound problems. Archie Hunter and several other members of the 1887 FA Cup-winning team were coming to the end of their careers, while off the field there were problems, too, with allegations of ill discipline and even corruption. The 1888-89 league season started brightly enough for Villa, who drew their first two games before beating champions Preston 5-3 at Perry Barr. However, after losing eight of their final 12 games, there was no disguising the malaise that had taken hold of the side that had claimed the FA Cup only two years previously.

The only bright spot for Villa was that, despite finishing eighth in the table, they were spared the ignominy of having to apply for re-election to the league. Under league rules, the bottom four clubs had to go through this humbling experience, but because Villa and Bolton had finished level on points, the powers that be did not insist upon it, and both teams kept their place in the league for the following season.

Scandal at the 1892 Cup Final

Villa's fortunes took an unexpected turn into the ascendant in 1892 with an impressive run in the FA Cup. However, despite progressing to the final, the Midlanders could not silence the rumourmongers, and whispered allegations of corruption surfaced after controversy dogged the match at The Oval. Villa's progress to the final had been impressive, with victories over three league teams – Darwen, Wolves and the season's eventual champions, Sunderland – setting up a repeat of the 1887 final and a clash with local rivals West Bromwich Albion.

Villa had already beaten Albion twice in the league during 1891-92 and were clear favourites to lift the cup. One Birmingham shopkeeper was apparently so confident that he displayed a dead Throstle in his window in anticipation of a Villa victory. However, Albion had an excellent cup pedigree, having reached the final four times in seven seasons, and were keen to avenge their defeat of five years earlier.

Archie Hunter, Villa's star player from the 1887 final, had been forced to retire after suffering a stroke in a match against Everton in 1890, but several of his team-mates from that game still wore the Villa colours, most notably winger Dennis Hodgetts and goalkeeper Jimmy Warner. These Perry Barr stalwarts had been joined by a trio of new stars in the shape of Charlie Athersmith, James Cowan and John Devey, and the combination of experience and youth appeared to be working to good effect.

The week before the FA Cup final Aston Villa's confidence was buoyed by a record 12-2 victory against Accrington, with Devey scoring four goals and Louis Campbell and Billy Dickson each scoring hat-tricks. After their feast of goals against Accrington, Villa travelled to their regular retreat at Holt Fleet to prepare for the big game.

It was shirtsleeve weather on 19 March when Villa and Albion took to the field at The Oval. Villa began the brighter of the two teams, with Devey twice going close in the opening minutes. However, in the fifth minute, a swift Albion counterattack ended with an innocuous looking shot creeping past Warner to open the score for the Throstles. The Villa keeper was again at fault ten minutes later when he failed to meet a Geddes cross and let in Nicholls to give Albion a two-goal lead. Thereafter, Albion's wing halves, John Reynolds and Willie Groves, took control of the game and dictated the pace of play. More of the same followed after the interval with another goalkeeping error increasing Albion's winning margin to three goals without reply.

The match had been a disaster for Villa and the club's fans were in no doubt as to who was to blame for The Oval debacle. Goalkeeper Jimmy Warner was the man held culpable and the windows of his Birmingham pub were smashed by irate Villa supporters. However, worse would follow for a player who had kept goal for Villa with great skill for many years. Rumours quickly began to circulate that Warner had taken money in return for throwing the final. The keeper had apparently been seen after the game taking money from a dubious character who was known to the Villa committee. Warner denied the allegation and put his team's defeat down to the over confidence of his team-mates. Nevertheless, a catalogue of misdemeanours, which included insulting members of the committee in the run-up to the final, resulted in Warner being dropped for the next game and that effectively brought the curtain down on his hitherto glorious career with the Perry Barr club.

Fred Rinder's determination to move Villa forward led to great changes at Villa Park.

Rinder Takes Charge

The 1892 FA Cup final had re-ignited Villa's ambitions, but there was much work to be done off the field as the club attempted to shake itself out of the malaise that had taken hold during the dark days of the previous three years. Frederick W. Rinder, a committee member since 1881, was the man who would take the initiative in a period of great change at Perry Barr. Rinder, who hailed from Liverpool and had moved to Birmingham to work in the city's surveyor's office, had no great knowledge of the game, but his organizational skills were to prove invaluable. By 1892 he had grown frustrated at the direction and management of the club, and he was particularly concerned by allegations that gatemen were defrauding the club on sales of match tickets and admission.

Rinder called a special meeting of club members on 24 February 1893 and launched a tirade against the men in control. He was especially damning of the Villa committee's tolerance of ill discipline and of players' drinking. His charismatic and compelling performance culminated in the resignation of the

Villa committee. Rinder himself took on the job of financial secretary and a new committee was formed, pledging itself to lead Villa out of its current decline.

Rinder immediately installed turnstiles at Perry Barr to prevent any further defrauding of the club. It was an action that was swiftly vindicated, as gate receipts immediately increased from around £75 to £250. Furious gatemen protested their innocence, but Rinder made no comment, pointing out that he had not accused any individual of criminal activity.

Changes were also made to the playing staff at Perry Barr ahead of the 1893-94 season. Most notably, Villa signed the two West Bromwich Albion wing halves, Groves and Reynolds, who had caused them so much trouble in the 1892 FA Cup final. The former Albion duo would join Scotsman James Cowan in a formidable half-back line.

The First League Championship

The league campaign of 1893-94 got off to an indifferent start, with Villa losing each of their first three away games and struggling to find any early-season consistency. An upturn in form followed during the winter of 1893 and a run of nine victories in ten games lifted Villa to the top of the table. A 9-0 win over Darwen on Boxing Day gave the Villans a six-point lead over second-placed Burnley and they remained on top of the table for the remainder of the season. The title was duly clinched with a 6-3 triumph at Burnley in the penultimate match of the season. For the first time in the club's history, the name Aston Villa FC was engraved upon the league championship trophy. It was a tremendous achievement for a club that had struggled to hang on to league status just two years earlier, and it owed much to the efforts of 20-goal top scorer John Devey who, in turn, was indebted to the skilful wing play of Hodgetts and Athersmith. Villa's forward combination had contributed fully to a season of high achievement and rich entertainment that had seen the Perry Barr Pets score an incredible 84 goals in their 30 league games.

Despite averaging almost three goals a game, the public were still not overly enamoured with the new league competition, and it was clear that the FA Cup remained the ultimate prize in the eyes of the supporters. Villa had been eliminated in the third round of the competition in 1894, losing out to Sheffield Wednesday on a quagmire of a pitch after defeating Sunderland's 'team of all talents' in the second round. It is interesting to note that Villa's two home games in the FA Cup attracted crowds in excess of 20,000, while the average attendance for a league fixture at Perry Barr was half that figure.

The Rinder-inspired renaissance continued during the 1894-95 season. A run of six consecutive wins in the closing months of 1894 had made amends for an indifferent start to the season, and a 1-0 victory over Preston on 12 January put Villa on top of the table level on points with Sunderland. A report in *The Grasshopper* underlined Villa's growing challenge: 'Aston Villa continue sailing along in their own sweet winning way, and though some members of the doubting heart family wagged their heads and said depressing things about what would be the outcome of the visit of the league cup holders to Preston, the Birmingham boys proved that the confidence in them by the major part of the public was not misplaced.'

However, despite the optimism of *The Grasshopper*'s reporter, Villa's title challenge was rather derailed by defeat in their next game at Everton. Around 2,500 Villa fans had travelled to Merseyside, taking advantage of a special 3/- offer from London & North-Western Railway, but a 4-2 reverse rather handed the initiative to Sunderland in the championship race. The Wearsiders were eventually crowned as league champions, with Villa finishing eight points adrift in third place. Sunderland had now won three of the seven league championships contested, and, along with Everton, were Villa's main rivals.

Cup Consolation for Resurgent Villa

Villa's disappointment at failing to successfully defend their league title, however, was tempered by a successful run in the FA Cup which saw the Midlanders dispose of Derby County, Newcastle United and Nottingham Forest with routine victories at Perry Barr. Having scored 15 goals and conceded just three, Villa were now in the competition's last four and, just as they had in 1892, they would face Sunderland in the semi-finals. It was a mouth-watering tie – the so-called 'team of all talents' against the reigning league champions.

A close game was inevitable between two such well-matched teams, but it was Villa who emerged victorious with a 2-1 win and a place in the FA Cup final. The Midlanders' fans were elated and *The Grasshopper* noted: 'The Villa had a great reception, and when they arrived at New Street Station on Sunday morning, they were met by a huge crowd of enthusiasts.'

Football fervour would continue to grip the Midlands throughout the early spring of 1895 as anticipation grew for a third Villa versus Albion FA Cup final in nine years. Villa were once again favourites, but after the events of 1892 it would have been folly to ignore the cup-fighting credentials of the Albion. 'The Throstles always play about two goals better than their ordinary form on these big occasions,' reminded one Birmingham-based pundit.

A crowd of 42,000 attended the final at the Crystal Palace and, to avoid the confusion of previous finals, they were directed to their places by a system of multi-coloured cards. However, despite the innovative new system, many fans were still shuffling into position when Villa scored the game's only goal after 39 seconds. Chatt appeared to be the scorer, but after the game, the Villa players confirmed that

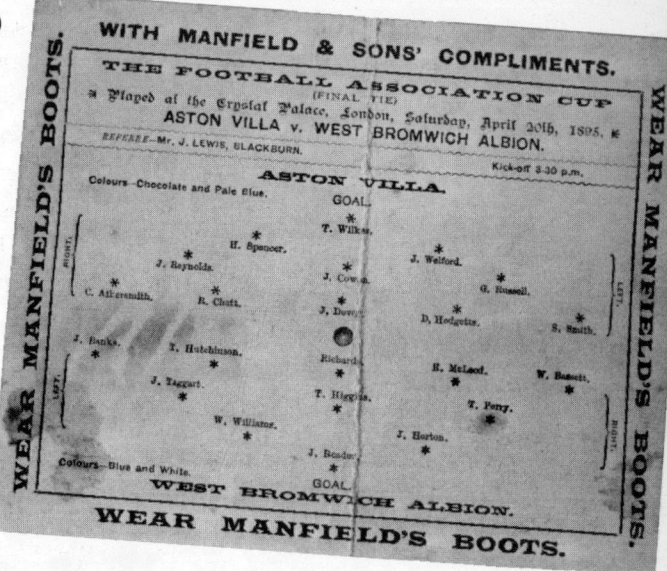

The match programme from the 1895 FA Cup final – it was the third time that Villa and Albion had met at this stage of the competition in nine years.

John Devey had netted after Chatt's shot had been blocked straight into the latter's path and had ricocheted off his knee. The Throstles never recovered from their early setback. 'The Villa men did not make the mistake of two or three years ago,' declared *The Grasshopper*, explaining, 'merely because they were men of a different calibre altogether, men who knew their powers.'

Villa had achieved the impressive feat of finishing third in the First Division and winning the FA Cup in 1894-95, and their success owed much to the work of Fred Rinder. The club's secretary had instigated a policy of scouting and signing talented young local players, and two rising stars had played their part in the FA Cup final victory over the Albion. Steve Smith was a young winger who Rinder was reported to have signed at the coalface of the Cannock and Rugeley Colliery in Hednesford, while Howard Spencer was a local lad who had come to Villa's attention with the Albert Road schoolboys' side. Both players would go on to play for England at senior level.

Villa Become a Limited Company

Rinder's continued modernization of Aston Villa gathered pace during the summer of 1895 following the publication of a committee report on the possible advantages that would 'be derived by the conversion of the club into a limited liability company, with subscribed capital'.

Aston Villa's victorious FA Cup side from 1895. Back row (l to r, in kit): Reynolds, Howard Spencer, John Devey, Wilkes, Welford; front row (l to r): Athersmith, Chatt, Cowan, Russell, Hodgetts, Smith.

The committee was wholeheartedly in favour of the conversion, which it said would: '(1) be conducive to and more firmly establish its financial position and stability; (2) will enable the club to secure and lay out a permanent ground; (3) will relieve the committee and officers from individual monetary responsibility.'

It was proposed that the existing club would be wound up and a new company launched, with a capital of £5,000, in 1,000 shares of £5 each. A meeting was called for 24 May 1895 at the Masonic Hall, New Street, to discuss the matter. The members agreed to accept the principle of limited liability and the decision was applauded by *The Grasshopper*, which rather patronizingly noted 'if they are a little limited company they will be able to fit up their own ground, have their own property, and be people of means'.

There was, however, some resistance to the proposal from what one member [a Fergus Johnston] described as 'our most rapacious members', who he explained were characterized by 'ignorance and flatulent egotism'. It seemed these members were keen to protect their own interests and cheap admission, and Johnston added: 'Which means to continue ever onwards the selfish privilege of attending all our matches for about twopence ... and thus may prevent many of our members from becoming shareholders in our new company, which means spoking the wheels of our onwards progress to a more satisfactory state of things for our club in the future'.

When the club formally accepted the proposal to become a limited company in January 1896, Rinder took the opportunity to take a swipe at those members still preoccupied with their own cheap admission. Following the change, members would have to pay 10s 6d per annum to protect their existing privileges, and Rinder noted: 'We hope the members are satisfied with this. If they are not … they must be very hard to please, for they have about the best value for their money of any footballers in the country. Indeed, we think their interests have been considered a little too much for the real benefit of the club, and we venture to say that very many of those who have been the most blatant critics will be the slowest to take up the shares when they are issued to the public.'

The Grasshopper offered the most pertinent question: 'Is it proposed to stop at Perry Barr, or will the club eventually migrate to the Aston Lower Grounds?' Adding, 'Don't let us have any half-hearted measures or it is possible that an unfortunate season or two may bring the club into that insignificance [from which] it is so hard to recover. There is nothing like striking the iron when it is hot, and it may be that the present opportunities will never recur.'

Prior to becoming a limited company, Villa had no ground and no capital to speak of – in effect they had no security. All the club possessed was its name and its reputation. Had they lost key players and gone on a run of poor results it would have been difficult to survive. Their situation was precarious, though not unique. Thankfully, it quickly became apparent that, as suggested by *The Grasshopper*, the motivation for Villa's share subscription was indeed to raise funds to finance a move to the Aston Lower Grounds.

FA Cup Stolen

While Rinder and the Aston Villa committee set about instigating the move to a new home, on the pitch the club continued its voracious quest for trophies. Unfortunately, it soon became apparent that Villa were not quite as good at looking after their silverware as they were at winning it. On the night of 11 September 1895 the FA Cup was stolen from the premises of Birmingham bootmaker Mr William Shillcock in Newton Road. Bills were posted offering a £10 reward for the return of the cup, but the trophy never resurfaced and a replacement had to be commissioned. Sixty-three years later, the *Sunday Pictorial* revealed what had happened to the original cup. An 83-year-old man named Harry Burge, then a patient in a Birmingham Corporation Welfare Hostel, confessed that it was he and two friends who had stolen the cup. He also revealed that they had melted down the cup and made counterfeit half-crowns, some of which the thieves had spent in a pub run by Villa player Dennis Hodgetts.

The theft of the cup aside, the 1895-96 season had begun brightly for Villa. Such was local interest in the progress of the cup holders, that the first pre-season trial game attracted a crowd of 6,000 to Perry Barr. Many came to see the club's new signings after the Villa committee had taken the decision to strengthen their already impressive team during the summer of 1895. Jimmy Crabtree, an England international full back, was signed from Burnley. Crabtree would spend nine seasons with Villa and collected a further 11 caps during his time at the club. The other notable new arrival was Celtic's Scottish international centre forward John Campbell. 'That the team is a most expensive one cannot be doubted,' declared *The Grasshopper*, 'and it behoves the players themselves, both for the credit of the club and their own reputations, to see that the club and public are not disappointed.'

With the new players settling in quickly and the considerable presence of James Cowan still exerting a major influence over the team from centre half, Villa made an impressive start to the season. They dropped just four points from their opening 12 fixtures and quickly established a lead over title rivals Everton and Derby. However, Villa's defence of the FA Cup was brought to an abrupt end in February 1896 when, before a crowd of 25,000 at the Baseball Ground, they went down 4-2 to Derby. The following weekend the two teams met again on Derby's ground, but this time the Villans had the last laugh, clawing back a 2-0 deficit to earn a significant point in the title race. At season's end Villa collected the league trophy for the second time in three years, finishing with a four-point lead over the Rams.

The Move to Villa Park

The off-the-field changes had continued apace, and, on 20 January 1896, Villa's committee ceased to exist when the club finally became a limited company. The directors of the new company were James Lees, Joshua Margoschis, Charles Johnstone and Fred Rinder. The stated aim of the new board was to secure the club its own ground and initially that meant negotiating a 21-year lease on the Aston Lower Grounds in Trinity Road.

The Grasshopper was among the biggest advocates of the move, and applauded the club's decision to relocate because, 'the means of access to the Lower Grounds are unrivalled in Birmingham, the double frontage gives entrances and exits which it would be practically impossible to obtain in connection with any other enclosure, whilst the buildings already erected and ready to hand will form the basis of club houses and offices, quite unique in their way. The hotel, too, will be most convenient for the use of visiting teams, and the adjacent Great Hall forms conveniences of no mean order'.

Contrary to the views of *The Grasshopper*, however, there was still much work needed to prepare the Aston Lower Grounds for the rigours of regular league football. According to optimistic predictions, the ground would not be ready until the spring of 1897, and so it was in the familiar environs of Perry Barr that Aston Villa kicked off what would become the most successful season in the club's history.

Villa's Double Quest Begins

With the exception of Dennis Hodgetts, who had moved on to Small Heath, all of the previous season's players were retained ahead of the 1896-97 season. The committee also saw fit to bring in two new signings in the shape of Grimsby goalkeeper Jimmy Whitehouse, who was signed for £200, then a record fee for a keeper, and winger Fred Wheldon from Small Heath. Confidence was high ahead of the curtain-raiser at home to Stoke City and a 2-1 victory served only to reinforce the belief that Villa would soon be adding to their rapidly growing collection of silverware. However, the form of the champions was somewhat stuttering in the opening weeks of the season, and after winning just two of their first six games they were left in mid-table.

The critics said that the Villa forwards were too willing to 'fiddle about in front of goal' and that they were given to complicating matters unnecessarily. It was a common line of criticism in the 1890s. In an era of muddy pitches, heavy leather balls and even heavier boots, intricate passing moves were both rare and often frowned upon. By contrast, virtues such as hard kicking, dribbling and barging were warmly applauded. It was, therefore, hardly surprising that, not for the first time, the critics had targeted Villa's relatively sophisticated attacking play as the cause of the team's problems. In reality, it was simply a combination of some difficult fixtures and the disruptive effects of injuries and the arrival of Fred Wheldon that had temporarily blunted the Villa attack. Furthermore, as one pundit pointed out, after six games Villa had six points, just as they had at the start of the previous, title-winning season.

Three successive victories in October lifted Villa to within two points of leaders Bolton, and by the end of November, having dropped just one point in nine games, they were on top of the table, boasting their own two-point lead. It was a position they would maintain for the remainder of the year. Villa's first match of 1897, however, brought a first league defeat for three months, with bottom club Burnley securing an improbable 3-0 win at Perry Barr. A second successive league defeat followed a week later, and once again it came at the hands of the bottom club, which was now Sunderland after the Wearsiders had been leapfrogged by Burnley following the previous week's result. It proved to be Villa's final defeat of the season and following a 2-1 victory in the return against Sunderland, their title challenge quickly regained its relentless momentum.

There were no more hiccups en route to the league championship and at the end of the season Aston Villa sat 11 points clear of second-placed Sheffield United. However, back-to-back league titles would not be sufficient to satisfy the ambitions of inspirational captain John Devey. His goal was to emulate the Double achieved by Preston North End's 'Invincibles' back in the first season of league football and he declared: 'I don't see why we shouldn't bring off the Double ... it has been done before and it will be done again.'

If ever there was a team capable of matching the achievements of the Invincibles, it was Devey's Villa. Fred Rinder had assembled a formidable collection of players although Devey, as captain, would also play a significant role in Villa's successes. Club trainer Joe Grierson was the man who ensured the players were all in peak condition, but it was left to Devey to motivate them and devise the tactics. In Villa's case the tactics were simple – keep the ball on the floor with a combination of quick, short passing and dribbling from the likes of Crabtree, Reynolds and Wheldon. And, if all else failed, there was always Athersmith's devastating pace and the reliable goal-scoring talents of both Devey himself and Campbell. Centre half James Cowan anchored the whole team, while the Perry Barr Pets were also indebted to the uncompromising duo of Spencer and Evans in defence.

Villans Close in on the Cup

With the league already looking like a forgone conclusion, Aston Villa began to focus their attention on the FA Cup in the opening months of 1897. Newcastle United were disposed of in the competition's first round, with goals from Fred Wheldon illuminating a resounding 5-0 win at Perry Barr. Wheldon was again on target in the next round, but this time Villa were run close by a determined Notts County team who, despite playing half the game with only ten men, were unfortunate to lose 2-1. For Villa, of course, the manner of the victory mattered little, although they had at least shown great persistence to beat County with a late goal from Campbell.

Persistence would also be needed to overcome Preston North End in the third round. The tie against the North Enders required two replays before

Villa emerged victorious after a keenly contested match at Bramall Lane ended 3-2. For their efforts, the Villa players were rewarded with a £3 bonus and a tie against Liverpool, also at Bramall Lane, in the semi-final. The Merseysiders, however, were no match for a determined Villa side who won through to the final with a 3-0 victory courtesy of a brace of goals from John Cowan and a typically stylish individual effort from England forward Charlie Athersmith.

Villa were in the final of the FA Cup for the fourth occasion, but for the first time they would not face West Bromwich Albion in the season's showpiece. Instead, it would be Everton who would provide the opposition for the match at Crystal Palace. George Ramsay was in confident mood ahead of the final, boldly declaring that: 'I think we shall win the game ... I made up my mind early in the season that we had a great chance of winning both the League and the English Cup this year, and I have never had any

50 Greatest Players

JAMES COWAN   **Centre half**

Born: Jamestown, Scotland, 17 October 1868

Joined Aston Villa: 1889   **From:** Vale of Leven

Appearances: 356   **Goals:** 26

Left Aston Villa: 1902 (retired)

Centre half James Cowan was the foundation upon which the successful Aston Villa teams of the 1890s were built. A formidable competitor and an imposing figure, his tackling was legendary for both its ferocity and accuracy. However, Jas, as he was affectionately known, was more than just a spoiler, and in addition to directing the Villa defence he was also an extremely constructive player. Jas, whose brother John also enjoyed a successful career with Villa in the 1890s, was an excellent passer of the ball and would berate any team-mate who lumped a hopeful ball forward in preference to playing a measured pass. Cowan was an ever-present during the 1896-97 Double season, but he famously missed six games during the previous campaign. In need of some money and being a player of good pace, Cowan decided to enter the Powderhall Sprint of 1896 in Edinburgh. He feigned injury, complaining of a bad back, to give himself time to train for the race, which he duly won, collecting £80 in prize money. The Villa committee got wind of his antics and fined him.

reason for changing my mind,' although the Villa secretary did offer a word of caution, adding, 'Mind, I am not under-rating Everton ... they are going well now, and we will meet their full strength.' Ramsay's words were to prove prophetic.

The 1897 final certainly captured the interest of the Birmingham public. More than 10,000 fans took advantage of a special Birmingham works' holiday and made the trip to London to join a record-breaking crowd of more than 65,000.

Villa captain John Devey won the toss and elected to take advantage of a fair breeze in the first half. The Midlanders began the final brightly and took the lead through Campbell's forceful drive after 15 minutes, but Everton rallied and scored two goals in quick succession to establish a lead of their own as the game approached the half-hour mark. The glut of goals continued

50 Greatest Players

CHARLIE ATHERSMITH   Winger

Born: Bloxwich, 1872
Joined Aston Villa: 1890   **From:** Unity Gas FC
Appearances: 311   **Goals:** 86
Left Aston Villa: 1901   **For:** Small Heath

Charlie Athersmith is arguably the fastest player ever to have played for Aston Villa. His speed was legendary, and the Bloxwich-born winger formed a formidable right-flank partnership with John Devey. Charlie was a renowned athlete before making his name as a footballer. He began his senior football career with Unity Gas FC, playing both as a half back and as a forward. However, after his move to Villa, the Amateur Athletic Association got to hear about his switch to professionalism and his career as a sprinter was at an end. Charlie, who won 12 England caps, was a great entertainer, but he was tough, too, a fact alluded to by Simon Tappertit in *The Grasshopper*, who stated: 'Once [opponents] get him off his groove by violent play, it is not so pleasant to see him perform; but as a rule he takes things equably and happily, and sometimes has the good sense to smile at spiteful opponents. He is one of those performers who can play equally well at home or abroad, and once on the run, he fears no foe; and he is remarkably skilful and well trained, it is seldom that a match passes without him doing some memorable things in it.'

and John Cowan struck home to draw the score level and the ever-reliable Wheldon then gave Villa a 3-2 lead with nine first-half minutes remaining. As the interval approached the pace of the game slowed and in the second period tension replaced the frenetic, cavalier football of the first 45 minutes. Late in the game Everton began to exert considerable pressure, but Villa held on to clinch victory and a third success in the FA Cup.

Double Celebrations for Devey and Co

Villa's FA Cup final triumph on 10 April 1897 had also coincided with a result that clinched the league championship for the Perry Barr club. Derby County had lost to Bury, giving Villa an unassailable lead at the top of the First Division table. Both legs of the Double had been completed on the same day, although John Devey was not aware of his team's 'other' achievement when he lifted the FA Cup aloft at the Crystal Palace after some kind words from the presenting dignitary, Lord Rosebury.

Back in Birmingham, Villa's supporters soon became aware of their team's great achievement and the celebrations commenced. The players themselves returned to join the party on the Monday after the final. A char-a-banc tour of the city was followed by a civic reception. It was no more than the returning heroes deserved. John Devey and his team-mates had achieved a feat that would not be equalled for 64 years. Still now, more than 105 years on, only five other teams have achieved the Double. The benchmark had been set for every Villa team to come. The fans would not be satisfied with second best – they would not make do with mediocrity.

However, even in the glorious Double season, it is interesting to note that the team did not enjoy the unconditional support of the Perry Barr crowd. Villa would, in fact, win more away games than home (11 to ten), and the situation was serious enough for George Ramsay to comment upon it in a pre-Cup final interview. 'I know our form in home matches has not been true,' explained Ramsay, 'The team feel that they are being unduly criticized throughout the match [at home], and it makes them positively unwilling to shoot as they are able to do... The Perry Barr crowd is undoubtedly rather too critical. When they are away they are indifferent as to what the crowd think of them, and they let fly at goal at every opportunity. This is what wins at football. A man must make some bad shots during an afternoon's football. It is undoubtedly an advantage to play at home, and the curious results we have had at Perry Barr make some explanation necessary.'

The good news for the players was that they would no longer have to play at Perry Barr, although it was doubtful that a move across the road to the

Great Matches

FA CUP FINAL   **Crystal Palace, 10 April 1897**

Aston Villa 3   Everton 2   **Attendance: 65,891**

Campbell	Bell
John Cowan	Boyle
Wheldon	

Aston Villa's cup-winning team included: (back row, l to r, in kit) Spencer, Whitehouse, Evans, Crabtree; (front row) Jas Cowan, Athersmith, Campbell, Devey, Weldon, John Cowan, Reynolds.

The 1897 FA Cup final was the climactic game of the most successful season in Aston Villa's history. By the time Cup final day came round, Villa had already built up a commanding lead over rivals Sheffield United and Derby in the championship race and, although they were not yet mathematically sure of the title, to all but the most pessimistic it was clear that they were playing for the Double at Crystal Palace. Villa were favourites, but their opponents were not to be underestimated. Everton had already beaten the Villans at Perry Barr in the League earlier that season, and the Midlanders would need to be on their best form to lift the cup at Crystal Palace. So the scene was set for this classic clash.

As you would expect of a Double-winning team, Aston Villa circa 1897 were a team of considerable quality. The Perry Barr Pets had a formidable forward line built around the powerful Scottish centre forward John Campbell and the trickery of Messrs Athersmith, Devey and Wheldon. At the other end, the uncompromising full-back duo of Spencer and Evans offered protection to the reliable Whitehouse in goal. However, between defence and attack lay Villa's greatest asset – the half-back line of Reynolds, Jas Cowan and Crabtree.

To use the parlance of the day, Villa 'played up well' in the opening exchanges of the 1897 final and after 15 minutes took the lead through Campbell. A flurry of goals followed as Everton came back strongly to hold a 2-1 advantage on the half-hour mark, but Villa came again and drew level through John Cowan's close-range effort. Shortly afterwards, another goal, the fifth goal in 21 breathtaking minutes, duly arrived, this time via the boot of Fred Wheldon. Chances came and went for both sides thereafter, but in the second period Aston Villa successfully closed down the game through the energetic play of their half-back line. John Devey collected the cup from Lord Rosebury who paid testimony to the 'Olympian struggle' that he had just witnessed. Soon, the news filtered through that events elsewhere on that sunny April day had given the Midlanders an unassailable lead at the top of the First Division. Aston Villa FC had clinched both legs of the Double on the same day.

Aston Villa: Whitehouse, Spencer, Evans, Reynolds, Cowan (Jas), Crabtree, Athersmith, Devey, Campbell, Wheldon, Cowan (John).

Everton: Menham, Meecham, Storrier, Boyle, Holt, Stewart, Taylor, Bell, Hartley, Chadwick, Milward.

Referee: J. Lewis.

Aston Lower Grounds would greatly improve the patience of the Villa fans. For Fred Rinder, the club's move there represented the successful culmination of several years of work. The club's secretary had toiled tirelessly towards his goal since taking charge of the club at that fateful meeting in 1893.

Aston Villa's first game at their new home came a week after the FA Cup final, and, despite a torrential downpour on the morning of the game, more than 15,000 fans came to see the Double holders defeat Blackburn Rovers 3-0, with John Campbell scoring the historic first goal at Villa's new headquarters. Many of the fans came merely to take a look at the new ground, particularly with its covered accommodation for around 17,000 Villa fans. The work at the Lower Grounds had cost the club almost £20,000, although many queried the wisdom of creating a 70,000-capacity stadium at a time when the average attendances for First Division games stood at less than 15,000.

Double Winners Struggle

With a new ground and an all-conquering team to entertain them, the fans anticipated another season of high achievement in 1897-98. However, the claret-and-blue band-wagon ground to an abrupt halt. Shortly after the close of the Double season Villa sold Campbell, Reynolds

50 Greatest Players

JOHN DEVEY   Forward

Born: Newtown, Birmingham, 26 December 1866
Joined Aston Villa: 1891   **From:** Mitchell's St George
Appearances: 308   **Goals:** 187
Left Aston Villa: 1902 (retired)

John Devey was the captain of Aston Villa's great teams of the 1890s and, during an 11-year spell as a Villan, he led the club to two FA Cup successes and five league championships. However, despite his conspicuous talent, for many years it appeared that the lad from Lozells would never get the chance to wear the colours of his local team.

Devey's big problem was Archie Hunter. He was a similar player to the Scotsman, and for many years it was thought that the two could not play together. Devey, like Hunter, possessed a rare combination of devastating pace and transcendental control, which in his youth had ensured he became a prominent local player. However, with Hunter providing Aston Villa with similar qualities in the 1880s, it was not until 1891 that John got the chance to join his Uncle Harry on the playing staff at Perry Barr. The critics said that at the age of 24 John was too old to make an impact in the Football League, but after scoring two goals on his debut he ended the season with a respectable haul of 13 goals and was soon picked to play for England against Ireland. He would also play first-class cricket for Warwickshire and took a seat on the Villa board after retiring in 1902.

and Welford to Celtic and none of the trio were adequately replaced. In Campbell's case the goals of Wheldon, who finished the 1897-98 season as the league's top scorer with 23 goals, helped paper over the cracks, but in defence Villa were short on quality and they immediately began to leak goals – five in the first two games.

In the League Villa finished a distant fifth, seven points adrift of champions Sheffield United, while in the FA Cup their defence ended ignominiously with a first-round defeat against Derby at the Baseball Ground.

Sports Argus commented at season's end: 'I venture to assert that a huge despondent sigh went up at the Aston Lower Grounds at the close of this afternoon's match, as the Villa supporters cast their minds back over what has transpired since 1 September last... Comparatively speaking, the Villa's record is one of the worst the club have ever experienced. Last season the club were at the top of the tree ... now they have fallen to a very low estate indeed ... their list of defeats runs into double figures.'

Fortunes Revive Despite Poor Start

The following campaign Villa again began poorly, and after a defeat at the hands of Bury in the second game of the season, pessimism got the better of Villa's critics: 'The Villa have started worse than they did last season,' commented a report in *Sports Argus*, 'In the first 11 days of the 1897-98 campaign they scored three victories... Now, the season is but ten days old, yet they have one victory neutralized by one defeat. This does not look very promising, does it? Points thrown away just now are desperately hard to make up later on.'

The critics had spoken too quickly, and Villa soon made up ground on their rivals. However, a first-round FA Cup elimination to Nottingham Forest was followed by a decline in form that saw Villa win just one league game in nine attempts between the end of January and mid-April. Nevertheless, with three games to go the Midlanders remained within striking distance of leaders Liverpool, who led by four points but had played a game more. Villa closed the gap to two points with an emphatic 6-1 victory over Notts County, courtesy of a hat-trick from 19-goal leading scorer Devey. Two days later, Villa won their game in hand with a 7-1 thrashing of West Brom to move to the top of the table.

'Thirteen goals to two was enough to take our breath away, wasn't it? Why, previous to that they had played in 11 matches or for 16-and-a-half hours, and had only chalked up an aggregate of 14 goals! No wonder the Villa spectators gasped at such unwanted proceedings,' declared an editorial in *Sports Argus*.

Final Day Drama against Liverpool

There was yet more excitement to come for the fans at Villa Park. The championship race would be decided on the final day of the season with a showdown meeting between the top two teams at the Trinity Road ground. A draw would be enough for Villa, but Liverpool had to win to clinch the title. A buzz of excitement swept around Birmingham as anticipation grew in the run up to the most climactic ending to a league season in the competition's 12-year history. The Villa directors decided to cash in on the unprecedented interest in the 1899 title decider and put up admission prices. It was a move that incensed both supporters and media alike, but nevertheless 41,000 fans turned up despite the ticket prices and the league trophy was put on view in the grandstand to whet their appetites.

Villa, who had spent the week before the game at Holt Fleet, overwhelmed Liverpool. After four minutes skipper John Devey scored to settle the home team's nerves and within a quarter of an hour he had doubled Villa's advantage. By half-time Villa had established an unassailable 5-0 lead and at the end of the game Devey collected the league trophy to rapturous applause. It was the fourth time in six seasons that Aston Villa had been crowned champions and, not for the first time, Devey had been the star of the team, scoring 21 goals in the 34-match league campaign.

The match against Liverpool brought in gate receipts of £1,558 – the next best during the season had been £825 from a crowd of 30,000 against Newcastle. A profit of around £3,000 was recorded for the season. However, despite the successes on the pitch and Villa's seemingly secure financial position, the summer of 1899 was dominated by wrangles over money between players and directors. As Villa closed in on the title, the club had sought to sign on its key players for the following season. Athersmith and Wheldon were both quick to re-sign, but the club found it more difficult to agree terms with James Cowan and Crabtree, who had got wind that the directors were paying certain players £6 per week – and therefore in excess of the £4.10s maximum standard wage that they had been offered.

Argus Junior commented: 'Whilst I have always been of the opinion that the wages of the average football professional have reached a ludicrously high and exorbitant standard, I must say that Crabtree is quite justified in holding out for as much money as he can get. If there is any man in the Villa team worth a tip-top wage, it is certainly the ex-Burnley man.'

Crabtree eventually got his £6 per week, and so it was that Villa opened the 1899-1900 campaign with the same team that had closed the previous season with that famous victory over Liverpool. Villa kicked off with a difficult trip to Wearside, but a 1-0 victory over Sunderland got the title defence off to a perfect start. A 9-0 thrashing of Glossop followed in the first home game of the season, and when Villa met early-season leaders Sheffield United at Bramall Lane in October, they sat just two points adrift of their opponents. A victory would have taken Villa to the top, but it was not to be, and the Blades won 2-0 to extend their lead to four points.

Injuries to the likes of Crabtree, Athersmith, Cowan and Johnson would further undermine Villa's challenge, which looked to have floundered in the winter of 1899-1900. However, Villa were not willing to give up their title without a fight and, in the absence of several of the club's more creative and attacking players, the Midlanders began to place a greater emphasis on defence. Howard Spencer's and Albert Evans' stoicism allied to the formidable

Great Matches

FOOTBALL LEAGUE   **Villa Park, 29 April 1899**

Aston Villa 5   **Liverpool 0**   **Attendance: 41,000**

Devey 2
Wheldon 3

Victorian football fans never truly took a shine to the league championship. They preferred the unpredictable drama and the glory of the FA Cup to the eight-month serial production of the League. However, in 1899, events conspired to leave the championship race with a truly climactic finish that would convert a few of the fans to the long-distance nature of the title chase.

First-placed Aston Villa took on second-placed Liverpool at Villa Park on the final Saturday of the season in a classic 'winner takes all' encounter. A week before the end of the season it had looked like Liverpool would cruise to the title with Villa seemingly in freefall after a run that had seen them win just once in their last nine games. However, when a morale-boosting 6-1 triumph over Notts County was followed, two days later, with a 7-1 win over local rivals West Bromwich Albion, Villa found themselves back at the top of the table, albeit on goal average. And so events led to Villa Park and that showdown meeting...

The championship trophy was put on display in the Whitton Road stand ready to present to the winning captain, and a crowd of 41,000 flocked to Villa Park in eager anticipation. Liverpool's supporters were hopeful that their team would be able to regain the form that had seen them beat the same opponents 3-0 at Anfield, while Villa's followers were looking forward to reacquainting themselves with a trophy that they had won four times in the 1890s.

Several members of the 1897 Double team still remained in the Villa line-up, and it was these experienced stars who proved decisive against Liverpool. A goal from captain John Devey after just four minutes eradicated any nerves and thereafter Villa played with the fluency that had seen them score 13 goals in their last two games. A second goal duly followed within a quarter of an hour, before Wheldon put the game beyond Liverpool with a five-minute hat-trick as half-time approached. Five-nil at the interval remained five-nil at the final whistle. Villa were champions again, and this time even the most curmudgeonly of Victorian Villans was moved to applaud.

Aston Villa: George, Spencer, Evans, Bowman, Jas Cowan, Crabtree, Athersmith, Devey, Garraty, Wheldon, Smith.

Liverpool: Perkins, Goldie, Dunlop, Howell, Raisbeck, Wilson, Cox, Walker, Allan, Morgan, Robertson.

presence of 6ft 2in goalkeeper Billy George, ensured Sheffield United remained in sight at the top of the table. By mid-February, Villa were back to something like full strength and a 6-2 victory over Notts County took them ahead of Sheffield United on points, although the Yorkshire side still had a game in hand.

Senior Players Disciplined

On 3 March the top two met at Villa Park and after going a goal behind, Villa struck back through Garraty to earn a 1-1 draw. Garraty would finish the season as the club's top scorer with 27 league goals and his youthful forward play hinted at a bright future for both the club and the player. By contrast three players of rather more experience found themselves facing disciplinary action from the Villa committee after being caught drinking and socializing to excess in the run up to the Sheffield United game. Messrs Cowan, Crabtree and Wheldon were all suspended for Villa's next game, a cup-tie against Southern League side Millwall. It was a decision that proved costly for all concerned, with the Londoners running out 2-1 winners. For Rinder it was particularly galling, since a successful cup run would have provided a welcome boost to the Villa Park coffers.

Consolation came in the league. Sheffield United lost two games in succession during March, handing the initiative to Villa who, despite dropping two points at Newcastle themselves, took advantage of their rival's failing form. The Midlanders were not playing with the fluency of years gone by, but they drew upon all their experience to win five of their last six games and clinch the title.

The *Birmingham Owl* was fulsome in its praise: 'Aston Villa have won the league championship again, and won it under conditions which entitle them to take a deal of credit for their triumph. At Christmas they did not seem to have the slightest chance of beating Sheffield United, but the consistency of the team since the second half of the season was entered upon has been remarkable.'

Villa were undeniably the team to beat at the turn of the 20th century, and the *Birmingham Owl* continued: 'I doubt if any team are played harder against than the Villa, and this makes their success all the more significant. Aston Villa have been the consistent XI in the country since the institution of the league.'

Villa would begin the first full season of the 20th century as champions, having collected eight major trophies in the 1890s. However, with the likes of Devey and Cowan now in their 30s, the question was, how long could Villa retain their place at the top of the tree?

Chapter Three: 1900-15
Building on Success

Aston Villa began the 20th century as champions. However, after a decade as the dominant force in English football, their rivals were beginning to close the gap. Everton, Sunderland, Liverpool, Sheffield Wednesday, Manchester United and Newcastle United would each taste championship success in the coming years, although none attained the pre-eminence that Villa enjoyed in the 1890s.

Villa remained a significant force in the game, but there was no escaping the fact that English football had become more competitive than ever before. To the new breed of contenders, the men in claret and blue remained the team to beat and, as was noted in the previous chapter, opponents invariably 'played up well' against Aston Villa. The situation was compounded by the inevitable decline of the great team of the 1890s. By the start of the 1900-01 season the team was in need of significant rebuilding.

An impressive start to the campaign, in which Villa won four games in succession, served only to paper over some rather deep and profound cracks. The quartet of wins was followed by a dismal run of form that saw the Villans finish the season fourth from bottom after closing the campaign with four consecutive defeats. It was clear that the 1899-1900 championship success had been the last great hurrah for Villa's all-conquering team of the 1890s. The summer of 1901 saw the departure of Charlie Athersmith, Steve Smith and Jimmy Crabtree, while James Cowan, whose influence was fading, ended his 13-year stint at Villa Park in 1902.

The team-building work began with the signing of Joe Bache from Stourbridge FC. Bache would go on to be the team's inspiration for many years to come, taking over the mantle of John Devey, and forming an excellent partnership with Albert Hall on the left of Villa's attack throughout the latter half of the decade.

The 1901-02 season brought a slight improvement in the league position, but a mid-table finish, some ten points adrift of champions Sunderland, was disappointing for a club that had grown used to success. However, league tables seemed of little consequence in April 1902 when 25 men lost their lives at the Ibrox Stadium disaster in Glasgow during a match between England and Scotland. Three Villa players – Billy George, Albert Wilkes and

Bobby Templeton – were among the England line-up, while former favourite John Campbell had been in the Scotland team on that fateful day.

A New Team Takes Shape

In 1902 Villa's team rebuilding gathered pace. Howard Spencer was soon the only member of the 1897 team still in situ at Villa Park. Most significantly, a new half-back line had been assembled. The renewal of the creative hub of the team was a bold but necessary move on the part of the Villa board. Joe Pearson took over at right half and would soon be joined by Alec Leake and Jack Windmill in a formidable combination. Leake had been at the club for several years, having been signed from Small Heath, whom he captained, in 1899. He would become an extremely popular figure with the Villa faithful, who appreciated his steady and dependable play. He also won five England caps between 1904 and 1906 as a Villa player.

50 Greatest Players

HOWARD SPENCER Full back

Born: Edgbaston, 23 August 1875

Joined Aston Villa: 1894   **From:** Birchfield Town (Juniors)

Appearances: 295   **Goals:** 2

Left Aston Villa: 1908 (retired)

Howard Spencer was the very antithesis of the modern day stereotype of the spoilt brat footballer. Howard was a one-club man who never caused problems on or off the pitch and retained a sense of humility despite a career of high achievement that saw him captain England and Aston Villa. Howard was known as the 'Prince of Full Backs' and was renowned for his sense of fair play and sportsmanship. That said, 'Gentle Howard' was nevertheless a fierce competitor and an extremely effective defender. At a time when defenders would frequently 'charge' opponents with little intention, or hope, of winning the ball, Spencer mastered the art of jockeying attackers away from goal. In 1897, Howard was a member of Villa's historic Double-winning team. However, by 1904 the club's directors believed he was past his best and set about replacing him with Bolton's Tom Brown. It proved a premature move. By season's end, Howard had won back his place in the team and it was he, rather than Brown, that led Villa to the 1905 FA Cup. Howard eventually hung up his boots in 1907 and became a Villa director, remaining on the board for 29 years.

The transitional Villa team faced inevitable teething troubles and began the 1902-03 league campaign poorly. By Christmas relegation worries had been largely set aside, and were replaced by an unfamiliar mid-table mediocrity. However, a revival in fortunes propelled Villa up the table from 13th place to the fringes of the title race by early spring. They would win 12 of their last 15 games to finish agonizingly just one point behind champions, Wednesday. Disappointment at missing out on the league title, however, was tempered by the realization that a promising new line-up was emerging at Villa Park.

The Pearson-Leake-Windmill half-back line was beginning to function effectively, assuming the mantle of the Reynolds-Cowan-Crabtree trio that had proved so devastating in the latter years of the 1890s. Villa's renewed attacking potency was also underlined by their goal-scoring exploits in 1903-04 when they outscored the champions by some 22 goals despite finishing fifth.

A Fifth Cup Final

Despite four trophyless seasons, Aston Villa had lost none of their popular appeal with English football followers. In 1904, they played Southern League side Tottenham Hotspur in the second round of the FA Cup at White Hart Lane and such was the interest in the visit of the Midlanders that Spurs attempted to accommodate extra fans on temporary benches and in every available nook and cranny. The result was that disgruntled fans spilled onto the pitch in a mood of protest and the match was abandoned. For the record, the FA fined the Londoners £350 and ordered the rescheduled match to be played at Villa Park, where Spurs won 1-0 with a late goal.

The following season's FA Cup programme brought better fortune to Aston Villa, who began impressively with a 5-1 victory over Leicester Fosse before disposing of the 1903 winners, Bury, to reach the third round and a tie against Southern League Fulham. A crowd of 42,000 turned up at Villa Park to see the Midlanders crush Fulham 5-0 en route to a semi-final meeting with league leaders Everton at Stoke on 25 March.

Everton and Villa were well matched and the game was keenly contested. However, as the game entered its final six minutes Villa held what appeared to be a decisive one-goal advantage. Everton's Sharp had other ideas, however, and struck a devastating equalizer to take the tie to a replay.

With polite confidence, the Villa captain Howard Spencer offered his prediction for the replay: 'I think we are certain to win the replay on Wednesday; I have never seen so much confidence among our men.' The *Sports Argus* added that: 'The general opinion of the Villa team was that Everton were a trifle lucky to make a draw.'

Villa's confidence was well placed and they won the replay 2-1 despite, according to the *Sports Argus*, being underdogs: 'Almost unanimously the quidnuncs favoured Everton … [even after the first match] the blue-shirted ones still carried the most money, as they say on the Turf.'

Victory over Everton meant Aston Villa were through to a fifth FA Cup final – their opponents would be championship-chasing Newcastle United, who had never before qualified for English football's showpiece.

Ten days before the FA Cup final the two teams played out a dress rehearsal at St James' Park. The match ended in a 2-0 defeat for Villa, but the *Sports Argus* seemed unperturbed and its buoyant editorial by *Argus Junior* was accompanied by a cartoon that represented the two teams as a pair of boxers (wearing appropriate colours). The Villa pugilist sported both a wry smile and a black eye, while Newcastle's boxer wore a smug grin. The caption read: 'That Northern Magpie appears to think he has a soft thing on!' 'Aston Villa: Don't worry. I'm alright. I've only been luring him on. Have your money on me for the final round!'

The 2-0 reverse at Newcastle was followed by a trip to Middlesbrough, but when that match also ended in defeat, concerns began to grow for Villa's cup prospects. However, against Boro the Midlanders had fielded a woefully understrength team. Brown, Miles, Garraty, Bache and Wilkes were all nursing injuries and the directors had struggled to name an experienced XI at Ayresome Park.

Thankfully a week at the Marine Hydro Hotel in Rhyl proved a welcome tonic to Villa's walking wounded and the team that Howard Spencer led out on a sunny day at Crystal Palace was encouragingly familiar. Twenty-nine-year-old Spencer had himself already won two FA Cup finals with Villa, although he had been dropped the previous season when his form had dipped. However, when his replacement, Brown from Bolton, was injured, Spencer was recalled and he greeted his reprieve with a rapid return to the form that had, to date, brought him four England caps. Such was Spencer's renaissance that he won back his place in the national team and twice more donned an England shirt, on both occasions as captain.

If Spencer was the established star of Villa's 1905 FA Cup team, then Harry Hampton was the emerging talent. The 20-year-old striker had taken over at centre forward from Garraty and had established himself as Villa's chief goal threat. Hampton had also become the focal point for Villa's attacking play. He was a courageous and determined leader of the line and his presence was instrumental in a switch to a more direct game. Wingers were still important to Villa's play, but there was now a definite focus for their endeavours and they were encouraged to put the ball into the penalty area at the earliest opportunity. Hampton would challenge for almost any cross, however unlikely he was to reach the ball first, and he was not averse to putting both the ball and the keeper into the back of the net.

'Appy 'Arry Strikes in Final

The 1905 FA Cup final captured the imagination of London's football fans, many of whom made the trip to Crystal Palace to be among the record-breaking crowd of 101,117. Villa remained a huge draw, having already contested four FA Cup finals, and trees and banking alongside the ground were filled with fans desperate to catch a glimpse of an eagerly anticipated match.

Newcastle won the toss and their captain, Aitkin, chose ends, leaving Villa to play into the sun and the wind for the first half. Newcastle's good fortune soon ended, however, and when the game kicked off they quickly found themselves under pressure. The Magpies had not anticipated Villa's new,

50 Greatest Players

HARRY HAMPTON   Centre forward

Born: Wellington, Shropshire, 21 April 1885

Joined Aston Villa: 1904   **From:** Wellington Town

Appearances: 373   **Goals:** 242

Left Aston Villa: 1920   **For:** Birmingham

In an age when burly centre forwards ruled the football fields of Britain and goalkeepers lived in fear of the lawful shoulder charge, Harry Hampton was the most deadly marksman in the Football League. In the words of Charlie Buchan, who played against Hampton in the 1913 FA Cup final, he was a great man '... to have on your side!' Harry, or 'Appy 'Arry 'Ampton as he was nicknamed, was the most significant player in the Villa story since Archie Hunter. The Wellington-born striker was instrumental in a switch to more direct tactics and was the pivotal figure in the FA Cup successes of 1905 and 1913, as well as the championship triumph of 1910. Hampton was no great ball player, but any shortcomings in his technical skills were made up for in his courage and determination. He was an aggressive, whole-hearted competitor who, though often unpopular with opposing fans, was adored by the Villa faithful. Harry won four England caps and moved on to Birmingham after 16 years at Villa Park in 1920. He died in 1963 at the age of 77.

more direct game and in the third minute they fell behind. A poor clearance from a panicking Newcastle defender gave Hampton possession, and the striker combined with Bache before netting the game's opening goal.

Villa's superiority continued throughout the first half and owed much to the probing passing of Billy Garraty, who had been withdrawn into midfield. Garraty it was who served the wingers, who, in turn, arrowed the ball in towards the Newcastle penalty area. However, a procession of chances came and went without further addition to the score and at the interval the Magpies were still in contention.

Buoyed by Villa's inability to kill off the game, Newcastle began the second half strongly, but they too were unable to score, despite a period of ascendancy. Defenders Spencer and Miles – a rare blend of youth and experience – held firm and played with great composure to see off the resurgent Magpies. With 15 minutes to go the score remained at 1-0. It seemed that Hampton's third-minute effort would be the only goal of the final. However, when Lawrence, the Newcastle keeper, was unable to hold a shot from Hall the ball fell invitingly into the path of Hampton, who duly smashed it home to complete the scoring and a 2-0 victory for Aston Villa.

Villa's fourth FA Cup success brought an abrupt end to Newcastle's hopes of becoming the third team to complete the Double. The Midlanders would, though, endear themselves to the North-easterners when they beat title-challenging Manchester City on the last day of the season, thereby ensuring Newcastle ended the campaign as champions. Villa finished fourth – six points adrift of the Magpies – and had themselves harboured quiet thoughts of the Double up until that league defeat at St James' Park ten days before the Cup final.

Harry Hampton pounces to score Villa's second goal in the 1905 FA Cup final after Newcastle keeper Jimmy Lawrence failed to hold on to a shot from Albert Hall.

After five seasons without a trophy Aston Villa had got back to winning ways in fine style, and their victory over the season's eventual champions had brought a welcome injection of cash into the club coffers at a time when the board was working on plans to buy Villa Park outright. It would take until 1911 for Rinder and his colleagues to negotiate the purchase of the seven-acre site for £8,250.

Mediocrity Returns

Hopes were high ahead of the 1905-06 season. Villa had re-signed all of their FA Cup heroes and all were fit for the commencement of the new league campaign. The *Sports Argus* was, as usual, optimistic: 'On the whole the prospects of the Villa for the coming season are as bright as at any time in the past, and barring unforeseen misfortune, the clubs that head the Villa in the field will be fine exponents of football.'

At season's end, however, seven teams were ahead of Villa in the league table after nine months of football which had been characterized by a frustrating level of inconsistency. The FA Cup had provided the main highlights, most notably in the shape of an 11-1 victory over King's Lynn. However, a truer picture of Villa's season can be gleaned from the FA Cup-tie against Plymouth Argyle, in which the Midlanders drew 0-0 at home, only to win 5-1, four days later, in the replay.

Four trophyless seasons followed the FA Cup success of 1905 and, although Villa were distant runners-up to Manchester United three years later, it was not until 1909-10 that they truly threatened to reclaim their position at the pinnacle of the English game. Spencer, Pearson, Leake, Windmill, Brawn and Garraty had all departed the club in the four seasons following the 1905 FA Cup final, and it was a much-changed team that kicked off the campaign with an emphatic 5-1 win at home to Woolwich Arsenal.

A new half-back line had been formed, utilizing the talents of George Tranter and George Hunter either side of centre half Chris Buckley, but alongside these relative newcomers there was at least the consolation of the continued presence of Messrs Hampton, Bache and Hall from the 1905 team.

Back on the Championship Trail

Villa performed well enough during the early months of the 1909-10 season, but it was their acceleration up the table in December and January that was most impressive. At the start of 1910 the Midlanders sat in fifth position, two points off the lead but with games in hand on all of their rivals. Four weeks later, and after dropping just one point from their last seven games, Villa were on top of the table and in unstoppable form.

Harry Hampton had scored a hat-trick in the 4-3 victory over Blackburn Rovers that took Villa top, and the Wellington-born striker had become a target for 'special attention' from both opposition defenders and supporters. In the 2-1 FA Cup victory at Oldham, 'Appy 'Arry had been struck by a spectator as he went off to change his shorts, and on his return he was kicked by Oldham's Cook, who was sent off for his efforts. It would, however, be wrong to paint the combative Hampton as an innocent victim of sporting envy – a fact evidenced by a report in *Sports Argus* of his performance against Derby in the second round of the FA Cup. Villa had beaten the Rams 6-1 and Hampton had scored one of the goals by barging the Derby keeper over the line, or as the *Sports Argus* politely put it: 'His [Hampton's] "brotherly" attention to Scattergood [the Derby keeper] resulted in the second goal.' The same match report also notes how at one point Hampton's challenge for a cross ended with a Derby defender turning a 'somersault into the goal'.

Villa were knocked out of the FA Cup in the third round in 1910, falling to Manchester City at Villa Park. However, by now the league championship was regarded as equally important as the FA Cup, which had previously been held up as English football's premier competition, and with Villa heading the table there was no time to reflect on the defeat against City.

A week after their FA Cup elimination Aston Villa reclaimed their position at the top of the table with a 7-1 demolition of Manchester United at Villa Park. All seven goals were shared among Villa's rampant forward line, with Hampton (two goals) for once outscored by his colleague Walters, who hit a hat-trick. 'The match will be long remembered for the magnificent form shown by the Villa,' reported the *Sports Argus*. 'There was nothing wrong at all with the United. They were simply overcome by the superlative brilliance of the home team.'

Villa Regain the Title

Villa extended their unbeaten run to 11 games two weeks later with another emphatic victory, this time it was Sheffield Wednesday who fell victim to the in-form Midlanders. Wednesday were destroyed with five second-half goals after holding Villa to 0-0 at half-time, and their centre half, McConnell, played out the last minutes of the game with his arms folded in a gesture of resignation. 'They danced and jigged around us ... made us regular laughing stocks,' moaned McConnell.

It had been ten years since Villa last won the title, but their unrelenting path to the championship remained on course throughout the spring and by mid-April they were just one win away from an unassailable lead. All Villa had to do was beat Notts County away to clinch the title ahead of their only potential rivals, Newcastle United, who had a game in hand. The match against County proved a dramatic encounter and at half-time Villa trailed 2-0. Eleven minutes after the interval Villa were back on level terms, and ten minutes before the end, Wallace scored to clinch both the victory and the championship. Aston Villa had now won the title a record six times. However, few who watched that game at Meadow Lane would still be around to witness Villa's seventh championship success 71 years later.

In 1910, though, there was little reason to suspect that Villa were set for anything but a period of sustained success. William McGregor noted in his column in the *Sports Argus*: 'Aston Villa have, in most decisive fashion, proved themselves to be champions of the country. They have not only carried off the league championship, but the championship of the Birmingham and District League as well.'

Aston Villa travelled to Liverpool for the final game of the season chasing a record points' total, having already equalled a club record by scoring 84 goals during the season. However, Villa lost 2-0 to second-placed Liverpool and their disappointment was compounded when they were attacked by yobs on their way home.

'As the Aston Villa players, the champions of the League, were leaving the Liverpool ground they had a hostile reception from a crowd of 2,000 roughs and hooligans,' explained the *Sports Argus*' reporter, adding: 'For some reason or other Hampton was the centre of the crowd's wrath, and he was loudly hooted and jeered. There was some stone-throwing but no one was hurt, but as the Villa players were mounting the char-a-banc which conveyed them to the city more stones were thrown. 'The char-a-banc was stopped and a number of the Villa players got off. A disgraceful melee ensued during which Hunter, the Villa half back, received a severe blow in the face. By this time a number of police arrived on the scene and dispersed the crowd.'

The ugly scenes that marred the final day of the season could not, however, undermine the achievements of an impressive Villa team. Confidence was justifiably high as the champions prepared to defend their title in the summer of 1910 and William McGregor offered his view on the season past and the one to come in his column in the *Sports Argus*: 'To two causes I attribute Villa's greatness last season: they dropped a good deal of their pattern-weaving, and they put more vim into their work. One or two of the men were accused of over-indulgence in the former, and one or two were considered guilty of an excess of the latter. Well, we have not reached the pinnacle of football skill yet.' On Villa's prospects for 1910-11, he declared: 'Again, from goalkeeper to centre forward, Villa are a talented side, and I am looking forward to their upholding their own reputation and the reputation of the Midlands.'

The championship defence began with a disappointing 1-1 draw against newly promoted Oldham, although the result was undoubtedly influenced by an injury to Harry Hampton in the second half that put Villa down to ten men. The *Sports Argus* somewhat dramatically explained that: '... his opponent's knee caught him [Hampton] under the heart and he was carried off the field in a virtually unconscious condition'.

Villa were still without the injured Hampton when they lost their next match, away to Sunderland. It was suggested that they, like FA Cup-holders Newcastle, were paying the price for attractive football that was ineffective against the 'rush-and-force' methods that were coming into vogue with certain other teams. Crowds, however, were still good at Villa Park, and 20,000 turned up to watch the Midlanders earn their first win of the season with a 3-0 victory over Woolwich Arsenal.

A run of nine successive victories between mid-October and mid-December compensated for Villa's indifferent start to the season and propelled them back into the title race. By early spring the Midlanders appeared to have the title in the bag. On the penultimate Saturday of the season Villa had beaten their main challengers, Manchester United, 4-2, in an ill-tempered game at Villa Park before a crowd of 47,000. They were now top of the table on goal average with a game in hand over United. That game in hand came two days later against Blackburn Rovers at Ewood. However, a goalless draw handed United a lifeline.

Final-Day Heartache

The title race would go down to the final weekend of the season. Villa would play Liverpool at Anfield while United took on third-placed Sunderland at home. If Villa won against the Merseysiders the title was theirs, providing United did not score the hatful of goals they needed to recover a goal-average disadvantage. However, with a second successive title within their reach, Villa blew it. They lost to Liverpool 3-1 while United crushed Sunderland 5-1. Villa had faced stern opposition against a Liverpool team that was clearly delighted to take their prized scalp.

The agonizing finale to the 1910-11 campaign left an inevitable hangover at Villa Park that proved impossible to shake off the following season. Villa finished sixth, eight points behind Blackburn, and were knocked out of the FA Cup by lowly Reading in a replay. Action was clearly required to shake Villa out of their relative malaise and in the summer of 1912 the club's board invested

£2,200 to sign three new players of impressive pedigree. Liverpool's Sam Hardy and Jimmy Harrop arrived for combined fees of £1,200. Hardy had already won ten England caps and was widely regarded as the best goalkeeper in the First Division. The former Liverpool duo were joined by Andrew Ducat, who was signed from Woolwich Arsenal for £1,000.

The new, improved Villa team made an immediate impact and enjoyed a season of high achievement that evoked memories of the glory years of the 1890s. In the league, the Midlanders were beaten just seven times all season and their record of 86 goals was a club record. Both Villa and Sunderland would chase the Double in one of the most engaging seasons in the history of English football.

Villa won five of their first eight games in the League to establish themselves as contenders for the title, underlining their return to grace with a stunning 10-0 victory over The Wednesday at home. Further evidence of the growing confidence at Villa Park was provided by Villa's impressive progress in the FA Cup.

A 3-1 victory over Derby County at the Baseball Ground got the campaign off to a good start, but it was a trio of 5-0 wins over West Ham, Crystal Palace and Bradford Park Avenue that caught the eye and prompted the Villa crowd to adopt the count of five as a chant for many years to come. Eighteen goals scored and just one conceded was a staggering record even allowing for the fact that the Midlanders had only met First Division opposition once (Derby County) en route to a semi-final against Oldham Athletic at Ewood Park. However, the seemingly unstoppable claret-and-blue machine encountered a rare glitch a week before the showdown with the Latics. A 4-0 league reverse at Manchester United was Villa's first defeat for three months and brought an end to a six-match winning run. The FA Cup semi-final provided Villa with the perfect opportunity to make amends and they did not disappoint – Clem Stephenson striking the game's only goal to book his team a place in the final.

Stephenson's Dream Final

Aston Villa's opponents in the final would be championship-chasing Sunderland. Just as they had in 1905, the Midlanders faced North-eastern opponents pursuing the Double, while they too harboured dreams of a clean sweep themselves. It was the dream FA Cup final – the two top teams contesting the first leg of a potential Double and the attendance of just under 122,000 was a record. Fans were everywhere and there was no room inside Crystal Palace. Several people were even injured when they fell to ground from the top of a refreshment stand, which they had climbed upon to gain an improved view of the action.

Villa's Cup final team was built around the skilful half-back line of Barber, Harrop and Leach. Harrop was particularly instrumental to Villa's progress, providing the vital link to a forward line in which Hampton still dominated, ably supported now by Bache and Stephenson.

The final itself was dominated by over zealous defending, though there was some good football, too. Clem Stephenson, according to legend, had dreamt about the final the night before and had foreseen the result of the game. Early on, the young Villa forward turned to Charlie Buchan as the duo waited for a throw-in and said, '1-0. Dreamt it last night. Tommy Barber with a header.' Buchan paid little attention.

Stephenson himself seemed to have undermined his own prediction when he fell to the ground in the Sunderland 18-yard box and won a penalty. His team-mate Charlie Wallace stepped up to take the kick. However, Wallace, the only Sunderland-born player on the pitch, dragged his shot hopelessly wide. At half-time the hapless Villa man was inconsolable, locking himself in the toilet and refusing to speak to his team-mates.

Soon after the interval Hampton had a goal disallowed for offside. Hampton would have a running battle with Sunderland's bald-headed defender Charlie Thomson throughout the game. However, the referee took a lenient view of their scuffling. The official was probably influenced by the fact that this was the first FA Cup final attended by royalty, and he opted to

The 1913 FA Cup-winning team. Back row (l to r, in kit): Tommy Lyons, Tommy Weston, Sam Hardy; middle row (l to r): Joe Bache, Harold Halse, Harry Hampton, Clem Stephenson; front row (l to r): Charlie Wallace, Tommy Barber, Jimmy Harrop, Jimmy Leach.

leave both men on the field. The two combatants were later charged, along with the referee, with failing to maintain order and all three were suspended for a month at the start of the following season.

A missed penalty, a disallowed goal and nothing to show for their superiority – it looked as though Villa's chance had gone, particularly when goalkeeper Hardy went off the field to receive treatment for around ten minutes after a clash with Sunderland's Harry Martin. Harrop went in goal, Hampton moved back to centre half and, predictably, the Wearsiders enjoyed a dangerous spell of pressure. It was Villa's turn to enjoy good fortune as Sunderland twice hit the woodwork as well as having a shot cleared off the line.

With 15 minutes remaining the score remained at 0-0 when Wallace took a corner from the right. The Villa man topped his kick and sent the ball into the box at waist height. Barber ghosted in from midfield and, with the Sunderland defence caught out, stooped to head home from the edge of the penalty area. Stephenson's prophecy had come true. The game ended 1-0 and Sunderland's hopes of becoming the third team to win the Double were at an end. Now it was Villa who harboured hopes of emulating their legendary team of 1897.

Double Chance

Victory over Sunderland meant that Villa had emulated the feat of the Wanderers and Blackburn Rovers in winning the FA Cup five times. The players were taken by open coach from New Street to a reception at the Grand Hotel in Colmore Row. However, the celebrations were modest, as, four days later, Villa faced Sunderland again – this time in a crucial league match at Villa Park.

A record crowd of 60,000 turned up to cheer on their FA Cup-winning heroes – minus the still-injured Hardy. If Villa could beat Sunderland the pressure would be on the Wearsiders and the title race would be alive. However, the league leaders spoilt the party by taking a first-half lead and, though Harold Halse struck back with an equalizer after good work from Joe Bache, Villa could not find a winner. At the end of the season, Aston Villa were four points adrift of Sunderland, in second place. It had, nevertheless, been a season of exceptional achievement at Villa Park.

A year on Villa were again runners-up – the third time in four years that the Midlanders had finished in second place. It seemed that while Villa could not claim to have re-attained the dominant status they had enjoyed in the 1890s, they were now firmly back among English football's elite and were

50 Greatest Players

SAMUEL HARDY   **Goalkeeper**

Born: Newbold, Chesterfield, 26 August 1883

Joined Aston Villa: 1912   **From:** Liverpool

Appearances: 183

Left Aston Villa: 1921   **For:** Nottingham Forest

There can be few men left alive who ever saw Sam Hardy keep goal for Aston Villa, but those who remain will probably contend that the popular custodian was the greatest net minder in the club's history. In a 14-year international career, Hardy won 21 senior caps for England, and despite the interruption of the Great War, in which he served in the Royal Navy, he played more than 600 first-team games.

   Hardy was a goalkeeper not given to acrobatics and he never embellished his work with unnecessary leaps and rolls. Instead, he kept goal with an economy of effort that had the effect of making him look as though he was always playing well within himself. 'There was nothing spectacular about Sam,' explained his former team-mate Billy Walker, 'but what a goalkeeper he was!' He arrived at Villa Park in 1912, just in time to help the club to the FA Cup final in 1913. Sam would play his part in another run to the cup final, this time in 1920, but a year later he brought down the curtain on his spell at Villa Park after a dispute over his continued residence away from Birmingham.

genuine contenders for major honours. Fred Rinder's ambitions for the club matched this status. In the summer of 1914 the cycling track was removed from around the pitch at Villa Park and the plans to expand the ground's capacity were moving on apace.

However, by the time the 1914-15 season reached its conclusion, with Villa in a disappointing 14th place, World War One was under way. It was the first time Villa had finished in the bottom half of the table since 1901 and to make matters worse attendances were well down.

The FA Cup went ahead as planned in 1915, but afterwards Lord Derby of the FA declared: 'The clubs and their supporters have seen the cup played for and it was now everybody's duty to play a sterner game for England.' League football was duly suspended for four seasons as Europe embarked upon the most bloody and depressing conflict it had seen for centuries.

Chapter Four: 1918-45
A Period of Transition

The resumption of league football after World War One found Aston Villa in a parlous financial state. Redevelopment work at Villa Park and the loss of gate receipts for the duration of the conflict had left the directors to contend with an overdraft of more than £2,500. The introduction of a controversial entertainment tax contributed still further to this monetary malaise and, unsurprisingly, admission prices rose as a result. The cheapest admission was now a shilling.

By way of consolation for the increased expense of watching Aston Villa, the team served up a season of rich entertainment and great drama, climaxing with a record-breaking seventh FA Cup final appearance. Two players, however, who would not share in this glorious campaign were Arthur Dobson and Tommy Barber. Both men had lost their lives during the war. Dobson was a young defender, while Barber was a wing half who had starred in the 1913 FA Cup-winning team.

The remaining members of the 1913 team had survived the war, although several had seen their careers enter a sharp decline after spending their best years in olive green rather than claret and blue. Joe Bache, Tommy Lyons and Harold Halse were among those who suffered this fate as a new Villa team, built around the likes of Sam Hardy, Jimmy Harrop and Clem Stephenson, emerged.

Harry Hampton, who was by now 34, remained the darling of the Villa faithful and was one of six survivors of the 1913 FA Cup-winning team who took to the field for the opening fixture against Sunderland. Hardy, Weston, Harrop, Wallace and Stephenson were the other cup heroes in the team that day, but Villa went down 2-1 at Roker Park. It was the start of an appalling run that brought just one point from the first seven games.

Barson Revives Flagging Villa

Hampton's powers were clearly declining and a new hero was soon acquired. Frank Barson, a centre half signed from Barnsley, was the man who would revive Villa's fortunes. Barson, an unyielding and uncompromising Yorkshireman, remains arguably the most competitive footballer to wear the famous claret and blue shirt. He joined a Villa team that had collected just three points from a possible 20 and was marooned at the foot of the table as October drew to a close. Barson was an inspirational figure and his arrival filled his team-mates with a hitherto unseen confidence. His debut coincided with a 4-1 win over Middlesbrough and inspired an unexpected and meteoric revival in Villa's fortunes.

New Heroes Emerge

Ten victories in 11 games saw the Midlanders climb out of the relegation places and into the relative security of mid-table. Barson's impact had been immense, although it must be said that others had also played their part. Another new signing, centre forward Walter Boyman, had scored a hat-trick in the 4-1 win over Boro. In defence, Villa had also found a player who was almost Barson's equal in terms of both power and aggression in the shape of the giant full back Tommy Smart, who would go on to win five England caps. Villa also signed Billy Kirton from Leeds City for a modest fee of £500 when the Yorkshire club were forced to auction off their players after being found guilty of various financial irregularities.

The man who many believe to have been the greatest Villa player of the inter-war years, however, waited until January to make his mark. Billy Walker was a 22-year-old forward who few Villa fans had heard of when he made his debut in an FA Cup first-round tie against Queens Park Rangers in the first week of 1920. Walker scored a goal in each half against Rangers and helped Villa to a 2-1 win. The *Sports Argus* commented: 'Walker was a capital leader, and his display gave promise that Villa have found the man required to fill this important position [centre forward]. Despite a strong cross-wind, he controlled the ball well and passed to the wings with accuracy, while no one excelled him in a dash. He never missed a chance of racing in with the hope of adding to the score.'

Walker had played because Boyman and Young, who were the regular centre forwards, were cup-tied. The directors now had to decide whether or not to keep faith with their young striker. Walker had come to the fore with excellent performances for Wednesbury Old Park as a junior and the Villa Park officials had clearly seen enough of him to know that his goal-scoring debut was no fluke. He kept his place in the team for the next game, a league match against Burnley, while both Boyman and Young turned out for the reserves in their Central League fixture against the same opponents. Within a year Walker had won not only an FA Cup-winner's medal but also a senior England cap.

As one England star arrived another departed. Walker's rapid progress hastened Harry Hampton's exit, although after 16 years of service, his days as a rampaging No. 9 were coming to an end anyway, and it was as a wing half that he played out the remainder of his career with Birmingham.

With Walker now established in the forward line, Villa took on Manchester United in the second round of the FA Cup. *Argus Junior* was uncharacteristically pessimistic: 'Aston Villa have unquestionably the most difficult task... I cannot see Villa winning at Manchester,' declared the *Sports Argus*' football expert. A 1-0 victory over Arsenal, courtesy of Clem Stephenson's 40-yard effort, helped raise confidence ahead of the trip to Lancashire, and after the in-form Stephenson struck an equalizer at Old Trafford, it was left to Walker to provide the coup de grace with a winning goal nine minutes from time. *Argus Junior* changed his tune, after a sudden attack of optimism on Villa's behalf, ahead of the Sunderland game in round three. 'The cup is the laurel wreath of the intelligent men and teams,' he explained. 'In modern times Aston Villa have taken the cup to their possession more often than others, and I attribute their success to the fact that included in their ranks have been men of more than average intelligence.'

Frank Barson had been one of Villa's best players against Manchester United, despite a slightly unorthodox journey to the game. Since he lived in Yorkshire, Barson was left to make his own way to Old Trafford along with another non-Midlander, Sam Hardy. However, when their train stalled and sat motionless on the rails, the intrepid duo elected to run seven miles across country to reach Stalybridge, from where they found alternative transportation. They arrived at the ground with only 15 minutes before kickoff.

There would be no transportation problems ahead of the third-round meeting with Sunderland at Villa Park, but the club's directors could have done with Barson's stoicism and resourcefulness as they attempted to defend themselves against allegations of profiteering from disgruntled fans. The clash with Sunderland was a high-profile game and was eagerly anticipated, but when ticket prices were put up to half a guinea many regular fans were left furious. The directors countered that they had only put up the prices to prevent dangerous levels of overcrowding on the terraces. In the end a disappointing crowd of 32,000 turned up to see Clem Stephenson score the only goal on a day when the half-back line of Ducat, Barson and Harrop was infinitely superior to that of Sunderland.

Villa's FA Cup campaign was fast gathering momentum, and when an own goal from Tommy Clay gave the Midlanders victory over Spurs in the quarter-final, many began to believe that this was going to be their year. The early months of 1920 were good for football in the West Midlands. Villa were in the semi-finals of the Cup, West Bromwich Albion were top of the League and Birmingham were vying for promotion. Not that Villa fans cared much for the successes of their neighbours – their only concern was that the men in claret and blue made it to the FA Cup final.

The final was scheduled to be held at Stamford Bridge. However, there was one potential problem with this plan – Chelsea were still in the FA Cup. The Londoners were Villa's semi-final opponents, and, if they won, the FA would either have to let them play the FA Cup final on their own ground – which was against the competition's rules – or find an alternative venue. Much to the relief of the FA, Villa solved the problem by eliminating the Blues with a 3-1 victory at Bramall Lane. Billy Walker was the star of the semi-final, scoring twice, despite having earlier been carried off the field after a painful collision with a Chelsea defender.

Final Meeting with Terriers

Aston Villa's opponents for the 1920 FA Cup final were Huddersfield Town, who were chasing a Double of promotion and the FA Cup. It was a feat that had never been achieved, but the Terriers were confident of victory and went into the final on the back of a fine run of league form. Nevertheless, Villa's cup pedigree and First Division status ensured that they were favourites to win the trophy for a sixth time.

The Villa XI that lifted the 1920 FA Cup to deny Huddersfield Town a unique Double. Back row (l to r, in kit): Smart, Sam Hardy, Moss; middle row (l to r): Kirton, Andy Ducat, Billy Walker, Stephenson; front row (l to r): Wallace, Frank Barson, Weston, Dorrell.

Despite their status and position among English football's elite, financial problems meant that there would be no week of rest and recuperation for Villa ahead of the final. Walker and Co would have to make do with an excursion to the brine baths at Droitwich instead of the usual trip to Rhyl.

If Villa had hoped that their appearance in the FA Cup final would make a significant impact on their finances, they would have been disappointed to see a relatively modest crowd of 50,000 make the trip to Stamford Bridge for the season's showpiece final. However, with economic recession round the corner and World War One still fresh in the public's mind, it is unsurprising that many football followers elected to stay at home.

Strict disciplinarian Jack Howcraft was the referee and before the game began he came into the Villa dressing room and cautioned Villa's Barson, warning him that he would send him off for the slightest indiscretion. Even the normally unflappable Barson was taken aback and his performance was uncharacteristically cautious for much of the game. Villa were also handicapped by the absence of James Harrop (thigh injury) and Harold Edgely, who had broken his leg in a league match against Chelsea three weeks earlier. Andy Ducat, who had missed the 1913 final with a broken leg, captained Villa in place of Harrop.

The 1920 final was played on a wet, greasy surface and developed into a cagey affair. For most of the match the two midfields cancelled each other out, with Moss and Ducat particularly impressive for Villa. After 90 minutes neither team had managed to break the deadlock, and for the first time an FA Cup final went to extra-time. Six minutes into added time, Villa finally found a way past Huddersfield goalkeeper Mutch. The Midlanders won a corner and Arthur Dorrell swung over the ball from the right. As the ball came down, Kirton challenged Huddersfield's centre half Wilson and the ball flew into the net. It seems likely that Wilson got the decisive touch, but in these days before video replays, nobody cared to dispute Kirton's claims that the goal was his, least of all the Huddersfield man.

The record books still show that it was Kirton who scored the only goal of the 1920 FA Cup final. For the remainder of the game, Huddersfield pressed forward only to be foiled by Hardy on each occasion that they managed to get a shot on goal. At the final whistle Andy Ducat collected the cup from Prince Henry and Villa celebrated their sixth FA Cup win.

Billy Walker had been the undoubted star of the 1920 cup team, and years later he recalled how he felt after the victory over Huddersfield: 'I came to the conclusion that football was the most glorious thing on earth. I was a youngster and the day of the victory was wonderful. Villa fans were the

50 Greatest Players

CLEM STEPHENSON Inside forward

Born: Blyth, 6 February 1891

Joined Aston Villa: 1910   **From:** West Stanley

Appearances: 216   **Goals:** 96

Left Aston Villa: 1921   **For:** Huddersfield Town

Aside from front-line centre forwards, only a handful of players have scored more goals for Aston Villa than Clem Stephenson. In many ways, Clem remains somewhat overlooked in the Villa story. His goals and inventive forward play were instrumental in the FA Cup successes in 1913 and 1920, but he has long been cast in the shadow of more famous team-mates like Harry Hampton and Billy Walker. Clem was a skilful dribbler who packed a powerful shot, and it remains something of a mystery as to why he was capped only once by England. In addition to his skills with a football, Clem is also remembered as something of a psychic. In 1913, he predicted – correctly – that Villa would win the FA Cup final against Sunderland with a headed goal from Tommy Barber. Apparently Stephenson had seen it all in a dream the night before. Unfortunately for Aston Villa, the club's directors were not blessed with such foresight and, in 1921, they let Clem leave for Huddersfield Town. A dispute over his continued residency in Newcastle had precipitated the transfer, although there was also a growing feeling that he was past his best. Clem soon made a mockery of such suggestions, winning three consecutive championships with the Terriers.

proudest people on earth, and I felt the proudest of them all. The day after our triumph we were taken to Brighton, where we found "everything in the garden lovely". The weather was ideal. The sun shone and the seaside was top hole.'

Everything was 'top hole' for Walker the following autumn, too, with the talented young forward kicking off the new season with four goals in a 5-0 win over Arsenal before a crowd of 47,000 at Villa Park. In October he made his England debut and, predictably, scored in a 2-1 win over Ireland.

Walker's arrival had given Villa's forward line a welcome injection of quality, but defensively the reigning FA Cup holders were not quite so impressive. The Midlanders finished the 1920-21 season in tenth place and conceded 70 goals, 12 more than relegated Derby County. There had been more reason to celebrate in the club's defence of the FA Cup, with victories over Bristol City, Notts County and Huddersfield preceding elimination in the quarter-finals against Spurs. Defeat at White Hart Lane had seen Sam Hardy make his final appearance in Villa's colours – Tommy Jackson would succeed him.

Villa's defensive frailties disappeared, albeit temporarily, in 1921-22. The Midlanders finished fifth in the league, having conceded 15 goals fewer than the previous season and were the First Division's top scorers with 74 goals. However encouraging these statistics were, though, more significant events were taking place off the pitch.

Controversy Takes Hold

In 1921 there had been boardroom grumblings about Fred Rinder's activities and an attempt was made to oust him over allegations that he had been 'cornering' shares. A year later, Rinder, having apparently weathered the storm, was still in situ for the opening of the Trinity Road Stand. He had overseen the development of the stand himself and soon came under pressure because of its unexpectedly high cost. The stand had ended up a much grander construction from that which had appeared in the original plans of architect Archibald Leitch. Plush fixtures and fittings abounded, and shortly after its official opening in 1924 it was revealed that it had cost almost £90,000 and that Villa had been left around £55,000 in debt as a result. Soon afterwards Rinder resigned, though he would return to the club in 1936.

Another significant figure parted company with Aston Villa due to a dispute with directors in 1922. Frank Barson had been an immensely influential figure on the pitch for Villa since his arrival from Barnsley three years earlier, but he still resided in Yorkshire and his employers did not approve. The directors wanted him to move to Birmingham, but he had business interests in Sheffield and declined. Andy Ducat, Sam Hardy, Clem Stephenson and Jimmy Harrop had all left the club for similar reasons, and shortly after the start of the 1922-23 season, Barson departed for Manchester United.

The controversy did not end there. Barson's successor was a young centre half called Tommy Ball and, not long after establishing himself in the Villa first team, Ball was shot dead in the street after a dispute with his landlord. No lesser man than John Devey had just weeks before described Ball as a 'young man with a future', adding, 'he will make a great player.'

The death of Ball had coincided with Aston Villa's Golden Jubilee season. Fifty years after the club's formation, Villa could point to a host of trophies

50 Greatest Players

FRANK BARSON   Centre half

Born: Grimesthorpe, Sheffield, 10 April 1891

Joined Aston Villa: 1919   **From:** Barnsley

Appearances: 108   **Goals:** 10

Left Aston Villa: 1922   **For:** Manchester United

When Frank Barson arrived at Villa Park in the winter of 1919 he provided much-needed backbone to a team that was floundering hopelessly at the foot of Division One. Barson was a 1920s Stuart Pearce – feared for his biting tackles and competitive spirit, but admired for his ability on the ball. In his first season at Villa Park, he helped to lift the Midlanders to the safety of mid-table and played his part in the FA Cup success, too. Barson was widely booed and bated by opposing supporters, but was adored by the Villa faithful. His strong-arm approach and abrasive personality meant that controversy was always close at hand, and he was frequently suspended and was often in dispute with directors. A former blacksmith's apprentice, Barson arrived at Villa Park after a dispute with the Barnsley board over travelling expenses from his home in Sheffield, which he was unwilling to move from. Three years later, a similar disagreement over his residence away from Birmingham led to his departure from Villa.

and successes, but history mattered little to the fans, who were desperate to see their team celebrate the Jubilee with some fresh silverware.

The 1923-24 league campaign got off to an ignominious start, with a 3-0 defeat against Birmingham at St Andrews, and Villa failed to mount a serious challenge for the championship. They did, at least, improve on the previous season's performance, finishing sixth. More significantly, they had also tightened up their defence and conceded 14 fewer goals than in 1922-23. Villa's resolute rearguard was built around centre half Dr Victor Milne, a Scot who was a qualified physician. He was flanked by the energetic combination of George Blackburn and Frank Moss, with Tommy Smart and Tommy Mort as the full backs. It was a line-up that would also contribute to a successful FA Cup campaign in 1924.

Jubilee Cup Run

Ten goals scored and just one conceded, saw Villa safely past Ashington, Swansea Town and Leeds United and to a quarter-final against West Bromwich Albion at the Hawthorns. A 2-0 victory over the Throstles delighted the Villa fans and inspired confidence, which was reinforced with an impressive 3-0 win against Burnley in the semi-final. Aston Villa had made it to Wembley for the first time. The new stadium had played host to its first FA Cup final the previous season, when Bolton Wanderers had beaten West Ham in the famous 'White Horse Final'.

Villa's opponents for the 1924 final were Newcastle United – the team the Midlanders had beaten at Crystal Palace 15 years earlier. Five days before the Cup final, on Easter Monday, Newcastle came to Villa Park for a league meeting that was billed as a dress rehearsal for the final. However, the Magpies fielded only one of the XI that would take to the field at Wembley. Against this Newcastle reserve team Villa won 6-1. It was not the first time Newcastle had rested key players in the run up to the final, but it was the most blatant. The FA would later fine them £750 for deliberately fielding a weakened team.

Aside from the distraction of the league match against Newcastle, Villa prepared for the final with two weeks training at Rhyl. There was little to choose between the finalists in terms of their respective league positions, but because of their superior FA Cup record the Villans were installed as favourites. The pundits also believed that Newcastle's aging defence would not be able to stand up to Villa's dynamic forward line. Len Capewell was now playing at centre forward, and he had scored seven of the 15 goals that had got Villa to Wembley. The two Billys, Walker and Kirton, were the inside forwards, while Dickie York and Arthur Dorrell were the wingers.

On the day of the final, Villa's players and officials had all got cabs from Paddington Station to Wembley. The car containing Len Capewell, Tommy Jackson and Tommy Mort got lost en route and ended up stuck in traffic. They arrived half an hour late and were met by anxious and glowering faces when they walked through the officials' entrance.

Villa duly took the field on a rainy day in north London and had much the better of the first half. The Midlanders should have established a good lead, but they found the Newcastle keeper, Bradley, in top form and, despite twice hitting the woodwork, it was 0-0 at the interval. Newcastle would make the Villa pay for their profligacy.

For most of the second half it was defences rather than forward lines that were most impressive. However, as the game neared its conclusion, Newcastle began to enjoy their best spell. Seven minutes from the end, the Villa defence was slow to react when Tommy Jackson palmed out a shot from Cowan. The ball spun loose and was netted by Harris. Villa threw everything forward in search of an equalizer, but were hit with a sucker punch 90 seconds later when Seymour added a second.

Frank Moss, the Villa captain, put it succinctly: 'We had 20 chances, they had two. They accepted theirs, we missed ours.' The editorial in the following weekend's *Sports Argus* offered a somewhat partisan view of the final: 'By their play and not their failure in the 1924 final, Villa added to their fame. They can be great in their failures, as well as in their triumphs, and that is why they are so popular.'

It was not a view shared by Billy Walker. The Villa inside forward, who had played and scored for England at Wembley against Scotland a week before the FA Cup final, had collided with a goalpost and knocked himself out on what he regarded as a thoroughly miserable afternoon against Newcastle. Four years earlier Walker had tasted FA Cup final glory and had celebrated with his team mates on a post-final excursion in Brighton – this time the emotions were rather different. 'We went to Brighton and found the weather – well, simply rotten. It rained in torrents and there was a vigorous gale. A disappointed crowd and the Brighton weather conditions made us dejected and miserable,' explained Walker some years later. 'That day, at any rate, I had a different opinion of both football and Brighton.'

Tommy Smart, who had also played in the 1920 cup-winning team, apparently took defeat rather more easily and told his team-mates: 'You don't think I wanted another winner's medal did you? I've already got one of they [sic]!' Smart was lucky. It would be 34 years before another Villa player would play in an FA Cup final, much less collect a full set of medals.

After 37 years that had brought six league championships and eight FA Cup final appearances, Aston Villa were on the verge of a rather more challenging and infinitely less successful era.

The 1924-25 season offered a foretaste of the struggles that lay ahead for Villa, and despite welcoming back the same squad of players that had got them to the previous season's FA Cup final, the Midlanders slipped to 15th in the table. Not for the first time since the war, defensive frailties were the cause of Aston Villa's problems and a record of 71 goals conceded (34 more than the previous season) was woeful. Financial problems also continued to dog Villa, and by 1925 the club owed the bank around £30,000, while other creditors were owed £25,000. Fred Rinder departed the club on 25 September 1925, having tendered his resignation as a result of the disquiet caused by the cost of the Trinity Road stand.

Rinder, however, was in no mood to apologize for a stand that he regarded as a symbol of Aston Villa's greatness rather than an ill-advised folly. The former chairman defended his actions in sanctioning the extra cost, explaining defiantly: '… no one can hope to receive money unless they spend money.' He regarded the ground as the best in the country and he denied the suggestion that the club's finances were in a parlous state. 'Don't believe it,' he countered. 'The club is in a better position today than it was 12 months ago.'

Rule Change Leads to Goals Bonanza

Boardroom changes, of course, were of little interest to most Villa followers, who were more intrigued by a change in the offside rule ahead of the 1925-26 season. The amended rule meant that two rather than three defenders now had to be between a player and the goal when the ball was played forward. The change had been much overdue. The game was becoming blighted by offside traps, most notably in games involving Newcastle who appeared to have mastered the offside trap, which made it virtually impossible for attacking sides to break through.

Villa began the season with a 10-0 victory over Burnley at Villa Park. The Midlanders had never indulged in the offside trap themselves, and their quick, incisive forward line had worked hard in pre-season to ensure that they profited from the rule change. Len Capewell scored five, while Walker also grabbed a hat-trick against Burnley. Villa finished the season in a respectable sixth place. However, the Midlanders were unable to sustain their upward trend and slipped to tenth a year later. The club's directors attempted to avert the slide and could not be faulted for their bold transfer dealings.

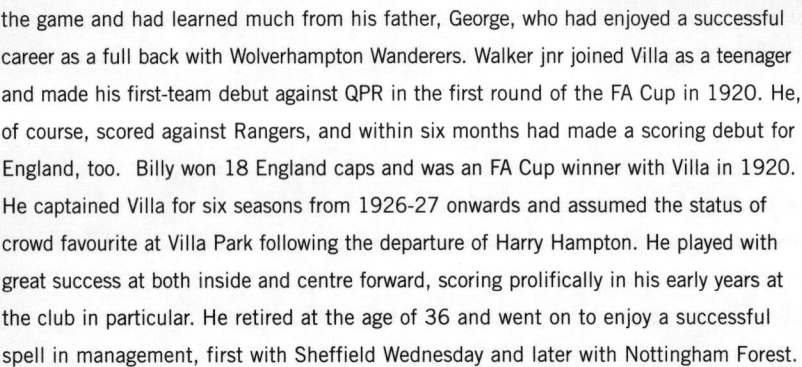

50 Greatest Players

BILLY WALKER   Forward

Born: Wednesbury, Staffordshire, 29 October 1897

Joined Aston Villa: 1919   **From:** Wednesbury Old Athletic

Appearances: 531   **Goals:** 244

Left Aston Villa: 1934 (retired)

It is not difficult to present a compelling argument as to why Billy Walker was among the greatest players to have graced the claret and blue shirt of Aston Villa FC. Walker was all the things we are told footballers should be: charismatic, committed, loyal, professional and, most of all, prodigiously talented. He was, in many ways, the benchmark for the modern footballer – certainly for the modern Aston Villa player.

It was not entirely a surprise that Walker should turn out to be such a success as a footballer. He had grown up around the game and had learned much from his father, George, who had enjoyed a successful career as a full back with Wolverhampton Wanderers. Walker jnr joined Villa as a teenager and made his first-team debut against QPR in the first round of the FA Cup in 1920. He, of course, scored against Rangers, and within six months had made a scoring debut for England, too. Billy won 18 England caps and was an FA Cup winner with Villa in 1920. He captained Villa for six seasons from 1926-27 onwards and assumed the status of crowd favourite at Villa Park following the departure of Harry Hampton. He played with great success at both inside and centre forward, scoring prolifically in his early years at the club in particular. He retired at the age of 36 and went on to enjoy a successful spell in management, first with Sheffield Wednesday and later with Nottingham Forest.

In April 1927, Villa signed Jimmy Gibson from Partick Thistle for a record fee. Gibson was a six-foot-tall wing half and a Scottish international who would form a successful wing-half combination with Alec Talbot. The former Partick man was one of Scotland's Wembley Wizards of 1928, and he remained at Villa Park for 13 years. Alec Talbot was later switched to centre half following the departure of Dr Milne. A new half-back line was taking shape, with Gibson at right half, Joe Tate (who would go on to win three England caps) at left half and Talbot in the centre.

Another new arrival was Eric Houghton, who joined the club as a 17-year-old in 1927. He would enjoy a 20-year playing career at Villa Park, building a reputation as a goal-scoring winger and a deadball specialist. According to legend, Houghton turned up for a trial at Villa Park in August 1927 carrying a heavy suitcase and was greeted by Billy Smith, the club secretary, who said: 'How long do you think you're staying for … a month?'

The following year Aston Villa bolstered their forward line still further by signing arguably the club's greatest-ever player. Tranmere Rovers striker Tom 'Pongo' Waring cost the club £4,700 – a record fee for a Third Division player – but in his five years at Villa Park, he would prove astoundingly good value for money. He was a tall, powerful frontman and a natural finisher. His goals and his personality – he was extremely charismatic if unorthodox – endeared him to the Villa fans like only Archie Hunter and Harry Hampton had done before him.

Villa had assembled a formidable new line-up, and in Waring's first full season they finished third, just two points behind champions Sheffield Wednesday and only a single point adrift of runners-up Leicester. They also reached the semi-final of the FA Cup, losing out to Portsmouth who profited from a dubious penalty to win 1-0.

Villa finished third again in 1929-30, and it now seemed that the Midlanders were getting back on track. The fans were also getting behind their team, and an FA Cup fourth-round tie against Walsall attracted a record crowd of 74,600 to Villa Park. The home team won 3-1, but the scoreline would have been more emphatic had it not been for Saddlers' keeper Fred Biddlestone, who signed for Villa later in the season.

One player, however, who Villa missed out on was Preston's Alex James. The Midlanders had been keen on the mercurial inside forward, but it was Arsenal's manager Herbert Chapman who won the race for his signature. The Gunners would also sign Bolton's David Jack and it soon became evident that Chapman was on a ruthless quest to assemble the greatest club side English football had ever seen.

Goals Galore but No Trophies

Unfortunately for Aston Villa, the advent of Arsenal's great team coincided with the emergence of an excellent team at Villa Park – a team that might ordinarily have expected to have been challenging for the silverware. The most frustrating season of all, in this respect, came in 1930-31, when Villa finished as runners-up seven points behind the Gunners. Had the prize been awarded for aggregate goals, Villa would have been champions. They scored 128 times in the League, once more than Arsenal, and it remains the club's record season for goals. Villa scored in all of their home games and all but three of their away matches, and netted four or more goals on 20 occasions. Waring scored 49 league goals, Houghton scored 30 from the wing, while Walker and Beresford both made double figures.

Gibson, Tate and Talbot formed the half-back line that provided the platform for a formidable Villa attack, and the Villa Park crowd were treated to a season of high entertainment. They watched their team beat Manchester United 7-0, which remains United's record defeat, and Arsenal 5-1. There were other high points, too, most notably the 4-0 derby victory over Birmingham at St Andrews and the 8-1 demolition of Middlesbrough at Villa Park. However, the season ended with no addition to the Villa Park trophy cabinet and it was Arsenal who proved Villa's nemesis, not only in the league but also in the cup, with Alex James scoring twice in a third-round replay.

50 Greatest Players

TOM 'PONGO' WARING   Centre forward

Born: Birkenhead, 12 October 1906

Joined Aston Villa: 1928   **From:** Tranmere Rovers

Appearances: 226   **Goals:** 167

Left Aston Villa: 1933   **For:** Barnsley

If Billy Walker was the consummate professional and all-round good guy of Aston Villa's successful inter-war team, then Pongo Waring was the inspirational, and at times unpredictable, maverick of the side. There was, however, one thing that this charismatic Merseysider did with stunning predictability – he scored goals, and lots of them. Waring remains the greatest goalscorer in the history of Aston Villa FC. His average of more than two goals in every three games is nothing short of staggering. It is a ratio that is unlikely ever to be bettered.

Pongo was a tall and powerful man and he used his formidable physical presence to good effect on the football field. He was, though, an extremely skilful player and his link play was renowned. Pongo arrived at Villa Park for £4,700 in February 1928 and scored a hat-trick on his first appearance in claret and blue – albeit in a Central League match. The goals continued to flow throughout the next five years. However, his temperament did not always make him the easiest of players to manage. Billy Walker remembered that his striking partner was, '... a funny lad indeed,' adding that: 'There were no rules for Pongo ... nobody on the staff ... could do anything with him.' To the fans, of course, this mattered little. Pongo Waring scored goals for Villa, and for them that was good enough.

50 Greatest Players

ERIC HOUGHTON   Winger

Born: Billingborough, 29 June 1910

Joined Aston Villa: 1929   **From:** Billingborough

Appearances: 392   **Goals:** 170

Left Aston Villa: 1947   **For:** Notts County

Goalscoring wingers are highly valued and much sought after by football managers and Villa have had no more prolific outside forward than Lincolnshire-born Eric Houghton. In 20 years as a Villa man he scored more than 200 goals (including wartime competitions), averaging close to a goal every two games from his position out on the left wing. Houghton's greatest gift was a sledgehammer shot, which he deployed to devastating effect from both free kicks and penalties. At a time when heavy, often waterlogged, leather balls and cumbersome boots were still the norm, the ability to strike a powerful shot was much prized. Houghton, it is reckoned, scored from 30 free kicks and netted 72 times from the penalty spot, missing just nine. One of his seven failures came on his debut against Leeds United in 1930, but the young winger did not let this setback affect him and he soon became the most feared spot-kick expert in the League. Houghton brought the curtain down on his playing days at Villa Park after World War Two, but he returned to the club as manager in 1953, leading them to the 1957 FA Cup.

Two seasons later, Villa were again runners-up to Arsenal, finishing four points behind the Gunners. The Midlanders had begun the season brightly and sat on top of the table after remaining unbeaten in their first 11 games. However, despite beating Arsenal 5-3 at home in the autumn of 1931, defensive frailties soon returned to undermine the efforts of the Villa forwards. Nevertheless, as the season reached its climax, the Midlanders were still contenders. A 5-0 defeat at Highbury on 1 April, when Villa were just three points behind the north Londoners, scuppered any lingering hopes of lifting the championship trophy.

The 1932-33 season represented the last hurrah for the impressive Villa team of the early 1930s, and shortly afterwards the team entered a sharp decline. A run to the semi-final of the FA Cup helped disguise the club's problems in the spring of 1934, but at season's end Villa sat 13th in the League and had been eliminated from the FA Cup in humiliating style, via a 6-1 drubbing from Manchester City.

Villa's First 'Manager'

The directors needed to take action – and fast. For the first time in the club's history, Aston Villa appointed a team manager. The directors had controlled and selected the team for more than 60 years, but now they would hand that responsibility to Jimmy McMullan, the manager of Oldham and a former Scotland international.

McMullan was charged with averting Aston Villa's downward trend, and he made several quick raids on the transfer market. McMullan signed Jimmy Allen from Portsmouth and Jimmy McLuckie from Manchester City to bolster Villa's failing defence, although it was a junior player called Frank Broome, who arrived from Berkhamstead Town, that would make the greatest contribution to the Villa story.

The signing of Allen was immensely significant. The big centre half cost a record fee of £10,500, and his arrival was an attempt by the Villa directors to buy a player who could fulfil the role that Herbie Roberts had made famous at Arsenal. His arrival was a break with the club's tradition of playing with constructive centre halves like Barson, Milne and Talbot. Allen was to play the stopper role in the new third-back game, which had been popularized by Arsenal and Roberts.

However, Aston Villa did not find it easy to adapt to the new formation, and the inclusion of Allen served, initially, to confuse the players and worsen their palpable defensive record. Villa were eliminated by Bradford City in the third round of the FA Cup at home and in the League they leaked 88 goals, two more than a side that was heading for Division Two, Leicester City.

Villa's defensive problems had not been resolved by the start of the 1935-36 season and, after an appalling start to the league programme, it soon became apparent that avoiding relegation would be the goal for the Midlanders. Twice they conceded seven goals at home, and after nine defeats in their first 14 games, Villa's situation was desperate. The club's porous backline was simply not up to the task of repelling First Division forward lines. By the end of October, McMullan had resigned as Villa team manager. Former Villa favourite, Frank Barson, returned to the club to help take over some of McMullan's duties, although the directors stopped short of giving him the job of manager – he was simply to be called a coach.

The directors then tried to extricate Aston Villa from the relegation mire by embarking on an unprecedented spending spree as they gambled heavily to keep the famous old club in the First Division. In three months during the winter of 1935-36, Villa spent more than £35,000 on transfers (all of which are listed below).

Player	Position	Fee	Selling club
Charlie Phillips	Forward	£9,000	Wolverhampton Wanderers
George Cummings	Left back	£8,000	Partick Thistle
Alex Massie	Wing half	£6,000	Hearts
Tommy Griffiths	Centre half	£5,000	Middlesbrough
Gordon Hodgson	Wing half	£3,000	Liverpool
Jack Palethorpe	Centre forward	£2,500	Sheffield Wednesday
Jackie Williams	Winger	£2,000	Northampton

The gamble did not pay off. Several of the new arrivals, most notably Massie and Cummings, would make a significant impact at Villa Park in the coming seasons, but none proved the catalyst for an instant revival in the way that Barson had done in 1919. Villa were still capable of pulling off the occasional good result – witness the New Year's Day victory over champions-elect Sunderland at Roker Park – but they remained defensively flawed and were unable to establish any consistently good form.

The pressure grew steadily in the second half of the season and eventually Villa wilted. The club's relegation stunned football and post-mortems swiftly began. Money had been spent, good players had been bought, so how had this happened? The answer was simple. Villa had leaked 110 goals in 42 games. The club had also been guilty of complacency – of believing that they were too good to go down.

Argus Junior asked: 'Who is to blame for Villa's fate? ... There has been trifling team work for two seasons. And the directors? Candidly they were late in sensing the collapse. Their policy of developing young talent was left too late. They will be accused of blundering.'

It was certainly true that the Villa board had been slow to recognize the importance of developing players through an organized junior section. Following his return to the club, Frank Barson took charge of the youth teams and oversaw a marked improvement in their performances. Ironically, as the first team contemplated life in Division Two, the club's juniors were celebrating a host of trophy successes.

Hogan Takes Charge

Relegation brought with it an inevitable boardroom reshuffle. The transfer gamble had failed and the club had lost around £11,000 in one year. Fred Rinder was recalled to the board, which was now headed by Fred Normansell, who had taken over from the previous chairman, Jack Jones. Rinder's first action on returning to the board was to seek out and secure the services of an experienced coach. The man he targeted was Jimmy Hogan.

Hogan was a progressive coach with an impressive resumé. He had previously coached in Austria and Hungary, had played for Fulham, Swindon and Bolton, and he proclaimed himself to be a '… teacher and lover of constructive football with every pass, every kick, every movement an object'. After a great deal of effort on Rinder's part, he took charge of Villa, having led Austria's national team at the 1936 Olympics in Berlin. However, like McMullan before him, he would not be given the full title of manager. Nevertheless, he would shake things up impressively at Villa Park, where ill-discipline and complacency had begun to undermine attempts to recapture former glories.

Hogan's arrival sounded the death knell on numerous Villa careers, most notably those of 'Pongo' Waring, Jimmy Gibson and Joe Beresford. Also on the way out were Danny Blair, Frank Butcher, Norman Young, Jimmy McLuckie, Billy Simpson, Bob Brocklebank and Arthur Cuncliffe, as Hogan set about clearing the way for a new generation of Villa stars. However, team-building was for the future. In the short term, all that mattered was regaining First Division status.

Villa made a good start to the season and dropped just two points from their opening six games. However they soon realized they would not have things all their own way in the quest for promotion. Two defeats were followed by three draws, and a 5-1 reverse at Sheffield United on 31 October demonstrated how tough things could be in the Second Division. Villa revived their fortunes briefly with an impressive run of seven wins in eight games in February and March, but their challenge faltered and they finished the campaign with six consecutive defeats.

The following season, 1937-38, Hogan and his players were better prepared for the demands of a promotion campaign and, this time, they did not disappoint the club's supporters. The summer break saw two significant new arrivals at Villa Park. Bob Iverson, a left half, arrived from Wolves, while Sheffield Wednesday's acclaimed inside forward, Ronnie Starling, was signed as the belated successor to Billy Walker.

Villa started the season steadily but were not among the league leaders until the start of January. However, thereafter they remained among the contenders for promotion – vying with Manchester United, Coventry City and Sheffield United for top-flight status. By mid-April Villa had secured promotion, and with five victories in their final six games they also clinched the Second Division championship. A solid defence had provided the foundation for Villa's success, with Jimmy Allen now showing his true form as both captain and centre half. The Midlanders had also been impressive going forward, and Frank Broome and Frank Shell had led the line superbly, scoring 47 goals between them. The two Franks were ably assisted by both Houghton and Haycock, who each made it into double figures.

Success in the League had also ensured an impressive average crowd of more than 40,000 at Villa Park. At the end of the season, the fans engulfed the pitch to celebrate the championship and victory over Norwich City. The Canaries had also been Villa's victims in the third round of the FA Cup. Goals from Houghton and Haycock had inspired a 3-2 victory over the East Anglians, but it was an epic fifth-round tie against Charlton Athletic that proved most memorable.

The clash with the Addicks ran to three games, and more than 200,000 fans paid to watch the trilogy unfold. The first game ended in a 1-1 draw at Villa Park, while the second match, which was watched by a record crowd of 75,031 at the Valley, saw Villa clinch a draw with a late Shell equalizer after being outplayed by the Londoners. Finally Villa emerged victorious after beating ten-man Charlton, who had been left short after their striker Harold Hobbis broke a leg early in the game. A hat-trick from Broome helped the Midlanders to a 4-1 win. Broome was also among the scorers in the quarter-final victory against Manchester City. However, Preston North End proved Villa's FA Cup nemesis, inflicting a 2-1 defeat on the Midlanders in the semi-final at Bramall Lane.

Promotion and a run to the last four of the FA Cup was, however, a feat worth celebrating and the Villa players were taken on a summer tour of Germany. Little did they know that many of them would be fighting against the Germans in continental Europe within two years. The Nazis were already in power and the Villa players were advised by the British ambassador that they should follow the lead of the FA and give a Nazi salute to the crowd both before and after each game. However, to their credit the Villa players refused, and they were jeered throughout their first game as a result.

Great Managers – 1936-44

JIMMY HOGAN

Upon first inspection, Jimmy Hogan's reign at Villa Park looks far from 'great'. The former Fulham player won no cups, no league championships and was in charge for just three seasons of meaningful football. However, despite all this, Hogan's tenure was a significant one, for under his tutelage Villa finally shook themselves out of a deep-rooted malaise and began looking forward after 16 years of steady decline. Hogan was appointed manager by Fred Rinder following relegation in 1936 and he faced a massive task to turn the club around. He took to the job with both energy and, most importantly, a clear mind. The Villa playing staff was burgeoning with swollen egos and players past their best. Hogan quickly cleared the decks.

Rinder had targeted Hogan to lead the club to promotion after learning of his feats with various clubs and international sides in continental Europe. Born in Lancashire, he had enjoyed a modest playing career with Fulham, Swindon and Bolton, but had excelled as a coach. By the time he arrived at Villa Park, Hogan had coached in Austria, Hungary, Italy and France. Rinder had to use all his considerable powers of persuasion to secure Hogan's services. However, despite the new man's impressive resumé – he had led Austria's national team at the 1936 Olympics in Berlin – and the club's need for a clear redirection, like Jimmy McMullan before him, Hogan was never given the full title of manager.

Hogan's first season in charge was one of transition, but the following campaign ended with promotion and the assembly of a promising new line-up. However, after just one campaign back in Division One, World War Two interrupted Hogan's work at Villa Park. When league football resumed in 1946, the club and Hogan decided that it would be best for a younger man to take charge and the job passed to Alex Massie.

Back on home soil, Villa returned to the First Division and gave a good account of themselves, finishing in the relative comfort of mid-table. The season would, though, be marred by the death of Fred Rinder on Christmas Day 1938. Rinder's role in the Villa story is immense, and it was his vision and foresight that lay behind many of the club's successes both on and off the field.

By the start of the 1939-40 season, the Germans were preparing to march into Poland and Europe was bracing itself for a return to war. The Football League programme was just three games old when it was suspended. Wartime football commenced the following season, by which time Villa Park had taken on a new role. The Trinity Road stand was now a store for ARP materials and a TA regiment had taken up residence in the home dressing room. For the next five years sport would seem insignificant.

Chapter Five: 1946-67
Postwar Drama

By the time league football resumed on a rain-sodden August day in 1946, seven seasons and many blossoming careers had been lost to World War Two. Aston Villa had fared better than many clubs during the years of conflict and had shown up well in the various wartime competitions. However, the serious business of league football would present an all together more taxing proposition.

In 1946, Villa had finished as runners-up in the Wartime League South and had reached the sixth round of the cup, losing out to a Raich Carter-inspired Derby County before 76,588 fans at Villa Park. The club had enjoyed a settled line-up throughout the war, and had benefited from the continued service of many of its pre-war stars. Alex Massie, George Cummings, Bob Iverson, Frank Broome and Eric Houghton had all regularly turned out in claret and blue. However, the presence of these experienced stars served only to build false optimism. Impressive results against opponents who frequently had to field guest players of varying ages and dubious quality were no indication of how Villa would fare once they were playing against teams with settled, professional line-ups.

The truth was that Villa's team was past its best. Players like Houghton and Broome were coming to the end of their careers, while the 40-year-old Massie had more pressing concerns. The Scotsman was the man chosen to take over as team manager from Jimmy Hogan, who had left the club at the end of the war. Massie faced a major rebuilding job, although he did at least have one or two emerging talents with which to work.

Harry Parkes was one of Massie's young hopefuls. He had joined Villa as an amateur in 1939 and would enjoy a 15-year stint with the Midlanders, playing in every outfield position before finally settling in defence. George Edwards, a goal-scoring winger who had scored 39 times in the final season of war-restricted football, was also a promising talent.

League Football Resumes

Back to that rainy day in the late summer of 1946. After seven seasons of making do with the football equivalent of B-movies, a little rain was not going to keep the fans away, and a crowd of 50,000 packed into Villa Park for some proper league football at last.

50 Greatest Players

ALEX MASSIE   Right half/Inside forward

Born: Glasgow, 1 March 1906

Joined Aston Villa: 1935   **From:** Heart of Midlothian

Appearances: 152   **Goals:** 5

Left Aston Villa: 1939 (became team manager at Villa Park)

Alex Massie was one of a host of new signings made during the winter of 1935 as the club tried to avert the slide towards relegation. Massie was already a Scotland international and was one of the most expensive of the newcomers, costing £6,000 from Hearts. Much was expected of Massie. However, he was no Frank Barson, and he was not the right type of player to lead a team through a relegation dogfight. Massie was a footballing thoroughbred – a football purist, who played with patience and skill rather than passion and urgency.

It was not until the 1937-38 promotion season that Aston Villa's fans saw the best of him. Massie was a mesmeric dribbler and a superb passer of the ball, and he provided the driving force in Villa's Division Two championship-winning team.

He eventually succeeded Jimmy Allen as captain. However, the war cut short his playing career. When league football finally resumed in 1946, Alex was 40 and, as a reward for his efforts on the field, he was appointed manager in succession to Jimmy Hogan.

Middlesbrough were the visitors in a repeat of the opening fixture of the abandoned 1939 season, but only three names survived from the Villa teamsheet that had been submitted six years previously. Broome, Callaghan and Cummings were the returning heroes, but Villa's largely unfamiliar line-up failed to illuminate the grey Birmingham sky and it was Middlesbrough's Wilf Mannion who scored the only goal of the game.

The poor start to the season continued two days later against Everton, with Villa going down to a second consecutive 1-0 defeat at home. However, just when it seemed that Massie's team was set for a season of struggle they began to find some form and climbed into the safety of mid-table. There would be no challenge for trophies, but there would also be no battle against relegation. Eighth place at the end of the season represented a respectable performance.

Massie had also attempted to bolster his team's attacking options, and in January began his team rebuilding work with the bold signing of 23-year-old

Wales international forward Trevor Ford from Swansea for the sizeable fee of £9,500. Ford had scored just nine league goals in his career, all of which had come in the first 16 games of the 1946-47 season, and his prolific start to the campaign convinced Massie to invest the bulk of his transfer fund in the Swansea-born forward. It proved to be a wise decision. Ford would score 60 times in his four seasons in claret and blue, before departing for Sunderland for a record fee of £30,000 in 1950.

Another forward making his way at Aston Villa in the mid-1940s was Johnny Dixon, a young winger from Durham who had first appeared in a Villa shirt as a wartime guest in 1944. Dixon was signed as a professional in 1946 and soon became a favourite with the postwar crowd at Villa Park. He would remain at the club for 15 years, captaining the team to FA Cup success in 1957.

Massie's young team achieved a respectable sixth-place finish in 1948, but it was an FA Cup-tie against Manchester United on 10 January that lived longest in the memory from an otherwise unspectacular campaign. United, who had already beaten Villa 2-0 at Old Trafford earlier in the season, were the clear favourites for a cup-tie played out before a crowd of nearly 60,000 lucky souls. The breathless action began when Villa took the lead after just 14 seconds, but by half-time United's superior attacking play had seen them stride into a 5-1 lead. It was clear that Villa could not match United's quick, short-passing game, so instead Massie instructed his team to opt for a more direct approach. The plan worked – to an extent – and the Midlanders had closed the gap to just a single goal as the game entered its final ten minutes. The Villa Park crowd urged their team on in the desperate quest for an equalizer. Caution was thrown to the wind, and in the dying minutes Ford hit the bar. However, United held on and it was they who scored the game's tenth goal with virtually the final kick of the game to bring down the curtain on an exhilarating encounter that left all who had witnessed it exhausted.

Villa Buy their Way to Safety

The following season started catastrophically for Villa. They lost six of their first eight games and relegation quickly became a realistic proposition. The Villa directors acted to resolve the situation and, just as they had in 1935, attempted to buy their way out of trouble. Around £50,000 was spent to bring in Ivor Powell (from QPR), Colin Gibson (from Newcastle United) and Irishman Con Martin (from Leeds United). This time the board's strategy worked, but not before Massie had made a few key tactical switches.

On New Year's Day, after another run of six defeats in eight games, Villa were cast adrift at the bottom of the table following a 5-2 reverse at home against

Blackpool. Massie went back to the drawing board and finally found the solution to his team's problems. Firstly, and most significantly, he switched to a more direct game that saw Villa make better use of the predatory instincts of Trevor Ford. Secondly, Martin was withdrawn to centre half and became the pivotal figure in a half-back line that included Ivor Powell and Frank Moss. Welshman Powell was a tough and confident competitor and proved the perfect foil for the laid-back Irishman alongside him.

Villa's revival was as dramatic as their decline had been sudden. Having lost 15 of their first 25 games, they lost just one of their remaining 17 fixtures, taking 26 points to finish snugly in the comfort of mid-table obscurity. Villa's only defeat thereafter was away to the eventual league champions, Portsmouth.

Trevor Ford, like both Martin and Powell, was instrumental in Villa's New Year renaissance. The Welshman was top scorer the following season, too, by which time he was benefiting from the wing play of Dixon on a regular basis. Villa, however, slipped to 12th place in 1949-50, and there was no disguising their declining fortunes.

As the 1940s drew to a close, Villa set up a fourth team. It was an initiative that brought them in line with most of their rivals, who already had junior teams in which they could bring on young players. At first-team level, though, Villa were no longer among the leading lights of the English game – a fact underlined by two heavy defeats to Manchester United in 1949-50.

Alex Massie soon paid the price for his failure to return Villa to the heights of their former glories, and, after a poor start to the 1950-51 season, he departed Villa Park. Another Scot, George Martin from Newcastle United, was appointed as Massie's successor. By early in 1951 it was clear that the new manager faced a battle to keep his team in Division One. Villa eventually extricated themselves from the mire with four victories over Easter, including back-to-back wins against Wolves, although it was not until 21 April, with only two games to play, that Villa were mathematically safe from relegation, following the 2-1 away victory over struggling Everton.

Martin's first season in charge may have ended in relief rather than elation, but he had at least added several impressive new players to the Villa squad. Forward Tommy Thompson was signed from Martin's former club Newcastle for £15,000 and proved an instant success. Within a year Thompson had broken into the senior England team, and he would score 67 league goals in 149 games for Villa before moving to Preston for £13,500 in 1955.

The most influential of the newcomers was wing half Danny Blanchflower, an expensive signing from Barnsley. Over the next three years, Blanchflower would add much-needed craft to a youthful Villa line-up. However, he took his time settling in as he attempted to curb his natural attacking tendencies in order to contribute fully to the club's survival bid. Blanchflower's transfer was largely financed by the controversial sale of Trevor Ford the previous October.

The Irish Connection

By the start of the following season, Villa had something of an Irish theme running down the middle of the team, with Eire international Walsh in attack, Blanchflower in midfield and, somewhat bizarrely, Con Martin in goal. It seems incredible today, in an era of specialist, giant keepers, but at the start of the 1951-52 campaign, Villa's manager switched his centre half to goal.

'Last season I noticed that after practice matches he would go into goal and invite the lads to shoot at him. He obviously revelled in it and it struck me more and more forcibly that he was a natural,' explained George Martin. 'Not only has he had a psychological effect on the defence, he has solved two positions in one. We had two centre halves in Moss and Martin of equal ability. I felt that when one was playing he knew that he had only to make a mistake and waiting to take his place was the other man. It was a vicious circle. Now they tell me that Frank Moss is playing better at centre half than he ever has done for Villa.' George Martin already had something of a track record for switching players, having re-deployed the great Jackie Milburn from the wing to centre forward during his time as manager at Newcastle. Con Martin duly made his debut between the posts in a 4-1 win over Derby. An impressive victory over Arsenal followed, with Thompson scoring the goal that earned both points. Villa were now playing a more direct game that proved more effective than Arsenal's 'fiddling game'.

After eight games, Villa were second with a game in hand over leaders Manchester United. It was the Midlander's best start to the season for 19 years, but George Martin was not getting carried away: 'We're doing alright, but I shall not be content until we have football and football and more football.'

However, Villa had slipped out of the championship race by Christmas and were down to tenth place. Martin's team eventually finished in a respectable sixth position. It was Villa's best finish for four seasons and their improved showing owed much to the presence of a settled midfield and, in particular, the form of Blanchflower, whose creative talents were perfectly complemented by team-mates Frank Moss and Dick Dorsett.

Villa trod water in 1952-53, finishing in mid-table with neither the threat of relegation nor the promise of a championship challenge to stir their fans. In the autumn of 1953, however, things began to get a little livelier at Villa Park. The new season kicked off with two defeats and, although Villa recovered somewhat with a run of seven wins in eight games, they collected just one point from five games in October. The board took immediate action and Martin departed the club to be replaced by Eric Houghton, who was in charge at Notts County. Houghton had been an immensely popular player, and his return to the club gave cause for renewed optimism among the Villa fans.

The new manager further endeared himself to his old supporters by introducing 19-year-old Irishman Peter McParland to the Villa first team. The teenage outside left made an instant impact, and by the end of the season he had broken into the Northern Ireland team, scoring twice on his debut in a victory over Wales. Houghton's policy of blooding new talent soon saw Ken Roberts, Joe Tyrrell and Derek Pace, all 21 or under, get their chance in the first team. In April, a Villa team imbued with the enthusiasm of youth trounced West Bromwich Albion 6-1 in a match that did much to deny the Throstles the league championship.

Villa eventually finished the season in 13th place, although it must be said that their league position owed much to a late run of victories over teams

---

50 Greatest Players

CON MARTIN — Defender/Goalkeeper

Born: Dublin, 20 March 1923

Joined Aston Villa: 1948   **From:** Leeds United

Appearances: 213   **Goals:** 1

Left Aston Villa: 1956   **For:** Waterford

Con Martin was the original 'utility player'. He made his Republic of Ireland debut as a goalkeeper, began his time with Villa at left back and played by choice at centre half. His unconventional career also took in international appearances for two countries – Northern Ireland (six caps) and Eire (30 caps). He arrived at Villa Park during Alex Massie's reign, having lost form towards the end of his time with his previous club, Leeds. The Dubliner quickly regained his confidence and spent two good seasons as Villa's defensive linchpin.

Under George Martin, Con was switched to goalkeeper where he played 26 times in the early 1950s. By all accounts, he was an accomplished keeper and had no problems making the transition from outfield player. After eight seasons he returned home to Ireland, where he is regarded as something of a sporting hero. His son Mick also played football professionally, enjoying spells with both Manchester United and Newcastle United.

with little to play for. Nevertheless, Houghton had done well to guide a transitional Villa team to ta respectable position in Division One. He had inherited a disaffected and struggling squad, which soon afterwards had lost its star player. Danny Blanchflower's decision to ask for a transfer rocked the club, but after much deliberation the board agreed and invited offers for their midfield general. An auction duly began. Arsenal wanted Blanchflower, but it was Spurs who matched Villa's record transfer valuation, and so it was to White Hart Lane that the Irishman went for £30,000. At the end of the season Tommy Thompson followed him out of Villa Park, joining Preston for £25,000. Villa had boosted their bank balance, but had lost two of their best players at a time when they could ill afford to do so.

Welshman Vic Crowe was signed to replace Blanchflower at right half, and Roy Chapman and Eddie Follan also arrived to boost Houghton's squad. However, all was not right at Villa Park. Defensive frailties had returned in 1954-55, and Villa were the only team in the top ten to finish with a negative goal difference. A year later, and now without Thompson, the Midlanders would again have cause to stare long and hard at the goals 'for and against' columns, as goal average was all that separated them from relegation.

Villa began the season poorly, winning just one of their first ten games. The board, as they had on two previous occasions, attempted to buy their way out of trouble. On this occasion the bill came to around £50,000 as the likes of Everton's Dave Hickson, Jackie Sewell, Jimmy Dugdale, Les Smith and Nigel Sims arrived at Villa Park. The gamble paid off, but only just. Villa collected 15 points from their final 11 games to pull clear of the relegation places, although it was not until they beat West Brom 3-0 at Villa Park that they were assured of safety. The six-time champions had escaped relegation at the expense of Huddersfield Town, courtesy of a 0.2 goal advantage over the Terriers.

Villa Return to Wembley

The board's mid-season investment had brought a marked improvement in Villa's defensive play which carried through to the following campaign. Houghton's team would finish tenth in the league in 1956-57, but it was their performances in the FA Cup that were most memorable.

Under Houghton's stewardship, a different type of Villa team had emerged. No longer trying to excel with pure football, as they had done for so many years, they had now become both more pragmatic and more competitive. Club captain Johnny Dixon was the embodiment of the new energetic approach, and he was ably supported by Peter McParland. Villa had become a difficult team to beat, but in the early months of 1956-57 they were also

50 Greatest Players

DANNY BLANCHFLOWER Wing half

Born: Belfast, 10 February 1926

Joined Aston Villa: 1951   **From:** Barnsley

Appearances: 155   **Goals:** 10

Left Aston Villa: 1954   **For:** Tottenham Hotspur

It is undoubtedly true that Aston Villa did not see the best of Danny Blanchflower – that privilege was reserved for Tottenham Hotspur, the team he led to the Double in 1961. Nevertheless, the mercurial Ulsterman's skilful midfield play illuminated Villa Park for the better part of four seasons and gave great entertainment at a time when there was precious little to cheer.

Danny's stay at Villa Park straddled the managerial reigns of George Martin and Eric Houghton, but neither was able to grant him licence to fully reveal his considerable talents in claret and blue. He arrived from Barnsley in 1951 to join a team threatened by relegation, so he attempted to help his new club avoid the drop. His first full season as a Villan coincided with the club's best postwar league showing, and Danny was undeniably the creative force behind a youthful and seemingly improving Villa team that finished sixth. However, the team failed to progress and two seasons of mediocrity followed at Villa Park. Danny's frustrations grew and in 1954 he asked for a transfer. The board reluctantly agreed and the Irishman headed for Spurs for a record fee of £30,000.

finding it difficult to score themselves. They had no real cutting edge to their attacking play and were without a genuine No. 9. In the absence of a specialist centre forward, it was left to Billy Myerscough to lead the forward line for much of the season.

In the early rounds of the FA Cup, Dixon dominated Villa's scoring. The captain struck four times in four games to help the club progress to the sixth round. Luton were disposed of in round three, after a replay, and Middlesbrough fell next, with Villa winning 3-2 and Dixon predictably scoring the winner. Dixon was also on target in the quarter-finals, scoring in a 2-0 replay win against Burnley at Villa Park. Now came the serious business.

Villa were drawn against West Bromwich Albion in the semi-final, which would be played at neutral Molineux. It was a Midlands derby with the added incentive of a place in the FA Cup final for the winners. With five minutes remaining, the Throstles were deservedly 2-1 up. McParland had scored Villa's goal, and as the game neared its conclusion, the left winger struck again – finishing from Billy Myerscough's cross to keep Villa's cup hopes alive.

The two sides reconvened at St Andrews before a crowd of 58,000 five days later and Myerscough scored the game's only goal with a header from a McParland cross to send the Villans through to a record-equalling ninth FA Cup final. However, Villa's victory owed as much to good fortune as it did to the goal scoring of Myerscough. Albion had been forced to play most of the game with only ten men after Ronnie Allen sustained an injury in the 20th minute, and they had also contrived to miss an open net after Sims had been beaten and was left stranded out of his goal. Albion skipper Ray Barlow bemoaned his team's luck, saying: 'I think if we had played all day, the luck and the run of the ball would have continued to go against us.'

Villa's opponents in the 1957 FA Cup final would be Matt Busby's much-fabled and extremely talented Manchester United team. The Busby Babes were challenging for a treble of league, FA Cup and European Cup in the spring of 1957, while Villa were simply basking in the comfortable obscurity of mid-table as they warmed up for the Wembley showdown with their glamorous opponents. United were, of course, favourites for the FA Cup, but Villa had good reason for optimism. Since the previous season's flirtation with relegation, Eric Houghton and his coaching staff, which now included Jimmy Hogan once more, had turned Villa into a difficult team to beat. Defensively they were much stronger than in recent years. They were a fit team, too, and both morale and confidence was high.

Villa prepared for the FA Cup final with a trip to the Lancashire coast. 'The Villa lads have spent most of this week tuning up at Blackpool,' explained Johnny Dixon in his newspaper column, adding: 'But it has been anything but a rest cure. Trainer Bill Moore has kept us hard at it. Even when it rained we did our training in a nursery – and that wasn't child's play.'

Busby's team would be without their talented inside left, Dennis Viollet, for the final. They did, however, manage to find an able deputy. Nineteen-year-old Bobby Charlton, who had scored for United in the semi-final, came into the team in Viollet's place. For Villa, Stan Crowther kept his place in the line-up, having got his chance because of a knee injury that had sidelined Bill Baxter.

On FA Cup final day Eric Houghton wore the same lucky Abercrombie overcoat and green trilby hat he had worn for each of Villa's cup-ties. The coat and hat were not enough to dispel Jimmy Dugdale's anxieties, however, and the centre half was apparently sick with nerves just 30 minutes before kickoff.

The familiarity of Houghton's attire was also in stark contrast to the kits worn by his players. A clash between the claret of Villa's shirts and United's red tops saw the Midlanders adopt a new striped kit. It did not meet with everybody's approval. Former player Billy Walker would later confess: 'Those claret and blue stripes just didn't seem like the Aston club for which I had played so long.'

The problems of nerves and fashion soon disappeared at kickoff. Jimmy Dugdale, Villa's centre half, kept a close rein on the dangerous Tommy Taylor throughout the early exchanges. However, the game's turning point would arrive at the other end, in a blaze of controversy, after just six minutes.

Sewell sent over a hopeful and overhit cross that McParland met with a weak header that United's Ray Wood caught cleanly. The danger had apparently passed for the team in red, whose keeper had the ball in both hands. However, Villa's McParland followed up and shoulder-charged Wood, sending him sprawling to the ground. The United players were incensed, but the referee took no action, and in this era before the advent of substitutes, the Red Devils were down to ten men. Wood was stretchered off and, though he came on for spells on the wing, he made little impact. Duncan Edwards was pulled back to centre half to take the place of Jackie Blanchflower, who spent most of the remainder of the game in goal.

A Controversial Cup Performance

The score was 0-0 at half-time, but after 66 minutes McParland struck, heading in Dixon's cross. McParland added a second six minutes later to ensure a monopoly on the following day's backpages. This time the Irishman profited when Dixon's shot was parried into his path. The dangerous Taylor pulled a goal back as United rallied late in the game. Wood returned to goal as Busby's men pushed for an equalizer, but Villa held on and Dixon duly lifted the cup. It was Aston Villa's first piece of silverware since 1920. However, the controversy of Wood's injury would dominate the story of the 1957 FA Cup final.

If you look at McParland's challenge today, in the 21st century, it seems indefensible, but, of course, 45 years ago, football was a different and far more physical game. Although undoubtedly partisan, Johnny Dixon said of the McParland-Wood collision: 'To my mind it was purely accidental ... we would have much rather beaten 11 fit Manchester United men – but it just wasn't meant to be.'

The celebratory issue of the *Sports Argus* had an interview with 78-year-old Villa fan Arthur Shelton who had watched six FA Cup finals and remembered the opening game at the Aston Lower Grounds in 1897. When asked about the game against United, he commented: 'Footballers are too pampered these days. Busby's Babes... pah!'

Billy Walker was similarly dismissive and, with all the objectivity of a former Villa legend, declared: 'Both players were at fault. McParland raced in, but the goalkeeper saw him coming and had plenty of time to get out of the way.' Just a year after narrowly avoiding relegation, Aston Villa had finished tenth in the league and had beaten the league champions in the FA Cup final. Villa's wingers were the key to their unexpected success. The duo of McParland and Les Smith scored 32 goals between them. Smith netting 13 times, with McParland reaching an impressive total of 19.

Confidence was high after the high jinks of the FA Cup final success, and the *Daily Mail*'s preview ahead of the 1957-58 season reckoned: 'Great days are in store for Villa, for out of the faded and dusty traditions of the past has come a new spirit. Vive Villa!'

Alas, the FA Cup success of 1957 proved not to be the start of a new era for Aston Villa, but merely an anomalous break from postwar mediocrity and a reminder of previous glories. Eric Houghton attempted to build a positive new momentum after the cup win, telling the press: 'We've got the same players and they've still got that deadly keen spirit and super-fitness. I can't see why we shouldn't improve on last year's performance ... We're confident ... Yes, quietly confident.'

Confidence quickly evaporated after a poor start to the 1957-58 season, and soon Houghton made it known that he was in the market for a new striker. A host of players were linked, but it became clear that Cardiff's Gerry Hitchens was the man Houghton wanted. Hitchens was a Midlander who had grown up on Villa's doorstep and had played for Kidderminster before being picked up by a Cardiff scout. He was still on national service when Villa eventually signed him for £22,500, and it would be some time before he was available for full-time training and even longer still before they saw the best of him.

In December, local rivals Birmingham completed the Double over Villa, the first time they had done so since 1905-06, with a 2-0 win before a crowd of 40,000 at Villa Park. Villa were now three points above relegation, having played a game more than most of the clubs beneath them. After the high jinks of the previous season's FA Cup final, reality was taking hold. At the end of the season Aston Villa sat a disappointing 14th in the table, seven points above relegation.

Mediocrity was replaced by crisis the following season, and, by mid-September, Villa's plight was apparent. They had lost six of their first

Great Matches

FA CUP FINAL

Aston Villa 2　　**Manchester United 1**

McParland 2　　Taylor

Wembley Stadium, 4 May 1957

Attendance: 100,000

Aston Villa were overwhelming underdogs for the 1957 FA Cup final. The Villans went into the game having not won a major trophy for 37 years, while Manchester United, had claimed the latest in a string of successes just a few weeks before, with a second successive league championship. The Reds were the dominant force in English football and had clinched the title by Easter in 1957. On a balmy day in north London, the Double was in their sights and Matt Busby's fabled Babes looked odds on to emulate Villa's great team of 1897. However, Eric Houghton's team had taken heart from a draw against the champions-elect three weeks before and although they could not match United's star-studded line-up they had several top-class players and it was Villa's combative and talented forward, Peter McParland, who took centre stage.

Villa began the stronger of the two teams, and United's players had not been able to make a significant impact by the time the game's pivotal moment arrived after six minutes. McParland met a cross from Sewell and pushed the ball goalward. United keeper Ray Wood took the ball cleanly, but as it nestled in his hands Villa's outside left came steaming in. It looked as though they would clash shoulder-to-shoulder, but at the last moment Wood stopped. McParland kept on going and crashed into the Reds' keeper, sending him sprawling to the ground concussed. Wood was stretchered off though he later returned to play ineffectively on the wing. To all intents and purposes, United were down to ten men, and had centre half Jackie Blanchflower between the posts as an emergency goalkeeper.

Frustratingly, Villa rarely got close enough to test Blanchflower's goalkeeping skills in a first half of few chances. United came out the stronger of the two teams after the interval, and for the most part it was Nigel Sims who was the busier of the two keepers. However, after resisting United's pressure for the first 12 minutes of the second half, Villa broke forward through captain Johnny Dixon. McParland sniffed a chance, careered into the area and got across Duncan Edwards to head home from the penalty spot. Four minutes later the same two players combined again to extend Villa's lead. This time the goal was not quite as impressive, but it proved to be nonetheless decisive. McParland was once again the scorer, striking home after Dixon's shot had bounced down off the crossbar. The dangerous Tommy Taylor, who had hitherto been well policed by the impressive Jimmy Dugdale, pulled back a goal for United after 84 minutes, but it proved to be no more than a consolation goal. Sims and his defenders held out in the face of a late United onslaught and Dixon collected the cup to bring an end to 37 years of trophyless frustration.

Aston Villa: Sims, Lynn, Aldis, Crowther, Dugdale, Saward, Smith, Sewell, Myerscough, Dixon, McParland.

Manchester United: Wood, Foulkes, Byrne, Colman, Blanchflower, Edwards, Berry, Whelan, Taylor, Charlton, Pegg.

Referee: Frank Coultas.

The turning point of the 1957 FA Cup final? Villa's Peter McParland charges United keeper Ray Wood – the result saw Wood stretchered off the field and the fabled Busby Babes were effectively reduced to ten men for the rest of the game.

Peter McParland proved the pivotal figure in the 1957 final. Here he scores the second of his two goals to clinch a 2-1 victory for the Midlanders.

50 Greatest Players

JOHNNY DIXON   Inside forward

Born: Hebburn-on-Tyne, 10 December 1923

Joined Aston Villa: 1945   **From:** Spennymoor United

Appearances: 430   **Goals:** 144

Left Aston Villa: 1961 (retired)

Every football manager craves a player like Johnny Dixon. A loyal, versatile, dependable and, above all else, talented footballer who scores and creates goals but never gets consumed by ego or taken in by hyperbole. In 15 years as a Villa man, Dixon was the consummate professional, and his efforts did not go unnoticed. The likeable North-easterner was a massive favourite with the club's supporters, who held him up as their champion throughout the 1950s.

Dixon made his first appearances in claret and blue as a wartime guest, but it was not until 1946 and the resumption of league football that he signed a permanent, professional contract. By then he was already 23, but despite losing his formative footballing years to the war, he still racked up an impressive total of more than 400 appearances for Villa. Although by preference a left winger, Johnny played right across the forward line and also at left half on occasions. The zenith of Dixon's Villa days came in 1957 when he captained the club to the FA Cup, bringing an end to 37 trophyless years. The skipper scored four times in the cup during 1957 and, although it was Peter McParland who struck both of Villa's goals in the final, his contribution was recognized by the supporters who voted him their Player of the Year.

eight games, conceding 27 goals in the process, and relegation was becoming a realistic prospect. Problems on the field were mirrored in the boardroom, too, with the Shareholders' Association keen to get a voice on the board. They would fail in their attempts in 1958, but power struggles and the like would continue to undermine Villa's progress over the next 20 years.

With Villa languishing in the lower reaches of Division One, Houghton paid the inevitable price. The board invited him to resign. He declined and was sacked. On the night of his dismissal he was negotiating with Hearts for wing half Dave Mackay for a fee of £15,000. Villa would be relegated at season's end, while Mackay would go on to win the Double with Spurs two seasons later.

Houghton's relationship with the directors had been soured somewhat after a dispute over FA Cup final bonuses, and he later confessed that he wished he had departed sooner. He also claimed to have left the club with 'many good young players including Harry Burrows, Kevin Keelan, Mike Tindall and Alan Deakin'. Houghton had also brought the not-inconsiderable talents of Gerry Hitchens to Villa Park – something for which the Villa directors would later be very grateful.

Mercer Moves In

Sheffield United manager Joe Mercer was given the job of replacing Houghton and attempting to avert a seemingly inevitable drop into Division Two. Houghton had been a popular and extremely likeable man, but he was perhaps too nice, and the suspicion was that he did not put enough pressure on the board to open their purse strings, hence Villa were unable to build on their 1957 FA Cup final success and sustain their progress. Nevertheless, Houghton did bequeath a squad with several top-quality players to Mercer; albeit one that was bottom of Division One.

Mercer's reign began poorly with three consecutive defeats, which did not help the club's parlous position. He then oversaw a win at home to Chelsea and addressed the problem of Villa's woeful defence by signing Scottish full back Doug Winton from Burnley. Mercer placed great stock by defence and instigated a new policy of doubling up on opponents, encouraging his players to press the ball and work hard to win back possession. Defensive fundamentals now, but revolutionary stuff back in 1959.

Mercer later explained the situation that greeted him upon taking charge at Villa Park: 'The impression when I first arrived at Villa Park was that the place was morbid and lifeless. The club seemed to be choked by tradition. Tradition can be a wonderful friend but a dangerous enemy.'

Double Disappointment

The FA Cup provided the only highlights in a season of great upheaval at Villa Park. With their new-found defensive fortitude, Mercer's men battled past Rotherham, Chelsea, Everton and Burnley en route to the semi-finals. Sims had been his usual reliable self throughout the cup run, playing with particular assurance in the quarter-final against Burnley, while both McParland and Wylie had been impressive in attack. However, in the semi-final, the Villa forward line misfired and was unable to take advantage of several good passages of play. Villa eventually paid the price for their profligacy when Forest's Quigley struck the game's only goal.

Great Managers – 1953-58

ERIC HOUGHTON

It may have only been a brief and fleeting taste of glory, but the 1957 FA Cup success provided a much-needed fillip to Aston Villa's success-starved, postwar supporters. And the man behind the cup success that ended 37 trophyless years was Eric Houghton. As a player, Eric had been a popular figure with the Villa faithful, and his return to the club as manager was greeted warmly in 1953. He had served his managerial apprenticeship at Notts County.

Eric did his best to reinvigorate a Villa team that had gone somewhat stale, and he endeared himself to the fans by introducing promising young winger Peter McParland. The Irishman was an instant hit, scoring goals and terrorizing opposing full backs with his powerful wing play. McParland was one of several young players who would rise to prominence at Villa Park in the 1950s. The pinnacle of Houghton's managerial tenure came with that FA Cup final victory against Manchester United, when, of course, his own prodigy, McParland, proved the match winner. However, Villa continued to struggle for consistency in the League and, after a change of chairman which left the manager without an ally in the boardroom, and with relations soured over the treatment of trainer Billy Moore, Houghton parted company with the club he had served with such distinction. He left Villa in a perilous position in the league table, and they were relegated at the end of the season. However, his true legacy came in the shape of a squad full of promising young stars, most notably Gerry Hitchens, Harry Burrows and Alan Deakin.

Against Forest, Mercer was convinced his team had had a perfectly good McParland goal ruled out. 'I still think that the referee had given him offside and not seen the Forest full back on the line! The ref's subsequent explanation was that Peter had handled the ball a few moments before. But how that was possible with the ball on the ground all the time, I just don't know.'

Villa's FA Cup run of 1959 may have ended in disappointment, but the confidence induced by cup progress had proved the catalyst for an improvement in league form, and a run of five wins in seven games saw Villa move up the table and into relative safety, five points above the relegation zone. However, the Easter programme brought a disastrous downturn in Villa's fortunes. They collected just one point from five games and were in freefall. The relegation battle went down to the final game of the season – with Manchester City and Villa battling for their Division One status. City won at home to Leicester to give themselves a lifeline, but Villa would still survive if they could beat West Brom at the Hawthorns. Villa took the lead through Hitchens with 14 minutes remaining, but in the 88th minute Ronnie Allen scored for Albion to send Mercer's men down. It was an agonizing moment for Villa fans and it could not have happened at a worse place.

Mercer remained sanguine: 'Relegation will not mean we have to change our policy ... we didn't want it, [but] we may find it easier to rebuild in Division Two where the pressure may not be so intense.'

Mercer remained upbeat after the summer break: 'We've got a football empire here,' he told journalists. 'We have average gates of 36,000. The ground is here – the name Aston Villa arouses more enthusiasm wherever we go than even Arsenal did when I was at Highbury. And the directors are right behind me – I am in sole charge. I have a free hand. Aston Villa will rise again.'

He had been promised around £25,000 to spend on players when he joined the club, but instead decided the money would be better spent on a training ground and on developing young players. The result was a state-of-the-art floodlit facility with two full-size pitches at the Hercules Sports Ground. It was among the best in the country. However, following Mercer's departure in the mid-1960s, the club sold the ground and the players were left without a proper training facility. 'We had to beg, steal and borrow training pitches from all the local factories,' remembered Charlie Aitken.

Promoted as Champions

Mercer's enthusiasm for a strong defence and counter-attacking tactics remained undimmed despite Villa's relegation. Dugdale was the strong man at the back, the foundation around which the rest of the team was built for the promotion campaign of 1959-60. In attack McParland had become vital and he would frequently wander in from his nominal position out on the wing to join the central attackers. The Irishman, who scored 25 goals in 1959-60, was joint top scorer with Gerry Hitchens.

Hitchens was still not a complete player, but when his confidence was high he was unstoppable, as Charlton Athletic found to their cost in November. Villa's prodigious young striker scored five goals in an 11-1 win against the Addicks, who had their keeper taken off with an arm injury early in the game.

By midway through the season, Villa were four points clear of second-placed Cardiff, having played a game more. However, controversy remained close at hand in the boardroom, where the Shareholders' Association was still struggling to make its voice heard. The Association wanted to know how the club had been allowed to get into debt to the tune of £87,000, while allegations were also made about share dealings.

Villa breezed to the Division Two title ahead of Cardiff – their only wobble coming after their FA Cup dreams came to an end at the hands of Wolves at the semi-final stage. Mercer no doubt took great pride from the resoluteness of his defence and goalkeeper. Sims, Lynn, Neal, Crowe, Dugdale and Saward conceded just 43 goals in the league to provide the platform for promotion. Saward, a Republic of Ireland international, was particularly impressive, having taken over as captain after being on the fringes of the first team prior to Joe Mercer's arrival.

In the FA Cup, Villa had cast aside Leeds, Chelsea, Port Vale and Preston prior to their disappointing defeat to Wolves in the semi-final at the Hawthorns. The junior section was faring well, too, and had reached the last eight of the FA Youth Cup. There had also been impressive progress off the field. The Trinity Road stand had been decorated, and a new medical room had been installed. Refreshment bars were added to various stands. The signs were encouraging. Perhaps Villa were, at last, ready to reclaim their position among English football's top sides.

Mercer's Minors Go up a Class

The ascendant trend continued on Villa's return to Division One. Mercer guided his team to an impressive ninth-place finish in the league, while in the FA Cup they fell to eventual Double winners Tottenham Hotspur at the quarter-final stage. However, Villa's greatest triumph of the season came in the newly created and much-maligned League Cup.

Several teams snubbed the new competition and many Villa players thought it was an ill-advised idea to enter – although they later changed their minds when they began to pick up bonuses to supplement their £20-a-week wages. Villa played seven games en route to the competition's last-four and met only one Division One side, in the shape of Preston North End, before clashing with Division Two side Burnley in the semi-finals. A play-off match was needed to separate the two sides, but by then the league season was over, and only 7,000 were in attendance at Old Trafford to see Villa win 2-1, courtesy of a late goal from Gerry Hitchens.

With Villa already committed to an end-of-season tour to Russia, there was no time to play the final in the spring of 1961 and it was scheduled to be played in the first two weeks of the next season. By then, however, Villa would be without their leading scorer. Hitchens had fulfilled his never-doubted potential in 1960-61, scoring 42 goals and breaking into the England team as a result. Italian giants Inter Milan soon came to learn of the fast and powerful striker in Villa's frontline and made both the club and the player offers that they could not turn down. For Hitchens, the package was reported to include a car, a flat, bonuses and a signing-on fee of around £12,000. For Villa the fee was £60,000, almost three times the price Eric Houghton had paid for the striker three-and-a-half years before.

It would not be easy for Villa to replace a player who had scored 96 goals in 160 appearances in claret and blue. For Mercer the loss was particularly frustrating, as Hitchens had been something of a personal prodigy. The Villa manager had analysed the young striker's game at close quarters, playing alongside him in Villa's forward line on a tour of Scandinavia. Mercer had assessed Hitchens' strengths and weaknesses and had helped him to improve his game.

Hitchens was one of a number of young players to make impressive progress under Mercer's tutelage at Villa Park. Charlie Aitken, Alfie Hale, Alan Baker, Harry Burrows and Jimmy McMorran would all be given their chance in the team nicknamed 'Mercer's Minors' by the press. By contrast, stalwarts like Johnny Dixon, Nigel Sims and Peter McParland were coming to the end of their Villa Park careers. Dixon would, in fact, make his final appearance for the club on the same spring day in 1961 that saw Aitken, then just a promising full back, make his debut.

To supplement his young stars and fill the void left by Hitchens' departure, Mercer signed Derek Dougan from Blackburn for £15,000 in July 1961. Dougan, however, was cup-tied for the League Cup final against Rotherham United, which was to be played over two legs in the late summer of 1961, so it was left to 17-year-old Ralph Brown to lead the line in the first leg at Millmoor. Villa were poor and deservedly lost 2-0, which prompted Mercer to put his players on a £90 bonus to win the final.

Whether it was due to financial incentive or perhaps just professional pride, Villa produced a much-improved display in the second leg. Mercer left out Brown and switched McParland to centre forward, bringing in Harry Burrows in the Irishman's usual outside-left position. Two goals in two second-half minutes – the first by Alan O'Neill, the second by Burrows – brought Villa back on terms and forced extra-time. The Midlanders had 30 minutes to beat their Division Two opponents, and early in the second period McParland netted after a goalmouth scramble to clinch the new League Cup.

Shortly after the win over Rotherham, Aston Villa reported a profit of almost £20,000, which was a marked improvement on the £16,000 loss

50 Greatest Players

GERRY HITCHENS   Centre forward

Born: Rawnsley, 8 October 1934

Joined Aston Villa: 1957   **From:** Cardiff City

Appearances: 160   **Goals:** 96

Left Aston Villa: 1961   **For:** Inter Milan

The football career of Gerry Hitchens is one that is ripe for a sporting biopic. It is a tale that begins in the modest environs of Kidderminster Harriers, following a stint as a miner, and takes in spells with six clubs in three countries, including a season with the mighty Internazionale of Milan, not to mention a spell in the army and national service of a different kind with the England football team. In the midst of this varied career, Gerry arrived at Aston Villa in 1957 as an unproven hopeful after three seasons with Cardiff City. He was fast and strong, but his touch was erratic and his finishing unreliable. Villa fans were quick to question Eric Houghton's judgement for investing the sum of £22,500 in a raw recruit who was unavailable for full-time training due to his National Service commitments.

It was not until 1959, with Villa in Division Two and after much hard work on the training ground with Joe Mercer, that Gerry finally began to fulfil his obvious potential. Villa were promoted at the end of the season and the blond-haired Midlander, who had evaded Villa's scouts as a youngster, was top scorer. With his confidence high, Gerry took Division One by storm the following season, netting 42 times and guiding Villa to the League Cup final. A call-up to England colours duly followed and with it the attention of Internazionale, who made both player and club an offer too good to refuse.

of the previous year. With Mercer apparently making progress with his young team, the future looked bright. However, success in football is never more than transient, and after finishing seventh in 1962, Villa entered a downturn over the next two years. Fifteenth place was followed by an even worse showing that saw the Midlanders end the 1963-64 campaign fourth from bottom. In between, Villa had reached a second League Cup final, but defeat to Birmingham City did not go down well with the fans, who grew increasingly disgruntled with both their club and its manager. In December 1963, Mercer's five-year contract expired and after extended negotiations the two parties eventually agreed a new deal. However, defeat to Fourth Division

50 Greatest Players

NIGEL SIMS   Goalkeeper

Born: Coton-in-the-Elms, 9 August 1931

Joined Aston Villa: 1954   **From:** Wolverhampton Wanderers

Appearances: 310

Left Aston Villa: 1964   **For:** Peterborough United

For the better part of seven seasons, Nigel Sims was Aston Villa's regular and reliable No. 1. He was a powerfully built, brave and agile goalkeeper who was regarded by many as Villa's best custodian since the days of Sam Hardy before World War One. Sims was one of a clutch of emergency signings made by Eric Houghton as he attempted to steer his team away from the relegation places in the spring of 1956. For Sims it was the chance to play regular first-team football, having spent the previous six years as understudy to Bert Williams at Molineux. Nigel took his chance with gusto and played a full role in Villa's successful fight against relegation. The following season he was instrumental in success of another kind, helping his new team to FA Cup honours against Manchester United at Wembley.

Aldershot in the FA Cup left the fans irate. Shortly afterwards Mercer found himself walking round the pitch at a Villa home match and was shocked by the abuse being hurled his way: 'Apples and orange peel hit me. I had never had the bird in my life before and it hurt,' recounted Mercer some years later. 'Should I turn and argue with them? No. I just kept plodding on, praying they would not knock my hat off.'

Despite his problems at Villa, Mercer remained popular both with the press and the FA. He was England's U-23 manager and Alf Ramsay's right-hand man. However, at Villa Park the pressures were getting to him and, in July 1964, he resigned on grounds of ill health. Mercer had been frustrated by Villa's lack of progress, but it was also clear that, tactically, the team had stagnated, too. They had failed to move with the times, and in particular the advent of new tactical systems like 4-4-2. Under Mercer, Villa still persisted with the WM formation and would frequently find themselves outmanoeuvred by teams who employed four midfielders and overlapping full backs.

Dick Taylor replaced Mercer as manager, but he was unable to lift the malaise that had taken hold at Villa Park in the early 1960s. In Tony Hateley

50 Greatest Players

PETER McPARLAND Outside left

Born: Newry, County Down, 25 April 1934

Joined Aston Villa: 1952   **From:** Dundalk

Appearances: 341   **Goals:** 120

Left Aston Villa: 1962   **For:** Wolverhampton Wanderers

Peter McParland will forever be remembered as the player who got away with the most controversial challenge in FA Cup final history. The Irishman's shoulder charge on Ray Wood left the Manchester United keeper poleaxed and effectively meant the Reds were down to ten men. What is often forgotten, however, is that the Villa forward also scored both his team's goals in a 2-1 win. McParland played both at centre forward and inside forward, but it was from the left wing that he was most effective. Fast over the ground and with a powerful shot in either foot, he was the scourge of Division One defences during the 1950s and early 1960s. A favourite tactic was for his wing partner, Les Smith, to deliver the ball right across the pitch, whereupon the Irishman would pounce at the far post. His heading ability was unusually good for a winger and he was strong enough to withstand the physical challenges of the most brutal of 1950s full backs.

McParland joined Villa from Irish side Dundalk in 1952 for a fee of around £4,000, and by the time he departed for Wolves ten years later he had scored 120 goals and played his part in the Division Two title of 1960 and the League Cup triumph a year later.

the club had, at least, managed to find a worthy successor to Gerry Hitchens. Hateley scored 20 goals in 1964-65 as he helped Villa climb to Division One safety after an appalling start to the season. However, there was no disguising the problems at Villa Park, and it was revealing that, at season's end, Ron Wylie chose to join relegated Birmingham City despite being a highly valued player at the peak of his game.

Relegation Becomes Reality

Villa finished in 16th place in the spring of 1966, but more worryingly the club continued to lose its best players. Phil Woosnam – a Wales international wing half, headed for America and Hateley left for Chelsea in a £100,000 deal. Taylor would get only a small fraction of these fees to buy replacements.

In their last season together at Villa Park, Hateley had scored 28 league and cup goals, while Woosnam had netted 20.

Without their two most reliable goalscorers, Villa unsurprisingly found themselves in trouble during the opening weeks of the 1966-67 season, and by Christmas the Midlanders were struggling down in 17th place. Sprint coach Mike Rawson was taken on to improve the players' fitness, and for a time in the spring it looked as though Villa would avoid relegation.

Victory over rivals Stoke left Villa five points clear of the drop zone towards the end of March. However, just when it seemed as though the Midlanders' luck had changed, their rivals ran into form and the Easter results all went against Taylor's team. By 1 April Villa were back in the relegation places and, after collecting just two points from their final seven games, they closed their campaign with a 4-2 defeat against Everton that

Great Managers – 1958-64

JOE MERCER

Joe Mercer's reign at Villa Park was not an easy one. He joined a club facing relegation, where ambition was high but success, aside from the 1957 FA Cup final, had been elusive. The former Arsenal star had already enjoyed modest success in charge at Sheffield United, but he was unable to avert Villa's slide toward Division Two in the spring of 1959. It was a huge disappointment to the fans, but it gave Mercer the opportunity to rebuild his team away from the limelight. New players arrived, mostly defenders, and old ones were taught new tricks ... most notably the importance of disciplined defending throughout the team.

Mercer placed great importance upon defending and insisted on players covering and closing down. However, it would be wrong to paint Mercer as an overly conservative manager and he greatly improved Villa's attacking potency by personally nurturing the considerable, but previously erratic, talents of Gerry Hitchens. The manager's efforts proved worthwhile. Hitchens' goals combined with an improved defence to propel Villa to promotion and the Division Two championship at the first attempt. The following season brought further success, with a ninth-place finish and victory in the inaugural League Cup final. Joe also earned praise for continuing the trend started by Eric Houghton of blooding young talent, and the likes of Charlie Aitken, Harry Burrows and Alan Baker all rose to prominence during his reign.

However, the League Cup success proved to be the major achievement of Joe Mercer's Villa Park sojourn, and when a largely uneventful 1962-63 season was followed by a worrying drop to 15th place, his critics set to work. An embarrassing FA Cup defeat against Aldershot gave the snipers ammunition, and soon Villa's manager lost the support of the crowd. Mercer began to suffer ill health and in 1964 he left the club.

50 Greatest Players

TONY HATELEY Centre forward

Born: Derby, 13 June 1941

Joined Aston Villa: 1963   **From:** Notts County

Appearances: 148   **Goals:** 86

Left Aston Villa: 1966   **For:** Chelsea

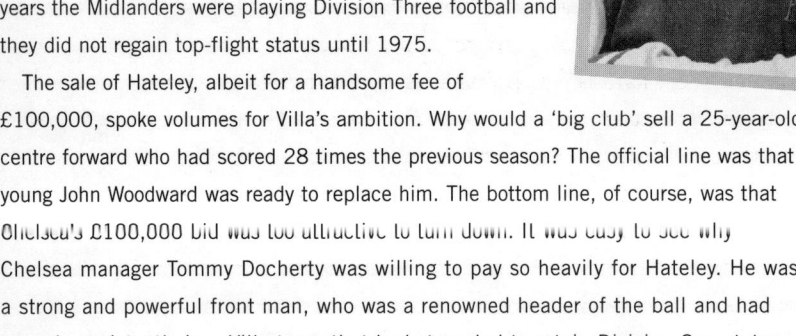

Tony Hateley won nothing at Villa but the striker's contribution to the Villa story is significant, although his importance only truly became apparent when he left the club in the autumn of 1966. Hateley's departure left Villa without a reliable goalscorer and, predictably, the club was relegated six months after. It was the start of a disastrous spell for Aston Villa. Within three years the Midlanders were playing Division Three football and they did not regain top-flight status until 1975.

The sale of Hateley, albeit for a handsome fee of £100,000, spoke volumes for Villa's ambition. Why would a 'big club' sell a 25-year-old centre forward who had scored 28 times the previous season? The official line was that young John Woodward was ready to replace him. The bottom line, of course, was that Chelsea's £100,000 bid was too attractive to turn down. It was easy to see why Chelsea manager Tommy Docherty was willing to pay so heavily for Hateley. He was a strong and powerful front man, who was a renowned header of the ball and had scored consistently in a Villa team that had struggled to retain Division One status.

confirmed their demotion. Taylor soon departed, paying the price for the mistakes of others as well as his own.

After the Everton game, Tom Duckworth in the *Sports Argus* said: 'On this performance there is a tremendous rebuilding job to be done at Villa Park and the present side certainly would not get far in Division Two.' The fans directed their protests at the board, booing the directors who they blamed for the demise of their club.

The truth, of course, was that Villa had simply stagnated. The club had neither a truly modern and effective scouting network nor an effective coaching system. They needed a high-profile manager, too, not to mention a more ruthless attitude towards business and transfers. A complete overhaul both on and off the field was required before Aston Villa Football Club would be in a position to move forward again. And that ... would take time.

Chapter Six: 1967-80
From Bournemouth to Barcelona

After seven seasons of relative struggle in the rarefied air of English football's top flight, Aston Villa prepared to reacquaint themselves with Division Two in the summer of 1967. On the eve of their return below stairs, chairman Mr Norman L. Smith declared: 'I appreciate that the fans have had little to enthuse over in recent times... I make no rash promises, but I pledge the wholehearted efforts of everyone connected with Aston Villa to put the club back in its rightful position as quickly as possible.'

The trouble was, that after a half a century characterized as much by disappointment and mediocrity as by success and silverware, nobody was entirely sure where Aston Villa's rightful place was any longer. The glory days of the 1890s and early 20th century were a distant memory in the minds of only the oldest supporters by now, while there were plenty of fans for whom the last major success, in 1957, was ancient history.

The unenviable task of rebuilding Villa's fortunes fell to Tommy Cummings, who was appointed as Dick Taylor's successor. Cummings had caught the eye after leading Mansfield Town into Division Three, and he quickly formulated a plan to bring success back to Villa inside five years. However, after successive defeats in his first two games in charge, Cummings may have wanted to revise his forecast. His first task was to rebuild a forlorn squad that was low on morale.

New players duly arrived, with Preston duo Brian Greenhalgh and Brian Godfrey among the first to sign for Cummings. John Dunn, Tommy Mitchison and Dick Edwards further boosted the squad, and a mid-season revival helped move Villa away from trouble at the foot of the table. However, despite their relative resurgence, Villa remained both inconsistent and defensively flawed. At the end of the season the Midlanders sat an embarrassing 16th in the table. Improvement was needed and fast, although it would not be easy, since the club was in a precarious financial position and trouble was simmering in the boardroom once more.

Cummings attempted to improve his attacking options by signing Blackburn winger Mike Ferguson for £50,000 in the summer of 1968. It was a deal that took the manager's spending to £200,000 in a year, but there was no instant return on this sizeable investment. Villa began the 1968-69 season appallingly.

Five points were taken from the first ten games, and when an own goal gave Preston victory at Villa Park on 9 November, Villa were sent to the foot of the table and Cummings was given his cards.

Sacking the manager, however, could not provide a cure for the deep-seated problems that had been allowed to fester for too long at Villa Park, and Cummings' dismissal cut little ice with the fans, who pointed the finger of blame unerringly in the direction of the directors' box. The club's chairman, Norman Smith, sat at the head of an aging five-man board, which included several members in their 70s. The Shareholders' Association had long campaigned for representation on the board, and they finally got their way when 40-somethings Bob Mackay and Roy Ladbroke were granted directorships. However, an injection of relative youth could not solve the club's financial malaise and it was clear that radical action was required.

Former player George Edwards gave his view on the current crisis: 'Once the air at Villa Park used to be electric and the whole place was alive. Now match days seem like an afternoon out for the directors, while the fans feel like interlopers ... all this is going to take a lot to put right.'

It was becoming increasingly obvious that a share issue was Villa's best chance of salvation. It was something the club had successfully avoided since the original issue of 2,000 five-pound shares back in 1896. The directors had, of course, resisted the idea, since they did not want to relinquish control of the club. On 21 November 1968, however, a board meeting ended in controversy when 71-year-old George Robinson resigned his seat. Following Robinson's resignation the board had announced that they would 'make available, by their resignation, such seats as new financial arrangements might require'. A supporters' meeting was called and Mr Brian Evans explained: 'I interpret this as meaning that Villa is up for sale. I now ask for someone among the shareholders and the industrialists of the Midlands to seize this opportunity.'

Speculation about who might effectively buy control of Villa was rife. The names in the frame were many and varied, and they included the chairmen of both Walsall FC and Atlanta Chiefs from America's NFL. The eventual buyer was London financier Mr Pat Matthews, who paid the Villa directors a reported £60 per share. Matthews would provide £50,000 to meet immediate needs and would refinance the club with a loan and a share issue. He also wanted to bring in Tommy Docherty as manager and Doug Ellis as chairman. Docherty had conveniently resigned as manager of Queens Park Rangers on 5 December, while Ellis was a successful businessman and a director of Birmingham City FC.

The potential appointment of Ellis met with disapproval from some supporters, who were less than happy about a man with Birmingham City associations taking charge at Villa Park. Despite the misgivings of the Shareholders' Association, Ellis was given the job of chairman when the new board was formed on 16 December 1968. The other directors were Harry Parkes, Bob Mackay and Harry Kartz. Parkes was a former Villa player who had made more than 300 appearances for the club in the first nine seasons of league football after the war.

The Doc Takes Charge

While Matthews and Ellis were busying themselves in the boardroom, the job of taking charge of the team had passed temporarily to coach Arthur Cox. The caretaker boss faced a thankless task, but did his best to rally his beleaguered troops. 'I want a team of fighters,' said Cox. 'Men who will give their all for Villa. Given this spirit I believe that we can avoid relegation.'

Unfortunately, such spirit was not immediately forthcoming from one of the club's most expensive players, Barrie Hole. Cox dropped the £60,000 midfielder for his first game in charge, and Hole walked out on the club. The Wales international would return, but his next appearance would be under a different manager.

The fans may have been reticent about Ellis' arrival, but they were buzzing with uncontainable anticipation at the announcement of the second half of Matthews' dream team on 18 December. Glaswegian Tommy Docherty had enjoyed a successful spell in charge at Chelsea and brought both hope and charisma in equal measure to Villa Park. It was the Doc's third club in a season that was not yet four months old, but he told reporters: 'I shall be quite happy to spend the rest of my football life with Villa, although you never can tell in this game... I have been presented with what I regard as my greatest challenge... Villa have been too long in the background.'

Docherty's first game in charge ended in a 2-1 victory over Norwich City, with Hole scoring on his return to the line-up after a club-imposed suspension. The win over the Canaries lifted Villa off the bottom of the table and was the first of five successive victories. Docherty's impact was instant. His charisma lifted the club and he became the figurehead of the new regime, with his media-friendly persona attracting great publicity. Crowds were on the increase, too, and for his first game in charge the attendance was 8,000 up on the previous home game. The fans showed their appreciation for the man who they hoped would lead them to safety with a massive ovation, and he duly obliged by guiding the club to the security of 18th place at season's end.

Bound for Division Three

The turnaround in Villa's fortunes appeared to be complete when the long-awaited share issue brought in around £200,000 in the summer of 1969. Docherty duly invested much of the money in new players, as Villa assembled a squad that, on paper at least, was too strong for Division Two. The summer newcomers were: Neil and Bruce Rioch (Luton Town, combined fee of £100,000); Ian 'Chico' Hamilton (Southend United, £40,000); and Pat McMahon (Celtic, free).

However, Villa started the new season poorly, losing five of their first six games. There was a suggestion that a taxing tour of North America in the summer of 1969 had left the team fatigued and ill prepared for the rigours of the new season. It took Villa ten attempts to register their first win of the season, but even that did not kick-start a run of good form, and by the turn of the year the Midlanders were still sat at the foot of Division Two. Despite the new players and Docherty's much-feted powers of motivation, Villa were in trouble once more. The Doc had tried tinkering with different systems and tactical approaches, but all to no avail.

Villa's biggest problem was that they were still without a genuine No. 9, having consistently failed to find a replacement for the long-departed Tony Hateley. Only three goals had come from the centre-forward position by January, and Villa were linked with a host of forwards, including Bobby Gould, Frank Clarke and Andy Lochhead. On 17 January, Aston Villa were beaten 5-3 by struggling Portsmouth at Villa Park. It was a disastrous result against a team just five points ahead of Villa, and the fans vented their spleen having watched their team surrender a game that had been there to win at half-time with the score at 2-2. Villa sat at the foot of the table. 'Walsall, Walsall, here we come!' chanted the Holte End.

Two days after the Portsmouth debacle Docherty was sacked. However, the fans were disgruntled at the departure of the charismatic Scot, and many of the 3,500 supporters who attended the reserve team game against Newcastle at Villa Park, came only to express their dissatisfaction with the board. Some fans chanted 'Ellis must go' and 'Bring back Docherty'. Others were less polite. Just to compound matters, there were even rumours of a dressing-room revolt, though Villa captain George Curtis refuted this suggestion and explained that the players were professionals: 'I know that we will buckle down to the job of making the club safe from relegation.'

The job of succeeding Docherty went to Vic Crowe, who had returned to the club as a coach the previous summer. The former Villa skipper, who had experienced management in America with Atlanta Chiefs, brought in

Great Managers – 1968-70

TOMMY DOCHERTY

Tommy Docherty may not have led Villa to any great success, but he is nonetheless a significant figure in the club's story. He came with a big reputation and a high media profile and departed after just over a year in which ambitions had been briefly re-ignited, even if there had been minimal progress on the field. Docherty was, in many ways, the figurehead of the brave new order that had been ushered in at Villa Park by businessman Pat Matthews and chairman Doug Ellis in the winter of 1968-69. He inherited a team that was struggling and gave it an immediate lift. Results improved, crowds increased and what had seemed like inevitable relegation was avoided. After the Doc's instant tonic had revived Villa in his first few months in charge, the fans were filled with optimism as they looked forward to the 1969-70 season.

However, things began badly and as hard as the Villa manager tried to shake the Midlanders out of their malaise, the deeper they sank. A 5-3 defeat against struggling Portsmouth at Villa Park on 17 January brought the curtain down on Tommy Docherty's brief reign with the Villans. At the end of the season Villa were relegated, although Docherty contended that it was not his fault and that he would have averted the decline if given a few more weeks. It was a view shared by many disappointed Villa fans.

Ron Wylie as first-team trainer and coach. 'Getting out of a position which causes such concern presents a great challenge to all of us at Villa Park, but there are 16 games to play and 32 points to be won,' explained an optimistic Crowe, adding: 'We shall be out to win every one, treating them as if they were all vital and I feel sure we can avoid relegation.'

Crowe's first game in charge ended with a creditable 1-1 draw, after Villa fought back from a goal down against fellow strugglers Preston in a fiercely contested game at Deepdale. Soon afterwards, the manager attempted to solve his team's palpable lack of a reliable centre forward by signing 28-year-old Leicester striker Andy Lochhead for £35,000. He was an experienced player who had tasted both relegation and FA Cup final defeat in one season with Leicester, and was desperate not to sample yet more footballing ignomiry.

However, as March reached its conclusion, Aston Villa were still stuck at the foot of the table and concern was growing about the imminent arrival of

Division Three football at Villa Park. Despite their appalling form, the men in claret and blue were still attracting respectable crowds of around 27,000 to their home games. As a result, Division Three chairmen began to contemplate the cash windfall that would come their way if Villa – complete with Division One-size gates – entered their league. 'I realize it's a tragedy for them,' said Mansfield's Joe Eaton, 'but frankly we'll be delighted to see them.'

Crowe's men gave themselves some hope with two victories in their final two league games, but to avoid the drop they still needed both Preston and Charlton to lose. Alas, the Addicks won and Villa were down. The new management team had made progress, but not enough to avoid relegation. At the end of the season, Tommy Docherty told the *Sports Argus* he was not to blame. 'If I had not been sacked the team would have been out of trouble two or three weeks ago ... sacking me when they did was one of Villa's mistakes. They should have let me go through to the end of the season and then sacked me if things had not worked out. As it was, the Villa board let me off the hook. I cannot be held responsible.'

Whoever was or was not to blame mattered little. The problem now was for Vic Crowe and his staff to extricate Aston Villa Football Club from the mire of Division Three. It would not be easy, particularly since confidence was at an all-time low. Thankfully, Villa had at least reached their nadir, and they began the season relatively brightly, beating Chesterfield 3-2 on their Division Three debut. Bruce Rioch scored two of the goals, but the influential midfielder was injured against Mansfield two weeks later and underwent two cartilage operations and a lengthy period on the sidelines.

Centre forward Chico Hamilton was also coming good after a difficult start to his career at Villa Park. He had been heavily criticized for his profligacy following his arrival from Southend. However, as his confidence grew his speed and powerful shot came to the fore, and an uncanny knack of scoring match-winning goals endeared him to the Villa faithful. Hamilton's form had improved markedly towards the end of the relegation season, and he began the Division Three campaign impressively.

By early December, Villa were challenging for promotion and were through to the semi-finals of the League Cup against Manchester United. The Midlanders prepared for the clash with their 1957 FA Cup final opponents by taking a trip to Spain. Morale was good, and during one practice session, directors Doug Ellis and Harry Parkes even joined in a five-a-side game. Back home, the build-up to the semi-final showdown with United was attracting backpage headlines, and George Best incensed the Villa players by declaring that the Red Devils were already 'through to the League Cup final…' Best added, 'I know we've still got to meet Aston Villa in the semi-final, but I'd be lying if I didn't say that, so far as I am concerned, we must be there already.'

Best's words provided all the team-talk Villa needed, and an Andy Lochhead goal at Old Trafford in the first leg gave the Midlanders a deserved lead. Ten thousand Villa fans began chanting 'Easy, easy!' and although United pulled back a goal through Brian Kidd, the Division Three side were in a strong position ahead of the return at Villa Park. A crowd of 62,500 attended and most watched in delight as goals from Lochhead and McMahon cancelled out Kidd's effort for United. Villa were through to a third League Cup final and would face Tottenham Hotspur at Wembley in the New Year.

Wembley Showdown with Spurs

Spurs were a strong side in the early 1970s, and they included Martin Peters, Martin Chivers and the considerable physical presence of Alan Gilzean in their line-up. Together this trio had already shared 61 goals by the time they took on Villa on 27 February. However, for most of the game the Midlanders matched their more illustrious opponents.

Villa hassled and harried, denying Spurs space in midfield, while in attack Chico Hamilton and Andy Lochhead were lively. In truth, Villa should have taken the lead. They had the better chances and even had a shot from Lochhead cleared off the line. Alas, in the final analysis, Tottenham's superior finishing proved to be decisive, and Chivers scored twice in three second-half minutes (78 and 81) to give his team a 2-0 victory.

Soon after the League Cup final, Crowe bought Birmingham Geoff Vowden for £14,000 as he attempted to inspire a final push towards promotion. Vowden was a 29-year-old forward who had been at the Blues for seven years. 'Villa appears to be a club who can only go one way – forward,' declared the 30-year-old striker. 'The next few years would seem to be an exciting period for them and I hope to be able to share in it.' Despite the addition of Vowden, Villa's promotion challenge floundered and they eventually finished fourth, seven points off promotion. It was a disappointing end to an otherwise encouraging season that had seen the club return record profits.

In the summer of 1971 Vic Crowe made just one major addition to his squad, signing 23-year-old winger Ray Graydon from Bristol Rovers in a deal that cost Villa £55,000 plus the services of Brian Godfrey. Graydon proved an inspired signing and his direct wing play and eye for a goal were to prove major assets to Villa for the next six seasons. Graydon would join skipper Bruce Rioch in a midfield that was simply too good for Division Three.

Villa began the season with a 3-1 home win over Plymouth before a crowd of 26,000, but in truth the Midlanders' early season form was stuttering. Nevertheless, they remained in touch with the league leaders, even rising to the summit of the table briefly in mid-October. It was, however, a glorious run of 13 wins in 15 games between mid-November and mid-March that propelled Villa back into Division Two as champions.

The green shoots of recovery were also evident at junior level, with Villa's youngsters lifting the FA Youth Cup after beating Liverpool 4-2 following extra-time in the final at Anfield. Frank Upton had been in charge of the club's youth section for two years, and he had produced an impressive team that had Brian Little as its star player. Upton had successfully converted the skilful North-easterner from a midfielder to a striker, and Little's season of success continued with a memorable first-team debut when he came into Crowe's team to score one goal and set up two more in a 5-1 win against Torquay that ensured Villa finished with a record 70 points. The Midlanders had also set an attendance record for Division Three when 48,110 supporters watched them beat Bournemouth 2-1 with goals from Lochhead and Vowden.

Back in Division Two

The momentum that had swept Villa to promotion in the spring of 1972 continued the following autumn, and after ten games Vic Crowe's men sat on top of Division Two. However, a dip in form followed and the next ten games brought just two victories. The remainder of the season would follow a similar pattern, with Villa winning spurts of games before enduring frustratingly barren spells. For the fans it was too much to bear – each time their hopes of promotion were raised, they were dashed by an inexplicable run of poor form, and when things went badly it was Crowe who inevitably got the blame. The Villa manager was mercilessly berated by disappointed fans, most notably when his team was defeated by promotion rivals Burnley in January.

At season's end Aston Villa sat in a creditable third place in Division Two, but with only two teams promoted and without the consolation of the play-offs, it mattered little. In any case, whatever the final league standings suggested, Villa were still some way off promotion, since they had finished 11 points behind runners-up Queens Park Rangers.

The battle for promotion had been overshadowed at Villa Park by yet more boardroom upheaval in the autumn of 1972. The season had begun in a blaze of controversy as reports emerged of a dispute between Doug Ellis and fellow director Harry Parkes. Rumours soon began to circulate that Alan Smith, the Warwickshire cricketer and England Test selector, would be

50 Greatest Players

ANDY LOCHHEAD   Centre forward

Born: Lenzie, Scotland, 9 March 1941

Joined Aston Villa: 1969   **From:** Leicester City

Appearances: 154   **Goals:** 44

Left Aston Villa: 1973   **For:** Oldham Athletic

Even back in the 1970s Andy Lochhead was considered an 'old fashioned' centre forward – a player from a bygone era when strength and stamina were as important as speed and skill. Lochhead arrived at Villa Park after suffering both relegation and FA Cup final defeat with Leicester, and he quickly found his new club heading for Division Three. However, the powerful Scotsman could find neither the goals nor the inspiration to stir a revival at Villa Park in the spring of 1970. He did, though, show commendable spirit and no little talent, and his efforts were greatly appreciated by both manager and team-mates. During his three-and-a-half seasons as a Villan, he earned the respect of both supporters and opponents.

He was a powerful player, who took his fair share of knocks and was particularly strong in the air. He was, however, a decent footballer with the ball at his feet, too, and could be unselfish, frequently making space for his more skilful team-mates. His best season in claret and blue came in 1971-72, when he was voted the Supporters' Player of the Year and Midland Footballer of the Year after a campaign that ended with Villa winning promotion to Division Two. 'Andy has done a tremendous job,' explained Ray Graydon who had formed a productive attacking combination with Lochhead. 'Besides being a fine target man you can be sure he will always be up there in the middle of it, fighting even for bad balls. He has taken some stick, but has helped the rest of us no end.'

put forward as a possible replacement for Parkes at a forthcoming AGM. However, Ellis' plans hit an unexpected glitch when his fellow directors turned on him and replaced him with Jim Hartley as their chair.

The ousted Villa chairman was down but not defeated, and he struck back at his former colleagues in spectacular fashion at an EGM soon afterwards. Ellis had two powerful allies.

Firstly, the supporters were behind him because of his modernizing programme that had seen the arrival of a succession of new players and the development of an impressive training facility at Bodymoor Heath. Secondly, and most significantly, Ellis was backed by Villa's most powerful shareholder and the man behind the 1968 take-over, Pat Matthews. Forty-three days after being apparently cast aside by his fellow directors, Ellis returned to power after receiving the backing of the shareholders. He also saw his four nominees replace the directors who had voted against him back in August.

Crowe Road Comes to an End

For most of the late 1960s and early 1970s, boardroom battles and takeovers would dominate events at Villa Park. However, the 1973-74 season was relatively free from such upheaval. Alas, it was also bereft of success, and after raising hopes with a good start to the campaign, which saw Villa in second place, just a point behind leaders Middlesbrough after 15 games, they fell away to finish a disappointing 14th. Gates were falling, too, and attendances of around 12,000 were not uncommon. The board steeled themselves for action, and shortly after the end of the season Vic Crowe and Ron Wylie were dismissed.

Speculation over Crowe's successor began instantly, with Brighton's controversial manager Brian Clough and recently dismissed England boss Sir Alf Ramsey among the leading contenders. Clough was, initially at least, the favourite to land the job, but his high media profile did little to endear him to the Villa board, and after some deliberation they decided to resist the temptation to give the job to the supporters' choice. Instead, Ellis and his colleagues chose to employ Ron Saunders, who had been sacked by Manchester City three weeks before.

The start of Saunders' reign at Villa Park coincided with the club's centenary season and a renewed determination to get back among English football's elite. The new manager made just one major signing in the summer of 1974, returning to his former club, Manchester City, to sign winger Frank Carrodus. However, after a somewhat insipid start to the season, which saw Villa draw each of their first three games 1-1, it looked as though Saunders may have underestimated the task at hand.

Villa were up against Manchester United in the battle for promotion, and the Old Trafford club were the early season pace-setters. Despite their difficult start, Saunders' team remained in touch with the leaders and after winning their first league game of the season with an emphatic 6-0 trouncing of Hull City, their promotion push soon gathered momentum. Having steadily climbed the table throughout the autumn, Villa were handily placed in third position at the start of November.

Saunders' methodical and pragmatic approach was paying dividends, and in addition to their ascendant path in Division Two, Villa were also making good progress in the League Cup. An impressive 3-0 win over Everton proved the highlight of the early rounds, and, by Christmas, Villa were in the semi-finals of what was fast becoming their favourite competition.

Back in the League Villa's form began to wobble and a run of consecutive defeats was extended to three matches with an undeserved reverse at Old Trafford in mid-November. Despite controlling the game and taking the lead, Villa went down 2-1 to their rivals, and by the turn of the year they were lagging behind the Red Devils in seventh place.

League Cup and Promotion Double

Saunders took drastic and innovative action to avert his team's slide down the table. He made the players follow a pre-season style training programme ahead of the FA Cup third-round tie against Oldham. It was a fresh start, a clean slate, and the players responded positively. Oldham were defeated, as were each of Villa's next three league opponents. In the midst of this fine run of form, the Midlanders took on Chester City in the first leg of the League Cup semi-final at Sealand Road.

Villa drew 2-2 against the Division Four side, with Graydon and teenage midfielder Bobby McDonald the scorers for the men in claret and blue. Graydon had become a major player in Saunders' team. He had scored the first goal of the new manager's reign and his direct style made him an integral part of a midfield that had been bolstered by the signing of Leighton Phillips from Cardiff for £100,000 in the autumn.

A crowd of 47,000 turned up at Villa Park for the second leg of the League Cup semi-final, which proved to be a nervous encounter. For a time it seemed that Villa had the game sewn up, with Keith Leonard scoring twice to put them into a 4-2 aggregate lead. However, the Villans lost concentration and conceded twice to hand Chester a lifeline. Thankfully, with ten minutes left on the clock, Brian Little struck the game's decisive goal, firing home after good work from McDonald to send Villa to Wembley.

Saunders' team was rapidly growing in confidence, and Villa warmed up for their League Cup final showdown with Norwich City by beating Manchester United in the league. This time the Villans had got their just reward for their superior team-play, with goals from Graydon and Aitken earning a deserved 2-0 victory over Tommy Docherty's team. Villa sat third in Division Two, with a game in hand over the leaders, as they made the trip to Wembley to take on the Canaries.

In truth, the all-Division Two showdown with Norwich proved, for the most part, to be decidedly forgettable. Villa were the slight favourites against their promotion rivals, and they started the stronger, dominating the game for long periods. However, it took until the 80th minute for the Midlanders to find a way past Norwich's former Villa keeper, Kevin Keelan. As the game entered its final ten minutes, Chris Nicholl directed a header past Keelan and towards the goal, but as the ball was about to cross the line, City defender Mel Machin repelled it with his hand. Graydon took the resultant penalty, which was saved by Keelan who pushed the ball onto the post. However, as the ball came back off the woodwork, Graydon closed in and scored at the second attempt. Skipper Ian Ross later confessed that he could not watch the penalty being taken. It proved to be the only goal of the game and Ross duly lifted the cup, while Saunders began to look forward to Aston Villa's debut in the UEFA Cup the following season.

Victory in the League Cup was only half of the story, and for Villa's centenary season to be a success Saunders would have to guide the Midlanders back into the top flight, too. The club's new manager did not disappoint, and 11 of the next 13 league games ended in victory. Promotion was assured when Villa beat Sheffield Wednesday 4-0 on 23 April, and they finished the season as runners-up to Manchester United.

Saunders declared: 'I came to Villa Park last June hoping to get the breaks and knowing that I would have to graft. I found the best supporters in the world and this is the best team and the best group of players I have ever been

in charge of. This has been the happiest season of my life. The Villa supporters are a truly incredible bunch of people.

'Before Christmas we used over 20 players, but from January onwards I think we had found our best team, I needed to call on only a minimum to see the season through. By then we had sorted ourselves out and really got to know each other ... we not only scored goals but were usually creating an abundance of chances.'

Saunders remained loyal to the players who had won promotion

In 1975, Villa's centenary season, captain Ian Ross, carried by keeper Jim Cumbes, holds aloft the League Cup.

when Villa returned to Division One after an absence of eight seasons in the autumn of 1975. The Midlanders were 50-1 to win the league, and the bookmakers looked to have the odds about right when, after three games, Villa had just one point and a goal difference of minus three. Things improved with back-to-back wins against Manchester City and Coventry City, but, as autumn turned to winter, indifferent results returned and it became apparent that Division One survival would represent a successful season.

A European Debut

Amid the battle for league points, there was at least the distraction of a European debut for Villa to look forward to in September 1975. Belgian side Royal Antwerp provided the opposition for a historic match played in unseasonably cold conditions in continental Europe. Villa were without both Carrodus and Little against Antwerp, but nevertheless dominated much of

50 Greatest Players

RAY GRAYDON   **Winger**

Born: Bristol, 21 July 1947

Joined Aston Villa: June 1971 **From:** Bristol Rovers

Appearances: 231 **Goals:** 81

Left Aston Villa: 1977 **For:** Coventry City

Ray Graydon was one of the few constants in the ever-changing Villa team of the mid-1970s. The diligent and skilful Bristolian played in three divisions, two League Cup finals and two promotion-winning teams during a six-year stay at Villa Park that took in the reigns of both Vic Crowe and Ron Saunders. Graydon was a fast and direct winger whose greatest gift was an unerring eye for goal. However, despite his conspicuous talent, he arrived at Villa Park at a relatively low ebb after a difficult spell that had seen his career stall somewhat following a bright start that had brought him England honours at youth level.

The £55,000 move from Villa's Third Division rivals Bristol Rovers soon revived Ray's fortunes, and he became an integral part of Crowe's team which won the Third Division championship in his first season at the club. However, his best spell as a Villan coincided with Ron Saunders' debut campaign of 1974-75. It was Villa's centenary season, and it ended in not only promotion but also League Cup success. Graydon was the club's top scorer with 27 goals; a total that included the only goal of the League Cup final win.

the first half and enjoyed the better of the early chances. However, against the run of play, Antwerp took the lead when Jos Heylighen struck a 30-yard free kick past Jim Cumbes. The home team's confidence grew markedly, and within minutes Austrian striker Karl Kodat had put them 2-0 up with a deflected shot from distance.

Two more Kodat strikes, both from distance, found the net to put the Belgians 4-0 up at half-time. Ray Graydon reduced the deficit with a potentially valuable away goal in the second half, but it proved no more than a consolation as Villa lost the return leg 1-0.

Aston Villa's first European campaign had faltered at the first hurdle, but both club and players had learned vital tactical lessons from defeat. For Jim Cumbes, the goalkeeper who was widely held culpable for Villa's away reverse, there would be no opportunity to make amends. Saunders had already invested £90,000 in Blackpool keeper John Burridge, who took charge of Villa's No. 1 jersey soon after the Antwerp defeat.

Gray Adds Colour to Villa Attack

Saunders' team building continued in 1975 with the signing of Scotland U-23 international Andy Gray from Dundee United for £110,000. Gray was still only 19 years old, but he had already shown himself to be a reliable and accomplished goalscorer. He had netted 26 times in his last full season in Scotland and he wasted little time making his mark south of the border. He opened his Villa account with a goal in a League Cup match against Manchester United at Villa Park and kept scoring for the remainder of the season.

Another important figure in the Villa story arrived at the club during the first half of the 1975-76 season. Dennis Mortimer was a 23-year-old midfielder of immense promise when he arrived from Coventry City for £175,000 in December 1975. However, like Gray, his youth was matched by an unusual wealth of experience, and he had already clocked up more than 200 appearances for the Sky Blues.

With his team now reinforced with a new goalkeeper, centre forward and midfielder, Saunders guided Aston Villa to a relatively comfortable 16th-place finish at the end of their first season back in Division One. It was a good start, but ambition had been stirred by the previous season's Double of League Cup and promotion.

The summer of 1976 was reported to be the hottest on record, but the high temperatures and drought warnings clearly did not affect Aston Villa's pre-season preparations. Saunders' team kicked off the 1976-77 with a torrent of goals, putting four past West Ham on the opening day of the season, and

50 Greatest Players

CHARLIE AITKEN   Defender

Born: Edinburgh, 1 May 1942

Joined Aston Villa: 1959   **From:** Edinburgh Thistle

Appearances: 660   **Goals:** 16

Left Aston Villa: 1976   **For:** New York Cosmos

Words like 'stalwart' and 'loyal servant' hardly do justice to the record-breaking Villa career of Charlie Aitken who arrived at Villa Park in 1959 and his 17-year stay took in 660 first-team appearances and six managers. Aitken joined Aston Villa from Hibernian junior side Edinburgh Thistle, and he was one of a number of young players to benefit from Joe Mercer's policy of giving youth its chance. Having progressed through the reserves at Villa Park, he made the breakthrough into the first team as an 18-year-old against Sheffield Wednesday in April 1961.

For most of his career Charlie played at left back, providing a stoic presence in an ever-changing backline. His greatest assets were his pace and stamina, and it was rare to find a winger who could match his athleticism. Having helped Villa to promotion in 1975, Charlie headed for America after one last season in Division One. He saw out his playing days with New York Cosmos playing alongside Pele.

going one better against Ipswich Town two weeks later. Three wins in the first four games took Villa to the top of the table, albeit briefly, in early September.

The Villans also made good progress in the League Cup during the late summer of 1976, and it was fast becoming clear that Saunders was assembling a team of considerable potential at Villa Park. Having already breezed past Manchester City 3-0, Villa defeated Norwich City 2-1 at Villa Park in a match that saw the debut of 17-year-old midfielder Gordon Cowans, who had risen through the junior ranks at Villa Park. Saunders' line-up was rapidly taking shape and was by now built around the central spine of Burridge, Chris Nicholl, Mortimer and Gray. In attack Villa were also now benefiting from the fit-again Brian Little, who had overcome the knee problems that had dogged him throughout the previous campaign and had formed an impressive partnership with Gray. Saunders continued to add to his promising young team, signing Scotland international Alex Cropley from Arsenal for £100,000 and drafting in teenage forward John Deehan during 1976.

Villa remained in touch with the league leaders throughout the early months of the season, but when they took on early pace-setters Liverpool at Villa Park on 15 December, it appeared that their chance had gone. The Merseysiders had a six-point lead over Villa, although they had played a game more, and Bob Paisley's team were the reigning league champions and UEFA Cup holders. However, when Andy Gray gave the home side an early lead with a trademark header, Villa's confidence ballooned. A brace of goals from Deehan and one from Little gave Villa a 4-0 lead after half an hour and, though Liverpool pulled a goal back, Gray struck again to close the scoring. Villa had beaten the leading lights of English football 5-1. It was an astonishing scoreline. Liverpool, who would win the European Cup at season's end, had only conceded three or more goals on seven occasions since 1962. Ron Saunders applauded the efforts of his players, but tried to avoid raising undue expectations: 'I'm hoping we'll be able to continue our challenge,' was all that the Villa manager would say.

However, Saunders' playing resources were wafer thin, and as good as his first XI was, there was little depth to his squad. An injury to an expensive signing like Gray or Mortimer invariably meant a call up for a teenage hopeful. By the end of the demanding Christmas programme, Saunders' team had slid down the table and were nine points adrift of Liverpool. An injury to Andy Gray, who had been Division One's top scorer during the first half of the season, undoubtedly played a part in Villa's mid-season crisis.

In the FA Cup, Villa enjoyed their best showing since 1957, progressing to the quarter-finals, where they lost 2-1 to Manchester United at Old Trafford. However, by then the Midlanders had already made it to one domestic Cup final. Victory over Queens Park Rangers, courtesy of a Brian Little hat-trick at Highbury, in a twice-replayed semi-final had earned Villa a place in the League Cup final for the third time in six years. However, the Wembley meeting with Everton on 12 May turned out to be something of a damp squib and ended goalless. The most memorable aspect on an otherwise forgettable day came when Andy Gray chose not to join Villa's lap of honour because he felt he hadn't played well enough. A day later, the 21-year-old Glaswegian became the first player to win both the PFA Young Player of the Year and Player of the Year awards.

The two League Cup finalists reconvened at Hillsborough four days after their first meeting and once more served up disappointing fare. This time there were at least two goals for the 55,000 assembled fans to enjoy, although Villa's goal in a 1-1 draw was scored by an Everton player. The Midlanders were making hard work of beating a team they had already defeated twice in the league without conceding a goal. When the two teams met for a third time there would have to be a winner, even if it meant the match at Old Trafford being decided by penalties.

Villa were without Gray for the League Cup final part 3, so Deehan filled in at centre forward and Graydon came in on the right of the attack and the reshuffled line-up fared reasonably well through the first half. Shortly before the interval, Bob Latchford fired home after team-mate Ken McNaught headed the ball into his path from a free kick. It looked for a long time as though the goal would prove to be decisive, and as the Everton rearguard stood firm in the face of relentless Villa pressure, tension began to build. With ten minutes remaining, the Midlanders got the goal their dominance deserved when Chris Nicholl fired home after a surging run.

Villa sensed victory, and when Brian Little profited from confusion in the Everton defence to fire home from a narrow angle two minutes later, it looked as though the job was done. However, an equalizer from Mick Lyons within a minute, took the game into extra-time. Penalties loomed as the game entered its 119th minute. Fortunately, the players and supporters were spared the tension of a spot-kick shoot-out when Brian Little made the most of hesitant Everton defending to net from Gordon Smith's cross. A 3-2 victory was no more than Villa deserved for their exertions in an epic cuptie that had finally sprung to life after five hours of football.

The demands of a marathon League Cup run undoubtedly took their toll on Villa's league performances, although once the cup was safely ensconced in the Villa Park trophy cabinet, the Villans focused their attentions back on the First Division, winning each of their next three games. Villa closed the campaign with a 4-0 win over West Brom to finish the season in a creditable fourth place. It was a commendable achievement for a young and emergent team who were the top flight's leading scorers with 14 more goals than champions Liverpool.

Barca Come to Villa Park

After finishing in the top four and winning the League Cup, Villa were now back in Europe, although for Saunders the league championship remained the primary goal. To this end, the Villa manager was given a transfer fund of more than £300,000, which he spent on three players in the summer of 1977. Since Villa already had a formidable attack, it came as no surprise that the new arrivals were all bought to reinforce a defence that had conceded 50 goals in the previous campaign. The new arrivals were goalkeeper Jimmy Rimmer from Arsenal; utility player John Gregory from Northampton Town; and defender Ken McNaught from Everton.

Despite the club's commendable investment in players, the 1977-78 domestic season proved a relative disappointment for Aston Villa. The league campaign got off to a mixed start, with victories and defeats in equal measure, while progress in both cups faltered in the early stages. A run of five victories in the final six games did at least haul Villa up the table to finish in a respectable eighth place, but it was in the UEFA Cup that the men in claret and blue produced their best performances.

Villa began their second campaign of European football with a tie against Fenerbahce of Turkey, and the Midlanders showed that they had learned much from the painful defeat to Antwerp two years earlier. Saunders' team overcame the Turks with relative ease, winning 4-0 at home and 2-0 in Istanbul. A brace of headers from Ken McNaught, his first goals for the club, earned Villa a 2-0 win at home to Polish side Gornik Zabrze in the next round, while in the return leg Villa played with commendable composure after conceding a first-half goal to the Poles. Despite a period of relentless pressure the defence held firm and an Andy Gray header eased tension and clinched a 3-1 aggregate victory.

It was, however, not until the third round that Villa faced a team with true European pedigree. Athletic Bilbao had been runners-up in the previous season's UEFA Cup and had a formidable record at home in Europe. The first leg was played on a rain-sodden Villa Park and, after 30 minutes of stalemate, Villa made the breakthrough when Alex Cropley's corner was palmed into the net by former Spanish international goalkeeper José Irabar. Late in the second half Deehan doubled Villa's lead when he headed home Gidman's cross. In the return, Villa played with an assurance that belied their inconsistent domestic form. The Midlanders deservedly took the lead via a Mortimer header shortly before half-time and the tie was effectively over. Bilbao now had to score four times in little over 45 minutes. They managed just one, and even that did not arrive until the game's dying minutes.

Victory over Bilbao took Villa into the quarter-finals of the UEFA Cup, which were to be played in March after a winter break. Saunders had wanted to test his team against the best and now he would get the chance, as Villa were drawn against Catalan giants Barcelona.

Saunders and his men faced a Barca team that included the incomparable Johan Cruyff as its creative fulcrum, and the Dutchman scored the opening goal in a 2-2 draw at Villa Park. A crowd of 80,000 attended the second leg in the giant Nou Camp stadium, and for 20 minutes Villa held their own. Alas, just as it seemed as though the Midlanders were in with a chance of snatching an unlikely victory, John Gidman was sent off for aiming a retaliatory kick at Barca's Jesus de la Cruz, and, as he left the field, it seemed that so too did

Great Matches

UEFA CUP QUARTER-FINAL   **Villa Park, 1 March 1978**

Aston Villa 2   **Barcelona 2**   **Attendance: 50,000**

McNaught   Cruyff
Deehan   Zuviria

On 1 March 1978 Aston Villa FC exorcized the last of the ghosts from their nightmare spell as a 'lower division side' in the early 1970s as they clashed with the mighty Barcelona in a UEFA Cup quarter-final. The Villa were back. Ron Saunders' team had already defeated Spanish opposition en route to the last eight, having disposed of Athletic Bilbao in impressive fashion in the previous round. A Barcelona team which had Johan Cruyff as its playmaker would, of course, be a rather different proposition. For Saunders the game offered the chance for him to test his skills against one of football's greatest coaches, Rinus Michels – the man behind 'total football' and the great Dutch teams of the 1970s.

Cruyff had already announced his intention to quit European football at the end of the season, so the match at Villa Park would be his last in England. Cruyff scored the game's opening goal, firing a shot past Rimmer from the edge of the box. A second Barca goal arrived late in the second half, and with his team two goals up and with only 11 minutes remaining Cruyff left the field. However, as the Dutch maestro took his place on the bench, Villa pulled a goal back through McNaught and with three minutes left, the home side grabbed an equalizer. A crowd of 80,000 attended the second leg and for 20 minutes Villa held their own. However, when John Gidman was sent off for retaliation it seemed as though Villa's chance had gone. The ten men rallied and took the lead early in the second half. Thereafter, the Catalans laid siege to Jimmy Rimmer's goal and Villa's resistance was broken in the 66th minute. The home side won the match 2-1 and the tie 4-3 on aggregate. Defeat was no disgrace, and Villa had gained valuable experience which they would put to good use during their next foray into Europe in 1981-82.

Aston Villa: Rimmer, D. Evans (A. Evans), Smith, Phillips, McNaught, Mortimer, Gregory, Little, Deehan, Cowans, Carrodus.

Barcelona: Artola, Ramos, Migueli, Olmo, De La Cruz, Costas, Zuviria, Rexach, Cruyff (Juanjo), Asensi, Fortes.

Villa's hopes of glory. However, to their credit, Saunders' team rallied and early in the second half they took the lead when Brian Little profited from hesitancy in the Barca rearguard. At the other end Jimmy Rimmer had been offering stoic resistance, but having held the lead for ten minutes Villa's defence was finally breached in the 66th minute. The giants of Barcelona had won through to the semi-finals, but they had been pushed all the way by a promising Aston Villa team that emerged with not only credit but also with valuable experience.

The 1978-79 season proved something of an anti-climax for a Villa side unable to replicate either the drama of the clash with Barca or the satisfaction of the 1977 League Cup success. To all intents and purposes the Midlanders trod water, finishing eighth in Division One with 46 points, just as they had in 1977-78. Off the field there had been the now-perennial boardroom changes and ructions, with the topic of a new, improved and extended contract for Ron Saunders dividing the directors in the summer of 1978. Saunders had wanted a six-year contract and had been tempted to take the vacant manager's job at Leeds rather than wait around. In the end he stayed and chairman Harry Kartz granted the manager a new deal.

Saunders also found himself at the centre of a dispute with one of his leading players. John Gidman was an England international and a popular figure with the crowd. However, he reacted badly to public criticism from Ron Saunders after a League Cup defeat to Luton and handed in a transfer request. The request was eventually withdrawn, but Gidman would soon be on his way out of Villa Park, together with a host of high-profile stars.

Saunders Rebuilds

By the summer of 1979, Saunders had begun a massive team-rebuilding programme, as he attempted to inject new life into his team. In several cases the players departing had struggled to get on with Saunders and his disciplined ways, while in others it was simply a case of a good offer for a player the manager considered to be expendable. John Gidman, Brian Little, Andy Gray, John Gregory and John Deehan would all soon depart during a year of considerable change at Villa Park.

Gray was the most high profile of the departees, and his move to Wolves for a British record £1.4 million represented a huge gamble on Saunders' part. The controversial Villa manager put his faith in youth, signing 24-year-old Tony Morley from Burnley and introducing the likes of Gary Shaw, Lee Jenkins and Brendan Ormsby to first-team action. In addition, Grimsby striker Terry Donovan arrived for £80,000 and, once Gray completed his move to Wolves, more money was invested in the likes of Everton's Mike Pejic, Hibs midfielder Des Bremner and Ipswich forward David Geddis. Saunders had also brought in young keeper Nigel Spink from Southern League Chelmsford, and the 19-year-old became the official reserve keeper following the departure of Jake Findlay. 'If Jimmy [Rimmer] ever does get injured, then I have every

50 Greatest Players

BRIAN LITTLE   Forward

Born: Peterlee, 25 November 1953

Joined Aston Villa: 1971   **From:** Durham Boys

Appearances: 302   **Goals:** 82

Left Aston Villa: 1980 (retired)

Brian Little was a skilful and elegant forward who possessed a sublime touch and a rare ability to both create and score goals. Had he played ten years earlier, he would have been described as an inside forward, while had he played 20 years later he would have been a withdrawn- or split-striker, playing in the 'hole' behind the front man. He was, in essence, the Dennis Bergkamp of his day. Little arrived at Villa Park as an apprentice, moving to Birmingham as a teenager along with his brother Alan, who was a promising midfielder. However, it soon became evident that Brian was the more talented of the Little brothers, and though Alan did make three first-team appearances for Villa, it was his older sibling who made the greatest impact in a claret and blue shirt.

Brian made his senior debut in the penultimate game of the 1971-72 season, coming in to Vic Crowe's Third Division championship-winning team for the clash with Torquay at Villa Park. It proved to be a memorable occasion, with the young player scoring once and setting up two goals in a 5-1 win. Little, who had been the star of Frank Upton's FA Youth Cup-winning team of 1972, had an injury-curtailed career, but still clocked up 60 league goals at Villa, many of which arrived via a fruitful partnership with Andy Gray in the mid-1970s.

confidence that Nigel will be an adequate replacement,' explained a prophetic Saunders.

As the Villa manager set about his team restructuring, changes were also afoot in the boardroom. Doug Ellis found himself at odds with chairman Harry Kartz and the powerful Bendalls, Ron and Donald. Ellis brought a resolution to have his trio of opponents removed from the board. However, despite support from shareholders, his plan failed, largely due to the Bendalls' own sizeable shareholding. Ellis resigned and sold the bulk of his own shares to Ron Bendall. He explained that he had done so in the best interests of the club, but he pledged that he would set the money aside in case Aston Villa needed him again in the future.

50 Greatest Players

ANDY GRAY **Centre forward**

Born: Glasgow, 20 November 1955

Joined Aston Villa: 1975, 1985 **From:** Dundee United, Everton

Appearances: 210 **Goals:** 78

Left Aston Villa: 1979, 1987 **For:** Wolves, WBA

Andy Gray is among the most talented centre forwards ever to have worn the famous claret and blue jersey. The charismatic Scot became an instant hero at Villa Park, where his rugged, all-action style made him a firm favourite with supporters following his move from Dundee United in 1975. However, when it seemed that both player and club were on the verge of great things, Gray left for Wolves in a record-breaking transfer.

Andy's move to Molineux stunned the fans, but it earned Villa a £1.3 million profit on a player they had paid just £110,000 for four years earlier. Gray had been signed by Ron Saunders as a 19-year-old, having caught the eye with 26 goals in his last full season in Scotland, and he wasted little time making his mark south of the border. He opened his Villa account with a goal against Manchester United at Villa Park and such was his progress that 18 months later he became the first player to win both the PFA Young Player of the Year and Player of the Year awards in the same year.

Full Scotland caps followed, and with Villa enjoying a good run in the UEFA Cup in 1977-78, Andy's reputation and experience grew immeasurably. However, at the end of the following season came the move to Wolves. He would return to Villa Park after an absence of six years, but in the interim he had missed out on the club's greatest success of the 20th century with the championship and European Cup triumphs of 1981 and 1982. Andy's scoring potency had also diminished during his years away from Villa Park and he scored just five times in 54 appearances before moving to West Brom.

Despite all of the changes of personnel, both on the field and in the boardroom, Villa finished a creditable seventh in Division One in the spring of 1980. However, their tally of 51 goals in 42 league games was far from impressive, and it was clear that neither Geddis nor Donovan was going to be Villa's long-term No. 9. Saunders would have to find a new striker if he was to fulfil his ambitions at Villa Park.

Chapter Seven: 1980-87
From Success to Despair

The first full season of the new decade heralded only one major signing, but little did Villa fans realize what an impact that player would have on their lives. Peter Withe, a 28-year-old striker who had won the league title with Nottingham Forest in 1978, was lured away from Newcastle United for a club-record £500,000 fee. He would prove to be worth every penny.

Villa enjoyed a good start to the season, winning three and drawing one of their first four fixtures. Withe had already proved that he would be a handful for opposition defences and he found the ideal strike partner in the light-footed Gary Shaw. With his team in second place after 12 matches, Saunders refused to make any rash predictions about their fate. 'We have got off to a good start,' he told reporters in Birmingham. 'But it is far too early to start making forecasts. We must wait and see.'

Wary though the manager was, Villa continued to tag the Division One front-runners. By the beginning of January they were jostling for the leadership with the country's two best teams, Liverpool and Ipswich Town, although defeat by the latter in the third round of the FA Cup was not the most encouraging way to see in the New Year.

It hardly mattered. A similarly early exit from the League Cup enabled Saunders to concentrate his men on the league campaign, and the reward for their focus was a splendid run of seven victories – beginning with a win over Liverpool. The champions boasted a wealth of international talent that had been responsible for stocking the Anfield trophy cabinet in recent seasons, but they were no match for a Villa side rock solid at the back. Ken McNaught was outstanding that day, playing Kenny Dalglish off the park. Withe scored once, but certainly the more memorable was Dennis Mortimer's goal, a brilliant strike which flew into the back of the net after the captain's solo run scythed Liverpool in two.

Villa also beat Coventry City, Manchester City, Everton, Crystal Palace, Wolves and Sunderland before

Peter Withe joined the Villans in a £500,000, club record transfer.

a 3-3 draw with Manchester United put a halt to the winning run. By now they were the league's clear leaders, with Ipswich running them a close second. Excitement was mounting among the supporters, who could see that this was the club's best chance in years to reclaim the league championship they last won in 1910.

A crowd of 47,988 turned up to watch the midweek derby against West Bromwich Albion at Villa Park – the biggest attendance of the season – and they were treated to an 88th-minute goal by Withe after a poor back pass by Brendan Batson. It may not have been the prettiest of victories, but it kept the team on the right track as they approached the fixture many thought would be the season's title decider – the home match against Ipswich Town.

Ipswich manager Bobby Robson had already conceded that, should Villa win on 14 April, the title would almost certainly bypass Portman Road. The fixture's importance was not lost on the fans either, as 47,495 turned up to watch, although the vast majority of them would go home with leaden hearts, as one of Villa's weakest defensive displays of the season allowed Ipswich to take a 2-0 lead. Although the players had several opportunities to re-establish themselves, Gary Shaw's goal in the dying minutes was too late to save the game, and Ipswich were now just a point behind with a game in hand.

Nervous Wait for the Title

Saunders refused to admit defeat. He was interviewed after the match by a television reporter, who opened with the ill-advised line: 'Well, you've probably lost the title, how do you feel?' The typically deadpan response from Villa's manager did much to lift local spirits: 'Do you want to bet against us? We gave Ipswich a goal start, but then we created enough chances to win by a street. It's our own fault, but it makes it interesting, doesn't it?' Saunders' exterior may have been cool, but the supporters were getting distinctly edgy. The attendance dropped dramatically for Villa's match against Nottingham Forest four days later, although by this time the players had rediscovered their missing form and cruised to a 2-0 victory. After gaining another valuable point away to Stoke City, goals from Evans, Shaw and Withe ensured the last home game of the season was an occasion to savour with a 3-0 destruction of Middlesbrough. It meant the team required just one point from their final encounter, against Arsenal, to secure the title.

Half of Birmingham seemed to decamp to North London on 2 May to watch in hope. They were within touching distance of the title, so close that just a final kick would pull them away from the outstretched arms of Ipswich, but the plot was to take one final twist. Villa produced one of their most impotent displays of the season – rarely did it look as though they would score – and went down 2-0. It was a desperately disappointing result, but no sooner had heads begun to drop than the news filtered through that Ipswich had lost to Middlesbrough. It meant they were out of contention – and Aston Villa had won the league title for the first time in 71 years.

The players were lauded, with Tony Morley in particular winning handsome praise for his contribution to the campaign. The skilful winger had baffled the opposition all season, with his silky skills, scored a hatful of goals and set up many more for Shaw and Withe. Of course, Saunders was also paid his due for completing an incredible transformation at Villa Park. David Harrison, writing in the *Evening Mail*, said: 'The popular image of the team chief is a teak-hard disciplinarian who rules by fear. But there is more substance to the man than that. He can motivate players with encouragement and knows that sympathy and compassion also have their place in football.'

Harrison's colleague, Ray Matts, wrote: 'Villa have won more matches than anyone else, lost fewer than most, scored about the same as their main rivals and conceded fewer. They have been one of the most entertaining and exciting sides to watch, home and away. They have done the second city proud and struck a magnificent blow for West Midlands football in general.'

A crowd of around 100,000 greeted the open-topped bus carrying the triumphant Villa squad as it toured Birmingham city centre with the Division One trophy. It was a glorious day for everybody connected with the club – in fact the only worrying development seemed to be Manchester United's interest in Saunders. Short of a manager, the Old Trafford directors were known to be keen on the Villa boss, but he was quick to put a stop to speculation that he might leave. 'I have repeated all along that I wanted to spend the rest of my managerial career at Villa Park and I will say it again,' he said. 'Although I am flattered by United's approach, my feelings about my future at Villa have not changed.'

It had been the perfect end to a perfect season. And if there was ever a year to become a sports fan, this was it. While the country struggled to clamber out of its worst economic recession since World War Two, the back pages of newspapers provided a

The Villa players celebrate the club's first title success in 71 years.

welcome diversion from preceding tomes of discontent. As a nation, millions were enthralled by the summer-time heroics of Ian Botham as the England cricket team came from behind to win the Ashes. Football drifted from consciousness, for a few weeks at least, but the feel-good factor lingered and Birmingham was abuzz as temperatures rose.

The days were still warm when the new season arrived on 29 August. Shirtsleeved supporters, hopeful of witnessing a keen defence of the title, were already looking forward to the following summer when many of them would be travelling to Spain to enjoy a month of football, as England qualified for their first World Cup in 12 years. What price glory on a hot night in Europe?

Taking Success One Step Further

Well, best-laid plans and all that. From finding themselves perched at the top of the domestic game, Villa embarked on the season in which they would go one better. Twenty years later, the fans remember it all as if it was yesterday and wonder if they will ever see the like again.

A damaged instep and ankle injury suffered by Gary Shaw meant that Villa were already without their speediest striker when newly promoted Notts County arrived to test their mettle. Still, a crowd of 30,000 expected no more than the formality of victory against the whippersnappers from Meadow Lane. By the arrival of the final whistle, the Holte End's rendition of 'One Man went to Mow' was distinctly off key, a performance to match that of their team's 1-0 defeat, but Villa had lost more than three points. Ken McNaught had been forced to leave the pitch after just ten minutes with a knee injury, and joined Shaw as a spectator for much of the early league programme.

There was a sense that the bubble of optimism had been pricked, and even those who failed to notice at the time were left deflated by a second successive defeat, this time to Sunderland at Roker Park. Terry Donovan stood in for Shaw and scored, but it was not enough to prevent Villa from completing the worst conceivable start to their season. By the time of the visit to White Hart Lane, on 5 September, the team were desperate for a kick-start that would regain the momentum of their previous campaign. A change in the Football League's regulations meant that three points rather than two were now available for a win, and the players wanted to total as many as possible before supporters became accustomed to the new scheme.

Of course, with Villa yet to score a point this neat little psychology was having the reverse effect. Table-studiers twitched as Ron Saunders took his team to face Tottenham Hotspur, the FA Cup holders and host to the prodigious talents of Glenn Hoddle, Osvaldo Ardiles and Ricky Villa. This was a far more important match than the Charity Shield final, which the two teams had shared after a 2-2 draw a few weeks earlier. The first leg of a first-round European Cup match against Valur Reykjavik loomed in just 11 days, and Villa's defeats had to be halted before they became habitual. The relief was palpable as the in-form Donovan scored twice and Villa came away with a 3-2 victory in North London. Three points out of nine may not have been the perfect start to the season, but at least the champions were under way, and a 1-1 draw at home to Manchester United the following Saturday meant that some degree of stability had been restored. Villa were still in the lower half of Division One, but at least their fortunes had been reversed in time for the first European Cup-tie in the club's history.

Valur Reykjavik. Hardly a name synonymous with the giants of European football. Were it not for the fact that the club plays out of a capital city, even the more educated fan would be reaching for the atlas with a pin in one hand and a blindfold in the other. By 16 September 1981, however, Holte Enders were well aware that there was more to a geyser than a dodgy cockney accent and a couple of episodes of *Minder*.

If Villa did suffer from nerves ahead of their match against the champions of Iceland, they hid them well. A 5-0 victory was even more comfortable than they had expected against a team consisting largely of part-timers, and a modest crowd of 20,481 left well satisfied with a goal from Morley, two from Withe and yet another brace from Donovan.

Although McNaught was entering hospital for knee surgery when the return leg took place two weeks later, Shaw's fitness was giving the most cause for concern. He returned to the starting line-up for the match, but an appalling, pockmarked pitch provided clear danger to his healing ankle, while an Arctic wind made these 90 of the most arduous minutes any of the players had experienced on a football pitch. Shaw overcame the conditions to score both goals as Villa completed a 7-0 aggregate win, although years later he recalled he had never been so cold. 'Most of us wore long sleeves and quite a few of us had T-shirts underneath,' he said. 'The wind was strong, too. One of my goals was wind-assisted as it flew past their goalkeeper. The guy never moved!'

All Quiet on the Domestic Front

Back in the bread and butter business of the league, Villa were finding victories a lot more difficult to come by. Successive draws against Liverpool, Stoke City,

Birmingham City, Leeds United and Coventry City left the club with nine points from the opening nine fixtures – hardly the sort of form that would retain the title. A 3-2 win over West Ham United on 17 October was important not just because it brought to an end the run of deadlocks, but because four days later much stiffer opposition awaited in the second round of the European Cup.

If Ron Saunders' players knew nothing of the polarized politics that split Germany for four decades, they were at least about to peek around the Iron Curtain. An away draw to Dynamo Berlin in the first leg of the second round ensured a sizeable reception from the East German army, although it was the military precision of Morley that proved by far the more deadly weapon. He stunned Dynamo after just four minutes when his volley seared into the back of the net and, roared on by 20,000 fans starved of everything but on-field success, the Germans came right back at Villa. The Sportspark stadium erupted when Dynamo's persistence paid off with a goal from Hans Jurgen Riediger shortly after half-time, and it took a brilliant penalty save by Rimmer to keep the weary visitors in the tie.

Then, in the 85th minute, something very special happened. Morley, back in Villa's penalty area helping an exhausted defence, collected the ball from a corner headed clear by Withe and took off on a journey that would provide him with a hero's status. Neatly sidestepping a German lunge, he ran like an asylum seeker headed for the infamous wall, and only when he reached the edge of the Dynamo penalty area did he release the ball, firing it low and to the left of Bodo Rudwaleit to secure a famous victory for Villa and a place in the history books for himself.

Back in Birmingham, the importance of the goal to Morley became clear. After his crucial role the year before, he had struggled with a lack of consistency and confidence for much of the early part of the season. Boasting probably the most technically perfect goal in Villa's history was a fillip, to say the least. 'There wasn't much to aim at, so I decided to hit it low and close to his body,' he said later. 'Once I start getting goals I have the confidence to keep trying with shots from any range with either foot.'

Confidence was high at Villa Park. Supporters knew by this stage that there was little chance of retaining the league championship, as a 3-0 victory at Molineux on 24 October had been followed by successive home defeats to Ipswich Town and Arsenal. But there was a good feeling about the European Cup. This was long before the concept of the Champions League, and the only obstacle blocking the path to the quarter-final stage was a Dynamo team already 2-1 down. Saunders made a tactical change to his central defence in selecting Gary Williams to replace an out-of-sorts Brendan

Ormsby, but must have been wondering if he had got it right after 14 minutes when Frank Terletzki, the Germans' skipper, sent a low shot skimming past Rimmer to bring the tie level on aggregate. The remaining 75 minutes were played on a knife edge as both teams searched for the deciding goal without the freedom to fully commit, but in the end Villa's away tally proved decisive and, in front of a relieved crowd of just 28,175, they went through to the last eight of the competition.

Villa may have had four months to prepare for their next match in Europe, but there was no respite from domestic commitments. The League Cup campaign was already under way and victories over Wolves, Leicester and Wigan ensured Christmas arrived with the promise of success in another knock-out competition. In the league, however, the exertions of such a demanding campaign were already beginning to take their toll. A 3-1 victory over Nottingham Forest preceded three straight defeats and, despite the win away to Brighton on 28 December, all hopes of defending the title had evaporated.

Saunders Shocks the Villans

Notts County were made to suffer for the impudence of their first-day victory when a David Geddis hat-trick spurred Villa to a 6-0 victory in the first round of the FA Cup. Although Shaw's goal ensured Bristol City were eliminated in the second round to set up yet another meeting with Spurs, all anticipation was geared towards the European Cup matches to come. Then,

a hammer blow. Five weeks before his team were due to face Dynamo Kiev, Ron Saunders resigned.

It emerged that Ron Bendall, the chairman, had altered the terms of Saunders' employment. The rollover contract he previously enjoyed would now be modified to become a straightforward three-year deal, meaning a decreased pay-off if the manager was dismissed. It was an offer he felt unable to agree to.

'I have always said that I wanted to spend the rest of my life with Villa,' Saunders told reporters in Birmingham, 'but the present situation means that the odds of this

Tony Morley provided the impetus in Villa's march through Europe in 1981-82.

127

happening are stacked against me. I am now worse off than I was three years ago when I was originally given a six-year contract, which became a permanent three-year agreement on their suggestion. The players need to know that their manager is on a long-term contract because that helps to engender confidence throughout the club.'

Saunders handed in his resignation to an apparently bemused Bendall on 9 February 1982, complete with parting shot. 'If Villa want me to be their paid manager then I will have to be the manager,' he said. 'I will not be the office boy.' The fans' frustration at losing a popular boss during the most important campaign in the club's history was only increased by Bendall's decision to adopt a stance that could be described, at best, as non-committal. After a sincere, but unemotional farewell to his players at the Bodymoor Heath training ground near Tamworth, Saunders handed the team over to Tony Barton, his number two at the club since 1976. Less than two weeks later he was back at Villa Park as a manager, although this time as the new boss of Birmingham City, with a three-year rollover contract to boot. Blues were beaten 1-0, but it was a difficult day for supporters to stomach.

Victory against their cross-city rivals signalled something of a revival in Villa's league fortunes, but not before the resolution of more international matters. Having conquered opposition in a communist republic already that season, the players were being asked to do so once again, although this time against even tougher opposition. Dynamo Kiev were Soviet Union champions at a time when the superpower enjoyed football excellence on a par with its military. The match would be a harsh examination in itself, although it was nothing in comparison to conditions off the field.

The tie had been switched to Simferopol, the little-known capital of Crimea, days before Villa's arrival – a decision mainly due to a winter-ravaged pitch in Kiev, but compounded by the tactics of clandestine Russian officials. Many of them would have been more at home among the pages of a best-selling espionage thriller, and they certainly attempted every trick in the book once Barton's team had landed. First they altered the visitors' accommodation from a relatively plush Black Sea resort to the unwelcoming Hotel Moscow in Simferopol, an establishment so archaic in standards of both comfort and hygiene that Satan's bottom lip would have trembled had he had the misfortune to visit. Then Villa were informed that the kickoff time was being brought forward by two hours to suit local broadcasting requirements. By the time kickoff arrived on 3 March at 5pm local time, 90 minutes seemed like a short trip to civilization.

There were a few more challenges to overcome on the pitch that night, too, as Oleg Blokhin ran Villa's defence ragged in the first half. A 0-0 draw represented a highly creditable performance in difficult circumstances, although nobody could have predicted what was to come in the second leg.

A crowd of 38,579 crammed into Villa Park two weeks later, expecting to witness a performance of grit from the home team. What they got instead was a performance of such polish that the dream of football's ultimate club prize was materializing into reality. Goals from Shaw and McNaught won it on the night, but Villa were worth far more than a 2-0 victory. This was the night that they signalled their intentions, as Gordon Cowans confirmed. 'Once we got past Dynamo Kiev we began thinking we could go all the way,' he remembered. 'Deep down we knew that we were a good side.'

The heroic endeavours of their European campaign made Villa's inconsistent form in the League even harder to fathom. Defeats against

Great Managers – 1974-82

RON SAUNDERS

He may not have been in charge when his Aston Villa players secured their greatest prize – the European Cup – but Ron Saunders' contribution towards the achievement is undeniable. Over the course of eight years at the helm he took a group of footballers that had been languishing outside Division One since 1967 and transformed them into one of the leading teams in the country. He may never have got the chance to perform such feats had the Villa directors stuck with their original intention of appointing a higher profile manager.

Sir Alf Ramsey had recently been dismissed as England boss and Brian Clough was among the other contenders for the position, but in the end they went with Saunders, whose previous managerial experience had taken in the likes of Oxford United, Norwich City and Manchester City. It was the right decision. Saunders took the club back into the top flight at the first time of asking and set about building a team capable of challenging for major honours.

Tactically astute, a disciplinarian who was respected by his players, he led Villa to their first league title for 71 years in 1980-81, having already secured two League Cups, and proved he was a man of principle when he resigned over a disagreement with the board as the team was in the middle of its European campaign. A week later, much to the dismay of Villa supporters, he took charge of Birmingham City.

Ipswich and Arsenal were Barton's first as manager, although by the time of the semi-final, against Anderlecht, the trend had been reversed with successive victories against West Bromwich Albion and Southampton. The Belgian champions were offering somewhat tougher opposition, however.

Closing in on European Glory

Arriving in Birmingham to play the first leg on 7 April, a week after Barton had been confirmed as manager, they had already seen off the likes of Juventus and Red Star Belgrade by exploiting a system of counterattack allied to perhaps the most well-executed offside trap in the history of the sport.

They had an abundance of talent and a team full of internationals, but Tomislav Ivic, the Anderlecht coach, seemed unwilling to utilize them. Villa's defence had a relatively easy night, despite Rimmer's fine early save from Frank Vercauteren, and it was at the other end of the pitch that they were frustrated, as the Belgians' spoiling tactics ruined the game as a spectacle. It made Morley's goal after 28 minutes, when he latched onto a pass from Cowans and found the only square of space on the field, all the more vital. Ivic endured heavy criticism from the media for his approach, but the fact remained that, two weeks later, Barton would have to take his team to Brussells and avoid defeat if Villa were to be sure of reaching the European Cup final.

They achieved their objective, but a 0-0 draw was the only positive result that could be taken away from the Belgian capital. A match that was to be a stepping-stone to the most important night in the club's history was overshadowed long before it ended by the behaviour of both sets of supporters. Football hooliganism was rife at the time, both in England and on the continent, and it was only when riot police began to beat offenders with their batons that the supporters were separated, although this course of action prompted one Villa fan, a soldier, to run onto the pitch and lie down inside the penalty area.

The fact that the first bouts of fighting broke out on the Villa terraces did not escape the attention of Barton, who complained that his team's achievement had been 'ruined'. It really could have been had Anderlecht's calls for Villa to be expelled from the competition been sustained. In truth, the Belgian club was at least partly culpable because of the lack of planned security, but 88 arrests and 18 injuries are figures that speak for themselves. That the players managed to perform so professionally in such trying circumstances spoke volumes. 'We were magnificent,' said Barton, and his comments were underlined by Cowans. 'Getting through that leg in Brussels was the most difficult task we faced on the way to the final,' he said. 'Realizing you had got to the European Cup final was nearly as good as winning it.'

The worrying hurdle of a UEFA Control and Disciplinary Committee hearing had to be cleared before Villa were assured of their place in the final. Although elimination from the competition had been mooted, it was never seriously considered and, ultimately, the club endured no more than a rap on the knuckles when the European governing body hit them with a £14,500 fine and ordered their next home match in the competition to be played behind closed doors. So fans were free to take up Villa's 14,000 ticket allocation for the final, in Rotterdam, although they knew they would be segregated from supporters of the one team that barred their path to glory – Bayern Munich.

Villa's form in the run-up to Rotterdam was abysmal. Confidence boosting had been prescribed and a single win alongside two draws and defeats, to Leeds, Stoke and Everton, hardly met the required dose. The hope had to be that they were saving the best for last, and at least Uli Hoeness, Bayern's general manager, was given food for thought when he watched the champions sign off their league campaign with a 3-0 victory over Swansea City. Goals from Withe, Bremner and Morley saw Villa finish in 11th place in Division One, and prospects brightened further when Shaw, who had missed the Swansea game, was passed fit to play in the final on 26 May.

Villa's Biggest Night

Bayern were emerging from a quiet period in European football after winning the European Cup three times during the mid-1970s. They had come back with a bang that season though, putting seven goals past CSKA Sofia in their semi-final and boasting the talents of Karl-Heinz Rummenigge, the European Footballer of the Year and West Germany captain, at centre forward. At least Villa could prepare in comfort for the challenge, and it was clear that Barton was putting his faith in familiarity when he named a line-up that had played together eight times since his appointment: Rimmer, Swain, Williams, Evans, McNaught, Mortimer, Bremner, Shaw, Withe, Cowans and Morley. Their names had appeared many times in match-day programmes – now they were about to be written into the history books, as was that of another.

Nigel Spink, the 23-year-old substitute goalkeeper who had made only one other senior appearance, was forced into action in the ninth minute when Rimmer retired with a cricked neck, the result of a training injury. Reeling off save after outstanding save, he produced the performance of a lifetime just when it was needed most. Although Villa seemed determined to take the game to Bayern, the Germans were feeling their way into the game and Spink was soon in the thick of things, cleanly catching Durnberger's strike after half an hour. A minute later he was required again when Rummenigge found himself with space in front of goal, only to discover Spink was more than ready for his well-hit shot.

Once the second half had started, Bayern were determined to exert their authority and a header from Augenthaler, desperately headed off the line by Swain, suggested it would only be a matter of time before they scored. Villa stood firm, and Morley signalled his intent with a 20-yard shot that flew high over the crossbar. Moments later his contribution was to prove far more valuable. Mortimer, the captain, crossed to Shaw, who evaded the attention of Wolfgang Dremmler and passed to Morley. Grateful to find himself with space, Morley set off on a darting run that bamboozled Hans Weiner in the centre of the Bayern defence, before sending a low, left-footed cross to Withe, on the edge of the six-yard box. The ball bobbled as it approached the centre forward right in front of Villa's massed supporters. With what can only be described as a mis-hit, Withe left Augenthaler helpless, and the goalkeeper watched in horror as the ball hit the inside of the post and went in. Sixty-seven minutes gone: Bayern Munich 0, Aston Villa 1.

'I remember it as if it happened yesterday,' Withe recalled many years later. 'Tony drove the ball across, but it seemed to happen in slow motion. The ball hit a divot as it reached me and it half hit my shin and half hit my ankle. If I'd struck it properly, the keeper would have saved it!'

Luckily for Villa he didn't. The goal eased their defensive jitters and, if anything, they looked the better side as the match sped towards its climax. At the final whistle, the players raced towards their celebrating fans, who then watched awestruck as Mortimer became the first captain in the club's history to lift the European Cup. The celebrations that followed that night were bettered still by the reception the Villa players enjoyed when they embarked on another open-topped bus tour of Birmingham two days later, and nothing the club has done since has come close to the sight of club football's most prestigious trophy on display in the Council House. For the first time in decades, Aston Villa was a force to be reckoned with, not just at home, but all over the world.

Emerging from the shadow of their East Midlands rivals, Nottingham Forest, Villa had won the English championship and European Cup in successive years. How could the players possibly follow such an achievement? 'The one thing I'm pleased about is that we'll always be part of the club,' said Mortimer some years later. 'I'd have hated to have played for the number of years I did

Great Matches

EUROPEAN CUP FINAL   **Feyenoord Stadium, Rotterdam, 26 May 1982**

Bayern Munich 0   Aston Villa 1   **Attendance: 39,776**

Withe

The greatest night in the history of Aston Villa Football Club was notable for an apparent lack of nerves among the players. Despite facing opponents who were used to the pressure-cooker situation of European competition, Villa looked relaxed as they took to the pitch in Rotterdam and had the best of the early skirmishes with both Allan Evans and Peter Withe going close. The loss of an experienced goalkeeper in Jimmy Rimmer after only nine minutes might have put them on the back foot, but it was not long before Nigel Spink proved he was a more than adequate replacement, saving to his right from Bernhard Durnberger when the defence was under pressure. As the first half progressed the Germans grew more confident, with Reinhold Mathy going close and Karl-Heinz Rummenigge causing palpitations among Villa supporters with an overhead kick that flashed past the post. Bayern stepped up the pressure in the second half, when Villa's penalty area was under almost constant siege, but in the 67th minute the watching millions were shocked. Gary Shaw dumbfounded the Bayern defence with a brilliant turn before sending the ball through to Tony Morley, whose pace was too much for Wolfgang Dremmler. Firing in a low cross, the ball made contact with Withe's shin before flying into the back of the net – not the cleanest of his finishes, but certainly one of the most important! The final 20 minutes of the match were spent repelling more German attacks, but Villa's defence stood firm and at the whistle their opponents wore

vanquished expressions as Dennis Mortimer lifted the cup, and his team was bestowed the status of legends.

Bayern Munich: Muller, Dremmler, Horsemann, Weiner, Augenthaler, Kraus (Niedermayer), Durnberger, Breitner, Hoeness, Mathy (Guttler), Rummenigge.

Aston Villa: Rimmer (Spink), Swain, G. Williams, Evans, McNaught, Mortimer, Bremner, Shaw, Withe, Cowans, Morley.

Referee: G. Kpnrath (France).

Peter Withe scuffs home the ball to earn Villa an historic European Cup win.

and not have won anything. To have won the two big ones was immense.' If the honours were going to be difficult to sustain, at least fans could be assured of seeing some flamboyant football once the summer of celebration was over. In addition to the domestic competitions and their defence of the European Cup, Villa were playing in the European Super Cup and the World Club Cup, which meant there was the prospect of some of the stars of the 1982 World Cup taking on their heroes. Everything in the garden looked rosy – and then the new season began.

Back to Reality

If Villa's opening encounters in the defence of their league title the previous season had been a trifle disappointing, their first competitive matches as champions of Europe were nothing short of abysmal. After losing the opening game at home to Sunderland, 3-1, Barton's men crumbled in humiliating style at Goodison Park, conceding five goals on their way to the club's heaviest defeat in more than a decade. By the time Southampton had inflicted another wound with victory by a single goal at the Dell, the team had taken root at the foot of the Division One table.

Successive 4-1 victories over Luton Town and Nottingham Forest ensured Villa could claw their way to a respectable position, but it was clear from the jittery start that all was not as it should be among the players. In fact, the 11 men who had committed themselves so valiantly in Rotterdam a few months earlier would never play together again. Kenny Swain was seeking a transfer and would soon be off to Forest, while both Evans and McNaught were unsettled, feelings which were clearly reflected through their performances.

Villa knew they would have to find their resolve before their first game in defence of the European Cup, at home to Besiktas, and although Williams, Withe and Mortimer scored as they breezed to a 3-1 victory, the players were forced to compete in the most bizarre atmosphere – or lack of it – of their careers. There were no Villa supporters inside the ground – the punishing result of the shocking events in Brussels – and with no crowd to accommodate, the match was played in mid-afternoon. It was all in sharp contrast to the return leg at the Inonu Stadium in Istanbul, where a 0-0 draw ensured a meeting with Dynamo Bucharest. Around 70,000 Romanian fans packed the home stadium for the first leg of the second-round clash, but Villa were undaunted and produced a super-smooth performance. Gary Shaw, who continued to attract the attention of top coaches, scored both goals in a 2-0 victory that Barton described as his best in Europe. 'We have never received the praise we deserved for winning the European Cup,' he said, 'but we are a good team

50 Greatest Players

DENNIS MORTIMER Midfielder

Born: Liverpool, 5 April 1952

Joined Aston Villa: 1975 **From:** Coventry City

Appearances: 405 **Goals:** 36

Left Aston Villa: 1985 **For:** Brighton & Hove Albion

The only Villa captain ever to have held the European Cup aloft, not to mention the most recent to have led his team to the league championship, Mortimer's legacy has been written indelibly into the record books. As well as being the skipper, he was also the chief engineer on his side's journey to success, squeezing every last drop of effort from his team-mates while running himself into the ground with constant forays among opposition defenders. He will always be remembered as a servant of Villa, but Mortimer began his career with Coventry, who he joined as an apprentice in 1967. Turning professional less than two years later, he played more than 200 times for the Highfield Road club before signing for Villa in 1975. Mortimer won his first honours with a League Cup medal in 1977, before adding league and European medals to his haul. After leaving Villa in 1985, he spent a season at Brighton before moving back to the Midlands to play for Birmingham. When Mortimer retired in 1987, he had amassed more than 700 league and cup appearances.

and if we can defeat Dynamo to reach the quarter-finals I am sure it will make our opponents respect us even more.'

Normal service had returned on the pitch, with wins over Brighton, Manchester United and Stoke strengthening Villa's run up the table. Off it, however, the club's financial problems were beginning to mount. At the AGM in October 1982, debts totalling £1.6 million were revealed, mainly the result of escalating wages and costly building work. In pre-Premiership days, when the BBC enjoyed the majority of television rights at a low cost, this represented a significant overdraft for a top-flight club and the problems went a long way towards shaping Villa's future.

At the end of November, Ron and Donald Bendall resigned from the board. Although there was much speculation over who would take over as chairman, one candidate was always going to be too strong for the competition. Three years after bowing his head for 'the sake of harmony', Doug Ellis returned

50 Greatest Players

TONY MORLEY   Midfielder

Born: Ormskirk, 26 August 1954

Joined Aston Villa: 1979   **From:** Burnley

Appearances: 180   **Goals:** 34

Left Aston Villa: 1984   **For:** West Bromwich Albion

If Peter Withe hit the right note, he had Tony Morley to thank for providing the sheet music when Villa won the European Cup – it was his perfect centre that set up the winner, the trademark of a career spent worrying defenders with his pace on the wing, his crossing and his scoring ability. Morley cost Ron Saunders £200,000 when he arrived from Burnley in 1979. Although his talent was already obvious, Villa Park would become the stage on which he would hone his skills, providing the ammunition with which Withe and Shaw would fire the club to the Division One title in 1980-81. Morley scored ten times during that campaign, and was Villa's leading marksman in the European Cup the following season with four goals from eight games. Although he was also a member of the team that beat Barcelona to win the European Super Cup, Morley's appearances became limited under Tony Barton and he was sold to West Bromwich Albion for £75,000 during the 1983-84 season.

to Villa Park and promptly bought Ron Bendall's 42 per cent shareholding. The deal gave him a vice-like grip on the club that, 20 years and many managers later, would show no sign of weakening.

A Shot at the World Title

Ellis rejoined Villa at one of the most exciting points in their history, a few days before the club was due to contest the World Club Cup in Tokyo against the South American champions. Peñarol of Uruguay boasted some top-class talent, but the *Birmingham Evening Mail* reported Barton in bullish mood prior to the game, declaring: 'We are here to win.' Sixty-two thousand fans packed into Japan's National Stadium to watch the game, but they saw a shadow of Villa's usual style as the players struggled to come to terms with a grassless pitch and lighter ball. Jair and Siba scored for Peñarol as Villa failed their audition on the world stage, but it would not be long before they had the chance to redeem themselves against another footballing giant.

The European Super Cup was a two-legged play-off between the holders of the European Cup and the European Cup-Winners' Cup. Although in reality it was little more than an international version of the Charity Shield, the competition itself provided obvious benefits – attendance figures and television deals for the clubs and high-quality football for the supporters. Opposition did not come with much more quality than Barcelona, and after Villa had suffered nothing worse than a 1-0 defeat in the first leg at the Nou Camp, Birmingham was in a state of anticipation again when the Catalan side arrived to contest the return match.

Those who had come expecting flair were left feeling disappointed. Barcelona were determined to make the encounter as physical as possible – whether they played within the rules or not – and a night of vicious tackles almost over-shadowed Villa's utter supremacy. A crowd of 31,500 saw the home side win 3-0 and add another medal to the cabinet, but Barton described his feelings afterwards as 'bittersweet'. 'I thought my players showed remarkable restraint,' he said, 'though they faced the most severe provocation.'

The Super Cup represented Villa's final piece of international silverware. A month later the players faced Juventus in the quarter-final of the European Cup, but they could not get a grip in either tie of the double-legged match, losing 2-1 at Villa Park and 3-1 in Turin. It was no disgrace – Juventus boasted a line-up that included Michel Platini, Zbigniew Boniek, Paolo Rossi, Dino Zoff and four other Italian World Cup winners – and after so many cup-ties, ensuring another season of European football by finishing sixth in the league was an achievement in itself. By now, however, the team's finest results were behind them.

The 1983-84 season would again be a decisive one for Villa, though not through the positive effect of the team's performances. In fact this was to be the most disappointing campaign in several years, despite some transfer movement over the summer. McNaught and Rimmer left the club, to go to West Bromwich Albion and Swansea City respectively, and Barton quickly brought in Steve McMahon, a future England player, from Everton for £375,000, and Paul Rideout, who arrived from Swindon Town at a cost of £75,000.

Start of a Downward Spiral

Things started badly when Cowans broke a leg in a pre-season tournament in Spain, which ruled him out of action for almost a year, but Villa at least overturned a 1-0 defeat in the first leg of the UEFA Cup match against Vitoria Guimaraes, triumphing 5-0 over the Portuguese in Birmingham. It looked as though the team might be on course for another epic run on the continent when they held Spartak Moscow to a commendable 2-2 draw in

Great Matches

EUROPEAN SUPER CUP, SECOND LEG   Villa Park, 26 January 1983

Aston Villa 3   Barcelona 0   Attendance: 31,500

Shaw
Cowans
McNaught

Villa were 1-0 down after the first leg of the European Super Cup, a two-legged play-off between the European Cup holders and the winners of the European Cup-Winners' Cup. A goal from Marcos had put the Spaniards in front at the Nou Camp, but Villa held their own for most of the match and that gave the players some cause for optimism for the return tie at Villa Park. They were right to be hopeful. Villa were by far the more potent attacking force, causing Barcelona's Alberto to be sent off for deliberate handball before, with ten minutes of normal time left, Gary Shaw scored to take the match into extra-time. In the 99th minute Mark Walters, who was on as a substitute for Tony Morley, was tripped in the penalty area. Gordon Cowans saw his spot-kick saved, but followed up on the rebound to ease the ball over the line, a success which irked the Barcelona keeper to such an extent that he aimed a flying kick at the Villa man, taking his legs from underneath him. Ken McNaught sealed a 3-1 aggregate victory with a diving header, but the night had been marred by some gruesome tackling from the Catalan team. Shaw had warned before the game that Barcelona would be physical, but even he was unprepared for a real horror show as the visitors were reduced to nine men and Allan Evans also got his marching orders for a second bookable offence. Tony Barton, the Villa manager, praised his players for their collective show of restraint over the course of the game, but they took solace from securing another European trophy.

Aston Villa: Spink, G. Williams, Gibson, Evans, McNaught, Blair, Bremner, Shaw (Birch), Withe, Cowans, Morley (Walters).

Barcelona: Urruti, Gerardo, Migueli, Alescano, Manola, Sanchez, Moratalla, Esterban, Simonsen, Quini, Carrasco.

the heart of the Soviet Union. Despite being outplayed for much of the second leg, at 1-1 with only seconds of the match remaining, Villa were on course for the third round via the away-goals' rule. Then Fyodor Cherenkov slipped inside the defence to score with a deflection off the leg of Mortimer. After promising so much, the UEFA Cup journey had come to an abrupt end.

Barton knew that Villa's only chance of getting back into Europe would be through a drastic improvement in domestic form. His efforts were hampered by the inconsistency that had haunted the club's league performances since the title-winning season of 1980-81, and after losing an FA Cup third-round replay to Norwich City, only the Milk Cup [the re-named League Cup] offered an escape route. Villa beat Norwich on their way to the semi-final stage, but lost over two legs to Everton and completed their first barren season for three years. Tenth place in Division One was nowhere near good enough for European qualification – after the glitz and glory of recent times, it was clear supporters were going to have to get used to much more mundane fare.

Such a prospect did not entice Ellis, whose efforts to reduce the club's debts had succeeded only so far as stability. Faced with spiralling costs off the pitch and diminishing returns on it, he demanded the manager cut back significantly on a playing staff of 29. Barton, loyal to his men, insisted he would take his time over the reductions, phasing out players over a period of his making, but after Villa's disappointing season the folly of playing the stalling game with Ellis became all too evident. Refusing to agree to cuts in the summer of 1984, he was sacked on 18 June. 'I want only the best for Villa and our supporters and that means we have to make progress,' said the chairman.

'Deadly Doug' Springs a Surprise

It was no secret that Ellis wanted Ron Atkinson, the former West Brom manager, who was by this time in charge of Manchester United, to succeed Barton. That particular vision would take several more years to materialize, but instead of searching for someone with similar experience, the chairman chose a young man at the other end of the managerial spectrum. Graham Turner, a 36-year-old who had enjoyed some success with Shrewsbury Town in the lower divisions, was seen by some as an inspired and imaginative choice. To others, his appointment was symptomatic of the confusion about how best to take the team forward. Turner, who signed an optimistic five-year contract with the club, only had to examine Barton's fate to realize he would not have much money to play with. History has probably judged him harshly because he broke up the remnants of a European Cup-winning side, many of whom

50 Greatest Players

KEN McNAUGHT   Defender

Born: Kirkcaldy, 11 January 1955

Joined Aston Villa: 1977   **From:** Everton

Appearances: 260   **Goals:** 13

Left Aston Villa: 1983   **For:** West Bromwich Albion

A solid central defender, McNaught was Villa's rock over a six-year period during which he made 260 appearances for the club. The son of Willie, a Scottish international, he started his career with Everton, turning professional in 1972 and playing every match during the 1976-77 season. Part of the Toffeemen team which lost the League Cup final to Villa in 1977, he joined Ron Saunders' side weeks later and immediately cemented his place. An ever-present in the championship-winning line-up of 1980-81, injury caused McNaught to miss almost half of the following season. He returned to play in the European Cup final though, and missed only one match the following year before being sold to West Bromwich Albion for £125,000. Uncapped, the nearest he came to playing for Scotland was prior to the squad announcement for the 1982 World Cup, but the trip to Spain was not to be.

would have argued they still had some good seasons ahead of them, but the team was clearly descending from its pinnacle. Besides, the only way the manager could fund the arrival of fresh talent was by selling players he felt had passed their expiry dates.

Given the conflict between ambition and financial reality, Turner deserved credit for having the patience to embark on a watchful first season in charge. Buoyed by the return from injury of Cowans, he received a further boost when Shaw, whom Atkinson himself had coveted for some time, signed a two-year contract with Villa. That delight turned sour in September when the injury-cursed forward underwent yet another operation to an injured right knee, leaving him hospitalized and out for the rest of the season.

The new manager was not enjoying much more luck on the field. Despite victories over Coventry and Stoke in the first two games of the season, horrible defeats at the hands of Newcastle, Nottingham Forest, Spurs, Ipswich and Leicester – to name but a few – quickly quelled the optimism generated by a

50 Greatest Players

JIMMY RIMMER   Goalkeeper

Born: Southport, 10 February 1948

Joined Aston Villa: 1977   **From:** Arsenal

Appearances: 287

Left Aston Villa: 1983   **For:** Swansea City

Already an established top-flight goalkeeper by the time he joined
Villa in 1977, Rimmer started all nine of Villa's European Cup
matches but lasted only nine minutes of the final before having
to be replaced by Nigel Spink. Despite the bad luck, he collected
his second medal in the competition, having been on the bench
for the 1968 final as a Manchester United rookie. Rimmer had
made his first-team debut at Old Trafford at the age of 19, but
spent much of his early career as understudy to Alex Stepney.
After transferring to Arsenal, he won an England cap against
Italy in New York before signing for Villa in a deal worth £65,000. Although he missed
most of the club's famous night in Rotterdam, Rimmer was part of the side that won the
European Super Cup shortly afterwards. He moved to Swansea City in 1983.

new man at the helm. By the end of the first week in January, Villa were out of
both cup competitions and languishing in the nether regions of the table. To date
Turner had made only two notable first-team additions, that of Tony Dorigo,
an 18-year-old left back who would go on to enjoy a highly successful career,
and Didier Six, a French striker who, by any standards, had already had one.

Six had been a member of the brilliant France team that lost controversially
to West Germany in the 1982 World Cup semi-final, and his arrival on a free
transfer was greeted enthusiastically by supporters. He soon discovered,
however, that his panache amid the rough and tumble of the English league
blended with all the ease of a Versace shirt and Burton cufflinks. With two goals
to his name he pronounced himself dissatisfied with the contract offered to him
at the end of the 1984-85 season and returned from whence he came, the French
Second Division club Mulhouse, again on a free.

A slight improvement in form – though by no means anything spectacular –
saw Villa finish the season in tenth position. The team had missed out on a place
in Europe once again, although the tragic events at Belgium's Heysel Stadium a
couple of weeks later, when 39 Italian fans died in the European Cup final

between Liverpool and Juventus, meant the failure was academic. English clubs received an indefinite ban from European competition as a result of the disaster, a punishment that would remain in force for five years.

Turner Rebuilds

This was Turner's time to rebuild, but after waiting so long for his chance, his decisions proved mystifying. Rideout, who had top scored with 15 goals over the season, was transferred to the Italian Serie A club Bari along with Cowans, a key midfielder and a firm favourite with the Holte End. McMahon, who had also made his mark at Villa Park, joined Liverpool in a £375,000 deal, and Withe, the man who had scored the most important goal in the club's history a couple of seasons before, left for Sheffield United on a free transfer. In came Steve Hodge, the Nottingham Forest midfielder, and Andy Gray, a Scotland international already well known in the area and an FA Cup winner with Everton. They completed a young team that had been moulded by Turner's hands alone. He knew now that he would have to take Villa to a season of achievement.

Great Managers – 1982-84

TONY BARTON

If Ron Saunders had a huge part to play in Villa's success, Tony Barton's contribution was at least the equal. A quiet man, he was there for the majority of his predecessor's reign, advising him on transfer dealings and developing a more personal relationship with the players. Some history books suggest that when he took charge of the team in the aftermath of Saunders' sudden departure, the hard work was already done. In fact, it was just about to begin, as Barton regrouped the players ahead of their European Cup quarter-final and ensured they remained focused. The antithesis to Saunders, whom he played alongside at Portsmouth in the early 1960s, Barton was placid and understated, but he knew his players inside out and had a shrewd football brain. He lost the faith of the board at the end of the 1983-84 season when, having repeatedly refused requests to trim the playing  staff, he took the team no higher than 11th in Division One – hardly a disastrous achievement, but grounds enough for Doug Ellis to sack the man who had led Villa to both the European Cup and European Super Cup. Barton died aged 57 in 1993, and many fans feel his work has still not been fully recognized by the club's administration.

50 Greatest Players

DES BREMNER   Midfielder

Born: Kirkcaldy, 7 September 1952

Joined Aston Villa: 1979   **From:** Hibernian

Appearances: 227   **Goals:** 10

Left Aston Villa: 1984   **For:** Birmingham City

An experienced utility player by the time he joined Villa, Bremner's versatility proved invaluable throughout five years with the club. He started his career as a defender with Hibernian in 1971, but after turning professional the following year he soon converted to midfield, scoring 22 goals in 255 games for the Scottish club. After the £250,000 move to Villa Park, he would occupy the right side of midfield, but also stood in at full back and in the centre of defence, notably in the away leg of the European Cup quarter-final against Dynamo Kiev.

Bremner had already completed his international career by the time he signed for Villa, a sign of the strength of the Scotland team at that time. He won nine U-23 caps but appeared only once for the senior side, as a substitute, against Switzerland in 1976. At Villa, Bremner helped to win the Division One title, the European Cup and the European Super Cup. He was signed again by Saunders, this time at Birmingham City, in 1984.

It was not to be. The popularity of football in the mid-1980s was as far removed from today as possible. Those disastrous scenes in Brussels had poisoned the general public's perception of the national game and its followers, and it was understandable that many supporters walked away from the sport, temporarily at least, rather than leave themselves open to association with a rampant community of hooligans. Clearly Villa had no involvement with the events surrounding the European Cup final, but the malaise was all-pervading and it was no surprise to see attendances well down on the annual average. Had circumstances differed, it is debatable whether Villa Park would have been packed to the rafters anyway. It was unsurprising that the first home match of the season, against much-maligned Liverpool, drew an audience of only 20,000, but an average of just over 15,000 for the season – with barely 8,000 in the ground for the league meeting with Southampton – tells its own story. Such a lack of atmosphere can only have made an insipid season that much more difficult to endure.

Graham Turner may have been the surprise replacement for Tony Barton, but it was clear that he had the full support of Doug Ellis in a way that few Villa managers have enjoyed.

Certainly that was the impression the players gave, struggling to impose themselves against all but the weakest opposition after setting the tone with a 4-0 defeat at Old Trafford. Arsenal, West Ham and Spurs all recorded comfortable victories over Villa, who failed again in the FA Cup, but at least enjoyed another respectable run in the Milk Cup. The nadir was unmistakable though. A 3-0 defeat at home to Birmingham City, bound for relegation after one season back in the top flight, is still ranked by fans as one of the most humiliating results in Villa's history. It was made all the worse by the fact that the Blues were still managed by Ron Saunders, the man many believed should never have been allowed to leave the club.

It was clear that Villa's midfield was not up to scratch, which made Turner's decision to sell both Cowans and McMahon all the more difficult to understand, but the manager's only purchases during the 1985-86 season were Paul Elliott, a central defender who transferred from Luton Town for £400,000, and Simon Stainrod, a forward, from Sheffield Wednesday. The latter scored some important goals, most notably in the Milk Cup, but even he could not prevent Villa from sliding dangerously close to the relegation zone. A 4-2 defeat to Spurs on the final day of the season left the club in 16th place in Division One. The players had managed to avoid relegation – by the margin of just three points – but this was clearly not the bright new dawn Ellis had dreamt of. Some commentators wondered if Turner would last until the beginning of the new campaign, and, if anything, the fact that he did spoke volumes of the high regard in which he was held by the chairman. Many managers, before and since, have learned the hard way that Ellis' patience is

50 Greatest Players

GORDON COWANS   Forward

Born: Durham, 27 October 1958

Joined Aston Villa: 1970, 1988, 1993

From: Schoolboy, Bari, Blackburn Rovers

Appearances: 528   **Goals:** 59

Left Aston Villa: 1985, 1991, 1993

For: Bari, Blackburn Rovers, Derby County

The closest thing to a prodigal son at Villa Park, Cowans enjoyed three spells with the club over two decades. Destined to wear the famous strip after signing schoolboy forms at the age of 12, Cowans – or Sid as he was affectionately known – graduated through the youth and reserve sides after leaving school before making his first-team debut against Norwich City at the age of 17. By the beginning of the 1977-78 season he was a regular in the first team, and he went on to be an integral member of the team that won the league championship and European Cup in successive years. Perhaps the most astonishing statistic of his long career is that he failed to miss a single match between 1979 and 1983. Cowans won eight England caps under Bobby Robson before being sold to Serie A club Bari in 1985. He returned three years later when Graham Taylor was in charge of Villa, was sold by Ron Atkinson to Blackburn Rovers in 1991 and enjoyed one more spell at the club before joining Derby.

something of a smouldering fuse. Turner was being given every opportunity to turn results around.

Turner Lives on Borrowed Time

In his search for a winning formula the manager signed players to strengthen each key department on the field in time for the beginning of the 1986-87 season. Garry Thompson became the second Sheffield Wednesday player to join Villa in a year, partnering Stainrod in attack, but the long journey south of Neale Cooper, who transferred from Aberdeen, was the only addition to a below-strength midfield. By far the most interesting signing was that of a young central defender from Arsenal who would go on to captain England in a World Cup qualifying match and win top honours in both the League and FA Cup. His name was Martin Keown. If Turner was to have any chance of keeping the job, he needed Villa to sprint out of the starting blocks. By the definition of anybody who watched, what he got was two false starts and a disqualification. The tone was set on the first day when the team went down 3-0 at home to Spurs, a result followed three days later by a 3-2 defeat by Wimbledon at Plough Lane. Keown's introduction helped to shore up the defence the following weekend, but even he could not prevent Queens Park Rangers from snatching victory by a single goal at Loftus Road. The visit of Luton Town offered Turner brief respite as Villa got off the mark with their first win of the season, but what gloom was lifted quickly descended once more, only this time ever more choking, as Oxford United headed back down the M40 with all three points in the bag.

Dragging his team through pre-match training and post-match inquests, Turner by this time had about as much need to plan for the future as a hedgehog with a home on the M6. For once Ellis lingered in his decision when any good

50 Greatest Players

PETER WITHE **Centre forward**

Born: Liverpool, 30 August 1951

Joined Aston Villa: 1980 **From:** Newcastle United

Appearances: 233 **Goals:** 92

Left Aston Villa: 1985 **For:** Sheffield United

A record signing when Ron Saunders agreed to buy him from Newcastle United for £500,000, Withe wasted no time in making an impact at Villa. Already a league championship winner under Brian Clough at Nottingham Forest, he was hungry for more success and 20 league goals in his first season helped the club to its first league title in 71 years. Of all the times he found the back of the net in a claret and blue shirt, none will be more fondly remembered than the mis-hit shot which led Villa to a 1-0 victory over Bayern Munich in the European Cup final on 26 May 1982. It was a moment fans have been replaying in their minds ever since, and raised his stature from popular to legendary in the blink of an eye. Withe had a habit of collecting a bag of sweets from supporters in the Holte End after each home match, and his relationship with them was equally as sweet throughout his time with the club. At the age of 34, and after winning 11 England caps, he joined Sheffield United on a free transfer in 1985, returning to the club as assistant manager to Josef Venglos five years later.

fight referee would have stepped in to remove the gum shield and the result, as has often been witnessed in boxing, was a final, brutal annihilation from which dignity was lost and recovery impossible. A 6-0 defeat away at Nottingham Forest was every bit as much of a capitulation as it sounds – Turner's team had disintegrated in front of his eyes. It was painful to watch, and with Villa now firmly rooted to the foot of the Division One table, it left Ellis with no choice but to sack his young manager.

Despite appalling results and the fact that he was clearly doing the right thing, this was a difficult decision for Ellis to take. He liked Turner and had imbued him with much faith when taking him on from Shrewsbury. Indeed, Turner's comments at the time of his dismissal indicate he was regarded in the same light as perhaps only Brian Little, of his successors, went on to enjoy. 'I always had a good relationship with the chairman,' he said. 'He sacked me and then we talked about my successor. If I had a choice it would be Billy McNeill – I feel he is the right man for the job.'

Whether or not the appointment of McNeill was Turner's idea or an original thought by Ellis, it was this route the directors decided to explore as the club scrambled for an escape route from their dire surroundings. By the end of the season the chairman would have cause to question Turner's judgement once more, and he may even have paused to wonder at his own. 'There isn't an awful lot wrong with the appetite and attitude of the players in training,' McNeill announced during one of his early press conferences. 'Their confidence has simply taken an awful hammering because of the results.'

These words had a welcome confidence to them, not least because the new manager was respected and admired. Where Turner had been fresh faced and full of promise, McNeill arrived with a reputation as a motivator and boasting a resumé, as both a player and manager, that most would give their right arm for. Many Villa fans who had enjoyed their own club's success at the highest level a few years previously could also remember McNeill lifting the European Cup, as captain of the Celtic team managed by Jock Stein, way back in 1967. He had managed the same club to league and cup success over the course of five seasons and, upon moving south in the early 1980s, took Manchester City into Division One in only his second year at Maine Road. 'It's a new experience for me to arrive when the season has started,' McNeill said, 'without the benefit of summer preparations. During the close season you can get to know the players much better, but my first impressions have been encouraging.'

As it turned out, they were also misleading. A handful of victories, over Coventry, Southampton, Newcastle and Leicester, eased the pressure and helped Villa to rise a few places in the table, and supporters were encouraged by

McNeill's willingness to experiment, most notably by using Keown's attacking instincts in a sweeper position rather than playing him as a conventional central defender. But even this temporary recovery, very much the blip in the season, could not mask the truth – Villa were a mediocre team without the resources to buy new talent. A player had to be sold before another could be bought and under such conditions the manager found himself hamstrung.

Not least among McNeill's worries was a run of toothless performances in front of goal. A 4-0 defeat to Arsenal on 29 November was the signal for the slide to recommence and it would be Boxing Day before the team won again in the league with Birch and Tony Daley, a young winger who would go on to be one of Villa's most popular players, finding the net. By this time the team had lost in the League Cup, now sponsored by Littlewoods, and early in the New Year they were knocked out of the FA Cup in a third-round replay with Chelsea. Injuries to Gray and the luckless Shaw meant the team were without their first-choice attack for much of the time, and it was not until the departure of Hodge, who moved to Spurs around Christmas for £400,000, that McNeill could even begin finding replacements. His choice of player was a strange one – the inexperienced Everton centre forward Warren Aspinall arrived in a £200,000 deal when Villa were crying out for a player with the appetite for a scrap. There was little he could do to reverse the decline.

A total of five defeats out of the final six matches meant that the season had ended exactly as it had started. It also meant that Villa, who had been staving off the threat of relegation for two years, were in Division Two for the first time in 12 years. McNeill was not present to witness the final ignominy, a 3-1 defeat by Manchester United at Old Trafford, because with the team guaranteed bottom spot in the division he had been sacked the day before. With a mere eight months under his belt, he endured the briefest spell of any manager in the club's history, and even his pedigree and experience had failed to leave him immune to the underlying financial problems at Villa Park. 'When a big club like Villa starts to slide,' mused McNeill, 'it is difficult to stop. I always knew there would not be a quick and simple solution.'

Although McNeill was not blameless for his role in the relegation season, there was some sympathy for a man who was asked to transform a team at its lowest ebb without the basic assistance of finance. That said, with the credentials he brought to the job, the supporters at least had the right to expect light at the end of the tunnel. Having seen their own abject team limp to the championship wooden spoon, they instead found themselves staring into the abyss.

Chapter Eight: 1987-92
Back to the Drawing Board

Confidence was low at Villa. Since the departure of Barton, two managers at either end of the spectrum had tried their best to restore the club to loftier heights, but both had been found wanting. Ellis was still keen to appoint Ron Atkinson, a manager whose perfect team could be moulded from his philosophy of life – brash and expensive. Again he was unavailable, so the search went on for a suitable replacement.

What the board really needed was a tactician with business sense – somebody who would make the best use of the resources on offer, but who would understand the restrictions within which he would have to operate. And so it was that the directors of Aston Villa initiated one of the most astute business dealings in the history of the club. They acquired the services of Graham Taylor.

Taylor will forever be remembered for his lack of success as an international manager. He was the man who took charge of an England team that had just reached the semi-final stage of the World Cup, saw them through a disastrous European Championship, then failed to get them to USA '94. Vilified and humiliated for much of his time as the national coach, he was written and talked about as though he didn't have a clue about football.

It wasn't always like this. Injury forced Taylor to quit playing at the age of just 28, but he used his missed opportunities on the pitch to forge a successful career off of it. In the late 1980s he was best known for having taken Watford from the depths of the old Division Four to the giddy summit of Division One, and all in the space of five years. Along the way the club narrowly missed out on the championship, finishing as runners-up in the 1982-83 season, and lost to Everton in the 1984 FA Cup final, when Andy Gray had been one of the goalscorers. Now Villa had hired his services he seemed like a shrewd bet to get the club back into Division One.

Taylor was aware of the task ahead of him and spoke intelligently when asked what he hoped he could achieve at Villa Park. 'Managers often take a job and ask supporters to be patient. How can I do that when Villa were European champions only five years ago? The Second Division will be tough, but we must have the desire and the passion. The supporters will take us the rest of the way.' There were practical matters to attend to first, of course. The first team needed to be rebuilt, not least in defence where both Dorigo and

50 Greatest Players

GARY SHAW   **Forward**

Born: Birmingham, 1 January 1961

Joined Aston Villa: 1977   **From:** Coleshill Town

Appearances: 212   **Goals:** 80

Left Aston Villa: 1988   **For:** BK Copenhagen

A perfect example of what might have been, Gary Shaw had everything a young striker should need to achieve success – pace, anticipation and a natural appetite for goal scoring. Born in Kingshurst, his local roots helped to endear him to the Holte End when he turned professional a year after beginning an apprenticeship at Villa Park. Shaw became a first-team regular in the 1979-80 season, missing just two matches throughout Villa's league title campaign the following year. One of the true stars of the team that progressed to the European Cup, Shaw scored a memorable goal in the quarter-final against Dynamo Kiev, and his outstanding displays helped to win the honour of European Young Footballer of the Year. A formidable partner to Peter Withe, Shaw was also a regular member of the 1982-83 team, but then a succession of injuries almost certainly robbed him of an international career as well as a chance to extend his already impressive club record.

Williams were leaving. Taylor brought in David Hunt from Notts County, Steve Sims from Watford, and Mark Lillis from Derby County, and also added Kevin Gage, a Wimbledon full back, without breaking the bank. Gray and Stainrod both left the club before the new season began, so to bolster his attack Taylor snapped up Alan McInally in a £225,000 deal with Celtic.

He also instilled a discipline in the side that had been sadly lacking for a number of years. Working the players harder than ever in practice, and insisting that they arrived at Villa Park no later than 10am on home match days, he was able to spend more time getting to know his squad and working through their problems. If achieving promotion at the first attempt was even a slight opportunity, Taylor wanted to grasp it with both hands.

The approach paid off. Two defeats in the first three matches of the new league campaign was an inauspicious start, especially as one of them was against Birmingham at home, but after the first few, faltering steps, Taylor's new-look Villa began to find their feet, particularly during a three-month spell between November and February when they won nine matches in a spectacular unbeaten run. Although promotion was a distinct possibility, the manager's mind was already turning to the following season and the requirements for Villa to consolidate their resurgence in fortunes. Into the club came the Crystal Palace midfielder Andy Gray and his Barnsley namesake Stuart, but the new arrival destined to make the biggest impact was David Platt, an attacking midfielder signed from Crewe Alexandra for £200,000. Platt scored on his debut for the club, against Blackburn Rovers at Ewood Park, and established himself as a favourite with the fans when he found the net in his second and third games too, against Plymouth and Bournemouth.

A run of three defeats at the beginning of April left Villa with an uphill task to secure one of the automatic promotion berths. When the team could manage only a 0-0 draw away to Swindon on the last day of the season, it seemed almost certain that they would finish in third place and be forced into the new play-off system as one of four clubs battling it out for a single slot in Division One. Then news filtered through that Middlesbrough had been beaten in their final match, meaning that Villa had risen to second place. Thanks to Taylor's measured and disciplined approach, not to mention the shrewd signings of McInally and Platt, the club were back up at the first time of asking.

50 Greatest Players

ALLAN EVANS   **Defender**

Born: Edinburgh, 12 October 1956

Joined Aston Villa: 1977   **From:** Dunfermline Athletic

Appearances: 473   **Goals:** 63

Left Aston Villa: 1989   **For:** Leicester City

Evans stood firm at the heart of Villa's defence for a decade, but had far more attacking ambition when he began his career. As a 15-year-old at Dunfermline Athletic he turned heads with a natural prowess in front of goal but endured a nightmare debut in the first team when he broke his leg against Rangers, but he went on to play more than 120 games before joining Villa in 1977. Evans played his first three games in attack, scoring against Newcastle, but it was not long before he switched to the centre of defence. He lost his place during the season of 1986-87, but Graham Taylor's arrival gave his career a new lease of life. Evans moved to Leicester, but he returned to Villa as Brian Little's assistant manager at the end of 1994.

Consolidation was to prove a more difficult task than promotion. Many 21st century clubs find the chasm between Division One and the Premiership too wide to bridge and, although the difference around the time of the 1988-89 season was somewhat less extreme, Villa were given an instant reminder that this was going to be a tough campaign. After the euphoria of the previous 12 months, many supporters thought this would be the year in which their club reached for the skies once more, some even predicting a place in Europe – as it was, that second goal would be a few more months coming.

Villa beat Arsenal at Highbury on 3 September, with a goal from Gray and a brace from McInally, but this was the team's only victory during the first two months of the season. They were drawing too many games and losing to the likes of Derby and Coventry. The side had more resilience about it than the one which had been relegated two years before, but the results were a clear indication that safety was as much as Villa could hope for this time.

Taylor spent much of the season searching for the upturn in fortunes that would see his team through to a respectable finish, but Villa were not scoring enough. Both McInally and Platt had been in marvellous form early on, contributing bagfuls of goals, but unfortunately too many were being conceded and once the new-look attack began to run out of steam, the problems mounted. Again the team failed in the cup competitions, although supporters did enjoy the spectacle of a 7 0 aggregate thrashing of Birmingham in the Littlewoods Cup, and another crisis loomed fast when an appalling two-month run saw the players pick up two points out of a possible 24.

Vital victories over Luton Town and Newcastle were to prove the last of the season, a shame, because defeat by Derby in the penultimate game meant that Villa required three points against Coventry to guarantee their survival. They managed only a 1-1 draw as the tension became unbearable for many of the fans. Police made more than 50 arrests, but any effort expended through frustration was even more futile than usual – with other clubs still having to complete their programmes it would be more than a week before Villa knew their fate. On 23 May 1989, the club breathed a collective sigh of relief. West Ham United, who had been vying with Villa for that unwanted relegation spot, were trounced 5-1 by Liverpool at Anfield. The Hammers went down, Villa stayed up, and Taylor now knew what he would have to do to make his team a force to be reckoned with. As expected, the summer break was a busy one for the financiers. Changes were made all over the pitch, but it was the defence in which Taylor knew he had to make the greatest investment and, accordingly, he signed an international who became the best-paid player in Villa's history.

50 Greatest Players

PAUL McGRATH Defender

Born: Ealing, 4 December 1959

Joined Aston Villa: 1989 **From:** Manchester United

Appearances: 323 **Goals:** 10

Left Aston Villa: 1996 **For:** Derby County

Alex Ferguson's decision to sell 29-year-old Paul McGrath to Aston Villa for £400,000 was one of his rare errors. A succession of knee injuries and his well-documented social life had caused his relationship with Ferguson to deteriorate, and in the summer of 1989 he switched to Villa Park. Much credit goes to Graham Taylor whose foresight landed Aston Villa a player who is regarded by many as the greatest defender of his generation. Despite the condition of his knees, which latterly prevented him from training, he maintained an astonishing level of consistency, was quick, powerful, strong in the air, formidable in the tackle and composed in possession. He was a player who invited hyperbole. His best season as a Villan came in 1992-93 when he starred in Ron Atkinson's side that pushed United all the way in the race for the inaugural Premiership crown. United eventually won the race, but McGrath had the consolation of being voted Player of the Year by fellow professionals.

Search for the Right Formula

It says something for the way footballers' salaries have snowballed since. Paul McGrath, a Republic of Ireland central defender who would take part in a World Cup quarter-final 12 months later, had agreed to the princely sum of £2,000 a week after agreeing to a transfer from Manchester United. Nowadays he would be demanding a figure closer to 15 times that amount, even though he was the proud owner of the most famous dodgy knees in the business. At 29 he was just reaching his prime and would become the rock among Taylor's solid new foundation of a three-man central defence.

There was to be no room in this triumvirate for Keown, who was sold to Everton for £750,000. His place had been taken by Derek Mountfield, who had moved in the opposite direction from Goodison Park a few months earlier. He had been part of the team that beat Taylor's Watford in the 1984 FA Cup final, and also boasted league and European Cup-Winners' Cup medals among the glinting shelves of his trophy cabinet.

The final berth was to be occupied by another polished and experienced player. Kent Nielsen, an international with Denmark, arrived from Brondby to add yet more solidity at the back. Described by Taylor at the time as 'the nearest thing to what you might call an old-fashioned centre half', it was his dependability that was to allow his two more adventurous colleagues to mix defence with attack on a regular basis.

Recent months had also seen changes to Villa's attack. McInally's goal-scoring exploits had attracted the attention of German giants Bayern Munich, who paid £1.1 million to take him to the Bundesliga, although any disappointment the fans felt in losing him had already been tempered by the return of Gordon Cowans after his spell with Bari. The Villa Park stalwart would form a prosperous relationship with his new manager, whose approach suited his talents perfectly.

Ian Olney, a lively 19-year-old, took over from McInally at centre forward for his first season of top-class football. The other key players were to be Platt, whose stock was to rise at stellar speed over the next couple of years, and the two wide players – Ian Ormondroyd and Tony Daley, the latter by now a winger in the true footballing sense of the word and with a 240-volt kick in his heels.

The defence undoubtedly looked more reliable, but three draws from the opening three encounters, against Nottingham Forest, Liverpool and Charlton, hardly lifted Villa off the ground. Three defeats from the next four games prompted another re-jig from Taylor, and although personnel would switch around with regularity over the next few weeks, it worked an immediate trick. A 1-0 win over Derby County heralded a five-match winning streak, in itself part of a five-month run that would see the team win all but three of its matches in the League.

By the time Villa completed a routine 2-0 victory at Spurs on 21 February 1990, the team sat proudly on top of Division One. But the players' style, rather than their short inhabitancy of the summit of English football, would prove to be the most notable achievement of Taylor's initial reign as manager. This was a formation bent on attack, with five front men surging forward in the knowledge that they had reliable cover at the back. Platt, as well as possessing wonderful control and exceptional power, could cut through from midfield to danger areas like a shark's fin through water. During the season as a whole he scored 19 goals from 37 games – statistics which supported the statement of Dario Grady, the Crewe Alexandra manager, who had suggested Taylor had got his man for a 'bargain' at £200,000 the previous year.

Daley had found his feet in every sense, frightening opposition players when he ran at them with the ball, neatly sidestepping challenges and righting himself in an instant on the rare occasion he lost any balance. Olney, despite the fact that he was not scoring that many goals, was proving a distraction to defenders with his probing runs in the centre-forward position. All of this, combined with Cowans' ability to pick out his target man and hit him with the perfect pass, made Villa a formidable opposition. In a season Arsenal and Liverpool were expected to dominate as they fought it out for the championship once more, the West Midlands had managed to offer up something for sports writers to think about.

A two-week stutter in the resurgence saw Villa let Liverpool back in with a sniff at the top of Division One, crashing 3-0 in a shocking home performance against Wimbledon, and going down 2-0 away to Coventry. Defeat at the hands of Oldham Athletic meant that the club progressed no further than the sixth round of the FA Cup, so by mid-March it was clear that all attention needed to be focused on top spot in the league. Villa still led the way, albeit now without the advantage of games in hand, and they recovered the initiative by beating Luton and Derby.

Tony Cascarino became Villa's record signing when he joined from Millwall for £1.5 million, but the big Irish striker was unable to help his new team-mates sustain their title challenge. A lifeless performance at Selhurst Park, resulting in defeat by a single goal, allowed Liverpool to leapfrog Villa. Taylor's men could not manage to overhaul the Merseyside team again and stalemates in the final two games of the season meant that they finished nine points behind the champions.

Overall, the campaign could hardly have been described as a disappointment. With a radical alteration to both team and tactics, Taylor had transformed Villa from a side relegated only three seasons before. Now they had beaten the previous year's champions, Arsenal, into second place, and gained the reward of entry into the UEFA Cup as a result. Not only would it be the fans' first taste of European football in seven years, it would also both guarantee bigger gate receipts and television money to the club.

International Recognition

It was no surprise that Taylor's success had been noted in other quarters. Impressed by his work at Villa Park, and searching for a replacement for Bobby Robson, who had announced he would be leaving the position after the 1990 World Cup, the Football Association asked him to become the new manager of England. It was an offer he could hardly refuse and he left with the support of a good percentage of Birmingham, if not the country, to take up the toughest job in football management.

It was still two years before the formation of the Premiership, but Ellis could see that football was big business once more. With Villa having qualified for

European competition as English club's re-entered the international arena, it was vital that he hired a forward-thinking coach. Not for the first time, he showed surprising imagination with the appointment of Dr Josef Venglos, a multi-lingual expert in philosophy and physical education, twice manager of the Czechoslovakia national team, and the first foreign coach to take charge of a top-flight club in England.

Venglos, who soon became affectionately known as Gentleman Jo around Villa Park, had achieved much with the Czech national side, having been no mean player himself with Slovan Bratislava. He took them to two World Cups and the semi-finals of the 1980 European Championships, and had rounded his coaching skills with jobs in the Far East, Australia and Portugal. Having coached some precocious talents, he saw much that he liked at Villa. 'Our boys have confidence that they're able to compete with the best in England,' he told the *Birmingham Post*. 'Players such as Platt and Daley are more flexible, skilful players. Through our training sessions we can try to adapt, bring something that is different to them. I was in charge for 76 games with Czechoslovakia, so I know about pressure.'

Which was handy, because Villa won only three of the first eight games of the new season, leaving the team tottering around the mid-table region by the time it had to face Banik Ostrava in the two-legged first round of the UEFA Cup. Goals from Mountfield, Olney and Platt ensured the players had a comfortable 3-1 platform to take away to the second leg, but they had to rely on an own goal from Ivo Stas to win the return match 2-1. Now came the greater test – a second-round showdown with Inter Milan.

Venglos had introduced a number of innovations to his players' regular preparations in anticipation of such games. He insisted that they cut out half-time cups of tea and made sure they received vitamin and mineral supplements so as to be in peak physical condition. When Villa took on an Internazionale team bursting with Italian internationals in the first leg on 24 October, it looked as though his theories were beginning to bear fruit. Using the explosive pace of Daley and Platt to pin their opponents back, they stormed to a 2-0 victory worthy of mention alongside the club's finest European endeavours. Nielsen and Platt himself, with a goal in either half, were the scorers, but every player and the manager himself were heroes for having beaten Inter at their own game.

All of this made Villa's second leg performance that much harder to fathom. Perhaps the team was undone by the thought of playing in front of 75,000 fans at the San Siro. Certainly the players were a pale shadow of their former selves, and by the time a contested third Inter goal was allowed they were hurtling out of the competition. Platt, a star in his own right on the international stage after

50 Greatest Players

DAVID PLATT   **Midfielder**

Born: Oldham, 10 June, 1966

Joined Aston Villa: 1988   **From:** Crewe Alexandra

Appearances: 155   **Goals:** 68

Left Aston Villa: 1991   **For:** Bari

Still the best investment Villa have made, Dario Grady spotted Platt's potential, and when he transferred from Gresty Road to Villa Park in 1988 the Crewe manager referred to the £200,000 price tag as a bargain. Platt established himself as one of the leading midfielders of his generation, combining exceptional pace and power with scoring as many goals as a manager would expect from an out-and-out striker. His defining moment came at the 1990 World Cup, when he latched onto Paul Gascoigne's free kick in the 119th minute of a second-round match against Belgium, spinning and volleying into the net to give England a dramatic 1-0 victory. Platt was sold to the Serie A club Bari the following year for £5.5 million – a staggering fee at the time – and went on to play for Sampdoria and Juventus before returning to England to win the domestic Double with Arsenal. With combined transfer fees topping £22 million, he was once the world's most expensive footballer, and followed up 62 international caps by becoming England U-21 manager at the age of 35.

his last-minute World Cup goal for England against Belgium a few months before, summed it up simply: 'We know we didn't play well.'

Slide Down the Table

Not for the first time, it was as if a bubble had been burst at Villa Park. All the optimism that had built up prior to the second match with Inter had suddenly dissipated, as though the performers had been handed the wrong script. Villa managed just one more victory prior to Christmas, a 2-1 win over Sheffield United, and then just five between the New Year and end of the season, finishing four points and one place above the relegation zone, in 17th position. Along the way the *Evening Mail* had run with a backpage splash demanding: 'For God's sake go, Dr Jo!' Cascarino had suffered another miserable season with nine league goals hardly justifying his price tag, Platt appeared to be on his way out of the club, and the relevance of a

19-year-old Trinidadian called Dwight Yorke scoring in the penultimate match of the season was lost on just about everybody.

As it turned out, Platt would never play for Villa again. With another 24 goals to add to his previous tally and an increasingly good international strike rate for a midfielder, he was a man in demand. Bari won the race for his services, the Serie A club paying Villa £5.5 million to take him to Italy, and in doing so beating the record transfer of Andy Gray to Wolves, some 11 years earlier, by £4 million.

Venglos was to be denied the chance to use the proceeds from Platt's sale when, a couple of weeks after the season ended, his contract was terminated. Despite his disappointing season, many felt sorry for a coach considered to be ahead of his time. His methods on both technical and dietary levels paved the way for the likes of Wenger and Houllier in English football, and who is to say that, given another season, he might not have been successful? Either way, his valedictory speech was typically gracious. 'To have been at the epicentre of English football has been an honour and a privilege,' he said. 'I am wiser for the experience. I have been widely described as an honest, gentlemanly person. This is very nice, but I would much prefer to make an impression as a successful coach here.' Perhaps if his players had been as forward thinking as he, he may have had the chance.

Ellis Finally Gets His Man

New season, new manager needed – hardly the first time the chairman had found himself in this position (and not exactly the last), but again Ellis had a definite idea of the man he wanted to take charge. This time he was determined to get him, too. Announcing that he was looking for 'an experienced British manager', his train of thought having taken something of an about-turn, he set about securing the services of the larger-than-life figure who had escaped his attentions twice before – Ron Atkinson.

'Big Ron' was already well known in the Midlands. His highest profile jobs had been as manager of Manchester United and Atletico Madrid, but he had also served two spells as manager of West Bromwich Albion. In recent years he had been in charge of Sheffield Wednesday, steering the Yorkshire club to its first postwar trophy with the capture of the Littlewoods Cup in 1990-91, but throughout that time he had maintained his local connections, living with his wife, Maggie, in the plush Birmingham suburb of Barnt Green. Wednesday directors were far from keen to let their manager go and Ellis' initial approach failed when, after a lengthy meeting with his chairman at Hillsborough, Atkinson turned down a substantial offer. Days later, however, he was on his way to Villa Park, citing the 200-mile round trip from Birmingham as the main reason for his departure, but declining to discuss the details of the improved offer of £750,000 over four years.

Atkinson was quick off the mark, bringing Andy Gray back to the club for a third spell – this time as assistant manager – and splashing out £1.1 million on the Liverpool and Republic of Ireland left back Steve Staunton, and £1.6 million – a club record – on Dalian Atkinson, a former Wednesday striker who had been playing for Real Sociedad in Spain. Paul Mortimer was signed from Charlton Athletic to help out on the left side of midfield, and veteran striker Cyrille Regis arrived from Coventry City to add some wile to the attack.

A change in tactics was in the offing, too. Villa reverted to a 4-4-2 formation for the first time in four years – a traditional British system which suited Atkinson's direct and attacking style. Early results were inconclusive, with the usual spattering of draws and defeats comprising the first month of his reign, but five straight league victories on the trot throughout October were a sign that the players were becoming accustomed to one another. The £1.7 million signing of right back Earl Barrett from Oldham Athletic broke Villa's transfer record for the second time in months, and with the £650,000 addition of

50 Greatest Players

KENT NIELSEN   Defender

Born: Denmark, 28 December 1961

Joined Aston Villa: 1989   **From:** Brondby

Appearances: 100   **Goals:** 5

Left Aston Villa: 1992   **For:** AGF

A brilliant stopper, Nielsen slotted into the central defence with consummate ease when he arrived at Villa Park for £500,000. He formed one third of an imposing partnership alongside Paul McGrath and Derek Mountfield when Graham Taylor's 3-5-2 system took Villa to the runners-up position in Division One. Best remembered by supporters for a magnificent UEFA Cup goal against Inter Milan, it was actually his ability to stand almost on top of defenders that helped to resettle Taylor's team after the initial traumas of life back in the top flight. Nielsen's talents did not go unrecognized at home either – he was a member of Denmark's surprise European Championships-winning side in 1992 – and many fans were unhappy when Ron Atkinson, having recently been appointed as manager, took the decision to sell him to AGF.

50 Greatest Players

STEVE STAUNTON   Defender

Born: Droghedra, Ireland, 19 January 1969

Joined Aston Villa: 1991, 2000	**From:** Liverpool (both times)
Appearances: 278	**Goals:** 18
Left Aston Villa: 1998	**For:** Liverpool

Steve Staunton was one of a host of expensive new signings made by Ron Atkinson after his appointment as Villa manager in the summer of 1991. Staunton, who had already collected league and FA Cup winner's medals with the Reds, was the pick of the new arrivals, and at £1.1m was a bargain. He wasted little time settling in, scoring on his debut against Sheffield Wednesday, before adding to his tally with a goal in the 3-1 win over Arsenal a week later. The defender, who now holds the appearance record for the Republic of Ireland, remains a reliable goalscorer, thanks in no small part to a venomous left-footed shot from either open play or a deadball situation. His other great asset is his versatility, and he has played at left back, left midfield and centre back. He was a member of the victorious 1994 League Cup-winning team, but missed the 1996 final, and a year later returned to Anfield on a Bosman-style free transfer. After two years, John Gregory brought the competitive Irishman back to Villa Park.

Garry Parker to midfield, fans found themselves pleasantly surprised that the board had kept its promise to re-invest some of the proceeds of Platt's sale.

The sixth round of the FA Cup was as far as Villa got in any of the knock-out competitions, but Atkinson enjoyed an encouraging first campaign in the League. Gone was the uncertainty and unfamiliarity that had marked Venglos' tenure, and some increasingly assured performances elevated the team to seventh position at the end of the season. Dalian Atkinson had been a big disappointment, largely due to injury problems that forced him to miss far too many matches, but Regis had more than made up for his young colleague's absence with some wonderful touches and a bagful of goals. Daley also enjoyed a telling year, continuing to worry opposition defences with his pace from wide midfield, but the real find was that young striker who had scored for the first time at the end of the previous season. Dwight Yorke was simply spectacular, finishing with 17 goals in 35 games and displaying the confident touch and decisive finishing that would make him a Holte End hero for a long time to come.

Chapter Nine: 1992-2000
A New Premiership Start

Villa's re-acquaintance with successful traditions had come in the nick of time. The summer of 1992 became the most important for the Football League since its inception in 1888 (although not to the advantage of the organization itself) and the most tangible result was money. Pots of it. It was, of course, the creation of the FA Premiership, formed when the Division One clubs resigned from the league. They would take part in a new competition that guaranteed them some of the proceeds from Sky's pay-for-view television coverage, for which Rupert Murdoch, the chairman, had agreed to pay £304 million over five years. It would usher in a new era where the most successful clubs – and therefore the richest – would pull away from the strugglers to effectively create a league within a league.

Club chairmen knew that the stakes, and rewards, had been raised. The race was on for the top spots in the Premiership's first season, and Ellis, adamant that Villa would be among the front-runners, delved into his pocket yet again when, a few weeks into the season, it became obvious that a new striker was needed to partner the fit-again Dalian Atkinson. At 34, Regis could not be expected to cope with the pace, so the manager went for Welsh international Dean Saunders who, at £2.3 million, became the latest to break Villa's increasingly fragile transfer record. He was joined by another Ireland international, Ray Houghton, who arrived from Liverpool for £850,000, and Mark Bosnich, an Australian goalkeeper who would replace Nigel Spink between the posts.

Although three draws from the opening three fixtures was a modest return, opposition teams soon found that this was, at least, a sign that Villa were difficult to beat. Atkinson's team was winning new fans with a tight defence and a balanced, attractive and attacking approach, and victories over Liverpool, Manchester United and Arsenal were confirmation of their credentials. Yorke and Saunders, in particular, were running into form and a 5-1 victory over Middlesbrough on 17 January 1993 put Villa on top of the fledgling Premiership for the first time in the club's history. Although they had suffered another disappointing season in the cups, the real target – the inaugural Premiership crown – was still very much an option.

Faltering form saw Atkinson's charges slip to third within a few weeks, but with two months of the season left they were still in contention. A 1-1 draw against the leaders, Manchester United, had been given the showcase treatment by Sky and Villa had lived up to the billing with aplomb – Staunton firing his team in front before a header from Mark Hughes levelled the scores. After such a display it was a disappointment that the players allowed inconsistency to creep in, although they did reclaim top spot when McGrath scored the only goal in the early-April win over Nottingham Forest.

A draw against Coventry, followed by wins over Arsenal and Manchester City, meant Villa were neck-and-neck with United going into the final stage of the season. Supporters prayed that they would finish the season with a sprint, so a 3-0 defeat at the hands of Blackburn Rovers was the last thing anybody expected. Worse still, the best player on show at Ewood Park that day was Gordon Cowans, who had moved to the Lancashire club 18 months earlier.

Now it was critical. Atkinson knew that Villa needed at least a point from the penultimate game against Oldham Athletic to take the title race to the last day of the season. The disappointment at losing 1-0, therefore, was acute. It had been a horrible performance on the day, gifting the Premiership crown to United. Although he did not mention it, the irony of the result was not lost on a manager who had been sacked from the Old Trafford post for failing in much the same way a few years earlier. 'We haven't scored enough in the run-in,' he told reporters. 'It's been nip and tuck with United, but now it looks as though they might win it by a street, which won't be a fair reflection on us.' Atkinson was correct. Villa lost their final match against QPR and finished ten points behind the new champions.

At least a second top-two finish in the space of four years guaranteed more European football. In the days prior to the Champions League, the runners-up position was good enough only for a place in the UEFA Cup, but this was a satisfying return from the first season of the Premiership and ensured that the club could plan for the future with the knowledge of a certain level of income. An early sign was the opening of the new Doug Ellis Stand, a 10,000-seater structure that lacked modesty in both appearance and name.

Push for the Top

The build-up to the 1993-94 season was as busy as ever, with striker Guy Whittingham and yet another Ireland international, midfielder Andy Townsend, joining the club for a combined fee of £3.3 million. The prodigal Gordon Cowans was also welcomed back to the Midlands after completing his spell at Blackburn. Unusually for Villa, it was to be a season in which the players' achievements in cup competitions outshone their performances in the league. They would not enjoy a lengthy run in Europe, though. A comfortable

50 Greatest Players

ANDY TOWNSEND Midfielder

Born: Maidstone, 23 July 1963

Joined Aston Villa: 1993 **From:** Chelsea

Appearances: 176 **Goals:** 11

Left Aston Villa: 1997 **For:** Middlesbrough

When Andy Townsend made the switch to Villa Park from Chelsea in 1993 he came with a reputation as one of the most complete and coveted midfielders in the Premier League. The effervescent Republic of Ireland international had been courted by all of England's top clubs, and his signing, for a fee of £2.5m, was something of a coup for Villa boss Ron Atkinson. Andy quickly proved his worth to Villa with a series of action-packed displays from the left-hand side, bringing both skill and industry to an already impressive Villa midfield. In his first season as a Villan, Andy collected a League Cup-winner's medal after a Man-of-the-Match performance in the 3-0 victory over Manchester United. Two years later Andy was back at Wembley in the same competition, but this time he was captain for the 3-0 triumph over Leeds United. By the time he moved on to Middlesbrough in the summer of 1997, Andy Townsend had firmly established himself in the affections of the Villa faithful. His competitive spirit, his accomplished range of passing and his ability to strike the ball with power from distance, marked him out as the latest in a long line of top-class midfielders to have graced the claret and blue jersey.

2-1 aggregate victory over Slovan Bratislava in the first round pitched them against Deportivo La Coruña, a brilliant team from northern Spain for whom Brazilian World Cup striker Bebeto was a regular. Despite a 1-1 draw on foreign turf, Villa flopped at home and lost by a single goal. Atkinson was left seething. 'There were a lot of my most experienced players out there who let themselves, the club and the fans down,' he stormed. 'We were a very poor advert for English football and I wish I knew why.'

Villa's form in the Premiership also took a knock after the UEFA Cup defeat. The team were booed off the pitch after losing at home to Southampton in late November, but this was only the beginning of a dire run which yielded just three points from a possible 18. From second place in the table they plummeted to tenth by the turn of the year, and just six victories throughout the remainder of the season was nowhere near enough to get them near a European slot.

All was not lost, however. After many seasons of underachievement, Villa were enjoying something of a renaissance in cup competitions – or the League Cup, at least. Coca-Cola had taken over the marketing and the backing of such a major sponsor had helped to restore some of the trophy's previous gloss. Villa started off in the best possible way, beating Birmingham 2-0 on aggregate in the first round. Then an emphatic victory over Sunderland, followed by the completion of the North London double of Arsenal and Spurs, booked a place in the semi-final. Atkinson knew that appearing at Wembley would be a stepping-stone to Europe, but by the end of the first leg, on 16 February, his plans had been sunk. A 3-1 defeat by Tranmere Rovers at Prenton Park was unexpected, and leading up to the return leg at Villa Park he proclaimed that it was a time for his highly paid stars to 'stand up and be counted'.

Original it may not have been, effective it certainly was. In a nail-biting match, goals from Saunders and Shaun Teale fired Villa to a 2-0 lead in less than half an hour, before a penalty from John Aldridge rested the initiative back with Tranmere. With two minutes remaining, Villa were 4-3 down on aggregate until Dalian Atkinson scored one of his most vital goals for the club to level the tie. Both teams tired visibly in extra-time and a penalty shoot-out was inevitable as the final whistle approached. The teams remained deadlocked, 4-4, by the time sudden death arrived, and the hearts of Villa supporters died a little when Kevin Richardson sent his strike soaring over the crossbar. Liam O'Brien stepped up to take the kick that could send Tranmere through, but this time it was Bosnich who performed heroically, diving to his right to stop the shot. Tony Daley converted Villa's next penalty and then it was Tranmere spirits that were shattered, as Bosnich again saved from Ian Nolan to seal the match. Villa were at Wembley for the first time in 17 years.

It was ironic that Manchester United should lie in wait for the manager once more, having caused him to come to grief on more than one occasion. This time Big Ron would emerge with a big smile. Two goals from Saunders – one a penalty after Kanchelskis handled on the line in the dying minutes – helped Villa to a 3-1 win in front of a crowd of 77,231. A season that had looked as though it was drifting towards mediocrity had delivered spectacularly and, after three years in charge, Atkinson was as popular as ever.

Facing the Future with Confidence

As the club looked towards the 1994-95 season, it could take heart in the knowledge that it was a stable organization. Atkinson had delivered silverware

Great Matches

LEAGUE CUP FINAL		Wembley Stadium, 27 March 1994

Aston Villa 3   **Manchester United 1**   Attendance: 77,231

Atkinson   Hughes
Saunders 2 (1 pen)

The first trophy Villa had won since the European Super Cup 11 years earlier was savoured all the more for the identity of the opposition they overcame. United had become established as the country's leading club, and possessed a team which, in Ron Atkinson's words, was 'better than when they won the Premiership title last season'. Dean Saunders was Villa's sole striker in a 4-5-1 formation designed specifically to put a stranglehold on United's midfield freedom, meaning that their attackers – Eric Cantona, Ryan Giggs and Andrei Kanchelskis – had to toil to find space in which to operate. Alex Ferguson's team grabbed the early initiative with both Roy Keane and Mark Hughes going close, but his defenders found themselves being constantly pulled out of position by Villa's midfield. After 25 minutes Andy Townsend pushed the ball forward to Saunders, whose first-time pass found Atkinson in space. The Villa striker took the ball out of the path of Steve Bruce before firing a shot below Les Sealey – a brilliant goal with which to take the lead. United continued to be suffocated by Villa's tactics and found chances few and far between, and they were made to suffer further when Paul Parker fouled Tony Daley on the left wing. From the resultant free kick, Villa captain Kevin Richardson crossed into United's penalty area where Saunders prodded the ball into the net from six yards. Mark Hughes pulled one back after 83 minutes to give the Reds a glimmer of hope, but in the dying seconds of the match Kanchelskis was sent off for deliberately handling an Atkinson shot in the area, and the match was Villa's. Saunders slapped the penalty into the back of the net and the celebrations began.

Aston Villa: Bosnich, Barrett, McGrath, Teale, Staunton (Cox), Richardson, Daley, Townsend, Fenton, Atkinson, Saunders.

Manchester United: Sealey, Parker, Bruce (McClair), Pallister, Irwin, Kanchelskis, Keane, Ince, Giggs (Sharpe), Cantona, Hughes.

and a second promise of European spoils since taking over from Venglos, helping the club to build impressively at the forefront of the Premiership revolution. Within months the outlook would change dramatically, although that transformation began in the most positive style. In the light of Lord Justice Taylor's report into ground safety, commissioned after the 1989 Hillsborough disaster, Villa had agreed to demolish its terraces to build an all-seater stadium. Planning permission had been granted for a new two-tier stand at the Holte End, to allow the ground to hold just under 40,000 fans.

The final game in front of the terraces had been an emotional occasion, attracting a crowd of over 45,000 as Villa beat Liverpool 2-1 in the last match of the 1993-94 season. Yorke scored both in front of the Holte End, but then it was in with the bulldozers for a project which, in tandem with other redevelopment work, would cost Villa around £14 million.

It was a cost reflected by a relatively modest series of transfer activities over the summer. John Fashanu was the best-known arrival, costing £1.2 million from Wimbledon, but players already at the club signed most of the important deals. Bosnich, the hero of Wembley, agreed a five-year extension to his contract, while Staunton did almost as well with a four-year agreement. Thirty-four-year-old McGrath, having long since established himself as one of the club's greatest defenders, was given another year. Tony Daley closed the chapter on his Villa story by agreeing to a £1.25 million transfer to Wolves. Despite the rivalry between the two clubs, he left nothing but fond memories and plenty of friends.

50 Greatest Players

TONY DALEY   **Winger**

Born: Birmingham, 18 October 1967

Joined Aston Villa: 1985 (as apprentice)

Appearances: 290   **Goals:** 38

Left Aston Villa: 1994   **For:** Wolverhampton Wanderers

If supporters held a straw poll for the title of 'Fastest Thing On Two Legs Ever To Have Worn A Villa Shirt', Tony Daley would win by a landslide. Certainly one of the most popular players the club has produced, he was signed as an apprentice after his talent was spotted at an early age, and made his first-team debut in a 5-2 home victory over Queens Park Rangers in 1985. With his exquisite balance and control, Daley was one of the shining lights in an often indifferent team in the mid- and late 1980s, with the sort of pace on the wing that would terrify opposition full backs. Actually told to slow down by Graham Taylor in an attempt to work on his crossing, Daley flourished in the side that finished runners-up for the title in 1989-90. His unpredictable running could throw defences into chaos, and he carried that form into Ron Atkinson's reign as manager, winning seven England caps before leaving for Wolves.

Great Matches

UEFA CUP FIRST ROUND, SECOND LEG   **Villa Park, 29 September 1994**

Aston Villa 1   **Internazionale 0***   **Attendance: 30,533**

Houghton
*Aggregate score 1-1. Villa won 4-3 on penalties

Villa have been blessed with some comfortable UEFA Cup first-round draws over the years
– not so in 1994-95, when Ron Atkinson's team found itself up against Internazionale,
the holders, just a few weeks into the season. Dennis Bergkamp had scored in the first
leg at the San Siro to give Inter a 1-0 lead, but Villa's bombardment of their opponents'
defence suggested there would still be plenty to play for in Birmingham. That theory
was proved when Ray Houghton levelled the aggregate scores, but 90 minutes of normal
time plus an extra half-hour failed to provide a winning goal for either side so, for the
first time, Villa took part in a penalty shoot-out. Bia, Bergkamp and Seno scored the first
three penalties for Inter, but each one of their efforts was matched by a Villa opponent
– Parker, Staunton and Townsend. By the time Fontolan stepped up to take the fourth
penalty for the Italians, the fans at Villa Park were praying for something to go their way
before sudden death ensued. Fontolan missed – but Whittingham failed to take advantage,
leaving the teams deadlocked at 3-3. Villa might have thought they had blown it, but got
an unexpected second chance when Ruben Sosa struck the underside of the crossbar with
his kick to make it three misses in a row. Up stepped Phil King, an accomplished, but
unheralded, left back, to take the penalty that could send his team into the second
round. With exceptional composure, he sent Gianluca Pagliuca the wrong way with a
well-hit shot and won the tie for Villa. Atkinson's men had knocked out the champions.
Aston Villa: Spink, Barrett, King, Ehiogu, McGrath, Richardson (Parker), Houghton,
Townsend, Saunders (Whittingham), Atkinson, Staunton.
Internazionale: Pagliuca, Bergomi, Festa, Paganin, Bia, Conte (Orlandini), Berti,
Bergkamp, Seno, Pancev (Fontolan), Sosa.

Villa began the season in time-honoured fashion – with three draws – before
rediscovering winning ways against Coventry City and Ipswich Town. An
unbeaten start in the League was the perfect fillip for a UEFA Cup campaign
that began with the sternest of tests, against their old rivals Internazionale,
who had won the tournament four months earlier. Although a penalty from
a young Dennis Bergkamp helped Inter to a 1-0 win, Villa's stoic defence gave
them every chance of overturning the score in the second leg at Villa Park.

Ray Houghton, who had scored in Ireland's shock 1-0 win over Italy in the World Cup a few months before, delighted supporters by putting the home side in front, but his was the only goal in two hours of open play. With the scores at 1-1 on aggregate and no away goals for either side, the players were consigned to the drama of another penalty shoot-out – and when Phil King, a left back who had recently joined Villa from Sheffield Wednesday, swept the decisive kick into the back of the net, the stadium shook with delight. The success was to be short-lived. Having disposed of the champions, Villa were expected to overcome Trabzonspor without too many problems in the second round, but having lost the first leg in Turkey by a single goal, they could manage no more than a 2-1 win at home and went out of the competition on the away-goals rule.

Perhaps the defeat should not have been so surprising. Atkinson claimed he 'could not believe it' when Trabzonspor scored, but during the UEFA Cup run Villa's form had hit rock bottom. They had secured one point from a possible 18, and the situation became critical when further defeats to Manchester

Great Managers – 1991-94

RON ATKINSON

Long admired by Doug Ellis, Atkinson would have been manager of Aston Villa many years before he actually took over had the chairman had his way. An average player, Atkinson had been on Villa's books as a teenager but he failed to break into the first team. In a long managerial career he had taken charge of Kettering Town, Cambridge United, West Bromwich Albion (twice), Manchester United, Atletico Madrid and Sheffield Wednesday before moving to Villa Park to accept a challenge he had coveted for years. When he arrived he was quick to dismantle the remnants of the Taylor regime, which had begun to crumble under Josef Venglos anyway, and play a more direct game.

Building a beautifully balanced side, he established Villa as a front-runner in the early days of the Premiership, and led the club to its first silverware in more than a decade

with victory in the 1994 League Cup. A flamboyant character who, with his perpetual tan and sunglasses always looked as though he had just spent two weeks on a beach in Marbella, Atkinson took his job seriously and was devastated when Ellis sacked him on the back of a poor run of results. If Villa owe him anything, it is that he ensured they did not lag at the birth of the Premiership revolution.

50 Greatest Players

RAY HOUGHTON   Midfielder

Born: Glasgow, 9 January 1962
Joined Aston Villa: 1992   **From:** Liverpool
Appearances: 121   **Goals:** 11
Left Aston Villa: 1995   **For:** Crystal Palace

Ray Houghton was a player who fizzed with energy, packing
more enterprise and endeavour into one match than many of his
team-mates managed in an entire season. His Villa career was
similarly intense, with the Republic of Ireland international
playing his part in three dramatic seasons at Villa Park in
the 1990s. Ray was signed by Ron Atkinson from Liverpool
in a somewhat surprising and relatively inexpensive transfer in
the summer of 1992, and having collected a raft of trophies
during a glittering five-season stay on Merseyside his
£825,000 switch came as a huge disappointment to many Liverpool fans.

Once installed at Villa Park, Ray wasted no time in making his mark. He began his
debut campaign in the centre of midfield, but enjoyed his best performances on the
right-hand side, from where he contributed three goals in a season that saw Villa push
Manchester United all the way in the race for the championship. In his second term as
a Villan, Ray helped the Midlanders on the road to Wembley in the League Cup, but he
missed the final against Manchester United due to injury. The following autumn, Ron
Atkinson's tenure as Villa boss came to an end, and the arrival of Brian Little –
complete with tactical switch to 3-5-2 – left Ray surplus to requirements and he was
sold to Crystal Palace for a small fee on transfer deadline day.

United and Wimbledon left the club contemplating relegation. Twenty four
hours after watching his team lose at Selhurst Park, Atkinson was sacked.

Clearly devastated by the decision, he wasted no time with media-driven
protests. 'I have always had a great desire to manage Villa and take them to
the top,' he said. 'Something drastic had to be done, but I don't think my
head had to roll to help the revival.' Atkinson has never forgiven Ellis for the
decision to remove him from office, but such is the chairman's thick skin it
is not an animosity that has worried him unduly. He has never been afraid
to tread on toes, as Leicester City were about to discover. Having had three
seasons out of an experienced manager, Ellis turned his attention to an

50 Greatest Players

NIGEL SPINK   Goalkeeper

Born: Chelmsford, 8 August 1958

Joined Aston Villa: 1979   **From:** Chelmsford City

Appearances: 454

Left Aston Villa: 1996   **For:** West Bromwich Albion

Spink might never have had a part to play in the most famous
night in Villa's history but for an injury to Jimmy Rimmer which
meant he joined the fray in the European Cup final against
Bayern Munich after only nine minutes of the match. Just 21,
he proved his mettle immediately with a series of superb saves,
every one worth as much as Peter Withe's match-winning goal.
Even after his heroic performance, however, Spink had to wait
until Rimmer's transfer to Swansea before becoming first-
choice goalkeeper. Having made his full debut on Boxing Day,
1979, he saw off a variety of challengers during more than a decade between the posts,
and it was only the arrival of Mark Bosnich in the early 1990s that signalled the
beginning of the end of his spell at Villa Park. After 454 appearances he transferred to
West Bromwich Albion in 1996, but will forever be regarded as a hero of the Holte End.

up-and-coming star once more. This one was well known to Villa fans – Brian
Little, the brilliant young forward who had delighted them in the 1970s.

Little Hopes for Big Things

Little's contract with Leicester still had three years to run when Villa's
interest became apparent. Ellis had been refused permission to talk to him by
the Filbert Street board, but that technicality failed to prevent the resignation
of their manager on 22 November 1994. The directors were stunned further
when, although he denied any personal contact with Villa at the time of his
departure, Little was unveiled as Atkinson's successor three days later. It was
news that annoyed everybody associated with Leicester, including the fans,
who would subject him to hostile abuse when he returned as an opposition
manager less than two weeks later.

Although hurt by the criticism, managing Villa had been such an ambition
for Little that he brushed the catcalls aside and threw himself into his new
job. Dispensing with Atkinson's flat back four and employing a 3-5-2

formation based on a trio of central defenders and quick wing backs, he adopted a more adventurous policy in the bid for Premiership survival. Alan Wright and Gary Charles joined for a combined fee of £1.8 million and immediately settled into the flanking roles, while lifelong Villa fan, Ian Taylor, transferred from Sheffield Wednesday to beef up the midfield.

The team's form was anything but consistent for the rest of the season, but Little's main priority was safety and Ellis understood the need for the new players to settle. Their fate was not to be decided until the last match of the season. Although a draw against Norwich was insufficient in itself to guarantee Villa's place in the Premiership, Newcastle United's 3-2 victory over Crystal Palace sent the London club through the trap door instead. Stage one of the latest revival had been completed.

As with all managers about to start their first full season in charge of a club, Little was keen to buy in his own men. The Villa career of former captain Kevin Richardson had ended more or less when Atkinson left, as had that of Ray Houghton, but for some players at smaller clubs Little's arrival signalled a new phase. Among them was Gareth Southgate, then the 24-year-old captain of Crystal Palace, and the first major signing at a cost of £2.5 million.

Little had long been an admirer of Southgate, who would also break into the England team within a few months, but he had a different role in mind for him within his reshaped team. If his 3-5-2 formation was to work he needed three reliable centre backs. He had two already in McGrath, who agreed to a further 12-month extension to his contract, and Ugo Ehiogu, who Atkinson had virtually stolen from West Bromwich Albion for £40,000. Now Southgate would complete a solid, impressive triumvirate with his calm authority on the ball, and it would be a role that would help his international career to get off the ground.

Little returned to Filbert Street to sign Mark Draper, a midfielder, for £3.25 million, but the deal that excited most Villa fans was forged abroad. Savo Milosevic, the Partizan Belgrade and Yugoslavia forward, had been turning heads in Europe with an impressive strike rate. Now 21, he yearned for a move to a bigger stage. After secret talks with a British manager and his chairman, and a cheque for £3.5 million to his club, he got it.

The first match of the new season pitched Villa against their old rivals Manchester United. After finishing a close second to Blackburn Rovers in the Premiership a few months earlier, Alex Ferguson's side were determined to reclaim their familiar place at the top of the League, but they reckoned without the fresh optimism at Villa Park. The new team of Bosnich, Wright, Southgate, McGrath, Ehiogu, Charles, Taylor, Draper, Townsend, Yorke and Milosevic played with wonderful flair – so much so that Villa were more than good for their 3-1 victory. The solid form continued with wins over Spurs, Bolton Wanderers, Wimbledon and Coventry so that, by the first week of October, Little's team lay in second place, having lost just once since the beginning of the campaign.

Although the first few weeks had raised hopes that the club might be in a position from which to challenge for the title once more, they proved to be something of a false dawn. Little was still unable to shed Villa of the annoying inconsistency that had blighted results since the early 1980s and, as usual, not enough goals were being scored. Yorke had continued to give nightmares to goalkeepers, but Milosevic, as was to become his trademark, disappointed. For all his physical stature, powerful running and undoubted skill, he was finding English football a tough proposition.

Villa finished fourth in the Premiership, a position that confirmed the status of a very good team, but not an outstanding one. For the second time in three years the players would enjoy more success in the knock-out competitions, reaching the quarter-finals of the FA Cup and triumphing once more in the Coca Cola Cup.

An away-goals victory over Arsenal had granted Villa a place in the final, and they would use the match against Leeds United to produce one of their finest performances at Wembley. A crowd of 77,056 had travelled to watch the clash between two clubs with proud histories, but whose recent aspirations had been dashed more often than not by the growing might of Manchester United. On the day there was only one team in it, and the most impressive player, ironically, was Milosevic.

The Yugoslav's best performance in a Villa shirt began when he scored one of the best goals in a major final. Midway through the first half he took control of the ball from almost level with the centre circle, evading opposition players until, from 25 yards out, he unleashed an unstoppable shot into the top of the Leeds net. Taylor scored the second after some neat build-up play by Wright, but it was Milosevic who created the third, totally deceiving the Leeds defenders as he passed for Yorke to complete the job. It was a brilliant performance from the team, and a day Milosevic said he would not forget either. 'I have been disappointed at not scoring more goals this season,' he said afterwards, 'but this was a great occasion for the team and one I shall always remember. My goal made up for a lot.'

Villa's victory put them level with Liverpool as the most successful clubs, with five wins each, in League Cup finals, but it was Little's ambition to make them a mighty force in the Premiership. Having been something of a flair player himself, it was no surprise that he should try to attract similar

Great Matches

LEAGUE CUP FINAL   **Wembley Stadium, 24 March, 1996**

Aston Villa 3   **Leeds United 0**   **Attendance: 77,056**

Milosevic
Taylor
Yorke

Two years after winning the League Cup under Ron Atkinson, Villa were back at Wembley to contest the final of their favourite competition. Brian Little was the manager by this time and had built his own team, full of attacking potential and pressing for a place in Europe through its form in the Premiership. One of the few disappointments of Little's first full season in charge had been the form of Savo Milosevic, the £3.5 million signing from Partizan Belgrade. He had scored only 12 goals in the league, but would make his mark in this match after just 20 minutes. Sauntering forward after taking possession just inside the Leeds half, he reached 25 yards from goal before drawing back his left leg and dispatching a rocket of a shot high into the net. Villa were one up, and they doubled their lead ten minutes into the second half with another top-class piece of finishing. Alan Wright's cross to the back post was only half-cleared by Lucas Radebe and Ian Taylor made no mistake in volleying first time past John Lukic. By now there was only one team in contention for the cup and Villa fans were getting ready to celebrate as the final whistle approached. They had a treat still to come in the final minute, though, when a careful build-up by Mark Draper gave Milosevic the ball. The Yugoslav duped Leeds' defenders and whipped a pass to Yorke, whose shot went in off the underside of the crossbar to make it 3-0. One of their easiest victories at Wembley had guaranteed Villa a place in Europe, and added a fifth League Cup to the trophy cabinet.

Aston Villa: Bosnich, Charles, Southgate, McGrath, Ehiogu, Wright, Taylor, Draper, Townsend, Yorke, Milosevic.

Leeds United: Lukic, Kelly, Radebe (Brolin), Wetherall, Parker, Pemberton, Gray, Ford (Deane), Speed, McAllister, Yeboah.

exponents of the sport, but this is where the problem lay with his reign as manager. Milosevic had been a worthwhile gamble, but a few eyebrows were raised when the manager paid even more for the talents of Sasa Curcic, another former Partizan Belgrade player who had spent the previous season at Bolton. Also joining the club were Julian Joachim, a striker whose pace, if not touch, was undeniable, and Fernando Nelson, the Portugal international, who would take the place of an injured Gary Charles at right wing back.

Football's Popularity at All-Time High

The success of Euro '96, during which Villa Park had been one of the venues, ensured English football's popularity was higher than it had ever been, and hearts were gladdened further by the club's encouraging start to the 1996-97 season. After an opening-day defeat by Sheffield Wednesday, Villa remained unbeaten for a month, notching up wins against Blackburn, Derby and Everton. They were the victims of a first-round shock in the UEFA Cup, losing on away goals to the Swedish part-timers Helsingborgs, but such was the general optimism that, having estimated its value at around £130 million, the board voted to make Aston Villa a public limited company, hoping to raise millions of pounds in share issues as a result.

It would not take long for matters to go awry. Shareholders soon found that the predictability of the London Stock Exchange could not be relied upon, and the manager discovered that much the same could be said of his foreign imports. Milosevic continued to flatter to deceive, while Curcic became an embarrassment, publicly voicing his dissatisfaction with his new club and hardly doing anything to enamour himself to the fans when playing. Little could at least rely on the confidence of Ellis, having signed a five-year contract with Villa when the team was still in touch with the leaders at the beginning of 1997, but a final position of fifth in the Premiership was something of a disappointment – even if it did grant the players another shot in Europe.

Little was still not convinced that he had the perfect pairing up front as he prepared for the 1997-98 season. While Yorke was the first name on his team sheet, Milosevic had continued to underachieve and Joachim had struggled to get into the first team because of persistent injury problems. Rumours had been rife some months earlier that Little was interested in bringing home one of the Holte End's favourite 'sons', and there was mass coverage in the local media when eventually he did announce the signing of Stan Collymore.

Having made his name at Nottingham Forest, Cannock-born Collymore spent two seasons at Liverpool, where he had endured both highs and lows. A prolific tally in his first season had been followed by problems on and off the pitch, and it was no secret that his relationship with certain Anfield regulars had disintegrated. For Villa fans, though, his arrival was the best possible news. A quick and powerful centre forward, he was seen by many supporters as an ideal player to decrease the weight of the burden on Yorke's shoulders, and it was all to the good that he had stood among them on the terraces as a boy.

Little was also on the look-out for a midfielder to replace Townsend, who was nearing the end of his career and had moved to Middlesbrough, but it was a surprise when he plumped for Simon Grayson, a reliable but unspectacular acquisition from Leicester. All the talent on the pitch could not fail to disguise an insipid start to the season, with three defeats and a draw from the first four matches, but there was some relief when the players strung together successive victories over Leeds United, Barnsley and Derby County. After that their league form would fluctuate between hideous and pretty damn ugly, a fact that looked quite incongruous alongside the results they produced in the UEFA Cup. Having defended resolutely away from home in the first leg of the first-round tie against Bordeaux, a 1-0 victory at Villa Park saw them progress. Much the same ensured the team's success over Athletic Bilbao in the second round, save for the fact that it was a 2-1 victory in the second leg. The third-round, second-leg clash with Steaua Bucharest prompted some of the best football of Villa's season, when goals from Taylor and Milosevic helped overturn a 2-1 deficit, putting the team into the quarter-finals, three months later.

By the time they were ready for that match, the players would be punch drunk. While Villa's UEFA run had cast a ray of light on the season, all else was pitched in darkness. Despite the odd flash of genius, Collymore had struggled to find his form, and even Yorke's goal return was beginning to look disappointing as Little's system began to fail him.

A handful of wins dotted around a succession of defeats and draws was not enough to pull Villa away from the wrong end of the table, and matters reached an all-time low on 17 January. Having seen their team capitulate to Blackburn Rovers, losing 5-0 at Ewood Park, the supporters let rip, and Milosevic took the brunt of the criticism. He had suffered another poor game, but nothing could excuse his reaction when, upon hearing the abuse of some of the fans, he spat in their direction. Vilified in Birmingham's newspapers, Milosevic was placed on the transfer list the following week. He would leave at the end of the season, but not before the departure of yet another manager.

Little Leaves

Villa managed a 4-0 victory over West Bromwich Albion in the FA Cup the following week, a result which lifted spirits temporarily, but further defeats in the Premiership to Newcastle, Manchester United and Wimbledon raised speculation that Little was on the verge of being sacked. Instead, he resigned. 'There were certain things going on behind the scenes which were affecting my own managerial position,' he told reporters. 'My decision was not taken lightly or on the spur of the moment. It was made with the well-being of Aston Villa uppermost in my mind.'

Although it looked as though Ellis had offered him the chance to fall on his sword, the chairman has always denied he was close to sacking Little. Indeed he claims he had already talked his young manager out of quitting, days before the announcement. 'Whatever else has been said or written about Brian's departure, no dispute, no mysterious happening behind the scenes, no abrasive comment from myself or anyone else prompted his leaving,' he said. 'Brian left Aston Villa because he chose voluntarily to do so and because a variety of pressures had brought him to the conclusion that it would be in the best interests of the club and himself.'

In his autobiography, *Deadly*, Ellis went further, suggesting that Little's decision was largely based on abuse directed not just at himself, but also towards his family. 'It is fair to say that he had been directly affected by abuse suffered by his children who no longer wished to be taken to school because of it,' wrote the chairman, '[and also] by personal, foul-mouthed abuse he was receiving from members of the public seated near his dug-out place.'

Gregory Takes Charge

Speculation as to who would take charge began immediately, but Ellis wasted no time in announcing the appointment of John Gregory as the new manager. Gregory had been first-team coach under Little until 16 months before, when he had taken up an offer to manage Wycombe Wanderers, and results bear out the theory that his departure precipitated Villa's slide. Confident upon his return, arrogant in the eyes of some, he was quick to announce his intention. 'I'm here to keep us up,' he said. 'I know the staff, I know everybody connected with Aston Villa – and I'm quite cheap.'

Morale was low, so it was a big task for Gregory to turn things around. Despite losing out to Atletico Madrid in the UEFA Cup quarter-finals, he and Steve Harrison, who became assistant manager for the second time, transformed an unhappy troop with new ideas in training and fresh tactics on the pitch. Out of ten Premiership matches between his appointment and the end of the season, Villa won eight, an astonishing run that took them to seventh place. With Chelsea – who finished above them in the League – winning the European Cup-Winners' Cup, the team had qualified for Europe again. Not bad for your first three months in charge.

If Gregory thought his management could maintain the stability of its first three months, he was in for a shock. Most of his problems in the run-up to the new season concerned Collymore, who proceeded to compound his ineffectiveness on the pitch by courting controversy off of it. The worst incident, and certainly the most public, was an altercation with his girlfriend,

50 Greatest Players

DWIGHT YORKE   Forward

Born: Tobago, 3 November 1971

Joined Aston Villa: 1989   **From:** Signal Hill (Tobago)

Appearances: 287   **Goals:** 97

Left Aston Villa: 1998   **For:** Manchester United

One of the most talented strikers of his generation, Dwight Yorke was an unknown teenager when he made his debut for Aston Villa. He was brought to the club by Graham Taylor, who had heard promising reports of an exciting young forward plying his trade in the West Indies. With a wonderful first touch and an instinctive finishing ability, Yorke soon endeared himself to supporters, and his goals-to-games ratio would have been higher but for the fact that, towards the end of his spell at Villa Park, he was played out of position. Nor did he benefit from having to carry the attack almost single-handedly throughout the mid-1990s. He became the club's most expensive export when he was sold to Manchester United in August 1998 for £12.6 million. 'If I'd had a gun I would have shot him,' said John Gregory at the time of his transfer request. He was only too aware of the talent he was losing – the predatory skills that would soon win Yorke a new legion of fans as he helped to secure the Treble for United.

the television celebrity Ulrika Jonsson, in which he assaulted her in a Paris bar full of Scotland fans during France '98. The media were whipped into a frenzy by pictures of a miserable Jonsson in the back of a car, apparently concealing her injuries with dark sunglasses, but after releasing a statement deploring his behaviour, Villa stuck by the striker.

Days before the beginning of the new Premiership campaign, the *Sports Argus* reported that Collymore would miss the first three weeks of the season after suffering a thigh strain during training. It was the worst news a manager with limited ammunition could have imagined, particularly as Manchester United were pursuing a particularly aggressive bid to sign Yorke, but the injury had worse ramifications for Collymore, who had been keen to knuckle down after a disappointing first year. He was to suffer another tortuous campaign as his relationship with Gregory, who could not bring himself to understand the striker's fragile personality and flickering form, disintegrated.

Collymore's absence was injurious enough to Villa's hopes of scoring a bagful of goals in the opening fixtures – the next blow was all but mortal. The fact that Alex Ferguson wanted to take Yorke to Old Trafford was hardly little known, but the fans that had cheered him throughout the 1990s at Villa clung desperately to the hope that the Manchester United manager would fail to match Ellis and Gregory's asking price. Such hope evaporated with barely a week of the season gone when Ferguson tabled a bid of £12.6 million – a record for both clubs – and the Trinidadian headed north M6.

'If I'd had a gun I would have shot him,' said Gregory, in a typically honest response to the question of how he had felt when Yorke informed him of his decision to leave, although it would have taken a brave businessman to turn down the type of money United were offering. Without either of his first-choice strikers to pick it was not as though he had the time to harbour a grudge anyway, and replacements would be hard to come by as he grew used to the frustration of waiting for transfer money to be reinvested in the squad. Most of the goals in the opening fixtures would come from midfield, and it was in this area that Gregory made his first major acquisition with the signing of Paul Merson.

Controversy, Success and Anticlimax

A member of the famous title-winning Arsenal team of 1989, Merson had overcome much-publicized drink, drugs and gambling addictions before moving to Middlesbrough in the mid-1990s. Under the management of Bryan Robson, however, he became increasingly unsettled and jumped at the chance of a move to Villa after voicing his own fears that he would slip back into bad old ways in the Northeast. The £6.75 million signing made an immediate impact with a goal against Wimbledon on his debut, a feat that would soon be repeated by the man brought in to fill Yorke's shoes. Dion Dublin's £5.75 million transfer from Coventry City gave Villa some real firepower up front. What he lacked in pace, Dublin more than made up for in presence and he challenged Julian Joachim for the title of top scorer for the season, despite missing the last few games due to a hernia operation and chipped cartilage.

Steve Watson, Colin Calderwood and Mark Delaney were all added to boost the defence during the season, while Gregory made another high-profile signing with the purchase of Steve Stone, the England midfielder, from Nottingham Forest for £5.5 million. The new-look team soon bore all the hallmarks of Gregory's organizational skills, proving difficult to break down if not precocious in attack. Results were solid rather than spectacular as the club reached the fourth round of the FA Cup, third in the Worthington Cup and second in the UEFA Cup, and despite blips along the way – Merson threw his shirt off in disgust after he was substituted in the 4-1 defeat against Coventry City – Gregory's approach ensured Villa took sixth place in the Premiership.

After completing his first full season in charge, Gregory was confident his team could press for honours in 1999-2000. George Boateng, the Dutch midfielder, was signed from Coventry for £4.5 million, and David James arrived from Liverpool for £1.7 million to take over the goalkeeping duties from Mark Bosnich. The Australian shot-stopper quit Villa to follow his old pal Yorke to Manchester United, departing on a free transfer under the Bosman ruling to take Peter Schmeichel's place in the Old Trafford goalmouth. His career with the Treble winners was to be both frustrating and short – but at least he provided Villa fans with one more memorable performance when he was arrested outside of a Birmingham lap-dancing club on the night before his wedding. Police released him without charge before the service got under way…

Villa won a pre-season tournament in New York against stiff opposition from the likes of Fiorentina, so Gregory could not be accused of fostering misplaced hopes, and the team went on to give the manager his best season at the club. Again vying for a place in Europe, they managed sixth place in the Premiership once more, but it was the players' form in the knock-out competitions that so nearly had the shelves of the club's trophy cabinet creaking. A tremendous run in the Worthington Cup saw them reach the semi-finals, but their progress was bizarre to say the least.

Villa were favourites to beat West Ham United in the quarter-finals. Taylor and Dublin scored in a pulsating match at Upton Park, but the team appeared to be eliminated after the match finished 2-2 after extra-time and West Ham won the penalty shoot-out 5-4. Villa were resigned to concentrating on the remaining competitions when it was revealed that West Ham had fielded an ineligible substitute during the tie – and after urgent meetings between the club chairmen and representatives of both the FA and Football League, a replay was ordered. The London club was furious but went along with the ruling, and on 11 January 2000, the teams met again in front of 25,000 supporters at Upton Park. Villa won 3-1, with two goals from Ian Taylor and another courtesy of Joachim.

After seemingly etching the club's name on the trophy, the players were frustrated by their inability to score against Leicester City in the semi-final, and went out after losing 1-0 on aggregate at Filbert Street. However, they were to have another stab at glory in a far more prestigious competition – the steady progress made under Gregory had been reflected in Villa's FA Cup results, and his team chose this competition in which to produce its performance of the season.

The fifth round 3-2 victory against Leeds, televised live on Sky Sports, was remarkable for more than just the fact that it was a classic cup encounter. It was also the day on which a little Italian propelled himself into the national consciousness with a display that defined audacity. Benito Carbone had been brought in on loan from Sheffield Wednesday after Dion Dublin suffered a freak injury, breaking his neck just before Christmas. Happily, Dublin was to make a full recovery, but not before Carbone's scintillating hat-trick sent David O'Leary's team crashing out of the tournament. One of his goals – a 35-yard effort – went on to win a goal of the month competition, and it persuaded Gregory that he should attempt to sign the former Inter Milan striker permanently, despite his struggle to score throughout earlier performances.

'The hat-trick convinced me,' said the Villa manager. 'Before then I had needed persuading and we had the perfect arrangement with Sheffield Wednesday – sale or return. He integrated himself into the dressing room exceptionally well, contrary to the rumours that we had heard about his problems at Hillsborough.' Gregory's hopes of clinching the Carbone deal would eventually be dashed – although his services were secured until the end of the season, face-blanching wage demands of £45,000 per week caused more than the odd ripple in the boardroom and the Italian started the following season with Bradford City.

Villa went on to beat Everton and Bolton, the latter on penalties after a 0-0 draw, to reach the FA Cup final for the first time in 43 years. It was the last time the showpiece event would be held in the old Wembley stadium, and as surely as the stands were to be pulled down a few months later, so the club's fervent supporters were to be brought back to Earth with a bump. Although David James was blamed for the decisive goal – he could only palm Gianfranco Zola's free kick against Gareth Southgate and Roberto Di Matteo scored from the rebound – the other Villa players did themselves no favours in a final that went down as one of the poorest in living memory. Unbeaten in 18 Premiership games leading up to the event, they came up against a Chelsea team just as uncompromising, some said as unimaginative on the day, and the result was woeful. After an anti-climax to a year that had promised so much, serious issues had to be addressed ahead of the first complete season of the 21st century.

Chapter Ten: 2000-02
Challenging Times Ahead

The nature of the FA Cup final defeat to Chelsea only served to support the fears Gregory had been voicing for months. Villa were in desperate need of a goalscorer and it was time for the board to prove their commitment to supporters by financing a heavyweight deal. Dublin, who had averaged a goal every two games before breaking his neck, had yet to fully recover, but the other strikers had failed to seize upon the chance he had inadvertently handed them. 'We were unlucky losing Dion,' said Gregory, 'but you still need someone else who can bang in 12 or 14 [goals] and we have not got that. Julian Joachim has failed to come up with the goals to match his work rate, Ian Taylor has not scored enough, Lee Hendrie has not scored enough and the same can be said for [the others].' In an era during which more and more managers recognized a basic requirement for four top-class finishers to choose from, it was difficult not to feel some sympathy for Gregory. He was already suspicious that the rumours of Villa's 'lack of ambition' might be true, or at least that the chairman believed that a championship-challenging team could be built while balancing the books. Gregory's mood would darken further within months, as disenchantment began to cloak key members of the squad.

The necessary evil of the InterToto Cup, Villa's only means of entry into senior European competition, meant that players had barely removed their boots before being ordered into training in preparation for their first fixture, on 19 July. By 2 August they had been eliminated, victims of a 3-1 home defeat at the hands of Celta Vigo, but at least there could be no complaints of lack of practice by the time the new Premiership season arrived.

Heading out of Villa Park were Steve Watson, who joined Everton for £2.5 million, Mark Draper, sold to Southampton for £1.25 million, and the out-of-favour Alan Thompson, who would go on to greater success after his sale to Celtic for £2.75 million. Stan Collymore's miserable spell had already come to an end with a transfer to Leicester City, although it was to be another ill-fated move. Joining the club were Alpay Ozalan, an international central defender with Fenerbahce and Turkey, and, to a mixture of hoots and hoorahs, the mercurial David Ginola.

Feted by Newcastle United fans during the managerial reign of Kevin Keegan, Ginola had enjoyed three successful seasons with Tottenham

50 Greatest Players

UGO EHIOGU   Defender

Born: London, 3 November 1972

Joined Aston Villa: 1991   **From:** West Bromwich Albion

Appearances: 303   **Goals:** 15

Left Aston Villa: 2000   **For:** Middlesbrough

When he was signed by Ron Atkinson for £40,000, Ugo Ehiogu joined a club with one great central defender and two very good ones. Although Atkinson dispensed with the remnants of Graham Taylor's 3-5-2 system and went with a flat back four, Ehiogu would watch and learn as Paul McGrath commanded the defence, and when in 1993-94 he began to play more regularly for the first team, he became assured of both his responsibilities and his place in the side. Alongside Gareth Southgate he blossomed further, showing the sort of form that led to his full England debut under Glenn Hoddle. A thinking fan's central defender, he also added potency up front when coming forward. Ehiogu's appearances became limited under John Gregory, and he made the move to unfashionable Middlesbrough in 2000. He was recalled to the England squad, but he soon lost out to the preferred pairing of Rio Ferdinand and Sol Campbell.

Hotspur, and, at the time, there was doubt as to whether his heart – or that of Gregory, for that matter – was truly set on the £3 million move. At least it meant a surge in shirt sales, however, and for a while Ellis was all but swooning with the Birmingham housewives as his new acquisition flicked his luxurious fringe this way and that for assorted press corps. In September, Gregory finally got the quality striker he craved, albeit on a free transfer. Luc Nilis, the Belgian international, was an exciting addition to the squad, having played in Euro 2000 a few months before and also boasting World Cup experience.

It took only days for things to go disastrously wrong. In his third match, a Premiership clash with Ipswich Town on 9 September, Nilis went for a 50-50 ball with Richard Wright, the opposition goalkeeper. In a sickening collision which brought to mind the horrific injury to Coventry City's David Busst a few years earlier, the Villa player suffered a double fracture of his leg. Stomach-churning photographs in the following day's newspapers only partially revealed the extent of his injuries – for a time afterwards there were fears over whether he would ever again have the ability to walk normally. As it was, it was enough to end his career. Villa physio Jim Walker said: 'I had an inkling when I first saw it that perhaps he would never play again. What he suffered was not unlike something you may see in a bad car accident.'

Nilis returned to Belgium to recuperate after undergoing an operation on his leg, but was forced to retire some months later. He absolved Wright from any blame for what happened, adding: 'It was just one of those things and he didn't do it deliberately. It was a case of me not seeing him as I went for the ball and it all happened in a few split seconds. There is still some pain, but I can handle it now.'

Gregory might have thought matters could hardly worsen, but at much the same time he was facing the prospect of losing another of his senior players. Ugo Ehiogu, a regular feature in the centre of defence throughout the 1990s, had struggled to hold down his place. On the fringe of the England setup and desperate for first-team football, it was only a matter of time before his departure to a club he hoped would be better able to challenge for trophies. On 20 October, he signed for Middlesbrough for £8 million. On the face of it a hefty sum for a redundant defender might seem like a good deal, but Ehiogu's transfer was perceived as a negative by those whose fears of

---

50 Greatest Players

GARETH SOUTHGATE **Defender**

Born: Watford, 3 September 1972

Joined Aston Villa: 1995	**From:** Crystal Palace
Appearances: 243	**Goals:** 9
Left Aston Villa: 2001	**Goals:** Middlesbrough

One of the classiest central defenders in football, Gareth Southgate will leave an unjustified legacy if all the game remembers him for is a penalty miss in the Euro '96 semi-final. He had broken into the England side after his transfer from Palace, where he was captain, to Villa, where he would soon assume the same role, and it was a measure of his maturity that he managed to put such a well-publicized 'failure' behind him. In many of Villa's more mediocre performances Southgate would stand out as an example to his team-mates, intelligent and calm on the ball. He fell out with John Gregory before his move to Middlesbrough and his departure was a big loss to the club.

50 Greatest Players

IAN TAYLOR   **Midfielder**

Born: Birmingham, 4 June 1968

Joined Aston Villa: 1994   **From:** Sheffield Wednesday

Appearances: 272*   **Goals:** 41*

* Up to end of 2001-02 season

Although he had spent a season playing in Sheffield, there was only one club Ian Taylor ever wanted to appear for. When he was signed by Brian Little to beef up the midfield early in his reign as manager, at a cost of £1.3 million, there was no player more proud to wear the famous claret and blue. A tremendous ball winner, he has protected Villa's defence on countless occasions down the seasons and boasts a healthy scoring record of his own. Taylor invariably ends a campaign having scored some vital goals, a reflection of his intelligent running and powerful finishing. His efforts down the years have earned him the tag of 'Villa stalwart', a journeyman tag that perhaps fails to do justice to his game, although he was known to be disappointed with the contract terms offered to him when Graham Taylor was reappointed as manager towards the end of the 2001-02 season.

stagnation at Villa Park were growing steadily. Gareth Southgate's frustration was no secret either, and the image of a club from which international players could not wait to get away hardly lifted the spirits.

Indifferent results in the league left the club to flit between seventh and 11th place for much of the early season. Defeat to Manchester City at the beginning of November ended League Cup hopes, and by the New Year it was beginning to look – yet again – like just another average season. Gregory blew his top.

Disappointed to preside over a campaign that bore all the hallmarks of mediocrity, he unleashed a withering assault on his chairman, accusing Ellis of 'living in a time-warp' when it came to finances and effectively holding the club back. Whether or not his outburst was considered, rather than spontaneous, was open to debate – what was without question was the fury it provoked. Within days Gregory had been forced to publicly apologize for his comments – a decision which probably saved him from being sacked – and it was clear that the relationship between the two had taken an irrevocable turn for the worse.

Ironically, Gregory chose to criticize his chairman just as the most expensive signing in the history of the club was about to be sanctioned. The purchase of the Colombia striker Juan Pablo Angel, from River Plate of Argentina, was as protracted as the average £9.5 million deal – but if the player believed his transfer to be tortuous, he was in for worse yet. Angel, little-known to most Villa fans but with a reputation as a world-class striker, was unveiled before the Premiership match at home to Liverpool on 13 January 2001. Two goals from Danny Murphy and another from Steven Gerrard dampened any enthusiasm inside Villa Park as he watched his new team slump to a 3-0 defeat.

More losses against Manchester United and Leeds pushed Villa further out of contention, and although the players finally rediscovered winning ways, beating Bradford 3-0 at Valley Parade and knocking Newcastle out of the FA Cup, Angel's form was a worry. His difficulties on the pitch were being compounded by the problems of settling in a new country far from home. Later the club admitted it had made a mistake by not employing a welfare officer, but in the meantime it was left to Gregory to appeal for public support for his stricken signing.

50 Greatest Players

DARIUS VASSELL   Forward

Born: Birmingham, 13 June 1980

Joined Aston Villa: 1998 (as apprentice)

Appearances: 102*   **Goals:** 21*

* Up to end of 2001-02 season

Straight out of the book of modern strikers, Darius Vassell's football is about pace and more pace. Electrifying when surging forward, he can be deadly if allowed to collect the ball in space before running at the defence, and possesses an equally adept instinct for poaching goals. Given his first-team debut by John Gregory in the 1998-99 season, it took Vassell two years to score his first goal in the Premiership, and by the end of the 2000-01 campaign he had the unflattering statistic of four goals from 46 appearances. His potential had already been seen with a scoring debut against Stromsgodset in the UEFA Cup, however, when two goals helped Villa recover from a 2-0 deficit. A longer run in the team followed the next season and he gained a place in England's U-21 side. Soon after, Sven-Goran Eriksson handed Vassell his full international debut and he repaid him with a breathtaking goal against Holland and took him to Japan for the finals of the 2002 World Cup.

Although a few spirits were raised by the reunification of the 1981 championship-winning side at a celebratory 20th anniversary dinner in March, it was a rare high point as the season drew to an end. Knocked out of the FA Cup by Leicester City, a desperately disappointing 0-0 draw against Southampton heralded a cacophony of booing in the Villa Park rafters. Angel eventually scored his first goal for the club in a 3-2 victory that relegated Coventry City for the first time in 34 years, but the 3-0 defeat against Newcastle on the final day of the campaign, during which Ian Taylor was sent off and the ineffective Ginola substituted two minutes before half-time, was a suitably morose note on which to finish. To chants of 'Ellis out', Villa closed the door on the season in eighth place in the Premiership and looked forward to yet another InterToto cup campaign.

The last thing Gregory needed after such a disappointing end to the season was to lose his captain, but he could not hold onto Gareth Southgate any longer.

50 Greatest Players

DION DUBLIN **Forward**

Born: Leicester, 22 April 1969

Joined Aston Villa: 1998 **From:** Coventry City

Appearances: 127* **Goals:** 42*

* Up to end of 2001 02 season

An old-fashioned centre forward, Dublin made an immediate impact after signing for Villa, scoring twice on his debut against Spurs in a 3-2 victory in November 1998. Brought in to add some much-needed firepower to the attack after the departure of Dwight Yorke, Dublin scored a hat-trick in the next match, against Southampton, and two more against Liverpool the following weekend. Things had not always been so easy. Dublin had been released by Manchester United after just a handful of games at the end of the 1993-94 season. Impressed by his versatility – Dublin has also played in central defence – Coventry signed him and he became an instant hero, scoring 61 goals in 145 matches for the club and winning his first England cap. An integral part of John Gregory's attack in the first couple of years of his contract, Dublin's progress was interrupted when he broke his neck. Gregory kept faith, despite the striker's struggle to recapture his form after his recovery, but it seemed his Villa days were numbered when Graham Taylor took over and loaned him to Millwall. Ever keen to prove his critics wrong, he returned from the New Den in time for the final match of the 2001-02 season – and scored.

The disgruntled England defender followed Ehiogu to Middlesbrough for £6.5 million, prompting an unhappy manager to say: 'I wanted him to continue being captain as he is the best man for the job, but he doesn't want it.'

Other important transfer dealings included the signing of the midfielder Moustapha Hadji from Coventry, with Julian Joachim moving in the opposite direction, and the £5.7 million capture of Sweden and Racing Santander defender Olof Mellberg to take Southgate's place.

The surprise of the summer arrived when David James, who had regained his England place during his two years at Villa Park, was sold for £3.5 million to West Ham United. The goalkeeper made it clear that he had not instigated the transfer, although the club's reasoning became evident when Peter Schmeichel, who had left Manchester United two years earlier, joined for free from Sporting Lisbon. 'I'm looking forward to the atmosphere,' he said upon his arrival. 'The whole thing with the crowd and the tempo – I want to be part of that again.'

Schmeichel's first task would arrive in the InterToto Cup, the tournament that offers Premiership also-rans the opportunity to gain a place in the UEFA Cup. Gregory made no secret of his dislike for the competition, as it required pre-season training to begin in June. He needed his players to be fresh, particularly as boardroom pressure was beginning to tell. Mark Ansell, the deputy chief executive, chose a surprising method of encouragement when he informed the local media that eighth place in the Premiership 'isn't good enough', but Gregory responded by stating his desire to get Villa into the top four.

Ginola was doing his best to dent Gregory's bravado – the Frenchman may well have been an exciting addition to the squad 12 months earlier, but his lacklustre performances in a Villa shirt reinforced popular opinion that he had been foisted upon the manager by Ellis. His early substitution against Newcastle had ended any chance of a workable relationship, and the 33-year-old went as far as to threaten legal action when Gregory made comments about his weight. The tactic backfired – Villa fans were unhappy at such mutinous behaviour and booed him throughout the first Premiership match of the new season, a 0-0 draw against his old club, Tottenham.

For a while, Villa supporters enjoyed the most successful period in recent memory. Completion of a 5-2 aggregate victory over FC Basle secured the InterToto Cup on 21 August and a stunning 3-1 victory over Liverpool at Anfield, with goals from Dublin, Hendrie and Vassell, boded well for the coming months. The defence looked solid throughout a 1-1 draw with Manchester United and Gregory picked up the Manager of the Month award for September, despite watching his team fall to Varteks in the first round of

50 Greatest Players

PAUL MERSON   Midfielder

Born: London, 20 March 1968

Joined Aston Villa: 1998   **From:** Middlesbrough

Appearances: 143   **Goals:** 21

Left Aston Villa: 2002   **For:** Portsmouth

A footballer for the modern age, this 21-year-old attacking midfielder was part of Arsenal's brilliant championship-winning team of 1989, on the fast track to millionaire status. More medals followed, then, in 1994, came his confession that he had a £150-per-day cocaine habit. An alcoholic drug taker with a gambling problem, it seemed that Merson had become the first Premiership footballer to be choked by the hand that fed him, but a sympathetic response from both the FA and the public encouraged his recuperation. After a miserable spell at Middlesbrough, Merson moved to Villa so that he could be nearer to his children, and the transfer paid off as he began to produce the sort of form that made him a hero at Highbury. A sublime passer of the ball with unparalleled vision, Merson won the first of his two Player of the Year awards in 1999-2000 and might have made the England squad for Euro 2000 had he not already announced his international retirement after 21 caps. After Gregory's departure, his relationship with Graham Taylor soured and he moved to First Division Portsmouth.

the UEFA Cup. Results began to fluctuate again towards the end of the year – although Angel enjoyed a much more profitable season, goals were still hard to come by and the situation was summed up by a goal from Schmeichel, of all people, during the 3-2 defeat at Everton. The final match of 2001 – a 1-1 draw with Tottenham – saw Villa lodged in eighth place once again.

Gregory's Patience Runs Out

After almost four years with the club, time was not on Gregory's side. When asked about the task of fulfilling supporters' expectations, in the third week of the New Year, he defiantly insisted: 'I will never walk away.' Understandably, then, news of his resignation on 24 January dominated the backpages of the national press. Shackled by financial restraints, the final threads of Gregory's patience had snapped. A face-to-face confrontation with Ellis preceded 48 hours of soul searching before he confirmed his decision, safe in the knowledge that he was likely to be offered a job at another of his old clubs. As always with the relationship between the manager and his chairman, there was to be a final twist.

Announcing Gregory's departure, Ellis said: 'John's resignation is sad, was most unexpected but has been amicable. I can understand how he feels regarding his need for a break and that is a reflection of the pressures that managers endure in modern-day Premier League football.' Gregory was unhappy with this version of events, so his solicitor, Julian Middleton, issued a statement confirming his client's enjoyment of 'football management at the highest level'.

Turning to an Old Face

A parting of the ways had been on the cards for months, probably as far back as Gregory's public criticism of Ellis a year earlier, but the announcement was still a shock when it arrived. Paul Merson said he was 'gutted', while the fans were dismayed to see the manager they hoped would lead them into the Champions League heading off in exasperation to take charge of Derby County, a club the fraction of the size of Villa and heading for relegation. The net value of Gregory's transfer dealings amounted to no more than £17 million, a miserly sum, and yet again the fans vented their feelings through the local media. The years have rewarded Ellis with a thick skin, however, and he still had one more trick up his sleeve to appease the supporters. Two weeks later, he reappointed the man he never wanted to lose in the first place, and Graham Taylor became the manager.

Taylor had rejoined Villa as a non-executive director after 'retiring' from management following a second spell with Watford. He had made his mind up that his days on the training pitch were over, until Ellis offered him the one job he could not refuse. 'I would have regretted turning down an opportunity I did not think would come, managing a leading Premiership club,' he told reporters. 'When I left Villa we'd finished runners-up and we were in Europe. I've come back to finish the job.'

Three days after Taylor's appointment was confirmed, Ginola moved to Everton on a free transfer, but the new boss was also to have limited opportunities to add to the squad. Peter Crouch signed from Portsmouth for £5 million to share the attacking duties with Angel, with Dion Dublin spending much of the final part of the season on loan to Millwall, but the team was entrenched in mediocrity and managed only to scrape another shot at the InterToto Cup. Their final place in the Premiership? Eighth.

Great Managers – 1987-90, 2002-

GRAHAM TAYLOR

While readers of the *Sun* may always remember Graham Taylor as a failed England manager with a turnip for a head, his achievements at club level tell another story. Having built his reputation with unprecedented success at Watford, he took charge of an ailing Villa side that, besides having been relegated to Division Two, had just lost its second manager in less than a year. He then set about reshaping the team, employing a new formation and fresh tactics, and bringing footballers to Villa Park that would stand alongside the finest to have played at the ground. Building his team on the foundation of three central defenders, Taylor employed frighteningly quick wingers to terrorize opposition full backs and packed in a midfield full of pace and gusto. Among others he was responsible for bringing to the club were David Platt, who went on to become the world's most expensive footballer, and Dwight Yorke, and it was no surprise when, having taken Villa to second place in the old Division One, he was offered the England manager's job. Taylor returned to the club as a director in 2001 and was re-appointed manager when John Gregory resigned the following year. After a shaky start, it remains to be seen if he can have a similar effect this time around.

It has been a difficult period for Villa. Anybody can wishfully hark back 20 years and wonder if the club will ever recapture the glory of that unforgettable night in Rotterdam, but, in truth, most fans would happily accept only a fraction of those celebrations right now, perhaps even another League Cup win just to remind them what it feels like to win a major competition. This is the least the club's short-changed supporters deserve for their loyalty – now that they have been joined in the Premiership by their rivals Birmingham City and West Bromwich Albion, success has become all the more imperative. Graham Taylor has already delivered once to this club – the jury is out as to whether he can do it again.

THE ESSENTIAL HISTORY OF
ASTON VILLA

CLUB STATISTICS

The Aston Villa Directory

Origins

- Formed by cricket-playing members of the Villa Cross Wesleyan Chapel, Aston, in 1874. The young Midlanders were looking for a sporting pursuit to occupy themselves during the long winter months of the cricket close season.
- Villa struggled to find opponents in their early days, and their first game was a 15-a-side encounter against Aston Brook St Mary's Rugby team.
- Scotsman George Ramsay is the man credited with turning Villa into a first-class team. Ramsay was an ambitious man and an experienced player, and under his tutelage Villa rose from obscurity to become Birmingham's premier club.
- Villa were one of the founder members of the Football League and have won the competition seven times.

Honours

- Division 1 Champions: 1893-94, 1895-96, 1896-97, 1898-99, 1899-1900, 1909-10, 1980-81
- Division 1 Runners-up: 1888-89, 1902-03, 1907-08, 1910-11, 1912-13, 1913-14, 1930-31, 1932-33, 1989-90
- Premier League Runners-up: 1992-93
- FA Cup winners 1887, 1895, 1897, 1905, 1913, 1920, 1957
- FA Cup finalists: 1892, 1924, 2000
- Football League Cup winners: 1961, 1975, 1977, 1994, 1996
- Football League Cup finalists: 1963, 1971
- European Cup winners: 1981-82
- European Super Cup winners: 1982-83

League and Premiership Record

- Division One (old): 1888-1936, 1938-59, 1960–67, 1975-87, 1988-92
- Division Two (old): 1936-38, 1959-60, 1967-70, 1972-75, 1987-88
- Division Three (old): 1970-72
- FA Premier League: 1992-

Club Information

- Villa Park, Trinity Road, Birmingham, B6 6HE
- Tel: 0121 327 2299 Fax: 0121 322 2107
- Ticket Information: 0121 327 5353
- Website: www.avfc.co.uk
- Ground capacity: 42,584
- Pitch measurements: 115 x 72 yards
- Chairman: H.D. Ellis
- Year formed: 1874
- Turned professional: 1885
- Club nickname: The Villans
- Previous grounds: 1874 Wilson Road and Aston Park; 1876 Wellington Road, Perry Barr; 1897–present Villa Park (Note: some games were also played on the Aston Lower Grounds in the 1870s)
- Colours: Claret shirts with sky blue and green trim; white shorts with claret and blue trim; sky blue and claret socks with white turnover
- Change colours: Silver shirts with navy and yellow trim; navy blue and grey shorts with green trim; navy blue and green socks with grey turnover

Managers

George Ramsay (Secretary-manager)
  (1884–1926)

W.J. Smith (1926–34)

Jimmy McMullan (1934–35)

Jimmy Hogan (1936–44)

Alex Massie (1945–50)

George Martin (1950–53)

Eric Houghton (1953–58)

Joe Mercer (1958–64)

Dick Taylor (1964–67)

Tommy Cummings (1967–68)

Tommy Docherty (1968–70)

Vic Crowe (1970–74)

Ron Saunders (1974–82)

Tony Barton (1982–84)

Graham Turner (1984–86)

Billy McNeill (1986–87)

Dr Jozef Venglos (1990–91)

Ron Atkinson (1991–94)

Brian Little (1994–98)

John Gregory (1998–2002)

Graham Taylor (2002–)

Records

- Highest attendance: 76,588 v Derby County, FA Cup 6th Round, 2 March 1946
- Highest League position: Champions, Division One, (seven times): 1893-94, 1895-96, 1896-97, 1898-99, 1899-1900, 1909-10, 1980-81
- Record League victory (H): 12-2 v Accrington Stanley, Division One, 12 March 1892
- Record Cup victory: 8-1 v Exeter City, League Cup, 9 October 1985
- Record Cup defeat: 1-8 v Blackburn Rovers, FA Cup 3rd Round, 16 February 1889
- Most League points (2 for a win): 70, Division Three, 1971-72
- Most League points (3 for a win): 78, Division Two, 1987–88
- Most League goals: 128, Division One, 1930–31
- Record League appearances: Charlie Aitken, 561, 1959–76

- Most League goals for club: Harry Hampton, 215, 1904–20
- Most League goals in one season: Pongo Waring, 49, 1930-31
- Most capped player: Steve Staunton (Republic of Ireland), 64 caps out of 102 won while a Villa Player
- Record transfer fee paid: £9.5m, Juan Pablo Angel (River Plate), January 2001
- Record transfer fee received: £12.6m, Dwight Yorke (Manchester United), August 1998

Steve Staunton is No. 39 in our Great Players listing and holds the Villa record for the most capped player with 64 Republic of Ireland caps.

50 Greatest Players

This list is not intended to be definitive. Not many fans would agree on exactly the same choice of the greatest players ever to have donned a Villa shirt. The 50 listed here are our choices, taking into consideration their respective performances, their achievements as players and their dedication to the club. Whether or not you agree with our selection, it shows what a great variety of incredible talent has represented Aston Villa Football Club over the years.

No. 1 Tom 'Pongo' Waring (Centre forward) – 226 appearances, 167 goals. The greatest goalscorer ever to play for Villa, Pongo averaged better than two goals in every three games (see page 68).

No. 2 Billy Walker (Centre forward) – 531 appearances, 244 goals. Billy spent 18 years at Villa Park, captaining the team for six of them (see page 66).

No. 3 Andy Gray (Centre forward) – 210 appearances, 78 goals. Talented and brave to the point of foolhardiness, he was adored by the Villa fans during his first stint at the club in the mid-70s (see page 120).

No. 4 Archie Hunter (Forward) – 73 appearances, 42 goals. Aston Villa's first truly great footballer who led the club to victory in its first FA Cup final in 1887 (see page 16).

No. 5 Harry Hampton (Centre forward) – 373 appearances, 242 goals. An aggressive, whole-hearted competitor who was adored by the fans (see page 45).

No. 6 Gordon Cowans (Forward) – 528 appearances, 59 goals. Elegant and assured, Gordon was a member of both league and European Cup-winning teams of the early 1980s (see page 145).

No. 7 Paul McGrath (Defender) – 323 appearances, 10 goals. Powerful and intelligent, composed in possession and deceptively quick over the ground, Paul McGrath remains the most complete defender to have donned an Aston Villa jersey (see page 153).

No. 8 John Devey (Forward) – 308 appearances, 187 goals. Captain of Aston Villa's great team of the 1890s and also a reliable source of goals (see page 36).

No. 9 George Ramsay (Forward) – A central figure in the Villa story, both on and off the pitch (see page 8).

No. 10 Dennis Mortimer (Midfielder) – 405 appearances, 36 goals. Captain and midfield general of the 1982 European Cup-winning team. His energy and commitment were greatly admired by the Villa faithful (see page 135).

No. 11 Peter McParland (Outside left) – 341 appearances, 120 goals. Pacy and with a powerful shot in either foot, he was the scourge of Division One defences in the 1950s and early 1960s (see page 96).

No. 12 Charlie Aitken (Defender) – 660 appearances, 16 goals. Record-breaking defender was an athletic and reliable defender who wore the claret and blue jersey for 17 years (see page 113).

No. 13 Charlie Athersmith (Winger) – 311 appearances, 86 goals. Champion sprinter who put his pace to good use on Villa's right flank in the 1890s (see page 32).

No. 14 Howard Spencer (Full back) – 295 appearances, 2 goals. Brought a rare blend of fair play and competitive spirit to the successful Villa team of the 1890s (see page 42).

No. 15 James Cowan (Centre half) – 356 appearances, 26 goals. Tough-tackling, ball winner and hardman of the glorious team of the 1890s (see page 31).

No. 16 Johnny Dixon (Inside forward) – 430 appearances, 144 goals. Captain of the 1957 FA Cup-winning team, a player who displayed loyalty and skill in equal measure during a Villa career spanning 15 years (see page 88).

No. 17 Samuel Hardy (Goalkeeper) – 183 appearances. Perhaps the greatest of Villa's 20th century goalkeepers. His calm, no-frills keeping saw him amass an impressive haul of 21 England caps (see page 54).

No. 18 Tony Morley (Midfielder) – 180 appearances, 34 goals. Tony Morley brought pace and trickery to a Villa midfield that had been carefully constructed by Ron Saunders in the late 1970s (see page 136).

No. 19 Clem Stephenson (Inside forward) – 216 appearances, 96 goals. An inventive and prolific goal-scoring inside forward who helped Villa to FA Cup successes in both 1913 and 1920 (see page 60).

No. 20 Gary Shaw (Forward) – 212 appearances, 80 goals. A modern Villa legend, having played a pivotal role in the successes of the early 1980s, and only the impact of a succession of injuries prevented him taking that status onto the international stage (see page 150).

No. 21 Tony Daley (Midfielder) – 290 appearances, 38 goals. The high-velocity winger terrified opposing defences with his direct running and his incredible balance (see page 166).

No. 22 Eric Houghton (Winger) – 392 appearances, 170 goals. With a cannonball shot and a prodigious appetite for hard work, left winger Eric Houghton was a huge favourite with Villa fans during the inter-war years (see page 69).

No. 23 Dwight Yorke (Forward) – 287 appearances, 97 goals. Illuminated Villa Park with his bright and inventive forward play throughout the mid-1990s (see page 177).

No. 24 David Platt (Midfielder) – 155 appearances, 68 goals. He came from Crewe, he scored goals aplenty, won himself a place in the England team and moved to Italian Serie A side Bari for a then-massive £5.5 million in 1991 (see page 157).

No. 25 Frank Barson (Centre half) – 108 appearances, 10 goals. With a strong personality and playing skills to match this tough centre half brought much-needed backbone to Villa in the early 1920s (see page 62).

No. 26 Danny Blanchflower (Wing half) – 155 appearances, 10 goals. The Irishman brought a refreshing injection of quality to a mediocre Villa team in the 1950s (see page 82).

No. 27 Nigel Sims (Goalkeeper) – 310 appearances. An agile and fearless custodian, Nigel was the team's regular keeper for the best part of seven seasons (see page 95).

No. 28 Gerry Hitchens (Centre forward) – 160 appearances, 96 goals. Arrived at Villa Park as a promising, but unreliable centre forward – left three-and-a-half years later as the finished article (see page 94).

No. 29 Andy Townsend (Midfielder) – 176 appearances, 11 goals. Gave Aston Villa the best years of a career characterized by performances of consistently high quality (see page 163).

No. 30 Darius Vassell (Forward) – 102 appearances, 21 goals. Burst onto the first-team stage at Villa Park with a memorable goal-scoring debut against Stromsgodset in the UEFA Cup in 1998 (see page 185).

No. 31 Brian Little (Forward) – 302 appearances, 82 goals. A deep-lying forward who scored and created goals in equal measure. He returned to Villa Park as manager in 1994 (see page 119).

No. 32 Ray Graydon (Winger) – 231 appearances, 81 goals. A hard-working and skillful winger who played in three divisions, two League Cup finals and two promotion-winning teams during a six-year stay at Villa Park (see page 111).

No. 33 Jimmy Rimmer (Goalkeeper) – 287 appearances. The former Arsenal goalkeeper was an ever-present for Villa during the 1980-81 championship-winning season (see page 141).

No. 34 Peter Withe (Centre forward) – 233 appearances, 92 goals. His goal against Bayern Munich in the European Cup final propelled him to the status of legend at Villa Park (see page 146).

No. 35 Ian Taylor (Midfielder) – 272 appearances, 41 goals. A local boy, a supporter and a wholehearted competitor who gives his all for the claret and blue jersey (see page 184).

No. 36 Ugo Ehiogu (Defender) – 303 appearances, 15 goals. Tall, powerful, quick and constructive in possession, Ugo Ehiogu is a centre half without obvious weakness (see page 182).

No. 37 Ken McNaught (Defender) – 260 appearances, 13 goals. Few more reliable and diligent defenders have graced the claret and blue jersey (see page 140).

No. 38 Con Martin (Defender/Goalkeeper) – 213 appearances, 1 goal. Won caps for both Eire and Northern Ireland, and played both at centre half and in goal for the Villans in the 1950s (see page 80).

No. 39 Steve Staunton (Defender) – 278 appearances, 18 goals. Versatile, the Irishman, who holds the appearance record for the Republic, can always be replied upon to play with both tenacity and skill (see page 160).

No. 40 Nigel Spink (Goalkeeper) – 454 appearances. His career spanned 17 years and more than 400 appearances, but he will be forever remembered for one 81-minute substitute appearance in the 1982 European Cup final (see page 170).

No. 41 Des Bremner (Midfielder) – 227 appearances, 10 goals. A versatile and tough competitor who brought valuable commitment and energy to the successful team of the early 1980s (see page 143).

No. 42 Alex Massie (Right half/Inside forward) – 152 appearances, 5 goals. A cultured and patient midfielder who led the club to promotion before becoming manager after the war (see page 76).

No. 43 Tony Hateley (Centre forward) – 148 appearances, 86 goals. Tony Hateley was a talented and dependable goalscorer who was sold too soon and too cheaply, joining Chelsea for £100,000 in 1965 (see page 98).

No. 44 Ray Houghton (Midfielder) – 121 appearances, 11 goals. Discarded by Liverpool, his energetic midfield play enlivened proceedings at Villa Park for three years (see page 169).

No. 45 Gareth Southgate (Midfielder) – 243 appearances, 9 goals. Transformed himself from a utility player to an international-class central defender during his six years as a Villan (see page 183).

No. 46 Andy Lochhead (Centre forward) – 154 appearances, 44 goals. 'Cult hero' who worked tirelessly as a targetman (see page 107).

No. 47 Paul Merson (Forward) – 143 appearances, 21 goals. Provided a welcome injection of quality and midfield-invention to the all-too-predictable Villa team of the last few years (see page 188).

No. 48 Kent Nielsen (Defender) – 100 appearances, 5 goals. Showed real quality during his three-year stay at Villa Park (see page 159).

No. 49 Allan Evans (Defender) – 473 appearances, 63 goals. A reassuringly consistent presence in the Villa defence for more than a decade (see page 151).

No. 50 Dion Dublin (Forward) – 127 appearances, 42 goals. A reliable scorer and a popular figure with the supporters (see page 186).

Results and Tables 1888-2002

The following pages include details of every official match played by Aston Villa. Each season has its own page and is dated at the top. The opponents played at home are written in capital letters and appear in upper and lower case for away games. The date of the match, the score, Aston Villa goalscorers and the match attendance are also included. Full league and cup appearances and the goalscorers are featured separately. The final league table is included at the bottom of each page as well as a Fact File which notes particularly interesting facts and figures for the season as well as any notable transfers etc.

The results of matches played during the war years, 1914-18 and 1939-45, are not included. During these years the official Football League programme was suspended.

In both the League & Cup Appearances and Goalscorers tables the category 'other' includes matches in the UEFA Cup, European Cup, FA Charity Shield, European Cup, World Club Championship, Full Members' Cup, Simod Cup, Zenith Data Systems Cup and the Intertoto Cup.

Key: Rd – round; R – replay; 2nd R – second replay; L – leg; FL – first leg; F – final; SF – semi-final; SF FL – semi-final first leg; QF – quarter-final.

Season 1888-89

Football League

DATE	OPPONENTS	SCORE	GOALSCORERS	ATTENDANCE
Sep 8	Wolverhampton Wanderers	D 1-1	Green	2,500
Sep 15	STOKE CITY	W 5-1	Dixon, Brown, Hunter, Allen, Green	2,000
Sep 22	EVERTON	W 2-1	Hodgetts 2	5,000
Sep 29	NOTTS COUNTY	W 9-1	Allen 3, Hunter 2, Green 2, Hodgetts, Widdowson o.g.	4,000
Oct 6	Everton	L 0-2		10,000
Oct 13	Blackburn Rovers	W 6-1	Hunterm Green, Goodall, Brown, Allen 2	5,000
Oct 20	Bolton Wanderers	W 3-2	Hodgetts, Allen, Hunter	7,000
Oct 27	Accrington	W 4-3	Allen, Hodgetts, Brown 2	600
Nov 3	Stoke City	D 1-1	Allen	3,000
Nov 10	Preston North End	D 1-1	Green	2,000
Nov 17	Blackburn Rovers	L 1-5	Allen	9,000
Nov 24	WOLVERHAMPTON WANDERERS	W 2-1	Goodall 2	6,000
Dec 8	Notts County	W 4-2	Brown, Green, Goodall 2	2,000
Dec 15	Accrington	D 1-1	Brown	5,000
Dec 22	BURNLEY	W 4-2	Green, Goodall, Allen, Hunter	2,000
Dec 29	DERBY COUNTY	W 4-2	Green 2, Allen, Goodall	4,000
Jan 5	Burnley	L 0-4		6,000
Jan 12	BOLTON WANDERERS	W 6-2	Allen, Hunter, Brown, Green 2, Hodgetts	2,000
Jan 19	WEST BROMWICH ALBION	W 2-0	Hodgetts, Allen	10,000
Jan 26	West Bromwich Albion	D 3-3	Allen 2, Green	8,515
Feb 9	PRESTON NORTH END	L 0-2		12,000
Mar 9	Derby County	L 2-5	Allen 2	2,500

FA Cup

Feb 2	WITTON	(Rd 1) W 3-2	Allen, Hunter, Green	1,500
Feb 16	DERBY COUNTY	(Rd 2) W 5-3	Hunter 2, Hodgetts 2, Brown	2,000
Mar 2	Blackburn Rovers	(Rd 3) L 1-8	Hodgetts	12,000

League & Cup Appearances

PLAYER	LEAGUE	CUP COMPETITION FA CUP	TOTAL
Allen	21	3	24
Ashmore	1		1
Brown A	22	3	25
Burton J	16	3	19
Coulton	19	2	21
Cox	22	3	25
Dawson	3		3
Devey H	21	3	24
Dickson W	3	3	6
Garvey	2		2
Goodall	14		14
Green	21	3	24
Harrison	2		2
Hodgetts	17	3	20
Hunter	19	3	22
Thomas	1		1
Warner	21	3	24
Woollaston	4	1	5
Yates	13	2	15

Goalscorers

PLAYER	LEAGUE	CUP COMPETITION FA CUP	TOTAL
Allen	18	1	19
Green	13	1	14
Hodgetts	7	3	10
Hunter	7	3	10
Brown A	7	1	8
Goodall	7		7
Dickson W	1		1
Opps' o.gs.	1		1

MANAGER: Committee

CAPTAIN: D Hodgetts, A Hunter

TOP SCORER: A Allen, 19 (18 league)

BIGGEST WIN: 9-1 v Notts County (H), Football League, 29 September 1888

HIGHEST ATTENDANCE: 12,000 v Preston NE (H), Football League, 9 February 1889; v Blackburn Rovers (A), FA Cup, 2 March 1889

MAJOR TRANSFERS IN: A Goodall from Preston North End, W Dickson from Sunderland, H Devey from Small Heath

Final Football League Table

		P	W	D	L	F	A	Pts
1	PRESTON NE	22	18	4	0	74	15	40
2	ASTON VILLA	22	12	5	5	61	43	29
3	WOLVERHAMPTON W	22	12	4	6	50	37	28
4	BLACKBURN R	22	10	6	6	66	45	26
5	BOLTON W	22	10	2	10	63	59	22
6	WBA	22	10	2	10	40	46	22
7	ACCRINGTON	22	6	8	8	48	48	20
8	EVERTON	22	9	2	11	35	46	20
9	BURNLEY	22	7	3	12	42	62	17
10	DERBY CO	22	7	2	13	41	61	16
11	NOTTS CO	22	5	2	15	40	73	12
12	STOKE	22	4	4	14	26	51	12

Season 1889-90

Football League

DATE	OPPONENTS	SCORE	GOALSCORERS	ATTENDANCE
Sep 7	BURNLEY	D 2-2	Hodgetts 2	4,000
Sep 14	NOTTS COUNTY	D 1-1	Dickson	6,500
Sep 21	PRESTON NORTH END	W 5-3	Cowan 2, Dickson, Brown, Allen	11,500
Sep 28	West Bromwich Albion	L 0-3		10,122
Oct 5	Burnley	W 6-2	Allen 3, Hunter 2, Hodgetts	8,000
Oct 12	Derby County	W 7-1	Allen 2, Dickson 2, Hodgetts, Brown 2	5,000
Oct 19	Blackburn Rovers	L 0-7		7,000
Oct 26	WEST BROMWICH ALBION	W 1-0	Brown	8,000
Nov 2	WOLVERHAMPTON WANDERERS	W 2-1	Moore 2	5,000
Nov 9	Notts County	D 1-1	Dickson	4,000
Nov 16	Bolton Wanderers	L 0-2		5,000
Nov 23	EVERTON	L 1-2	Brown	6,000
Nov 30	Accrington	L 2-4	Hodgetts 2	2,000
Dec 7	STOKE CITY	W 6-1	Dickson 2, Allen, Garvey 3	4,000
Dec 21	Wolverhampton Wanderers	D 1-1	Hodgetts	8,000
Dec 25	Preston North End	L 2-3	Moore, Dickson	9,000
Dec 26	ACCRINGTON	L 1-2	Garvey	2,000
Dec 28	Derby County	L 0-5		5,000
Jan 4	Everton	L 0-7		10,000
Jan 25	BOLTON WANDERERS	L 1-2	Brown	5,000
Mar 17	Stoke City	D 1-1	Allen	2,000
Mar 31	BLACKBURN ROVERS	W 3-0	Campbell, Hodgetts, Brown	6,000

FA Cup

Jan 18	South Shore	(Rd 1) W 4-2	Allen, Dickson, Hodgetts 2	1,500
Feb 1	Notts County	(Rd 2) L 1-4	Hodgetts	3,000

League & Cup Appearances

PLAYER	LEAGUE	CUP COMPETITION FA CUP	TOTAL
Aldridge	17		17
Allen	20	2	22
Brown A	22	2	24
Burton	10	2	12
Campbell L	2	1	3
Clarkson	10		10
Connor	1		1
Coulton	12	2	14
Cowan Jas	22	2	24
Cox	18	2	20
Davis	1		1
Devey H	19	1	20
Dickie	1		1
Dickson	19	2	21
Garvey	5		5
Graham	1		1
Grey S	2		2
Hickton	1		1
Hodgetts	19	2	21
Hunter	13		13
Moore	5	1	6
Patton	1		1
Warner	21	2	23
Yates	1		1

Goalscorers

PLAYER	LEAGUE	CUP COMPETITION FA CUP	TOTAL
Hodgetts	8	3	11
Allen	8	1	9
Dickson	8	1	9
Brown A	7		7
Garvey	4		4
Moore	3		3
Cowan Jas	2		2
Hunter	2		2
Campbell L	1		1

Fact File

Aston Villa were saved from having to apply for re-election to the Football League only by a decision to suspend the rules!

MANAGER: Committee

CAPTAIN: D Hodgetts, A Hunter

TOP SCORER: D Hodgetts, 11 (8 league)

BIGGEST WIN: 7-1 v Derby County (H), Football League, 12 October 1889

HIGHEST ATTENDANCE: 11,500 v Preston North End (H), Football League, 21 September 1889

MAJOR TRANSFERS IN: Jas Cowan from Vale of Leven

MAJOR TRANSFERS OUT: Tommy Green to Kidderminster Harriers, Archie Hunter – retired

Final Football League Table

		P	W	D	L	F	A	Pts
1	PRESTON NE	22	15	3	4	71	30	33
2	EVERTON	22	14	3	5	65	40	31
3	BLACKBURN R	22	12	3	7	78	41	27
4	WOLVERHAMPTON W	22	10	5	7	51	38	25
5	WBA	22	11	3	8	47	50	25
6	ACCRINGTON	22	9	6	7	53	56	24
7	DERBY CO	22	9	3	10	43	55	21
8	ASTON VILLA	22	7	5	10	43	51	19
9	BOLTON W	22	9	1	12	54	65	19
10	NOTTS CO	22	6	5	11	43	51	17
11	BURNLEY	22	4	5	13	36	65	13
12	STOKE	22	3	4	15	27	69	10

Season 1890-91

Football League

DATE	OPPONENTS	SCORE	GOALSCORERS	ATTENDANCE
Sep 6	Wolverhampton Wanderers	L 1-2	Brown A	4,000
Sep 13	NOTTS COUNTY	W 3-2	Brown A, Dickson, Graham	6,000
Sep 20	Burnley	L 1-2	Campbell L	10,000
Sep 27	WEST BROMWICH ALBION	L 0-4		12,000
Oct 4	Bolton Wanderers	L 0-4		10,000
Oct 11	EVERTON	D 2-2	Patton, Cowan	5,000
Oct 18	Derby County	L 4-5	Hodgetts, Cowan 2, Graham	3,000
Oct 25	DERBY COUNTY	W 4-0	Cowan, Brown A, Hodgetts 2	3,000
Nov 1	West Bromwich Albion	W 3-0	Brown A 2, Dickson	8,000
Nov 8	BURNLEY	D 4-4	Dickson, Brown A, Cowan, Graham	5,000
Nov 15	ACCRINGTON	W 3-1	Graham, Hodgetts, Brown A	3,000
Nov 22	BOLTON WANDERERS	W 5-0	Brown A 2, Campbell G, Dickson, Brown J	10,000
Nov 29	Notts County	L 1-7	Dickson	4,000
Dec 6	Blackburn Rovers	L 1-5	Dickson	5,000
Dec 13	BLACKBURN ROVERS	D 2-2	Allen, Brown A	4,000
Dec 26	SUNDERLAND	D 0-0		6,000
Jan 1	Everton	L 0-5		9,000
Jan 10	Sunderland	L 1-5	Graham	6,000
Jan 24	Preston North End	L 1-4	Brown A	2,000
Mar 9	PRESTON NORTH END	L 0-1		5,000
Mar 14	WOLVERHAMPTON WANDERERS	W 6-2	McKnight, Dickson 2, Athersmith 3	5,000
Mar 12	Accrington	W 3-1	Dickson 2, Burton JH	1,000

FA Cup

Jan 17	THE CASUALS	(Rd 1) W 13-1	Hodgetts 4, Campbell L 3, McKnight 2, Brown A 2, Graham 2	5,000
Jan 31	Stoke City	(Rd 2) L 0-3		7,000

League & Cup Appearances

PLAYER	LEAGUE	CUP COMPETITION FA CUP	TOTAL
Allen	4		4
Athersmith	2		2
Brown Alb	16	2	18
Brown J	15	2	17
Burton JH	2		2
Campbell G	15	2	17
Campbell L	9	2	11
Clarkson	6		6
Connor	3		3
Cowan Jas	20	1	21
Cox	20	2	22
Devey H	19	1	20
Dickson W	18		18
Evans W	21	2	23
Graham	16	2	18
Harley	1		1
Hodgetts	18	2	20
McKnight	10	2	12
Marshall	3		3
Paton	2		2
Warner	22	2	24

Goalscorers

PLAYER	LEAGUE	CUP COMPETITION FA CUP	TOTAL
Brown Alb	11	2	13
Dickson W	10		10
Hodgetts	4	4	8
Graham	5	2	7
Cowan Jas	5		5
Athersmith	3		3
Campbell L	1	2	3
McKnight	1	2	3
Allen	1		1
Brown J	1		1
Burton JH	1		1
Campbell G	1		1
Paton	1		1

Fact File

Villa scored 25 goals in seven league games between mid-October and late November before losing 7-1 at Notts County.

MANAGER: Committee

CAPTAIN: D Hodgetts

TOP SCORER: Albert Brown, 13 (11 league)

BIGGEST WIN: 13-1 v The Casuals (H), FA Cup First Round, 17 January 1891

HIGHEST ATTENDANCE: 12,000 v West Bromwich Albion (H), Football League, 27 September 1890

MAJOR TRANSFERS IN: George Campbell from Renton, W Evans from Bootle

MAJOR TRANSFERS OUT: Albert Aldridge (retired)

Final Football League Table

		P	W	D	L	F	A	Pts
1	EVERTON	22	14	1	7	63	29	29
2	PRESTON NE	22	12	3	7	44	23	27
3	NOTTS CO	22	11	4	7	52	35	26
4	WOLVERHAMPTON W	22	12	2	8	39	50	26
5	BOLTON W	22	12	1	9	47	34	25
6	BLACKBURN R	22	11	2	9	52	43	24
7	SUNDERLAND	22	10	5	7	51	31	23
8	BURNLEY	22	9	3	10	52	63	21
9	ASTON VILLA	22	7	4	11	45	58	18
10	ACCRINGTON	22	6	4	12	28	50	16
11	DERBY CO	22	7	1	14	47	81	15
12	WBA	22	5	2	15	34	57	12

SUNDERLAND TWO POINTS DEDUCTED FOR FIELDING AN INELIGIBLE PLAYER.

Season 1891-92

Football League

DATE	OPPONENTS	SCORE	GOALSCORERS	ATTENDANCE
Sep 5	BLACKBURN ROVERS	W 5-1	Hislop, Devey J 2; Dickson, Athersmith	6,000
Sep 12	WEST BROMWICH ALBION	W 5-1	Athersmith, Devey J 2, Hislop, Dickson	12,100
Sep 19	Preston North End	W 1-0	Devey J	10,000
Sep 28	SUNDERLAND	W 5-3	Hodgetts, Dickson, Devey J 2, Athersmith	6,000
Oct 3	Derby County	L 2-4	Dickson 2	6,500
Oct 10	BOLTON WANDERERS	L 1-2	Hislop	2,000
Oct 17	Burnley	L 1-4	Dickson	6,500
Oct 24	Stoke City	W 3-2	Campbell L, Devey J, Dickson	8,000
Oct 31	Darwen	W 5-1	Campbell L 2, Hare 2, Devey J	6,000
Nov 7	Notts County	W 5-1	Devey J, Hodgetts 2, Hare, Athersmith	3,000
Nov 14	West Bromwich Albion	W 3-0	Devey J, Campbell L, Hare	14,085
Nov 21	STOKE CITY	W 2-1	Campbell L, Brown J	5,000
Nov 28	EVERTON	L 1-5	Hodgetts	15,000
Dec 5	BURNLEY	W 6-1	Devey J 3, Dickson, Brown J, Campbell L	5,000
Dec 19	Wolverhampton Wanderers	L 0-2		8,000
Dec 26	DARWEN	W 7-0	Hodgetts 2, L Campbell L 2, Athersmith 2, Devey J	3,000
Dec 28	EVERTON	L 3-4	Devey J 2, Athersmith	14,000
Jan 2	Notts County	L 2-5	Athersmith, Devey J	3,000
Jan 4	Accrington	L 2-3	Devey J , Athersmith	3,500
Jan 9	DERBY COUNTY	W 6-0	Devey J 2, Dickson, Hodgetts, Campbell L , Athersmith	8,000
Mar 5	Blackburn Rovers	L 3-4	Campbell L 3	6,000
Mar 12	Accrington	W 12-2	Hodgetts, Devey J 4, Dickson 2, Campbell L 4, Athersmith	8,000
Mar 26	Sunderland	L 1-2	Devey J	7,000
Apr 2	Bolton Wanderers	W 2-1	Devey J 2	6,000
Apr 16	PRESTON NORTH END	W 3-1	Dickson 2, Devey H	5,000
Apr 18	WOLVERHAMPTON WANDERERS	L 3-6	Hodgetts, Dickson, Devey J	8,000

FA Cup

Jan 16	HEANOR T	(Rd 1) W 4-1	Hodgetts 3, Devey	2,000
Jan 30	DARWEN	(Rd 2) W 2-0	Devey J, Hodgetts	4,500
Feb 13	Wolverhampton Wanderers	(Rd 3) W 3-1	Campbell L, Athersmith, Devey J	22,000
Feb 27	Sunderland*	(SF) W 4-1	Devey 2, Hodgetts 2	25,000
Mar 19	West Bromwich Albion#	(F) L 0-3		32,810

*Played at Bramall Lane, Sheffield.
#Played at The Oval, London.

League & Cup Appearances

PLAYER	LEAGUE	CUP COMPETITION FA CUP	TOTAL
Athersmith	24	5	29
Baird J	15	5	20
Brown J	18	1	19
Campbell G	20	1	21
Campbell L	19	5	24
Coulton	3	2	5
Cowan Jas	25	4	29
Cox	17	3	20
Devey H	10	4	14
Devey J	25	5	30
Dickson	21	4	25
Diver	3		3
Dutton	1		1
Evans W	23	5	28
Graham	1		1
Hare	8	1	9
Hinchley	8	1	9
Hislop	11		11
Hodgetts	24	5	29
Warner	11	5	16

Goalscorers

PLAYER	LEAGUE	CUP COMPETITION FA CUP	TOTAL
Devey J	29	5	34
Campbell L	16	1	17
Hodgetts	9	6	15
Dickson	14		14
Athersmith	11	1	12
Hare	4		4
Hislop	3		3
Brown J	2		2
Devey H	1		1

Fact File

Jack Reynolds and Willie Groves helped WBA defeat Villa in the FA Cup final, but soon after they were both transferred to Villa!

MANAGER: Committee

CAPTAIN: Jack Devey, D Hodgetts

TOP SCORER: Jack Devey, 34 (29 league)

BIGGEST WIN: 12-2 v Accrington (H), Football League 12 March 1892

HIGHEST ATTENDANCE: 32,810 v West Bromwich Albion, FA Cup final at The Oval, 19 March 1892

MAJOR TRANSFERS IN: Howard Spencer from Birchfield Trinity, Jack Devey from Mitchell's St George

MAJOR TRANSFERS OUT: Albert Allen, retired

Final Football League Table

		P	W	D	L	F	A	Pts
1	SUNDERLAND	26	21	0	5	93	36	42
2	PRESTON NE	26	18	1	7	61	31	37
3	BOLTON W	26	17	2	7	51	37	36
4	ASTON VILLA	26	15	0	11	89	56	30
5	EVERTON	26	12	4	10	49	49	28
6	WOLVERHAMPTON W	26	11	4	11	59	46	26
7	BURNLEY	26	11	4	11	49	45	26
8	NOTTS CO	26	11	4	11	55	51	26
9	BLACKBURN R	26	10	6	10	58	65	26
10	DERBY CO	26	10	4	12	46	52	24
11	ACCRINGTON	26	8	4	14	40	78	20
12	WBA	26	6	6	14	51	58	18
13	STOKE	26	5	4	17	38	61	14
14	DARWEN	26	4	3	19	38	112	11

Season 1892-93

Football League Division One

DATE	OPPONENTS	SCORE	GOALSCORERS	ATTENDANCE
Sep 5	Burnley	W 2-0	Campbell L, Hodgetts	9,000
Sep 10	EVERTON	W 4-1	Hodgetts, Fleming 2, Devey J	12,000
Sep 12	Stoke City	W 1-0	Campbell L	6,000
Sep 17	SUNDERLAND	L 1-6	Hodgetts	16,000
Sep 19	West Bromwich Albion	L 2-3	Devey J, Davis	11,239
Sep 24	Bolton Wanderers	L 0-5		8,000
Oct 1	Everton	L 0-1		10,000
Oct 8	Wolverhampton Wanderers	L 1-2	Hodgetts	8,000
Oct 10	STOKE CITY	W 3-2	Brown A, Campbell L, Devey J	7,000
Oct 15	NOTTINGHAM FOREST	W 1-0	Brown A	11,000
Oct 22	Preston North End	L 1-4	Devey J	10,000
Oct 29	DERBY COUNTY	W 6-1	Brown A , Athersmith 2, Devey J 2, Dowds	5,000
Nov 5	WEST BROMWICH ALBION	W 5-2	Brown A 2, Hare, Burton G, Devey J	12,100
Nov 12	Nottingham Forest	W 5-4	Athersmith 3, Hare, Devey J	10,000
Nov 19	Newton Heath	L 0-2		7,000
Nov 26	PRESTON NORTH END	W 3-1	Hodgetts, Brown A , Dowds	7,000
Dec 3	Sheffield Wednesday	L 3-5	Dowds, Devey J 2	7,000
Dec 10	BLACKBURN ROVERS	W 4-1	Athersmith, Devey J 2, Brown A	6,000
Dec 17	Derby County	L 1-2	Logan	4,500
Dec 24	Bolton Wanderers	D 1-1	Logan	3,000
Dec 31	Notts County	W 4-1	Athersmith, Devey J, Logan, Skea	4,000
Jan 7	SHEFFIELD WEDNESDAY	W 5-1	Logan 2, Hodgetts 2, Devey W	6,000
Jan 14	Sunderland	L 0-6		7,500
Feb 11	Blackburn Rovers	D 2-2	Athersmith 2	3,000
Mar 6	NEWTON HEATH	W 2-0	Logan 2	6,000
Mar 18	NOTTS COUNTY	W 3-1	Devey W, Devey J 2	4,000
Mar 25	Accrington	W 6-4	Devey J 2, Brown A, Woolley 2 Athersmith	5,000
Apr 3	WOLVERHAMPTON WANDERERS	W 5-0	Hodgetts, Cowan, Woolley 2, Brown A	6,000
Apr 4	BURNLEY	L 1-3	Devey J	7,000
Apr 15	Accrington	D 1-1	Devey J	2,000

FA Cup

Jan 21	Darwen	(Rd 1) L 4-5	Cowan, Devey J, Athersmith, Brown J	6,000

League & Cup Appearances

PLAYER	LEAGUE	CUP COMPETITION FA CUP	TOTAL
Athersmith	26	1	27
Baird	12		12
Brown A	20	1	21
Brown J	18	1	19
Burton G	12		12
Campbell G	15		15
Campbell L	11		11
Chatt R	1		1
Clarkson	1		1
Cowan Jas	26	1	27
Cox	10	1	11
Davis	1		1
Devey H	4		4
Devey J	30	1	31
Devey W	6		6
Dowds	19	1	20
Dunning	26	1	27
Evans W	17		17
Fleming	4		4
Hare	6		6
Hodgetts	28	1	29
Logan	10	1	11
Paton	1		1
Ramsay	4		4
Roberts	4		4
Skea	1		1
Stokes	13	1	14
Woolley	4		4

Goalscorers

PLAYER	LEAGUE	CUP COMPETITION FA CUP	TOTAL
Devey J	19	1	20
Athersmith	10	1	11
Brown A	9		9
Hodgetts	8		8
Logan	7		7
Woolley	4		4
Campbell L	3		3
Dowds	3		3
Cowan Jas	1	1	2
Devey W	2		2
Fleming	2		2
Hare	2		2
Burton G	1		1
Davis	1		1
Skea	1		1

Fact File

Frederick W. Rinder became a director of Aston Villa. He later became chairman and remained in office for 27 years.

MANAGER: Committee

CAPTAIN: Jack Devey, Dennis Hodgetts

TOP SCORER: Jack Devey, 20 (19 league)

BIGGEST WIN: 6-1 v Derby County (H), Division One, 29 October 1892

HIGHEST ATTENDANCE: 16,000 v Sunderland (H), Division One, 17 September 1892

MAJOR TRANSFERS IN: G.F. Burton from Walsall Town, W. Dunning from Bootle, R. Chatt from Middlesbrough Ironopolis

MAJOR TRANSFERS OUT: F. Coulton (retired), J. Warner to Newton Heath

Final Division One Table

		P	W	D	L	F	A	Pts
1	SUNDERLAND	30	22	4	4	100	36	48
2	PRESTON NE	30	17	3	10	57	39	37
3	EVERTON	30	16	4	10	74	51	36
4	ASTON VILLA	30	16	3	11	73	62	35
5	BOLTON W	30	13	6	11	56	55	32
6	BURNLEY	30	13	4	13	51	44	30
7	STOKE	30	12	5	13	58	48	29
8	WBA	30	12	5	13	58	69	29
9	BLACKBURN R	30	8	13	9	47	56	29
10	NOTTINGHAM FOREST	30	10	8	12	48	52	28
11	WOLVERHAMPTON W	30	12	4	14	47	68	28
12	SHEFFIELD W	30	12	3	15	55	65	27
13	DERBY CO	30	9	9	12	52	64	27
14	NOTTS CO	30	10	4	16	53	61	24
15	ACCRINGTON	30	6	11	13	57	81	23
16	NEWTON HEATH	30	6	6	18	50	85	18

Football League Division One

DATE	OPPONENTS	SCORE	GOALSCORERS	ATTENDANCE
Sep 2	WEST BROMWICH ALBION	W 3-2	Reynolds (pen), Devey J, Woolley	15,100
Sep 9	Sunderland	D 1-1	Hodgetts	10,000
Sep 11	STOKE CITY	W 5-1	Hodgetts 2, Logan, Woolley 2	8,000
Sep 16	Everton	L 2-4	Woolley, Athersmith	15,000
Sep 23	EVERTON	W 3-1	Woolley 2, Athersmith	7,000
Sep 30	DERBY COUNTY	D 1-1	Reynolds	12,000
Oct 2	Sheffield United	L 0-3		8,000
Oct 7	Nottingham Forest	W 2-1	Devey J, Groves	12,000
Oct 14	Darwen	D 1-1	Devey J	3,000
Oct 16	Stoke City	D 3-3	Athersmith, Devey J, Clare o.g.	5,000
Oct 21	West Bromwich Albion	W 6-3	Devey J 2, Cowan, Athersmith, Hare, Woolley	14,000
Oct 28	BURNLEY	W 4-0	Smith, Hare, Devey J, Athersmith	8,000
Oct 30	Sheffield United	W 4-0	Hare 3, Reynolds	9,500
Nov 4	Blackburn Rovers	L 0-2		6,000
Nov 11	SUNDERLAND	W 2-1	Devey J, Reynolds (pen)	14,100
Nov 18	Bolton Wanderers	W 1-0	Hare	700
Nov 25	PRESTON NORTH END	W 2-0	Devey J, Hare	10,300
Dec 2	Derby County	W 3-0	Athersmith, Hodgetts 2	7,000
Dec 19	SHEFFIELD WEDNESDAY	W 3-0	Hodgetts, Athersmith, Brown RN o.g.	10,900
Dec 16	Newton Heath	W 3-1	Devey J, Mitchell 2 o.gs.	8,000
Dec 23	Wolverhampton Wanderers	L 0-3		14,000
Dec 26	DARWEN	W 9-0	Devey J 2, Brown 2, Smith, Hodgetts 2, Athersmith, Reynolds	12,500
Jan 6	Sheffield Wednesday	D 2-2	Reynolds, Woolley	8,000
Jan 18	Preston North End	W 5-2	Devey J 2, Hodgetts, Cowan 2	4,000
Feb 3	Newton Heath	W 5-1	Devey J 3, Hodgetts, Reynolds	5,800
Mar 3	BOLTON WANDERERS	L 2-3	Chatt 2	8,000
Mar 24	BLACKBURN ROVERS	W 2-1	Chatt 2	18,000
Mar 26	WOLVERHAMPTON WANDERERS	D 1-1	Athersmith	15,500
Apr 7	Burnley	W 6-3	Groves 2, Devey J 2, Hodgetts 2	7,000
Apr 14	NOTTINGHAM FOREST	W 3-1	Athersmith, Chatt, Devey J	4,700

FA Cup

DATE	OPPONENTS		SCORE	GOALSCORERS	ATTENDANCE
Jan 27	WOLVERHAMPTON WANDERERS	(Rd 1)	W 4-2	Devey J 2, Chatt, Cowan	22,981
Feb 10	Sunderland	(Rd 2)	D 2-2	Cowan, Hodgetts	22,000
Feb 21	SUNDERLAND	(R)	W 3-1	Athersmith, Hodgetts, Chatt	25,000
Feb 24	Sheffield Wednesday	(Rd 3)	L 2-3*	Chatt 2	20,000

*After extra-time.

League & Cup Appearances

PLAYER	LEAGUE	CUP COMPETITION FA CUP	TOTAL
Athersmith	25	4	29
Baird	29	4	33
Benwell	1		1
Brown A	6		6
Burton G	4		4
Chatt	13	4	17
Coulton	1		1
Cowan Jas	30	4	34
Devey J	29	4	33
Devey W	4		4
Dunning	28	4	32
Elliot	12	4	16
Gillan	3		3
Groves	22	4	26
Hare	10		10
Hodgetts	29	4	33
Logan J	4		4
Randall	1		1
Reynolds	26	4	30
Russell	5		5
Smith	15		15
Welford	19		19
Woolley	14	4	18

Goalscorers

PLAYER	LEAGUE	CUP COMPETITION FA CUP	TOTAL
Devey J	20	2	22
Hodgetts	12	2	14
Athersmith	10	1	11
Chatt	5	4	9
Woolley	8		8
Hare	7		7
Reynolds	7		7
Cowan Jas	3	2	5
Groves	3		3
Brown A	2		2
Smith	2		2
Logan J	1		1
Opps' o.gs.	4		4

Fact File

Right Winger Charlie Athersmith was earning £6 per week – one of the highest paid footballers in the game.

MANAGER: Committee

CAPTAIN: Jack Devey, D Hodgetts

TOP SCORER: Jack Devey, 22 (20 league)

BIGGEST WIN: 9-0 v Darwen (H), Division One, 26 December 1893

HIGHEST ATTENDANCE: 25,000 v Sunderland (H), FA Cup Second Round Replay, 21 February 1894

MAJOR TRANSFERS IN: Steve Smith from Hednesford Town, Willie Groves and Jack Reynolds from West Bromwich Albion, Jim Wellford from Bishop Auckland

MAJOR TRANSFERS OUT: George Campbell to Dundee, Harry Devey retired

Final Division One Table

		P	W	D	L	F	A	Pts
1	ASTON VILLA	30	19	6	5	84	42	44
2	SUNDERLAND	30	17	4	9	72	44	38
3	DERBY CO	30	16	4	10	73	62	36
4	BLACKBURN R	30	16	2	12	69	53	34
5	BURNLEY	30	15	4	11	61	51	34
6	EVERTON	30	15	3	12	90	57	33
7	NOTTINGHAM F	30	14	4	12	57	48	32
8	WBA	30	14	4	12	66	59	32
9	WOLVERHAMPTON W	30	14	3	13	52	63	31
10	SHEFFIELD U	30	13	5	12	47	61	31
11	STOKE	30	13	3	14	65	79	29
12	SHEFFIELD W	30	9	8	13	48	57	26
13	BOLTON W	30	10	4	16	38	52	24
14	PRESTON NE	30	10	3	17	44	56	23
15	DARWEN	30	7	5	18	37	83	19
16	NEWTON HEATH	30	6	2	22	36	72	14

Season 1894-95

Football League Division One

DATE	OPPONENTS	SCORE	GOALSCORERS	ATTENDANCE
Sep 1	SMALL HEATH	W 2-1	Smith, Gordon	20,000
Sep 8	Liverpool	W 2-1	Smith, Chatt	20,000
Sep 15	Sunderland	L 1-2	Smith	19,500
Sep 22	Derby County	W 2-0	Chatt, Devey	8,000
Sep 29	Stoke City	L 1-4	Chatt	5,000
Oct 6	Nottingham Forest	L 1-2	Devey	7,000
Oct 13	WEST BROMWICH ALBION	W 3-1	Hodgetts 2, Woolley	15,000
Oct 20	Small Heath	D 2-2	Gordon, Hodgetts	14,000
Oct 22	Sheffield United	L 1-2	Cowan	10,000
Oct 27	LIVERPOOL	W 5-0	Hodgetts, Dorrell, Cowan, Reynolds 2 (1 pen)	5,000
Nov 3	Sheffield Wednesday	L 0-1		15,000
Nov 10	PRESTON NORTH END	W 4-1	Devey, Hodgetts, Chatt, Dunn o.g.	7,000
Nov 17	West Bromwich Albion	L 2-3	Smith, Purslow	12,000
Nov 24	NOTTINGHAM FOREST	W 4-1	Hodgetts, Cowan, Devey 2	8,000
Dec 1	Blackburn Rovers	W 3-1	Smith 3	10,000
Dec 3	SHEFFIELD WEDNESDAY	W 3-1	Russell, Devey, Reynolds (pen)	5,000
Dec 8	BLACKBURN ROVERS	W 3-0	Athersmith, Devey 2	5,000
Dec 22	Wolverhampton Wanderers	W 4-0	Hodgetts 2, Athersmith, Devey	7,000
Dec 26	STOKE CITY	w 6-0	Athersmith 3, Reynolds, Devey, Chatt	11,000
Jan 2	Sunderland	D 4-4	Smith 2, Reynolds (pen) Devey	12,000
Jan 5	DERBY COUNTY	W 4-0	Hodgetts 2, Smith, Chatt	4,000
Jan 12	Preston North End	W 1-0	Devey	8,000
Jan 17	Everton	L 2-4	Dorrell, Smith	15,000
Jan 26	BOLTON WANDERERS	W 2-1	Jones o.g., Devey	5,000
Feb 23	Burnley	D 3-3	Chatt, Athersmith, Crabtree o.g.	7,000
Mar 23	Bolton Wanderers	L 3-4	Smith, Athersmith, Devey	6,000
Apr 6	BURNLEY	W 5-0	Dorrell 2, Athersmith, Hodgetts, Chatt	4,000
Apr 15	WOLVERHAMPTON WANDERERS	D 2-2	Spencer, Cowan	7,000
Apr 24	EVERTON	D 2-2	Athersmith, Smith	5,000

FA Cup

Feb 2	DERBY COUNTY	(Rd 1) W 2-1	Devey, Smith	6,000
Feb 16	NEWCASTLE UNITED	(Rd 2) W 7-1	Dorrell 2, Russell, Devey 2, Athersmith 2	9,000
Mar 2	NOTTINGHAM FOREST	(Rd 3) W 6-1	Chatt 2, Smith 2, Russell, Cowan	20,000
Mar 16	Sunderland*	(SF) W 2-1	Smith 2	14,000
Apr 20	West Bromwich Albion#	(F) W 1-0	Chatt	42,562

*Played at Ewood Park, Blackburn.
#Played at Crystal Palace, London.

League & Cup Appearances

PLAYER	LEAGUE	CUP COMPETITION	TOTAL
		FA CUP	
Athersmith	30	5	35
Baird	5		5
Burton	6	1	7
Chatt	27	3	30
Cowan Jas	30	5	35
Devey J	25	5	30
Dorrell W	9	1	10
Dunning	10		10
Elliott	6	2	8
Gordon	4		4
Hare	2		2
Hodgetts	25	5	30
Kinsey	3		3
Podmore	1		1
Purslow	1		1
Reynolds	24	4	28
Russell	27	5	32
Smith	26	5	31
Spencer	23	4	27
Wellford	26	4	30
Wilkes	20	5	25
Woolley	2		2

Goalscorers

PLAYER	LEAGUE	CUP COMPETITION	TOTAL
		FA CUP	
Devey J	16	3	19
Smith	13	5	18
Chatt	10	3	13
Athersmith	9	2	11
Hodgetts	11		11
Dorrell W	4	2	6
Reynolds	6		6
Cowan Jas	4	1	5
Russell	1	2	3
Gordon	2		2
Podmore		1	1
Purslow	1		1
Spencer	1		1
Woolley	1		1
Opps' o.gs.	3		3

Fact File

Bob Chatt scored the only goal of the 1895 FA Cup final after only 39 seconds.

MANAGER: Committee
CAPTAIN: Jack Devey, Jack Reynolds
TOP SCORER: Jack Devey, 19 (16 league)
BIGGEST WIN: 7-1 v Newcastle United (H), FA Cup Second Round, 16 February 1895
HIGHEST ATTENDANCE: 42,562 v West Bromwich Albion, FA Cup final at Crystal Palace, 20 April 1895
MAJOR TRANSFERS IN: W. Dorrell from Leicester City
MAJOR TRANSFERS OUT: Willie Groves to Hibernian, J. Logan to Notts County, A. Woolley to Derby County

Final Division One Table

		P	W	D	L	F	A	Pts
1	SUNDERLAND	30	21	5	4	80	37	47
2	EVERTON	30	18	6	6	82	50	42
3	ASTON VILLA	30	17	5	8	82	43	39
4	PRESTON NE	30	15	5	10	62	46	35
5	BLACKBURN R	30	11	10	9	59	49	32
6	SHEFFIELD U	30	14	4	12	57	55	32
7	NOTTINGHAM F	30	13	5	12	50	56	31
8	SHEFFIELD W	30	12	4	14	50	55	28
9	BURNLEY	30	11	4	15	44	56	26
10	BOLTON W	30	9	7	14	61	62	25
11	WOLVERHAMPTON W	30	9	7	14	43	63	25
12	SMALL HEATH	30	9	7	14	50	74	25
13	WBA	30	10	4	16	51	66	24
14	STOKE	30	9	6	15	50	67	24
15	DERBY CO	30	7	9	14	45	68	23
16	LIVERPOOL	30	7	8	15	51	70	22

Football League Division One

DATE	OPPONENTS	SCORE	GOALSCORERS	ATTENDANCE
Sep 2	WEST BROMWICH ALBION	W 1-0	Devey	18,150
Sep 7	SMALL HEATH	W 7-3	Campbell 4, Cowan Jas, Devey 2	13,000
Sep 14	Sheffield United	L 1-2	Hodgetts	10,000
Sep 21	DERBY COUNTY	W 4-1	Cowan J, Devey, Campbell Cowan Jas	12,000
Sep 28	Blackburn Rovers	D 1-1	Campbell	15,000
Sep 30	EVERTON	W 4-3	Athersmith, Devey, Campbell 2	15,000
Oct 5	SUNDERLAND	W 2-1	Campbell, Cowan J	20,000
Oct 12	West Bromwich Albion	D 1-1	Campbell	17,510
Oct 19	BLACKBURN ROVERS	W 3-1	Crabtree, Dorrell, Hodgetts	17,000
Oct 26	Small Heath	W 4-1	Devey 2, Reynolds, Campbell	10,000
Nov 2	BURNLEY	W 5-1	Athersmith 3, Smith, Devey	17,000
Nov 9	Sunderland	L 1-2	Hodgetts	15,000
Nov 16	SHEFFIELD UNITED	D 2-2	Chatt, Cowan J	12,000
Nov 23	Burnley	W 4-3	Athersmith 2, Devey, Reynolds	8,000
Dec 14	BOLTON WANDERERS	W 2-0	Welford, Campbell	6,000
Dec 21	Everton	L 0-2		30,000
Dec 28	BURY	W 2-0	Campbell 2	7,000
Jan 4	Stoke City	W 2-1	Campbell 2	14,000
Jan 11	Preston North End	W 1-0	Cowan J	10,000
Jan 18	Sheffield Wednesday	W 3-1	Cowan J, Devey, Crabtree	12,000
Jan 25	NOTTINGHAM FOREST	W 3-1	Chatt, Devey, Cowan J	10,000
Feb 8	Derby County	D 2-2	Devey, Athersmith	15,000
Feb 22	STOKE CITY	W 5-2	Chatt, Robertson o.g. Campbell 3	15,000
Mar 7	Bolton Wanderers	D 2-2	Devey, Campbell	15,000
Mar 14	SHEFFIELD WEDNESDAY	W 2-1	Cowan J, Campbell	10,000
Mar 21	Bury	L 3-5	Devey, Campbell, Cowan J	10,000
Apr 3	Nottingham Forest	W 2-0	Athersmith, Campbell	12,000
Apr 6	WOLVERHAMPTON WANDERERS	W 4-1	Cowan J, Crabtree, Campbell 2	15,000

FA Cup

Feb 1	Derby County	(Rd 1) L 2-4	Burton, Hodgetts	25,000

League & Cup Appearances

PLAYER	LEAGUE	CUP COMPETITION FA CUP	TOTAL
Athersmith	29	1	30
Burton	14	1	15
Campbell J	26	1	27
Chatt	17	1	18
Cowan Jas	23	1	24
Cowan J	22	1	23
Crabtree	28	1	29
Devey	30	1	31
Dorrell	2		2
Elliott	1		1
Griffiths	1		1
Harris	1		1
Hodgetts	21	1	22
Reynolds	22		22
Smith	11		11
Spencer	29	1	30
Welford	24		24
Wilkes	29	1	30

Goalscorers

PLAYER	LEAGUE	CUP COMPETITION FA CUP	TOTAL
Campbell J	26		26
Devey	16		16
Cowan J	9		9
Athersmith	8		8
Hodgetts	3	1	4
Chatt	3		3
Crabtree	3		3
Cowan Jas	2		2
Reynolds	2		2
Smith	2		2
Burton		1	1
Dorrell	1		1
Spencer	1		1
Welford	1		1
Opps' o.gs.	1		1

Fact File

On the night of 11 September 1895 the FA Cup – won by Villa the previous April – was stolen from the shop window of William Shillcock, a boot and shoe manufacturer in Newton Row, Birmingham.

MANAGER: Committee

CAPTAIN: Jack Devey, Jimmy Crabtree, Howard Spencer

TOP SCORER: Johnny Campbell, 26 (all league)

BIGGEST WIN: 7-3 v Small Heath (H), Division One, 7 September 1895

HIGHEST ATTENDANCE: 30,000 v Everton (A), Division One, 21 December 1895

MAJOR TRANSFERS IN: John Cowan from Glasgow Rangers, Jimmy Crabtree from Burnley

MAJOR TRANSFERS OUT: W. Dunning, retired, C. Hare to Arsenal

Final Division One Table

		P	W	D	L	F	A	Pts
1	ASTON VILLA	30	20	5	5	78	45	45
2	DERBY CO	30	17	7	6	68	35	41
3	EVERTON	30	16	7	7	66	43	39
4	BOLTON W	30	16	5	9	49	37	37
5	SUNDERLAND	30	15	7	8	52	41	37
6	STOKE	30	15	0	15	56	47	30
7	SHEFFIELD W	30	12	5	13	44	53	29
8	BLACKBURN R	30	12	5	13	40	50	29
9	PRESTON NE	30	11	6	13	44	48	28
10	BURNLEY	30	10	7	13	48	44	27
11	BURY	30	12	3	15	50	54	27
12	SHEFFIELD U	30	10	6	14	40	50	26
13	NOTTINGHAM F	30	11	3	16	42	57	25
14	WOLVERHAMPTON W	30	10	1	19	61	65	21
15	SMALL HEATH	30	8	4	18	39	79	20
16	WBA	30	6	7	17	30	59	19

Season 1896-97

Football League Division One

DATE	OPPONENTS	SCORE	GOALSCORERS	ATTENDANCE
Sep 2	STOKE CITY	W 2-1	Cowan J, Devey	6,000
Sep 5	West Bromwich Albion	L 1-3	Devey	10,000
Sep 12	SHEFFIELD UNITED	D 2-2	Wheldon, Brown	5,000
Sep 19	Everton	W 3-2	Campbell 2, Devey	20,000
Sep 26	EVERTON	L 1-2	Devey	20,000
Oct 3	Sheffield United	D 0-0		10,000
Oct 10	WEST BROMWICH ALBION	W 2-0	Wheldon, Campbell	15,500
Oct 17	Derby County	W 3-1	Cowan J, Campbell, Wheldon	8,500
Oct 24	DERBY COUNTY	W 2-1	Wheldon, Cowan J	7,500
Oct 31	Stoke City	W 2-0	Wheldon, Smith	6,000
Nov 7	BURY	D 1-1	Athersmith	5,000
Nov 14	Sheffield Wednesday	W 3-1	Wheldon, Campbell, Athersmith	8,000
Nov 21	SHEFFIELD WEDNESDAY	W 4-0	Smith, Devey, Wheldon, Athersmith	14,000
Nov 28	Blackburn Rovers	W 5-1	Devey, Smith, Wheldon 3	7,000
Dec 19	NOTTINGHAM FOREST	W 3-2	Devey, Athersmith, Reynolds	7,000
Dec 25	Liverpool	D 3-3	Cowan Jas, Wheldon, Athersmith	15,000
Dec 26	Wolverhampton Wanderers	W 2-1	Chatt, Athersmith	18,000
Jan 2	BURNLEY	L 0-3		14,000
Jan 9	Sunderland	L 2-4	Ferguson o.g., Campbell	8,000
Jan 16	SUNDERLAND	W 2-1	Devey, Wheldon	15,000
Feb 6	Bury	W 2-0	Campbell 2	10,000
Feb 8	Burnley	W 4-3	Devey 3, Campbell	4,000
Feb 22	PRESTON NORTH END	W 3-1	Devey 2, Athersmith	14,000
Mar 6	Nottingham Forest	W 4-2	Devey 2, Wheldon, Cowan J	8,000
Mar 13	LIVERPOOL	D 0-0		18,000
Mar 22	BOLTON WANDERERS	W 6-2	Athersmith, Reynolds, Devey, Campbell, Wheldon 2	8,000
Mar 27	Bolton Wanderers	W 2-1	Wheldon 2	7,000
Apr 17	BLACKBURN ROVERS	W 3-0	Campbell, Cowan J, Kelean o.g.	15,000
Apr 19	Wolverhampton Wanderers	W 5-0	Cowan J 2, Devey, Campbell 2	35,000
Apr 26	Preston North End	W 1-0	Wheldon	3,000

FA Cup

DATE	OPPONENTS		SCORE	GOALSCORERS	ATTENDANCE
Jan 30	NEWCASTLE UNITED	(Rd 1)	W 5-0	Athersmith Wheldon 2, Smith, White o.g.	6,000
Feb 13	NOTTS COUNTY	(Rd 2)	W 2-1	Wheldon, Campbell	4,000
Feb 27	Preston North End	(Rd 3)	D 1-1	Campbell	14,000
Mar 3	Preston North End	(R)	D 0-0		12,000
Mar 10	Preston North End*	(2nd R)	W 3-2	Athersmith 2, Campbell	22,000
Mar 20	Liverpool*	(SF)	W 3-0	Cowan J 2, Athersmith	30,000
Apr 10	Everton#	(F)	W 3-2	Campbell, Wheldon, Crabtree	65,891

*Played at Bramall Lane, Sheffield.
#Played at Crystal Palace, London.

League & Cup Appearances

PLAYER	LEAGUE	CUP COMPETITION FA CUP	TOTAL
Athersmith	30	7	37
Burton	8		8
Campbell J	29	7	36
Chatt	11	1	12
Cowan Jas	30	7	37
Cowan J	15	3	18
Crabtree	25	6	31
Devey J	29	7	36
Evans A	15	7	22
Griffiths	1	1	2
Reynolds	24	6	30
Smith	15	4	19
Spencer	28	7	35
Welford	10		10
Wheldon	30	7	37
Whitehouse	22	2	24
Wilkes	8	5	13

Goalscorers

PLAYER	LEAGUE	CUP COMPETITION FA CUP	TOTAL
Wheldon	18	4	22
Campbell J	13	4	17
Devey J	17		17
Athersmith	8	4	12
Cowan J	7	2	9
Smith	3	1	4
Reynolds	2		2
Burton	1		1
Cowan Jas	1		1
Chatt	1		1
Opps' o.gs.	2	1	3

Fact File

Villa emulated the feat of Preston North End (1888-89) by completing the Double – and they also played their first game at Villa Park, beating Blackburn Rovers 3-0 on 17 April 1897.

MANAGER: Committee

CAPTAIN: Jack Devey, Jimmy Crabtree

TOP SCORER: Fred Wheldon, 22 (18 league)

BIGGEST WIN: 6-2 v Bolton Wanderers (H), Division One, 22 March 1897

HIGHEST ATTENDANCE: 65,891 v Everton, FA Cup final at Crystal Palace, 10 April 1897

MAJOR TRANSFERS IN: G.F. Wheldon from Small Heath, A. Evans from Barnard Castle, J. Whitehouse from Grimsby Town

MAJOR TRANSFERS OUT: D. Hodgetts to Small Heath

Final Division One Table

		P	W	D	L	F	A	Pts
1	ASTON VILLA	30	21	5	4	73	38	47
2	SHEFFIELD U	30	13	10	7	42	29	36
3	DERBY CO	30	16	4	10	70	50	36
4	PRESTON NE	30	11	12	7	55	40	34
5	LIVERPOOL	30	12	9	9	46	38	33
6	SHEFFIELD W	30	10	11	9	42	37	31
7	EVERTON	30	14	3	13	62	57	31
8	BOLTON W	30	12	6	12	40	43	30
9	BURY	30	10	10	10	39	44	30
10	WOLVERHAMPTON W	30	11	6	13	45	41	28
11	NOTTINGHAM F	30	9	8	13	44	49	26
12	WBA	30	10	6	14	33	56	26
13	STOKE	30	11	3	16	48	59	25
14	BLACKBURN R	30	11	3	16	35	62	25
15	SUNDERLAND	30	7	9	14	34	47	23
16	BURNLEY	30	6	7	17	43	61	19

Season 1897-98

Football League Division One

DATE	OPPONENTS	SCORE	GOALSCORERS	ATTENDANCE
Sep 1	SHEFFIELD WEDNESDAY	W 5-2	Wheldon 3, Cowan J Athersmith	10,000
Sep 4	WEST BROMWICH ALBION	W 4-3	Wheldon 3, Fisher	20,950
Sep 11	Notts County	W 3-2	Cowan J 2, Devey	6,000
Sep 18	BURY	W 3-1	Fisher 2, Wheldon	18,000
Sep 25	Blackburn Rovers	L 3-4	Wheldon 2 (1 pen), Cowan J	10,000
Oct 2	BOLTON WANDERERS	W 3-2	Sharp J 2, Wheldon	20,000
Oct 9	West Bromwich Albion	D 1-1	Sharp J	12,244
Oct 16	Notts County	W 4-2	Devey, Wheldon, Sharp J 2	10,000
Oct 23	Sunderland	D 0-0		20,000
Oct 30	LIVERPOOL	W 3-1	Devey, Wheldon, Athersmith	20,000
Nov 6	Preston North End	L 1-3	Fisher	5,000
Nov 13	EVERTON	W 3-0	Wheldon 2 (1 pen), Sharp J	14,000
Nov 20	Bolton Wanderers	L 0-2		12,000
Nov 27	SUNDERLAND	W 4-3	Wheldon 2 (1 pen), Harvey 2	15,000
Dec 11	BLACKBURN ROVERS	W 5-1	Cowan Jas, Crabtree, Wheldon, Athersmith, Cowan J	22,000
Dec 18	Stoke City	D 0-0		10,000
Dec 25	Everton	L 1-2	Wheldon	18,000
Dec 27	Wolverhampton Wanderers	D 1-1	Athersmith	20,000
Jan 8	Sheffield United	L 0-1		25,000
Jan 15	SHEFFIELD UNITED	L 1-2	Wheldon (pen)	42,000
Jan 22	Derby County	L 1-3	Sharp J	12,000
Feb 5	PRESTON NORTH END	W 4-0	Suddick, Sharp J, Wheldon Athersmith	15,000
Mar 5	DERBY COUNTY	W 4-1	Smith, Sharp J 2, Fisher	11,900
Mar 12	Bury	W 2-1	Sharp J, Wheldon	9,000
Mar 26	Nottingham Forest	L 1-3	Wheldon	7,000
Apr 2	STOKE CITY	D 1-1	Harvey	8,000
Apr 11	WOLVERHAMPTON WANDERERS	L 1-2	Wheldon	9,000
Apr 16	Liverpool	L 0-4		20,000
Apr 30	NOTTINGHAM FOREST	W 2-0	Smith, Johnson	4,000

FA Cup

Jan 29	Derby County	(Rd 1) L 0-1		20,000

League & Cup Appearances

PLAYER	LEAGUE	CUP COMPETITION FA CUP	TOTAL
Aston	1		1
Athersmith	27	1	28
Bowman	15	1	16
Burton	8		8
Chatt	17		17
Cowan Jas	28	1	29
Cowan J	22	1	23
Crabtree	25	1	26
Devey J	17		17
Evans A	30	1	31
Fisher	18		18
Garraty	2		2
George	7		7
Harvey	11		11
Johnson	1		1
Sharp B	18	1	19
Sharp J	15	1	16
Smith	9	1	10
Spencer	6		6
Strange	2		2
Suddick	2		2
Wheldon	26	1	27
Whitehouse	18	1	19
Wilkes T	5		5

Goalscorers

PLAYER	LEAGUE	CUP COMPETITION FA CUP	TOTAL
Wheldon	23		23
Sharp J	11		11
Athersmith	5		5
Cowan J	5		5
Fisher	5		5
Harvey	3		3
Devey J	3		3
Smith	2		2
Cowan Jas	1		1
Crabtree	1		1
Johnson	1		1
Suddick	1		1

Fact File

Villa's average league attendance for home games was 16,323 – the highest in the competition at that time.

MANAGER: Committee

CAPTAIN: Jimmy Crabtree, Jack Devey

TOP SCORER: Fred Wheldon, 23 (all league)

BIGGEST WIN: 5-1 v Blackburn Rovers (H), Division One, 11 December 1897

HIGHEST ATTENDANCE: 42,000 v Sheffield United (H), Division One, 15 January 1898

MAJOR TRANSFERS IN: J. Fisher from St Bernard's, W. George via Army, W. Garraty form Aston Shakespeare

MAJOR TRANSFERS OUT: Jack Reynolds and J. Welford both to Celtic

Final Division One Table

		P	W	D	L	F	A	Pts
1	SHEFFIELD U	30	17	8	5	56	31	42
2	SUNDERLAND	30	16	5	9	43	30	37
3	WOLVERHAMPTON W	30	14	7	9	57	41	35
4	EVERTON	30	13	9	8	48	39	35
5	SHEFFIELD W	30	15	3	12	51	42	33
6	ASTON VILLA	30	14	5	11	61	51	33
7	WBA	30	11	10	9	44	45	32
8	NOTTINGHAM F	30	11	9	10	47	49	31
9	LIVERPOOL	30	11	6	13	48	45	28
10	DERBY CO	30	11	6	13	57	61	28
11	BOLTON W	30	11	4	15	28	41	26
12	PRESTON NE	30	8	8	14	35	43	24
13	NOTTS CO	30	8	8	14	36	46	24
14	BURY	30	8	8	14	39	51	24
15	BLACKBURN R	30	7	10	13	39	54	24
16	STOKE	30	8	8	14	35	55	24

Season 1898-99

Football League Division One

DATE	OPPONENTS	SCORE	GOALSCORERS	ATTENDANCE
Sep 3	STOKE CITY	W 3-1	Athersmith, Devey, Gaudie	25,000
Sep 10	Bury	L 1-2	Devey	10,000
Sep 19	Burnley	W 4-2	Smith, Athersmith, Johnson Wheldon	8,000
Sep 24	SHEFFIELD UNITED	D 1-1	Devey	24,521
Oct 1	Newcastle United	D 1-1	Devey	25,000
Oct 8	PRESTON NORTH END	W 4-2	Devey 2, Cowan Jas Johnson	20,000
Oct 15	Liverpool	W 3-0	Johnson, Devey, Wheldon	20,000
Oct 22	NOTTINGHAM FOREST	W 3-0	Devey, Sharp J 2	18,000
Oct 29	BOLTON WANDERERS	W 2-1	Devey, Wheldon	20,000
Nov 5	DERBY COUNTY	W 7-1	Devey 2, Johnson 2, Wheldon 2, Cowan J	20,000
Nov 12	West Bromwich Albion	W 1-0	Johnson	15,896
Nov 19	BLACKBURN ROVERS	W 3-1	Devey, Weldon 2	24,000
Nov 26	Sheffield Wednesday*	L 1-4	Bedingfield	10,000
Dec 3	SUNDERLAND	W 2-0	Sharp J 2	22,000
Dec 10	WOLVERHAMPTON WANDERERS	D 1-1	Crabtree	13,000
Dec 17	EVERTON	W 3-0	Wheldon, Devey, Johnson	25,000
Dec 24	Notts County	L 0-1		20,000
Dec 26	NEWCASTLE UNITED	W 1-0	Athersmith	25,000
Dec 31	Stoke City	L 0-3		8,000
Jan 7	BURY	W 3-2	Wheldon, Devey 2	18,000
Jan 14	BURNLEY	W 4-0	Wheldon, Taylor o.g. Bowman, Athersmith	22,000
Jan 21	Sheffield Wednesday	W 3-1	Wilkes A, Cowan J 2	10,000
Feb 4	Preston North End	L 0-2		10,000
Feb 18	Nottingham Forest	L 0-1		11,000
Mar 4	Derby County	D 1-1	Johnson	10,000
Mar 18	Blackburn Rovers	D 0-0		10,000
Mar 25	SHEFFIELD WEDNESDAY	W 3-1	Wheldon, Garraty, Johnson	15,000
Apr 1	Sunderland	L 2-4	Devey, Cowan J	20,000
Apr 4	Wolverhampton Wanderers	L 0-4		18,000
Apr 15	Everton	D 1-1	Smith	20,000
Apr 17	Bolton Wanderers	D 0-0		7,000
Apr 22	Notts County	W 6-1	Devey 3, Whedon, Garraty 2	8,000
Apr 24	WEST BROMWICH ALBION	W 7-1	Bowman, Wheldon 2, Cowan Jas, Garraty 3	10,000
Apr 29	LIVERPOOL	W 5-0	Devey 2, Wheldon 2, Crabtree	41,000

*Abandoned after 79 minutes. Football League made Villa travel back to Sheffield in March to play the remaining ten minutes. Bedingfield did not play the remaining ten minutes, his place going to Bill Garraty.

FA Cup

Jan 28	Nottingham Forest	(Rd 1) L 1-2	Johnson	32,000

Charity Shield

Mar 11	Queen's Park†	D 0-0	14,000

†Played at Crystal Palace, London.

League & Cup Appearances

PLAYER	LEAGUE	CUP COMPETITION FA CUP	OTHER	TOTAL
Aston	13		1	14
Athersmith	28	1	1	30
Bedingfield	1			1
Bowman	34	1	1	36
Cowan Jas	33	1	1	35
Cowan J	7			7
Crabtree	31	1	1	33
Devey	30	1		31
Evans J	29	1	1	31
Garraty	9		1	10
Gaudie	5			5
George	30	1	1	32
Haggart	1			1
Johnson	24	1	1	26
Leigh	1			1
Sharp B	4			4
Sharp J	8			8
Smith	27	1	1	29
Spencer	10			10
Templeton	1			1
Wheldon	33	1	1	35
Wilkes A	11	1		12
Wilkes T	4			4

Goalscorers

PLAYER	LEAGUE	CUP COMPETITION FA CUP	OTHER	TOTAL
Devey	21			21
Wheldon	16			16
Johnson	9	1		10
Garraty	6			6
Athersmith	4			4
Cowan J	4			4
Sharp J	4			4
Bowman	2			2
Cowan Jas	2			2
Crabtree	2			2
Smith	2			2
Bedingfield	1			1
Gaudie	1			1
Wilkes A	1			1
Opps' o.gs.	1			1

Fact File

Villa scored 18 goals in three home league games during the last week of April.

MANAGER: Committee

CAPTAIN: Jimmy Crabtree, Fred Wheldon, Jas Cowan

TOP SCORER: Jack Devey, 21 (all league)

BIGGEST WIN: 7-1 v Derby County (H), Division One, 5 November 1898; 7-1 v West Bromwich Albion (H), Division One, 24 April 1899

HIGHEST ATTENDANCE: 41,000 v Liverpool (H), Division One, 29 April 1899

MAJOR TRANSFERS IN: R. Templeton from Hibernian

MAJOR TRANSFERS OUT: R. Chatt to Stockton, J. Whitehouse to Newton Heath

Final Division One Table

		P	W	D	L	F	A	Pts
1	ASTON VILLA	34	19	7	8	76	40	45
2	LIVERPOOL	34	19	5	10	49	33	43
3	BURNLEY	34	15	9	10	45	47	39
4	EVERTON	34	15	8	11	48	41	38
5	NOTTS CO	34	12	13	9	47	51	37
6	BLACKBURN R	34	14	8	12	60	52	36
7	SUNDERLAND	34	15	6	13	41	41	36
8	WOLVERHAMPTON W	34	14	7	13	54	48	35
9	DERBY CO	34	12	11	11	62	57	35
10	BURY	34	14	7	13	48	49	35
11	NOTTINGHAM F	34	11	11	12	42	42	33
12	STOKE	34	13	7	14	47	52	33
13	NEWCASTLE U	34	11	8	15	49	48	30
14	WBA	34	12	6	16	42	57	30
15	PRESTON NE	34	10	9	15	44	47	29
16	SHEFFIELD U	34	9	11	14	45	51	29
17	BOLTON W	34	9	7	18	37	51	25
18	SHEFFIELD W	34	8	8	18	32	61	24

Season 1899 -1900

Football League Division One

DATE	OPPONENTS	SCORE	GOALSCORERS	ATTENDANCE
Sep 2	Sunderland	W 1-0	Garraty	27,000
Sep 4	GLOSSOP	W 9-0	Wheldon 2, Smith, Devey Garraty 4, Athersmith	15,000
Sep 9	WEST BROMWICH ALBION	L 0-2		17,482
Sep 16	Everton	W 2-1	Wheldon, Garraty	30,000
Sep 23	BLACKBURN ROVERS	W 3-1	Wheldon, Devey 2	20,000
Sep 30	Derby County	L 0-2		12,000
Oct 7	BURY	W 2-1	Johnson, Wheldon	20,000
Oct 14	Notts County	W 4-1	Johnson 3, Devey	10,000
Oct 21	MANCHESTER CITY	W 2-1	Wheldon (pen), Devey	25,000
Oct 28	Sheffield United	L 1-2	Smith	28,000
Nov 4	NEWCASTLE UNITED	W 2-1	Devey, Wheldon	20,000
Nov 11	WOLVERHAMPTON WANDERERS	D 0-0		8,000
Nov 13	Stoke City	W 2-0	Garfield, Devey	15,000
Nov 18	Liverpool	D 3-3	Storer o.g., Devey, Wilkes	20,000
Nov 25	BURNLEY	W 2-0	Templeton, Wheldon	10,000
Dec 2	Preston North End	W 5-0	Garraty, Dunn o.g., Smith 3	12,000
Dec 9	NOTTINGHAM FOREST	D 2-2	Garraty, Devey	15,000
Dec 16	Glossop	L 0-1		4,000
Dec 23	STOKE CITY	W 4-1	Smith, Garraty, Wheldon 2	6,000
Dec 30	SUNDERLAND	W 4-2	Garraty 3, Johnson	20,000
Jan 1	Bury	L 0-2		13,000
Jan 6	West Bromwich Albion	W 2-0	Garraty 2	6,575
Jan 13	EVERTON	D 1-1	Athersmith	17,000
Jan 20	Blackburn Rovers	W 4-0	Athersmith, Smith, Garraty 2	7,000
Feb 3	DERBY COUNTY	W 3-2	Garraty 2, Wheldon	6,000
Feb 17	NOTTS COUNTY	W 6-2	Athersmith, Cowan, Devey Garraty 3	22,000
Mar 3	SHEFFIELD UNITED	D 1-1	Garraty	50,000
Mar 10	Newcastle United	L 2-3	Devey, Garraty	19,549
Mar 19	Manchester City	W 2-0	Garraty 2	15,000
Mar 24	LIVERPOOL	W 1-0	Devey	12,000
Mar 31	Burnley	W 2-1	Devey, Woolfall o.g.	6,000
Apr 7	PRESTON NORTH END	W 3-1	Templeton, Garraty 2	18,000
Apr 14	Nottingham Forest	D 1-1	Templeton	12,000
Apr 16	Wolverhampton Wanderers	W 1-0	Templeton	18,000

FA Cup

Jan 27	Manchester City	(Rd 1) D 1-1	Devey	30,000
Jan 31	MANCHESTER CITY	(R) W 3-0	Garraty 2, Wheldon	20,000
Feb 10	Bristol City	(Rd 2) W 5-0	Garraty, Devey 4	12,000
Feb 24	Millwall	(Rd 3) D 1-1	Wheldon	25,000
Feb 28	MILLWALL	(R) D 0-0		15,000
Mar 5	Millwall*	(2nd R) L 1-2	Johnson	15,000

*Played at Elm Park, Reading.

Charity Shield

Nov 8	Corinthians†		L 1-2	Garraty	8,000

†Played at Crystal Palace, London.

League & Cup Appearances

PLAYER	LEAGUE	CUP COMPETITION FA CUP	OTHER	TOTAL
Aston	3			3
Athersmith	24	6	1	31
Bowman	27	5	1	33
Crabtree	17	4		21
Cowan Jas	25	5		30
Devey J	25	6	1	32
Evans J	26	6	1	33
Garfield	1			1
Garraty	33	6	1	40
George	34	6	1	41
Haggatt	1			1
Johnson	9	1		10
Mann	7		1	8
McEllery	1			1
Noon	15	2		17
Smith	31	5	1	37
Spencer	28	6	1	35
Templeton	11	1		12
Wheldon	34	5	1	40
Watkins	1			1
Wilkes	21	2	1	24

Goalscorers

PLAYER	LEAGUE	CUP COMPETITION FA CUP	OTHER	TOTAL
Garraty	27	3	1	31
Devey J	13	5		18
Wheldon	11	2		13
Smith	7			7
Johnson	5	1		6
Athersmith	4			4
Templeton	4			4
Cowan Jas	1			1
Garfield	1			1
Wilkes	1			1
Opps' o.gs.	3			3

Fact File

Villa gained 11 points from their last six matches to beat off a strong challenge from Sheffield Wednesday to regain the league championship.

MANAGER: Committee

CAPTAIN: Jimmy Crabtree, Jack Devey, Howard Spencer

TOP SCORER: W Garraty, 31 (27 league)

BIGGEST WIN: 9-0 v Glossop (H), Division One, 4 September 1899

HIGHEST ATTENDANCE: 50,000 v Sheffield United (H), Division One, 3 March 1900

MAJOR TRANSFERS IN: A. Watkins from Leicester Fosse

MAJOR TRANSFERS OUT: B. Sharp and J. Sharp both to Everton

Final Division One Table

		P	W	D	L	F	A	Pts
1	ASTON VILLA	34	22	6	6	77	35	50
2	SHEFFIELD U	34	18	12	4	63	33	48
3	SUNDERLAND	34	19	3	12	50	35	41
4	WOLVERHAMPTON W	34	15	9	10	48	37	39
5	NEWCASTLE U	34	13	10	11	53	43	36
6	DERBY CO	34	14	8	12	45	43	36
7	MANCHESTER C	34	13	8	13	50	44	34
8	NOTTINGHAM F	34	13	8	13	56	55	34
9	STOKE	34	13	8	13	37	45	34
10	LIVERPOOL	34	14	5	15	49	45	33
11	EVERTON	34	13	7	14	47	49	33
12	BURY	34	13	6	15	40	44	32
13	WBA	34	11	8	15	43	51	30
14	BLACKBURN R	34	13	4	17	49	61	30
15	NOTTS CO	34	9	11	14	46	60	29
16	PRESTON NE	34	12	4	18	38	48	28
17	BURNLEY	34	11	5	18	34	54	27
18	GLOSSOP	34	4	10	20	31	74	18

Season 1900-01

Football League Division One

DATE	OPPONENTS	SCORE	GOALSCORERS	ATTENDANCE
Sep 1	STOKE CITY	W 2-0	Athersmith, Smith	20,000
Sep 4	PRESTON NORTH END	W 4-0	Devey 3, Garraty	12,000
Sep 8	West Bromwich Albion	W 1-0	Johnson	35,417
Sep 10	BURY	W 1-0	Devey	23,000
Sep 15	EVERTON	L 1-2	Devey	27,000
Sep 22	Sunderland	D 0-0		22,000
Sep 29	DERBY COUNTY	W 2-1	Devey 2	20,000
Oct 6	Bolton Wanderers	L 0-1		10,000
Oct 13	NOTTS COUNTY	L 1-2	Johnson	13,000
Oct 20	Preston North End	W 2-0	Smith, Garraty	10,000
Oct 27	WOLVERHAMPTON WANDERERS	D 0-0		18,000
Oct 29	BLACKBURN ROVERS	D 3-3	Templeton, Athersmith 2	14,000
Nov 3	Sheffield Wednesday	L 2-3	Garraty, Johnson	22,000
Nov 10	Liverpool	L 1-5	Johnson	18,000
Nov 17	NEWCASTLE UNITED	D 2-2	Johnson, Wilkes	20,000
Nov 24	Sheffield United	D 2-2	Brown 2	18,000
Dec 1	MANCHESTER CITY	W 7-1	Johnson 4, Devey, Garraty Wilkes	15,000
Dec 8	Bury	L 1-3	Smith	4,000
Dec 15	NOTTINGHAM FOREST	W 2-1	Devey 2	10,000
Dec 22	Blackburn Rovers	D 2-2	Garraty, Smith	5,000
Dec 26	BOLTON WANDERERS	W 3-0	Devey 2, Athersmith	20,000
Dec 29	Stoke City	D 0-0		12,000
Jan 5	WEST BROMWICH ALBION	L 0-1		30,000
Jan 12	Everton	L 1-2	Garraty	18,000
Jan 19	SUNDERLAND	D 2-2	Devey, Garraty	10,000
Feb 16	Notts County	L 0-2		15,000
Mar 9	SHEFFIELD WEDNESDAY	W 2-1	Garraty, Lloyd	16,000
Mar 16	LIVERPOOL	L 0-2		14,000
Mar 30	SHEFFIELD UNITED	D 0-0		5,000
Apr 8	Wolverhampton Wanderers	D 0-0		7,000
Apr 17	Newcastle United	L 0-3		12,000
Apr 20	Nottingham Forest	L 1-3	Bache	5,000
Apr 22	Derby County	L 0-3		6,000
Apr 27	Manchester City	L 0-4		7,000

FA Cup

Jan 26	MILLWALL	(Rd 1) W 5-0	Devey, Smith, Johnson 3	24,000
Feb 23	NOTTINGHAM FOREST	(Rd 2) D 0-0		40,000
Feb 27	Nottingham Forest	(R) W 3-1	Athersmith, Cowan, Garraty	30,000
Mar 23	Small Heath	(Rd 3) D 0-0		18,000
Mar 27	SMALL HEATH	(R) W 1-0	Garraty	15,000
Apr 1	Sheffield United	(R) D 2-2	Garraty, Devey	30,000
Apr 11	Sheffield United#	(R) L 0-3		22,000

*Played at Nottingham. #Played at Baseball Ground, Derby.

Charity Shield

Mar 2	Corinthians†	W 1-0	Athersmith	10,000

†Played at Crystal Palace, London.

League & Cup Appearances

PLAYER	LEAGUE	CUP COMPETITION FA CUP	OTHER	TOTAL
Aston	6			6
Athersmith	24	7	1	32
Bache	7			7
Bowman	24	6	1	31
Brown	2			2
Cowan Jas	23	6	1	30
Crabtree	23	7	1	31
Devey	25	7	1	33
Evans	25	6	1	32
Garraty	33	7	1	41
George	31	7	1	39
Gilson	2			2
Johnson	21	3	1	25
Lloyd	2	1		3
McAulay	6			6
Mann	3			3
Miller	1			1
Murray	1			1
Noon	12	1		13
Pearson	6			6
Smith	28	6	1	35
Spencer	20	2		22
Templeton	17	4		21
Whitley	3			3
Wilkes	24	7	1	32
Wilson	1			1
Wood	4			4

Goalscorers

PLAYER	LEAGUE	CUP COMPETITION FA CUP	OTHER	TOTAL
Devey	13	2		15
Johnson	9	3		12
Garraty	8	3		11
Athersmith	4	1	1	6
Smith	4	1		5
Brown	2			2
Wilkes	2			2
Bache	1			1
Lloyd	1			1
Templeton	1			1

Fact File

Villa's final league position this season – 15th – was their lowest since the competition started in 1888.

MANAGER: Committee

CAPTAIN: Jack Devey, Jimmy Crabtree, Howard Spencer

TOP SCORER: Jack Devey, 15 (13 league)

BIGGEST WIN: 7-1 v Manchester City (H), Division One, 1 December 1900

HIGHEST ATTENDANCE: 40,000 v Nottingham Forest (H), FA Cup Second Round, 23 February 1901

MAJOR TRANSFERS IN: J. Pearson from Saltley College, Joe Bache from Stourbridge

MAJOR TRANSFERS OUT: F. Wheldon to West Bromwich Albion, S. Smith to Portsmouth

Final Division One Table

		P	W	D	L	F	A	Pts
1	LIVERPOOL	34	19	7	8	59	35	45
2	SUNDERLAND	34	15	13	6	57	26	43
3	NOTTS CO	34	18	4	12	54	46	40
4	NOTTINGHAM F	34	16	7	11	53	36	39
5	BURY	34	16	7	11	53	37	39
6	NEWCASTLE U	34	14	10	10	42	37	38
7	EVERTON	34	16	5	13	55	42	37
8	SHEFFIELD W	34	13	10	11	52	42	36
9	BLACKBURN R	34	12	9	13	39	47	33
10	BOLTON W	34	13	7	14	39	55	33
11	MANCHESTER C	34	13	6	15	48	58	32
12	DERBY CO	34	12	7	15	55	42	31
13	WOLVERHAMPTON W	34	9	13	12	39	55	31
14	SHEFFIELD U	34	12	7	15	35	52	31
15	ASTON VILLA	34	10	10	14	45	51	30
16	STOKE	34	11	5	18	46	57	27
17	PRESTON NE	34	9	7	18	49	75	25
18	WBA	34	7	8	19	35	62	22

Season 1901-02

Football League Division One

DATE	OPPONENTS	SCORE	GOALSCORERS	ATTENDANCE
Sep 7	Bury	D 0-0		14,000
Sep 9	NOTTS COUNTY	W 2-0	Bache, Garraty	15,000
Sep 14	BLACKBURN ROVERS	D 1-1	Bache	22,000
Sep 16	SHEFFIELD UNITED	L 1-2	Wilkes	12,000
Sep 21	Stoke City	L 0-1		5,000
Sep 28	EVERTON	D 1-1	Bache	20,000
Oct 5	Sunderland	L 0-1		12,000
Oct 12	Small Heath	W 2-0	Devey, Bache	23,000
Oct 19	Derby County	L 0-1		15,000
Oct 26	SHEFFIELD WEDNESDAY	W 4-1	Templeton, Bache, McLuckie 2	30,000
Nov 2	Notts County	W 3-0	McLuckie 2, Garraty	15,000
Nov 9	BOLTON WANDERERS	W 1-0	McLuckie	22,000
Nov 23	WOLVERHAMPTON WANDERERS	W 2-1	McLuckie 2	20,000
Nov 30	Liverpool	L 0-1		16,000
Dec 7	NEWCASTLE UNITED	D 0-0		25,000
Dec 14	GRIMSBY TOWN	W 4-1	McLuckie 3, Devey	10,000
Dec 25	Everton	W 3-2	Garraty, Wood, Clarke	18,000
Dec 26	SMALL HEATH	W 1-0	McLuckie	40,000
Dec 28	NOTTINGHAM FOREST	W 3-0	Clarke, Garraty, McLuckie	14,000
Jan 1	Sheffield United	L 0-6		26,000
Jan 4	BURY	W 2-0	McLuckie, Clarke	10,000
Jan 11	Blackburn Rovers	L 0-4		18,000
Jan 18	STOKE CITY	D 0-0		20,000
Feb 1	SUNDERLAND	L 0-1		23,000
Feb 15	DERBY COUNTY	W 3-2	Perry, Bache, Wood	15,000
Feb 17	Manchester City	L 0-1		15,000
Feb 22	Sheffield Wednesday	L 0-1		14,000
Mar 8	Bolton Wanderers	D 2-2	Johnson, McLuckie	10,000
Mar 22	Wolverhampton Wanderers	W 2-0	McLuckie, Bache	18,000
Mar 29	LIVERPOOL	L 0-1		20,000
Mar 31	MANCHESTER CITY	D 2-2	McLuckie, Johnson	16,000
Apr 1	Nottingham Forest	D 1-1	Niblo	12,000
Apr 5	Newcastle United	L 1-2	Niblo	14,000
Apr 12	Grimsby Town	L 1-4	Bache	8,000

FA Cup

DATE	OPPONENTS		SCORE	GOALSCORERS	ATTENDANCE
Jan 25	Stoke City	(Rd 1)	D 2-2	Garraty 2	20,000
Jan 29	STOKE CITY	(R)	L 1-2*	Garraty	22,000

*After extra-time.

League & Cup Appearances

PLAYER	LEAGUE	CUP COMPETITION FA CUP	TOTAL
Bache	34	2	36
Banks	5		5
Brawn	1		1
Clarke	15	1	16
Cooch	1		1
Cowan Jas	1		1
Crabtree	29	2	31
Devey	3	1	4
Evans	4		4
Garraty	26	2	28
George	25	2	27
Harris	3		3
Johnson	8		8
Lloyd	3		3
McLuckie	21	2	23
Marriott	8		8
Millar	9		9
Murray	1		1
Niblo	12		12
Noon	10		10
Pearson	5		5
Perry	23	2	25
Shutt	24	2	26
Smith G	5		5
Templeton	24	2	26
Whitley	8		8
Wilkes	29	2	31
Wood	33	2	35
Wilson	4		4

Goalscorers

PLAYER	LEAGUE	CUP COMPETITION FA CUP	TOTAL
McLuckie	16		16
Bache	8		8
Garraty	4	3	7
Clarke	3		3
Devey	2		2
Johnson	2		2
Niblo	2		2
Wood	2		2
Perry	1		1
Templeton	1		1
Wilkes	1		1

Fact File

Villa used 29 players in league and FA Cup football this season – a club record at the time.

MANAGER: Committee

CAPTAIN: Jimmy Crabtree, Joe Bache

TOP SCORER: Jasper McLuckie, 16 (all league)

BIGGEST WIN: 4-1 v Sheffield Wednesday (H), Division One, 26 October 1901; 4-1 v Grimsby Town (H), Division One, 14 December 1901

HIGHEST ATTENDANCE: 40,000 v Small Heath (H), Division One, 26 December 1901

MAJOR TRANSFERS IN: Billy Brawn from Sheffield United, J. McLuckie from Bury, T. Perry from West Brom, A. Wood from Stoke City, T. Niblo from Newcastle United

MAJOR TRANSFERS OUT: J. Devey – retired (to become a director), C. Athersmith to Birmingham, Jas Cowan – retired

Final Division One Table

		P	W	D	L	F	A	Pts
1	SUNDERLAND	34	19	6	9	50	35	44
2	EVERTON	34	17	7	10	53	35	41
3	NEWCASTLE U	34	14	9	11	48	34	37
4	BLACKBURN R	34	15	6	13	52	48	36
5	NOTTINGHAM F	34	13	9	12	43	43	35
6	DERBY CO	34	13	9	12	39	41	35
7	BURY	34	13	8	13	44	38	34
8	ASTON VILLA	34	13	8	13	42	40	34
9	SHEFFIELD W	34	13	8	13	48	52	34
10	SHEFFIELD U	34	13	7	14	53	48	33
11	LIVERPOOL	34	10	12	12	42	38	32
12	BOLTON W	34	12	8	14	51	56	32
13	NOTTS CO	34	14	4	16	51	57	32
14	WOLVERHAMPTON W	34	13	6	15	46	57	32
15	GRIMSBY T	34	13	6	15	44	60	32
16	STOKE	34	11	9	14	45	55	31
17	SMALL HEATH	34	11	8	15	47	45	30
18	MANCHESTER C	34	11	6	17	42	58	28

Season 1902-03

Football League Division One

DATE	OPPONENTS	SCORE	GOALSCORERS	ATTENDANCE
Sep 6	DERBY COUNTY	D 0-0		3,000
Sep 12	Nottingham Forest	L 0-2		7,000
Sep 20	BURY	D 2-2	Bache, Johnson	20,000
Sep 27	Blackburn Rovers	W 2-0	Bache, Johnson	10,000
Oct 4	SUNDERLAND	L 0-1		15,000
Oct 11	Stoke City	L 0-1		10,000
Oct 18	EVERTON	W 2-1	Noon, Garraty	21,000
Nov 1	WEST BROMWICH ALBION	L 0-3		35,128
Nov 8	Notts County	L 1-2	Garraty	7,000
Nov 15	BOLTON WANDERERS	W 4-2	Garraty 2, Bache, Wilkes	16,000
Nov 22	Middlesbrough	W 2-1	Clarke, Hogg o.g.	10,000
Nov 29	NEWCASTLE UNITED	W 7-0	Agnew o.g. Templeton, Leake, Bache 2, Johnson 2	10,000
Dec 6	Wolverhampton Wanderers	L 1-2	Bache	7,000
Dec 13	LIVERPOOL	L 1-2	Bache	19,500
Dec 20	Sheffield United	W 4-2	McLuckie 2, Garraty 2	15,000
Dec 26	SHEFFIELD WEDNESDAY	W 1-0	Garraty (pen)	40,000
Dec 27	GRIMSBY TOWN	D 2-2	Garraty 2	30,000
Jan 1	Sheffield Wednesday	L 0-4		28,000
Jan 3	Derby County	L 0-2		12,000
Jan 10	NOTTINGHAM FOREST	W 3-1	Garraty 2, McLuckie	25,000
Jan 17	Bury	W 1-0	McLuckie	12,000
Jan 24	BLACKBURN ROVERS	W 5-0	McLuckie 2, Garraty, Niblo, Brawn	17,000
Jan 31	Sunderland	L 0-1		25,000
Feb 14	Everton	W 1-0	Bache	20,000
Feb 28	West Bromwich Albion	W 2-1	McLuckie, Wood	28,536
Mar 14	Bolton Wanderers	W 1-0	Johnson	14,000
Mar 28	Newcastle United	L 0-2		20,000
Apr 4	WOLVERHAMPTON WANDERERS	W 3-1	McLuckie, Johnson, Garraty	18,000
Apr 11	Liverpool	L 1-2	Garraty (pen)	15,000
Apr 13	STOKE CITY	W 2-0	Clarke, Leake	10,000
Apr 15	NOTTS COUNTY	W 2-1	Brawn (pen) McLuckie	20,000
Apr 18	SHEFFIELD UNITED	W 4-2	Garraty, McLuckie 3	25,000
Apr 25	Grimsby Town	W 2-0	McLuckie 2	8,000
Apr 27	MIDDLESBROUGH	W 5-0	Wood, Leake, Johnson Clarke, McLuckie	20,000

FA Cup

DATE	OPPONENTS		SCORE	GOALSCORERS	ATTENDANCE
Feb 7	SUNDERLAND	(Rd 1)	W 4-1	Bache, Johnson 2, Pearson	47,000
Feb 21	BARNSLEY	(Rd 2)	W 4-1	McLuckie 3, Johnson	28,000
Mar 7	Tottenham Hotspur	(Rd 3)	W 3-2	Johnson, McLuckie 2	30,000
Mar 21	Bury*	(SF)	L 0-3		45,000

*Played at Goodison Park, Liverpool.

League & Cup Appearances

PLAYER	LEAGUE	CUP COMPETITION FA CUP	TOTAL
Brawn	16	4	20
Bache	25	3	28
Clarke	20		20
Cooch	5		5
Evans A	18		18
Evans O	2		2
Fisher	1		1
George	29	4	33
Griffin	1		1
Garraty	28	2	30
Harris	4		4
Johnson	20	4	24
Leake	28	4	32
Lockett	1		1
McLuckie	21	3	24
Noon	16	4	20
Niblo	17	4	21
Perry	4		4
Pearson	13	4	17
Shutt	15		15
Spencer	27	4	31
Templeton	11		11
Wilkes	21		21
Wood	31	4	35

Goalscorers

PLAYER	LEAGUE	CUP COMPETITION FA CUP	TOTAL
McLuckie	15	5	20
Garraty	15		15
Johnson	7	4	11
Bache	8	1	9
Clarke	3		3
Leake	3		3
Brawn	2		2
Wood	2		2
Niblo	1		1
Noon	1		1
Pearson		1	1
Templeton	1		1
Wilkes	1		1
Opps' o.gs.	2		2

Fact File

Despite winning their last five league matches, Villa were pipped for the championship by Sheffield Wednesday by a single point.

MANAGER: Committee

CAPTAIN: Howard Spencer, Albert Evans

TOP SCORER: Jasper McLuckie, 20 (15 league)

BIGGEST WIN: 7-0 v Newcastle Utd (H), Division One, 29 November 1929

HIGHEST ATTENDANCE: 47,000 v Sunderland (H) FA Cup First Round, 7 February 1903

MAJOR TRANSFERS IN: Albert Leake from Small Heath

MAJOR TRANSFERS OUT: R. Templeton to Newcastle United

Final Division One Table

		P	W	D	L	F	A	Pts
1	SHEFFIELD W	34	19	4	11	54	36	42
2	ASTON VILLA	34	19	3	12	61	40	41
3	SUNDERLAND	34	16	9	9	51	36	41
4	SHEFFIELD U	34	17	5	12	58	44	39
5	LIVERPOOL	34	17	4	13	68	49	38
6	STOKE	34	15	7	12	46	38	37
7	WBA	34	16	4	14	54	53	36
8	BURY	34	16	3	15	54	43	35
9	DERBY CO	34	16	3	15	50	47	35
10	NOTTINGHAM F	34	14	7	13	49	47	35
11	WOLVERHAMPTON W	34	14	5	15	48	57	33
12	EVERTON	34	13	6	15	45	47	32
13	MIDDLESBROUGH	34	14	4	16	41	50	32
14	NEWCASTLE U	34	14	4	16	41	51	32
15	NOTTS CO	34	12	7	15	41	49	31
16	BLACKBURN R	34	12	5	17	44	63	29
17	GRIMSBY T	34	8	9	17	43	62	25
18	BOLTON W	34	8	3	23	37	73	19

Season 1903-04

Football League Division One

DATE	OPPONENTS	SCORE	GOALSCORERS	ATTENDANCE
Sep 2	Newcastle United	D 1-1	Bache	8,000
Sep 5	Sunderland	L 1-6	McLuckie	21,000
Sep 12	WEST BROMWICH ALBION	W 3-1	Garraty, McLuckie 2	38,920
Sep 19	Small Heath	D 2-2	Pearson (pen), Garrraty	25,000
Sep 26	EVERTON	W 3-1	Johnson, McLuckie, Wilkes	35,000
Oct 3	Stoke City	L 0-2		10,000
Oct 10	DERBY COUNTY	W 3-0	Niblo, Bache, McLuckie	21,000
Oct 17	Manchester City	L 0-1		30,000
Oct 24	NOTTS COUNTY	W 4-0	Garraty, Lockett, Johnson, McLuckie	18,000
Oct 31	Sheffield United	W 2-1	Johnson, Bache	23,000
Nov 7	NEWCASTLE UNITED	W 3-1	Bache 3	20,000
Nov 14	WOLVERHAMPTON WANDERERS	W 2-0	Garraty 2 (1 pen)	10,000
Nov 21	Middlesbrough	L 1-2	Garraty (pen)	18,000
Nov 28	LIVERPOOL	W 2-1	Johnson, Brawn	15,000
Dec 5	Bury	D 2-2	Bache 2	9,000
Dec 12	BLACKBURN ROVERS	L 2-3	Bache, McLuckie	18,000
Dec 19	Nottingham Forest	W 7-3	Niblo 3, Hall, Bache 3	8,000
Dec 26	SHEFFIELD WEDNESDAY	W 2-1	Niblo, Brawn	49,500
Dec 28	Derby County	D 2-2	Hall 2	22,000
Jan 2	SUNDERLAND	W 2-0	Niblo, Lockett	28,000
Jan 9	West Bromwich Albion	W 3-1	Bache, Wood, Brawn (pen)	31,418
Jan 16	SMALL HEATH	D 1-1	Brawn	20,000
Jan 23	Everton	L 0-1		25,000
Jan 30	STOKE CITY	W 3-1	Harris, Watkins, Meredith o.g.	15,000
Feb 13	MANCHESTER CITY	L 0-1		20,000
Feb 27	SHEFFIELD UNITED	W 6-1	McLuckie 2, Hall, Wood, Brawn 2	7,000
Mar 12	Wolverhampton Wanderers	L 2-3	Hall 2	12,000
Mar 19	MIDDLESBROUGH	W 2-1	Bache 2	10,000
Mar 26	Liverpool	D 1-1	Leake	15,000
Apr 1	Notts County	D 0-0		15,000
Apr 2	BURY	L 0-2		7,000
Apr 9	Blackburn Rovers	W 3-0	Pearson, Garraty, Matthews	5,000
Apr 16	NOTTINGHAM FOREST	W 3-1	Garraty, Brawn, Matthews	4,500
Apr 23	Sheffield Wednesday	L 2-4	Matthews, Garraty	3,000

FA Cup

Feb 6	Stoke City	(Rd 1)	W 3-2	Brawn (pen) Leake, Bache	10,000
Feb 24	TOTTENHAM HOTSPUR	(Rd 2)	L 0-1		20,000

League & Cup Appearances

PLAYER	LEAGUE	CUP COMPETITION FA CUP	TOTAL
Bache	27	2	29
Brawn	32	2	34
Clarke	2		2
Cooch	9		9
Evans	14	1	15
Garraty	16	2	18
George	25	2	27
Hall	9	2	11
Harris	2		2
Johnson	13		13
Leake	28	2	30
Lockett	27		27
Matthews	8		8
Miles	16	1	17
McLuckie	15		15
Niblo	16	2	18
Noon	12		12
Pearson	26		26
Shutt	1		1
Spencer	23	2	25
Watkins	5		5
Wilkes	18	2	20
Windmill	1		1
Wood	29	2	31

Goalscorers

PLAYER	LEAGUE	CUP COMPETITION FA CUP	TOTAL
Bache	15	1	16
Garraty	9		9
McLuckie	9		9
Brawn	7	1	8
Hall	6		6
Niblo	6		6
Johnson	4		4
Matthews	3		3
Lockett	2		2
Pearson	2		2
Wood	2		2
Leake	1	1	2
Harris	1		1
Watkins	1		1
Wilkes	1		1
Opps' o.gs.	1		1

Fact File

In January 1904, Villa paid a club record fee of £400 for Martin Watkins from Stoke City.

MANAGER: Committee

CAPTAIN: Howard Spencer

TOP SCORER: Joe Bache, 16 (15 league)

BIGGEST WIN: 7-3 v Nottingham Forest (A), Division One, 19 December 1903

HIGHEST ATTENDANCE: 49,500 v Sheffield Wednesday (H), Division One, 26 December 1903

MAJOR TRANSFERS IN: Martin Watkins from Stoke City, Albert Hall from Stourbridge

MAJOR TRANSFERS OUT: Jimmy Crabtree to Plymouth Argyle

Final Division One Table

		P	W	D	L	F	A	Pts
1	SHEFFIELD W	34	20	7	7	48	28	47
2	MANCHESTER C	34	19	6	9	71	45	44
3	EVERTON	34	19	5	10	59	32	43
4	NEWCASTLE U	34	18	6	10	58	45	42
5	ASTON VILLA	34	17	7	10	70	48	41
6	SUNDERLAND	34	17	5	12	63	49	39
7	SHEFFIELD U	34	15	8	11	62	57	38
8	WOLVERHAMPTON W	34	14	8	12	44	66	36
9	NOTTINGHAM F	34	11	9	14	57	57	31
10	MIDDLESBROUGH	34	9	12	13	46	47	30
11	SMALL HEATH	34	11	8	15	39	52	30
12	BURY	34	7	15	12	40	53	29
13	NOTTS CO	34	12	5	17	37	61	29
14	DERBY CO	34	9	10	15	58	60	28
15	BLACKBURN R	34	11	6	17	48	60	28
16	STOKE	34	10	7	17	54	57	27
17	LIVERPOOL	34	9	8	17	49	62	26
18	WBA	34	7	10	17	36	60	24

Season 1904-05

Football League Division One

DATE	OPPONENTS	SCORE	GOALSCORERS	ATTENDANCE
Sep 1	PRESTON NORTH END	L 1-2	Brawn (pen)	15,000
Sep 3	STOKE CITY	W 3-0	Hall, Bache 2	25,000
Sep 10	Blackburn Rovers	L 0-4		12,000
Sep 12	EVERTON	W 1-0	Brawn	5,000
Sep 17	NOTTINGHAM FOREST	W 2-0	Matthews 2	12,000
Sep 24	Sheffield Wednesday	L 2-3	Bache, Matthews	20,000
Oct 1	SUNDERLAND	D 2-2	Bache, Wood	28,000
Oct 8	Woolwich Arsenal	L 0-1		7,500
Oct 15	DERBY COUNTY	L 0-2		22,000
Oct 22	Everton	L 2-3	Johnson, Garraty	25,000
Oct 29	SMALL HEATH	W 2-1	Brawn (pen), Garraty	40,000
Nov 19	Manchester City	L 1-2	Lockett	15,000
Nov 12	NOTTS COUNTY	W 4-2	Lockett, Brawn, Hampton Cantrell	15,000
Nov 19	Sheffield United	W 3-0	Bache, Hampton, Brawn (pen)	20,000
Nov 26	NEWCASTLE UNITED	L 0-1		14,000
Dec 3	Preston North End	W 3-2	Bache, Garraty, Hampton	12,000
Dec 10	MIDDLESBROUGH	D 0-0		8,000
Dec 17	Wolverhampton Wanderers	D 1-1	Hampton	12,000
Dec 24	BURY	W 2-0	Hampton 2	10,000
Dec 26	WOOLWICH ARSENAL	W 3-1	Leake, Hampton, Bache	17,000
Dec 31	Stoke City	W 4-1	Hampton 2, Bache, Garraty	10,000
Jan 7	BLACKBURN ROVERS	W 3-0	Leake, Matthews, Bache	8,000
Jan 14	Nottingham Forest	D 1-1	Garraty (pen)	12,000
Jan 21	SHEFFIELD WEDNESDAY	L 0-2		14,000
Jan 28	Sunderland	W 3-2	Brawn, Hall, Bache	27,000
Feb 11	Derby County	W 2-0	Bache, Leake	7,000
Feb 25	Small Heath	W 3-0	Pearson, Hampton, Windmill	35,000
Mar 11	Notts County	W 2-1	Garraty, Pearson	10,000
Mar 18	SHEFFIELD UNITED	W 3-0	Hall, Hampton, Bache	18,000
Apr 5	Newcastle United	L 0-2		25,000
Apr 8	Middlesbrough	L 1-3	Hall	10,000
Apr 22	Bury	W 3-2	Hampton 2, Brawn	7,000
Apr 26	WOLVERHAMPTON WANDERERS	W 3-0	Garraty, Hampton, Lockett	15,000
Apr 29	MANCHESTER CITY	W 3-2	Garraty, Hampton, Hall	10,000

FA Cup

Feb 4	LEICESTER FOSSE	(Rd 1) W 5-1	Bache 2, Hampton, Leake Hall	25,000
Feb 18	BURY	(Rd 2) W 3-2	Bache, Garraty, Hampton	32,000
Mar 4	FULHAM	(Rd 3) W 5-0	Pearson, Hampton 2, Bache, Hall	42,000
Mar 25	Everton*	(SF) D 1-1	Hall	35,000
Mar 29	Everton#	(R) W 2-1	Hampton, Garraty	25,000
Apr 15	Newcastle United†	(F) W 2-0	Hampton 2	101,117

*Played at Victoria Ground, Stoke. #Played at Nottingham.
†Played at Crystal Palace, London.

League & Cup Appearances

PLAYER	LEAGUE	CUP COMPETITION FA CUP	TOTAL
Bache	31	6	37
Brawn	30	6	36
Brown	12		12
Cooch	1		1
Cantrell	3		3
Clarke	5		5
Corbett	1		1
Evans	4	1	5
George	33	6	39
Garraty	31	6	37
Gray	7		7
Hall	22	6	28
Hampton	22	6	28
Johnson	3		3
Leake	30	6	36
Lockett	13		13
Matthews	7		7
Miles	29	6	35
Noon	5		5
Pearson	25	6	31
Spencer	19	5	24
Watkins	1		1
Wilkes	9	1	10
Windmill	25	5	30
Wood	6		6

Goalscorers

PLAYER	LEAGUE	CUP COMPETITION FA CUP	TOTAL
Hampton	15	7	22
Bache	12	4	16
Garraty	8	2	10
Hall	5	3	8
Brawn	7		7
Leake	3	1	4
Matthews	4		4
Lockett	3		3
Pearson	2		2
Cantrell	1		1
Johnson	1		1
Windmill	1		1
Wood	1		1

Fact File

The biggest crowd ever (101,117) to watch Villa (up to that time) attended the FA Cup final at Crystal Palace on 15 April 1905.

MANAGER: Committee

CAPTAIN: Howard Spencer, Joe Bache

TOP SCORER: Harry Hampton, 22 (15 league)

BIGGEST WIN: 5-0 v Fulham (H), FA Cup Third Round, 4 March 1905

HIGHEST ATTENDANCE: 101,117 v Newcastle United, FA Cup final at Crystal Palace, 15 April 1905

MAJOR TRANSFERS IN: Harry Hampton from Wellington

MAJOR TRANSFERS OUT: Jasper McLuckie to Plymouth Argyle, Tom Niblo to Nottingham Forest

Final Division One Table

		P	W	D	L	F	A	Pts
1	NEWCASTLE U	34	23	2	9	72	33	48
2	EVERTON	34	21	5	8	63	36	47
3	MANCHESTER C	34	20	6	8	66	37	46
4	ASTON VILLA	34	19	4	11	63	43	42
5	SUNDERLAND	34	16	8	10	60	44	40
6	SHEFFIELD U	34	19	2	13	64	56	40
7	SMALL HEATH	34	17	5	12	54	38	39
8	PRESTON NE	34	13	10	11	42	37	36
9	SHEFFIELD W	34	14	5	15	61	57	33
10	WOOLWICH ARSENAL	34	12	9	13	36	40	33
11	DERBY CO	34	12	8	14	37	48	32
12	STOKE	34	13	4	17	40	58	30
13	BLACKBURN R	34	11	5	18	40	51	27
14	WOLVERHAMPTON W	34	11	4	19	47	73	26
15	MIDDLESBROUGH	34	9	8	17	36	56	26
16	NOTTINGHAM F	34	9	7	18	40	61	25
17	BURY	34	10	4	20	47	67	24
18	NOTTS CO	34	5	8	21	36	69	18

Season 1905-06

Football League Division One

DATE	OPPONENTS	SCORE	GOALSCORERS	ATTENDANCE
Sep 2	Blackburn Rovers	D 1-1	Hampton	10,000
Sep 9	SUNDERLAND	W 2-1	Garraty 2	26,000
Sep 11	LIVERPOOL	W 5-0	Hampton 3, West o.g., Brawn	15,000
Sep 16	Birmingham	L 0-2		30,000
Sep 23	EVERTON	W 4-0	Bache, Garraty, Hall, Hampton	20,000
Sep 30	Derby County	L 0-1		8,000
Oct 7	SHEFFIELD WEDNESDAY	W 3-0	Brawn 2, Bache	24,000
Oct 14	Nottingham Forest	D 2-2	Millington, Garraty (pen)	12,000
Oct 21	MANCHESTER CITY	W 2-1	Bache, Garraty (pen)	22,000
Oct 28	Bury	W 1-0	Bache	7,000
Nov 4	MIDDLESBROUGH	W 4-1	Hampton, Allen, Bache, Garraty (pen)	21,000
Nov 11	Preston North End	L 0-2		16,000
Nov 13	Stoke City	W 1-0	Garraty	15,000
Nov 18	NEWCASTLE UNITED	L 0-3		23,000
Nov 25	WOLVERHAMPTON WANDERERS	W 6-0	Cantrell 3, Garraty 2, Hampton	20,000
Dec 2	Liverpool	L 0-3		20,000
Dec 9	SHEFFIELD UNITED	W 4-1	Hall, Garraty 2, Hampton	15,000
Dec 16	Notts County	L 1-2	Hampton	14,000
Dec 23	STOKE CITY	W 3-0	Hampton 2, Garraty	20,000
Dec 26	BOLTON WANDERERS	D 1-1	Bache	22,000
Dec 27	WOOLWICH ARSENAL	W 2-1	Garraty, Hampton	14,000
Dec 30	BLACKBURN ROVERS	L 0-1		8,000
Jan 2	Bolton Wanderers	L 1-4	Hampton	30,000
Jan 20	BIRMINGHAM	L 1-3	Bache	40,000
Jan 27	Everton	L 2-4	Hampton, Matthews	22,000
Feb 10	Sheffield Wednesday	D 2-2	Matthews, Hampton	25,000
Feb 17	NOTTINGHAM FOREST	W 3-1	Garraty, Hall, Bache	25,000
Feb 28	Sunderland	L 0-2		20,000
Mar 3	BURY	D 3-3	Hampton 2, Hall	10,000
Mar 10	Middlesbrough	W 2-1	Boden, Garraty	14,000
Mar 14	Manchester City	W 4-1	Hampton 2, Bache, Garraty	20,000
Mar 17	PRESTON NORTH END	L 0-1		20,000
Mar 24	Newcastle United	L 1-3	Matthews	18,000
Mar 31	Wolverhampton Wanderers	L 1-4	Bache	20,000
Apr 13	Woolwich Arsenal	L 1-2	Millington	30,000
Apr 14	Sheffield United	D 1-1	Bache	12,000
Apr 16	DERBY COUNTY	W 6-0	Millington, Garraty, Walters, Matthews, Bache, Boden	9,000
Apr 21	NOTTS COUNTY	W 2-1	Bache, Walters	4,000

FA Cup

Jan 13	KING'S LYNN	(Rd 1) W 11-1	Hall 3, Wilkes, Millington 4, Garraty 2, Pearson	23,000
Feb 3	PLYMOUTH ARGYLE	(Rd 2) D 0-0		30,823
Feb 7	Plymouth Argyle	(R) W 5-1	Garratt, Garraty 2, Bache, Hampton	22,843
Feb 24	Manchester United	(Rd 3) L 1-5	Hall	35,500

League & Cup Appearances

PLAYER	LEAGUE	CUP COMPETITION FA CUP	TOTAL
Allen	3		3
Bache	31	3	34
Boden	9	1	10
Brawn	15		15
Brown	1		1
Cantrell	8		8
Codling	3		3
Cooch	6		6
Corbett	4		4
Elston	1		1
Evans	14	1	15
Garratt	13	4	17
Garraty	33	4	37
George	32	4	36
Greenhalgh	12		12
Hadlee	11		11
Hall	30	4	34
Hampton	32	3	35
Harris	7	1	8
Hisbert	2		2
Kingaby	4		4
Leake	26		26
Logan J	7	4	11
Matthews	7		7
Miles	7		7
Millington	6	1	7
Noon	4	1	5
Pearson	26	4	30
Riley	4		4
Spencer	33	4	37
Walters	7	1	8
Wilkes	7	1	8
Windmill	13	3	16

Goalscorers

PLAYER	LEAGUE	CUP COMPETITION FA CUP	TOTAL
Garraty	17	4	21
Hampton	19	1	20
Bache	13	1	14
Hall	4	4	8
Millington	3	4	7
Matthews	4		4
Brawn	3		3
Cantrell	3		3
Boden	2		2
Walters	2		2
Allen	1		1
Garratt		1	1
Pearson		1	1
Wilkes		1	1
Opps' o.gs.	1		1

Fact File

As holders of the FA Cup, Villa were sensationally beaten 5-1 by Division Two side Manchester United at Old Trafford.

MANAGER: Committee

CAPTAIN: Howard Spencer

TOP SCORER: Bill Garraty, 21 (17 league)

BIGGEST WIN: 11-1 v Kings Lynn (H), FA Cup First Round, 13 January 1906

HIGHEST ATTENDANCE: 40,000 v Birmingham (H), Division One, 20 January 1906

MAJOR TRANSFERS IN: J. Walters from Stourbridge

MAJOR TRANSFERS OUT: Harry Hadley to Nottingham Forest, Billy Brawn to Middlesbrough

Final Division One Table

		P	W	D	L	F	A	Pts
1	LIVERPOOL	38	23	5	10	79	46	51
2	PRESTON NE	38	17	13	8	54	39	47
3	SHEFFIELD W	38	18	8	12	63	52	44
4	NEWCASTLE U	38	18	7	13	74	48	43
5	MANCHESTER C	38	19	5	14	73	54	43
6	BOLTON W	38	17	7	14	81	67	41
7	BIRMINGHAM	38	17	7	14	65	59	41
8	ASTON VILLA	38	17	6	15	72	56	40
9	BLACKBURN R	38	16	8	14	54	52	40
10	STOKE	38	16	7	15	54	55	39
11	EVERTON	38	15	7	16	70	66	37
12	WOOLWICH ARSENAL	38	15	7	16	62	64	37
13	SHEFFIELD U	38	15	6	17	57	62	36
14	SUNDERLAND	38	15	5	18	61	70	35
15	DERBY CO	38	14	7	17	39	58	35
16	NOTTS CO	38	11	12	15	55	71	34
17	BURY	38	11	10	17	57	74	32
18	MIDDLESBROUGH	38	10	11	17	56	71	31
19	NOTTINGHAM F	38	13	5	20	58	79	31
20	WOLVERHAMPTON W	38	8	7	23	58	99	23

Season 1906-07

Football League Division One

DATE	OPPONENTS	SCORE	GOALSCORERS	ATTENDANCE
Sep 1	BLACKBURN ROVERS	W 4-2	Hampton, Bache, Walters, Cantrell	40,000
Sep 3	Stoke City	W 2-0	Hampton 2 (1 pen)	12,000
Sep 8	Sunderland	L 1-2	Bache	20,000
Sep 10	STOKE CITY	W 1-0	Hall	14,000
Sep 15	BIRMINGHAM	W 4-1	Hall, Greenhalgh, Hampton (pen)	45,000
Sep 22	Everton	W 2-1	Hampton, Garraty	40,000
Sep 29	WOOLWICH ARSENAL	D 2-2	Hampton, Bache	40,000
Oct 6	Sheffield Wednesday	L 1-2	Hampton	22,000
Oct 13	BURY	W 3-1	Millington, Matthews, Walters	20,000
Oct 20	Manchester City	L 2-4	Bache, Hall	25,000
Oct 27	MIDDLESBROUGH	L 2-3	Hampton 2	20,000
Nov 3	Preston North End	L 0-2		11,000
Nov 10	NEWCASTLE UNITED	D 0-0		30,000
Nov 17	Derby County	W 1-0	Garraty	7,000
Nov 24	Liverpool	L 2-5	Walters, Hall	30,000
Dec 1	BRISTOL CITY	W 3-2	Bache, Cantrell, Millington	27,000
Dec 8	Notts County	D 1-1	Buckley	10,000
Dec 15	SHEFFIELD UNITED	W 5-1	Cantrell 3, Hall (pen) Millington	20,000
Dec 22	Bolton Wanderers	W 2-1	Millington, Walters	20,000
Dec 24	PRESTON NORTH END	W 3-0	Evans R, Millington	16,000
Dec 26	MANCHESTER UNITED	W 2-0	Cantrell, Chapple	25,000
Dec 29	Blackburn Rovers	L 1-2	Cantrell	10,000
Jan 1	Manchester United	L 0-1		40,000
Jan 5	SUNDERLAND	D 2-2	Bache, Evans	25,000
Jan 19	Birmingham	L 2-3	Chapple, Walters	49,900
Jan 26	EVERTON	W 2-1	Cantrell, Hampton	32,000
Feb 9	SHEFFIELD WEDNESDAY	W 8-1	Hampton 3, Bache 2, Cantrell 2, Millington	25,000
Feb 16	Bury	W 3-0	Hampton 2, Cantrell	16,000
Feb 23	MANCHESTER CITY	W 4-1	Hampton 2, Hall 2	18,000
Mar 2	Middlesbrough	L 0-1		20,000
Mar 16	Newcastle United	L 2-3	Hall (pen), Cantrell	50,000
Mar 23	DERBY COUNTY	W 2-0	Millington, Logan A	16,000
Mar 30	LIVERPOOL	W 4-0	Hampton, Chapple, Hall 2	28,000
Apr 1	Woolwich Arsenal	L 1-3	Hall	12,000
Apr 6	Bristol City	W 4-2	Hampton 3, Hall	18,000
Apr 13	NOTTS COUNTY	D 0-0		18,000
Apr 20	Sheffield United	D 0-0		12,000
Apr 27	BOLTON WANDERERS	L 0-2		10,000

FA Cup

DATE	OPPONENTS		SCORE	GOALSCORERS	ATTENDANCE
Jan 12	Burnley	(Rd 1)	W 3-1	Cantrell, Bache 2	16,242
Feb 2	Bolton Wanderers	(Rd 2)	L 0-2		40,367

League & Cup Appearances

PLAYER	LEAGUE	CUP COMPETITION FA CUP	TOTAL
Bache	29	2	31
Boden	8		8
Buckley	20	2	22
Cantrell	23	2	25
Chappel	8		8
Corbett	8		8
Codling	34	2	36
Cooch	2		2
Evans R	9	1	10
Garraty	5		5
George	36	2	38
Greenhalgh	30	2	32
Hall	26	1	27
Hampton	29	1	30
Harris	1		1
Leake	11	1	12
Logan A	3		3
Logan J	28	2	30
Matthews	4		4
Miles	30	1	31
Millington	28	2	30
Pearson	3		3
Riley	5		5
Spencer	9		9
Tainton	1		1
Walters	26	1	27
Wilkes	1		1
Windmill	1		1

Goalscorers

PLAYER	LEAGUE	CUP COMPETITION FA CUP	TOTAL
Hampton	21		21
Cantrell	12	1	13
Hall	12		12
Bache	8	2	10
Millington	7		7
Walters	6		6
Chapple	3		3
Evans R	3		3
Garraty	2		2
Buckley	1		1
Greenhalgh	1		1
Logan A	1		1
Matthews	1		1

Fact File

The average league attendance at Villa Park this season was 24,631 – a club record by over 4,000.

MANAGER: Committee

CAPTAIN: Joe Bache, Alf Miles

TOP SCORER: Harry Hampton, 21 (all league)

BIGGEST WIN: 8-1 v Sheffield Wednesday (H), Division One, 9 February 1907

HIGHEST ATTENDANCE: 50,000 v Newcastle United (A), Division One, 16 March 1907

MAJOR TRANSFERS IN: Chris Buckley from Brighton and Hove Albion

MAJOR TRANSFERS OUT: Michael Noon to Plymouth Argyle

Final Division One Table

		P	W	D	L	F	A	Pts
1	NEWCASTLE U	38	22	7	9	74	46	51
2	BRISTOL C	38	20	8	10	66	47	48
3	EVERTON	38	20	5	13	70	46	45
4	SHEFFIELD U	38	17	11	10	57	55	45
5	ASTON VILLA	38	19	6	13	78	52	44
6	BOLTON W	38	18	8	12	59	47	44
7	WOOLWICH ARSENAL	38	20	4	14	66	59	44
8	MANCHESTER U	38	17	8	13	53	56	42
9	BIRMINGHAM	38	15	8	15	52	52	38
10	SUNDERLAND	38	14	9	15	65	66	37
11	MIDDLESBROUGH	38	15	6	17	56	63	36
12	BLACKBURN R	38	14	7	17	56	59	35
13	SHEFFIELD W	38	12	11	15	49	60	35
14	PRESTON NE	38	14	7	17	44	57	35
15	LIVERPOOL	38	13	7	18	64	65	33
16	BURY	38	13	6	19	58	68	32
17	MANCHESTER C	38	10	12	16	53	77	32
18	NOTTS CO	38	8	15	15	46	50	31
19	DERBY CO	38	9	9	20	41	59	27
20	STOKE	38	8	10	20	41	64	26

Season 1907-08

Football League Division One

DATE	OPPONENTS	SCORE	GOALSCORERS	ATTENDANCE
Sep 2	MANCHESTER UNITED	L 1-4	Hampton (pen)	15,000
Sep 7	Blackburn Rovers	L 0-2		22,000
Sep 9	SUNDERLAND	W 1-0	Greenhalgh	18,000
Sep 14	BOLTON WANDERERS	W 2-0	Hampton 2	25,000
Sep 21	Birmingham	W 3-2	Cantrell, Evans, Hall	45,000
Sep 28	EVERTON	L 0-2		35,000
Oct 5	Sunderland	L 0-3		25,000
Oct 12	WOOLWICH ARSENAL	L 0-1		25,000
Oct 19	Sheffield Wednesday	W 3-2	Hampton 2, Hall (pen)	18,000
Oct 26	BRISTOL CITY	D 4-4	Bache 2, Hampton 2	22,000
Nov 2	Notts County	W 3-0	Logan A 2, Bache	12,000
Nov 9	MANCHESTER CITY	D 2-2	Hampton 2 (1 pen)	20,000
Nov 16	Preston North End	L 0-3		11,000
Nov 23	BURY	D 2-2	Hall, Logan A	15,000
Nov 30	NEWCASTLE UNITED	D 3-3	Logan A, Bache, Hall	24,000
Dec 7	Liverpool	L 0-5		30,000
Dec 14	MIDDLESBROUGH	W 6-0	Cantrell 2, Hall 2, Logan A 2	10,000
Dec 21	Sheffield United	D 1-1	Hall	17,000
Dec 25	NOTTINGHAM FOREST	W 4-0	Bache 4	20,000
Dec 26	Nottingham Forest	D 2-2	Cantrell 2	30,000
Dec 28	CHELSEA	D 0-0		25,000
Jan 4	BLACKBURN ROVERS	D 1-1	Bache	15,000
Jan 18	BIRMINGHAM	L 2-3	Logan A, Hall	39,500
Jan 25	Everton	L 0-1		30,000
Feb 8	Woolwich Arsenal	W 1-0	Bache	12,000
Feb 15	SHEFFIELD WEDNESDAY	W 5-0	Bache 3, Cantrell, Hampton	12,000
Mar 2	NOTTS COUNTY	W 5-1	Bache 3, Reeves, Hall (pen)	8,000
Mar 7	Manchester City	L 2-3	Reeves, Hampton	30,000
Mar 11	Bristol City	D 2-2	Hampton 2	7,000
Mar 14	PRESTON NORTH END	W 3-0	Reeves 2, Wallace	20,000
Mar 21	Bury	L 1-2	Bache	12,000
Apr 4	LIVERPOOL	W 5-1	Bache 3, Hampton 2	18,000
Apr 8	Newcastle United	W 5-2	Wallace 2, Bache 2, Hampton	15,000
Apr 11	Middlesbrough	W 1-0	Hampton	15,000
Apr 17	Bolton Wanderers	L 1-3	Bache	20,000
Apr 18	Sheffield United	W 1-0	Hampton	18,000
Apr 20	Manchester United	W 2-1	Hall 2 (1 pen)	10,000
Apr 25	Chelsea	W 3-1	Hall 2, Bache	22,000

FA Cup

Jan 11	STOCKPORT COUNTY	(Rd 1) W 3-0	Wallace, Bache, Logan A	16,000
Feb 1	HULL CITY	(Rd 2) W 3-0	Hampton, Hall 2 (1 pen)	35,000
Feb 22	MANCHESTER UNITED	(Rd 3) L 0-2		45,000

League & Cup Appearances

PLAYER	LEAGUE	CUP COMPETITION FA CUP	TOTAL
Bache	32	3	35
Buckley	1		1
Cantrell	14	1	15
Chapple	1		1
Codling	35	3	38
Cooch	1		1
Evans R	7		7
Garraty	8	2	10
George	30	3	33
Greenhalgh	4		4
Hall	37	3	40
Hampton	28	2	30
Harper	2		2
Harris	3		3
Kimberley	4		4
Kyle	4		4
Leake	4		4
Logan A	15	1	16
Logan J	37	3	40
Lyons	23	3	26
Miles	34	3	37
Millington	1		1
Reeves	12		12
Riley	7		7
Spencer	3		3
Trantor	27	3	30
Turner	7		7
Wallace	27	3	30
Walters	4		4
Wilcox	5		5
Windmill	1		1

Goalscorers

PLAYER	LEAGUE	CUP COMPETITION FA CUP	TOTAL
Bache	24	1	25
Hampton	18	1	19
Hall	13	2	15
Logan A	7	1	8
Cantrell	6		6
Reeves	4		4
Wallace	3	1	4
Evans R	1		1
Greenhalgh	1		1

Fact File

A crowd of 11,000 saw the Football League beat the Scottish League 2-0 at Villa Park.

MANAGER: Committee

CAPTAIN: Joe Bache, Alf Miles

TOP SCORER: Joe Bache, 25 (24 league)

BIGGEST WIN: 6-0 v Middlesbrough (H), Division One, 14 December 1907

HIGHEST ATTENDANCE: 45,000 v Birmingham (A), Division One, 21 September 1907; v Manchester United (H), FA Cup Third Round, 22 February 1908

MAJOR TRANSFERS IN: Tom Lyons from Bridgetown Amateurs, Charlie Wallace from Crystal Palace

MAJOR TRANSFERS OUT: Jimmy Cantrell to Notts County, Howard Spencer (retired)

Final Division One Table

		P	W	D	L	F	A	Pts
1	MANCHESTER U	38	23	6	9	81	48	52
2	ASTON VILLA	38	17	9	12	77	59	43
3	MANCHESTER C	38	16	11	11	62	54	43
4	NEWCASTLE U	38	15	12	11	65	54	42
5	SHEFFIELD W	38	19	4	15	73	64	42
6	MIDDLESBROUGH	38	17	7	14	54	45	41
7	BURY	38	14	11	13	58	61	39
8	LIVERPOOL	38	16	6	16	68	61	38
9	NOTTINGHAM F	38	13	11	14	59	62	37
10	BRISTOL C	38	12	12	14	58	61	36
11	EVERTON	38	15	6	17	58	64	36
12	PRESTON NE	38	12	12	14	47	53	36
13	CHELSEA	38	14	8	16	53	62	36
14	BLACKBURN R=	38	12	12	14	51	63	36
14	WOOLWICH ARSENAL=	38	12	12	14	51	63	36
16	SUNDERLAND	38	16	3	19	78	75	35
17	SHEFFIELD U	38	12	11	15	52	58	35
18	NOTTS CO	38	13	8	17	39	51	34
19	BOLTON W	38	14	5	19	52	58	33
20	BIRMINGHAM	38	9	12	17	40	60	30

The Essential History of Aston Villa

Season 1908-09

Football League Division One

DATE	OPPONENTS	SCORE	GOALSCORERS	ATTENDANCE
Sep 1	Liverpool	L 2-3	Logan J, Logan A	25,000
Sep 5	SHEFFIELD WEDNESDAY	D 1-1	Walters	20,000
Sep 12	Nottingham Forest	W 2-1	Bache, Hampton	17,000
Sep 19	SUNDERLAND	W 2-0	Hampton, Bache	26,000
Sep 26	Chelsea	W 2-0	Bache, Reeves	60,000
Oct 3	BLACKBURN ROVERS	D 1-1	Bache	25,000
Oct 10	Bradford City	D 1-1	Bache	30,000
Oct 17	MANCHESTER UNITED	W 3-1	Reeves 2, Hampton	42,000
Oct 24	Everton	L 1-3	Reeves	36,000
Oct 31	LEICESTER FOSSE	D 1-1	Bache	25,000
Nov 7	Woolwich Arsenal	W 1-0	Bache	20,000
Nov 14	NOTTS COUNTY	D 1-1	Tranter	15,000
Nov 21	Newcastle United	W 2-0	Wallace, Reeves	30,000
Nov 28	BRISTOL CITY	D 1-1	Bache	18,000
Dec 5	Preston North End	L 2-3	Wallace, Bache	10,000
Dec 12	MIDDLESBROUGH	L 0-3		15,000
Dec 19	Manchester City	L 0-2		12,000
Dec 25	LIVERPOOL	D 1-1	Logan A	20,000
Dec 26	BURY	W 3-0	Travers 3	20,000
Jan 1	Bury	W 2-1	Reeves, Eyre	16,000
Jan 2	Sheffield Wednesday	L 2-4	Buckley, Reeves	15,000
Jan 9	NOTTINGHAM FOREST	L 1-2	Hampton	15,000
Jan 23	Sunderland	L 3-4	Eyre, Logan J, Logan A	20,000
Jan 30	CHELSEA	D 0-0		18,000
Feb 6	Sheffield United	L 1-3	Hampton	15,000
Feb 13	BRADFORD CITY	L 1-3	Wallace	14,000
Feb 15	Blackburn Rovers	L 1-3	Hampton	15,000
Feb 27	EVERTON	W 3-1	Hampton 2, Walters	14,000
Mar 13	WOOLWICH ARSENAL	W 2-1	Eyre, Wallace (pen)	15,000
Mar 20	Notts County	D 1-1	Hall	6,000
Mar 27	Leicester Fosse	L 2-4	Walters 2	15,000
Mar 31	Manchester United	W 2-0	Walters, Hampton	10,000
Apr 3	Bristol City	D 0-0		16,000
Apr 9	SHEFFIELD UNITED	w 3-0	Walters, Bache, Eyre	20,000
Apr 10	PRESTON NORTH END	L 2-4	Wallace, Travers	18,000
Apr 17	Middlesbrough	L 0-1		8,000
Apr 24	MANCHESTER CITY	W 2-1	Walters, Wallace (pen)	15,000
Apr 26	NEWCASTLE UNITED	W 3-0	Wallace 2 (1 pen), Bache	7,500

FA Cup

Jan 16	Nottingham Forest	(Rd 1) L 0-2		14,000

League & Cup Appearances

PLAYER	LEAGUE	CUP COMPETITION FA CUP	TOTAL
Bache	31	1	32
Buckley	26	1	27
Cartlidge	3		3
Cooling	5		5
Corwan	16		16
Eyre	17	1	18
George	27		27
Gittins	1		1
Hall	23		23
Hampton	30	1	31
Hunter	15	1	16
Kearne	9		9
Kimberley	3		3
Kyle	1		1
Layton	9	1	10
Logan A	6		6
Logan J	28	1	29
Lyons	18		18
McKenzie	5		5
Miles	34		34
Reeves	23	1	24
Skiller	1	1	2
Tranter	21		21
Travers	4		4
Turner	7		7
Wallace	34	1	35
Walters	15		15
Whittaker	4		4
Wilcox	1		1
Windmill	1		1

Goalscorers

PLAYER	LEAGUE	CUP COMPETITION FA CUP	TOTAL
Bache	11		11
Hampton	9		9
Wallace	8		8
Reeves	7		7
Walters	7		7
Eyre	4		4
Travers	4		4
Logan A	3		3
Logan J	2		2
Buckley	1		1
Hall	1		1
Tranter	1		1

Fact File

Reserve defender George Harris was transferred to West Bromwich Albion for a record fee of £400.

MANAGER: Committee

CAPTAIN: Joe Bache, Alf Miles

TOP SCORER: Joe Bache, 11 (all league)

BIGGEST WIN: 3-0 v Bury (H), Division One, 26 December 1908; v Sheffield United (H), Division One, 9 April 1909

HIGHEST ATTENDANCE: 60,000 v Chelsea (A), Division One, 26 September 1908

MAJOR TRANSFERS IN: Arthur Cartlidge from Bristol Rovers

MAJOR TRANSFERS OUT: George Harris and Bill Garraty to West Bromwich Albion

Final Division One Table

		P	W	D	L	F	A	Pts
1	NEWCASTLE U	38	24	5	9	65	41	53
2	EVERTON	38	18	10	10	82	57	46
3	SUNDERLAND	38	21	2	15	78	63	44
4	BLACKBURN R	38	14	13	11	61	50	41
5	SHEFFIELD W	38	17	6	15	67	61	40
6	WOOLWICH ARSENAL	38	14	10	14	52	49	38
7	ASTON VILLA	38	14	10	14	58	56	38
8	BRISTOL C	38	13	12	13	45	58	38
9	MIDDLESBROUGH	38	14	9	15	59	53	37
10	PRESTON NE	38	13	11	14	48	44	37
11	CHELSEA	38	14	9	15	56	61	37
12	SHEFFIELD U	38	14	9	15	51	59	37
13	MANCHESTER U	38	15	7	16	58	68	37
14	NOTTINGHAM F	38	14	8	16	66	57	36
15	NOTTS CO	38	14	8	16	51	48	36
16	LIVERPOOL	38	15	6	17	57	65	36
17	BURY	38	14	8	16	63	77	36
18	BRADFORD C	38	12	10	16	47	47	34
19	MANCHESTER C	38	15	4	19	67	69	34
20	LEICESTER FOSSE	38	8	9	21	54	102	25

Season 1909-10

Football League Division One

DATE	OPPONENTS	SCORE	GOALSCORERS	ATTENDANCE
Sep 1	WOOLWICH ARSENAL	W 5-1	Bache 2, Hall, Gerrish, Walters	12,000
Sep 4	Bolton Wanderers	W 2-1	Wallace, Hall (pen)	25,000
Sep 11	CHELSEA	W 4-1	Gerrish 3, Bache	25,000
Sep 18	Blackburn Rovers	L 2-3	Gerrish, Wallace	25,000
Sep 25	NOTTINGHAM FOREST	D 0-0		25,000
Oct 2	Sunderland	D 1-1	Hall	20,000
Oct 9	Everton	W 3-1	Hampton 2, Hunter	35,000
Oct 16	Manchester United	L 0-2		20,000
Oct 23	BRADFORD CITY	W 3-1	Hampton, Hall, Gerrish	18,000
Oct 30	Sheffield Wednesday	L 2-3	Hampton 2	12,000
Nov 6	BRISTOL CITY	W 1-0	Gerrish	20,000
Nov 13	Bury	W 2-0	Bache 2	10,000
Nov 20	TOTTENHAM HOTSPUR	W 3-2	Gerrish, Bache, Hampton	20,000
Nov 27	Preston North End	L 0-1		10,000
Dec 4	NOTTS COUNTY	D 1-1	Hampton	8,000
Dec 11	Newcastle United	L 0-1		15,000
Dec 18	LIVERPOOL	W 3-1	Hampton, Bache 2	20,000
Dec 25	Sheffield United	W 1-0	Gerrish	25,000
Dec 27	SHEFFIELD UNITED	W 2-1	Hampton, Bache	43,000
Jan 1	Nottingham Forest	W 4-1	Hampton 3, Bache	8,000
Jan 8	BOLTON WANDERERS	W 3-1	Bache 2, Gerrish	18,000
Jan 22	Chelsea	D 0-0		33,000
Jan 29	BLACKBURN ROVERS	W 4-3	Bache, Hampton 3	20,000
Feb 12	SUNDERLAND	W 3-2	Walters, Buckley, Gerrish	25,000
Feb 26	MANCHESTER UNITED	W 7-1	Gerrish 2, Walters 3, Hampton 2	20,000
Mar 5	Bradford City	W 2-1	Bache, Robinson o.g.	22,000
Mar 12	SHEFFIELD WEDNESDAY	W 5-0	Hall 2, Wallace (pen), Bache 2	12,000
Mar 14	Everton	D 0-0		20,000
Mar 19	Bristol City	D 0-0		15,000
Mar 25	MIDDLESBROUGH	W 4-2	Hampton 3, Bache	30,000
Mar 26	BURY	W 4-1	Hampton 3, Walters	25,000
Mar 28	Middlesbrough	L 2-3	Wallace 2 (2 pens)	25,000
Apr 2	Tottenham Hotspur	D 1-1	Bache	35,000
Apr 9	Preston North End	W 3-0	Hampton, Gerrish, Bache	20,000
Apr 11	Woolwich Arsenal	L 0-1		9,000
Apr 16	Notts County	W 3-2	Wallace, Eyre, Hampton	13,000
Apr 27	NEWCASTLE UNITED	W 4-0	Bache, Wallace (pen), Eyre, Hampton	25,000
Apr 30	Liverpool	L 0-2		25,000

FA Cup

DATE	OPPONENTS		SCORE	GOALSCORERS	ATTENDANCE
Jan 15	Oldham Athletic	(Rd 1)	W 2-1	Bache, Hall	17,000
Feb 5	DERBY COUNTY	(Rd 2)	W 6-1	Wallace, Hampton 3, Bache, Scattergood o.g.	45,000
Feb 19	MANCHESTER CITY	(Rd 3)	L 1-2	Gerrish	45,000

League & Cup Appearances

PLAYER	LEAGUE	CUP COMPETITION FA CUP	TOTAL
Bache	32	3	35
Buckley	37	3	40
Cartlidge	35	2	37
Eyre	13		13
George	3	1	4
Gerrish	36	3	39
Hall	25	3	28
Hampton	32	3	35
Hunter	32	3	35
Kearns	10		10
Layton	4		4
Logan J	16		16
Lyons	35	3	38
Miles	27	3	30
Moss	1		1
Tranter	28	3	31
Wallace	38	3	41
Walters	14		14

Goalscorers

PLAYER	LEAGUE	CUP COMPETITION FA CUP	TOTAL
Hampton	26	3	29
Bache	20	2	22
Gerrish	14	1	15
Wallace	7	1	8
Hall	6	1	7
Walters	6		6
Eyre	2		2
Buckley	1		1
Hunter	1		1
Opps' o.gs.	1	1	1

Fact File

Villa finished five points ahead of runners-up Liverpool as they clinched their sixth league title.

MANAGER: Committee

CAPTAIN: Joe Bache, Chris Buckley, Alf Miles

TOP SCORER: Harry Hampton, 29 (26 league)

BIGGEST WIN: 7-1 v Manchester United (H), Division One, 26 February 1910

HIGHEST ATTENDANCE: 45,000 v Derby County (H), FA Cup Second Round, 5 February 1910; v Manchester City, FA Cup Third Round, 19 February 1910

MAJOR TRANSFERS IN: Clem Stephenson from Durham City, Bill Gerrish from Bristol Rovers

MAJOR TRANSFERS OUT: George Reeves to Bradford

Final Division One Table

		P	W	D	L	F	A	Pts
1	ASTON VILLA	38	23	7	8	84	42	53
2	LIVERPOOL	38	21	6	11	78	57	48
3	BLACKBURN R	38	18	9	11	73	55	45
4	NEWCASTLE U	38	19	7	12	70	56	45
5	MANCHESTER U	38	19	7	12	69	61	45
6	SHEFFIELD U	38	16	10	12	62	41	42
7	BRADFORD C	38	17	8	13	64	47	42
8	SUNDERLAND	38	18	5	15	66	51	41
9	NOTTS CO	38	15	10	13	67	59	40
10	EVERTON	38	16	8	14	51	56	40
11	SHEFFIELD W	38	15	9	14	60	63	39
12	PRESTON NE	38	15	5	18	52	58	35
13	BURY	38	12	9	17	62	66	33
14	NOTTINGHAM F	38	11	11	16	54	72	33
15	TOTTENHAM H	38	11	10	17	53	69	32
16	BRISTOL C	38	12	8	18	45	60	32
17	MIDDLESBROUGH	38	11	9	18	56	73	31
18	WOOLWICH ARSENAL	38	11	9	18	37	67	31
19	CHELSEA	38	11	7	20	47	70	29
20	BOLTON W	38	9	6	23	44	71	24

Season 1910-11

Football League Division One

DATE	OPPONENTS	SCORE	GOALSCORERS	ATTENDANCE
Sep 3	OLDHAM ATHLETIC	D 1-1	Gerrish	30,000
Sep 10	Sunderland	L 2-3	Logan J, Bache	30,000
Sep 17	WOOLWICH ARSENAL	W 3-0	Gerrish, Logan J, Renneville	26,000
Sep 24	Bradford City	W 2-1	Jones, Walters	25,000
Oct 1	BLACKBURN ROVERS	D 2-2	Eyre, Bache	28,000
Oct 8	Nottingham Forest	L 1-3	Hampton	18,000
Oct 15	MANCHESTER CITY	W 2-1	Bache, Walters	19,700
Oct 22	Everton	W 1-0	Walters	25,000
Oct 29	SHEFFIELD WEDNESDAY	W 2-1	Walters, Bache	20,000
Nov 5	Bristol City	W 2-1	Bache, Walters	16,000
Nov 12	NEWCASTLE UNITED	W 3-2	Hampton 2, Walters	30,000
Nov 19	Tottenham Hotspur	W 2-1	Hampton, Walters	25,000
Nov 26	MIDDLESBROUGH	W 5-0	Bache 3, Hampton 2	15,000
Dec 3	Preston North End	W 1-0	Wallace (pen)	8,000
Dec 10	NOTTS COUNTY	W 3-1	Bache 2, Hampton	12,000
Dec 17	Manchester United	L 0-2		20,000
Dec 24	LIVERPOOL	D 1-1	Hampton	18,000
Dec 26	BURY	W 4-1	Hampton, Henshall, Bache, Walters	30,000
Dec 28	Sheffield United	L 1-2	Walters	25,000
Dec 31	Oldham Athletic	D 1-1	Eyre	30,000
Jan 2	Bury	L 0-1		15,000
Jan 7	SUNDERLAND	W 2-1	Bache 2	18,000
Jan 28	BRADFORD CITY	W 4-1	Walters, Hampton 2, Henshall	24,000
Feb 11	NOTTINGHAM FOREST	W 3-1	Hampton, Henshall, Walters	18,400
Feb 18	Manchester City	D 1-1	Hampton	35,000
Feb 25	TOTTENHAM HOTSPUR	W 4-0	Wallace, Bache, Stephenson, Hampton	22,000
Mar 4	Sheffield Wednesday	L 0-1		12,000
Mar 11	BRISTOL CITY	W 2-0	Stephenson, Wallace	22,000
Mar 15	Woolwich Arsenal	D 1-1	Stephenson	5,000
Mar 18	Newcastle United	L 0-1		20,000
Mar 27	EVERTON	W 2-1	Walters, Hampton	11,000
Apr 1	Middlesbrough	W 1-0	Henshall	18,000
Apr 8	Preston North End	L 0-2		18,000
Apr 14	SHEFFIELD UNITED	W 3-0	Wallace (pen), Gerrish, Hampton	28,000
Apr 15	Notts County	W 2-1	Hampton 2	20,000
Apr 22	MANCHESTER UNITED	W 4-2	Henshall, Hampton, Bache, Wallace	50,855
Apr 24	Blackburn Rovers	D 0-0		20,000
Apr 29	Liverpool	L 1-3	Walters	35,000

FA Cup

Jan 14	Portsmouth	(Rd 1) W 4-1	Bache, Hampton 2, Thomson o.g.	17,500
Feb 4	Manchester United	(Rd 2) L 1-2	Henshall	65,100

FA Charity Shield

Aug 26	Brighton & Hove Albion*	L 0-1		15,000

*Played at Stamford Bridge, London.

League & Cup Appearances

PLAYER	LEAGUE	CUP COMPETITION FA CUP	OTHER	TOTAL
Anstey	9			9
Bache	32	2	1	35
Buckley	30	1	1	32
Cartlidge	14		1	15
Eyre	14			14
George	14	2		16
Gerrish	14		1	15
Hall	3		1	4
Hampton	33	2		35
Henshall	19	2		21
Hunter G	33	2	1	36
Jones	2			2
Kearns	15	1		16
Layton	3			3
Logan J	14	1		15
Lyons	28		1	30
Miles	30	2	1	33
Moss	1			2
Renneville	2			2
Stephenson	5			5
Tranter	36	2	1	39
Turner	1			1
Wallace	38	2	1	41
Walters	28	2	1	31

Goalscorers

PLAYER	LEAGUE	CUP COMPETITION FA CUP	OTHER	TOTAL
Hampton	19	2		21
Bache	15	1		16
Walters	13			13
Henshall	5	1		6
Wallace	5			5
Gerrish	3			3
Stephenson	3			3
Eyre	2			2
Logan J	2			2
Jones	1			1
Renneville	1			1
Opps' o.gs.		1		1

Fact File

Villa needed to win their final game of the season to become league champions ahead of Manchester United – they lost 3-1 at Liverpool.

MANAGER: Committee

CAPTAIN: Joe Bache, Chris Buckley, Freddie Miles

TOP SCORER: Harry Hampton, 21 (19 league)

BIGGEST WIN: 5-0 v Middlesbrough (H), Division One, 26 November 1910

HIGHEST ATTENDANCE: 65,100 v Manchester United (A), FA Cup Second Round, 4 February 1911

MAJOR TRANSFERS OUT: Edmund Eyre to Middlesbrough, Billy George to Birmingham (trainer)

Final Division One Table

		P	W	D	L	F	A	Pts
1	MANCHESTER U	38	22	8	8	72	40	52
2	ASTON VILLA	38	22	7	9	69	41	51
3	SUNDERLAND	38	15	15	8	67	48	45
4	EVERTON	38	19	7	12	50	36	45
5	BRADFORD C	38	20	5	13	51	42	45
6	SHEFFIELD W	38	17	8	13	47	48	42
7	OLDHAM ATH	38	16	9	13	44	41	41
8	NEWCASTLE U	38	15	10	13	61	43	40
9	SHEFFIELD U	38	15	8	15	49	43	38
10	WOOLWICH ARSENAL	38	13	12	13	41	49	38
11	NOTTS CO	38	14	10	14	37	45	38
12	BLACKBURN R	38	13	11	14	62	54	37
13	LIVERPOOL	38	15	7	16	53	53	37
14	PRESTON NE	38	12	11	15	40	49	35
15	TOTTENHAM H	38	13	6	19	52	63	32
16	MIDDLESBROUGH	38	11	10	17	49	63	32
17	MANCHESTER C	38	9	13	16	43	58	31
18	BURY	38	9	11	18	43	71	29
19	BRISTOL C	38	11	5	22	43	66	27
20	NOTTINGHAM F	38	9	7	22	55	75	25

Season 1911-12

Football League Division One

DATE	OPPONENTS	SCORE	GOALSCORERS	ATTENDANCE
Sep 2	Bradford City	L 1-2	Hampton	30,000
Sep 4	WEST BROMWICH ALBION	L 0-3		31,884
Sep 9	WOOLWICH ARSENAL	W 4-1	Walters, Hampton 2, Wallace (pen)	24,000
Sep 16	Manchester City	W 6-2	Bache 3, Henshall, Walters, Hampton	20,000
Sep 23	EVERTON	W 3-0	Hampton, Wallace (pen), Walters	28,000
Sep 30	West Bromwich Albion	D 2-2	Hampton, Henshall	46,203
Oct 7	SUNDERLAND	L 1-3	Wallace (pen)	28,000
Oct 14	Blackburn Rovers	L 1-3	Wallace (pen)	30,000
Oct 21	Sheffield Wednesday	L 2-3	Birch 2	13,570
Oct 23	Sheffield United	W 1-0	Walters	12,000
Oct 28	Bury	D 1-1	Walters	8,000
Nov 4	MIDDLESBROUGH	W 2-1	Wallace, Walters	24,120
Nov 18	TOTTENHAM HOTSPUR	D 2-2	Hampton 2	21,000
Nov 25	Manchester United	L 1-3	Whittaker	20,000
Dec 2	LIVERPOOL	W 5-0	Wallace 2 (1 pen), Goode 2, Bache	14,400
Dec 9	PRESTON NORTH END	W 1-0	Bache	15,000
Dec 16	Newcastle United	L 2-6	Bache, Hampton	30,000
Dec 23	SHEFFIELD UNITED	W 1-0	Wallace	14,500
Dec 26	OLDHAM ATHLETIC	W 6-1	Hampton 4, Stephenson 2	27,500
Dec 30	BRADFORD CITY	D 0-0		24,500
Jan 1	Bolton Wanderers	L 0-3		42,000
Jan 6	Woolwich Arsenal	D 2-2	Walters, Wallace	6,000
Jan 20	MANCHESTER CITY	W 3-1	Wallace 2 (1pen), Stephenson	11,760
Jan 27	Everton	D 1-1	Hampton	35,000
Feb 10	Sunderland	D 2-2	Stephenson, Henshall	12,000
Feb 17	BLACKBURN ROVERS	L 0-3		30,000
Feb 24	Sheffield Wednesday	L 0-3		20,000
Mar 2	BURY	W 5-2	Hampton 4, Wallace	13,000
Mar 9	Middlesbrough	W 2-1	Wallace, Bache	12,000
Mar 13	Notts County	L 0-2		6,000
Mar 16	NOTTS COUNTY	W 5-1	Hampton 2, Stephenson, Goode, Wallace	15,000
Mar 23	Tottenham Hotspur	L 1-2	Edgley	16,000
Mar 30	MANCHESTER UNITED	W 6-0	Stephenson 3, Wallace 2, Hampton	15,000
Apr 5	BOLTON WANDERERS	L 0-1		13,900
Apr 6	Liverpool	W 2-1	Hampton, Stephenson	30,000
Apr 8	Oldham Athletic	W 2-1	Hampton, Stephenson	7,000
Apr 13	Preston North End	L 1-4	Hampton	12,000
Apr 20	NEWCASTLE UNITED	W 2-0	Hampton, Hall	20,000

FA Cup

Jan 13	WALSALL	(Rd 1) W 6-0	Bache, Henshall 2, Hampton 2, Wallace	18,000
Feb 3	READING	(Rd 2) D 1-1	Hampton	25,000
Feb 7	Reading	(R) L 0-1		12,500

League & Cup Appearances

PLAYER	LEAGUE	CUP COMPETITION FA CUP	TOTAL
Anstey	21	3	24
Askew	2		2
Bache	34	3	37
Birch	3		3
Buckley	21		21
Edgley	2		2
Edwards	6	2	8
Gerrish	5		5
Goode	7		7
Hall	1		1
Hampton	33	3	36
Henshall	26	3	29
Hunter	11		11
Kearns	5		5
Lindin	1		1
Littlewood	3		3
Logan S	15	2	17
Lyons	28	1	29
Mann	1		1
Miles	25	3	28
Morris	1		1
Moss	3		3
Ralphs	1		1
Richards	6		6
Roose	10		10
Stephenson	20		20
Tranter	31	2	33
Wallace	35	3	38
Walters	19	3	22
Watson	3		3
Weston	15	2	17
Whittaker	24	3	27

Goalscorers

PLAYER	LEAGUE	CUP COMPETITION FA CUP	TOTAL
Hampton	25	3	28
Wallace	16	1	17
Stephenson	10		10
Bache	7	1	8
Walters	7		7
Henshall	3	2	5
Goode	3		3
Birch	2		2
Edgley	1		1
Hall	1		1
Whittaker	1		1

Fact File

Charlie Wallace scored six penalties in league games this season – he also missed three times from the spot.

MANAGER: Committee

CAPTAIN: Joe Bache, Freddie Miles, George Tranter

TOP SCORER: Harry Hampton, 28 (25 league)

BIGGEST WIN: 6-0 v Walsall (H), FA Cup First Round, 13 January 1912; v Manchester United (H), Division One, 30 March 1912

HIGHEST ATTENDANCE: 46,203 v West Bromwich Albion (A), Division One, 30 September 1911

MAJOR TRANSFERS IN: Leigh Richmond Roose from Woolwich Arsenal, Tommy Weston from Coombes Wood

MAJOR TRANSFERS OUT: Billy Gerrish to Preston North End, Joey Walters to Oldham Athletic

Final Division One Table

		P	W	D	L	F	A	Pts
1	BLACKBURN R	38	20	9	9	60	43	49
2	EVERTON	38	20	6	12	46	42	46
3	NEWCASTLE U	38	18	8	12	64	50	44
4	BOLTON W	38	20	3	15	54	43	43
5	SHEFFIELD W	38	16	9	13	69	49	41
6	ASTON VILLA	38	17	7	14	76	63	41
7	MIDDLESBROUGH	38	16	8	14	56	45	40
8	SUNDERLAND	38	14	11	13	58	51	39
9	WBA	38	15	9	14	43	47	39
10	WOOLWICH ARSENAL	38	15	8	15	55	59	38
11	BRADFORD C	38	15	8	15	46	50	38
12	TOTTENHAM H	38	14	9	15	53	53	37
13	MANCHESTER C	38	13	11	14	56	58	37
14	SHEFFIELD U	38	13	10	15	63	56	36
15	MANCHESTER C	38	13	9	16	56	58	35
16	NOTTS CO	38	14	7	17	46	63	35
17	LIVERPOOL	38	12	10	16	49	55	34
18	OLDHAM ATH	38	12	10	16	46	54	34
19	PRESTON NE	38	13	7	18	40	57	33
20	BURY	38	6	9	23	32	59	21

Season 1912-13

Football League Division One

DATE	OPPONENTS	SCORE	GOALSCORERS	ATTENDANCE
Sep 2	CHELSEA	W 1-0	Stephenson	25,000
Sep 7	BRADFORD CITY	W 3-1	Halse, Bache, Hall	33,000
Sep 9	Oldham Athletic	D 2-2	Bache, Wallace	10,000
Sep 14	Manchester City	L 0-1		40,000
Sep 16	Woolwich Arsenal	W 3-0	Hampton 2, Stephenson	6,000
Sep 21	WEST BROMWICH ALBION	L 2-6	Bache 2	55,064
Sep 28	Everton	W 1-0	Halse	35,000
Oct 5	SHEFFIELD WEDNESDAY	W 10-0	Hampton 6, Bache 2, Halse, Stephenson	30,000
Oct 12	Blackburn Rovers	D 2-2	Halse 2	40,000
Oct 19	DERBY COUNTY	W 5-1	Halse 5	30,000
Oct 26	Tottenham Hotspur	D 3-3	Halse 2, Stephenson	18,000
Nov 2	MIDDLESBROUGH	W 5-1	Hampton 2, Halse, Stephenson, Wallace (pen)	26,000
Nov 9	Notts County	D 1-1	Hampton	18,000
Nov 16	MANCHESTER UNITED	W 4-2	Bache, Hampton 2, Stephenson	28,000
Nov 23	Sunderland	L 1-3	Hampton	35,000
Nov 30	Liverpool	L 0-2		30,000
Dec 7	BOLTON WANDERERS	D 1-1	Wallace (pen)	21,000
Dec 14	Sheffield United	L 2-3	Halse 2	15,000
Dec 21	NEWCASTLE UNITED	W 3-1	Hampton, Bache, Wallace	24,000
Dec 26	OLDHAM ATHLETIC	W 7-1	Hampton 3, Halse 2, Stephenson 2	22,000
Dec 28	Bradford City	D 1-1	Stephenson	15,000
Jan 4	MANCHESTER CITY	W 2-0	Halse, Hampton	18,000
Jan 18	West Bromwich Albion	D 2-2	Hampton (pen), Harrop	40,589
Jan 25	EVERTON	D 1-1	Hampton	25,000
Feb 8	Sheffield Wednesday	D 1-1	Hall	41,000
Feb 15	BLACKBURN ROVERS	D 1-1	Barber	20,000
Mar 1	TOTTENHAM HOTSPUR	W 1-0	McLachlan	22,000
Mar 12	Derby County	W 1-0	Stephenson	6,000
Mar 15	NOTTS COUNTY	W 1-0	Stephenson	20,000
Mar 21	Chelsea	W 2-1	Hampton, Leach	65,000
Mar 22	Manchester United	L 0-4		30,000
Mar 24	WOOLWICH ARSENAL	W 4-1	Halse 2, Bache 2	25,000
Apr 5	LIVERPOOL	L 1-3	Doncaster	20,000
Apr 9	Middlesbrough	D 1-1	Halse	12,000
Apr 12	Bolton Wanderers	W 3-2	Barber, Hampton, Stephenson	20,000
Apr 23	SUNDERLAND	D 1-1	Halse	59,740
Apr 26	Newcastle United	W 3-1	Stephenson, Wallace, Hampton	20,000
Apr 28	SHEFFIELD UNITED	W 4-2	Wallace 2, McLachlan, Hampton	4,850

FA Cup

Jan 15	Derby County	(Rd 1) W 3-1	Halse 2, Hampton	15,000
Feb 1	WEST HAM UNITED	(Rd 2) W 5-0	Morris, Halse 2, Hampton, Stephenson	51,000
Feb 22	CRYSTAL PALACE	(Rd 3) W 5-0	Halse 2, Stephenson 2, Bache	44,500
Mar 8	Bradford	(Rd 4) W 5-0	Hampton 3, Halse, Stephenson	24,000
Mar 29	Oldham Athletic*	(SF) W 1-0	Stephenson	22,616
Apr 19	Sunderland#	(F) W 1-0	Barber	121,919

*Played at Ewood Park, Blackburn. #Played at Crystal Palace, London.

League & Cup Appearances

PLAYER	LEAGUE	CUP COMPETITION FA CUP	TOTAL
Anstey	5		5
Bache	35	6	41
Barber	15	5	20
Buckley	1		1
Dobson	1		1
Doncaster	2		2
Ducat	4		4
Hall	16		16
Halse	31	6	37
Hampton	33	6	39
Hardy	33	6	39
Harrop	35	4	39
Leach	10	4	14
Littlewood	5		5
Lyons	30	6	36
McLachlan	8		8
Miles	11		11
Morris	20		20
Stephenson	34	6	40
Tranter	10	1	11
Wallace	31	6	37
Weston	30	6	36
Whittaker	18	2	20

Goalscorers

PLAYER	LEAGUE	CUP COMPETITION FA CUP	TOTAL
Hampton	25	5	30
Halse	21	7	28
Stephenson	14	5	19
Bache	10	1	11
Wallace	7		7
Barber	2	1	3
Hall	2		2
McLachlan	2		2
Doncaster	1		1
Harrop	1		1
Leach	1		1
Morris		1	1

Fact File

Villa beat Sunderland in the FA Cup and Sunderland pipped Villa for the League. Charlie Wallace also became the first player to miss a penalty in an FA Cup final.

Final Division One Table

		P	W	D	L	F	A	Pts
1	SUNDERLAND	38	25	4	9	86	43	54
2	ASTON VILLA	38	19	12	7	86	52	50
3	SHEFFIELD W	38	21	7	10	75	55	49
4	MANCHESTER U	38	19	8	11	69	43	46
5	BLACKBURN R	38	16	13	9	79	43	45
6	MANCHESTER C	38	18	8	12	53	37	44
7	DERBY CO	38	17	8	13	69	66	42
8	BOLTON W	38	16	10	12	62	63	42
9	OLDHAM ATH	38	14	14	10	50	55	42
10	WBA	38	13	12	13	57	50	38
11	EVERTON	38	15	7	16	48	54	37
12	LIVERPOOL	38	16	5	17	61	71	37
13	BRADFORD C	38	12	11	15	50	60	35
14	NEWCASTLE U	38	13	8	17	47	47	34
15	SHEFFIELD U	38	14	6	18	56	70	34
16	MIDDLESBROUGH	38	11	10	17	55	69	32
17	TOTTENHAM H	38	12	6	20	45	72	30
18	CHELSEA	38	11	6	21	51	73	28
19	NOTTS CO	38	7	9	22	28	56	23
20	WOOLWICH ARSENAL	38	3	12	23	26	74	18

MANAGER: Committee

CAPTAIN: Joe Bache

TOP SCORER: Harry Hampton, 30 (25 league)

BIGGEST WIN: 10-0 v Sheffield Wednesday (H), Division One, 5 October 1912

HIGHEST ATTENDANCE: 121,919 v Sunderland FA Cup final at Crystal Palace, 19 April 1913

MAJOR TRANSFERS IN: Andy Ducat from Woolwich Arsenal, Harold Halse from Manchester United, Sam Hardy from Liverpool

MAJOR TRANSFERS OUT: Harry Henshall to Notts County

Season 1913-14

Football League Division One

DATE	OPPONENTS	SCORE	GOALSCORERS	ATTENDANCE
Sep 3	MANCHESTER CITY	D 1-1	Barber	10,000
Sep 6	Bradford City	D 0-0		30,000
Sep 13	BLACKBURN ROVERS	L 1-3	Stephenson	38,575
Sep 20	Sunderland	L 0-2		35,000
Sep 27	EVERTON	W 3-1	Whittaker, Bache 2	29,000
Oct 4	West Bromwich Albion	L 0-1		48,057
Oct 11	SHEFFIELD WEDNESDAY	W 2-0	Barber, Hampton	22,000
Oct 18	Bolton Wanderers	L 0-3		33,000
Oct 25	CHELSEA	L 1-2	Logan o.g.	27,000
Nov 1	Oldham Athletic	W 1-0	Stephenson	18,000
Nov 8	MANCHESTER UNITED	W 3-1	Hampton (pen), Whittaker, Hall	20,000
Nov 15	Burnley	L 0-4		20,000
Nov 22	PRESTON NORTH END	W 3-0	Hampton, Whittaker, Wallace	25,000
Nov 29	Newcastle United	D 2-2	Hampton, Stephenson	20,000
Dec 1	LIVERPOOL	W 2-1	Hampton 2 (1 pen)	15,000
Dec 13	TOTTENHAM HOTSPUR	D 3-3	Hampton, Whittaker, Harrop	24,500
Dec 20	Middlesbrough	L 2-5	Stephenson 2	15,000
Dec 25	Derby County	W 2-0	Hampton, Stephenson	9,500
Dec 26	SHEFFIELD UNITED	W 3-0	Hampton (pen), Barber, Wallace	21,000
Dec 27	BRADFORD CITY	L 0-1		35,000
Jan 1	Sheffield United	L 0-3		39,000
Jan 3	Blackburn Rovers	D 0-0		20,000
Jan 17	SUNDERLAND	W 5-0	Bache 2, Edgley 2, Hampton	32,000
Jan 24	Everton	W 4-1	Hampton, Stephenson 2, Fleetwood o.g.	35,000
Feb 7	WEST BROMWICH A	W 2-0	Wallace, Barber	48,000
Feb 14	Sheffield Wednesday	W 3-2	Stephenson, Hampton, Bache	30,000
Feb 25	BOLTON WANDERERS	W 1-0	Hampton	15,000
Feb 28	Chelsea	W 3-0	Stephenson, Hampton, Bache	55,000
Mar 14	Manchester United	W 6-0	Edgley, Bache 3, Hampton, Stephenson	30,000
Mar 18	OLDHAM ATHLETIC	D 0-0		20,000
Mar 21	BURNLEY	W 1-0	Edgley	30,000
Apr 1	Preston North End	L 2-3	Stephenson, Hampton (pen)	10,000
Apr 4	NEWCASTLE UNITED	L 1-3	Wallace (pen)	17,000
Apr 10	Manchester City	L 1-3	Edgley	35,000
Apr 11	Liverpool	W 1-0	Bache	40,000
Apr 13	DERBY COUNTY	W 3-2	Hampton 2 (1 pen), Bache	16,000
Apr 18	Tottenham Hotspur	W 2-0	McLachlan J, Hampton	25,000
Apr 25	MIDDLESBROUGH	L 1-3	Bache	19,500

FA Cup

DATE	OPPONENTS		SCORE	GOALSCORERS	ATTENDANCE
Jan 10	STOKE CITY	(Rd 1)	W 4-0	Stephenson 2, Hampton 2	18,000
Jan 31	Exeter City	(Rd 2)	W 2-1	Hampton 2	9,600
Feb 21	WEST BROMWICH ALBION	(Rd 3)	W 2-1	Bache, Hampton	57,293
Mar 7	Sheffield Wednesday	(Rd 4)	W 1-0	Edgley	56,991
Mar 28	Liverpool*	(SF)	L 0-2		27,464

*Played at White Hart Lane, London.

League & Cup Appearances

PLAYER	LEAGUE	CUP COMPETITION FA CUP	TOTAL
Anstey	6		6
Bache	28	4	32
Barber	28	5	33
Boyne	4		4
Chandler	1		1
Dyke	6		6
Edgley	19	5	24
Hall	3		3
Hampton	30	5	35
Hardy	30	5	35
Harrop	35	5	40
Laidlaw	2		2
Leach	28	5	33
Littlewood	7		7
Lyons	34	5	39
McLachlan A	3		3
McLachlan J	8		8
McLaverty	2		2
Miles	6		6
Morris	13		13
Richards	1		1
Slade	3		3
Smart H	1		1
Stephenson	36	5	41
Tranter	9		9
Wallace	32	5	37
Weston	28	5	33
Whittaker	14	1	15
Williams	1		1

Goalscorers

PLAYER	LEAGUE	CUP COMPETITION FA CUP	TOTAL
Hampton	19	5	24
Stephenson	12	2	14
Bache	12	1	13
Edgley	5	1	6
Barber	4		4
Wallace	4		4
Whittaker	4		4
Hall	1		1
Harrop	1		1
McLachlan J	1		1
Opps' o.gs.	2		2

Fact File

On 28 February 1914, Joe Bache became the first Villa player to reach the milestone of 400 league appearances and, to mark the event, he scored in a 3-0 victory at Chelsea.

MANAGER: Committee

CAPTAIN: Joe Bache, Clem Stephenson

TOP SCORER: Harry Hampton, 24 (19 league)

BIGGEST WIN: 6-0 v Manchester United (A), Division One, 14 March 1914

HIGHEST ATTENDANCE: 57,293 v West Bromwich Albion (H), FA Cup Third Round, 21 February 1914

MAJOR TRANSFERS OUT: Albert Hall to Millwall

Final Division One Table

		P	W	D	L	F	A	Pts
1	BLACKBURN R	38	20	11	7	78	42	51
2	ASTON VILLA	38	19	6	13	65	50	44
3	MIDDLESBROUGH	38	19	5	14	77	60	43
4	OLDHAM ATH	38	17	9	12	55	45	43
5	WBA	38	15	13	10	46	42	43
6	BOLTON W	38	16	10	12	65	52	42
7	SUNDERLAND	38	17	6	15	63	52	40
8	CHELSEA	38	16	7	15	46	55	39
9	BRADFORD C	38	12	14	12	40	40	38
10	SHEFFIELD U	38	16	5	17	63	60	37
11	NEWCASTLE U	38	13	11	14	39	48	37
12	BURNLEY	38	12	12	14	61	53	36
13	MANCHESTER C	38	14	8	16	51	53	36
14	MANCHESTER U	38	15	6	17	52	62	36
15	EVERTON	38	12	11	15	46	55	35
16	LIVERPOOL	38	14	7	17	46	62	35
17	TOTTENHAM H	38	12	10	16	50	62	34
18	SHEFFIELD W	38	13	8	17	53	70	34
19	PRESTON NE	38	12	6	20	52	69	30
20	DERBY CO	38	8	11	19	55	71	27

Season 1914-15

Football League Division One

DATE	OPPONENTS	SCORE	GOALSCORERS	ATTENDANCE
Sep 2	NOTTS COUNTY	W 2-1	Hampton 2	8,000
Sep 5	SUNDERLAND	L 3-1	Hampton	20,000
Sep 12	Sheffield Wednesday	L 2-5	Edgley, Humphries	10,000
Sep 19	WEST BROMWICH ALBION	W 2-1	Stephenson C, Harrop	29,000
Sep 26	Everton	D 0-0		20,000
Oct 3	CHELSEA	W 2-1	Hampton (pen), Stephenson C	20,000
Oct 10	Bradford City	L 0-3		22,000
Oct 17	BURNLEY	D 3-3	Barber 2, Ducat (pen)	16,000
Oct 24	Tottenham Hotspur	W 2-0	Stephenson C, Edgley	30,000
Oct 31	NEWCASTLE UNITED	W 2-1	Wallace, Whittaker	16,000
Nov 7	Middlesbrough	D 1-1	Bache	12,000
Nov 14	SHEFFIELD UNITED	W 1-0	Ducat	15,000
Nov 25	Manchester City	L 0-1		14,000
Nov 28	Liverpool	W 6-2	Stephenson C, Edgley, Hampton, Barber, Bache, Wallace	22,000
Dec 5	BRADFORD PARK AVENUE	L 1-2	Stephenson C	10,000
Dec 12	Oldham Athletic	D 3-3	Edgley, Bache, Hampton	7,000
Dec 19	MANCHESTER UNITED	D 3-3	Edgley, Hampton 2	10,000
Dec 25	Blackburn Rovers	W 2-1	Edgley, Leach	20,000
Dec 26	BOLTON WANDERERS	L 1-7	Stephenson C	27,000
Jan 1	Bolton Wanderers	D 2-2	Hampton, Edgley	18,000
Jan 16	SHEFFIELD WEDNESDAY	D 0-0		7,500
Jan 23	West Bromwich Albion	L 0-2		19,492
Feb 6	Chelsea	L 1-3	Stephenson C	22,000
Feb 10	EVERTON	L 1-5	Hampton	4,500
Feb 13	BRADFORD CITY	D 0-0		2,900
Feb 22	Burnley	L 1-2	Leach	8,000
Feb 27	TOTTENHAM HOTSPUR	W 3-1	Stephenson C, Hampton 2	13,000
Mar 13	MIDDLESBROUGH	W 5-0	Hampton 2, Harrop, Stephenson C 2	12,000
Mar 20	Sheffield United	L 0-3		17,000
Apr 2	Blackburn Rovers	W 2-1	Edgley, Stephenson C	10,000
Apr 3	LIVERPOOL	W 6-2	Hampton 3, Nash 3	12,000
Apr 5	Notts County	D 1-1	Bache	16,000
Apr 10	Bradford Park Avenue	D 2-2	Ducat (pen), Stephenson J	15,000
Apr 17	OLDHAM ATHLETIC	D 0-0		15,000
Apr 21	MANCHESTER CITY	W 4-1	Nash 2, Hampton 2 (1 pen)	15,000
Apr 26	Manchester United	L 0-1		8,000
Apr 28	Newcastle United	L 0-3		10,000

FA Cup

Jan 9	EXETER CITY	(Rd 1) W 2-0	Stephenson C, Bache	13,000
Jan 30	Manchester City	(Rd 2) L 0-1		29,661

League & Cup Appearances

PLAYER	LEAGUE	CUP COMPETITION FA CUP	TOTAL
Anstey	1		1
Bache	24	2	26
Barber	14	1	15
Boyne	4		4
Dobson	5	1	6
Ducat	26	2	28
Dyke	3		3
Edgley	35	1	36
Hampton G	3		3
Hampton H	30	2	32
Hardy	37	2	39
Harrop	32	2	34
Humphries	6	1	7
Leach	27		27
Littlewood	34	2	36
Lyons	21	1	22
McLachlan J	1		1
Morris	16	1	17
Moss	2		2
Nash	5		5
Stephenson C	37	2	39
Stephenson J	11		11
Wallace	30	2	32
Weston	12		12
Whittaker	2		2

Goalscorers

PLAYER	LEAGUE	CUP COMPETITION FA CUP	TOTAL
Hampton H	19		19
Stephenson C	11	1	12
Edgley	8		8
Bache	4	1	5
Nash	5		5
Barber	3		3
Ducat	3		3
Harrop	2		2
Leach	2		2
Wallace	2		2
Humphries	1		1
Stephenson J	1		1
Whittaker	1		1

Fact File

Harold Nash scored a hat-trick on his league debut for Villa in the 6-2 home win over Liverpool on 3 April 1915.

MANAGER: Committee

CAPTAIN: Joe Bache, Clem Stephenson

TOP SCORER: Harry Hampton, 19 (all league)

BIGGEST WIN: 6-2 v Liverpool (H), Division One, 3 April 1915

HIGHEST ATTENDANCE: 30,000 v Tottenham Hotspur (A), Division One, 24 October 1914

MAJOR TRANSFERS IN: Harold Nash from Pontypridd

MAJOR TRANSFERS OUT: Sammy Whittaker to Walsall

Final Division One Table

		P	W	D	L	F	A	Pts
1	EVERTON	38	19	8	11	76	47	46
2	OLDHAM ATH	38	17	11	10	70	56	45
3	BLACKBURN R	38	18	7	13	83	61	43
4	BURNLEY	38	18	7	13	61	47	43
5	MANCHESTER C	38	15	13	10	49	39	43
6	SHEFFIELD U	38	15	13	10	49	41	43
7	SHEFFIELD W	38	15	13	10	61	54	43
8	SUNDERLAND	38	18	5	15	81	72	41
9	BRADFORD PA	38	17	7	14	69	65	41
10	WBA	38	15	10	13	49	43	40
11	BRADFORD C	38	13	14	11	55	49	40
12	MIDDLESBROUGH	38	13	12	13	62	74	38
13	LIVERPOOL	38	14	9	15	65	75	37
14	ASTON VILLA	38	13	11	14	62	72	37
15	NEWCASTLE U	38	11	10	17	46	48	32
16	NOTTS CO	38	9	13	16	41	57	31
17	BOLTON W	38	11	8	19	68	84	30
18	MANCHESTER U	38	9	12	17	46	62	30
19	CHELSEA	38	8	13	17	51	65	29
20	TOTTENHAM H	38	8	12	18	57	90	28

Season 1919-20

Football League Division One

DATE	OPPONENTS	SCORE	GOALSCORERS	ATTENDANCE
Aug 30	Sunderland	L 1-2	Stephenson C	35,000
Sep 1	DERBY COUNTY	D 2-2	Bourne, Stephenson C	20,000
Sep 6	SUNDERLAND	L 0-3		40,000
Sep 8	Derby County	L 0-1		12,000
Sep 13	Liverpool	L 1-2	Bourne	40,000
Sep 20	LIVERPOOL	L 0-1		30,000
Sep 27	Bradford Park Avenue	L 1-6	Stephenson C	12,000
Oct 4	BRADFORD PARK AVENUE	W 1-0	Stephenson C	30,000
Oct 11	Preston North End	L 0-3		12,000
Oct 18	PRESTON NORTH END	L 2-4	Stephenson C, Dorrell	35,000
Oct 25	Middlesbrough	W 4-1	Boyman 3, Dorrell	18,000
Nov 1	MIDDLESBROUGH	W 5-3	Stephenson C 3, Dorrell, Boyman	30,000
Nov 10	West Bromwich Albion	W 2-1	Stephenson C, Boyman	43,121
Nov 15	WEST BROMWICH ALBION	L 2-4	Kirton, Boyman	58,273
Nov 22	Sheffield United	W 2-1	Kirton 2	25,000
Nov 29	SHEFFIELD UNITED	W 4-0	Stephenson C 4	16,000
Dec 6	MANCHESTER UNITED	W 2-0	Kirton, Boyman	31,000
Dec 13	Manchester United	W 2-1	Stephenson C 2	25,000
Dec 20	OLDHAM ATHLETIC	W 3-0	Edgley, Kirton, Stephenson C	35,000
Dec 25	CHELSEA	W 5-2	Stephenson C 2, Barson, Ducat, Kirton	35,000
Dec 27	Oldham Athletic	W 3-0	Young 2, Kirton	10,000
Jan 1	Newcastle United	L 0-2		50,000
Jan 3	BURNLEY	D 2-2	Stephenson C 2	33,000
Jan 17	Burnley	D 0-0		30,000
Jan 24	Arsenal	W 1-0	Stephenson C	55,000
Feb 7	Everton	D 1-1	Walker	45,000
Feb 11	ARSENAL	W 2-1	Stephenson C 2	20,000
Feb 14	EVERTON	D 2-2	Walker, Kirton	40,000
Feb 28	BRADFORD CITY	W 3-1	Walker, Stephenson C, Kirton	33,000
Mar 13	Bolton Wanderers	L 1-2	Kirton	14,000
Mar 17	Bradford City	L 1-3	Barson (pen)	13,000
Mar 20	BLACKBURN ROVERS	L 1-2	Walker	35,000
Apr 2	Chelsea	L 1-2	Kirton	70,000
Apr 3	NOTTS COUNTY	W 3-1	Boyman, Kirton, Barson (pen)	28,000
Apr 5	NEWCASTLE UNITED	W 4-0	Wallace, Walker 3	45,000
Apr 7	BOLTON WANDERERS	L 3-6	Stephenson C, Walker, Barson (pen)	26,000
Apr 10	Notts County	L 1-2	Davies	17,000
Apr 15	Blackburn Rovers	L 1-5	York	24,000
Apr 17	SHEFFIELD WEDNESDAY	W 3-1	Kirton, Stephenson C, Dorrell	25,000
Apr 26	MANCHESTER CITY	L 0-1		25,000
Apr 29	Sheffield Wednesday	W 1-0	Stephenson C	14,000
May 1	Manchester City	D 2-2	Kirton 2	32,000

FA Cup

Jan 10	QPR	(Rd 1) W 2-1	Walker 2	33,000
Jan 31	Manchester United	(Rd 2) W 2-1	Stephenson C, Walker	48,000
Feb 21	SUNDERLAND	(Rd 3) W 1-0	Stephenson C	31,784
Mar 6	Tottenham Hotspur	(Rd 4) W 1-0	Clay o.g.	52,179
Mar 27	Chelsea*	(SF) W 3-1	Walker 2, Edgley	37,771
Apr 24	Huddersfield Town#	(F) W 1-0†	Kirton	50,018

*Played at Bramall Lane, Sheffield.
#Played at Stamford Bridge, London. †After extra-time.

Fact File

Billy Walker, a future Villa captain and England international, scored twice on his debut in a 2-1 FA Cup win versus QPR on 10 January 1920.

MANAGER: Committee

CAPTAIN: Andy Ducat, Clem Stephenson

TOP SCORER: Clem Stephenson, 29 (27 league)

BIGGEST WIN: 5-2 v Chelsea (H), Division One, 25 December 1919

HIGHEST ATTENDANCE: 70,000 v Chelsea (A), Division One, 2 April 1920

MAJOR TRANSFERS IN: Tommy Ball from Newcastle United, Frank Barson from Barnsley, Tommy Smart from Halesowen, Billy Kirton from Leeds City, Dicky York via RAF

MAJOR TRANSFERS OUT: Harry Hampton to Birmingham

League & Cup Appearances

PLAYER	LEAGUE	CUP COMPETITION FA CUP	TOTAL
Ball	1		1
Barson	26	6	32
Blackburn	8	1	9
Bourne	6		6
Boyman	10		10
Davies	4		4
Dorrell	18	1	19
Ducat	20	6	26
Edgley	19	5	24
Hadley	4		4
Hampson	8	1	9
Hampton	7		7
Hardy	34	6	40
Harrop	31	4	35
Humphries	6		6
Kirton	32	6	38
Lawrence	13	1	14
Lee	8		8
Maiden	1		1
Moss	16	2	18
Nash	7		7
Pendleton	6		6
Sloley	2		2
Smart	11	4	15
Stephenson C	39	6	45
Stephenson J	5		5
Thompson	17		17
Walker	15	6	21
Wallace	31	6	37
Weston	30	5	35
Worrell	4		4
York	17		17
Young	6		6

Goalscorers

PLAYER	LEAGUE	CUP COMPETITION FA CUP	TOTAL
Stephenson C	27	2	29
Kirton	15	1	16
Walker	8	5	13
Boyman	8		8
Barson	4		4
Dorrell	4		4
Bourne	2		2
Edgley	1	1	2
Young	2		2
Davies	1		1
Ducat	1		1
Wallace	1		1
York	1		1
Opps' o.gs.		1	1

Final Division One Table

		P	W	D	L	F	A	Pts
1	WBA	42	28	4	10	104	47	60
2	BURNLEY	42	21	9	12	65	59	51
3	CHELSEA	42	22	5	15	56	51	49
4	LIVERPOOL	42	19	10	13	59	44	48
5	SUNDERLAND	42	22	4	16	72	59	48
6	BOLTON W	42	19	9	14	72	65	47
7	MANCHESTER C	42	18	9	15	71	62	45
8	NEWCASTLE U	42	17	9	16	44	39	43
9	ASTON VILLA	42	18	6	18	75	73	42
10	ARSENAL	42	15	12	15	56	58	42
11	BRADFORD PA	42	15	12	15	60	63	42
12	MANCHESTER U	42	13	14	15	54	50	40
13	MIDDLESBROUGH	42	15	10	17	61	65	40
14	SHEFFIELD U	42	16	8	18	59	69	40
15	BRADFORD C	42	14	11	17	54	63	39
16	EVERTON	42	12	14	16	69	68	38
17	OLDHAM ATH	42	15	8	19	49	52	38
18	DERBY CO	42	13	12	17	47	57	38
19	PRESTON NE	42	14	10	18	57	73	38
20	BLACKBURN R	42	13	11	18	64	77	37
21	NOTTS CO	42	12	12	18	56	74	36
22	SHEFFIELD W	42	7	9	26	28	64	23

The Essential History of Aston Villa

Football League Division One

DATE	OPPONENTS	SCORE	GOALSCORERS	ATTENDANCE
Aug 28	ARSENAL	W 5-0	Walker 4, Stephenson C (pen)	47,000
Aug 30	Manchester City	L 1-3	Walker	35,000
Sep 4	Arsenal	W 1-0	Walker	50,000
Sep 6	MANCHESTER CITY	W 3-1	Walker, Stephenson J, Dorrell	30,000
Sep 11	TOTTENHAM HOTSPUR	W 4-2	Dorrell, Kirton, Walker 2	55,000
Sep 15	Bolton Wanderers	L 0-5		45,000
Sep 18	Tottenham Hotspur	W 2-1	Dorrell, Kirton	45,000
Sep 25	OLDHAM ATHLETIC	W 3-0	Walker 2, Kirton	40,000
Oct 2	Oldham Athletic	D 1-1	Walker	20,000
Oct 9	PRESTON NORTH END	W 1-0	Walker	42,000
Oct 16	Preston North End	L 1-6	Walker	26,000
Oct 23	SHEFFIELD UNITED	W 4-0	Stephenson C 2, Barson, Kirton	40,000
Oct 30	Sheffield United	D 0-0		40,000
Nov 6	WEST BROMWICH ALBION	D 0-0		66,094
Nov 13	West Bromwich Albion	L 1-2	Stephenson C (pen)	42,334
Nov 20	BRADFORD PARK AVENUE	W 4-1	Kirton, Stephenson C, Walker 2	30,000
Nov 27	Bradford Park Avenue	L 0-4		20,000
Dec 4	Newcastle United	L 1-2	Kirton	25,000
Dec 11	NEWCASTLE UNITED	D 0-0		35,000
Dec 18	Liverpool	L 1-4	Walker	40,000
Dec 25	MANCHESTER UNITED	L 3-4	Walker, Stephenson C 2	40,000
Dec 27	Manchester United	W 3-1	Walker 2, Stephenson C	70,504
Jan 1	LIVERPOOL	L 0-2		30,000
Jan 15	EVERTON	L 1-3	Walker	35,000
Jan 23	Everton	D 1-1	Kirton	35,000
Feb 5	Burnley	L 1-7	Humphries	40,000
Feb 9	BURNLEY	D 0-0		40,000
Feb 12	SUNDERLAND	L 1-5	Boyman	40,000
Feb 23	Sunderland	W 1-0	Dorrell	40,000
Feb 26	BRADFORD CITY	L 1-2	Boyman	31,000
Mar 7	Bradford City	L 0-3		23,000
Mar 12	HUDDERSFIELD TOWN	D 0-0		20,000
Mar 19	Huddersfield town	L 0-1		20,000
Mar 26	Middlesbrough	W 4-1	Walker 2, Young 2	25,000
Mar 28	CHELSEA	W 3-0	Walker, Young, Dickson	30,000
Mar 29	Chelsea	L 1-5	Walker	25,000
Apr 2	MIDDLESBROUGH	L 0-1		30,000
Apr 9	Blackburn Rovers	W 1-0	Dickson	25,000
Apr 16	BLACKBURN ROVERS	W 3-0	Moss, Walker, Barson (pen)	20,000
Apr 23	Derby County	W 3-2	Walker, Young 2	14,000
Apr 30	DERBY COUNTY	W 1-0	Boyman	20,000
May 7	BOLTON WANDERERS	W 2-0	Wallace, York	15,000

FA Cup

Jan 8	BRISTOL CITY	(Rd 1) W 2-0	Stephenson C (pen), Walker	49,734
Jan 29	Notts County	(Rd 2) D 0-0		45,014
Feb 2	NOTTS COUNTY	(R) W 1-0	Walker	49,491
Feb 19	HUDDERSFIELD TOWN	(Rd 3) W 2-0	Walker 2	50,627
Mar 7	Tottenham Hotspur	(Rd 4) L 0-1		52,000

League & Cup Appearances

PLAYER	LEAGUE	CUP COMPETITION FA CUP	TOTAL
Ball	13		13
Barson	29	5	34
Blackburn E	4		4
Blackburn G	5		5
Bourne	1		1
Boyman	10		10
Dickson	8		8
Dorrell	34	5	39
Ducat	24	5	29
Hampson	6		6
Hardy	25	5	30
Harrop	20	3	23
Humphries	5		5
Jackson	3		3
Kirton	31	5	36
Leach	1		1
Lee	10		10
Moss	32	4	36
Price	8		8
Smart	37	5	42
Spiers	2		2
Stephenson C	21	5	26
Stephenson J	15	1	16
Thompson	9	2	11
Walker	37	5	42
Wallace	18	4	22
Weston	28	1	29
Wright	2		2
York	11		11
Young	13		13

Goalscorers

PLAYER	LEAGUE	CUP COMPETITION FA CUP	TOTAL
Walker	27	4	31
Stephenson C	8	1	9
Kirton	7		7
Young	5		5
Dorrell	4		4
Boyman	3		3
Barson	2		2
Dickson	2		2
Humphries	1		1
Moss	1		1
Stephenson J	1		1
Wallace	1		1
York	1		1

Fact File

The attendance of 70,504 for the league game away at Manchester United still stands as a record for Old Trafford.

MANAGER: Committee

CAPTAIN: Frank Barson, Andy Ducat, Frank Moss

TOP SCORER: Billy Walker, 31 (27 league)

BIGGEST WIN: 5-0 v Arsenal (H), Division One, 28 August 1920

HIGHEST ATTENDANCE: 70,504 v Manchester United (A), Division One, 27 December 1920

MAJOR TRANSFERS IN: Billy Dickson form Queen of the South, Cyril Spiers from Halesowen, George Blackburn via Army

MAJOR TRANSFERS OUT: Harold Nash to Coventry City

Final Division One Table

		P	W	D	L	F	A	Pts
1	BURNLEY	42	23	13	6	79	36	59
2	MANCHESTER C	42	24	6	12	70	50	54
3	BOLTON W	42	19	14	9	77	53	52
4	LIVERPOOL	42	18	15	9	63	35	51
5	NEWCASTLE U	42	20	10	12	66	45	50
6	TOTTENHAM H	42	19	9	14	70	48	47
7	EVERTON	42	17	13	12	66	55	47
8	MIDDLESBROUGH	42	17	12	13	53	53	46
9	ARSENAL	42	15	14	13	59	63	44
10	ASTON VILLA	42	18	7	17	63	70	43
11	BLACKBURN R	42	13	15	14	57	59	41
12	SUNDERLAND	42	14	13	15	57	60	41
13	MANCHESTER U	42	15	10	17	64	68	40
14	WBA	42	13	14	15	54	58	40
15	BRADFORD C	42	12	15	15	61	63	39
16	PRESTON NE	42	15	9	18	61	65	39
17	HUDDERSFIELD T	42	15	9	18	42	49	39
18	CHELSEA	42	13	13	16	48	58	39
19	OLDHAM ATH	42	9	15	18	49	86	33
20	SHEFFIELD U	42	6	18	18	42	68	30
21	DERBY CO	42	5	16	21	32	58	26
22	BRADFORD PA	42	8	8	26	43	76	24

Season 1921-22

Football League Division One

DATE	OPPONENTS	SCORE	GOALSCORERS	ATTENDANCE
Aug 27	Manchester City	L 1-2	Walker	35,000
Aug 29	CARDIFF CITY	W 2-1	Kirton, Young	30,000
Sep 3	MANCHESTER CITY	W 4-0	Young 2, Kirton, Moss	25,000
Sep 5	Cardiff City	W 4-0	Barson 2 Moss, Dorrell	45,000
Sep 10	Preston North End	L 0-1		30,000
Sep 12	BLACKBURN ROVERS	D 1-1	Walker	25,000
Sep 17	PRESTON NORTH END	W 2-0	Walker 2	28,000
Sep 24	Tottenham Hotspur	L 1-3	Dickson	42,000
Oct 1	TOTTENHAM HOTSPUR	W 2-1	Kirton, Dickson	42,000
Oct 8	West Bromwich Albion	W 1-0	Young	45,077
Oct 15	WEST BROMWICH ALBION	L 0-1		55,000
Oct 22	Middlesbrough	L 0-5		10,000
Oct 29	MIDDLESBROUGH	W 6-2	Dickson 2, York, Kirton Walker, Dorrell	32,000
Nov 5	Bradford City	L 2-3	Walker 2	20,000
Nov 12	BRADFORD CITY	W 7-1	Walker 3 (3 pens) Dickson 2, Dorrell 2	28,000
Nov 19	MANCHESTER UNITED	W 3-1	Walker, Barson Dickson	35,000
Nov 26	Manchester United	L 0-1		40,000
Dec 3	LIVERPOOL	D 1-1	Dickson	30,000
Dec 10	Liverpool	L 0-2		40,000
Dec 17	Newcastle United	W 2-1	Walker, Dickson	30,000
Dec 24	NEWCASTLE UNITED	W 1-0	Dorrell	34,000
Dec 26	Sheffield United	W 3-2	Dickson, York, Barson	40,000
Dec 27	SHEFFIELD UNITED	W 5-3	Dickson 3, Kirton, Walker	38,000
Dec 31	Burnley	L 1-2	Moss	20,000
Jan 14	BURNLEY	W 2-0	Kirton, Walker	35,000
Jan 21	Everton	L 2-3	Kirton 2	30,000
Feb 4	Sunderland	W 4-1	Dickson 2, Walker (pen), Kirton	16,000
Feb 8	EVERTON	W 2-1	Kirton, Dickson	30,000
Feb 11	SUNDERLAND	W 2-0	Walker, Dickson	30,000
Feb 25	HUDDERSFIELD TOWN	W 2-0	Kirton, Dickson	41,000
Mar 11	BIRMINGHAM	D 1-1	Dickson	52,000
Mar 15	Birmingham	L 0-1		34,190
Mar 18	ARSENAL	W 2-0	Dickson, Walker (pen)	21,500
Mar 25	Arsenal	L 0-2		40,000
Apr 1	Blackburn Rovers	W 2-1	Capewell, Dorrell	15,000
Apr 5	Huddersfield Town	L 0-1		17,000
Apr 14	Chelsea	L 0-1		59,557
Apr 15	BOLTON WANDERERS	W 2-1	Walker 2 (1 pen)	25,000
Apr 17	CHELSEA	L 1-4	Walker	20,000
Apr 22	Bolton Wanderers	L 0-1		20,000
Apr 29	OLDHAM ATHLETIC	W 2-0	Walker, Capewell	20,000
May 6	Oldham Athletic	L 1-3	Capewell	12,527

FA Cup

DATE	OPPONENTS		SCORE	GOALSCORERS	ATTENDANCE
Jan 7	DERBY COUNTY	(Rd 1)	W 6-1	Walker 3, Kirton 2, Dickson	41,000
Jan 28	LUTON TOWN	(Rd 2)	W 1-0	Walker	52,832
Feb 18	Stoke City	(Rd 3)	D 0-0		43,589
Feb 22	STOKE CITY	(R)	W 4-0	Dickson 3, Walker	53,385
Mar 4	Notts County	(Rd 4)	D 2-2	Dickson 2	41,375
Mar 8	NOTTS COUNTY	(R)	L 3-4	Dickson 2, Walker	40,161

League & Cup Appearances

PLAYER	LEAGUE	CUP COMPETITION FA CUP	TOTAL
Ball	11	2	13
Barson	37	5	42
Blackburn G	34	5	39
Blackburn E	20		20
Boyman	2		2
Capewell	5		5
Davies	1		1
Dickson	36	6	42
Dorrell	42	6	48
Harkus	1		1
Humphries	3		3
Jackson	39	6	45
Johnstone	6		6
Jones	7		7
Kirton	35	6	41
Leach	1		1
Mort	4		4
Moss	35	6	41
Price	2		2
Smart	39	6	45
Spiers	3		3
Stephenson G	3		3
Taylor	1		1
Walker	36	6	42
Weston	11	6	17
York	41	6	47
Young	7		7

Goalscorers

PLAYER	LEAGUE	CUP COMPETITION FA CUP	TOTAL
Dickson	20	8	28
Walker	21	6	27
Kirton	11	2	13
Dorrell	6		6
Barson	4		4
Young	4		4
Capewell	3		3
Moss	3		3
York	2		2

Fact File

Three Villa players – Frank Moss, Billy Walker and Dicky York – played for England against Scotland at Villa Park in April 1922.

MANAGER: Committee

CAPTAIN: Frank Moss

TOP SCORER: Billy Dickson, 28 (20 league)

BIGGEST WIN: 7-1 v Bradford City (H), Division One, 12 November 1921

HIGHEST ATTENDANCE: 59,557 v Chelsea (A), Division One, 14 April 1922

MAJOR TRANSFERS OUT: Harold Edgeley to QPR, Sam Hardy to Nottingham Forest, Ernie Blackburn to Bradford City, Tommy Weston to Stoke City

Final Division One Table

		P	W	D	L	F	A	Pts
1	LIVERPOOL	42	22	13	7	63	36	57
2	TOTTENHAM H	42	21	9	12	65	39	51
3	BURNLEY	42	22	5	15	72	54	49
4	CARDIFF C	42	19	10	13	61	53	48
5	ASTON VILLA	42	22	3	17	74	55	47
6	BOLTON W	42	20	7	15	68	59	47
7	NEWCASTLE U	42	18	10	14	59	45	46
8	MIDDLESBROUGH	42	16	14	12	79	69	46
9	CHELSEA	42	17	12	13	40	43	46
10	MANCHESTER C	42	18	9	15	65	70	45
11	SHEFFIELD U	42	15	10	17	59	54	40
12	SUNDERLAND	42	16	8	18	60	62	40
13	WBA	42	15	10	17	51	63	40
14	HUDDERSFIELD T	42	15	9	18	53	54	39
15	BLACKBURN R	42	13	12	17	54	57	38
16	PRESTON NE	42	13	12	17	42	65	38
17	THE ARSENAL	42	15	7	20	47	56	37
18	BIRMINGHAM	42	15	7	20	48	60	37
19	OLDHAM ATH	42	13	11	18	38	50	37
20	EVERTON	42	12	12	18	57	55	36
21	BRADFORD C	42	11	10	21	48	72	32
22	MANCHESTER U	42	8	12	22	41	73	28

Season 1922-23

Football League Division One

DATE	OPPONENTS	SCORE	GOALSCORERS	ATTENDANCE
Aug 26	BLACKBURN ROVERS	W 2-0	Kirton, Walker	40,000
Aug 28	Cardiff City	L 0-3		45,000
Sep 2	Blackburn Rovers	L 2-4	York, Kirton	25,000
Sep 4	CARDIFF CITY	L 1-3	Barnie-Adshead	25,000
Sep 9	WEST BROMWICH ALBION	W 2-0	Moss, Capewell	40,000
Sep 16	West Bromwich Albion	L 0-3		39,576
Sep 23	MIDDLESBROUGH	D 2-2	Dorrell, Dickson	27,000
Sep 30	Middlesbrough	D 2-2	Kirton, Walker	25,000
Oct 7	TOTTENHAM HOTSPUR	W 2-0	Dorrell 2	40,000
Oct 14	Tottenham Hotspur	W 2-1	Dickson, Walker	50,500
Oct 21	BOLTON WANDERERS	W 2-0	Walker (pen), York	27,000
Oct 28	Bolton Wanderers	L 0-3		25,000
Nov 4	Oldham Athletic	W 2-0	Kirton, Walker	12,464
Nov 11	OLDHAM ATHLETIC	W 3-0	York, Kirton 2	28,000
Nov 18	Liverpool	L 0-3		30,000
Nov 25	LIVERPOOL	L 0-1		42,000
Dec 2	Sheffield United	D 1-1	Walker	18,000
Dec 9	SHEFFIELD UNITED	L 0-1		20,000
Dec 16	NEWCASTLE UNITED	D 1-1	York	17,000
Dec 23	Newcastle United	D 0-0		30,000
Dec 25	Burnley	W 1-0	York	25,000
Dec 26	BURNLEY	W 3-1	York 3	50,000
Dec 30	PRESTON NORTH END	W 1-0	Walker	30,000
Jan 6	Preston North End	L 2-3	Walker 2	20,000
Jan 20	Nottingham Forest	L 1-3	Dorrell	20,000
Jan 27	NOTTINGHAM FOREST	W 4-0	Dorrell, Dickson 2, Walker	25,000
Feb 3	MANCHESTER CITY	W 2-0	Walker, York	22,000
Feb 10	Manchester City	D 1-1	Capewell	18,000
Feb 17	STOKE CITY	W 6-0	Dickson 3, Walker 2, Roxborough	30,000
Feb 24	Stoke City	D 1-1	Walker	20,000
Mar 3	HUDDERSFIELD TOWN	W 2-1	Roxborough, Moss	25,000
Mar 10	Huddersfield Town	W 5-3	Walker 3, Dorrell, Capewell	15,000
Mar 17	Birmingham	L 0-1		50,000
Mar 24	BIRMINGHAM	W 3-0	Capewell, Walker 2 (2 pens)	40,000
Mar 30	Chelsea	W 1-0	Walker (pen)	30,000
Mar 31	Arsenal	L 0-2		45,000
Apr 2	Chelsea	D 1-1	Walker	30,000
Apr 7	ARSENAL	D 1-1	Walker	18,000
Apr 14	Everton	L 1-2	Capewell	40,000
Apr 21	EVERTON	W 3-0	Walker 2, Kirton	18,000
Apr 28	Sunderland	L 0-2		10,000
May 5	SUNDERLAND	W 1-0	Dorrell	20,000

FA Cup

Jan 13	BLACKBURN ROVERS	(Rd 1)	L 0-1		47,000

League & Cup Appearances

PLAYER	LEAGUE	CUP COMPETITION FA CUP	TOTAL
Ball	35	1	36
Barnie-Adshead	2		2
Blackburn G	38	1	39
Capewell	17		17
Dickson	30	1	31
Dorrell	41	1	42
Harkus	3		3
Harris	5		5
Jackson	8		8
Johnstone	14		14
Jones	3		3
Kirton	31	1	32
Mort	34	1	35
Moss	32	1	33
Roxborough	12		12
Smart	42	1	43
Spiers	34	1	35
Stephenson G	5		5
Walker	40	1	41
York	36	1	37

Goalscorers

PLAYER	LEAGUE	CUP COMPETITION FA CUP	TOTAL
Walker	23		23
York	9		9
Dickson	7		7
Dorrell	7		7
Kirton	7		7
Capewell	5		5
Roxborough	3		3
Moss	2		2
Barnie-Adshead	1		1

Fact File

Frank Barson's transfer to Old Trafford in August 1922 was for a record fee of £5,000.

MANAGER: Committee

CAPTAIN: Frank Moss

TOP SCORER: Billy Walker, 23 (all league)

BIGGEST WIN: 6-0 v Stoke City (H), Division One, 17 February 1923

HIGHEST ATTENDANCE: 50,500 v Tottenham Hotspur (A), Division One, 14 October 1922

MAJOR TRANSFERS IN: John Roxborough from Leicester City, Alec Talbot from Hednesford Town

MAJOR TRANSFERS OUT: Frank Barson to Manchester United

Final Division One Table

		P	W	D	L	F	A	Pts
1	LIVERPOOL	42	26	8	8	70	31	60
2	SUNDERLAND	42	22	10	10	72	54	54
3	HUDDERSFIELD T	42	21	11	10	60	32	53
4	NEWCASTLE U	42	18	12	12	45	37	48
5	EVERTON	42	20	7	15	63	59	47
6	ASTON VILLA	42	18	10	14	64	51	46
7	WBA	42	17	11	14	58	49	45
8	MANCHESTER C	42	17	11	14	50	49	45
9	CARDIFF C	42	18	7	17	73	59	43
10	SHEFFIELD U	42	16	10	16	68	64	42
11	ARSENAL	42	16	10	16	61	62	42
12	TOTTENHAM H	42	17	7	18	50	50	41
13	BOLTON W	42	14	12	16	50	58	40
14	BLACKBURN R	42	14	12	16	47	62	40
15	BURNLEY	42	16	6	20	58	59	38
16	PRESTON NE	42	13	11	18	60	64	37
17	BIRMINGHAM	42	13	11	18	41	57	37
18	MIDDLESBROUGH	42	13	10	19	57	63	36
19	CHELSEA	42	9	18	15	45	53	36
20	NOTTINGHAM F	42	13	8	21	41	70	34
21	STOKE	42	10	10	22	47	67	30
22	OLDHAM ATH	42	10	10	22	35	65	30

Season 1923-24

Football League Division One

DATE	OPPONENTS	SCORE	GOALSCORERS	ATTENDANCE
Aug 25	Birmingham	L 0-3		41,300
Aug 29	MANCHESTER CITY	W 2-0	Walker, York	12,000
Sep 1	BIRMINGHAM	D 0-0		59,147
Sep 5	Manchester City	W 2-1	Capewell, Kirton	33,000
Sep 8	Chelsea	D 0-0		46,000
Sep 12	EVERTON	D 1-1	McBain o.g.	14,000
Sep 15	CHELSEA	D 0-0		22,000
Sep 19	Everton	L 0-2		10,000
Sep 22	Preston North End	D 2-2	Walker, Capewell	21,000
Sep 29	PRESTON NORTH END	W 5-1	Walker 3, Kirton, Capewell	23,000
Oct 6	Burnley	W 2-1	Capewell, Walker	17,000
Oct 13	BURNLEY	D 1-1	Kirton	20,000
Oct 20	West Bromwich Albion	L 0-1		42,096
Oct 27	WEST BROMWICH ALBION	W 4-0	Walker 3, York	52,550
Nov 3	NOTTS COUNTY	D 0-0		17,000
Nov 10	Notts County	W 1-0	Kirton	12,000
Nov 17	LIVERPOOL	D 0-0		27,000
Nov 24	Liverpool	W 1-0	Capewell	30,000
Dec 1	MIDDLESBROUGH	D 0-0		19,900
Dec 8	Middlesbrough	W 2-0	Dickson, Kirton	12,000
Dec 15	Sheffield United	L 1-2	Capewell	30,000
Dec 22	SHEFFIELD UNITED	D 2-2	Capewell 2	19,000
Dec 25	WEST HAM UNITED	D 1-1	Capewell	30,000
Dec 26	West Ham United	L 0-1		21,000
Dec 29	CARDIFF CITY	W 2-1	Capewell, Blair o.g.	54,775
Jan 1	Newcastle United	L 1-4	Dorrell	30,000
Jan 5	Cardiff City	W 2-0	Walker, Capewell	37,000
Jan 19	Bolton Wanderers	L 0-1		25,000
Jan 26	BOLTON WANDERERS	W 1-0	Capewell	56,000
Feb 9	SUNDERLAND	L 0-1		40,000
Feb 13	Sunderland	L 0-2		30,000
Feb 16	Arsenal	W 1-0	Dorrell	30,000
Mar 1	Blackburn Rovers	L 1-3	Capewell	15,000
Mar 12	ARSENAL	W 2-1	Dorrell, Kirton	25,000
Mar 15	TOTTENHAM HOTSPUR	D 0-0		20,000
Mar 22	Tottenham Hotspur	W 3-2	Capewell 3	30,000
Apr 2	BLACKBURN ROVERS	W 1-0	Stephenson	20,000
Apr 5	Huddersfield Town	L 0-1		27,000
Apr 12	Nottingham Forest	D 0-0		12,000
Apr 19	NOTTINGHAM FOREST	W 2-0	Capewell 2	20,000
Apr 21	NEWCASTLE UNITED	W 6-1	Capewell, York, Walker 3, Hunter o.g.	40,000
Apr 30	HUDDERSFIELD TOWN	W 3-1	Walker, Capewell, Dorrell	33,000

FA Cup

DATE	OPPONENTS		SCORE	GOALSCORERS	ATTENDANCE
Jan 12	Ashington	(Rd 1)	W 5-1	Walker 2, Page o.g., Capewell, Blackburn	11,837
Feb 2	Swansea Town	(Rd 2)	W 2-0	Capewell 2	19,036
Feb 23	LEEDS UNITED	(Rd 3)	W 3-0	Capewell 2, Walker	51,000
Mar 8	West Bromwich A	(Rd 4)	W 2-0	Capewell, Dorrell	43,743
Mar 29	Burnley*	(SF)	W 3-0	Kirton, Yorke 2	45,531
Apr 26	Newcastle United#	(F)	L 0-2		91,645

*Played at Bramall Lane, Sheffield. #Played at Wembley.

League & Cup Appearances

PLAYER	LEAGUE	CUP COMPETITION FA CUP	TOTAL
Armfield	3		3
Ball	14		14
Blackburn	35	5	40
Bowen	2		2
Campbell	1		1
Capewell	39	6	45
Corbett	1		1
Dickson	2		2
Dorrell	39	6	45
Harris	2		2
Jackson	35	6	41
Jones	5		5
Johnstone	12	2	14
Kirton	39	6	45
MacKay	2		2
McClure	5		5
Milne	24	5	29
Mort	36	6	42
Moss	33	4	37
Singleton	2		2
Smart	39	6	45
Spiers	5		5
Stephenson	9		9
Surtees	2		2
Talbot		1	1
Varco	2		2
Walker	36	6	42
York	37	6	43

Goalscorers

PLAYER	LEAGUE	CUP COMPETITION FA CUP	TOTAL
Capewell	20	6	26
Walker	14	3	17
Kirton	6	1	7
Dorrell	4	1	5
York	3	2	5
Blackburn		1	1
Dickson	1		1
Stephenson	1		1
Opps' o.gs.	3	1	4

Fact File

This season saw Frank Moss become the first player to captain Aston Villa and England at Wembley – leading his club in the FA Cup final and his country against Scotland.

MANAGER: Committee

CAPTAIN: Frank Moss

TOP SCORER: Len Capewell, 26 (20 league)

BIGGEST WIN: 6-1 v Newcastle United (H), Division One, 21 April 1924

HIGHEST ATTENDANCE: 91,645 v Newcastle, FA Cup final at Wembley, 26 April 1924

MAJOR TRANSFERS IN: Dr Vic Milne from Aberdeen

MAJOR TRANSFERS OUT: Bill Dickson to Middlesbrough, Tommy Ball – murdered (killed by neighbouring police officer)

Final Division One Table

		P	W	D	L	F	A	Pts
1	HUDDERSFIELD T	42	23	11	8	60	33	57
2	CARDIFF C	42	22	13	7	61	34	57
3	SUNDERLAND	42	22	9	11	71	54	53
4	BOLTON W	42	18	14	10	68	34	50
5	SHEFFIELD U	42	19	12	11	69	49	50
6	ASTON VILLA	42	18	13	11	52	37	49
7	EVERTON	42	18	13	11	62	53	49
8	BLACKBURN R	42	17	11	14	54	50	45
9	NEWCASTLE U	42	17	10	15	60	54	44
10	NOTTS CO	42	14	14	14	44	49	42
11	MANCHESTER C	42	15	12	15	54	71	42
12	LIVERPOOL	42	15	11	16	49	48	41
13	WEST HAM U	42	13	15	14	40	43	41
14	BIRMINGHAM	42	13	13	16	41	49	39
15	TOTTENHAM H	42	12	14	16	50	56	38
16	WBA	42	12	14	16	51	62	38
17	BURNLEY	42	12	12	18	55	60	36
18	PRESTON NE	42	12	10	20	52	67	34
19	ARSENAL	42	12	9	21	40	63	33
20	NOTTINGHAM F	42	10	12	20	42	64	32
21	CHELSEA	42	9	14	19	31	53	32
22	MIDDLESBROUGH	42	7	8	27	37	60	22

Season 1924-25

Football League Division One

DATE	OPPONENTS	SCORE	GOALSCORERS	ATTENDANCE
Aug 30	Liverpool	W 4-2	Walker 2, Kirton, Dorrell	45,000
Sep 1	BURY	D 3-3	York, Kirton, Capewell	30,000
Sep 6	NEWCASTLE UNITED	D 0-0		40,000
Sep 8	Bury	L 3-4	Moss, Dorrell, Walker	20,000
Sep 13	Sheffield United	D 2-2	Capewell, Walker	20,000
Sep 20	WEST HAM UNITED	D 1-1	Walker	25,000
Sep 27	Blackburn Rovers	D 1-1	Walker	30,000
Oct 2	Nottingham Forest	W 2-0	Kirton, Walker	12,000
Oct 4	HUDDERSFIELD TOWN	D 1-1	Walker	43,000
Oct 11	Birmingham	L 0-3		48,000
Oct 18	Arsenal	D 1-1	Walker	38,000
Oct 25	WEST BROMWICH ALBION	W 1-0	Dorrell	48,126
Nov 1	Tottenham Hotspur	W 3-1	Stephenson, Capewell, Moss	40,000
Nov 8	BOLTON WANDERERS	D 2-2	Kirton, Walker	25,000
Nov 15	Notts County	D 0-0		25,000
Nov 22	EVERTON	W 3-1	Walker, Dorrell, Varco	30,000
Nov 29	Sunderland	D 1-1	Blackburn	22,000
Dec 6	CARDIFF CITY	L 1-2	Walker	40,000
Dec 13	Preston North End	L 2-3	Walker, Dorrell	8,000
Dec 20	BURNLEY	W 3-0	Kirton, Surtees, Walker	30,000
Dec 25	Leeds United	L 0-6		24,000
Dec 26	LEEDS UNITED	W 2-1	Phoenix 2	50,000
Jan 3	Newcastle United	L 1-4	Kirton	28,000
Jan 17	SHEFFIELD UNITED	D 1-1	York	30,000
Jan 21	Liverpool	L 1-4	Capewell	21,000
Jan 24	West Ham United	L 0-2		25,000
Feb 7	Huddersfield Town	L 1-4	Walker	25,000
Feb 14	BIRMINGHAM	W 1-0	Capewell	60,000
Feb 28	West Bromwich Albion	L 1-4	York	22,123
Mar 7	TOTTENHAM HOTSPUR	L 0-1		20,000
Mar 14	Bolton Wanderers	L 0-4		15,000
Mar 21	NOTTS COUNTY	D 0-0		15,000
Mar 28	Everton	L 0-2		25,000
Apr 1	ARSENAL	W 4-0	York 2, Walker, Dorrell	12,000
Apr 4	SUNDERLAND	L 1-4	Dorrell	10,000
Apr 10	MANCHESTER CITY	W 2-1	Stephenson, Walker	12,500
Apr 11	Cardiff City	L 1-2	York	25,000
Apr 13	Manchester City	L 0-1		20,000
Apr 18	PRESTON NORTH END	W 1-0	Varco	12,000
Apr 25	Burnley	D 1-1	Walker	8,000
Apr 29	BLACKBURN ROVERS	W 4-3	Stephenson 2, Dorrell, Walker	7,000
May 2	NOTTINGHAM FOREST	W 2-0	Stephenson, Morgan o.g.	15,000

FA Cup

Jan 10	PORT VALE	(Rd 1)	W 7-2	Walker 3, Capewell 4	35,600
Jan 31	Swansea Town	(Rd 2)	W 3-1	York, Walker 2	20,000
Feb 21	West Bromwich Albion	(Rd 3)	D 1-1	Walker	64,612
Feb 25	WEST BROMWICH ALBION	(R)	L 1-2	Phoenix	60,015

League & Cup Appearances

PLAYER	LEAGUE	CUP COMPETITION FA CUP	TOTAL
Armfield	2		2
Blackburn G	18	1	19
Bowen	22	4	26
Campbell	3		3
Capewell	17	2	19
Clark	1		1
Corbett	2		2
Dennington	1		1
Dinsdale	5		5
Dorrell	41	4	45
Eccles	10		10
Harris C	15		15
Harris W	4		4
Jackson	8		8
Jakeman	3		3
Johnstone	23	3	26
Jones T	3		3
Kirton	33	4	37
McClure	17	2	19
Milne	21	4	25
Mort	19		19
Moss	19	3	22
Muldoon	17	1	18
Phoenix	3	1	4
Smart	28	4	32
Spiers	34	4	38
Stephenson	13	1	14
Surtees	9		9
Talbot	13		13
Varco	8		8
Walker	35	4	39
York	30	4	34

Goalscorers

PLAYER	LEAGUE	CUP COMPETITION FA CUP	TOTAL
Walker	19	6	25
Capewell	5	4	9
Dorrell	8		8
York	6	1	7
Kirton	6		6
Talbot	5		5
Phoenix	2	1	3
Moss	2		2
Varco	2		2
Blackburn G	1		1
Surtees	1		1
Opps' o.gs.	1		1

Fact File

The attendance of 64,612 at the FA Cup-tie with West Bromwich Albion at the Hawthorns on 21 February 1925 was a club record.

MANAGER: Committee

CAPTAIN: Frank Moss, Billy Walker

TOP SCORER: Billy Walker, 25 (19 league)

BIGGEST WIN: 7-2 v Port Vale (H), FA Cup First Round, 10 January 1925

HIGHEST ATTENDANCE: 64,612 v West Bromwich Albion (A), FA Cup Third Round, 21 February 1925

Final Division One Table

		P	W	D	L	F	A	Pts
1	HUDDERSFIELD T	42	21	16	5	69	28	58
2	WBA	42	23	10	9	58	34	56
3	BOLTON W	42	22	11	9	76	34	55
4	LIVERPOOL	42	20	10	12	63	55	50
5	BURY	42	17	15	10	54	51	49
6	NEWCASTLE U	42	16	16	10	61	42	48
7	SUNDERLAND	42	19	10	13	64	51	48
8	BIRMINGHAM	42	17	12	13	49	53	46
9	NOTTS CO	42	16	13	13	42	31	45
10	MANCHESTER C	42	17	9	16	76	68	43
11	CARDIFF C	42	16	11	15	56	51	43
12	TOTTENHAM H	42	15	12	15	52	43	42
13	WEST HAM U	42	15	12	15	62	60	42
14	SHEFFIELD U	42	13	13	16	55	63	39
15	ASTON VILLA	42	13	13	16	58	71	39
16	BLACKBURN R	42	11	13	18	53	66	35
17	EVERTON	42	12	11	19	40	60	35
18	LEEDS U	42	11	12	19	46	59	34
19	BURNLEY	42	11	12	19	46	75	34
20	ARSENAL	42	14	5	23	46	58	33
21	PRESTON NE	42	10	6	26	37	74	26
22	NOTTINGHAM F	42	6	12	24	29	65	24

Season 1925-26

Football League Division One

DATE	OPPONENTS	SCORE	GOALSCORERS	ATTENDANCE
Aug 29	BURNLEY	W 10-0	Capewell 5, Walker 3, York, Stephenson	43,000
Sep 2	Manchester United	L 0-3		41,717
Sep 5	Leeds United	D 2-2	Dorrell, Walker	30,000
Sep 7	MANCHESTER UNITED	D 2-2	Capewell, York	27,701
Sep 12	NEWCASTLE UNITED	D 2-2	Capewell, Walker (pen)	45,000
Sep 19	Bolton Wanderers	W 3-1	Capewell, York 2	16,000
Sep 26	NOTTS COUNTY	W 2-1	Capewell, Milne	25,000
Oct 3	West Bromwich Albion	D 1-1	Capewell	53,332
Oct 5	SUNDERLAND	W 4-2	Capewell 2, Walker 2	20,000
Oct 10	Leicester City	W 2-1	Capewell, Walker	37,483
Oct 17	BIRMINGHAM	D 3-3	Walker 2, Capewell	55,000
Oct 24	Bury	W 3-2	York 3	14,000
Oct 31	CARDIFF CITY	L 0-2		36,000
Nov 7	Sheffield United	L 1-4	Capewell	22,000
Nov 14	HUDDERSFIELD TOWN	W 3-0	Capewell 3	35,000
Nov 21	Everton	D 1-1	Capewell	27,000
Nov 28	MANCHESTER CITY	W 3-1	Walker, Capewell 2	25,000
Dec 5	Tottenham Hotspur	D 2-2	York 2	35,000
Dec 12	BLACKBURN ROVERS	L 1-2	Walker (pen)	30,000
Dec 19	Sunderland	L 2-3	Walker, Capewell	12,000
Dec 25	West Ham United	L 2-5	Walker, York	16,000
Dec 26	West Ham United	W 2-0	Capewell, Dorrell	50,000
Jan 1	Liverpool	L 1-3	Capewell	30,000
Jan 2	Burnley	W 3-2	Capewell, York 2	28,000
Jan 23	Newcastle United	D 2-2	York, Walker	40,000
Feb 3	LEEDS UNITED	W 3-1	Dorrell, Capewell 2	11,573
Feb 6	Notts County	L 0-1		17,000
Feb 13	WEST BROMWICH ALBION	W 2-1	Walker, Capewell	46,200
Feb 27	Birmingham	L 1-2	Walker	45,000
Mar 6	BURY	D 1-1	Mort	25,000
mar 10	LEICESTER CITY	D 2-2	York 2	10,000
Mar 13	Cardiff City	L 0-2		21,000
Mar 20	SHEFFIELD UNITED	D 2-2	Dorrell, Capewell	22,000
Mar 27	Huddersfield Town	L 1-5	York	32,000
Apr 2	ARSENAL	W 3-0	York, Stephenson, Walker	17,000
Apr 3	EVERTON	W 3-1	York 2, Walker	27,000
Apr 5	Arsenal	L 0-2		25,000
Apr 6	LIVERPOOL	W 3-0	Norris 2, Chester	15,000
Apr 10	Manchester City	L 2-4	Dorrell, Walker	42,000
Apr 17	TOTTENHAM HOTSPUR	W 3-0	Capewell 2, Stephenson	15,000
Apr 24	Blackburn Rovers	L 1-3	Walker (pen)	20,000
Apr 26	BOLTON WANDERERS	D 2-2	Capewell, Smart (pen)	10,000

FA Cup

Jan 9	Hull City	(Rd 1) W 3-0	York, Capewell 2	26,000
Jan 30	West Bromwich Albion	(Rd 2) W 2-1	Walker, Kirton	52,160
Feb 20	ARSENAL	(Rd 3) D 1-1	Kirton	71,446
Feb 24	Arsenal	(R) L 0-2		55,400

League & Cup Appearances

PLAYER	LEAGUE	CUP COMPETITION FA CUP	TOTAL
Armfield	3		3
Blackburn	3		3
Bowen	12		12
Capewell	34	4	38
Chester	3		3
Corbett	3		3
Dinsdale	3		3
Dorrell	38	4	42
Harris C	4		4
Harris W	2		2
Jackson	18	1	19
Jakeman	1		1
Johnstone	34	4	38
Jones T	2		2
Kirton	20	4	24
Milne	24	4	28
Mort	39	4	43
Moss	31	4	35
Muldoon	14		14
Norris	6		6
Smart	29	4	33
Spiers	24	3	27
Stephenson	25		25
Talbot	14		14
Walker	36	4	40
York	40	4	44

Goalscorers

PLAYER	LEAGUE	CUP COMPETITION FA CUP	TOTAL
Capewell	32	2	34
Walker	21	1	22
York	19	1	20
Dorrell	5		5
Stephenson	3		3
Norris	2		2
Chester	1		1
Milne	1		1
Mort	1		1
Smart	1		1

Final Division One Table

		P	W	D	L	F	A	Pts
1	HUDDERSFIELD T	42	23	11	8	92	60	57
2	ARSENAL	42	22	8	12	87	63	52
3	SUNDERLAND	42	21	6	15	96	80	48
4	BURY	42	20	7	15	85	77	47
5	SHEFFIELD U	42	19	8	15	102	82	46
6	ASTON VILLA	42	16	12	14	86	76	44
7	LIVERPOOL	42	14	16	12	70	63	44
8	BOLTON W	42	17	10	15	75	76	44
9	MANCHESTER U	42	19	6	17	66	73	44
10	NEWCASTLE U	42	16	10	16	84	75	42
11	EVERTON	42	12	18	12	72	70	42
12	BLACKBURN R	42	15	11	16	91	80	41
13	WBA	42	16	8	18	79	78	40
14	BIRMINGHAM	42	16	8	18	66	81	40
15	TOTTENHAM H	42	15	9	18	66	79	39
16	CARDIFF C	42	16	7	19	61	76	39
17	LEICESTER C	42	14	10	18	70	80	38
18	WEST HAM U	42	15	7	20	63	76	37
19	LEEDS U	42	14	8	20	64	76	36
20	BURNLEY	42	13	10	19	85	108	36
21	MANCHESTER C	42	12	11	19	89	100	35
22	NOTTS CO	42	13	7	22	54	74	33

Fact File

In this, the first season of the 'new' off-side rule, Aston Villa started off with a bang, firing ten past Burnley on the opening Saturday when Billy Walker (3) and Len Capewell (5) were on devastating form.

MANAGER: Committee

CAPTAIN: Frank Moss, Billy Walker

TOP SCORER: Len Capewell, 34 (32 league)

BIGGEST WIN: 10-0 v Burnley (H), Division One, 29 August 1925

HIGHEST ATTENDANCE: 71,446 v Arsenal (H), FA Cup Third Round, 20 February 1926

MAJOR TRANSFERS IN: Billy Kingdon from Kidderminster Harriers

MAJOR TRANSFERS OUT: Percy Varco to QPR

The Essential History of Aston Villa

Football League Division One

DATE	OPPONENTS	SCORE	GOALSCORERS	ATTENDANCE
Aug 28	Newcastle United	L 0-4		36,000
Aug 30	LIVERPOOL	D 1-1	Capewell	25,000
Sep 4	BURNLEY	D 1-1	Capewell	30,000
Sep 8	Liverpool	L 1-2	Stephenson	27,000
Sep 11	Cardiff City	W 3-2	York, Capewell, Kingdon	12,000
Sep 15	Leeds United	L 1-3	Kirton	13,792
Sep 18	BURY	L 1-2	Stephenson	16,000
Sep 25	BOLTON WANDERERS	L 3-4	York, Harris, Walker	15,000
Oct 2	Manchester United	L 1-2	Harris	31,234
Oct 16	Sunderland	D 1-1	Stephenson	25,000
Oct 23	WEST BROMWICH ALBION	W 2-0	Harris, Walker	49,952
Oct 30	Birmingham	W 2-1	Dorrell, Walker	48,500
Nov 6	TOTTENHAM HOTSPUR	L 2-3	Moss, Walker	23,000
Nov 13	West Ham United	L 1-5	Dorrell	13,000
Nov 20	SHEFFIELD WEDNESDAY	D 2-2	York, Kingdon	14,889
Nov 27	Leicester City	L 1-5	Walker	30,000
Dec 4	EVERTON	W 5-3	Capewell 3, Dorrell, Stephenson	25,000
Dec 11	Blackburn Rovers	W 2-0	Capewell 2	14,000
Dec 18	HUDDERSFIELD TOWN	W 3-0	Dorrell, Walker, Stephenson	25,000
Dec 25	SHEFFIELD UNITED	W 4-0	York, Capewell, Stephenson 2	37,000
Dec 27	Sheffield United	L 1-3	Capewell	50,000
Dec 28	LEEDS UNITED	W 5-1	Capewell, Dorrell, Walker, York, Stephenson	43,963
Jan 15	NEWCASTLE UNITED	L 1-2	Dorrell	50,000
Jan 22	Burnley	L 3-6	Capewell 2, Stephenson	15,000
Jan 29	BLACKBURN ROVERS	W 4-3	Walker 2, Capewell 2	16,000
Jan 31	CARDIFF CITY	D 0-0		10,000
Feb 5	Bury	W 1-0	Capewell	20,000
Feb 12	Bolton Wanderers	W 2-0	Yorke 2	20,000
Feb 19	MANCHESTER UNITED	W 2-0	Cook, York	32,467
Feb 26	Derby County	W 3-2	Stephenson, Cook 2	24,000
Mar 5	SUNDERLAND	W 3-1	Walker 2, Cook	35,000
Mar 12	West Bromwich Albion	L 2-6	York 2	50,392
Mar 19	BIRMINGHAM	W 4-2	Cook, Stephenson, York 2	52,000
Mar 26	Tottenham Hotspur	W 1-0	Cook	32,000
Apr 2	WEST HAM UNITED	L 1-5	Cook	9,020
Apr 15	Arsenal	L 1-2	Walker	42,000
Apr 16	Leicester City	W 2-0	Cook, Johnstone	34,000
Apr 18	ARSENAL	L 2-3	Walker, Stephenson	22,000
Apr 23	Everton	D 2-2	Walker 2	33,394
May 7	Huddersfield Town	D 0-0		17,000

FA Cup

Jan 8	Cardiff City	(Rd 3)	L 1-2	Dorrell	31,000

League & Cup Appearances

PLAYER	LEAGUE	CUP COMPETITION FA CUP	TOTAL
Armfield	1		1
Bowen	31	1	32
Capewell	21	1	22
Chester	4		4
Cook	13		13
Corbett	1		1
Dorrell	38	1	39
Gibson	1		1
Harris	13		13
Jackson	38	1	39
Jakeman	1		1
Johnson	2		2
Johnstone	16	1	17
Kingdon	26		26
Kirton	8		8
Milne	35	1	36
Mort	23	1	24
Moss	35	1	36
Muldoon	2		2
Nicholson	1		1
Norris	3		3
Smart	30		30
Spiers	2		2
Stephenson	36	1	37
Talbot	6		6
Walker	33	1	34
York	42	1	43

Goalscorers

PLAYER	LEAGUE	CUP COMPETITION FA CUP	TOTAL
Capewell	16		16
Walker	15		15
Stephenson	13		13
Yorke	12		12
Cook	9		9
Dorrell	7	1	8
Harris	4		4
Kingdon	2		2
Johnstone	1		1
Kirton	1		1
Moss	1		1

Fact File

In April 1927, Villa paid a record fee of £7,500 for Scottish international half back Jimmy Gibson from Partick Thistle.

MANAGER: Committee

CAPTAIN: Frank Moss

TOP SCORER: Len Capewell, 16 (all league)

BIGGEST WIN: 5-1 v Leeds United (H), Division One, 28 December 1926

HIGHEST ATTENDANCE: 52,000 v Birmingham (H), Division One, 19 March 1927

MAJOR TRANSFERS IN: Billy Cook from Huddersfield Town, Jimmy Gibson from Partick Thistle

MAJOR TRANSFERS OUT: George Blackburn to Cardiff City

Final Division One Table

		P	W	D	L	F	A	Pts
1	NEWCASTLE U	42	25	6	11	96	58	56
2	HUDDERSFIELD T	42	17	17	8	76	60	51
3	SUNDERLAND	42	21	7	14	98	70	49
4	BOLTON W	42	19	10	13	84	62	48
5	BURNLEY	42	19	9	14	91	80	47
6	WEST HAM U	42	19	8	15	86	70	46
7	LEICESTER C	42	17	12	13	85	70	46
8	SHEFFIELD U	42	17	10	15	74	86	44
9	LIVERPOOL	42	18	7	17	69	61	43
10	ASTON VILLA	42	18	7	17	81	83	43
11	ARSENAL	42	17	9	16	77	86	43
12	DERBY CO	42	17	7	18	86	73	41
13	TOTTENHAM H	42	16	9	17	76	78	41
14	CARDIFF C	42	16	9	17	55	65	41
15	MANCHESTER U	42	13	14	15	52	64	40
16	SHEFFIELD W	42	15	9	18	75	92	39
17	BIRMINGHAM	42	17	4	21	64	73	38
18	BLACKBURN R	42	15	8	19	77	96	38
19	BURY	42	12	12	18	68	77	36
20	EVERTON	42	12	10	20	64	90	34
21	LEEDS U	42	11	8	23	69	88	30
22	WBA	42	11	8	23	65	86	30

Season 1927-28

Football League Division One

DATE	OPPONENTS	SCORE	GOALSCORERS	ATTENDANCE
Aug 27	LEICESTER CITY	L 0-3		45,000
Aug 31	Portsmouth	L 1-3	Walker	30,000
Sep 3	Liverpool	D 0-0		35,000
Sep 5	PORTSMOUTH	W 7-2	Beresford 3 (1pen), Cook 2, Dorrell, Walker	22,000
Sep 10	ARSENAL	D 2-2	Beresford, Cook	45,000
Sep 17	Burnley	L 2-4	Cook 2	20,000
Sep 24	BURY	W 1-0	York	30,000
Oct 1	Sheffield United	W 3-0	Dorrell, Cook, Beresford	12,000
Oct 8	MIDDLESBROUGH	W 5-1	Walker, Dorrell, Cook 3	40,000
Oct 15	SUNDERLAND	W 4-2	York, Cook, Walker 2	40,000
Oct 22	Huddersfield Town	D 1-1	Cook	12,000
Oct 29	Newcastle United	W 3-0	Dorrell, Walker, Spencer o.g.	53,000
Nov 5	Birmingham	D 1-1	Walker	50,000
Nov 12	TOTTENHAM HOTSPUR	L 1-2	Cook	26,000
Nov 19	Manchester United	L 1-5	Cook	25,991
Nov 30	BLACKBURN ROVERS	W 2-0	Walker, Beresford	25,000
Dec 3	Cardiff City	L 1-2	Cook	25,000
Dec 10	EVERTON	L 2-3	Cook, Chester	40,353
Dec 17	Bolton Wanderers	L 1-3	Dorrell	15,000
Dec 24	SHEFFIELD WEDNESDAY	W 5-4	Beresford 3, Cook 2	12,345
Dec 26	Derby County	L 0-5		23,491
Dec 27	DERBY COUNTY	L 0-1		45,000
Dec 31	Leicester City	L 0-3		25,000
Jan 7	LIVERPOOL	L 3-4	Chester 2, Capewell	43,858
Jan 21	Arsenal	W 3-0	Dorrell, Smart (pen), Cook	22,000
Feb 4	Bury	D 0-0		8,000
Feb 8	Burnley	W 3-1	Cook, Capewell 2	22,000
Feb 11	SHEFFIELD UNITED	W 1-0	Cook	40,000
Feb 25	Sunderland	W 3-2	Cook, Waring, York	25,000
Mar 10	Newcastle United	L 5-7	Cook, Waring 2, Dorrell, York	25,000
Mar 17	BIRMINGHAM	D 1-1	Smart (pen)	62,000
Mar 21	Middlesbrough	D 0-0		12,000
Mar 24	Tottenham Hotspur	L 1-2	Capewell	40,000
Mar 31	MANCHESTER UNITED	W 3-1	Smart (pen), Waring, Cook	24,691
Apr 6	West Ham United	D 0-0		40,000
Apr 7	Blackburn Rovers	W 1-0	Armfield	13,000
Apr 9	WEST HAM UNITED	W 1-0	Dorrell	19,255
Apr 14	CARDIFF CITY	W 3-1	Beresford, Smart (pen), Waring	16,140
Apr 21	Everton	L 2-3	Waring, Gibson	39,825
Apr 28	BOLTON WANDERERS	D 2-2	Walker, Armfield	20,000
May 2	HUDDERSFIELD TOWN	W 3-0	Walker, Dorrell, Waring	35,000
May 5	Sheffield Wednesday	L 0-2		36,636

FA Cup

Jan 14	Burnley	(Rd 3) W 2-0	Walker, Beresford	26,150
Jan 28	Crewe A	(Rd 4) W 3-0	Cook 3	41,000
Feb 18	Arsenal	(Rd 5) L 1-4	Cook	58,505

League & Cup Appearances

PLAYER	LEAGUE	CUP COMPETITION FA CUP	TOTAL
Armfield	3		3
Beresford	31	3	34
Bowen	32	2	34
Brittleton	2		2
Capewell	6		6
Chester	11	1	12
Cook	35	3	38
Dorrell	36	3	39
Gibson	24		24
Goddard	1		1
Harris	1		1
Hickman	2		2
Jackson	17		17
Johnson	2		2
Kingdon	31	3	34
Milne	37	3	40
Mort	14	1	15
Moss	17	3	20
Olney	20	3	23
Smart	36	3	39
Stephenson	2		2
Talbot	2		2
Tate	4		4
Tully	6		6
Walker	38	3	41
Waring	13		13
Yates	11		11
York	28	2	30

Goalscorers

PLAYER	LEAGUE	CUP COMPETITION FA CUP	TOTAL
Cook	23	4	27
Beresford	10	1	11
Walker	10	1	11
Dorrell	9		9
Waring	7		7
Capewell	4		4
Smart	4		4
York	4		4
Chester	3		3
Armfield	2		2
Gibson	1		1
Opps' o.gs.	1		1

Fact File

In February 1928, a crowd of 23,667 attended Villa's reserve home game with Birmingham to witness the debut of 'Pongo' Waring who scored in a 6-2 win.

MANAGER: Committee

CAPTAIN: Vic Milne, Frank Moss, Billy Walker

TOP SCORER: Billy Cook, 27 (23 league)

BIGGEST WIN: 7-2 v Portsmouth (H), Division One, 5 September 1927

HIGHEST ATTENDANCE: 62,000 v Birmingham (H), Division One, 17 March 1928

MAJOR TRANSFERS IN: Joe Beresford from Mansfield Town, Tom Waring from Tranmere Rovers

MAJOR TRANSFERS OUT: Cyril Spiers to Tottenham Hotspur

Final Division One Table

		P	W	D	L	F	A	Pts
1	EVERTON	42	20	13	9	102	66	53
2	HUDDERSFIELD T	42	22	7	13	91	68	51
3	LEICESTER C	42	18	12	12	96	72	48
4	DERBY CO	42	17	10	15	96	83	44
5	BURY	42	20	4	18	80	80	44
6	CARDIFF C	42	17	10	15	70	80	44
7	BOLTON W	42	16	11	15	81	66	43
8	ASTON VILLA	42	17	9	16	78	73	43
9	NEWCASTLE U	42	15	13	14	79	81	43
10	ARSENAL	42	13	15	14	82	86	41
11	BIRMINGHAM	42	13	15	14	70	75	41
12	BLACKBURN R	42	16	9	17	66	78	41
13	SHEFFIELD U	42	15	10	17	79	86	40
14	SHEFFIELD W	42	13	13	16	81	78	39
15	SUNDERLAND	42	15	9	18	74	76	39
16	LIVERPOOL	42	13	13	16	84	87	39
17	WEST HAM U	42	14	11	17	81	88	39
18	MANCHESTER U	42	16	7	19	72	80	39
19	BURNLEY	42	16	7	19	82	98	39
20	PORTSMOUTH	42	16	7	19	66	90	39
21	TOTTENHAM H	42	15	8	19	74	86	38
22	MIDDLESBROUGH	42	11	15	16	81	88	37

Season 1928-29

Football League Division One

DATE	OPPONENTS	SCORE	GOALSCORERS	ATTENDANCE
Aug 25	Leeds United	L 1-4	York	26,588
Aug 27	MANCHESTER UNITED	D 0-0		30,356
Sep 1	LIVERPOOL	W 3-1	Beresford, York, Capewell	35,000
Sep 8	West Ham United	L 1-4	Capewell	38,000
Sep 15	NEWCASTLE UNITED	D 1-1	Chester	34,146
Sep 22	Burnley	L 1-4	Chester	15,000
Sep 29	CARDIFF CITY	W 1-0	York	30,000
Oct 6	Sheffield United	W 3-1	Waring 2, Dorrell	25,000
Oct 13	BURY	W 7-1	Walker, Waring 2, York 3, Dorrell	36,800
Oct 20	BOLTON WANDERERS	L 3-5	Walker 2, Dorrell	39,829
Oct 27	Birmingham	W 4-2	Waring, Walker 2, Beresford	40,000
Nov 3	DERBY COUNTY	L 2-3	Walker, Dorrell	38,000
Nov 10	Sunderland	W 3-1	Talbot, Walker 2	22,000
Nov 17	BLACKBURN ROVERS	W 2-1	Beresford 2	33,000
Nov 24	Arsenal	W 5-2	Waring 3, York, Talbot	30,491
Dec 1	EVERTON	W 2-0	Waring, Walker	50,000
Dec 8	Huddersfield Town	L 0-3		15,000
Dec 19	MANCHESTER CITY	W 5-1	Gibson, Beresford 2, York 2	13,002
Dec 22	Sheffield Wednesday	L 1-4	Gibson	24,822
Dec 25	Portsmouth	L 2-3	Dorrell, Beresford	25,000
Dec 26	PORTSMOUTH	W 3-2	Waring, Beresford, Walker	56,772
Dec 29	LEEDS UNITED	W 1-0	Waring	31,565
Jan 1	Manchester United	D 2-2	Waring 2	25,935
Jan 5	Liverpool	L 0-4		40,000
Jan 19	West Ham United	W 5-2	Beresford, Chester 2, Walker, York	30,000
Feb 2	BURNLEY	W 4-2	Waring 3, York	28,632
Feb 9	Cardiff City	W 2-0	Beresford, Cook	15,000
Feb 20	SHEFFIELD UNITED	W 3-2	Waring, York 2	15,044
Feb 23	Bury	D 2-2	Smart (pen), Walker	17,000
Mar 9	BIRMINGHAM	L 1-2	Waring	59,322
Mar 13	NEWCASTLE UNITED	L 1-2	York	35,000
Mar 16	Derby County	L 0-1		19,022
Mar 25	SUNDERLAND	W 3-1	England o.g., Cook, Waring	11,989
Mar 30	Blackburn Rovers	W 5-2	Walker 2, Dorrell, Waring, Cook	16,000
Apr 1	Leicester City	L 1-4	Capewell	21,000
Apr 2	LEICESTER CITY	W 4-2	Walker 2, Chester, Waring	26,000
Apr 6	ARSENAL	W 4-2	Beresford, York, Walker, Waring	35,067
Apr 13	Everton	W 1-0	Waring	20,594
Apr 17	Bolton Wanderers	L 1-3	Waring	15,000
Apr 20	HUDDERSFIELD TOWN	W 4-1	Chester 3, Walker	24,821
Apr 27	Manchester City	L 0-3		25,000
May 4	SHEFFIELD WEDNESDAY	W 4-1	Chester, York, Waring, Walker	12,510

FA Cup

Jan 12	CARDIFF CITY	(Rd 3) W 6-1	Tate, Dorrell, Waring, Beresford 2, York	51,242
Jan 26	CLAPTON ORIENT	(Rd 4) D 0-0		53,086
Jan 30	Clapton Orient	(R) W 8-0	Waring 3, Swales, Dorrell, York, Cook, Beresford	27,532
Feb 16	Reading	(Rd 5) W 3-1	Dorrell, Waring 2	23,703
Mar 2	ARSENAL	(Rd 6) W 1-0	Waring	73,686
Mar 23	Portsmouth*	(SF) L 0-1		36,147

*Played at Highbury, London.

Fact File

A record Villa Park crowd of 73,686 saw the sixth round FA Cup victory over Arsenal on 2 March 1929.

MANAGER: Committee

CAPTAIN: Billy Walker

TOP SCORER: Tom 'Pongo' Waring, 32 (25 league)

BIGGEST WIN: 7-1 v Bury (H), Division One, 13 October 1928

HIGHEST ATTENDANCE: 73,686 v Arsenal (H), FA Cup Sixth Round, 2 March 1929

MAJOR TRANSFERS IN: Fred Biddlestone from Walsall

MAJOR TRANSFERS OUT: Billy Kirton to Coventry City, Vic Milne (retired)

League & Cup Appearances

PLAYER	LEAGUE	CUP COMPETITION FA CUP	TOTAL
Beresford	38	6	44
Bowen	34	4	38
Brittleton	7		7
Capewell	5		5
Chester	17	2	19
Cook	9	1	10
Dorrell	25	4	29
Gibson	5		5
Jackson	5		5
Jakeman	3		3
Kingdon	38	6	44
Milne	16		16
Mort	12	3	15
Moss	2		2
Olney	37	6	43
Smart	31	5	36
Swales	5	2	7
Talbot	25	6	31
Tate	30	4	34
Tully	1		1
Walker	36	5	41
Waring	36	6	42
Yates	3		3
York	42	6	48

Goalscorers

PLAYER	LEAGUE	CUP COMPETITION FA CUP	TOTAL
Waring	25	7	32
Walker	19	5	24
York	16	2	18
Beresford	11	3	14
Chester	9		9
Dorrell	6	3	9
Cook	3	1	4
Capewell	3		3
Gibson	2		2
Talbot	2		2
Smart	1		1
Opps' o.gs.	1		1

Final Division One Table

		P	W	D	L	F	A	Pts
1	SHEFFIELD W	42	21	10	11	86	62	52
2	LEICESTER C	42	21	9	12	96	67	51
3	ASTON VILLA	42	23	4	15	98	81	50
4	SUNDERLAND	42	20	7	15	93	75	47
5	LIVERPOOL	42	17	12	13	90	64	46
6	DERBY CO	42	18	10	14	86	71	46
7	BLACKBURN R	42	17	11	14	72	63	45
8	MANCHESTER C	42	18	9	15	95	86	45
9	ARSENAL	42	16	13	13	77	72	45
10	NEWCASTLE U	42	19	6	17	70	72	44
11	SHEFFIELD U	42	15	11	16	86	85	41
12	MANCHESTER U	42	14	13	15	66	76	41
13	LEEDS U	42	16	9	17	71	84	41
14	BOLTON W	42	14	12	16	73	80	40
15	BIRMINGHAM	42	15	10	17	68	77	40
16	HUDDERSFIELD T	42	14	11	17	70	61	39
17	WEST HAM U	42	15	9	18	86	96	39
18	EVERTON	42	17	4	21	63	75	38
19	BURNLEY	42	15	8	19	81	103	38
20	PORTSMOUTH	42	15	6	21	56	80	36
21	BURY	42	12	7	23	62	99	31
22	CARDIFF C	42	8	13	21	43	59	29

Season 1929-30

Football League Division One

DATE	OPPONENTS	SCORE	GOALSCORERS	ATTENDANCE
Aug 31	BIRMINGHAM	W 2-1	Chester, York	38,000
Sep 4	Derby County	L 0-4		21,971
Sep 7	Leeds	L 1-4	Beresford	23,649
Sep 9	DERBY COUNTY	D 2-2	Brown, York	23,556
Sep 14	SHEFFIELD WEDNESDAY	L 1-3	Chester (pen)	36,209
Sep 21	Burnley	W 4-1	Brown 2, Chester, Walker (pen)	21,000
Sep 25	ARSENAL	W 5-2	Gibson, Brown 3, Beresford	37,465
Sep 28	SUNDERLAND	W 2-1	Chester, York	30,000
Oct 5	Bolton Wanderers	L 0-3		30,000
Oct 12	EVERTON	W 5-2	Brown 3, Chester (pen), Walker	35,243
Oct 19	LEICESTER CITY	W 3-0	Brown 2, Tate	40,000
Oct 26	Grimsby Town	W 2-0	Chester 2	22,000
Nov 2	MANCHESTER UNITED	W 1-0	Chester	24,292
Nov 9	Huddersfield Town	D 1-1	Walker	24,000
Nov 16	LIVERPOOL	L 2-3	Brown, Beresford	23,000
Nov 23	Middlesbrough	W 3-2	Brown 2, Beresford	25,000
Nov 30	BLACKBURN ROVERS	W 3-0	York, Brown, Beresford	27,000
Dec 7	Newcastle United	D 2-2	Chester, Brown	35,000
Dec 14	SHEFFIELD UNITED	W 5-1	Walker 4, Beresford	20,000
Dec 21	West Ham United	L 2-5	Smart (pen), Brown (pen)	18,000
Dec 25	MANCHESTER CITY	L 0-2		39,803
Dec 26	Manchester City	W 2-1	Brown, Heineman o.g.	70,000
Dec 28	Birmingham	D 1-1	Walker	40,000
Jan 4	LEEDS UNITED	L 3-4	Brown 2, Talbot	32,476
Jan 18	Sheffield Wednesday	L 0-3		34,911
Feb 1	Sunderland	L 1-4	Brown (pen)	28,000
Feb 5	BURNLEY	L 1-2	Beresford	14,672
Feb 12	BOLTON WANDERERS	W 2-0	Beresford, Brown	30,000
Feb 22	Leicester City	L 3-4	Houghton, York 2	17,000
Mar 5	Everton	W 4-3	Houghton 2, Waring, Brown	15,946
Mar 8	Manchester United	W 3-2	Waring 2, Beresford	25,407
Mar 15	HUDDERSFIELD TOWN	W 5-3	Mandley, Brown, Houghton, Waring 2	22,467
Mar 22	Liverpool	L 0-2		35,000
Mar 29	MIDDLESBROUGH	W 4-2	Waring 2, Brown 2	21,142
Apr 2	GRIMSBY TOWN	W 4-1	Houghton 2, Waring, Brown	18,068
Apr 5	Blackburn Rovers	L 0-2		20,000
Apr 12	NEWCASTLE UNITED	W 2-0	Houghton, Brown	35,066
Apr 15	Portsmouth	W 2-1	Houghton, Waring	17,000
Apr 19	Sheffield United	D 3-3	Beresford, Houghton 2	15,000
Apr 21	PORTSMOUTH	L 0-1		20,000
Apr 26	WEST HAM UNITED	L 2-3	Brown (pen), Houghton	21,650
May 3	Arsenal	W 4-2	Houghton, Brown, Waring 2	45,000

FA Cup

Jan 11	READING	(Rd 3) W 5-1	Houghton 2, Brown, Walker (pen) York	39,000
Jan 25	WALSALL	(Rd 4) W 3-1	Walker 2, Brown	74,626
Feb 15	BLACKBURN ROVERS	(Rd 5) W 4-1	Brown 3 (1 pen), Beresford	69,884
Mar 1	HUDDERSFIELD TOWN	(Rd 6) L 1-2	Brown (pen)	65,732

League & Cup Appearances

PLAYER	LEAGUE	CUP COMPETITION	TOTAL
		FA CUP	
Beresford	32	4	36
Biddlestone	14		14
Bowen	24	1	25
Brittleton	1		1
Brocklebank	1		1
Brown G	41	4	45
Chester	20		20
Dorrell	3		3
Gibson	26	3	29
Houghton	19	4	23
Jackson	1		1
Kingdon	21	1	22
Mandley	11		11
Mort	37	4	41
Olney	27	4	31
Smart	22	3	25
Swales	1		1
Talbot	39	4	43
Tate	40	4	44
Walker	31	4	35
Waring	23		23
York	28	4	32

Goalscorers

PLAYER	LEAGUE	CUP COMPETITION	TOTAL
		FA CUP	
Brown G	30	6	36
Houghton	12	2	14
Beresford	10	1	11
Walker	8	3	11
Waring	11		11
Chester	9		9
York	6	1	7
Gibson	1		1
Mandley	1		1
Smart	1		1
Talbot	1		1
Tate	1		1
Opps' o.gs.	1		1

Fact File

This season saw another record crowd at Villa Park – 74,626 against Walsall in the FA Cup – and 30 league goals in his first season for George Brown.

MANAGER: Committee

CAPTAIN: Jimmy Gibson, Billy Walker

TOP SCORER: George Brown, 36 (30 league)

BIGGEST WIN: 5-1 v Sheffield United (H), Division One, 14 December 1929; v Reading (H), FA Cup Third Round, 11 January 1930

HIGHEST ATTENDANCE: 74,626 v Walsall (H), FA Cup Fourth Round, 25 January 1930

MAJOR TRANSFERS IN: George Brown from Huddersfield Town, Jack Mandley from Port Vale

MAJOR TRANSFERS OUT: Len Capewell to Walsall

Final Division One Table

		P	W	D	L	F	A	Pts
1	SHEFFIELD W	42	26	8	8	105	57	60
2	DERBY CO	42	21	8	13	90	82	50
3	MANCHESTER C	42	19	9	14	91	81	47
4	ASTON VILLA	42	21	5	16	92	83	47
5	LEEDS U	42	20	6	16	79	63	46
6	BLACKBURN R	42	19	7	16	99	93	45
7	WEST HAM U	42	19	5	18	86	79	43
8	LEICESTER C	42	17	9	16	86	90	43
9	SUNDERLAND	42	18	7	17	76	80	43
10	HUDDERSFIELD T	42	17	9	16	63	69	43
11	BIRMINGHAM	42	16	9	17	67	62	41
12	LIVERPOOL	42	16	9	17	63	79	41
13	PORTSMOUTH	42	15	10	17	66	62	40
14	ARSENAL	42	14	11	17	78	66	39
15	BOLTON W	42	15	9	18	74	74	39
16	MIDDLESBROUGH	42	16	6	20	82	84	38
17	MANCHESTER U	42	15	8	19	67	88	38
18	GRIMSBY T	42	15	7	20	73	89	37
19	NEWCASTLE U	42	15	7	20	71	92	37
20	SHEFFIELD U	42	15	6	21	91	96	36
21	BURNLEY	42	14	8	20	79	97	36
22	EVERTON	42	12	11	19	80	92	35

Season 1930-31

Football League Division One

DATE	OPPONENTS	SCORE	GOALSCORERS	ATTENDANCE
Aug 31	Manchester United	W 4-3	Waring 4	18,004
Sep 1	SHEFFIELD WEDNESDAY	W 2-0	Waring, Brown	27,622
Sep 6	WEST HAM UNITED	W 6-1	Houghton, Walker, Waring 4	40,000
Sep 9	Grimsby Town	W 2-1	Waring, Houghton	10,000
Sep 13	Bolton Wanderers	D 1-1	Waring	15,500
Sep 15	GRIMSBY TOWN	W 2-0	Houghton, Waring	32,000
Sep 20	LIVERPOOL	W 4-2	Houghton, Brown, Walker Waring	34,000
Sep 27	Middlesbrough	L 1-3	Beresford	15,500
Oct 4	HUDDERSFIELD TOWN	W 6-1	Houghton 2, Walker 3, Waring	22,177
Oct 11	Sunderland	D 1-1	Houghton	35,000
Oct 18	BIRMINGHAM	D 1-1	Waring	59,787
Oct 25	Leicester City	L 1-4	Waring	37,483
Nov 1	BLACKBURN ROVERS	W 5-2	Waring 2, Houghton 2, Beresford	26,252
Nov 8	Arsenal	L 2-5	Waring 2	64,000
Nov 15	DERBY COUNTY	L 4-6	Houghton 2 (1 pen), Talbot, Waring	37,563
Nov 22	Blackpool	D 2-2	Chester, Mandley	14,000
Dec 3	PORTSMOUTH	D 2-2	Gibson, Mandley	28,000
Dec 6	Sheffield United	W 4-3	Waring 2, Houghton, Beresford	19,000
Dec 13	LEEDS UNITED	W 4-3	Mandley, Houghton, Waring, Walker	26,272
Dec 20	Manchester City	L 1-3	Waring	30,000
Dec 25	Chelsea	W 2-0	Waring, Walker	25,000
Dec 26	CHELSEA	D 3-3	Waring 2, Houghton (pen)	47,218
Dec 27	MANCHESTER UNITED	W 7-0	Mandley 2, Brown 2, Houghton 2 (pens), Beresford	32,505
Jan 1	Newcastle United	L 0-2		50,000
Jan 3	West Ham United	D 5-5	Beresford 2, Walker, Brown, Houghton (pen)	16,000
Jan 17	Bolton Wanderers	W 3-1	Houghton, Waring, Mandley	16,000
Jan 24	Liverpool	D 1-1	Walker	30,000
Jan 31	MIDDLESBROUGH	W 8-1	Houghton 2 (1 pen), Mandley Beresford, Waring 2, Walker 2	15,000
Feb 7	Huddersfield Town	W 6-1	Waring 2, Houghton 2, Gibson, Beresford	21,000
Feb 18	SUNDERLAND	W 4-2	Waring 4	23,500
Feb 21	Birmingham	W 4-0	Tate, Mandley, Houghton, Beresford	50,000
Feb 28	LEICESTER CITY	W 4-2	Waring, Beresford 3	24,000
Mar 7	Blackburn Rovers	W 2-0	Beresford, Waring	15,000
Mar 14	ARSENAL	W 5-1	Waring 2 , Walker, Houghton 2	40,000
Mar 21	Derby County	D 1-1	Houghton	24,466
Mar 28	BLACKPOOL	W 4-1	Waring 3, Houghton	20,000
Apr 4	Portsmouth	L 0-5		38,000
Apr 7	NEWCASTLE UNITED	W 4-3	Walker 2, Waring, Houghton	32,000
Apr 11	SHEFFIELD UNITED	W 4-0	Walker, Houghton (pen), Waring 2	30,000
Apr 18	Leeds United	W 2-0	Waring, Chester	10,388
Apr 25	MANCHESTER CITY	W 4-2	Chester, Beresford, Waring, Houghton	17,000
May 2	Sheffield Wednesday	L 0-3		12,419

FA Cup

Jan 10	Arsenal	(Rd 3) D 2-2	Brown, Walker	40,864
Jan 14	ARSENAL	(R) L 1-3	Waring	73,632

League & Cup Appearances

PLAYER	LEAGUE	CUP COMPETITION FA CUP	TOTAL
Beresford	28	2	30
Biddlestone	14		14
Bowen	26		26
Brown	16	1	17
Chester	8		8
Gibson	39	2	41
Houghton	41	2	43
Kingdon	2		2
Maggs	12	2	14
Mandley	32	2	34
Miles	16		16
Mort	35	2	37
Smart	23	2	25
Talbot	42	2	44
Tate	42	2	44
Walker	42	2	44
Waring	39	1	40
Wood	1		1
York	4		4

Goalscorers

PLAYER	LEAGUE	CUP COMPETITION FA CUP	TOTAL
Waring	49	1	50
Houghton	30	2	32
Walker	15	1	16
Beresford	14		14
Mandley	8		8
Brown	5	1	6
Chester	3		3
Gibson	2		2
Talbot	1		1
Tate	1		1

Fact File

Villa scored in every home game and they also netted 128 league goals (a record), yet only finished runners-up to Arsenal.

Final Division One Table

		P	W	D	L	F	A	Pts
1	ARSENAL	42	28	10	4	127	59	66
2	ASTON VILLA	42	25	9	8	128	78	59
3	SHEFFIELD W	42	22	8	12	102	75	52
4	PORTSMOUTH	42	18	13	11	84	67	49
5	HUDDERSFIELD T	42	18	12	12	81	65	48
6	DERBY CO	42	18	10	14	94	79	46
7	MIDDLESBROUGH	42	19	8	15	98	90	46
8	MANCHESTER C	42	18	10	14	75	70	46
9	LIVERPOOL	42	15	12	15	86	85	42
10	BLACKBURN R	42	17	8	17	83	84	42
11	SUNDERLAND	42	16	9	17	89	85	41
12	CHELSEA	42	15	10	17	64	67	40
13	GRIMSBY T	42	17	5	20	82	87	39
14	BOLTON W	42	15	9	18	68	81	39
15	SHEFFIELD U	42	14	10	18	78	84	38
16	LEICESTER C	42	16	6	20	80	95	38
17	NEWCASTLE U	42	15	6	21	78	87	36
18	WEST HAM U	42	14	8	20	79	94	36
19	BIRMINGHAM	42	13	10	19	55	70	36
20	BLACKPOOL	42	11	10	21	71	125	32
21	LEEDS U	42	12	7	23	68	81	31
22	MANCHESTER U	42	7	8	27	53	115	22

MANAGER: Committee

CAPTAIN: Billy Walker

TOP SCORER: Pongo Waring, 50 (49 league)

BIGGEST WIN: 8-1 v Middlesbrough (H), Division One, 31 January 1931

HIGHEST ATTENDANCE: 73,632 v Arsenal (H), FA Cup Third Round Replay, 14 January 1931

Season 1931-32

Football League Division One

DATE	OPPONENTS	SCORE	GOALSCORERS	ATTENDANCE
Aug 29	LEICESTER CITY	W 3-2	Houghton, Waring 2	21,000
Aug 31	Huddersfield Town	D 1-1	Waring	14,500
Sep 5	Liverpool	L 0-2		40,000
Sep 12	GRIMSBY TOWN	W 7-0	Beresford, Houghton 2, Mandley 2, Walker, Waring	20,000
Sep 19	Chelsea	W 6-3	Waring 4, Houghton 2	56,000
Sep 26	WEST HAM UNITED	W 5-2	Waring 4, Houghton	40,000
Oct 3	Sheffield Wednesday	L 0-1		28,798
Oct 10	BOLTON WANDERERS	W 2-1	Houghton, Walker	41,240
Oct 17	Portsmouth	W 3-0	Beresford, Walker, Astley	21,000
Oct 24	EVERTON	L 2-3	Houghton, Mandley	61,663
Oct 31	Arsenal	D 1-1	Waring	59,674
Nov 7	BLACKPOOL	W 5-1	Waring 3, Houghton, Beresford	42,000
Nov 14	West Bromwich Albion	L 0-3		59,674
Nov 21	BIRMINGHAM	W 3-2	Walker, Waring 2	49,900
Nov 28	Manchester City	D 3-3	Smart (pen), Waring 2	30,000
Dec 5	DERBY COUNTY	W 2-0	Houghton 2	32,871
Dec 12	Sheffield United	L 4-5	Gibson, Waring, Walker, Houghton	20,000
Dec 19	BLACKBURN ROVERS	L 1-5	Walker	29,540
Dec 25	MIDDLESBROUGH	W 7-1	Houghton 3, Beresford 3, Mort	35,000
Dec 26	Middlesbrough	D 1-1	Chester	30,000
Dec 28	NEWCASTLE UNITED	W 3-0	Chester, Waring, Houghton	45,000
Jan 1	Newcastle United	L 1-3	Beresford	46,000
Jan 2	Leicester City	W 8-3	Brown 5, Walker 2, Beresford	25,000
Jan 16	LIVERPOOL	W 6-1	Houghton, Brown 4, Stephenson	35,000
Jan 30	CHELSEA	L 1-3	Beresford	46,000
Feb 2	Grimsby Town	D 2-2	Mandley, Waring	12,000
Feb 6	West Ham United	L 1-2	Beresford	18,000
Feb 20	Bolton Wanderers	L 1-2	Waring	18,000
Feb 24	SHEFFIELD WEDNESDAY	W 3-1	Walker, Houghton, Waring	12,045
Feb 27	Portsmouth	L 0-1		17,000
Mar 5	Everton	L 2-4	Astley, Waring	39,190
Mar 19	Blackpool	W 3-1	Waring 2, Houghton (pen)	15,000
Mar 25	Sunderland	D 1-1	Astley	27,000
Mar 26	WEST BROMWICH ALBION	W 2-0	Astley, Houghton	51,000
Mar 28	SUNDERLAND	W 2-0	Brown, Houghton	35,000
Apr 2	Birmingham	D 1-1	Houghton	48,000
Apr 9	Manchester City	W 2-1	Chester (pen), Brown	30,000
Apr 16	Derby County	L 1-3	Chester	14,967
Apr 23	Sheffield United	W 5-0	Talbot, Waring, Astley 2, Mandley	20,000
Apr 25	ARSENAL	D 1-1	Mandley	24,000
Apr 30	Blackburn Rovers	L 0-2		12,000
May 7	Huddersfield Town	L 2-3	Waring, Moore	12,464

FA Cup

Jan 9	West Bromwich Albion	(Rd 3) W 2-1	Houghton, Brown	49,232
Jan 23	Portsmouth	(Rd 4) D 1-1	Beresford	36,946
Jan 27	PORTSMOUTH	(R) L 0-1		55,080

League & Cup Appearances

PLAYER	LEAGUE	CUP COMPETITION FA CUP	TOTAL
Astley	15		15
Beresford	31	3	34
Biddlestone	14		14
Blair	10		10
Bowen	5		5
Brown	14	3	17
Chester	13		13
Gibson	34	3	37
Houghton	36	3	39
Kingdon	1	1	2
Mandley	32	1	33
Moore	1		1
Mort	33	3	36
Morton	28	3	31
Simpson	2		2
Smart	36	3	39
Stephenson	2	2	4
Talbot	42	3	45
Tate	36		36
Walker	28	3	31
Waring	38		38
Wood	11		11

Goalscorers

PLAYER	LEAGUE	CUP COMPETITION FA CUP	TOTAL
Waring	30		30
Houghton	23	1	24
Brown	11	1	12
Beresford	9	1	10
Walker	9		9
Astley	6		6
Mandley	6		6
Chester	4		4
Gibson	1		1
Moore	1		1
Mort	1		1
Smart	1		1
Stephenson	1		1
Talbot	1		1

Final Division One Table

		P	W	D	L	F	A	Pts
1	EVERTON	42	26	4	12	116	64	56
2	ARSENAL	42	22	10	10	90	48	54
3	SHEFFIELD W	42	22	6	14	96	82	50
4	HUDDERSFIELD T	42	19	10	13	80	63	48
5	ASTON VILLA	42	19	8	15	104	72	46
6	WBA	42	20	6	16	77	55	46
7	SHEFFIELD U	42	20	6	16	80	75	46
8	PORTSMOUTH	42	19	7	16	62	62	45
9	BIRMINGHAM	42	18	8	16	78	67	44
10	LIVERPOOL	42	19	6	17	81	93	44
11	NEWCASTLE U	42	18	6	18	80	87	42
12	CHELSEA	42	16	8	18	69	73	40
13	SUNDERLAND	42	15	10	17	67	73	40
14	MANCHESTER C	42	13	12	17	83	73	38
15	DERBY CO	42	14	10	18	71	75	38
16	BLACKBURN R	42	16	6	20	89	95	38
17	BOLTON W	42	17	4	21	72	80	38
18	MIDDLESBROUGH	42	15	8	19	64	89	38
19	LEICESTER C	42	15	7	20	74	94	37
20	BLACKPOOL	42	12	9	21	65	102	33
21	GRIMSBY T	42	13	6	23	67	98	32
22	WEST HAM U	42	12	7	23	62	107	31

Fact File

Their emphatic 8-3 victory at Leicester in early January remains Villa's best ever away win in the Football League.

MANAGER: Committee

CAPTAIN: Billy Walker, Joe Tate

TOP SCORER: Pongo Waring, 30 (all League)

BIGGEST WIN: 8-3 v Leicester City (A), First Division, 2 January 1932

HIGHEST ATTENDANCE: 61,663 v Everton (H), Division One, 24 October 1931

MAJOR TRANSFERS IN: Dai Astley from Charlton Athletic, Danny Blair from Clyde

MAJOR TRANSFERS OUT: Percy Maggs to Torquay United

Season 1932-33

Football League Division One

DATE	OPPONENTS	SCORE	GOALSCORERS	ATTENDANCE
Aug 27	Middlesbrough	W 2-0	Brown, Walker	20,000
Aug 29	SUNDERLAND	W 1-0	Brown	26,000
Sep 3	BOLTON WANDERERS	W 6-1	Brown 4, Beresford 2	24,000
Sep 7	Sunderland	D 1-1	Brown	25,000
Sep 10	Liverpool	D 0-0		40,000
Sep 17	LEICESTER CITY	W 4-2	Brown 2, Walker, Houghton	25,000
Sep 24	Portsmouth	W 4-2	Brown 2, Astley 2	31,442
Oct 1	CHELSEA	W 3-1	Gibson, Astley 2	40,000
Oct 8	Huddersfield Town	D 0-0		22,000
Oct 15	SHEFFIELD UNITED	W 3-0	Walker, Brown, Houghton	18,000
Oct 22	BIRMINGHAM	W 1-0	Houghton	54,000
Oct 29	West Bromwich Albion	L 1-3	Houghton	42,093
Nov 5	BLACKPOOL	W 6-2	Houghton 2, Brown, Walker 2, Mandley	30,000
Nov 12	Everton	D 3-3	Astley, Brown, Mandley	38,769
Nov 19	ARSENAL	W 5-3	Houghton 2, Gibson, Mandley, Brown	58,640
Nov 26	Manchester City	L 2-5	Astley, Houghton	22,000
Dec 3	SHEFFIELD WEDNESDAY	L 3-6	Brown, Astley 2	31,518
Dec 10	Leeds United	D 1-1	Houghton (pen)	23,794
Dec 17	BLACKBURN ROVERS	W 4-0	Astley 2, Brown 2	25,000
Dec 24	Derby County	D 0-0		26,043
Dec 26	WOLVERHAMPTON WANDERERS	L 1-3	Astley	50,000
Dec 27	Wolverhampton Wanderers	W 4-2	Brown 2, Mandley, Beresford	40,000
Dec 31	MIDDLESBROUGH	W 3-1	Houghton (pen), Mandley, Beresford	22,000
Jan 7	Bolton Wanderers	W 1-0	Mandley	24,000
Jan 21	LIVERPOOL	W 5-2	Waring 2, Houghton, Gibson, Beresford	25,000
Feb 4	PORTSMOUTH	W 4-1	Brown, Watkins, Waring 2	27,000
Feb 9	Leicester City	L 0-3		16,000
Feb 11	Chelsea	W 1-0	Mandley	30,000
Feb 18	HUDDERSFIELD TOWN	L 0-3		24,000
Mar 8	Birmingham	L 2-3	Mandley, Brown	50,000
Mar 11	WEST BROMWICH ALBION	W 3-2	Astley 2, Brown	50,600
Mar 18	Blackpool	L 2-6	Chester, Simpson	12,000
Mar 25	EVERTON	W 2-1	Brown, Beresford	27,463
Apr 1	Arsenal	L 0-5		60,000
Apr 8	MANCHESTER CITY	D 1-1	Brown	20,000
Apr 15	Sheffield Wednesday	W 2-0	Wood, Brown	16,445
Apr 17	Newcastle United	L 1-3	Brown	22,000
Apr 18	NEWCASTLE UNITED	W 3-0	Wood, Brown 2	25,000
Apr 22	LEEDS UNITED	D 0-0		21,238
Apr 24	Sheffield United	L 0-1		17,700
Apr 29	Blackburn Rovers	W 5-0	Brown 4, Houghton	3,624
May 6	DERBY COUNTY	W 2-0	Cunliffe, Astley	32,738

FA Cup

Jan 14	Bradford City	(Rd 3) D 2-2	Mandley, Brown	26,852
Jan 18	BRADFORD CITY	(R) W 2-1	Brown, Tate	35,000
Jan 28	SUNDERLAND	(Rd 4) L 0-3		53,686

League & Cup Appearances

PLAYER	LEAGUE	CUP COMPETITION FA CUP	TOTAL
Astley	28		28
Beresford	18	3	21
Blair	37	3	40
Bowen	1		1
Brown	38	2	40
Callaghan	3	2	5
Chester	6		6
Cunliffe	1		1
Dix	1		1
Gibson	38	3	41
Houghton	42	3	45
Kingdon	18		18
Mandley	25	3	28
Mort	33	3	36
Morton	41	3	44
Nibloe	12		12
Simpson	13		13
Smart	2		2
Talbot	20	1	21
Tate	27	3	30
Tewkesbury	1		1
Tidman	1		1
Walker	30	3	33
Waring	5	1	6
Watkins A	8		8
Wood	13		13

Goalscorers

PLAYER	LEAGUE	CUP COMPETITION FA CUP	TOTAL
Brown	33	2	35
Astley	14		14
Houghton	13		13
Mandley	8	1	9
Beresford	6		6
Walker	5		5
Waring	4		4
Gibson	3		3
Wood	2		2
Chester	1		1
Dix	1		1
Simpson	1		1
Tate		1	1
Watkins A	1		1

Fact File

Fourteen goals out of centre forward George Brown's total of 33 in the league were scored against Lancashire clubs.

MANAGER: Committee

CAPTAIN: Joe Tate, Billy Walker

TOP SCORER: George Brown, 35 (33 league)

BIGGEST WIN: 6-1 v Bolton Wanderers (H), Division One, 3 September 1932

HIGHEST ATTENDANCE: 60,000 v Arsenal (A), Division One, 1 April 1933

MAJOR TRANSFERS IN: Arthur Cunliffe and Ronnie Dix from Blackburn Rovers, Joe Nibloe from Sheffield Wednesday

Final Division One Table

		P	W	D	L	F	A	Pts
1	ARSENAL	42	25	8	9	118	61	58
2	ASTON VILLA	42	23	8	11	92	67	54
3	SHEFFIELD W	42	21	9	12	80	68	51
4	WBA	42	20	9	13	83	70	49
5	NEWCASTLE U	42	22	5	15	71	63	49
6	HUDDERSFIELD T	42	18	11	13	66	53	47
7	DERBY CO	42	15	14	13	76	69	44
8	LEEDS U	42	15	14	13	59	62	44
9	PORTSMOUTH	42	18	7	17	74	76	43
10	SHEFFIELD U	42	17	9	16	74	80	43
11	EVERTON	42	16	9	17	81	74	41
12	SUNDERLAND	42	15	10	17	63	80	40
13	BIRMINGHAM	42	14	11	17	57	57	39
14	LIVERPOOL	42	14	11	17	79	84	39
15	BLACKBURN R	42	14	10	18	76	102	38
16	MANCHESTER C	42	16	5	21	68	71	37
17	MIDDLESBROUGH	42	14	9	19	63	73	37
18	CHELSEA	42	14	7	21	63	73	35
19	LEICESTER C	42	11	13	18	75	89	35
20	WOLVERHAMPTON W	42	13	9	20	80	96	35
21	BOLTON W	42	12	9	21	78	92	33
22	BLACKPOOL	42	14	5	23	69	85	33

Season 1933-34

Football League Division One

DATE	OPPONENTS	SCORE	GOALSCORERS	ATTENDANCE
Aug 26	LEICESTER CITY	L 2-3	Astley, Waring	42,000
Aug 28	Sheffield Wednesday	W 2-1	Houghton, Astley	19,185
Sep 2	Tottenham Hotspur	L 2-3	Waring, Astley	44,974
Sep 4	SHEFFIELD WEDNESDAY	W 1-0	Waring	22,581
Sep 9	LIVERPOOL	W 4-2	Astley, Talbot, Houghton 2	30,000
Sep 16	Chelsea	L 0-1		37,000
Sep 23	SUNDERLAND	W 2-1	Houghton, Astley	40,000
Sep 30	Portsmouth	L 2-3	Astley, Cunliffe	21,000
Oct 7	HUDDERSFIELD TOWN	W 4-3	Houghton 2, Astley, Waring	18,858
Oct 14	Stoke City	D 1-1	Cunliffe	37,511
Oct 21	Manchester City	L 0-1		35,000
Oct 28	ARSENAL	L 2-3	Waring 2	55,300
Nov 4	Leeds United	W 4-2	Astley, Houghton, Waring 2	20,148
Nov 11	MIDDLESBROUGH	W 3-0	Houghton, Beresford, Cunliffe	30,000
Nov 18	Blackburn Rovers	L 1-2	Cunliffe	20,000
Nov 25	NEWCASTLE UNITED	L 2-3	Astley, Waring	40,000
Dec 2	Birmingham	D 0-0		35,000
Dec 9	DERBY COUNTY	L 0-2		30,478
Dec 16	West Bromwich Albion	L 1-2	Astley	25,503
Dec 23	EVERTON	W 2-1	Astley, Houghton	24,438
Dec 25	WOLVERHAMPTON WANDERERS	W 6-2	Waring 2, Astley, Mandley 2, Dix	57,000
Dec 26	Wolverhampton Wanderers	L 3-4	Chester 2, Dix	42,000
Dec 30	Leicester City	D 1-1	Astley	15,140
Jan 1	Sheffield United	D 3-3	Houghton 2, Waring	20,000
Jan 9	TOTTENHAM HOTSPUR	L 1-5	Astley	31,770
Jan 20	Liverpool	W 3-2	Dix, Waring 2	40,000
Feb 3	Sunderland	L 1-5	Astley	24,000
Feb 7	CHELSEA	W 2-0	Astley, Houghton	26,000
Feb 10	PORTSMOUTH	D 1-1	Astley	21,450
Feb 21	Huddersfield Town	L 1-2	Cunliffe	23,000
Feb 24	STOKE CITY	L 1-2	Beresford	19,000
Mar 7	MANCHESTER CITY	D 0-0		20,000
Mar 10	Arsenal	L 2-3	Dix, Houghton	40,000
Mar 24	Middlesbrough	W 2-1	Houghton, Astley	13,000
Mar 31	BLACKBURN ROVERS	D 1-1	Talbot	16,400
Apr 2	SHEFFIELD UNITED	W 3-0	Astley, Houghton, Beresford	13,500
Apr 7	Newcastle United	D 1-1	Houghton	30,000
Apr 14	BIRMINGHAM	D 1-1	Dix	40,000
Apr 21	Derby County	D 1-1	Astley	14,149
Apr 28	WEST BROMWICH ALBION	D 4-4	Astley, Houghton 2 (1 pen), Beresford	20,050
Apr 30	LEEDS UNITED	W 3-0	Astley 3	9,849
May 5	Everton	D 2-2	Astley, Houghton	12,610

FA Cup

DATE	OPPONENTS		SCORE	GOALSCORERS	ATTENDANCE
Jan 13	Chesterfield	(Rd 3)	D 2-2	Cunliffe 2	23,878
Jan 17	CHESTERFIELD	(R)	W 2-0	Astley, Beresford	25,400
Jan 27	SUNDERLAND	(Rd 4)	W 7-2	Astley 4, Houghton 3	57,268
Feb 17	Tottenham Hotspur	(Rd 5)	W 1-0	Astley	44,365
Mar 3	Arsenal	(Rd 6)	W 2-1	Astley, Houghton	67,566
Mar 17	Manchester City*	(SF)	L 1-6	Astley	45,473

*Played at Leeds Road, Huddersfield.

League & Cup Appearances

PLAYER	LEAGUE	CUP COMPETITION FA CUP	TOTAL
Astley	38	6	44
Beresford	21	6	27
Blair	33	5	38
Bowen	2		2
Brocklebank	3		3
Brown	6	3	9
Callaghan	2		2
Chester	2		2
Cunliffe	33	6	39
Dix	28	5	33
Gardner	12		12
Gibson	27	1	28
Houghton	41	6	47
Kingdon	32	5	37
Mandley	6		6
Mort	13	6	19
Morton	42	6	48
Nibloe	36	4	40
Simpson	11		11
Talbot	27	6	33
Tate	1		1
Walker	5		5
Waring	27	1	28
Wood	14		14

Goalscorers

PLAYER	LEAGUE	CUP COMPETITION FA CUP	TOTAL
Astley	25	8	33
Houghton	19	4	23
Waring	14		14
Cunliffe	5	2	7
Beresford	4	1	5
Dix	5		5
Chester	2		2
Mandley	2		2
Talbot	2		2

Fact File

The lowest league attendance at Villa Park for nine years – 9,849 – saw Villa beat Leeds 3-0 on 30 April 1934.

MANAGER: Committee

CAPTAIN: Alec Talbot

TOP SCORER: Dai Astley 33, (25 league)

BIGGEST WIN: 7-2 v Sunderland (H), FA Cup Fourth Round, 27 January 1934

HIGHEST ATTENDANCE: 67,566 v Arsenal (A), FA Cup Sixth Round, 3 March 1934

MAJOR TRANSFERS IN: Tom Gardner from Hull City

MAJOR TRANSFERS OUT: Billy Walker (retired to become manager of Sheffield Wednesday)

Final Division One Table

		P	W	D	L	F	A	Pts
1	ARSENAL	42	25	9	8	75	47	59
2	HUDDERSFIELD T	42	23	10	9	90	61	56
3	TOTTENHAM H	42	21	7	14	79	56	49
4	DERBY CO	42	17	11	14	68	54	45
5	MANCHESTER C	42	17	11	14	65	72	45
6	SUNDERLAND	42	16	12	14	81	56	44
7	WBA	42	17	10	15	78	70	44
8	BLACKBURN R	42	18	7	17	74	81	43
9	LEEDS U	42	17	8	17	75	66	42
10	PORTSMOUTH	42	15	12	15	52	55	42
11	SHEFFIELD W	42	16	9	17	62	67	41
12	STOKE C	42	15	11	16	58	71	41
13	ASTON VILLA	42	14	12	16	78	75	40
14	EVERTON	42	12	16	14	62	63	40
15	WOLVERHAMPTON W	42	14	12	16	74	86	40
16	MIDDLESBROUGH	42	16	7	19	68	80	39
17	LEICESTER C	42	14	11	17	59	74	39
18	LIVERPOOL	42	14	10	18	79	87	38
19	CHELSEA	42	14	8	20	67	69	36
20	BIRMINGHAM	42	12	12	18	54	56	36
21	NEWCASTLE U	42	10	14	18	68	77	34
22	SHEFFIELD U	42	12	7	23	58	101	31

Season 1934-35

Football League Division One

DATE	OPPONENTS	SCORE	GOALSCORERS	ATTENDANCE
Aug 25	Birmingham	L 1-2	Waring	54,200
Aug 27	WOLVERHAMPTON WANDERERS	W 2-1	Astley, Dix	34,663
Sep 1	DERBY COUNTY	W 3-2	Houghton, Waring 2	44,267
Sep 3	Wolverhampton Wanderers	L 2-5	Dix, Houghton	25,000
Sep 8	Leicester City	L 0-5		30,000
Sep 15	SUNDERLAND	D 1-1	Astley	35,127
Sep 22	Tottenham Hotspur	W 2-0	Waring, Houghton	44,000
Sep 29	PRESTON NORTH END	W 4-2	Astley 3, Waring	29,000
Oct 6	Grimsby Town	L 1-5	Astley	15,000
Oct 13	EVERTON	D 2-2	Astley, Waring	37,707
Oct 20	Stoke City	L 1-4	Waring	34,000
Oct 27	MANCHESTER CITY	W 4-2	Astley, Waring 2, Houghton	27,000
Nov 3	West Bromwich Albion	D 2-2	Richardson o.g., Houghton	44,503
Nov 10	SHEFFIELD WEDNESDAY	W 4-0	Waring 2, Astley 2	25,300
Nov 17	Arsenal	W 2-1	Houghton, Brocklebank	57,000
Nov 26	PORTSMOUTH	W 5-4	Chester 2, Brocklebank, Houghton 2 (1pen)	17,500
Dec 1	Liverpool	L 1-3	Waring	20,000
Dec 8	LEEDS UNITED	D 1-1	Milburn o.g.	31,682
Dec 15	Middlesbrough	L 1-4	Astley	15,000
Dec 22	BLACKBURN ROVERS	D 1-1	Waring	25,000
Dec 25	Chelsea	L 0-2		50,000
Dec 26	CHELSEA	L 0-3		53,000
Dec 29	BIRMINGHAM	D 2-2	Astley, Waring	42,000
Jan 5	Derby County	D 1-1	Houghton	24,674
Jan 19	LEICESTER CITY	W 5-0	Astley 3, Cunliffe, Beresford	25,000
Feb 2	TOTTENHAM HOTSPUR	W 1-0	Dix	24,669
Feb 6	Sunderland	D 3-3	Cunliffe, Beresford, Dix	25,000
Feb 9	Preston North End	D 0-0		21,000
Feb 16	GRIMSBY TOWN	W 3-2	Houghton, Kingdon, Astley	20,000
Feb 23	Everton	D 2-2	Astley 2	30,772
Mar 2	STOKE CITY	W 4-1	Dix, Astley 3	35,000
Mar 9	Manchester City	L 1-4	Houghton	25,000
Mar 23	Sheffield Wednesday	L 1-2	Cunliffe	12,495
Mar 30	ARSENAL	L 1-3	Houghton	59,707
Apr 3	WEST BROMWICH ALBION	L 2-3	Dix, Watkin	55,067
Apr 6	Portsmouth	W 1-0	Watkin	20,000
Apr 13	LIVERPOOL	W 4-2	Cunliffe, Watkin, Broome 2	20,000
Apr 19	HUDDERSFIELD TOWN	D 1-1	Watkin	28,000
Apr 20	Leeds United	D 1-1	Kingdon	16,234
Apr 24	Huddersfield Town	D 1-1	Broome	9,000
Apr 27	Middlesbrough	L 0-3		15,000
May 4	Blackburn Rovers	L 0-5		4,700

FA Cup

Jan 12	BRADFORD CITY	(Rd 3)	L 1-3	Hamilton o.g.	30,795

League & Cup Appearances

PLAYER	LEAGUE	CUP COMPETITION FA CUP	TOTAL
Allen J	33	1	34
Astley	32	1	33
Beeson	40	1	41
Beresford	23		23
Blair	37	1	38
Broome	7		7
Brocklebank	11	1	12
Brown	1		1
Butcher	2		2
Callaghan	1		1
Chester	9	1	10
Cunliffe	26		26
Dix	24		24
Gardner	34	1	35
Gibson	9		9
Houghton	41	1	42
Kingdon	35	1	36
McLuckie	1		1
Mort	5		5
Morton	42	1	43
Simpson	3		3
Talbot	10		10
Waring	24	1	25
Watkin	11		11
Wood	1		1

Goalscorers

PLAYER	LEAGUE	CUP COMPETITION FA CUP	TOTAL
Astley	21		21
Waring	14		14
Houghton	12		12
Dix	6		6
Cunliffe	4		4
Watkin	4		4
Broome	3		3
Beresford	2		2
Brocklebank	2		2
Chester	2		2
Kingdon	2		2
Opps' o.gs.	2	1	3

Fact File

Harry Morton became the first Villa goalkeeper to be an ever-present in successive seasons.

MANAGER: Jimmy McMullan

CAPTAIN: Jimmy Allen, Eric Houghton

TOP SCORER: Dai Astley, 21 (all league)

BIGGEST WIN: 5-0 v Leicester City (H), Division One, 19 January 1935

HIGHEST ATTENDANCE: 59,707 v Arsenal (H), Division One, 30 March 1935

MAJOR TRANSFERS IN: George Beeson from Sheffield Wednesday, Frank Broome from Berkhampstead, Jimmy Allen from Portsmouth

MAJOR TRANSFERS OUT: Bowen to Norwich City, George Brown to Burnley

Final Division One Table

		P	W	D	L	F	A	Pts
1	ARSENAL	42	23	12	7	115	46	58
2	SUNDERLAND	42	19	16	7	90	51	54
3	SHEFFIELD W	42	18	13	11	70	64	49
4	MANCHESTER C	42	20	8	14	82	67	48
5	GRIMSBY T	42	17	11	14	78	60	45
6	DERBY CO	42	18	9	15	81	66	45
7	LIVERPOOL	42	19	7	16	85	88	45
8	EVERTON	42	16	12	14	89	88	44
9	WBA	42	17	10	15	83	83	44
10	STOKE C	42	18	6	18	71	70	42
11	PRESTON NE	42	15	12	15	62	67	42
12	CHELSEA	42	16	9	17	73	82	41
13	ASTON VILLA	42	14	13	15	74	88	41
14	PORTSMOUTH	42	15	10	17	71	72	40
15	BLACKBURN R	42	14	11	17	66	78	39
16	HUDDERSFIELD T	42	14	10	18	76	71	38
17	WOLVERHAMPTON W	42	15	8	19	88	94	38
18	LEEDS U	42	13	12	17	75	92	38
19	BIRMINGHAM	42	13	10	19	63	81	36
20	MIDDLESBROUGH	42	10	14	18	70	90	34
21	LEICESTER C	42	12	9	21	61	86	33
22	TOTTENHAM H	42	10	10	22	54	93	30

Season 1935-36

Football League Division One

DATE	OPPONENTS	SCORE	GOALSCORERS	ATTENDANCE
Aug 31	SHEFFIELD WEDNESDAY	L 1-2	Cunliffe	48,637
Sep 4	MIDDLESBROUGH	W 2-1	Waring, Houghton	16,000
Sep 7	Portsmouth	L 0-3		20,000
Sep 9	Middlesbrough	L 2-7	Dix 2	25,000
Sep 14	PRESTON NORTH END	W 5-1	Houghton, Astley 2, Waring, Kingdon	14,000
Sep 16	SUNDERLAND	D 2-2	Waring 2	32,000
Sep 21	Brentford	W 2-1	Waring, Astley	20,000
Sep 28	DERBY COUNTY	L 0-2		49,474
Oct 5	Everton	D 2-2	Broome 2	26,682
Oct 12	BOLTON WANDERERS	L 1-2	Houghton (pen)	36,000
Oct 19	WEST BROMWICH ALBION	L 0-7		38,037
Oct 26	Leeds United	L 2-4	Astley, Dix	35,000
Nov 1	GRIMSBY TOWN	L 2-6	McLuckie, Houghton	21,000
Nov 9	Liverpool	L 2-3	Houghton, Broome	40,000
Nov 16	CHELSEA	D 2-2	Drinkwater, Palethorpe	59,000
Nov 23	Birmingham	D 2-2	Astley 2	60,250
Nov 30	STOKE CITY	W 4-0	Dix, Williams 2, Houghton	44,000
Dec 7	Manchester City	L 0-5		35,000
Dec 14	ARSENAL	L 1-7	Palethorpe	60,891
Dec 21	Blackburn Rovers	L 1-5	Broome	5,000
Dec 25	HUDDERSFIELD TOWN	W 4-1	Astley 3, Houghton	45,000
Dec 26	Huddersfield Town	L 1-4	Dix	19,000
Dec 28	Sheffield Wednesday	L 2-5	Houghton, Williams	25,371
Jan 1	Sunderland	W 3-1	Dix 2, Massie	26,000
Jan 4	PORTSMOUTH	W 4-2	Astley 2, Houghton 2	17,000
Jan 18	Preston North End	L 0-3		15,000
Jan 25	BRENTFORD	D 2-2	Williams, Astley	40,000
Feb 1	Derby County	W 3-1	Phillips, Williams, Astley	30,087
Feb 8	EVERTON	D 1-1	Astley	53,837
Feb 15	Bolton Wanderers	L 3-4	Hodgson, Astley, Houghton	21,000
Feb 29	LIVERPOOL	W 3-0	Hodgson, Astley, Maund	19,000
Mar 7	Stoke City	W 3-2	Astley 2, Phillips	20,000
Mar 14	LEEDS UNITED	D 3-3	Astley, Massie, Maund	37,382
Mar 21	Chelsea	L 0-1		40,000
Mar 28	BIRMINGHAM	W 2-1	Broome, Hughes o.g.	50,000
Apr 1	West Bromwich Albion	W 3-0	Astley, Broome 2	28,821
Apr 6	Grimsby Town	L 1-4	Broome	12,324
Apr 10	WOLVERHAMPTON WANDERERS	W 4-2	Houghton, Broome 2, Astley	51,000
Apr 11	MANCHESTER CITY	D 2-2	Hodgson, Houghton	42,000
Apr 13	Wolverhampton Wanderers	D 2-2	Hodgson, Houghton	44,500
Apr 18	Arsenal	L 0-1		39,540
Apr 25	BLACKBURN ROVERS	L 2-4	Broome, Houghton	26,000

FA Cup

Jan 11	HUDDERSFIELD TOWN	(Rd 3)	L 0-1		62,620

League & Cup Appearances

PLAYER	LEAGUE	CUP COMPETITION FA CUP	TOTAL
Allen	22	1	23
Astley	38	1	39
Beeson	16		16
Beresford	2		2
Biddlestone	21		21
Blair	12		12
Brocklebank	4		4
Broome	16	1	17
Callaghan	13		13
Cummings	27	1	28
Cunliffe	9		9
Dix	26	1	27
Drinkwater	2		2
Gardner	5		5
Gibson	10		10
Griffiths	26	1	27
Hodgson	15		15
Houghton	40	1	41
Kingdon	19	1	20
McLuckie	14		14
Massie	24	1	25
Maund	4		4
Morton	21	1	22
Palethorpe	6		6
Phillips	11		11
Waring	10		10
Watkin	2		2
Williams	17		17
Wood	21	1	22
Young	9		9

Goalscorers

PLAYER	LEAGUE	CUP COMPETITION FA CUP	TOTAL
Astley	21		21
Houghton	15		15
Broome	11		11
Dix	7		7
Waring	5		5
Williams	5		5
Hodgson	4		4
Massie	2		2
Maund	2		2
Palethorpe	2		2
Phillips	2		2
Cunliffe	1		1
Drinkwater	1		1
Kingdon	1		1
McLuckie	1		1
Opps' o.gs.	1		1

Fact File

Villa were relegated from Division One for the first time along with another 'founder member' of the Football League – Blackburn Rovers.

MANAGER: Jimmy McMullan

CAPTAIN: Jimmy Allen, Eric Houghton

TOP SCORER: Dai Astley, 21 (all league)

BIGGEST WIN: 5-1 v Preston North End (H), Division One, 14 September 1935

HIGHEST ATTENDANCE: 62,620 v Huddersfield Town (H), FA Cup Third Round, 11 January 1936

MAJOR TRANSFERS IN: Jack Palethorpe from Sheffield Wednesday, George Cummings from Partick Thistle, Tom Griffiths from Middlesbrough, Gordon Hodgson from Liverpool, Alex Massie from Heart of Midlothian, Clarke Phillips from Wolves, Jackie Williams from Huddersfield Town

MAJOR TRANSFERS OUT: Arthur Cunliffe to Middlesbrough

Final Division One Table

		P	W	D	L	F	A	Pts
1	SUNDERLAND	42	25	6	11	109	74	56
2	DERBY CO	42	18	12	12	61	52	48
3	HUDDERSFIELD T	42	18	12	12	59	56	48
4	STOKE C	42	20	7	15	57	57	47
5	BRENTFORD	42	17	12	13	81	60	46
6	ARSENAL	42	15	15	12	78	48	45
7	PRESTON NE	42	18	8	16	67	64	44
8	CHELSEA	42	15	13	14	65	72	43
9	MANCHESTER C	42	17	8	17	68	60	42
10	PORTSMOUTH	42	17	8	17	54	67	42
11	LEEDS U	42	15	11	16	66	64	41
12	BIRMINGHAM	42	15	11	16	61	63	41
13	BOLTON W	42	14	13	15	67	76	41
14	MIDDLESBROUGH	42	15	10	17	84	70	40
15	WOLVERHAMPTON W	42	15	10	17	77	76	40
16	EVERTON	42	13	13	16	89	89	39
17	GRIMSBY T	42	17	5	20	65	73	39
18	WBA	42	16	6	20	89	88	38
19	LIVERPOOL	42	13	12	17	60	64	38
20	SHEFFIELD W	42	13	12	17	63	77	38
21	ASTON VILLA	42	13	9	20	81	110	35
22	BLACKBURN R	42	12	9	21	55	96	33

The Essential History of Aston Villa

Football League Division Two

DATE	OPPONENTS	SCORE	GOALSCORERS	ATTENDANCE
Aug 29	Swansea Town	W 2-1	Broome 2	26,000
Sep 2	Nottingham Forest	D 1-1	Broome	36,000
Sep 5	SOUTHAMPTON	W 4-0	Broome, Astley, Hodgson, Dix	45,000
Sep 7	NOTTINGHAM FOREST	D 1-1	Astley	28,000
Sep 12	Burnley	W 2-1	Broome, Hodgson	11,000
Sep 14	BRADFORD CITY	W 5-1	Dix, Astley, Hodgson 3	18,000
Sep 19	FULHAM	L 0-3		49,000
Sep 26	Doncaster Rovers	L 0-1		28,000
Oct 3	COVENTRY CITY	D 0-0		63,686
Oct 10	Plymouth Argyle	D 2-2	Broome, Astley	43,686
Oct 17	Bradford Park Avenue	D 3-3	Houghton, Broome, Johnstone o.g.	11,240
Oct 24	BARNSLEY	W 4-2	Broome 2, Astley, Houghton	38,000
Oct 31	Sheffield United	L 1-5	Houghton	30,000
Nov 7	TOTTENHAM HOTSPUR	D 1-1	Moralee	37,000
Nov 11	Bradford City	D 2-2	Griffiths, Dix	15,000
Nov 14	Blackpool	W 3-2	Houghton 2, Hodgson	10,000
Nov 21	BLACKBURN ROVERS	D 2-2	Dix, Houghton	33,000
Oct 28	Bury	L 1-2	Hodgson	25,000
Dec 5	LEICESTER CITY	L 1-3	Massie	30,000
Dec 19	NORWICH CITY	W 3-0	Broome, Dix, Maund	23,243
Dec 25	Chesterfield	L 0 1		20,000
Dec 26	SWANSEA TOWN	W 4-0	Dix 3, Allen	54,690
Dec 28	CHESTERFIELD	W 6-2	Broome 2, Dix 2, Iverson, Allen	29,177
Jan 2	Southampton	D 2-2	Dix 2	20,853
Jan 9	BURNLEY	D 0-0		40,000
Jan 23	Fulham	L 2-3	Haycock, Gardner	18,000
Jan 30	DONCASTER ROVERS	D 1-1	Phillips	9,986
Feb 6	Coventry City	L 0-1		40,000
Feb 13	PLYMOUTH ARGYLE	W 5-4	Houghton 3, Broome 2	41,000
Feb 20	BRADFORD PARK AVENUE	W 4-2	Houghton 2, Broome 2	20,000
Feb 27	Barnsley	W 4-0	Starling 2, Broome, Haycock	14,000
Mar 6	SHEFFIELD UNITED	W 2-1	Broome 2	30,000
Mar 13	Tottenham Hotspur	D 2-2	Haycock, Starling	36,000
Mar 20	BLACKPOOL	W 4-0	Broome 3, Haycock	54,579
Mar 26	Newcastle United	W 2-0	Broome 2	46,000
Mar 27	Blackburn Rovers	W 4-3	Broome 3, Houghton	27,000
Mar 30	Newcastle UNITED	L 0-2		65,500
Apr 3	BURY	L 0-4		47,000
Apr 10	Leicester City	L 0-1		39,127
Apr 17	WEST HAM UNITED	L 0-2		15,000
Apr 24	Norwich City	L 1-5	Broome	25,052
Apr 6	West Ham United	L 1-2	Starling	12,000

FA Cup

Jan 16	BURNLEY	(Rd 3) L 2-3	Houghton, Broome	43,568

League & Cup Appearances

PLAYER	LEAGUE	CUP COMPETITION FA CUP	TOTAL
Allen	11	1	12
Astley	14		14
Beeson	14		14
Biddleston	24		24
Broome	38	1	39
Callaghan	14		14
Cobley	34	1	35
Cummings	12		12
Dix	18	1	19
Gardner	23	1	24
Goss	2		2
Griffiths	39	1	40
Hardy	5		5
Haycock	22	1	23
Hodgson	13		13
Houghton	28	1	29
Iverson	22	1	23
Kerr	9		9
Massie	35		35
Martin	1		1
Maund	30		30
Moralee	12		12
Morton	18	1	19
Phillips	2		2
Pritty	1		1
Robey	3		3
Starling	17		17
Wood	1		1

Goalscorers

PLAYER	LEAGUE	CUP COMPETITION FA CUP	TOTAL
Broome	28	1	29
Houghton	12	1	13
Dix	12		12
Hodgson	7		7
Astley	5		5
Haycock	4		4
Starling	4		4
Allen	2		2
Gardner	1		1
Griffiths	1		1
Iverson	1		1
Massie	1		1
Maund	1		1
Moralee	1		1
Phillips	1		1
Opps' o.gs.	1		1

Fact File

Tom Griffiths scored his only goal for Villa in the 2-2 away draw at Bradford City.

MANAGER: Jimmy McMullan/Jimmy Hogan

CAPTAIN: Tom Griffiths

TOP SCORER: Frank Broome, 29 (28 league)

BIGGEST WIN: 6-2 v Chesterfield (H), Division One, 28 December 1936

HIGHEST ATTENDANCE: 65,500 v Newcastle United (H), Division Two, 30 March 1937

MAJOR TRANSFERS IN: Bob Iverson from Wolves, Ronnie Starling from Sheffield Wednesday

MAJOR TRANSFERS OUT: Dai Astley to Derby County, Billy Kingdon to Southampton, Danny Blair to Blackpool, Pongo Waring to Wolves, Jack Palethorpe to Crystal Palace, Gordon Hodgson to Leeds United, Ronnie Dix to Derby County

Final Division Two Table

		P	W	D	L	F	A	Pts
1	Leicester C	42	24	8	10	89	57	56
2	Blackpool	42	24	7	11	88	53	55
3	Bury	42	22	8	12	74	55	52
4	Newcastle U	42	22	5	15	80	56	49
5	Plymouth Arg	42	18	13	11	71	53	49
6	West Ham U	42	19	11	12	73	55	49
7	Sheffield U	42	18	10	14	66	54	46
8	Coventry C	42	17	11	14	66	54	45
9	Aston Villa	42	16	12	14	82	70	44
10	Tottenham H	42	17	9	16	88	66	43
11	Fulham	42	15	13	14	71	61	43
12	Blackburn R	42	16	10	16	70	62	42
13	Burnley	42	16	10	16	57	61	42
14	Barnsley	42	16	9	17	50	64	41
15	Chesterfield	42	16	8	18	84	89	40
16	Swansea T	42	15	7	20	50	65	37
17	Norwich C	42	14	8	20	63	71	36
18	Nottingham F	42	12	10	20	68	90	34
19	Southampton	42	11	12	19	53	77	34
20	Bradford PA	42	12	9	21	52	88	33
21	Bradford C	42	9	12	21	54	94	30
22	Doncaster R	42	7	10	25	30	84	24

Season 1937-38

Football League Division Two

DATE	OPPONENTS	SCORE	GOALSCORERS	ATTENDANCE
Aug 28	WEST HAM UNITED	W 2-0	Haycock, Maund	51,195
Sep 1	Luton Town	L 2-3	Maund, Massie	29,372
Sep 4	Southampton	D 0-0		25,560
Sep 11	BLACKBURN ROVERS	W 2-1	Haycock, Maund	41,805
Sep 16	Norwich City	L 0-1		23,039
Sep 18	Sheffield Wednesday	W 2-1	Haycock, Iverson	20,663
Sep 25	FULHAM	W 2-0	Broome, Haycock	42,333
Oct 2	Plymouth Argyle	W 3-0	Broome 2, Houghton	32, 936
Oct 9	CHESTERFIELD	L 0-2		50,605
Oct 16	NEWCASTLE UNITED	W 2-0	Houghton 2	50,459
Oct 23	Nottingham Forest	W 2-0	Broome, Houghton	24,846
Oct 30	COVENTRY CITY	D 1-1	Houghton	68,029
Nov 6	Bury	D 1-1	Haycock	16,947
Nov 13	BURNLEY	D 0-0		37,001
Nov 20	Manchester United	L 1-3	Iverson	33,193
Nov 27	SHEFFIELD UNITED	W 1-0	Clayton	35,000
Dec 4	Tottenham Hotspur	L 1-2	Houghton	37,396
Dec 11	STOCKPORT COUNTY	W 7-1	Shell 3, Houghton, Haycock, Broome 2	24,995
Dec 18	Barnsley	W 1-0	Shell	12,035
Dec 27	Bradford Park Avenue	W 2-1	Shell, Haycock	19,874
Dec 28	BARNSLEY	W 3-0	Massie, Broome 2	36,180
Jan 1	West Ham United	D 1-1	Weare o.g.	31,788
Jan 15	SOUTHAMPTON	W 3-0	Haycock 2, Houghton	31,705
Jan 27	Blackburn Rovers	L 0-1		11,872
Jan 29	SHEFFIELD WEDNESDAY	W 4-3	Starling 2, Broome, Houghton (pen)	35,603
Feb 5	Fulham	D 1-1	Houghton	37,690
Feb 19	Chesterfield	W 1-0	Broome	18,556
Feb 23	PLYMOUTH ARGYLE	W 3-0	Broome, Maund, Haycock	24,979
Feb 26	Newcastle United	L 0-2		47,782
Mar 9	NOTTINGHAM FOREST	L 1-2	Hardy	19,846
Mar 12	Coventry City	W 1-0	Starling	44,930
Mar 19	BURY	W 2-1	Broome, Haycock	50,115
Apr 2	MANCHESTER UNITED	W 3-0	Broome, Maund, Houghton (pen)	54,654
Apr 5	Burnley	L 0-3		14,660
Apr 9	Sheffield United	D 0-0		21,890
Apr 16	TOTTENHAM HOTSPUR	W 2-0	Broome 2	60,166
Apr 18	Swansea Town	L 1-2	Starling	25,446
Apr 19	SWANSEA TOWN	W 4-0	Iverson, Shell 2, Houghton	50,387
Apr 23	Stockport County	W 3-1	Haycock, Broome 2	20,452
Apr 27	BRADFORD PARK AVENUE	W 2-0	Broome, Haycock	40,020
May 7	NORWICH CITY	W 2-0	Shell, Haycock	42,337

FA Cup

Jan 8	Norwich City	(Rd 3) W 3-2	Houghton, Haycock, Iverson	33,346
Jan 22	BLACKPOOL	(Rd 4) W 4-0	Houghton, Broome, Shell, Starling	69,208
Feb 12	Charlton Athletic	(Rd 5) D 1-1	Shell	75,031
Feb 16	CHARLTON ATHLETIC	(R) D 2-2	Broome, Shell	61,530
Feb 21	Charlton Athletic*	(2nd R) W 4-1	Broome 3, Haycock	64,783
Mar 5	MANCHESTER CITY	(Rd 6) W 3-2	Broome, Shell, Haycock	75,540
Mar 26	Preston North End#	(SF) L 1-2	Shell	55,129

*Played at Highbury, London. #Played at Bramall Lane, Sheffield.

League & Cup Appearances

PLAYER	LEAGUE	CUP COMPETITION FA CUP	TOTAL
Allen	40	7	47
Barker	3		3
Biddlestone	39	6	45
Broome	38	7	45
Callaghan	40	7	47
Carey	3	1	4
Clayton	9		9
Cobley	8	1	9
Cummings	36	6	42
Gardner	3		3
Hardy	1		1
Haycock	39	7	46
Houghton	34	7	41
Iverson	39	6	45
Kerr	3		3
Martin	1		1
Massie	40	7	47
Maund	13		13
Phillips	9		9
Pritty	2	1	3
Shell	20	7	27
Starling	42	7	49

Goalscorers

PLAYER	LEAGUE	CUP COMPETITION FA CUP	TOTAL
Broome	20	6	26
Haycock	14	3	17
Houghton	12	2	14
Shell	8	5	13
Maund	5		5
Starling	4	1	5
Iverson	3	1	4
Massie	2		2
Phillips	2		2
Clayton	1		1
Hardy	1		1
Opps' o.gs.	1		1

Fact File

The highest ever average home league attendance – 41,856 – cheered Villa to the Second Division championship and subsequent promotion.

MANAGER: Jimmy Hogan

CAPTAIN: Alex Massie

TOP SCORER: Frank Broome, 26 (20 league)

BIGGEST WIN: 7-1 v Stockport County (H), Division Two, 11 December 1937

HIGHEST ATTENDANCE: 75,540 v Manchester City (H), FA Cup Sixth Round, 5 March 1938

MAJOR TRANSFERS IN: Frank Shell from Dagenham

MAJOR TRANSFERS OUT: George Beeson from Walsall

Final Division Two Table

		P	W	D	L	F	A	Pts
1	ASTON VILLA	42	25	7	10	73	35	57
2	MANCHESTER U	42	22	9	11	82	50	53
3	SHEFFIELD U	42	22	9	11	73	56	53
4	COVENTRY C	42	20	12	10	66	45	52
5	TOTTENHAM H	42	19	6	17	76	54	44
6	BURNLEY	42	17	10	15	54	54	44
7	BRADFORD PA	42	17	9	16	69	56	43
8	FULHAM	42	16	11	15	61	57	43
9	WEST HAM U	42	14	14	14	53	52	42
10	BURY	42	18	5	19	63	60	42
11	CHESTERFIELD	42	16	9	17	63	63	41
12	LUTON T	42	15	10	17	89	86	40
13	PLYMOUTH ARG	42	14	12	16	57	65	40
14	NORWICH C	42	14	11	17	56	75	39
15	SOUTHAMPTON	42	15	9	18	55	77	39
16	BLACKBURN R	42	14	10	18	71	80	38
17	SHEFFIELD W	42	14	10	18	49	56	38
18	SWANSEA T	42	13	12	17	45	73	38
19	NEWCASTLE U	42	14	8	20	51	58	36
20	NOTTINGHAM F	42	14	8	20	47	60	36
21	BARNSLEY	42	11	14	17	50	64	36
22	STOCKPORT CO	42	11	9	22	43	70	31

Season 1938-39

Football League Division One

DATE	OPPONENTS	SCORE	GOALSCORERS	ATTENDANCE
Aug 27	Grimsby Town	W 2-1	Broome 2	16,044
Aug 31	Middlesbrough	D 1-1	Houghton (pen)	25,000
Sep 3	DERBY COUNTY	L 0-1		49,604
Sep 5	EVERTON	L 0-3		34,105
Sep 10	Blackpool	W 4-2	Haycock, Kerr, Martin 2	20,000
Sep 17	BRENTFORD	W 5-0	Martin 2, Kerr 2, Houghton	49,462
Sep 24	Arsenal	D 0-0		70,000
Oct 1	PORTSMOUTH	W 2-0	Kerr, Starling	50,579
Oct 8	Huddersfield Town	D 1-1	Broome	20,639
Oct 16	Liverpool	L 0-3		41,224
Oct 22	LEICESTER CITY	L 1-2	Haycock	40,000
Oct 29	Birmingham	L 0-3		55,301
Nov 5	MANCHESTER UNITED	L 0-2		38,257
Nov 12	Stoke City	L 1-3	Kirton o.g.	27,000
Nov 19	CHELSEA	W 6-2	Broome, Haycock 2, O'Donnell 2, Houghton	40,306
Nov 26	Preston North End	L 2-3	Haycock, Broome	25,000
Dec 3	CHARLTON ATHLETIC	W 2-0	Iverson, O'Donnell	24,146
Dec 10	Bolton Wanderers	W 2-1	Houghton, Broome	22,600
Dec 17	LEEDS UNITED	W 2-1	O'Donnell, Houghton (pen)	28,990
Dec 24	GRIMSBY TOWN	L 0-2		21,773
Dec 26	Sunderland	W 5-1	Haycock, Broome 2, O'Donnell, Houghton	29,000
Dec 28	SUNDERLAND	D 1-1	Broome	40,351
Dec 31	Derby County	L 1-2	Houghton	25,759
Jan 14	BLACKPOOL	W 3-1	Houghton 2 (1 pen), Haycock	20,000
Jan 28	ARSENAL	L 1-3	O'Donnell	57,453
Feb 4	Portsmouth	D 0-0		25,000
Feb 8	Brentford	W 4-2	Broome 2, O'Donnell, Haycock	18,000
Feb 15	HUDDERSFIELD TOWN	W 4-0	Broome, O'Donnell 2, Martin	27,500
Feb 18	LIVERPOOL	W 2-0	Broome 2	40,000
Feb 25	Leicester City	D 1-1	O'Donnell	24,000
Mar 4	BIRMINGHAM	W 5-1	Martin 3, Houghton 2 (1 pen)	40,874
Mar 11	Manchester United	D 1-1	Broome	28,292
Mar 18	STOKE CITY	W 3-0	Broome, O'Donnell, Houghton	21,600
Mar 25	Chelsea	L 1-2	Haycock	30,000
Apr 1	PRESTON NORTH END	W 3-0	Martin, O'Donnell 2	25,000
Apr 8	Charlton Athletic	L 0-1		17,000
Apr 10	Wolverhampton Wanderers	L 1-2	O'Donnell	29,987
Apr 11	WOLVERHAMPTON WANDERERS	D 2-2	Iverson, Starling	35,500
Apr 15	BOLTON WANDERERS	L 1-3	Starling	24,000
Apr 22	Leeds United	L 0-2		14,241
Apr 29	Everton	L 0-3		23,667
May 6	MIDDLESBROUGH	D 1-1	Haycock	17,793

FA Cup

Jan 7	IPSWICH TOWN	(Rd 3) D 1-1	Allen	34,910
Jan 11	Ipswich Town	(R) W 2-1	Haycock 2	28,194
Jan 21	Preston North End	(Rd 4) L 0-2		37,548

League & Cup Appearances

PLAYER	LEAGUE	CUP COMPETITION FA CUP	TOTAL
Allen	41	3	44
Biddlestone	25	3	28
Broome	33	3	36
Callaghan	42	3	45
Clayton	2		2
Cobley	2		2
Cummings	40	3	43
Edwards	3		3
Haycock	38	3	41
Houghton	12	3	15
Iverson	42	3	45
Kerr	16		16
Martin	22		22
Massie	42	3	45
Moss F	2		2
O'Donnell	29	2	31
Rutherford	11		11
Shell	3	1	4
Starling	28	3	31
Wakeman	6		6

Goalscorers

PLAYER	LEAGUE	CUP COMPETITION FA CUP	TOTAL
Broome	16		16
O'Donnell	14		14
Haycock	10	2	12
Houghton	12		12
Martin	9		9
Kerr	4		4
Starling	3		3
Iverson	2		2
Allen		1	1
Opps' o.gs.	1		1

Fact File

A combined crowd of 127,453 people saw Aston Villa's league clashes against North London giants Arsenal.

MANAGER: Jimmy Hogan

CAPTAIN: George Cummings

TOP SCORER: Frank Broome, 16 (all league)

BIGGEST WIN: 6-2 v Chelsea (H), Division One, 19 November 1938

HIGHEST ATTENDANCE: 70,000 v Arsenal (A), Division One, 24 September 1938

MAJOR TRANSFERS IN: Frank O'Donnell from Blackpool

MAJOR TRANSFERS OUT: Tom Gardner to Burnley

Final Division One Table

		P	W	D	L	F	A	Pts
1	EVERTON	42	27	5	10	88	52	59
2	WOLVERHAMPTON W	42	22	11	9	88	39	55
3	CHARLTON ATH	42	22	6	14	75	59	50
4	MIDDLESBROUGH	42	20	9	13	93	74	49
5	ARSENAL	42	19	9	14	55	41	47
6	DERBY CO	42	19	8	15	66	55	46
7	STOKE C	42	17	12	13	71	68	46
8	BOLTON W	42	15	15	12	67	58	45
9	PRESTON NE	42	16	12	14	63	59	44
10	GRIMSBY T	42	16	11	15	61	69	43
11	LIVERPOOL	42	14	14	14	62	63	42
12	ASTON VILLA	42	15	11	16	71	60	41
13	LEEDS U	42	16	9	17	59	67	41
14	MANCHESTER U	42	11	16	15	57	65	38
15	BLACKPOOL	42	12	14	16	56	68	38
16	SUNDERLAND	42	13	12	17	54	67	38
17	PORTSMOUTH	42	12	13	17	47	70	37
18	BRENTFORD	42	14	8	20	53	74	36
19	HUDDERSFIELD T	42	12	11	19	58	64	35
20	CHELSEA	42	12	9	21	64	80	33
21	BIRMINGHAM	42	12	8	22	62	84	32
22	LEICESTER C	42	9	11	22	48	82	29

Season 1945-46

Football League South

DATE	OPPONENTS	SCORE	GOALSCORERS	ATTENDANCE
Aug 25	Luton Town	D 1-1	Edwards	12,000
Aug 29	West Bromwich Albion	L 0-1		15,898
Sep 1	LUTON TOWN	W 7-1	Broome 2, Gager o.g., Edwards 4	25,000
Sep 5	WEST BROMWICH ALBION	D 3-3	Edwards, Parkes, Goffin	36,103
Sep 8	SWANSEA TOWN	W 6-3	Iverson 2, Goffin, Kerr 2, Edwards	25,500
Sep 10	West Ham United	W 2-1	Edwards, Martin	23,000
Sep 15	Swansea Town	L 4-5	Goffin, Iverson 2, Kerr	15,000
Sep 22	Arsenal	W 4-2	Iverson 2, Edwards, Kerr	35,000
Sep 29	ARSENAL	W 5-1	Edwards 4, Broome	50,000
Oct 6	Charlton Athletic	D 0-0		50,000
Oct 13	CHARLTON ATHLETIC	L 0-2		48,000
Oct 20	FULHAM	W 3-0	Edwards, Broome, Iverson	15,000
Oct 27	Fulham	W 4-0	Edwards 2, Iverson 2	34,500
Nov 3	Plymouth Argyle	W 3-0	Edwards 3	33,038
Nov 10	PLYMOUTH ARGYLE	W 4-2	Martin 2, Iverson, Edwards	25,000
Nov 17	PORTSMOUTH	W 3-2	Iverson, Guthrie o.g., Edwards	20,000
Nov 24	Portsmouth	W 3-2	Edwards 2, Martin	30,000
Dec 1	NOTTINGHAM FOREST	W 3-1	Parkes, Smith, Edwards	30,000
Dec 8	Nottingham Forest	W 3-1	Martin, Edwards 2	30,224
Dec 19	NEWPORT COUNTY	W 5-2	Graham, Broome 2, Parkes, Edwards	20,000
Dec 22	Newport County	W 4-0	Iverson, Martin, Smith, Edwards	17,500
Dec 25	Wolverhampton Wanderers	W 2-1	Iverson, Edwards	30,000
Dec 28	WOLVERHAMPTON WANDERERS	D 1-1	Martin	59,970
Dec 29	WEST HAM UNITED	D 2-2	Martin, Iverson	34,000
Jan 12	BIRMINGHAM CITY	D 2-2	Jennings o.g., Edwards	63,820
Jan 19	Birmingham City	L 1-3	Edwards	40,000
Feb 2	TOTTENHAM HOTSPUR	W 5-1	Edwards 2, Broome 2, Cummings	25,000
Feb 16	Brentford	W 1-0	Iverson	27,000
Feb 20	Tottenham Hotspur	L 0-3		18,500
Feb 23	Chelsea	D 2-2	Goffin, Iverson	45,000
Mar 16	Millwall	D 2-2	Soo o.g., Broome	11,000
Mar 23	Southampton	W 5-3	Edwards 2, Goffin, Broome 2	23,000
Mar 27	CHELSEA	L 0-3		18,000
Mar 30	SOUTHAMPTON	W 2-0	Smith, Edwards	25,000
Apr 6	DERBY COUNTY	W 4-1	Broome 2, Edwards, Dixon	49,875
Apr 13	Derby County	W 1-0	Dixon	30,000
Apr 17	BRENTFORD	D 1-1	Broome	18,000
Apr 20	COVENTRY CITY	D 0-0		40,000
Apr 22	LEICESTER CITY	W 3-0	Dixon, Goffin 2	30,000
Apr 23	Leicester City	W 1-0	Martin	20,000
Apr 27	Coventry City	D 2-2	Edwards, Houghton (pen)	12,000
May 1	MILLWALL	W 2-0	Houghton (pen), Edwards	31,000

FA Cup

Jan 5	Coventry City	(Rd 3/FL) L 1-2	Smith	27,000
Jan 8	COVENTRY CITY	(Rd 3/SL) W 2-0	Smith, Goffin	20,000
Jan 26	Millwall	(Rd 4/FL) W 4-2	Goffin, Edwards 2, Smith	30,000
Jan 28	MILLWALL	(Rd 4/SL) W 9-1	Goffin 2, Parkes, Broome 3, Edwards, Smith, Iverson	28,000
Feb 9	Chelsea	(Rd 5/FL) W 1-0	Broome	60,000
Feb 12	CHELSEA	(Rd 5/SL) W 1-0	Goffin	56,000
Mar 2	DERBY COUNTY	(Rd 6/FL) L 3-4	Edwards, Iverson, Broome	76,588
Mar 9	Derby County	(Rd 6/SL) D 1-1	Broome	31,000

League & Cup Appearances

PLAYER	LEAGUE	CUP COMPETITION FA CUP	TOTAL
Beresford	1		1
Broome	27	6	33
Callaghan	26	4	30
Carey	1		1
Cummings	42	8	50
Dixon	5		5
Edwards	35	8	43
Godfrey	3		3
Goffin	17	7	24
Graham	4		4
Haycock	1		1
Houghton	14		14
Iverson	41	8	49
Kerr	9	2	11
Lowe	24	8	32
Massie	3		3
Martin	25	1	26
Morby	9	3	12
Moss	11	1	12
Parkes	30	8	38
Potts	39	8	47
Rutherford	9		9
Scott	2		2
Shell	4		4
Smith	22	8	30
Starling	28		28
Wakeman	30	8	38

Goalscorers

PLAYER	LEAGUE	CUP COMPETITION FA CUP	TOTAL
Edwards	39	4	43
Broome	14	6	20
Iverson	16	2	18
Goffin	7	5	12
Martin	9		9
Smith	3	4	7
Kerr	4		4
Parkes	3	1	4
Dixon	3		3
Houghton	2		2
Cummings	1		1
Graham	1		1
Opps' o.gs.	4		4

Fact File

The attendance of 76,588 for the FA Cup Sixth Round encounter with Derby County on 2 March 1946 is an all-time record for a game at Villa Park.

Final Football League South Table

		P	W	D	L	F	A	Pts
1	BIRMINGHAM C	42	28	5	9	96	45	61
2	ASTON VILLA	42	25	11	6	106	58	61
3	CHARLTON ATH	42	25	10	7	92	45	60
4	DERBY CO	42	24	7	11	101	62	55
5	WBA	42	22	8	12	104	69	52
6	WOLVERHAMPTON W	42	20	11	11	75	48	51
7	WEST HAM U	42	20	11	11	94	76	51
8	FULHAM	42	20	10	12	93	73	50
9	TOTTENHAM H	42	22	3	17	78	81	47
10	CHELSEA	42	19	6	17	92	80	44
11	ARSENAL	42	16	11	15	76	73	43
12	MILLWALL	42	17	8	17	79	105	42
13	COVENTRY C	42	15	10	17	70	69	40
14	BRENTFORD	42	14	10	18	82	72	38
15	NOTTINGHAM F	42	12	13	17	72	73	37
16	SOUTHAMPTON	42	14	9	19	97	105	37
17	SWANSEA T	42	15	7	20	90	112	37
18	LUTON T	42	13	7	22	60	92	33
19	PORTSMOUTH	42	11	6	25	66	87	28
20	LEICESTER C	42	8	7	27	57	101	23
21	NEWPORT CO	42	9	2	31	52	125	20
22	PLYMOUTH ARG	42	3	8	25	39	120	14

MANAGER: Alex Massie

CAPTAIN: George Cummings

TOP SCORER: George Edwards, 43 (39 league)

BIGGEST WIN: 9-1 v Millwall (H), Division One, 28 January 1946

HIGHEST ATTENDANCE: 76,588 v Derby County (H), FA Cup Sixth Round, 2 March 1946

MAJOR TRANSFERS IN: Eddie Lowe from Kynoch Works FC, Vic Potts from Doncaster Rovers, Les Smith from Brentford

MAJOR TRANSFERS OUT: Freddie Haycock to Wrexham

Season 1946-47

Football League Division One

DATE	OPPONENTS	SCORE	GOALSCORERS	ATTENDANCE
Aug 31	MIDDLESBROUGH	L 0-1		50,572
Sep 2	EVERTON	L 0-1		35,618
Sep 7	Derby County	W 2-1	Dixon, Edwards	28,454
Sep 11	Wolverhampton wanderers	W 2-1	Smith, Goffin	50,000
Sep 14	ARSENAL	L 0-2		42,000
Sep 16	WOLVERHAMPTON WANDERERS	W 3-0	Edwards 2, Smith	26,000
Sep 21	Blackpool	L 0-1		20,000
Sep 28	BRENTFORD	W 5-2	Smith o.g., Martin, Goffin 2, Graham	35,000
Oct 5	Blackburn Rovers	W 1-0	Edwards	24,000
Oct 12	PORTSMOUTH	D 1-1	Smith	40,500
Oct 19	CHARLTON ATHLETIC	W 4-0	Dorsett, Edwards, Dixon 2	43,500
Oct 26	Preston North End	L 1-3	Iverson	30,000
Nov 2	MANCHESTER UNITED	D 0-0		40,000
Nov 9	Stoke City	D 0-0		40,000
Nov 16	BOLTON WANDERERS	D 1-1	Dorsett	41,200
Nov 23	Chelsea	W 3-1	Edwards, Martin, Smith	65,815
Nov 30	SHEFFIELD UNITED	L 2-3	Edwards, Martin	30,000
Dec 7	Grimsby Town	W 3-0	Martin, Edwards, Dorsett	19,000
Dec 14	LEEDS UNITED	W 2-1	Smith, Dorsett	29,410
Dec 21	Liverpool	L 1-4	Dorsett	35,650
Dec 25	HUDDERSFIELD TOWN	D 2-2	Parkes, Martin	24,000
Dec 26	Huddersfield Town	L 0-1		32,000
Dec 28	Middlesbrough	W 2-1	Smith, Edwards	17,000
Jan 1	Everton	L 0-2		49,665
Jan 4	DERBY COUNTY	W 2-0	Martin, Graham	50,254
Jan 18	Arsenal	W 2-0	Smith, Dorsett	60,000
Jan 25	BLACKPOOL	D 1-1	Ford	35,000
Feb 1	Brentford	W 2-0	Ford 2	21,568
Feb 15	Portsmouth	L 2-3	Martin, Ford	25,000
Feb 22	Charlton Athletic	D 1-1	Campbell o.g.	30,000
Mar 8	Manchester United	L 1-2	Dorsett	36,965
Mar 22	Bolton Wanderers	L 1-2	Martin	25,000
Mar 29	CHELSEA	W 2-0	Ford, Dorsett	35,786
Apr 4	Sunderland	L 1-4	Dixon	54,000
Apr 5	Sheffield United	W 2-1	Dorsett 2	18,000
Apr 8	SUNDERLAND	W 4-0	Iverson, Dorsett, Ford 2	30,000
Apr 12	GRIMSBY TOWN	D 3-3	Ford 2, Edwards	34,000
Apr 19	Leeds United	D 1-1	Dorsett	22,291
Apr 26	LIVERPOOL	L 1-2	Evans	40,000
May 10	BLACKBURN ROVERS	W 2-1	Dorsett, Dixon	28,000
May 17	PRESTON NORTH END	W 4-2	Evans 2, Dixon, Iverson	31,640
May 26	STOKE CITY	L 0-1		41,902

FA Cup

Jan 3	Burnley	(Rd 3) L 1-5	Graham	38,532

League & Cup Appearances

PLAYER	LEAGUE	CUP COMPETITION FA CUP	TOTAL
Ashton	1		1
Broome	1		1
Callaghan	10	1	11
Cummings	31		31
Dixon	17		17
Dodds	1		1
Dorsett	31	1	32
Edwards	40	1	41
Evans	4		4
Ford	9		9
Goffin	9		9
Graham	7	1	8
Guttridge	11		11
Haynes	4		4
Houghton	4		4
Iverson	29		29
Kerr	1		1
Lowe	35		35
Martin	29	1	30
Moss A	8		8
Moss F	33	1	34
Parkes	26	1	27
Pulls	36	1	37
Rutherford	41	1	42
Smith	42	1	43
Starling	1	1	2
Wakeman	1		1

Goalscorers

PLAYER	LEAGUE	CUP COMPETITION FA CUP	TOTAL
Dorsett	13		13
Edwards	10		10
Ford	9		9
Martin	8		8
Smith	7		7
Dixon	6		6
Evans	3		3
Goffin	3		3
Graham	2	1	3
Iverson	3		3
Parkes	1		1
Opps' o.gs.	2		2

Fact File

The signing of Welshman Trevor Ford from Swansea Town, halfway through the season, cost Villa a record fee of £9,500.

MANAGER: Alex Massie

CAPTAIN: George Cummings, Bob Iverson

TOP SCORER: Dicky Dorsett, 13 (all league)

BIGGEST WIN: 5-2 v Brentford (H), Division One, 28 September 1946

HIGHEST ATTENDANCE: 65,815 v Chelsea (A), Division One, 23 November 1946

MAJOR TRANSFERS IN: Dicky Dorsett from Wolverhampton Wanderers, Trevor Ford from Swansea Town

MAJOR TRANSFERS OUT: Eric Houghton to Notts County, Frank Broome to Derby County

Final Division One Table

		P	W	D	L	F	A	Pts
1	LIVERPOOL	42	25	7	10	84	52	57
2	MANCHESTER U	42	22	12	8	95	54	56
3	WOLVERHAMPTON W	42	25	6	11	98	56	56
4	STOKE C	42	24	7	11	90	53	55
5	BLACKPOOL	42	22	6	14	71	70	50
6	SHEFFIELD U	42	21	7	14	89	75	49
7	PRESTON NE	42	18	11	13	76	74	47
8	ASTON VILLA	42	18	9	15	67	53	45
9	SUNDERLAND	42	18	8	16	65	66	44
10	EVERTON	42	17	9	16	62	67	43
11	MIDDLESBROUGH	42	17	8	17	73	68	42
12	PORTSMOUTH	42	16	9	17	66	60	41
13	ARSENAL	42	16	9	17	72	70	41
14	DERBY CO	42	18	5	19	73	79	41
15	CHELSEA	42	16	7	19	69	84	39
16	GRIMSBY T	42	13	12	17	61	82	38
17	BLACKBURN R	42	14	8	20	45	53	36
18	BOLTON W	42	13	8	21	57	69	34
19	CHARLTON ATH	42	11	12	19	57	71	34
20	HUDDERSFIELD T	42	13	7	22	53	79	33
21	BRENTFORD	42	9	7	26	45	88	25
22	LEEDS U	42	6	6	30	45	90	18

Season 1947-48

Football League Division One

DATE	OPPONENTS	SCORE	GOALSCORERS	ATTENDANCE
Aug 23	Grimsby Town	L 0-3		14,000
Aug 27	Sunderland	D 0-0		42,253
Aug 30	MANCHESTER CITY	D 1-1	Dorsett	50,296
Sep 1	SUNDERLAND	W 2-0	Goffin, Ford	27,000
Sep 6	Blackburn Rovers	D 0-0		24,000
Sep 8	EVERTON	W 3-0	Edwards, Ford, Dixon	28,764
Sep 13	BLACKPOOL	L 0-1		54,826
Sep 17	Everton	L 0-3		32,537
Sep 20	Derby County	W 3-1	Edwards, Ford, Lowe	32,891
Sep 27	HUDDERSFIELD TOWN	W 2-1	Ford, Dixon	36,000
Oct 4	Chelsea	L 2-4	Dixon, Ford (pen)	64,503
Oct 11	Arsenal	L 0-1		61,700
Oct 18	SHEFFIELD UNITED	W 2-0	Ford 2	45,176
Sep 25	Manchester United	L 0-2		47,078
Nov 1	PRESTON NORTH END	W 4-1	Brown, Martin 2, Dorsett	32,606
Nov 8	Portsmouth	W 4-2	Brown 2, Ford 2	41,000
Nov 15	BOLTON WANDERERS	W 3-1	Edwards 2, Smith	29,200
Nov 22	Stoke City	W 2-1	Brown, Goffin	24,250
Nov 29	BURNLEY	D 2-2	Moss F, Martin	33,467
Dec 6	Liverpool	D 3-3	Ford, Martin, Brown	37,732
Dec 13	MIDDLESBROUGH	D 1-1	Smith	38,000
Dec 20	GRIMSBY TOWN	D 2-2	Brown, Dorsett (pen)	25,000
Dec 26	WOLVERHAMPTON WANDERERS	L 1-2	Edwards	68,099
Dec 27	Wolverhampton wanderers	L 1-4	Smith	50,000
Jan 3	Manchester City	W 2-0	Dorsett, Dixon	50,080
Jan 31	Blackpool	L 0-1		24,233
Feb 14	Huddersfield Town	W 1-0	Ford	20,571
Feb 21	CHELSEA	W 3-0	Smith, Edwards, Ford	32,140
Feb 28	ARSENAL	W 4-2	Dixon, Smith, Ford 2	66,045
Mar 6	Sheffield United	L 1-3	Dorsett (pen)	26,000
Mar 20	Preston North End	L 0-3		30,000
Mar 22	MANCHESTER UNITED	L 0-1		52,368
Mar 26	Charlton Athletic	D 1-1	Brown	29,500
Mar 27	PORTSMOUTH	W 2-1	Brown, Edwards	26,571
Mar 30	CHARLTON ATHLETIC	W 2-1	Smith, Phipps o.g.	27,170
Apr 3	Bolton Wanderers	L 0-1		28,000
Apr 7	DERBY COUNTY	D 2-2	Vinall, Edwards	30,736
Apr 10	STOKE CITY	W 1-0	Smith	29,763
Apr 14	BLACKBURN ROVERS	W 3-2	Edwards, Smith, Goffin	20,500
Apr 17	Burnley	L 0-1		25,000
Apr 24	LIVERPOOL	W 2-1	Ford 2	20,000
May 1	Middlesbrough	W 3-1	Ford 2, Goffin	23,000

FA Cup

Jan 10	MANCHESTER UNITED	(Rd 3) L 4-6	Edwards 2, Smith, Dorsett (pen)	58,683

League & Cup Appearances

PLAYER	LEAGUE	CUP COMPETITION FA CUP	TOTAL
Brown	23	1	24
Chapman	6		6
Cummings	30		30
Dixon	12		12
Dorsett	40	1	41
Edwards	42	1	43
Evans	2		2
Ford	35	1	36
Goffin	15		15
Graham	1		1
Guttridge	4		4
Iverson	3		3
Jones	18	1	19
Lowe	37	1	38
Martin	23	1	24
Moss F	34	1	35
Parkes	40	1	41
Potts	26	1	27
Rutherford	23		23
Smith	42	1	43
Vinall	5		5
Wakeman	1		1

Goalscorers

PLAYER	LEAGUE	CUP COMPETITION FA CUP	TOTAL
Ford	18		18
Edwards	9	2	11
Smith	8	1	9
Brown	8		8
Dorsett	5	1	6
Dixon	5		5
Goffin	4		4
Martin	4		4
Lowe	1		1
Moss	1		1
Vinall	1		1
Opps' o.gs.	1		1

Fact File

George Edwards put Villa ahead after just 13 seconds' play of the home FA Cup-tie with Manchester United on 10 January 1948.

MANAGER: Alex Massie

CAPTAIN: George Cummings/Harry Parkes

TOP SCORER: Trevor Ford, 18 (all league)

BIGGEST WIN: 4-1 v Preston North End (H), Division One, 1 November 1947

HIGHEST ATTENDANCE: 68,099 v Wolves (H), Division One, 26 December 1947

MAJOR TRANSFERS IN: Albert 'Sailor' Brown from Nottingham Forest

MAJOR TRANSFERS OUT: Ronnie Starling and Bob Iverson retired

Final Division One Table

		P	W	D	L	F	A	Pts
1	ARSENAL	42	23	13	6	81	32	59
2	MANCHESTER U	42	19	14	9	81	48	52
3	BURNLEY	42	20	12	10	56	43	52
4	DERBY CO	42	19	12	11	77	57	50
5	WOLVERHAMPTON W	42	19	9	14	83	70	47
6	ASTON VILLA	42	19	9	14	65	57	47
7	PRESTON NE	42	20	7	15	67	68	47
8	PORTSMOUTH	42	19	7	16	68	50	45
9	BLACKPOOL	42	17	10	15	57	41	44
10	MANCHESTER C	42	15	12	15	52	47	42
11	LIVERPOOL	42	16	10	16	65	61	42
12	SHEFFIELD U	42	16	10	16	65	70	42
13	CHARLTON ATH	42	17	6	19	57	66	40
14	EVERTON	42	17	6	19	52	66	40
15	STOKE C	42	14	10	18	41	55	38
16	MIDDLESBROUGH	42	14	9	19	71	73	37
17	BOLTON W	42	16	5	21	46	58	37
18	CHELSEA	42	14	9	19	53	71	37
19	HUDDERSFIELD T	42	12	12	18	51	60	36
20	SUNDERLAND	42	13	10	19	56	67	36
21	BLACKBURN R	42	11	10	21	54	72	32
22	GRIMSBY T	42	8	6	28	45	111	22

Season 1948-49

Football League Division One

DATE	OPPONENTS	SCORE	GOALSCORERS	ATTENDANCE
Aug 21	LIVERPOOL	W 2-1	Ford 2	36,157
Aug 25	Bolton Wanderers	L 0-3		25,000
Aug 28	Blackpool	L 0-1		30,000
Aug 30	BOLTON WANDERERS	L 2-4	Martin JR, Graham	48,228
Sep 4	DERBY COUNTY	D 1-1	Dorsett (pen)	50,791
Sep 8	Newcastle United	L 1-2	Dixon	58,000
Sep 11	Arsenal	L 1-3	Edwards	62,000
Sep 13	NEWCASTLE UNITED	L 2-4	Dixon, Edwards	35,824
Sep 18	HUDDERSFIELD TOWN	D 3-3	Edwards, Brown, Smith L	44,523
Sep 25	Manchester United	L 1-3	Edwards	53,820
Oct 2	SHEFFIELD UNITED	W 4-3	Ford 2, Edwards 2	49,840
Oct 9	PORTSMOUTH	D 1-1	Mulraney	60,157
Oct 16	Manchester City	L 1-4	Smith L	38,024
Oct 23	CHARLTON ATHLETIC	W 4-3	Dorsett 2, Mulraney, Edwards	46,732
Oct 30	Stoke City	L 2-4	Dorsett (pen), Edwards	37,300
Nov 6	BURNLEY	W 3-1	Dorsett, Smith L, Ford	46,981
Nov 13	Preston North End	W 1-0	Edwards	20,000
Nov 20	EVERTON	L 0-1		43,382
Nov 27	Chelsea	L 1-2	Smith L	32,920
Dec 4	BIRMINGHAM CITY	L 0-3		61,632
Dec 11	Middlesbrough	L 0-6		25,000
Dec 18	Liverpool	D 1-1	Lowe	28,000
Dec 25	Wolverhampton Wanderers	L 0-4		40,000
Dec 27	WOLVERHAMPTON WANDERERS	W 5-1	Howarth, Ford 4	63,572
Jan 1	BLACKPOOL	L 2-5	Edwards, Goffin	28,722
Jan 22	ARSENAL	W 1-0	Goffin	64,190
Feb 12	Huddersfield Town	W 1-0	Ford	15,401
Feb 19	MANCHESTER UNITED	W 2-1	Dixon, Ford	68,354
Feb 26	Sheffield United	W 1-0	Howarth	32,000
Mar 5	Portsmouth	L 0-3		42,000
Mar 12	MANCHESTER CITY	W 1-0	Goffin	48,158
Mar 19	Everton	W 3-1	Gibson, Dixon 2	50,201
Mar 26	CHELSEA	D 1-1	Dorsett (pen)	47,446
Apr 2	Burnley	D 1-1	Dorsett	24,699
Apr 9	PRESTON NORTH END	W 2-0	Smith L, Ford	34,853
Apr 15	Sunderland	D 0-0		51,000
Apr 16	Charlton Athletic	W 2-0	Edwards, Dorsett	32,146
Apr 19	SUNDERLAND	D 1-1	Ford	35,298
Apr 23	STOKE CITY	W 2-1	Edwards, Dixon	34,820
Apr 27	Derby County	D 2-2	Dixon, Dorsett	23,405
Apr 30	Birmingham City	W 1-0	Craddock	45,000
May 7	MIDDLESBROUGH	D 1-1	Dorsett	40,882

FA Cup

Jan 8	BOLTON WANDERERS	(Rd 3) D	1-1*	Ford	53,459
Jan 15	Bolton Wanderers	(R) D	0-0*		38,706
Jan 17	BOLTON WANDERERS	(2nd R) W	2-1*	Edwards, Smith H	49,709
Jan 29	CARDIFF CITY	(Rd 4) L	1-2	Dorsett	70,718

*After extra-time.

League & Cup Appearances

PLAYER	LEAGUE	CUP COMPETITION FA CUP	TOTAL
Ashton	7		7
Brown	7		7
Canning	2		2
Craddock	3		3
Cummings	34	4	38
Dixon	25	1	26
Dorsett	38	3	41
Edwards	29	4	33
Evans	1		1
Ford	31	4	35
Gibson	11		11
Goffin	16	4	20
Graham	2		2
Howarth	7	1	8
Jones	13		13
Lowe	26	1	27
Martin C	31	4	35
Martin JR	5		5
Moss A	1		1
Moss F	34	3	37
Mulraney	12		12
Parkes	40	4	44
Powell	20	4	24
Rutherford	29	4	33
Smith H		2	2
Smith L	38	1	39

Goalscorers

PLAYER	LEAGUE	CUP COMPETITION FA CUP	TOTAL
Ford	13	1	14
Edwards	12	1	13
Dorsett	10	1	11
Dixon	7		7
Smith L	5		5
Goffin	3		3
Howarth	2		2
Mulraney	2		2
Brown	1		1
Craddock	1		1
Gibson	1		1
Graham	1		1
Lowe	1		1
Martin JR	1		1
Smith H		1	1

Final Division One Table

		P	W	D	L	F	A	Pts
1	PORTSMOUTH	42	25	8	9	84	42	58
2	MANCHESTER U	42	21	11	10	77	44	53
3	DERBY CO	42	22	9	11	74	55	53
4	NEWCASTLE U	42	20	12	10	70	56	52
5	ARSENAL	42	18	13	11	74	44	49
6	WOLVERHAMPTON W	42	17	12	13	79	66	46
7	MANCHESTER C	42	15	15	12	47	51	45
8	SUNDERLAND	42	13	17	12	49	58	43
9	CHARLTON ATH	42	15	12	15	63	67	42
10	ASTON VILLA	42	16	10	16	60	76	42
11	STOKE C	42	16	9	17	66	68	41
12	LIVERPOOL	42	13	14	15	53	43	40
13	CHELSEA	42	12	14	16	69	68	38
14	BURNLEY	42	12	14	16	43	50	38
15	BLACKPOOL	42	11	16	15	54	67	38
16	BIRMINGHAM C	42	11	15	16	36	38	37
17	EVERTON	42	13	11	18	41	63	37
18	MIDDLESBROUGH	42	11	12	19	46	57	34
19	HUDDERSFIELD T	42	12	10	20	40	69	34
20	PRESTON NE	42	11	11	20	62	75	33
21	SHEFFIELD U	42	11	11	20	57	78	33

Fact File

The average league attendance record for Villa Park of 47,168 was set this season – beating the previous best by more than 5,000.

MANAGER: Alex Massie

CAPTAIN: George Cummings, Harry Parkes

TOP SCORER: Trevor Ford, 14 (13 league)

BIGGEST WIN: 5-1 v Wolves (H), Division One, 27 December 1948

HIGHEST ATTENDANCE: 70,718 v Cardiff City (H), FA Cup Fourth Round, 29 January 1949

MAJOR TRANSFERS IN: Colin Gibson from Newcastle United, Jock Mulraney from Kidderminster Harriers, Con Martin from Leeds United

MAJOR TRANSFERS OUT: Albert Brown to Gorleston (player-coach)

Season 1949-50

Football League Division One

DATE	OPPONENTS	SCORE	GOALSCORERS	ATTENDANCE
Aug 20	Manchester City	D 3-3	Smith L, Goffin 2	39,594
Aug 23	DERBY COUNTY	D 1-1	Ford	53,080
Aug 27	FULHAM	W 3-1	Smith L, Goffin, Ford	46,635
Aug 31	Derby County	L 2-3	Ford, Goffin	31,748
Sep 3	Newcastle United	L 2-3	Lowe, Ford	59,700
Sep 5	PORTSMOUTH	W 1-0	Powell	48,000
Sep 10	BLACKPOOL	D 0-0		42,000
Sep 17	Middlesbrough	W 2-0	Goffin 2	30,000
Sep 24	EVERTON	D 2-2	Goffin, Ford	47,186
Oct 1	Huddersfield Town	L 0-1		20,636
Oct 8	West Bromwich Albion	D 1-1	Ford	53,690
Oct 15	MANCHESTER UNITED	L 0-4		47,483
Oct 22	Chelsea	W 3-1	Ford, Dixon, Craddock	44,704
Oct 29	Stoke City	D 1-1	Dixon	24,031
Nov 5	Burnley	L 0-1		24,130
Nov 12	SUNDERLAND	W 2-0	Ford, Craddock	36,868
Nov 19	Liverpool	L 1-2	Dixon	50,293
Nov 26	ARSENAL	D 1-1	Ford	47,048
Dec 3	Bolton Wanderers	D 1-1	Harrison	34,772
Dec 10	BIRMINGHAM CITY	D 1-1	Ford	44,520
Dec 17	MANCHESTER CITY	W 1-0	Moss F	30,223
Dec 24	Fulham	L 0-3		21,462
Dec 26	Wolverhampton Wanderers	W 3-2	Powell, Edwards, Ford	51,986
Dec 27	WOLVERHAMPTON WANDERERS	L 1-4	Dixon	69,492
Dec 31	NEWCASTLE UNITED	L 0-1		39,803
Jan 14	Blackpool	L 0-1		25,016
Jan 21	MIDDLESBROUGH	W 4-0	Ford, Craddock, Goffin 2	30,460
Feb 4	Everton	D 1-1	Gibson	43,634
Feb 18	HUDDERSFIELD TOWN	W 2-1	Ford 2	24,560
Feb 25	WEST BROMWICH ALBION	W 1-0	Gibson	40,132
Mar 8	Manchester United	L 0-7		22,149
Mar 11	LIVERPOOL	W 2-0	Goffin, Dixon	39,035
Mar 25	BURNLEY	L 0-1		30,122
Mar 29	Arsenal	W 3-1	Gibson, Dixon 2	23,700
Apr 1	Sunderland	L 1-2	Edwards	37,906
Apr 7	Charlton Athletic	W 4-1	Ford, Martin (pen), Goffin, Dixon	39,700
Apr 8	CHELSEA	W 4-0	Powell, Goffin, Ford, Dixon	35,147
Apr 11	CHARLTON ATHLETIC	D 1-1	Smith L	25,580
Apr 15	Stoke City	L 0-1		34,029
Apr 22	BOLTON WANDERERS	W 3-0	Goffin, Dixon 2	29,897
Apr 29	Birmingham City	D 2-2	Ford 2	26,144
May 6	Portsmouth	L 1-5	Dorsett (pen)	42,295

FA Cup

DATE	OPPONENTS		SCORE	GOALSCORERS	ATTENDANCE
Jan 7	MIDDLESBROUGH	(Rd 3)	D 2-2	Gibson, Dorsett (pen)	49,225
Jan 11	Middlesbrough	(R)	D 0-0		49,876
Jan 16	Middlesbrough*	(2nd R)	L 0-3		43,011

*Played at Elland Road, Leeds.

League & Cup Appearances

PLAYER	LEAGUE	CUP COMPETITION FA CUP	TOTAL
Craddock	16		16
Daly	3	1	4
Dixon	37	3	40
Dorsett	39	2	41
Edwards	13		13
Ford	36	3	39
Gibson	32	2	34
Goffin	33	1	34
Harrison	8		8
Howarth	1		1
Jones	10		10
Lowe	6	3	9
Martin	40	3	43
Moss A	2		2
Moss F	42	3	45
Parkes	40	3	43
Powell	42	3	45
Rutherford	28	3	31
Smith H	1		1
Smith L	29	3	32
Wakeman	4		4

Goalscorers

PLAYER	LEAGUE	CUP COMPETITION FA CUP	TOTAL
Ford	18		18
Goffin	13		13
Dixon	11		11
Gibson	3	1	4
Craddock	3		3
Powell	3		3
Smith L	3		3
Dorsett	1	1	2
Edwards	2		2
Harrison	1		1
Lowe	1		1
Martin	1		1
Moss F	1		1

Fact File

Charlie Mitten scored a hat-trick of penalties for Manchester United in their 7-0 league victory over Villa at Old Trafford on 8 March 1950.

MANAGER: Alex Massie

CAPTAIN: Dicky Dorsett

TOP SCORER: Trevor Ford, 18 (all league)

BIGGEST WIN: 4-0 v Middlesbrough (H), Division One, 21 January 1950; v Chelsea (H), Division One, 8 April 1950

HIGHEST ATTENDANCE: 69,492 v Wolves (H), Division One, 27 December 1949

MAJOR TRANSFERS IN: Jimmy Harrison from Leicester City, Stan Lynn from Accrington Stanley

MAJOR TRANSFERS OUT: Eddie Lowe to Fulham

Final Division One Table

		P	W	D	L	F	A	Pts
1	PORTSMOUTH	42	22	9	11	74	38	53
2	WOLVERHAMPTON W	42	20	13	9	76	49	53
3	SUNDERLAND	42	21	10	11	83	62	52
4	MANCHESTER U	42	18	14	10	69	44	50
5	NEWCASTLE U	42	19	12	11	77	55	50
6	ARSENAL	42	19	11	12	79	55	49
7	BLACKPOOL	42	17	15	10	46	35	49
8	LIVERPOOL	42	17	14	11	64	54	48
9	MIDDLESBROUGH	42	20	7	15	59	48	47
10	BURNLEY	42	16	13	13	40	40	45
11	DERBY CO	42	17	10	15	69	61	44
12	ASTON VILLA	42	15	12	15	61	61	42
13	CHELSEA	42	12	16	14	58	65	40
14	WBA	42	14	12	16	47	53	40
15	HUDDERSFIELD T	42	14	9	19	52	73	37
16	BOLTON W	42	10	14	18	45	59	34
17	FULHAM	42	10	14	18	41	54	34
18	EVERTON	42	10	14	18	42	66	34
19	STOKE C	42	11	12	19	45	75	34
20	CHARLTON ATH	42	13	6	23	53	65	32
21	MANCHESTER C	42	8	13	21	36	68	29
22	BIRMINGHAM C	42	7	14	21	31	67	28

Season 1950-51

Football League Division One

DATE	OPPONENTS	SCORE	GOALSCORERS	ATTENDANCE
Aug 19	WEST BROMWICH ALBION	W 2-0	Dixon, Gibson	65,036
Aug 21	SUNDERLAND	W 3-1	Craddock, Gibson, Dixon	36,200
Aug 26	Derby County	L 2-4	Craddock, Smith L	26,865
Aug 30	Sunderland	D 3-3	Powell, Dixon, Craddock	40,893
Sep 2	LIVERPOOL	D 1-1	Moss F	45,870
Sep 4	MANCHESTER UNITED	L 1-3	Ford	42,724
Sep 9	Fulham	L 1-2	Goffin	29,086
Sep 13	Manchester United	D 0-0		33,021
Sep 16	BOLTON WANDERERS	L 0-1		34,783
Sep 23	Blackpool	D 1-1	Goffin	32,691
Sep 30	TOTTENHAM HOTSPUR	L 2-3	Thompson, Smith L	49,664
Oct 7	NEWCASTLE UNITED	W 3-0	Thompson, Powell, Craddock	44,240
Oct 14	Huddersfield Town	L 2-4	Edwards, Ford	25,903
Oct 21	ARSENAL	D 1-1	Canning	53,455
Oct 28	Burnley	L 0-2		27,171
Nov 4	MIDDLESBROUGH	L 0-1		37,582
Nov 11	Sheffield Wednesday	L 2-3	Craddock, Gibson	37,160
Nov 18	CHELSEA	W 4-2	Dixon 2, Craddock, Thompson	29,185
Nov 25	Portsmouth	D 3-3	Dixon 2, Thompson	39,112
Dec 2	EVERTON	D 3-3	Smith L 2, Dorsett (pen)	27,133
Dec 9	Stoke City	L 0-1		28,125
Dec 16	West Bromwich Albion	L 0-2		28,796
Dec 23	DERBY COUNTY	D 1-1	Lynn	28,129
Dec 25	Charlton Athletic	D 2-2	Thompson, Smith L	24,016
Dec 26	CHARLTON ATHLETIC	D 0-0		33,247
Jan 13	FULHAM	W 3-0	Lynn (pen), Dixon, Quested o.g.	30,228
Jan 20	Bolton Wanderers	L 0-1		24,425
Feb 3	BLACKPOOL	L 0-3		54,140
Feb 17	Tottenham Hotspur	L 2-3	Dixon, Gibson	47,942
Mar 3	HUDDERSFIELD TOWN	L 0-1		34,882
Mar 10	Arsenal	L 1-2	Lynn (pen)	43,747
Mar 17	BURNLEY	W 3-2	Canning, Pace, Dixon	27,232
Mar 24	Middlesbrough	L 1-2	Dixon	27,063
Mar 26	Wolverhampton Wanderers	W 3-2	Dixon, Parkes (pen), Short o.g.	50,139
Mar 27	WOLVERHAMPTON WANDERERS	W 1-0	Thompson	48,057
Mar 31	SHEFFIELD WEDNESDAY	W 2-1	Walsh, Thompson	29,321
Apr 4	Newcastle United	W 1-0	Thompson	38,543
Apr 7	Chelsea	D 1-1	Smith H	28,696
Apr 14	PORTSMOUTH	D 3-3	Parkes (pen), Smith H, Dixon	39,258
Apr 21	Everton	W 2-1	Dixon, Smith H	45,245
Apr 25	Liverpool	D 0-0		23,061
May 5	STOKE CITY	W 6-2	Thompson 2, Walsh 2, Dixon, Sellers o.g.	24,033

FA Cup

Jan 6	BURNLEY	(Rd 3) W 2-0	Thompson, Smith L	37,806
Jan 27	Wolverhampton Wanderers	(Rd 4) L 1-3	Dixon	53,148

League & Cup Appearances

PLAYER	LEAGUE	CUP COMPETITION FA CUP	TOTAL
Aldis	12		12
Blanchflower	11		11
Canning	18	2	20
Craddock	15		15
Dixon	34	2	36
Dorsett	39	1	40
Edwards	11		11
Ford	9		9
Gibson	25	2	27
Goffin	24	1	25
Hindle	15		15
Jeffries	2		2
Jones	13	2	15
Lynn	9	1	10
Martin	31	2	33
Moss A	9	2	11
Moss F	32		32
Pace	2		2
Parkes	41	2	43
Powell	17		17
Rutherford	14		14
Sellers	2		2
Smith H	11		11
Smith L	22	2	24
Thompson	31	2	33
Walsh	13	1	14

Goalscorers

PLAYER	LEAGUE	CUP COMPETITION FA CUP	TOTAL
Dixon	15	1	16
Thompson	10	1	11
Craddock	6		6
Smith L	5	1	6
Gibson	4		4
Lynn	3		3
Smith H	3		3
Walsh	3		3
Canning	2		2
Ford	2		2
Goffin	2		2
Parkes	2		2
Powell	2		2
Dorsett	1		1
Edwards	1		1
Moss F	1		1
Pace	1		1
Opps' o.gs.	3		3

Fact File

The sale of centre forward Trevor Ford to Sunderland in October 1950 was for a British record fee of £30,000.

MANAGER: Alex Massie, George Martin

CAPTAIN: Dicky Dorsett, Con Martin

TOP SCORER: Johnny Dixon, 16 (15 league)

BIGGEST WIN: 6-2 v Stoke City (H), Division One, 5 May 1951

HIGHEST ATTENDANCE: 65,036 v West Bromwich Albion (H), Division One, 19 August 1950

MAJOR TRANSFERS IN: Dave Walsh from West Bromwich Albion

MAJOR TRANSFERS OUT: Trevor Ford to Sunderland

Final Division One Table

		P	W	D	L	F	A	Pts
1	TOTTENHAM H	42	25	10	7	82	44	60
2	MANCHESTER U	42	24	8	10	74	40	56
3	BLACKPOOL	42	20	10	12	79	53	50
4	NEWCASTLE U	42	18	13	11	62	53	49
5	ARSENAL	42	19	9	14	73	56	47
6	MIDDLESBROUGH	42	18	11	13	76	65	47
7	PORTSMOUTH	42	16	15	11	71	68	47
8	BOLTON W	42	19	7	16	64	61	45
9	LIVERPOOL	42	16	11	15	53	59	43
10	BURNLEY	42	14	14	14	48	43	42
11	DERBY CO	42	16	8	18	81	75	40
12	SUNDERLAND	42	12	16	14	63	73	40
13	STOKE C	42	13	14	15	50	59	40
14	WOLVERHAMPTON W	42	15	8	19	74	61	38
15	ASTON VILLA	42	12	13	17	66	68	37
16	WBA	42	13	11	18	53	61	37
17	CHARLTON ATH	42	14	9	19	63	80	37
18	FULHAM	42	13	11	18	52	68	37
19	HUDDERSFIELD T	42	15	6	21	64	92	36
20	CHELSEA	42	12	8	22	53	65	32
21	SHEFFIELD W	42	12	8	22	64	83	32
22	EVERTON	42	12	8	22	48	86	32

Season 1951-52

Football League Division One

DATE	OPPONENTS	SCORE	GOALSCORERS	ATTENDANCE
Aug 18	Bolton Wanderers	L 2-5	Smith H, Thompson	35,592
Aug 25	DERBY COUNTY	W 4-1	Smith L, Dixon 2, Walsh	37,548
Aug 27	Sunderland	W 2-1	Dixon, Pace	44,805
Sep 1	Manchester City	D 2-2	Pace, Smith L	31,503
Sep 5	Sunderland	W 3-1	Dixon, McLain o.g., Hudgell o.g.	49,776
Sep 8	ARSENAL	W 1-0	Thompson	59,850
Sep 10	HUDDERSFIELD TOWN	W 1-0	Goffin	38,046
Sep 15	Blackpool	W 3-0	Dixon 2, Thompson	34,867
Sep 19	Huddersfield Town	L 1-3	Moss A	29,146
Sep 22	LIVERPOOL	W 2-0	Goffin, Thompson	38,150
Sep 29	Portsmouth	L 0-2		37,283
Oct 6	Stoke City	L 1-4	Dixon	25,118
Oct 13	MANCHESTER UNITED	L 2-5	Smith H, Goffin	47,795
Oct 20	Tottenham Hotspur	L 0-2		49,246
Oct 27	PRESTON NORTH END	W 3-2	Smith L, Dixon, Gibson	27,907
Nov 3	Burnley	L 1-2	Thompson	17,770
Nov 10	CHARLTON ATHLETIC	L 0-2		33,450
Nov 17	Fulham	D 2-2	Lynn, Dixon	24,607
Nov 24	MIDDLESBROUGH	W 2-0	Dixon 2	30,120
Dec 1	West Bromwich Albion	W 2-1	Gibson 2	47,782
Dec 8	NEWCASTLE UNITED	D 2-2	Thompson, Dixon	32,884
Dec 15	BOLTON WANDERERS	D 1-1	Goffin	28,257
Dec 22	Derby County	D 1-1	Thompson	21,833
Dec 25	WOLVERHAMPTON WANDERERS	D 3-3	Walsh, Dixon, Goffin	49,525
Dec 26	Wolverhampton Wanderers	W 2-1	Smith H, Thompson	50,393
Dec 29	MANCHESTER CITY	L 1-2	Dixon	39,427
Jan 5	Arsenal	L 1-2	Dixon	53,540
Jan 19	BLACKPOOL	W 4-0	Thompson 2, Dixon, Walsh	38,990
Jan 26	Liverpool	W 2-1	Dixon, Gibson	39,774
Feb 9	PORTSMOUTH	W 2-0	Walsh, Dixon	54,763
Feb 16	STOKE CITY	L 2-3	Martin o.g., Walsh	35,106
Mar 1	Manchester United	D 1-1	Dixon	39,910
Mar 8	TOTTENHAM HOTSPUR	L 0-3		56,475
Mar 15	Preston North End	D 2-2	Thompson, Dixon	30,008
Mar 22	BURNLEY	W 4-1	Dixon, Roberts, Walsh, Thompson	29,173
Apr 5	FULHAM	W 4-1	Dixon, Goffin, Thompson, Walsh	15,500
Apr 12	Middlesbrough	L 0-2		18,000
Apr 14	Chelsea	D 2-2	Dorsett, Dixon	39,446
Apr 17	CHELSEA	W 7-1	Gibson 2, Dixon, Goffin 3, Walsh	29,882
Apr 19	WEST BROMWICH ALBION	W 2-0	Dixon 2	50,137
Apr 24	Charlton Athletic	W 1-0	Smith H	23,305
Apr 26	Newcastle United	L 1-6	Goffin	36,852

FA Cup

Jan 12	Newcastle United	(Rd 3) L 2-4	Dixon 2	56,177

League & Cup Appearances

PLAYER	LEAGUE	CUP COMPETITION FA CUP	TOTAL
Aldis	17		17
Blanchflower	42	1	43
Canning	1		1
Cordell	3		3
Dixon	42	1	43
Dorsett	38	1	39
Gibson	19	1	20
Goffin	35	1	36
Jones	11		11
Lynn	25	1	26
Martin	27	1	28
Moss A	11		11
Moss F	39	1	40
Pace	7		7
Parkes	42	1	43
Roberts	8		8
Rutherford	2		2
Smith H	26	1	27
Smith L	8		8
Thompson	36	1	37
Walsh	23		23

Goalscorers

PLAYER	LEAGUE	CUP COMPETITION FA CUP	TOTAL
Dixon	26	2	28
Thompson	13		13
Goffin	10		10
Walsh	8		8
Gibson	6		6
Smith H	4		4
Smith L	3		3
Pace	2		2
Dorsett	1		1
Lynn	1		1
Moss	1		1
Roberts	1		1
Opps' o.gs.	3		3

Fact File

The Republic of Ireland defender Con Martin played in goal for Villa this season!

MANAGER: George Martin

CAPTAIN: Danny Blanchflower, Frank Moss

TOP SCORER: Johnny Dixon, 28 (26 league)

BIGGEST WIN: 7-1 v Chelsea (H), Division One, 17 April 1952

HIGHEST ATTENDANCE: 59,850 v Arsenal (H), Division One, 8 September 1951

MAJOR TRANSFERS OUT: Ivor Powell to Port Vale

Final Division One Table

		P	W	D	L	F	A	Pts
1	Manchester U	42	23	11	8	95	52	57
2	Tottenham H	42	22	9	11	76	51	53
3	Arsenal	42	21	11	10	80	61	53
4	Portsmouth	42	20	8	14	68	58	48
5	Bolton W	42	19	10	13	65	61	48
6	Aston Villa	42	19	9	14	79	70	47
7	Preston NE	42	17	12	13	74	54	46
8	Newcastle U	42	18	9	15	98	73	45
9	Blackpool	42	18	9	15	64	64	45
10	Charlton Ath	42	17	10	15	68	63	44
11	Liverpool	42	12	19	11	57	61	43
12	Sunderland	42	15	12	15	70	61	42
13	WBA	42	14	13	15	74	77	41
14	Burnley	42	15	10	17	56	63	40
15	Manchester C	42	13	13	16	58	61	39
16	Wolverhampton W	42	12	14	16	73	73	38
17	Derby Co	42	15	7	20	63	80	37
18	Middlesbrough	42	15	6	21	64	88	36
19	Chelsea	42	14	8	20	52	72	36
20	Stoke C	42	12	7	23	49	88	31
21	Huddersfield T	42	10	8	24	49	82	28
22	Fulham	42	8	11	23	58	77	27

The Essential History of Aston Villa

Season 1952-53

Football League Division One

DATE	OPPONENTS	SCORE	GOALSCORERS	ATTENDANCE
Aug 23	ARSENAL	L 1-2	Walsh	54,516
Aug 30	Derby County	W 1-0	Gibson	22,010
Sep 1	SUNDERLAND	W 3-0	Smith, Aldis, Dixon	39,241
Sep 6	BLACKPOOL	L 1-5	Dixon	53,927
Sep 8	Wolverhampton Wanderers	L 1-2	Pace	37,952
Sep 13	Chelsea	L 0-4		56,653
Sep 15	WOLVERHAMPTON WANDERERS	L 0-1		29,141
Sep 20	MANCHESTER UNITED	D 3-3	Lockhart, Pace, Roberts	43,490
Sep 27	Portsmouth	D 1-1	Roberts	35,935
Oct 4	BOLTON WANDERERS	D 1-1	Moss A	29,868
Oct 11	MIDDLESBROUGH	W 1-0	Gibson	30,035
Oct 18	Liverpool	W 2-0	Hughes o.g., Roberts	42,573
Oct 25	MANCHESTER CITY	D 0-0		29,114
Nov 1	Stoke City	W 4-1	Dixon 3, Blanchflower	26,651
Nov 8	PRESTON NORTH END	W 1-0	Gibson	39,554
Nov 15	Burnley	L 0-1		24,609
Nov 22	TOTTENHAM HOTSPUR	L 0-3		33,108
Nov 29	Sheffield Wednesday	D 2-2	Lynn, Pace	30,153
Dec 13	Newcastle United	L 1-2	Dixon	38,046
Dec 20	Arsenal	L 1-3	Thompson	32,064
Dec 26	CHARLTON ATHLETIC	D 1-1	Thompson	34,512
Jan 1	Sunderland	D 2-2	Dixon, Thompson	37,786
Jan 3	DERBY COUNTY	W 3-0	Thompson, Dixon, Roberts	27,425
Jan 17	Blackpool	D 1-1	Gibson	21,258
Jan 24	CHELSEA	D 1-1	Thompson	31,860
Feb 7	Manchester United	L 1-3	Walsh	34,339
Feb 18	PORTSMOUTH	W 6-0	Stephens o.g., Dixon, Thompson, Goffin, Walsh 2	31,700
Feb 21	Bolton Wanderers	D 0-0		15,000
Mar 4	Middlesbrough	L 0-1		18,478
Mar 7	LIVERPOOL	W 4-0	Walsh, Dorsett, Dixon, Thompson	29,656
Mar 14	Manchester City	L 1-4	Thompson	32,566
Mar 18	Charlton Athletic	L 1-5	Walsh	10,529
Mar 25	STOKE CITY	D 1-1	Roberts	24,667
Mar 28	Preston North End	W 3-1	Pace 2, Walsh	28,525
Apr 4	BURNLEY	W 2-0	Moss A, Canning	24,037
Apr 6	West Bromwich Albion	L 2-3	Blanchflower, Walsh (pen)	34,310
Apr 7	WEST BROMWICH ALBION	D 1-1	Walsh	49,150
Apr 11	Tottenham Hotspur	D 1-1	Blanchflower	39,133
Apr 18	SHEFFIELD WEDNESDAY	W 4-3	Dixon 2, Gibson, Thompson	26,654
Apr 25	Cardiff City	W 2-1	Dixon, Moss A	23,779
Apr 29	CARDIFF CITY	W 2-0	Blanchflower, Walsh	17,603
May 1	NEWCASTLE UNITED	L 0-1		19,387

FA Cup

Jan 10	MIDDLESBROUGH	(Rd 3) W 3-1	Dixon, Thompson, Gibson	49,358
Jan 31	BRENTFORD	(Rd 4) D 0-0		40,625
Feb 4	Brentford	(R) W 2-1	Walsh, Thompson	21,735
Feb 14	Rotherham United	(Rd 5) W 3-1	Goffin, Walsh 2	19,964
Feb 28	EVERTON	(Rd 6) L 0-1		60,658

League & Cup Appearances

PLAYER	LEAGUE	CUP COMPETITION FA CUP	TOTAL
Aldis	23	4	27
Blanchflower	41	5	46
Canning	9		9
Cordell	2		2
Dixon	27	5	32
Dorsett	32	5	37
Gibson	30	2	32
Goffin	23	3	26
Jones	20		20
Lockhart	14	2	16
Lynn	18	1	19
McParland	1		1
Martin	10		10
Moss A	12		12
Moss F	33	5	38
Pace	11		11
Parkes	40	5	45
Parsons	20	5	25
Roberts	29	4	33
Smith H	12		12
Thompson	22	5	27
Vinall	3		3
Walsh	30	4	34

Goalscorers

PLAYER	LEAGUE	CUP COMPETITION FA CUP	TOTAL
Dixon	13	1	14
Walsh	10	3	13
Thompson	9	2	11
Gibson	5	1	6
Pace	5		5
Roberts	5		5
Blanchflower	4		4
Moss A	3		3
Goffin	1	1	2
Aldis	1		1
Canning	1		1
Dorsett	1		1
Lockhart	1		1
Lynn	1		1
Smith	1		1
Opps' o.gs.	2		2

Fact File

Peter Aldis, the Villa left back, scored with a header from 35 yards when Sunderland were beaten 3-0 in a home league game on 1 September 1952.

MANAGER: George Martin

CAPTAIN: Danny Blanchflower

TOP SCORER: Johnny Dixon, 14 (13 league)

BIGGEST WIN: 6-0 v Portsmouth (H), Division One, 18 February 1953

HIGHEST ATTENDANCE: 60,658 v Everton (H), FA Cup Sixth Round, 28 February 1953

MAJOR TRANSFERS IN: Norman Lockhart from Coventry City, Peter McParland from Dundalk

MAJOR TRANSFERS OUT: Leslie Smith to Brentford

Final Division One Table

		P	W	D	L	F	A	Pts
1	ARSENAL	42	21	12	9	97	64	54
2	PRESTON NE	42	21	12	9	85	60	54
3	WOLVERHAMPTON W	42	19	13	10	86	63	51
4	WBA	42	21	8	13	66	60	50
5	CHARLTON ATH	42	19	11	12	77	63	49
6	BURNLEY	42	18	12	12	67	52	48
7	BLACKPOOL	42	19	9	14	71	70	47
8	MANCHESTER U	42	18	10	14	69	72	46
9	SUNDERLAND	42	15	13	14	68	82	43
10	TOTTENHAM H	42	15	11	16	78	69	41
11	ASTON VILLA	42	14	13	15	63	61	41
12	CARDIFF C	42	14	12	16	54	46	40
13	MIDDLESBROUGH	42	14	11	17	70	77	39
14	BOLTON W	42	15	9	18	61	69	39
15	PORTSMOUTH	42	14	10	18	74	83	38
16	NEWCASTLE U	42	14	9	19	59	70	37
17	LIVERPOOL	42	14	8	20	61	82	36
18	SHEFFIELD W	42	12	11	19	62	72	35
19	CHELSEA	42	12	11	19	56	66	35
20	MANCHESTER C	42	14	7	21	72	87	35
21	STOKE C	42	12	10	20	53	66	34
22	DERBY CO	42	11	10	21	59	74	32

250

Season 1953-54

Football League Division One

DATE	OPPONENTS	SCORE	GOALSCORERS	ATTENDANCE
Aug 19	Tottenham Hotspur	L 0-1		50,202
Aug 22	Cardiff City	L 1-2	Dixon	28,156
Aug 24	MANCHESTER CITY	W 3-0	Blanchflower, Thompson 2	34,549
Aug 29	ARSENAL	W 2-1	Walsh, Dixon	36,028
Sep 2	Manchester City	W 1-0	Walsh	24,918
Sep 5	Portsmouth	L 1-2	Walsh	31,810
Sep 12	BLACKPOOL	W 2-1	Thompson, Walsh	31,434
Sep 14	SUNDERLAND	W 3-1	Thompson, Dixon 2	32,751
Sep 19	Chelsea	W 2-1	Walsh, Lockhart	47,487
Sep 26	SHEFFIELD UNITED	W 4-0	Walsh 2, Thompson, Lockhart	39,750
Oct 4	Huddersfield Town	L 0-4		36,645
Oct 10	Liverpool	L 1-6	Walsh	37,759
Oct 17	NEWCASTLE UNITED	L 1-2	Thompson	29,556
Oct 24	Manchester United	L 0-1		30,266
Oct 31	BOLTON WANDERERS	D 2-2	Roberts K, Walsh	26,572
Nov 7	Sheffield Wednesday	L 1-3	Thompson	31,124
Nov 14	MIDDLESBROUGH	W 5-3	Thompson 3, Walsh, Chapman	29,214
Nov 21	Burnley	L 2-3	Chapman 2	26,948
Nov 28	CHARLTON ATHLETIC	W 2-1	Dixon, Thompson	26,325
Dec 5	Preston North End	D 1-1	Thompson	19,440
Dec 12	TOTTENHAM HOTSPUR	L 1-2	Blanchflower	39,983
Dec 19	CARDIFF CITY	L 1-2	Dixon	21,226
Dec 24	Wolverhampton Wanderers	W 2-1	Dixon, McParland	49,286
Dec 26	WOLVERHAMPTON WANDERERS	L 1-2	Thompson	48,561
Jan 1	Sunderland	L 0-2		45,227
Jan 16	PORTSMOUTH	D 1-1	Thompson	28,930
Jan 23	Blackpool	L 2-3	Thompson 2	16,629
Feb 6	CHELSEA	D 2-2	Roberts KO, Blanchflower (pen)	29,452
Feb 20	HUDDERSFIELD TOWN	D 2-2	Thompson 2	24,118
Feb 27	LIVERPOOL	W 2-1	Thompson, Roberts KO	25,241
Mar 6	Newcastle United	W 1-0	Walsh	36,847
Mar 13	MANCHESTER UNITED	D 2-2	Thompson, Baxter	26,023
Mar 20	Bolton Wanderers	L 0-3		25,024
Mar 31	SHEFFIELD WEDNESDAY	W 2-1	Thompson, Dixon	9,609
Apr 3	Middlesbrough	L 1-2	McParland	21,552
Apr 6	Arsenal	D 1-1	McParland	14,899
Apr 10	BURNLEY	W 5-1	McParland, Baxter, Gibson, Pace 2	21,564
Apr 17	Charlton Athletic	D 1-1	Pace	22,143
Apr 19	West Bromwich Albion	D 1-1	McParland	45,972
Apr 20	WEST BROMWICH ALBION	W 6-1	Pace 2, Tyrell 2, Dixon, Blanchflower	45,557
Apr 24	PRESTON NORTH END	W 1-0	Tyrell	31,998
Apr 26	Sheffield United	L 1-2	Pace	23,872

FA Cup

Jan 9	Arsenal	(Rd 3) L 1-5	McParland	50,990

League & Cup Appearances

PLAYER	LEAGUE	CUP COMPETITION FA CUP	TOTAL
Aldis	38	1	39
Baxter	23		23
Blanchflower	40	1	41
Canning	9		9
Chapman	4		4
Dixon	39	1	40
Gibson	22	1	23
Goffin	1		1
Jones	33	1	34
Lockhart	18		18
Lynn	3	1	4
McParland	19	1	20
Martin	4		4
Moss A	21	1	22
Moss F	39	1	40
Pace	8		8
Parkes	39		39
Parsons	9		9
Roberts K	5		5
Roberts KO	16		16
Smith H	1		1
Thompson	34	1	35
Tyrrell	4		4
Vinall	3		3
Walsh	30	1	31

Goalscorers

PLAYER	LEAGUE	CUP COMPETITION FA CUP	TOTAL
Thompson	21		21
Walsh	11		11
Dixon	9		9
McParland	5	1	6
Pace	6		6
Blanchflower	4		4
Chapman	3		3
Tyrell	3		3
Baxter	2		2
Lockhart	2		2
Roberts KO	2		2
Gibson	1		1
Roberts K	1		1

Fact File

Peter McParland scored with his second kick in international football for Northern Ireland against Wales. He went on to win 33 full caps while a Villa player.

MANAGER: Eric Houghton

CAPTAIN: Danny Blanchflower, Frank Moss

TOP SCORER: Tommy Thompson, 21 (all league)

BIGGEST WIN: 6-1 v West Bromwich Albion (H), Division One, 20 April 1954

HIGHEST ATTENDANCE: 50,990 v Arsenal (A), FA Cup Third Round, 9 January 1954

MAJOR TRANSFERS IN: Billy Baxter from Wolverhampton Wanderers

Final Division One Table

		P	W	D	L	F	A	Pts
1	WOLVERHAMPTON W	42	25	7	10	96	56	57
2	WBA	42	22	9	11	86	63	53
3	HUDDERSFIELD T	42	20	11	11	78	61	51
4	MANCHESTER U	42	18	12	12	73	58	48
5	BOLTON W	42	18	12	12	75	60	48
6	BLACKPOOL	42	19	10	13	80	69	48
7	BURNLEY	42	21	4	17	78	67	46
8	CHELSEA	42	16	12	14	74	68	44
9	CHARLTON ATH	42	19	6	17	75	77	44
10	CARDIFF C	42	18	8	16	51	71	44
11	PRESTON NE	42	19	5	18	87	58	43
12	ARSENAL	42	15	13	14	75	73	43
13	ASTON VILLA	42	16	9	17	70	68	41
14	PORTSMOUTH	42	14	11	17	81	89	39
15	NEWCASTLE U	42	14	10	18	72	77	38
16	TOTTENHAM H	42	16	5	21	65	76	37
17	MANCHESTER C	42	14	9	19	62	77	37
18	SUNDERLAND	42	14	8	20	81	89	36
19	SHEFFIELD W	42	15	6	21	70	91	36
20	SHEFFIELD U	42	11	11	20	69	90	33
21	MIDDLESBROUGH	42	10	10	22	60	91	30
22	LIVERPOOL	42	9	10	23	68	97	28

Season 1954-55

Football League Division One

DATE	OPPONENTS	SCORE	GOALSCORERS	ATTENDANCE
Aug 21	TOTTENHAM HOTSPUR	L 2-4	Blanchflower (pen), Baxter	40,394
Aug 23	SUNDERLAND	D 2-2	McParland, Pace	36,135
Aug 28	Sheffield Wednesday	L 3-6	Dixon 2, Pace	34,243
Sep 1	Sunderland	D 0-0		50,562
Sep 4	PORTSMOUTH	W 1-0	Pace	27,854
Sep 8	Newcastle United	L 3-5	Pace, Dixon, Cowell o.g.	39,960
Sep 11	Blackpool	W 1-0	Pace	31,417
Sep 13	NEWCASTLE UNITED	L 1-2	Blanchflower (pen)	27,330
Sep 18	CHARLTON ATHLETIC	L 1-2	Chapman	24,766
Sep 25	Bolton Wanderers	D 3-3	Dixon 2, Pace	29,165
Oct 2	HUDDERSFIELD TOWN	D 0-0		20,435
Oct 9	EVERTON	L 0-2		30,702
Oct 16	Manchester City	W 4-2	Thompson 3, Walsh	36,384
Oct 23	ARSENAL	W 2-1	Lockhart, Lynn (pen)	39,520
Oct 30	West Bromwich Albion	W 3-2	Thompson 2, McParland	51,833
Nov 6	LEICESTER CITY	L 2-5	Walsh, Lockhart	26,875
Nov 13	Burnley	L 0-2		18,761
Nov 20	PRESTON NORTH END	L 1-3	Follan	24,683
Nov 27	Sheffield United	W 3-1	Dixon, Follan, Pace	26,824
Dec 4	CARDIFF CITY	L 0-2		26,490
Dec 11	Chelsea	L 0-4		36,162
Dec 18	Tottenham Hotspur	D 1-1	Dixon	29,242
Dec 27	Manchester United	W 1-0	Dixon	49,136
Dec 28	MANCHESTER UNITED	W 2-1	Dixon, Lockhart	48,718
Jan 1	SHEFFIELD UNITED	D 0-0		22,990
Jan 22	BLACKPOOL	W 3-1	Thompson 2, Pace	29,360
Feb 5	Charlton Athletic	L 1-6	Gibson	24,008
Feb 12	BOLTON WANDERERS	W 3-0	Lynn (pen), Dixon, Southren	19,226
Feb 23	Huddersfield Town	W 2-1	Lynn (pen), Gibson	5,287
Mar 5	CHELSEA	W 3-2	Walsh 2, McParland	24,822
Mar 12	Arsenal	L 0-2		30,136
Mar 19	WEST BROMWICH ALBION	W 3-0	Walsh, Lynn, Dixon	40,175
Mar 26	Leicester City	L 2-4	Southren, Dixon	18,897
Apr 2	BURNLEY	W 3-1	Follan, Dixon, McParland	24,263
Apr 9	Cardiff City	W 1-0	Follan	24,993
Apr 11	Wolverhampton Wanderers	L 0-1		33,765
Apr 12	WOLVERHAMPTON WANDERERS	W 4-2	Thompson 3, Follan	30,457
Apr 16	SHEFFIELD UNITED	W 3-1	Lynn, Thompson, Gibson	20,066
Apr 23	Preston North End	W 3-0	Thompson 2, Follan	15,169
Apr 27	Portsmouth	D 2-2	Gibson, Follan	17,255
Apr 30	MANCHESTER CITY	W 2-0	Lynn 2	25,133
May 4	Everton	W 1-0	Thompson	20,503

FA Cup

Jan 8	Brighton & Hove Albion	(Rd 3) D 2-2	Thompson 2		25,291
Jan 10	BRIGHTON & HOVE ALBION	(R) W 4-2	Lockhart 2, Southren, Thompson		13,609
Jan 29	Doncaster Rovers	(Rd 4) D 0-0			27,707
Feb 2	DONCASTER ROVERS	(R) D 2-2*	Thompson 2		26,872
Feb 7	Doncaster Rovers†	(2nd R) D 1-1*	Thompson		16,366
Feb 14	Doncaster Rovers§	(3rd R) D 0-0			15,339
Feb 19	Doncaster Rovers‡	(4th R) L 1-3	Dixon		17,155

*After extra-time. †Played at Maine Road, Manchester.
§Played at Hillsborough, Sheffield. Abandoned after 90 minutes.
‡Played at the Hawthorns, West Bromwich.

League & Cup Appearances

PLAYER	LEAGUE	CUP COMPETITION FA CUP	TOTAL
Aldis	33	7	40
Baxter	25	7	32
Birch	1		1
Blanchflower	4		4
Chapman	1		1
Clark	1		1
Crowe	25	3	28
Dixon	36	7	43
Follan	25	2	27
Gibson	12	1	13
Hogg	1		1
Jones	34	7	41
Lockhart	25	7	32
Lynn	39	7	46
McParland	32	3	35
Martin	32	6	38
Moss A	17	4	21
Moss F	9	1	10
Pace	18	1	19
Parkes	12		12
Parsons	7		7
Pinner	1		1
Proudler	1		1
Roberts KO	8		8
Southren	13	7	20
Thompson	26	7	33
Tyrrell	2		2
Walsh	12		12

Goalscorers

PLAYER	LEAGUE	CUP COMPETITION FA CUP	TOTAL
Thompson	14	6	20
Dixon	13	1	14
Pace	8		8
Follan	7		7
Lynn	7		7
Walsh	5		5
Lockhart	3	2	5
Gibson	4		4
McParland	4		4
Southren	2	1	3
Blanchflower	2		2
Baxter	1		1
Chapman	1		1
Opps' o.gs.	1		1

Fact File

The FA Cup Fourth Round tie against Doncaster Rovers in January/February 1955 lasted for a total of 510 minutes, covering five matches.

MANAGER: Eric Houghton

CAPTAIN: Danny Blanchflower, Johnny Dixon

TOP SCORER: Tommy Thompson, 20 (14 league)

BIGGEST WIN: 4-2 v Manchester City (A), Division One, 16 October 1954; v Brighton & Hove Albion (H), FA Cup Third Round Replay, 10 January 1955; v Wolves (H), Division One, 12 April 1955

HIGHEST ATTENDANCE: 51,833 v West Bromwich Albion (A), Division One, 30 October 1954

MAJOR TRANSFERS IN: Tommy Southren from West Ham United

MAJOR TRANSFERS OUT: Herbie Smith to Moor Green, Danny Blanchflower to Tottenham Hotspur

Final Division One Table

		P	W	D	L	F	A	Pts
1	CHELSEA	42	20	12	10	81	57	52
2	WOLVERHAMPTON W	42	19	10	13	89	70	48
3	PORTSMOUTH	42	18	12	12	74	62	48
4	SUNDERLAND	42	15	18	9	64	54	48
5	MANCHESTER U	42	20	7	15	84	74	47
6	ASTON VILLA	42	20	7	15	72	73	47
7	MANCHESTER C	42	18	10	14	76	69	46
8	NEWCASTLE U	42	17	9	16	89	77	43
9	ARSENAL	42	17	9	16	69	63	43
10	BURNLEY	42	17	9	16	51	48	43
11	EVERTON	42	16	10	16	62	68	42
12	HUDDERSFIELD T	42	14	13	15	63	68	41
13	SHEFFIELD U	42	17	7	18	70	86	41
14	PRESTON NE	42	16	8	18	83	64	40
15	CHARLTON ATH	42	15	10	17	76	75	40
16	TOTTENHAM H	42	16	8	18	72	73	40
17	WBA	42	16	8	18	76	96	40
18	BOLTON W	42	13	13	16	62	69	39
19	BLACKPOOL	42	14	10	18	60	64	38
20	CARDIFF C	42	13	11	18	62	76	37
21	LEICESTER C	42	12	11	19	74	86	35
22	SHEFFIELD W	42	8	10	24	63	100	26

Season 1955-56

Football League Division One

DATE	OPPONENTS	SCORE	GOALSCORERS	ATTENDANCE
Aug 20	Manchester City	D 2-2	Dixon 2	38,099
Aug 24	Sunderland	L 1-5	Dixon	32,460
Aug 27	CARDIFF CITY	W 2-0	Dixon, McParland	25,672
Aug 29	SUNDERLAND	L 1-4	Lockhart	26,385
Sep 3	Huddersfield Town	D 1-1	McParland	19,805
Sep 5	BIRMINGHAM CITY	D 0-0		57,690
Sep 10	BLACKPOOL	D 1-1	Kelly o.g.	53,864
Sep 17	Chelsea	D 0-0		34,643
Sep 21	Birmingham City	D 2-2	Merrick o.g., Baxter	32,642
Sep 24	BOLTON WANDERERS	L 0-2		27,538
Oct 1	Arsenal	L 0-1		43,748
Oct 8	West Bromwich Albion	L 0-1		37,395
Oct 15	MANCHESTER UNITED	D 4-4	Dixon 2, Hickson, Saward	29,478
Oct 22	Everton	L 1-2	Dixon	55,431
Oct 29	NEWCASTLE UNITED	W 3-0	Dixon, Crowe, Lockhart	26,851
Nov 5	Burnley	L 0-2		20,392
Nov 12	LUTON TOWN	W 1-0	Dixon	24,647
Nov 19	Charlton Athletic	L 1-3	Lockhart	19,919
Nov 26	TOTTENHAM HOTSPUR	L 0-2		23,806
Dec 3	Sheffield United	D 2-2	Sewell, Pace	22,044
Dec 10	PRESTON NORTH END	W 3-2	Baxter, Moss, Lockhart	25,714
Dec 17	MANCHESTER CITY	L 0-3		19,852
Dec 24	Cardiff City	L 0-1		21,789
Dec 26	PORTSMOUTH	L 1-3	Dixon	23,246
Dec 27	Portsmouth	D 2-2	McParland, Sewell	31,316
Dec 31	HUDDERSFIELD TOWN	W 3-0	Dixon 2, Lynn	24,993
Jan 14	Blackpool	L 0-6		21,840
Jan 21	CHELSEA	L 1-4	Lynn (pen)	24,732
Feb 11	ARSENAL	D 1-1	Dixon	27,898
Feb 18	Bolton Wanderers	L 0-1		19,512
Feb 25	Manchester United	L 0-1		36,277
Mar 3	CHARLTON ATHLETIC	D 1-1	Pace	25,696
Mar 10	Newcastle United	W 3-2	McParland, Pace, Dixon	34,647
Mar 19	BURNLEY	W 2-0	Dixon, Smith	22,158
Mar 24	Luton Town	L 1-2	Southren	17,102
Mar 31	EVERTON	W 2-0	Pace, Dixon	28,052
Apr 2	Wolverhampton Wanderers	D 0-0		33,633
Apr 3	WOLVERHAMPTON WANDERERS	D 0-0		38,460
Apr 7	Tottenham Hotspur	L 3-4	Smith, Pace, Dugdale	36,352
Apr 14	SHEFFIELD UNITED	W 3-2	Pace 3	25,147
Apr 21	Preston North End	W 1-0	Pace	16,176
Apr 28	WEST BROMWICH ALBION	W 3-0	Smith 2, Millard o.g.	45,120

FA Cup

Jan 7	HULL CITY	(Rd 3) D 1-1	McParland	33,284
Jan 12	Hull City	(R) W 2-1	Dixon, Sewell	24,253
Jan 28	Arsenal	(Rd 4) L 1-4	Dixon	43,052

League & Cup Appearances

PLAYER	LEAGUE	CUP COMPETITION FA CUP	TOTAL
Aldis	41	3	44
Ashfield	1		1
Baxter	38	3	40
Birch	9		9
Crowe	33	3	36
Dixon	37	3	40
Dugdale	14		14
Follan	9		9
Gibson	7		7
Hickson	12		12
Hogg	8		8
Jones	32	3	35
Lockhart	17	2	19
Lynn	35	3	38
McParland	29	3	32
Martin	19	3	22
Moss A	21		21
Pace	19	1	20
Pinner	1		1
Pritchard	1		1
Roberts KO	3	1	4
Saward	6		6
Sewell	15	3	18
Sims	9		9
Smith L	14		14
Southren	31	2	33
Tyrrell	1		1

Goalscorers

PLAYER	LEAGUE	CUP COMPETITION FA CUP	TOTAL
Dixon	16	2	18
Pace	9		9
McParland	4	1	5
Lockhart	4		4
Smith L	4		4
Sewell	2	1	3
Baxter	2		2
Lynn	2		2
Crowe	1		1
Dugdale	1		1
Hickson	1		1
Moss A	1		1
Saward	1		1
Southren	1		1
Opps' o.gs.	3		3

Fact File

The 4-4 draw at Old Trafford against Manchester United on 15 October 1955 was Villa's first such scoreline since 28 April 1934 when they shared eight goals with West Bromwich Albion at Villa Park.

MANAGER: Eric Houghton

CAPTAIN: Johnny Dixon

TOP SCORER: Johnny Dixon, 18 (16 league)

BIGGEST WIN: 3-0 v Newcastle United (H), Division One, 29 October 1955; v Huddersfield Town (H), Division One, 31 December 1955; v West Bromwich Albion (H), Division One, 28 April 1956

HIGHEST ATTENDANCE: 57,690 v Birmingham City (H), Division One, 5 September 1955

MAJOR TRANSFERS IN: Jackie Sewell from Hull City, Jimmy Dugdale from West Bromwich Albion, Pat Saward from Millwall, Dave Hickson from Everton

MAJOR TRANSFERS OUT: Dave Walsh to Walsall, Dave Hickson to Huddersfield Town

Final Division One Table

		P	W	D	L	F	A	Pts
1	MANCHESTER U	42	25	10	7	83	51	60
2	BLACKPOOL	42	20	9	13	86	62	49
3	WOLVERHAMPTON W	42	20	9	13	89	65	49
4	MANCHESTER C	42	18	10	14	82	69	46
5	ARSENAL	42	18	10	14	60	61	46
6	BIRMINGHAM C	42	18	9	15	75	57	45
7	BURNLEY	42	18	8	16	64	54	44
8	BOLTON W	42	18	7	17	71	58	43
9	SUNDERLAND	42	17	9	16	80	95	43
10	LUTON T	42	17	8	17	66	64	42
11	NEWCASTLE U	42	17	7	18	85	70	41
12	PORTSMOUTH	42	16	9	17	78	85	41
13	WBA	42	18	5	19	58	70	41
14	CHARLTON ATH	42	17	6	19	75	81	40
15	EVERTON	42	15	10	17	55	69	40
16	CHELSEA	42	14	11	17	64	77	39
17	CARDIFF C	42	15	9	18	55	69	39
18	TOTTENHAM H	42	15	7	20	61	71	37
19	PRESTON NE	42	14	8	20	73	72	36
20	ASTON VILLA	42	11	13	18	52	69	35
21	HUDDERSFIELD T	42	14	7	21	54	83	35
22	SHEFFIELD U	42	12	9	21	63	77	33

Season 1956-57

Football League Division One

DATE	OPPONENTS	SCORE	GOALSCORERS	ATTENDANCE
Aug 18	CHARLTON ATHLETIC	W 3-1	Dixon, Baxter, O'Linn o.g.	32,869
Aug 22	West Bromwich Albion	L 0-2		37,255
Aug 25	Manchester City	D 1-1	Smith	24,326
Aug 27	WEST BROMWICH ALBION	D 0-0		33,052
Sep 1	Blackpool	W 3-2	McParland 2, Sewell	46,246
Sep 5	Luton Town	D 0-0		21,388
Sep 8	Everton	W 4-0	Sewell 2, Dixon, Smith	43,762
Sep 15	TOTTENHAM HOTSPUR	L 2-4	Pace, McParland	44,847
Sep 22	Leeds United	L 0-1		35,388
Sep 29	BOLTON WANDERERS	D 0-0		34,632
Oct 6	Portsmouth	L 1-5	Smith	23,613
Oct 13	NEWCASTLE UNITED	W 3-1	Sewell, Smith 2	35,038
Oct 27	BIRMINGHAM CITY	W 3-1	Lynn, Roberts, Sewell	54,862
Nov 3	Arsenal	L 1-2	McParland	40,045
Nov 10	BURNLEY	W 1-0	Sewell	23,097
Nov 17	Preston North End	D 3-3	Smith, Lynn (pen), McParland	19,270
Nov 24	CHELSEA	D 1-1	Sewell	27,006
Dec 1	Sheffield Wednesday	L 1-2	McParland	24,353
Dec 8	MANCHESTER UNITED	L 1-3	Saward	42,530
Dec 15	Charlton Athletic	W 2-0	Dixon, McParland	13,552
Dec 25	Sunderland	L 0-1		18,223
Dec 29	Blackpool	D 0-0		16,777
Jan 12	EVERTON	W 5-1	Dixon, Pace 2, Sewell, Smith	25,274
Jan 19	Tottenham Hotspur	L 0-3		38,934
Feb 2	LEEDS UNITED	D 1-1	Pace	39,432
Feb 4	MANCHESTER CITY	D 2-2	Smith, McParland	10,554
Feb 9	Bolton Wanderers	D 0-0		21,012
Feb 18	PORTSMOUTH	D 2-2	Sewell 2	11,963
Mar 9	Manchester United	D 1-1	Dixon	55,484
Mar 13	CARDIFF CITY	W 4-1	Sewell 2, McParland, Lynn (pen)	11,834
Mar 16	ARSENAL	D 0-0		39,503
Mar 30	PRESTON NORTH END	W 2-0	Myerscough, Sewell	30,151
Apr 3	Cardiff City	L 0-1		14,820
Apr 6	Chelsea	D 1-1	Sewell	28,025
Apr 8	SUNDERLAND	D 2-2	Pace, Myerscough	8,252
Apr 10	Birmingham City	W 2-1	Chapman 2	29,893
Apr 13	SHEFFIELD WEDNESDAY	W 5-0	Sewell, Myerscough, Smith, McParland 2	28,134
Apr 15	Burnley	L 1-2	Pace	17,371
Apr 20	Newcastle United	W 2-1	Sewell, McParland	27,850
Apr 22	WOLVERHAMPTON WANDERERS	W 4-0	Dixon, Sewell, Smith 2	36,085
Apr 23	Wolverhampton Wanderers	L 0-3		35,585
Apr 27	LUTON TOWN	L 1-3	Smith	26,146

FA Cup

Jan 5	Luton Town	(Rd 3) D 2-2	Dixon, McParland	20,094
Jan 7	LUTON TOWN	(R) W 2-0	Dixon 2	28,356
Jan 26	Middlesbrough	(Rd 4) W 3-2	Pace, Smith, Dixon	42,396
Feb 16	BRISTOL CITY	(Rd 5) W 2-1	Pace, Sewell	63,099
Mar 2	Burnley	(Rd 6) D 1-1	McParland	49,346
Mar 6	BURNLEY	(R) W 2-0	Dixon, McParland	46,531
Mar 23	West Bromwich Albion*	(SF) D 2-2	McParland 2	55,549
Mar 28	West Bromwich Albion†	(R) W 1-0	Myerscough	58,067
May 4	Manchester United‡	(F) W 2-1	McParland 2	99,225

*Played at Molineux, Wolverhampton. †Played at St Andrew's, Birmingham.
‡Played at Wembley.

Fact File

Villa's 2-1 victory over Manchester United in the FA Cup final was their first success in the competition for 37 years – since beating Huddersfield 1-0 in 1920.

MANAGER: Eric Houghton

CAPTAIN: Johnny Dixon

TOP SCORER: Peter McParland, 19 (12 league)

BIGGEST WIN: 5-0 v Sheffield Wednesday (H), Division One, 13 April 1957

HIGHEST ATTENDANCE: 99,225 v Manchester United, FA Cup final at Wembley, 4 May 1957

MAJOR TRANSFERS OUT: Con Martin to Waterford (player-manager)

League & Cup Appearances

PLAYER	LEAGUE	CUP COMPETITION FA CUP	TOTAL
Aldis	41	9	50
Baxter	12		12
Birch	7		7
Chapman	6		6
Crowe	1		1
Crowther	24	9	33
Dixon	39	9	48
Dugdale	40	9	49
Hogg	12		12
Jackson	2		2
Jones	1		1
Lynn	30	9	39
McParland	36	9	45
Myerscough	13	3	16
Pace	21	6	27
Pinner	2		2
Pritchard	1		1
Roberts KO	9		9
Salvin	1		1
Saward	41	9	50
Sewell	39	9	48
Sims	38	9	47
Smith	39	9	48
Southren	7		7

Goalscorers

PLAYER	LEAGUE	CUP COMPETITION FA CUP	TOTAL
McParland	12	7	19
Sewell	17	1	18
Smith	12	1	13
Dixon	6	5	11
Pace	6	2	8
Myerscough	3	1	4
Lynn	3		3
Chapman	2		2
Baxter	1		1
Roberts KO	1		1
Saward	1		1
Opps' o.gs.	1		1

Final Division One Table

		P	W	D	L	F	A	Pts
1	MANCHESTER U	42	28	8	6	103	54	64
2	TOTTENHAM H	42	22	12	8	104	56	56
3	PRESTON NE	42	23	10	9	84	56	56
4	BLACKPOOL	42	22	9	11	93	65	53
5	ARSENAL	42	21	8	13	85	69	50
6	WOLVERHAMPTON W	42	20	8	14	94	70	48
7	BURNLEY	42	18	10	14	56	50	46
8	LEEDS U	42	15	14	13	72	63	44
9	BOLTON W	42	16	12	14	65	65	44
10	ASTON VILLA	42	14	15	13	65	55	43
11	WBA	42	14	14	14	59	61	42
12	BIRMINGHAM C=	42	15	9	18	69	69	39
12	CHELSEA=	42	13	13	16	73	73	39
14	SHEFFIELD W	42	16	6	20	82	88	38
15	EVERTON	42	14	10	18	61	79	38
16	LUTON T	42	14	9	19	58	76	37
17	NEWCASTLE U	42	14	8	20	67	87	36
18	MANCHESTER C	42	13	9	20	78	88	35
19	PORTSMOUTH	42	10	13	19	62	92	33
20	SUNDERLAND	42	12	8	22	67	88	32
21	CARDIFF C	42	10	9	23	53	88	29
22	CHARLTON ATH	42	9	4	29	62	120	22

Season 1957-58

Football League Division One

DATE	OPPONENTS	SCORE	GOALSCORERS	ATTENDANCE
Aug 24	Birmingham City	L 1-3	McParland	50,807
Aug 26	LEEDS UNITED	W 2-0	McParland, Sewell	25,693
Aug 31	EVERTON	L 0-1		37,759
Sep 4	Leeds United	L 0-4		22,685
Sep 7	Sunderland	D 1-1	Chapman	43,905
Sep 14	LUTON TOWN	W 2-0	McParland, Dixon	24,139
Sep 16	Wolverhampton Wanderers	L 1-2	McParland	26,033
Sep 21	Blackpool	D 1-1	McParland	30,057
Sep 23	WOLVERHAMPTON WANDERERS	L 2-3	Wright o.g., Chapman	21,336
Sep 28	LEICESTER CITY	W 5-1	Sewell 2, Southren, Lynn (pen), McParland	30,851
Oct 2	Arsenal	L 0-4		18,472
Oct 5	Manchester United	L 1-4	McParland	43,102
Oct 12	Chelsea	L 2-4	Sewell, McParland	40,769
Oct 19	NEWCASTLE UNITED	W 4-3	Dixon, Pace, Scott o.g., Myerscough	27,660
Oct 26	Burnley	L 0-3		19,846
Nov 2	PORTSMOUTH	W 2-1	Southren, Pace	29,023
Nov 9	West Bromwich Albion	L 2-3	Hazelden, Crowther	41,454
Nov 16	TOTTENHAM HOTSPUR	D 1-1	Sewell	27,796
Nov 23	Nottingham Forest	L 1-4	Crowther	30,232
Nov 30	PRESTON NORTH END	D 2-2	Lynn (pen), McParland	24,713
Dec 7	Sheffield Wednesday	W 5-2	Hazelden 2, Crowther 2, McParland	16,144
Dec 14	MANCHESTER CITY	L 1-2	McParland	24,017
Dec 21	BIRMINGHAM CITY	L 0-2		39,889
Dec 26	ARSENAL	W 3-0	Lynn, Evans o.g., Hitchens	40,638
Dec 28	Everton	W 2-1	Hitchens 2	41,195
Jan 11	SUNDERLAND	W 5-2	Lynn 3 (2 pens), Sewell, Myerscough	25,535
Jan 18	Luton Town	L 0-3		16,602
Feb 1	BLACKPOOL	D 1-1	McParland	44,715
Feb 8	Leicester City	L 1-6	Southren	27,140
Feb 22	CHELSEA	L 1-3	McParland	19,893
Mar 1	Newcastle United	W 4-2	Smith, Dugdale, Hitchens 2	40,135
Mar 8	BURNLEY	W 3-0	McParland 2, Lynn (pen)	34,740
Mar 15	Portsmouth	L 0-1		23,164
Mar 29	Tottenham Hotspur	L 2-6	Sewell, McParland	31,192
Mar 31	MANCHESTER UNITED	W 3-2	Myerscough, Hitchens, Sewell	16,631
Apr 4	Bolton Wanderers	L 0-4		19,026
Apr 5	WEST BROMWICH ALBION	W 2-1	Myerscough, McParland	32,010
Apr 8	BOLTON WANDERERS	W 4-0	Lynn, Hitchens, Sewell, Higgins o.g.	30,093
Apr 12	Preston North End	D 1-1	Myerscough	21,043
Apr 19	SHEFFIELD WEDNESDAY	W 2-0	Hitchens 2	25,955
Apr 26	Manchester City	W 2-1	Smith, Sewell	28,278
Apr 30	NOTTINGHAM FOREST	D 1-1	Hitchens	20,046

FA Cup

Jan 4	Stoke City	(Rd 3)	D 1-1	McParland	49,066
Jan 8	STOKE CITY	(R)	D 3-3	Sewell, Lynn, Hitchens	38,939
Jan 13	Stoke City*	(2nd R)	L 0-2		36,554

*Played at Molineux, Wolverhampton.

FA Charity Shield

Oct 19	Manchester United	L 0-4		27,923

Fact File

Stan Lynn became the first full back ever to score a hat-trick in First Division football when he netted three times in the home win over Sunderland on 11 January 1958.

MANAGER: Eric Houghton

CAPTAIN: Johnny Dixon, Pat Saward, Vic Crowe

TOP SCORER: Peter McParland 17 (16 League)

BIGGEST WIN: 5-1 v Leicester City (H), Division One, 28 September 1957

HIGHEST ATTENDANCE: 50,807 v Birmingham City (A), Division One, 24 August 1957

MAJOR TRANSFERS IN: Gerry Hitchens from Cardiff City

MAJOR TRANSFERS OUT: Stan Crowther to Manchester United

League & Cup Appearances

PLAYER	LEAGUE	CUP COMPETITION FA CUP	OTHER	TOTAL
Aldis	30	2	1	33
Ashfield	8	1		9
Birch	2			2
Chapman	8			8
Crowe	23	3		26
Crowther	26	2	1	29
Dixon	14			14
Dugdale	38	2	1	41
Hazelden	9	2		11
Hinchcliffe	2			2
Hitchens	20	2		22
Jackson	1			1
Jones	5			5
Lynn	40	3	1	44
McParland	41	3	1	45
Myerscough	22	2	1	25
Pace	12		1	13
Pritchard	1			1
Roberts	2			2
Sabin	1			1
Saward	40	2	1	43
Sewell	36	3	1	40
Sims	41			41
Smith	29	3	1	33
Southren	11			11

Goalscorers

PLAYER	LEAGUE	CUP COMPETITION FA CUP	OTHER	TOTAL
McParland	16	1		17
Hitchens	10	1		11
Sewell	10	1		11
Lynn	8	1		9
Myerscough	5			5
Crowther	4			4
Hazelden	3			3
Pace	3			3
Southren	3			3
Chapman	2			2
Dixon	2			2
Smith	2			2
Dugdale	1			1
Opps' o.gs.	4			4

Final Division One Table

		P	W	D	L	F	A	Pts
1	WOLVERHAMPTON W	42	28	8	6	103	47	64
2	PRESTON NE	42	26	7	9	100	51	59
3	TOTTENHAM H	42	21	9	12	93	77	51
4	WBA	42	18	14	10	92	70	50
5	MANCHESTER C	42	22	5	15	104	100	49
6	BURNLEY	42	21	5	16	80	74	47
7	BLACKPOOL	42	19	6	17	80	67	44
8	LUTON T	42	19	6	17	69	63	44
9	MANCHESTER U	42	16	11	15	85	75	43
10	NOTTINGHAM F	42	16	10	16	69	63	42
11	CHELSEA	42	15	12	15	83	79	42
12	ARSENAL	42	16	7	19	73	85	39
13	BIRMINGHAM C	42	14	11	17	76	89	39
14	ASTON VILLA	42	16	7	19	73	86	39
15	BOLTON W	42	14	10	18	65	87	38
16	EVERTON	42	13	11	18	65	75	37
17	LEEDS U	42	14	9	19	51	63	37
18	LEICESTER C	42	14	5	23	91	112	33
19	NEWCASTLE U	42	12	8	22	73	81	32
20	PORTSMOUTH	42	12	8	22	73	88	32
21	SUNDERLAND	42	10	12	20	54	97	32
22	SHEFFIELD W	42	12	7	23	69	92	31

The Essential History of Aston Villa

Football League Division One

DATE	OPPONENTS	SCORE	GOALSCORERS	ATTENDANCE
Aug 23	BIRMINGHAM CITY	D 1-1	Lynn (pen)	53,028
Aug 25	PORTSMOUTH	W 3-2	Myerscough, Dixon, McParland	34,797
Aug 30	West Ham United	L 2-7	Sewell, Smith	30,506
Sep 3	Portsmouth	L 2-5	Hitchens, Smith	24,209
Sep 6	NOTTINGHAM FOREST	L 2-3	Smith, Hitchens	29,036
Sep 8	WOLVERHAMPTON WANDERERS	L 1-3	Hitchens	41,845
Sep 13	Chelsea	L 1-2	Hazelden	44,023
Sep 17	Wolverhampton Wanderers	L 0-4		41,845
Sep 20	BLACKPOOL	D 1-1	Myerscough	22,970
Sep 27	Blackburn Rovers	W 3-2	McParland, Hitchens, Smith	27,376
Oct 4	NEWCASTLE UNITED	W 2-1	Barrett 2	29,335
Oct 11	WEST BROMWICH ALBION	W 1-0	Barrett	47,124
Oct 18	Leeds United	D 0-0		21,088
Oct 22	ARSENAL	L 1-2	McParland	31,862
Oct 25	BOLTON WANDERERS	W 2-1	McParland, Lynn	24,708
Nov 1	Luton Town	L 1-2	Hitchens	18,040
Nov 8	EVERTON	L 2-4	Sewell, Hitchens	27,649
Nov 15	Leicester City	L 3-6	Sewell, Hitchens 2	25,079
Nov 22	PRESTON NORTH END	W 2-0	Smith (pen), McParland	24,830
Nov 29	Burnley	L 1-3	Hitchens	15,023
Dec 6	MANCHESTER CITY	D 1-1	Myerscough	19,018
Dec 13	Arsenal	W 2-1	Myerscough, McParland	32,170
Dec 20	Birmingham City	L 1-4	Hazelden	31,829
Dec 26	Manchester United	L 1-2	Myerscough	63,098
Dec 27	MANCHESTER UNITED	L 0-2		56,450
Jan 3	WEST HAM UNITED	L 1-2	McParland	33,360
Jan 31	CHELSEA	W 3-1	Myerscough, Lynn, McParland	33,360
Feb 7	Blackpool	L 1-2	McParland	13,704
Feb 18	BLACKBURN ROVERS	W 1-0	Sewell	29,903
Feb 21	Newcastle United	L 0-1		20,182
Mar 7	LEEDS UNITED	W 2-1	Sewell, Hitchens	27,631
Mar 18	Bolton Wanderers	W 3-1	Hitchens 3	20,038
Mar 21	LUTON TOWN	W 3-1	Smith (pen), Hitchens 2	24,675
Mar 27	Tottenham Hotspur	L 2-3	McParland 2	45,059
Mar 28	Everton	L 1-2	McParland	34,986
Mar 30	TOTTENHAM HOTSPUR	D 1-1	McParland	34,660
Apr 4	LEICESTER CITY	L 1-2	Dixon	40,795
Apr 11	Preston North End	L 2-4	Myerscough, Sewell	12,244
Apr 18	BURNLEY	D 0-0		25,866
Apr 20	Nottingham Forest	L 0-2		18,803
Apr 25	Manchester City	D 0-0		39,661
Apr 29	West Bromwich Albion	D 1-1	Hitchens	48,281

FA Cup

Jan 10	ROTHERHAM UNITED	(Rd 3) W 2-1	Sewell, Hitchens	33,923
Jan 24	Chelsea	(Rd 4) W 2-1	Hitchens, Myerscough	55,944
Feb 14	Everton	(Rd 5) W 4-1	Wylie 3, McParland	60,225
Feb 28	BURNLEY	(Rd 6) D 0-0		60,145
Mar 3	Burnley	(R) W 2-0	McParland 2	39,066
Mar 14	Nottingham Forest*	(SF) L 0-1		64,882

*Played at Hillsborough, Sheffield.

League & Cup Appearances

PLAYER	LEAGUE	CUP COMPETITION FA CUP	TOTAL
Aldis	27	6	33
Barrett	5		5
Beaton	1		1
Birch	2		2
Crowe	33	6	39
Dixon	28	6	34
Dugdale	41	6	47
Hazelden	8		8
Hitchens	35	6	41
Jackson	5		5
Lee	14		14
Lynn	25	2	27
McParland	41	6	47
Myerscough	29	4	33
Saward	14		14
Sewell	31	6	37
Sharples	13		13
Sims	41	6	47
Smith	33	2	35
Southren	1		1
Willis	1		1
Winton	14	4	18
Wylie	20	6	26

Goalscorers

PLAYER	LEAGUE	CUP COMPETITION FA CUP	TOTAL
Hitchens	16	2	18
McParland	13	3	16
Myerscough	7	1	8
Sewell	6	1	7
Smith	6		6
Barrett	3		3
Lynn	3		3
Wylie		3	3
Dixon	2		2
Hazelden	2		2

Fact File

Ron Wylie's hat-trick against Everton on St Valentine's Day was the first by a Villa player in the FA Cup since Frank Broome's treble against Millwall in 1946. And it was to be another 23 years before it was repeated.

MANAGER: Eric Houghton, Joe Mercer

CAPTAIN: Vic Crowe, Johnny Dixon

TOP SCORER: Gerry Hitchens, 18 (16 league)

BIGGEST WIN: 4-1 v Everton (A), FA Cup Fifth Round, 14 February 1959

HIGHEST ATTENDANCE: 64,882 v Nottingham Forest, FA Cup semi-final at Hillsborough, 14 March 1959

MAJOR TRANSFERS IN: Doug Winton from Burnley, Ron Wylie from Notts County

MAJOR TRANSFERS OUT: Billy Myerscough to Rotherham United

Final Division One Table

		P	W	D	L	F	A	Pts
1	WOLVERHAMPTON W	42	28	5	9	110	49	61
2	MANCHESTER U	42	24	7	11	103	66	55
3	ARSENAL	42	21	8	13	88	68	50
4	BOLTON W	42	20	10	12	79	66	50
5	WBA	42	18	13	11	88	68	49
6	WEST HAM U	42	21	6	15	85	70	48
7	BURNLEY	42	19	10	13	81	70	48
8	BLACKPOOL	42	18	11	13	66	49	47
9	BIRMINGHAM C	42	20	6	16	84	68	46
10	BLACKBURN R	42	17	10	15	76	70	44
11	NEWCASTLE U	42	17	7	18	80	80	41
12	PRESTON NE	42	17	7	18	70	77	41
13	NOTTINGHAM F	42	17	6	19	71	74	40
14	CHELSEA	42	18	4	20	77	98	40
15	LEEDS U	42	15	9	18	57	74	39
16	EVERTON	42	17	4	21	71	87	38
17	LUTON T	42	12	13	17	68	71	37
18	TOTTENHAM H	42	13	10	19	85	95	36
19	LEICESTER C	42	11	10	21	67	98	32
20	MANCHESTER C	42	11	9	22	64	95	31
21	ASTON VILLA	42	11	8	23	58	87	30
22	PORTSMOUTH	42	6	9	27	64	112	21

Season 1959-60

Football League Division Two

DATE	OPPONENTS	SCORE	GOALSCORERS	ATTENDANCE
Aug 22	Brighton & Hove Albion	W 2-1	MacEwan, Sewell	31,828
Aug 26	Sunderland	L 0-1		29,860
Aug 29	SWANSEA TOWN	W 1-0	McParland	34,666
Aug 31	SUNDERLAND	W 3-0	Hitchens 2, Thomson	23,188
Sep 5	Bristol Rovers	D 1-1	Hitchens	26,162
Sep 9	Portsmouth	W 2-1	Hitchens, Thomson	19,910
Sep 12	IPSWICH TOWN	W 2-1	McParland, Wylie	36,608
Sep 15	PORTSMOUTH	W 5-2	Thomson, McParland 2, MacEwan 2	36,776
Sep 19	Huddersfield Town	W 1-0	McParland	22,522
Sep 26	LEYTON ORIENT	W 1-0	Hitchens	39,467
Sep 30	Stoke City	D 3-3	Thompson o.g., McParland 2	27,155
Oct 3	Lincoln City	D 0-0		13,850
Oct 10	Sheffield United	D 1-1	Hitchens	25,146
Oct 17	MIDDLESBROUGH	W 1-0	Lynn	34,773
Oct 24	Derby County	D 2-2	McParland 2	26,394
Oct 31	PLYMOUTH ARGYLE	W 2-0	MacEwan, McParland	35,531
Nov 7	Liverpool	L 1-2	McParland	49,981
Nov 14	CHARLTON ATHLETIC	W 11-1	Hitchens 5, Wylie, Thomson 2, MacEwan, McParland 2	21,997
Nov 21	Bristol City	W 5-0	Hitchens 3, Wylie, McParland	29,738
Nov 28	SCUNTHORPE UNITED	W 5-0	McParland 2, Hitchins 2, Thomson	39,185
Dec 5	Rotherham United	L 1-2	Adam	20,545
Dec 12	CARDIFF CITY	W 2-0	Adam, Hitchens	54,763
Dec 19	BRIGHTON & HOVE ALBION	W 3-1	McParland 2, Hitchens	29,875
Dec 26	Hull City	W 1-0	McParland	29,399
Dec 28	HULL CITY	D 1-1	Lynn (pen)	34,160
Jan 2	Swansea Town	W 3-1	Thomson 2, Hitchens	25,653
Jan 16	BRISTOL ROVERS	W 4-1	Thomson 2, Crowe, Adam	29,110
Jan 23	Ipswich Town	L 1-2	Dugdale	19,185
Feb 6	HUDDERSFIELD TOWN	W 4-0	Thomson 3, Hitchens	44,879
Feb 13	Leyton Orient	D 0-0		16,993
Feb 27	SHEFFIELD UNITED	L 1-3	Thomson	43,830
Mar 1	LINCOLN CITY	D 1-1	Thomson	33,868
Mar 5	Middlesbrough	W 1-0	Hitchens	39,071
Mar 15	DERBY COUNTY	W 3-2	Lynn (pen), Crowe, McParland	37,672
Mar 19	Scunthorpe United	W 2-1	Hitchens 2	13,084
Mar 30	LIVERPOOL	D 4-4	McParland, Thomson 2, Lynn (pen)	27,048
Apr 2	Charlton Athletic	L 0-2		28,068
Apr 9	BRISTOL CITY	W 2-1	Lynn 2 (2 pens)	33,682
Apr 16	Cardiff City	L 0-1		54,769
Apr 18	STOKE CITY	W 2-1	Lynn (pen), Thomson	25,939
Apr 23	ROTHERHAM UNITED	W 3-0	Thomson 2, Wylie	31,932
Apr 30	Plymouth Argyle	L 0-3		29,895

FA Cup

Jan 9	LEEDS UNITED	(Rd 3)	W 2-1	McParland, Wylie	43,474
Jan 30	Chelsea	(Rd 4)	W 2-1	McParland, Thomson	66,671
Feb 20	Port Vale	(Rd 5)	W 2-1	Hitchens, Thomson	48,749
Mar 12	PRESTON NORTH END	(Rd 6)	W 2-0	Hitchens, McParland	69,732
Mar 26	Wolverhampton Wanderers*	(SF)	L 0-1		55,596

*Played at the Hawthorns, West Bromwich.

MANAGER: Joe Mercer

CAPTAIN: Vic Crowe

TOP SCORER: Gerry Hitchens, 25 (23 league); Peter McParland, 25 (22 league)

BIGGEST WIN: 11-1 v Charlton Athletic (H), Division Two, 14 November 1959

HIGHEST ATTENDANCE: 69,732 v Preston North End (H), FA Cup Sixth Round, 12 March 1960

MAJOR TRANSFERS IN: Jimmy MacEwan from Raith Rovers, John Neal from Swansea Town, Bobby Thomson from Wolverhampton Wanderers

MAJOR TRANSFERS OUT: Jackie Sewell to Hull City

League & Cup Appearances

PLAYER	LEAGUE	CUP COMPETITION FA CUP	TOTAL
Adam	21		21
Ashe	1		1
Birch	1		1
Burrows	1		1
Crowe	41	5	46
Deakin	1		1
Dixon	4		4
Dugdale	39	5	44
Handley	3		3
Hitchens	36	5	41
Keelan	3		3
Lynn	42	5	47
MacEwan	28	5	33
McParland	41	5	46
Morrall	3		3
Neal	41	5	46
Saward	40	5	45
Sewell	2		2
Sims	39	5	44
Thomson	34	5	39
Tindall	2		2
Winton	1		1
Wylie	38	5	43

Goalscorers

PLAYER	LEAGUE	CUP COMPETITION FA CUP	TOTAL
Hitchens	23	2	25
McParland	22	3	25
Thomson	20	2	22
Lynn	7		7
MacEwan	5		5
Wylie	4	1	5
Adam	3		3
Crowe	2		2
Dugdale	1		1
Sewell	1		1
Opps' o.gs.	1		1

Fact File

Villa's 11-1 win over Charlton was the first time they had reached double figures in a league game since 29 August 1925 when they beat Burnley 10-0 on the opening day of the season.

Final Division Two Table

		P	W	D	L	F	A	Pts
1	ASTON VILLA	42	25	9	8	89	43	59
2	CARDIFF C	42	23	12	7	90	62	58
3	LIVERPOOL	42	20	10	12	90	66	50
4	SHEFFIELD U	42	19	12	11	68	51	50
5	MIDDLESBROUGH	42	19	10	13	90	64	48
6	HUDDERSFIELD T	42	19	9	14	73	52	47
7	CHARLTON ATH	42	17	13	12	90	87	47
8	ROTHERHAM U	42	17	13	12	61	60	47
9	BRISTOL R	42	18	11	13	72	78	47
10	LEYTON ORIENT	42	15	14	13	76	61	44
11	IPSWICH T	42	19	6	17	78	68	44
12	SWANSEA T	42	15	10	17	82	84	40
13	LINCOLN C	42	16	7	19	75	78	39
14	BRIGHTON & HA	42	13	12	17	67	76	38
15	SCUNTHORPE U	42	13	10	19	57	71	36
16	SUNDERLAND	42	12	12	18	52	65	36
17	STOKE C	42	14	7	21	66	83	35
18	DERBY CO	42	14	7	21	61	77	35
19	PLYMOUTH ARG	42	13	9	20	61	89	35
20	PORTSMOUTH	42	10	12	20	59	77	32
21	HULL C	42	10	10	22	48	76	30
22	BRISTOL C	42	11	5	26	60	97	27

Season 1960-61

Football League Division One

DATE	OPPONENTS	SCORE	GOALSCORERS	ATTENDANCE
Aug 20	CHELSEA	W 3-2	McParland, Hitchens, Thomson	43,776
Aug 22	West Ham United	L 2-5	Thomson, Hitchens	28,884
Aug 27	Blackpool	L 3-5	McParland, Hitchens 2	16,821
Aug 29	WEST HAM UNITED	W 2-1	Hitchens, Thomson	32,121
Sep 3	Everton	W 3-2	Hitchens 2, Thomson	37,036
Sep 7	Cardiff City	D 1-1	Crowe	35,000
Sep 10	Blackburn Rovers	L 1-4	Hitchens	22,300
Sep 12	CARDIFF CITY	W 2-1	Thomson, Burrows	32,958
Sep 17	MANCHESTER UNITED	W 3-1	Burrows, Thomson, MacEwan	35,493
Sep 24	Tottenham Hotspur	L 2-6	MacEwan, Hitchens	61,356
Oct 1	LEICESTER CITY	L 1-3	McParland	29,623
Oct 8	NEWCASTLE UNITED	W 2-0	Wylie, Crowe	25,336
Oct 15	Arsenal	L 1-2	MacEwan	34,048
Oct 22	BIRMINGHAM CITY	W 6-2	O'Neill 2, McParland, Hitchens 3	46,306
Oct 29	West Bromwich Albion	W 2-0	Hitchens, O'Neill	41,903
Nov 5	BURNLEY	W 2-0	Hitchens 2	35,772
Nov 12	Preston North End	D 1-1	McParland	11,093
Nov 19	FULHAM	W 2-1	MacEwan, Wylie	32,140
Nov 26	Sheffield Wednesday	W 2-1	Megson o.g., Hitchens	27,939
Dec 3	MANCHESTER CITY	W 5-1	O'Neill, Hitchens 2 (1 pen), McParland, Wylie	25,093
Dec 10	Nottingham Forest	L 0-2		23,178
Dec 17	Chelsea	W 4-2	Thomson 2, Wylie, MacEwan	23,805
Dec 24	WOLVERHAMPTON WANDERERS	L 0-2		48,795
Dec 26	Wolverhampton Wanderers	L 2-3	Hitchens 2	43,161
Dec 31	BLACKPOOL	D 2-2	Hitchens 2	30,037
Jan 21	BLACKBURN ROVERS	D 2-2	Hitchens 2	31,885
Feb 4	Manchester United	D 1-1	Thomson	33,525
Feb 11	TOTTENHAM HOTSPUR	L 1-2	Lynn (pen)	50,810
Feb 25	Newcastle United	L 1-2	McParland	21,275
Mar 4	ARSENAL	D 2-2	McParland, MacEwan	34,646
Mar 11	Birmingham City	D 1-1	Hitchens	41,645
Mar 22	Everton	W 2-1	Deakin, Thomson	28,115
Mar 25	Burnley	D 1-1	Hitchens	17,726
Mar 28	WEST BROMWICH ALBION	L 0-1		42,800
Apr 1	Nottingham Forest	L 1-2	McParland	25,780
Apr 3	Bolton Wanderers	L 0-3		20,334
Apr 4	BOLTON WANDERERS	W 4-0	MacEwan 2, McParland, O'Neill	15,990
Apr 8	Fulham	D 1-1	Hitchens	23,042
Apr 15	PRESTON NORTH END	W 1-0	Thomson	25,703
Apr 19	Leicester city	L 1-3	Hale	21,219
Apr 22	Manchester City	L 1-4	Crowe	25,235
Apr 29	SHEFFIELD WEDNESDAY	W 4-1	Hitchens 2, Thomson, Dixon	26,034

FA Cup

Jan 7	Bristol Rovers	(Rd 3) D 1-1	Thomson	34,061
Jan 9	BRISTOL ROVERS	(R) W 4-0	Thomson 2, Hitchens 2	26,542
Jan 28	Peterborough United	(Rd 4) D 1-1	Banham o.g.	28,266
Feb 1	PETERBOROUGH UNITED	(R) W 2-1	McParland	64,531
Feb 18	TOTTENHAM HOTSPUR	(Rd 5) L 0-2		69,672

League Cup

Oct 12	HUDDERSFIELD TOWN	(Rd 2) W 4-1	Wylie 2, Hitchens, Burrows	17,057
Nov 15	Preston North End	(Rd 3) W 3-0	O'Neill, Thomson, Hitchens	7,677
Nov 23	PRESTON NORTH END	(R) W 3-1	Hitchens, Wylie, MacEwan	15,000
Dec 13	Plymouth Argyle	(Rd 4) D 3-3	McParland 2, MacEwan	12,117
Dec 19	Plymouth Argyle	(R) D 0-0*		11,906
Feb 6	Plymouth Argyle	(2nd R) W 5-3	Burrows, O'Neill, Hitchens 3	13,548
Feb 22	WREXHAM	(Rd 5) W 3-0	Thomson, Hitchens 2	19,500
Apr 10	Burnley	(SF) D 1-1	Hitchens	16,094
Apr 26	BURNLEY	(R) D 2-2†	Hitchens, Thomson	24,000
May 2	Burnley§	(2nd R) W 2-1	Lynn (pen), Hitchens	7,953
Aug 2	Rotherham United‡	(F/FL) L 0-2		12,226
Sep 5	Rotherham United‡	(F/SL) W 3-0§	O'Neill, Burrows, McParland	30,765

*Abandoned at 90 minutes. †After extra-time. §Played at Old Trafford, Manchester.
‡Two-legged final played at the start of the 1961-62 season.

MANAGER: Joe Mercer

CAPTAIN: Vic Crowe

TOP SCORER: Gerry Hitchens, 42 (29 league)

BIGGEST WIN: 6-2 v Birmingham City (H), Division One, 22 October 1960

HIGHEST ATTENDANCE: 69,672 v Tottenham Hotspur (H), FA Cup Fifth Round, 18 February 1961

MAJOR TRANSFERS IN: Alan O'Neill from Sunderland

MAJOR TRANSFERS OUT: Gerry Hitchens to Inter Milan, Johnny Dixon retired

League & Cup Appearances

PLAYER	LEAGUE	CUP COMPETITION		TOTAL
		FA CUP	LC	
Adam	3			3
Aitken	1			1
Baker A	1			1
Brown			1	1
Burrows	11		6	17
Crowe	39	5	11	55
Deakin	23	2	9	34
Dixon	1			1
Dugdale	36	5	11	52
Hale	2			2
Hitchens	41	5	10	56
Keelan	2			2
Kenning	3			3
Lee	11		5	16
Lynn	14	3	5	22
MacEwan	37	5	11	53
McMorran	2			2
McParland	32	5	8	45
Morrall	5		1	6
Neal	36	5	7	48
O'Neill	15	3	6	24
Potter	3	2	1	6
Saward	11		1	12
Sidebottom	7	1	2	10
Simms	30	2	9	41
Sleeuwenhoek	1			1
Thomson	39	5	11	55
Winton	22	2	7	31
Wylie	34	5	10	49

Goalscorers

PLAYER	LEAGUE	CUP COMPETITION		TOTAL
		FA CUP	LC	
Hitchens	29	2	11	42
Thomson	12	3	3	18
McParland	10	2	3	15
MacEwan	8		2	10
O'Neill	5		3	8
Wylie	4		3	7
Burrows	2		3	5
Crowe	3			3
Deakin	1			1
Lynn	1		1	2
Dixon	1			1
Hale	1			1
Opps' o.gs.	1	1		2

Fact File

Ralph Brown's only first-team appearance for Villa was in the first leg of the League Cup final at Rotherham.

Final Division One Table

		P	W	D	L	F	A	Pts
1	TOTTENHAM H	42	31	4	7	115	55	66
2	SHEFFIELD W	42	23	12	7	78	47	58
3	WOLVERHAMPTON W	42	25	7	10	103	75	57
4	BURNLEY	42	22	7	13	102	77	51
5	EVERTON	42	22	6	14	87	69	50
6	LEICESTER C	42	18	9	15	87	70	45
7	MANCHESTER U	42	18	9	15	88	76	45
8	BLACKBURN R	42	15	13	14	77	76	43
9	ASTON VILLA	42	17	9	16	78	77	43
10	WBA	42	18	5	19	67	71	41
11	ARSENAL	42	15	11	16	77	85	41
12	CHELSEA	42	15	7	20	98	100	37
13	MANCHESTER C	42	13	11	18	79	90	37
14	NOTTINGHAM F	42	14	9	19	62	78	37
15	CARDIFF C	42	13	11	18	60	85	37
16	WEST HAM U	42	13	10	19	77	88	36
17	FULHAM	42	14	8	20	72	95	36
18	BOLTON W	42	12	11	19	58	73	35
19	BIRMINGHAM C	42	14	6	22	62	84	34
20	BLACKPOOL	42	12	9	21	68	73	33
21	NEWCASTLE U	42	11	10	21	86	109	32
22	PRESTON NE	42	10	10	22	43	71	30

Season 1961-62

Football League Division One

DATE	OPPONENTS	SCORE	GOALSCORERS	ATTENDANCE
Aug 19	Everton	L 0-2		52,293
Aug 26	CHELSEA	W 3-1	Thomson, Burrows, MacEwan	35,840
Aug 28	Wolverhampton Wanderers	D 2-2	Dougan 2	31,703
Sep 2	Sheffield United	W 2-0	Burrows, Dougan	18,500
Sep 9	WEST HAM UNITED	L 2-4	Crowe, McParland	31,903
Sep 16	Blackburn Rovers	L 2-4	Tindall, Burrows	14,000
Sep 18	MANCHESTER UNITED	D 1-1	McParland	38,837
Sep 23	BLACKPOOL	W 5-0	Burrows 2, McParland 3	34,035
Sep 30	Tottenham Hotspur	L 0-1		37,920
Oct 2	WOLVERHAMPTON WANDERERS	W 1-0	MacEwan	39,823
Oct 7	Fulham	L 1-3	MacEwan	25,000
Oct 16	SHEFFIELD WEDNESDAY	W 1-0	McParland	38,767
Oct 21	West Bromwich Albion	D 1-1	Jones o.g.	39,071
Oct 28	BIRMINGHAM CITY	L 1-3	McParland	39,790
Nov 4	Burnley	L 0-3		22,000
Nov 11	ARSENAL	W 3-1	Burrows, McParland, Thomson	35,000
Nov 18	Bolton Wanderers	D 1-1	Thomson	13,198
Nov 25	MANCHESTER CITY	W 2-1	Burrows, McParland	26,606
Dec 2	Leicester City	W 2-0	Wylie, Dougan	21,000
Dec 9	IPSWICH TOWN	W 3-0	McParland 2, Thomson	33,000
Dec 16	EVERTON	D 1-1	Thomson	34,939
Dec 23	Chelsea	L 0-1		21,000
Dec 26	Cardiff City	L 0-1		16,140
Jan 13	SHEFFIELD UNITED	D 0-0		28,000
Jan 15	Manchester United	L 0-2		20,807
Jan 20	West Ham United	L 0-2		20,000
Feb 3	BLACKBURN ROVERS	W 1-0	Dougan	25,740
Feb 10	Blackpool	W 2-1	MacEwan, McMorran	13,039
Feb 21	TOTTENHAM HOTSPUR	D 0-0		49,727
Feb 24	FULHAM	W 2-0	MacEwan, Burrows	19,598
Mar 3	Sheffield Wednesday	L 0-3		23,896
Mar 14	WEST BROMWICH ALBION	W 1-0	Burrows	35,104
Mar 17	Birmingham City	W 2-0	Burrows, Wylie	45,885
Mar 24	BURNLEY	L 0-2		36,772
Mar 31	Arsenal	W 5-4	Thomson 2, Crowe, Dougan, Ewing	20,107
Apr 7	BOLTON WANDERERS	W 3-0	Ewing, Thomson, Dougan	24,690
Apr 14	Manchester City	L 0-1		18,564
Apr 21	LEICESTER CITY	W 8-3	Thomson 3, Dougan 2, Burrows, Baker, Chalmers o.g.	24,184
Apr 23	NOTTINGHAM FOREST	W 5-1	Burrows 2 (1 pen), Ewing, McKinley o.g., Thomson	25,000
Apr 24	Nottingham Forest	L 0-2		24,890
Apr 28	Ipswich Town	L 0-2		29,000
May 1	CARDIFF CITY	D 2-2	Rankmore o.g., Dougan	21,446

FA Cup

Jan 6	CRYSTAL PALACE	(Rd 3) W 4-3	Burrows 2, McParland, Dougan	45,147
Jan 27	HUDDERSFIELD TOWN	(Rd 4) W 2-1	Hale, Crowe	38,013
Feb 17	CHARLTON ATHLETIC	(Rd 5) W 2-1	Dougan, Burrows	44,663
Mar 10	Tottenham Hotspur	(Rd 6) L 0-2		63,879

League Cup

Sep 13	Bradford City	(Rd 1) W 4-3	MacEwan, Wylie 2, Burrows	9,768
Oct 9	West Ham United	(Rd 2) W 3-1	McParland, Burrows, Bond o.g.	17,775
Nov 21	IPSWICH TOWN	(Rd 3) L 2-3	Burrows 2 (1 pen)	22,704

MANAGER: Joe Mercer

CAPTAIN: Vic Crowe

TOP SCORER: Harry Burrows 20 (13 league)

BIGGEST WIN: 8-3 v Leicester City (H), Division One, 21 April 1962

HIGHEST ATTENDANCE: 63,879 v Tottenham Hotspur (A), FA Cup Third Round, 10 March 1962

MAJOR TRANSFERS IN: Derek Dougan from Blackburn Rovers, Tommy Ewing from Partick Thistle

MAJOR TRANSFERS OUT: Jimmy Dugdale to Queens Park Rangers, Peter McParland to Wolverhampton Wanderers, Stan Lynn to Birmingham City

League & Cup Appearances

PLAYER	LEAGUE	CUP COMPETITION		TOTAL
		FA CUP	LC	
Aitken	35	4	3	42
Ashe	4			4
Baker	14		1	15
Briggs	1			1
Burrows	34	4	3	41
Crowe	42	4	2	48
Deakin	40	4	2	46
Dougan	23	4		27
Dugdale	7		1	8
Ewing	12			12
Fencott	1			1
Hale	3	2		5
Jones	1			1
Lee	32	4	1	37
Lynn	1		1	2
MacEwan	24	3	2	29
McMorran	9		1	12
McParland	21	1	3	25
Neal	15		1	16
O'Neill	3		1	4
Sidebottom	14	1	2	17
Sims	28	3	1	32
Sleeuwenhoek	35	4	2	41
Thomson	28	1	1	30
Tindall	10	1	2	13
Wylie	25	2	3	30

Goalscorers

PLAYER	LEAGUE	CUP COMPETITION		TOTAL
		FA CUP	LC	
Burrows	13	3	4	20
McParland	11	1	1	13
Thomson	12			12
Dougan	10	2		12
MacEwan	5		1	6
Wylie	2		2	4
Ewing	3			3
Crowe	2	1		3
Baker	1			1
McMorran	1			1
Tindall	1			1
Hale		1		1
Opps' o.gs.	4		1	5

Fact File

During September and October Villa were without the services of Derek Dougan and Bobby Thomson who were both involved in a serious road accident.

Final Division One Table

		P	W	D	L	F	A	Pts
1	IPSWICH T	42	24	8	10	93	67	56
2	BURNLEY	42	21	11	10	101	67	53
3	TOTTENHAM H	42	21	10	11	88	69	52
4	EVERTON	42	20	11	11	88	54	51
5	SHEFFIELD U	42	19	9	14	61	69	47
6	SHEFFIELD W	42	20	6	16	72	58	46
7	ASTON VILLA	42	18	8	16	65	56	44
8	WEST HAM U	42	17	10	15	76	82	44
9	WBA	42	15	13	14	83	67	43
10	ARSENAL	42	16	11	15	71	72	43
11	BOLTON W	42	16	10	16	62	66	42
12	MANCHESTER C	42	17	7	18	78	81	41
13	BLACKPOOL	42	15	11	16	70	75	41
14	LEICESTER C	42	17	6	19	72	71	40
15	MANCHESTER U	42	15	9	18	72	75	39
16	BLACKBURN R	42	14	11	17	50	58	39
17	BIRMINGHAM C	42	14	10	18	65	81	38
18	WOLVERHAMPTON W	42	13	10	19	73	86	36
19	NOTTINGHAM F	42	13	10	19	63	79	36
20	FULHAM	42	13	7	22	66	74	33
21	CARDIFF C	42	9	14	19	50	81	32
22	CHELSEA	42	9	10	23	63	94	28

The Essential History of Aston Villa

Football League Division One

DATE	OPPONENTS	SCORE	GOALSCORERS	ATTENDANCE
Aug 18	WEST HAM UNITED	W 3-1	Dougan, MacEwan, Thomson	39,556
Aug 20	TOTTENHAM HOTSPUR	W 2-1	Dougan 2	64,751
Aug 25	Manchester City	W 2-0	Thomson, Burrows	29,524
Aug 29	Tottenham Hotspur	L 2-4	Dougan, Deakin	55,650
Sep 1	BLACKPOOL	D 1-1	MacEwan	36,012
Sep 4	Arsenal	W 2-1	Thomson 2	33,861
Sep 8	Blackburn Rovers	L 1-4	Burrows	12,100
Sep 10	ARSENAL	W 3-1	Thomson, Burrows (pen), MacEwan	36,705
Sep 15	SHEFFIELD UNITED	L 1-2	Shaw o.g.	32,339
Sep 22	Nottingham Forest	L 1-3	Burrows	32,046
Sep 29	IPSWICH TOWN	W 4-2	Wylie, Thomson 2, Dougan	36,242
Oct 6	WEST BROMWICH ALBION	W 2-0	Burrows (pen), Baker	43,613
Oct 13	Everton	D 1-1	Baker	53,045
Oct 20	LEYTON ORIENT	W 1-0	Burrows	25,208
Oct 27	Birmingham City	L 2-3	O'Neill, Burrows (pen)	42,207
Nov 3	FULHAM	L 1-2	Burrows (pen)	28,009
Nov 10	Sheffield Wednesday	D 0-0		20,574
Nov 17	BURNLEY	W 2-1	Burrows, Dougan	34,154
Nov 24	Manchester United	D 2-2	Cantwell o.g., Dougan	36,852
Dec 1	BOLTON WANDERERS	W 5-0	Burrows, MacEwan 2, Thomson, Dougan	34,114
Dec 8	Leicester City	D 3-3	Chalmers o.g., MacEwan, Burrows	26,773
Dec 15	West Ham United	D 1-1	Thomson	21,532
Jan 19	BLACKBURN ROVERS	D 0-0		21,340
Feb 13	Liverpool	L 0-4		46,374
Mar 9	Leyton Orient	W 2-0	Woosnam, Wylie	11,509
Mar 16	BIRMINGHAM CITY	W 4-0	Woosnam, Baker, Deakin, Burrows (pen)	46,680
Mar 23	Fulham	L 0-1		22,508
Mar 29	Blackpool	L 0-4		10,690
Apr 1	EVERTON	L 0-2		31,377
Apr 6	Burnley	L 1-3	Crowe	19,406
Apr 9	MANCHESTER UNITED	L 1-2	Thomson	26,867
Apr 13	SHEFFIELD WEDNESDAY	L 0-2		23,898
Apr 15	Wolverhampton Wanderers	L 1-3	Thomson o.g.	26,299
Apr 16	WOLVERHAMPTON WANDERERS	L 0-2		31,506
Apr 20	Bolton Wanderers	L 1-4	Burrows	13,316
May 1	Sheffield United	L 1-2	Burrows	17,111
May 4	NOTTINGHAM FOREST	L 0-2		23,927
May 8	MANCHESTER CITY	W 3-1	Baker, Burrows 2 (2 pens)	17,707
May 11	West Bromwich Albion	L 0-1		25,500
May 15	LEICESTER CITY	W 3-1	Lee, Fraser, Dougan	20,720
May 18	LIVERPOOL	W 2-0	Graham, Thomson	18,848
May 21	Ipswich Town	D 1-1	Thomson	17,222

FA Cup

Jan 16	Bristol City	(Rd 3) D 1-1	Burrows (pen)	22,176
Mar 7	BRISTOL CITY	(R) W 3-2	Burrows, Baker, Thomson	21,632
Mar 11	Manchester United	(Rd 4) L 0-1		52,265

League Cup

Sep 24	PETERBOROUGH UNITED	(Rd 2) W 6-1	Dougan 3, Ewing, Wylie, Burrows	17,372
Oct 17	STOKE CITY	(Rd 3) W 3-1	Thomson, Ewing, Burrows (pen)	24,990
Nov 12	PRESTON NORTH END	(Rd 4) W 6-2	Baker 2, O'Neill 2, Burrows 2 (1 pen)	18,815
Dec 3	NORWICH CITY	(Rd 5) W 4-1	Thomson 2, MacEwan, Dougan	13,826
Jan 12	Sunderland	(SF/FL) W 3-1	Crowe, Thomson, Dougan	32,237
Apr 22	SUNDERLAND	(SF/SL) D 0-0		21,550
May 23	Birmingham City	(F/FL) L 1-3	Thomson	31,580
May 27	BIRMINGHAM CITY	(F/SL) D 0-0		37,921

MANAGER: Joe Mercer

CAPTAIN: Vic Crowe

TOP SCORER: Harry Burrows, 22 (16 league)

BIGGEST WIN: 6-1 v Peterborough United (H), League Cup Second Round, 24 September 1962

HIGHEST ATTENDANCE: 64,751 v Tottenham Hotspur (H), Division One, 20 August 1962

MAJOR TRANSFERS IN: Cammie Fraser from Dunfermline Athletic

MAJOR TRANSFERS OUT: Derek Dougan to Peterborough United

League & Cup Appearances

PLAYER	LEAGUE	CUP COMPETITION		TOTAL
		FA CUP	LC	
Aitken	42	3	8	53
Baker	30	1	7	38
Briggs	1			1
Burrows	39	3	8	50
Chatterley	6		1	7
Crowe	36	3	8	47
Deakin	27	3	3	33
Dougan	28	1	4	33
Ewing	13		3	16
Fencott	1		2	3
Fraser	22	2	5	29
Gavan	4			4
Graham	2		2	4
Lee	24	1	5	30
MacEwan	19	3	2	24
Neal	4			4
O'Neill	5		1	6
Sidebottom	25	3	6	34
Sims	13		2	15
Sleeuwenhoek	35	2	7	44
Thomson	34	3	6	43
Tindall	15	1	3	19
Woosnam	18		3	21
Wylie	20	1	5	26

Goalscorers

PLAYER	LEAGUE	CUP COMPETITION		TOTAL
		FA CUP	LC	
Burrows	16	2	4	22
Thomson	12	1	5	18
Dougan	9		5	14
Baker	4	1	2	7
MacEwan	6		1	7
O'Neill	1		2	3
Wylie	2		1	3
Crowe	1		1	2
Deakin	2			2
Ewing			2	2
Woosnam	2			2
Fraser	1			1
Graham	1			1
Lee	1			1
Opps' o.gs.	4			4

Fact File

Harry Burrows had the chance of scoring a hat-trick of penalties in the home league game against Manchester City in May – but he missed from the spot, having scored from two earlier efforts.

Final Division One Table

		P	W	D	L	F	A	Pts
1	EVERTON	42	25	11	6	84	42	61
2	TOTTENHAM H	42	23	9	10	111	62	55
3	BURNLEY	42	22	10	10	78	57	54
4	LEICESTER C	42	20	12	10	79	53	52
5	WOLVERHAMPTON W	42	20	10	12	93	65	50
6	SHEFFIELD W	42	19	10	13	77	63	48
7	ARSENAL	42	18	10	14	86	77	46
8	LIVERPOOL	42	17	10	15	71	59	44
9	NOTTINGHAM F	42	17	10	15	67	69	44
10	SHEFFIELD U	42	16	12	14	58	60	44
11	BLACKBURN R	42	15	12	15	79	71	42
12	WEST HAM U	42	14	12	16	73	69	40
13	BLACKPOOL	42	13	14	15	58	64	40
14	WBA	42	16	7	19	71	79	39
15	ASTON VILLA	42	15	8	19	62	68	38
16	FULHAM	42	14	10	18	50	71	38
17	IPSWICH T	42	12	11	19	59	78	35
18	BOLTON W	42	15	5	22	55	75	35
19	MANCHESTER U	42	12	10	20	67	81	34
20	BIRMINGHAM C	42	10	13	19	63	90	33
21	MANCHESTER C	42	10	11	21	58	102	31
22	LEYTON ORIENT	42	6	9	27	37	81	21

Season 1963-64

Football League Division One

DATE	OPPONENTS	SCORE	GOALSCORERS	ATTENDANCE
Aug 24	Nottingham Forest	W 1-0	Hateley	28,687
Aug 26	STOKE CITY	L 1-3	Hateley	39,041
Aug 31	BLACKBURN ROVERS	L 1-2	England o.g.	21,522
Sep 4	Stoke City	D 2-2	Burrows, Hateley	36,649
Sep 7	Blackpool	W 4-0	Deakin, Burrows 3	16,885
Sep 10	Arsenal	L 0-3		29,198
Sep 14	CHELSEA	W 2-0	MacEwan, Hateley	23,720
Sep 16	TOTTENHAM HOTSPUR	L 2-4	Baker P o.g., Baker A	36,170
Sep 21	West Ham United	W 1-0	Burrows	20,346
Sep 28	SHEFFIELD UNITED	L 0-1		22,228
Oct 5	Liverpool	L 2-5	Hateley 2	39,106
Oct 7	EVERTON	L 0-1		27,540
Oct 12	West Bromwich Albion	L 3-4	Crawford o.g., Tindall, Hateley	28,602
Oct 19	ARSENAL	W 2-1	Hateley 2 (1 pen)	22,981
Oct 26	Sheffield Wednesday	L 0-1		20,616
Nov 2	BOLTON WANDERERS	W 3-0	Ewing, Burrows 2	18,833
Nov 9	Fulham	L 0-2		15,060
Nov 16	MANCHESTER UNITED	W 4-0	Hateley 2, Deakin, Burrows	36,276
Nov 23	Burnley	L 0-2		13,595
Nov 30	IPSWICH TOWN	D 0-0		16,333
Dec 7	Leicester City	D 0-0		21,402
Dec 14	NOTTINGHAM FOREST	W 3-0	Burrows, MacEwan, Whitefoot o.g.	14,182
Dec 21	Blackburn Rovers	L 0-2		17,095
Dec 26	Wolverhampton Wanderers	D 3-3	Pountney, Crowe, Hateley	27,569
Dec 28	WOLVERHAMPTON WANDERERS	D 2-2	Burrows 2	
Jan 11	BLACKPOOL	W 3-1	Woosnam 2, Hateley	14,232
Jan 18	Chelsea	L 0-1		23,968
Jan 25	Tottenham Hotspur	L 1-3	Burrows	35,877
Feb 1	WEST HAM UNITED	D 2-2	Burrows, Woosnam	16,550
Feb 8	Sheffield United	D 1-1	Wylie	14,740
Feb 19	LIVERPOOL	D 2-2	Burrows, Wylie	13,729
Feb 22	WEST BROMWICH ALBION	W 1-0	Woosnam	27,633
Feb 28	Everton	L 2-4	Burrows (pen), Graham	50,092
Mar 7	SHEFFIELD WEDNESDAY	D 2-2	Hateley, Aitken	13,922
Mar 21	FULHAM	D 2-2	Burrows, Tindall	11,436
Mar 28	Bolton Wanderers	D 1-1	Hateley	8,327
Mar 30	BIRMINGHAM CITY	L 0-3		25,890
Mar 31	Birmingham City	D 3-3	Chatterley 2, Tindall	28,048
Apr 4	BURNLEY	W 2-0	Hateley 2	14,296
Apr 6	Manchester United	L 0-1		25,858
Apr 11	Ipswich Town	L 3-4	Pountney 2, Wylie	11,660
Apr 18	LEICESTER CITY	L 1-3	Deakin	17,886

FA Cup

Jan 4	ALDERSHOT	(Rd 3)	D 0-0		21,912
Jan 8	Aldershot	(R)	L 1-2	Hateley	13,566

League Cup

Sep 25	BARNSLEY	(Rd 2)	W 3-1	Hateley, Baker, Burrows	10,679
Oct 16	West Ham United	(Rd 3)	L 0-2		11,194

League & Cup Appearances

PLAYER	LEAGUE	CUP COMPETITION		TOTAL
		FA CUP	LC	
Aitken	34	2	1	37
Baker	15		2	17
Burrows	40	2	1	43
Chatterley	4			4
Crowe	21	2	2	25
Deakin	36	2	1	39
Ewing	14	2	1	17
Fencott	2			2
Fraser	11			11
Graham	6			6
Hateley	35	2	2	39
Home	6			6
Lee	13		1	14
MacEwan	27	2	1	30
Parker	1			1
Pountney	18	1		19
Sidebottom	8			8
Sims	25	2	2	29
Sleeuwenhoek	40	2	2	44
Thomson	5			5
Tindall	18	1	1	20
Wilson	9			9
Woosnam	23		2	25
Wright	31	2	2	35
Wylie	20		1	21

Goalscorers

PLAYER	LEAGUE	CUP COMPETITION		TOTAL
		FA CUP	LC	
Hateley	17	1	1	19
Burrows	16		1	17
Woosnam	4			4
Deakin	3			3
Pountney	3			3
Tindall	3			3
Wylie	3			3
Baker	1		1	2
Chatterley	2			2
MacEwan	2			2
Aitken	1			1
Crowe	1			1
Ewing	1			1
Graham	1			1
Opps' o.gs.	4			4

Fact File

The attendance of 8,327 at Bolton on 28 March 1964 was the lowest for a Villa league game (home or away) for seven years.

MANAGER: Joe Mercer

CAPTAIN: Vic Crowe, Alan Deakin, Charlie Aitken

TOP SCORER: Tony Hateley, 19 (17 league)

BIGGEST WIN: 4-0 v Blackpool (A), Division One, 7 September 1963; v Manchester United (H), Division One, 16 November 1963

HIGHEST ATTENDANCE: 50,092 v Everton (A), Division One, 28 February 1964

MAJOR TRANSFERS IN: Tony Hateley from Notts County, Phil Woosnam from West Ham United

MAJOR TRANSFERS OUT: Vic Crowe to Peterborough United, Bobby Thomson to Birmingham City

Final Division One Table

		P	W	D	L	F	A	PTS
1	LIVERPOOL	42	26	5	11	92	45	57
2	MANCHESTER U	42	23	7	12	90	62	53
3	EVERTON	42	21	10	11	84	64	52
4	TOTTENHAM H	42	22	7	13	97	81	51
5	CHELSEA	42	20	10	12	72	56	50
6	SHEFFIELD W	42	19	11	12	84	67	49
7	BLACKBURN R	42	18	10	14	89	65	46
8	ARSENAL	42	17	11	14	90	82	45
9	BURNLEY	42	17	10	15	71	64	44
10	WBA	42	16	11	15	70	61	43
11	LEICESTER C	42	16	11	15	61	58	43
12	SHEFFIELD U	42	16	11	15	61	64	43
13	NOTTINGHAM F	42	16	9	17	64	68	41
14	WEST HAM U	42	14	12	16	69	74	40
15	FULHAM	42	13	13	16	58	65	39
16	WOLVERHAMPTON W	42	12	15	15	70	80	39
17	STOKE C	42	14	10	18	77	78	38
18	BLACKPOOL	42	13	9	20	52	73	35
19	ASTON VILLA	42	11	12	19	62	71	34
20	BIRMINGHAM C	42	11	7	24	54	92	29
21	BOLTON W	42	10	8	24	48	80	28
22	IPSWICH T	42	9	7	26	56	121	25

The Essential History of Aston Villa

Football League Division One

DATE	OPPONENTS	SCORE	GOALSCORERS	ATTENDANCE
Aug 22	LEEDS UNITED	L 1-2	Woosnam	27,623
Aug 26	Chelsea	L 1-2	Hateley	30,839
Aug 29	Arsenal	L 1-3	Hateley	28,732
Aug 31	CHELSEA	D 2-2	Hateley, Wylie	19,740
Sep 5	BLACKBURN ROVERS	L 0-4		21,798
Sep 9	Sunderland	D 2-2	Burrows, Hateley	44,099
Sep 12	Blackpool	L 1-3	Hateley	22,795
Sep 14	SUNDERLAND	W 2-1	Aitken, Hateley	18,243
Sep 19	SHEFFIELD WEDNESDAY	W 2-0	Burrows, Hateley	18,859
Sep 26	Liverpool	L 1-5	Hateley	38,940
Oct 5	EVERTON	L 1-2	Pountney	20,141
Oct 10	West Ham United	L 0-3		20,600
Oct 17	WEST BROMWICH ALBION	L 0-1		28,030
Oct 24	Manchester United	L 0-7		35,807
Oct 31	FULHAM	W 2-0	MacEwan (pen), Lee	14,668
Nov 7	Nottingham Forest	L 2-4	Hateley, Burrows (pen)	25,204
Nov 14	STOKE CITY	W 3-0	Burrows 2, Tindall	19,309
Nov 21	Tottenham Hotspur	L 0-4		29,104
Nov 28	BURNLEY	W 1-0	Stobart	18,182
Dec 5	Sheffield United	L 2-4	Pountney, Burrows	12,892
Dec 12	Leeds United	L 0-1		27,339
Dec 19	ARSENAL	W 3-1	Baker 2, MacLeod	11,780
Dec 26	Wolverhampton Wanderers	W 1-0	Baker	30,829
Jan 2	Blackburn Rovers	L 1-5	Stobart	18,292
Jan 16	BLACKPOOL	W 3-2	Hateley, Baker, MacLeod	17,403
Feb 6	LIVERPOOL	L 0-1		24,396
Feb 13	Birmingham City	W 1-0	Stobart	32,491
Feb 27	West Bromwich Albion	L 1-3	Stobart	24,040
Mar 13	Everton	L 1-3	Hateley	32,525
Mar 15	Sheffield Wednesday	L 1-3	Chatterley	12,223
Mar 20	NOTTINGHAM FOREST	W 2-1	Hateley 2	14,445
Mar 22	WOLVERHAMPTON WANDERERS	W 3-2	Chatterley 2, Baker	28,892
Mar 27	Stoke City	L 1-2	Hateley	20,375
Mar 31	WEST HAM UNITED	L 2-3	Hateley, Aitken	19,906
Apr 3	TOTTENHAM HOTSPUR	W 1-0	Baker	25,025
Apr 10	Burnley	D 2-2	Hateley, Aitken	10,106
Apr 12	BIRMINGHAM CITY	W 3-0	Woosnam, Chatterley, Hateley	37,003
Apr 13	SHEFFIELD CITY	W 2-1	Hateley 2 (1 pen)	13,920
Apr 19	Leicester City	D 1-1	Woosnam	14,607
Apr 20	LEICESTER CITY	W 1-0	Chatterley	22,290
Apr 24	Fulham	D 1-1	Hateley	13,494
Apr 28	MANCHESTER UNITED	W 2-1	Baker, Park	36,081

FA Cup

Jan 9	COVENTRY CITY	(Rd 3)	W 3-0	Hateley 2, MacLeod	47,656
Jan 30	Sheffield United	(Rd 4)	W 2-0	Hateley, Stobart	31,655
Feb 20	WOLVERHAMPTON WANDERERS	(Rd 5)	D 1-1	Hateley	52,010
Feb 24	Wolverhampton Wanderers	(R)	D 0-0*		47,920
Mar 1	Wolverhampton Wanderers†	(2nd R)	L 1-3	Park	37,534

*After extra-time. †Played at the Hawthorns, West Bromwich.

League Cup

Sep 23	Luton Town	(Rd 2)	W 1-0	Park	9,011
Oct 14	Leeds United	(Rd 3)	W 3-2	Burrows, Park, Hateley	10,656
Nov 4	READING	(Rd 4)	W 3-1	Hateley 2, Burrows	7,964
Nov 23	BRADFORD CITY	(Rd 5)	W 7-1	Hateley 4, Wylie, Chatterley, Burrows	7,882
Jan 20	CHELSEA	(SF/FL)	L 2-3	Hateley 2	12,022
Feb 10	Chelsea	(SF/SL)	D 1-1	Hateley	17,425

MANAGER: Joe Mercer

CAPTAIN: Alan Deakin, Ron Wylie

TOP SCORER: Tony Hateley, 34 (20 league)

BIGGEST WIN: 7-1 v Bradford City (H), League Cup Fifth Round, 23 November 1964

HIGHEST ATTENDANCE: 52,010 v Wolves (H), FA Cup Fifth Round, 20 February 1965

MAJOR TRANSFERS IN: Johnny MacLeod from Arsenal, Barry Stobart from Manchester City

MAJOR TRANSFERS OUT: Nigel Sims to Peterborough United, Harry Burrows to Stoke City, Ron Wylie to Birmingham City

League & Cup Appearances

PLAYER	LEAGUE	CUP COMPETITION		TOTAL
		FA CUP	LC	
Aitken	42	5	6	53
Baker	24	3	2	29
Bloomfield	1			1
Bradley	7	1		8
Burrows	22	2	5	29
Chatterley	16		2	18
Deakin	21	3	1	25
Gavan	1		1	2
Hateley	42	5	6	53
Lee	24	3	4	31
MacEwan	4	2	2	8
MacLeod	33	3	1	37
Martin	1			1
Park	6	1	3	10
Parken	3		1	4
Pountney	36	5	5	46
Roberts			2	2
Sidebottom	16		3	19
Sleeuwenhoek	23	2	4	29
Stobart	12	4	1	17
Tindall	16		3	19
Withers	25	5	2	32
Woosnam	30	5	4	39
Wright	18	1	3	22
Wylie	39	5	5	49

Goalscorers

PLAYER	LEAGUE	CUP COMPETITION		TOTAL
		FA CUP	LC	
Hateley	20	4	10	34
Burrows	6		3	9
Baker	7			7
Chatterley	5		1	6
Stobart	4	1		5
Park	1	1	2	4
Aitken	3			3
MacLeod	2	1		3
Woosnam	3			3
Pountney	2			2
Wylie	1		1	2
Lee	1			1
MacEwan	1			1
Tindall	1			1

Fact File

Tony Hateley became the first Villa player to score four goals in a cup-tie for 30 years – since Dai Astley's feat against Sunderland on 27 January 1934 in the FA Cup.

Final Division One Table

		P	W	D	L	F	A	Pts
1	MANCHESTER U	42	26	9	7	89	39	61
2	LEEDS U	42	26	9	7	83	52	61
3	CHELSEA	42	24	8	10	89	54	56
4	EVERTON	42	17	15	10	69	60	49
5	NOTTINGHAM F	42	17	13	12	71	67	47
6	TOTTENHAM H	42	19	7	16	87	71	45
7	LIVERPOOL	42	17	10	15	67	73	44
8	SHEFFIELD W	42	16	11	15	57	55	43
9	WEST HAM U	42	19	4	19	82	71	42
10	BLACKBURN R	42	16	10	16	83	79	42
11	STOKE C	42	16	10	16	67	66	42
12	BURNLEY	42	16	10	16	70	70	42
13	ARSENAL	42	17	7	18	69	75	41
14	WBA	42	13	13	16	70	65	39
15	SUNDERLAND	42	14	9	19	64	74	37
16	ASTON VILLA	42	16	5	21	57	82	37
17	BLACKPOOL	42	12	11	19	67	78	35
18	LEICESTER C	42	11	13	18	69	85	35
19	SHEFFIELD U	42	12	11	19	50	64	35
20	FULHAM	42	11	12	19	60	78	34
21	WOLVERHAMPTON W	42	13	4	25	59	89	30
22	BIRMINGHAM C	42	8	11	23	64	96	27

Season 1965-66

Football League Division One

DATE	OPPONENTS	SCORE	GOALSCORERS	ATTENDANCE
Aug 21	Sheffield United	L 0-1		15,575
Aug 23	LEEDS UNITED	L 0-2		33,836
Aug 28	LEICESTER CITY	D 2-2	Hateley (pen), Aitken	21,052
Sep 1	Leeds United	L 0-2		33,575
Sep 4	Blackburn Rovers	W 2-0	Hateley 2	9,367
Sep 6	SUNDERLAND	W 3-1	Hamilton, Park, Hateley	21,998
Sep 11	BLACKPOOL	W 3-0	Hamilton, Woosnam, Park	21,615
Sep 15	Sunderland	L 0-2		37,961
Sep 18	Fulham	W 6-3	Hateley 2, Woosnam, Tindall, MacLeod, Hamilton	12,634
Sep 25	TOTTENHAM HOTSPUR	W 3-2	Park, Woosnam, Hamilton	27,890
Oct 2	Liverpool	L 1-3	Woosnam	43,959
Oct 9	Newcastle United	L 0-1		31,382
Oct 16	WEST BROMWICH ALBION	D 1-1	Pountney	41,455
Oct 23	Nottingham Forest	W 2-1	Woosnam, Hateley	20,833
Oct 30	SHEFFIELD WEDNESDAY	W 2-0	Hateley, Scott	23,247
Nov 6	Northampton Town	L 1-2	Park	18,836
Nov 13	STOKE CITY	L 0-1		21,654
Nov 20	Burnley	L 1-3	Hateley	14,279
Nov 27	CHELSEA	L 2-4	Scott, Pountney	16,355
Dec 4	Arsenal	D 3-3	Hateley, Parker, Hamilton	25,880
Dec 11	EVERTON	W 3-2	Woosnam, Hateley 2	18,712
Jan 1	NEWCASTLE UNITED	W 4-2	Woosnam 2, MacLeod, Hamilton	19,402
Jan 8	Everton	L 0-2		34,641
Jan 15	NOTTINGHAM FOREST	W 3-0	Hamilton, Woosnam 2	14,846
Jan 29	SHEFFIELD UNITED	L 0-2		15,302
Feb 5	Leicester City	L 1-2	Hateley	21,073
Feb 7	WEST HAM UNITED	L 1-2	Hateley (pen)	13,440
Feb 11	West Bromwich Albion	D 2-2	Hateley 2	17,089
Feb 19	BLACKBURN ROVERS	W 3-1	Deakin, Hateley, MacLeod	15,281
Feb 26	Blackpool	W 1-0	Hamilton	11,075
Mar 5	West Ham United	L 2-4	MacLeod, Hateley	22,058
Mar 12	FULHAM	L 2-5	Hateley, Deakin	13,829
Mar 19	Tottenham Hotspur	D 5-5	Hateley 4, Deakin	28,290
Mar 26	LIVERPOOL	L 0-3		23,625
Apr 2	NORTHAMPTON TOWN	L 1-2	Hamilton	10,431
Apr 6	MANCHESTER UNITED	D 1-1	MacEwan	28,211
Apr 9	Stoke City	L 0-2		15,186
Apr 16	BURNLEY	W 2-1	Hateley, Woosnam	14,101
Apr 27	Sheffield Wednesday	L 0-2		28,008
Apr 30	ARSENAL	W 3-0	Hateley 2, Woosnam	18,866
May 9	Manchester United	L 1-6	Woosnam	23,034
May 16	Chelsea	W 2-0	Hateley (pen), Woosnam	16,232

FA Cup

Jan 22	LEICESTER CITY	(Rd 3) L 1-2	Woosnam	38,015

League Cup

Sep 21	Swansea Town	(Rd 2) W 3-2	Woosnam 2, MacLeod	9,858
Oct 13	Sunderland	(Rd 3) W 2-1	Tindall, Woosnam	19,723
Nov 3	Fulham	(Rd 4) D 1-1	Stobart	10,083
Nov 8	FULHAM	(R) W 2-0	Woosnam 2	18,536
Nov 17	West Bromwich Albion	(Rd 5) L 1-3	Hateley	40,694

League & Cup Appearances

PLAYER	LEAGUE	CUP COMPETITION		TOTAL
		FA CUP	LC	
Aitken	42	1	5	48
Baker	8		1	9
Bloomfield	2			2
Bradley	5			5
Chatterley	4			4
Deakin	26		3	29
Gavan	4		2	6
Hamilton	37	1	4	42
Hateley	39	1	4	44
MacEwan	4			4
MacLeod	36	1	4	41
Park	13		3	16
Parker	8	1	2	11
Poutney	30	1	3	34
Roberts	1			1
Scott	25	1	3	29
Sleeuwenhoek	38	1	5	44
Stobart	5		1	6
Tindall	26		3	29
Withers	38	1	3	42
Woosnam	35	1	4	40
Wright	36	1	5	42

Goalscorers

PLAYER	LEAGUE	CUP COMPETITION		TOTAL
		FA CUP	LC	
Hateley	27		1	28
Woosnam	14	1	5	20
Hamilton	9			9
MacLeod	4		1	5
Park	4			4
Deakin	3			3
Pountney	2			2
Scott	2			2
Tindall	1		1	2
Aitken	1			1
MacEwan	1			1
Parker	1			1
Stobart			1	1

Fact File

Villa played no fewer than eight competitive league and cup games during the month of September, six of which were won.

MANAGER: Dick Taylor

CAPTAIN: Charlie Aitken, Alan Deakin

TOP SCORER: Tony Hateley, 28 (27 league)

BIGGEST WIN: 6-3 v Fulham (A), Division One, 18 September 1965

HIGHEST ATTENDANCE: 43,959 v Liverpool (A), Division One, 2 October 1965

MAJOR TRANSFERS IN: Willie Hamilton from Heart of Midlothian, Tony Scott from West Ham United

MAJOR TRANSFERS OUT: Alan Baker to Walsall

Final Division One Table

		P	W	D	L	F	A	Pts
1	LIVERPOOL	42	26	9	7	79	34	61
2	LEEDS U	42	23	9	10	79	38	55
3	BURNLEY	42	24	7	11	79	47	55
4	MANCHESTER U	42	18	15	9	84	59	51
5	CHELSEA	42	22	7	13	65	53	51
6	WBA	42	19	12	11	91	69	50
7	LEICESTER C	42	21	7	14	80	65	49
8	TOTTENHAM H	42	16	12	14	75	66	44
9	SHEFFIELD U	42	16	11	15	56	59	43
10	STOKE C	42	15	12	15	65	64	42
11	EVERTON	42	15	11	16	56	62	41
12	WEST HAM U	42	15	9	18	70	83	39
13	BLACKPOOL	42	14	9	19	55	65	37
14	ARSENAL	42	12	13	17	62	75	37
15	NEWCASTLE U	42	14	9	19	50	63	37
16	ASTON VILLA	42	15	6	21	69	80	36
17	SHEFFIELD W	42	14	8	20	56	66	36
18	NOTTINGHAM F	42	14	8	20	56	72	36
19	SUNDERLAND	42	14	8	20	51	72	36
20	FULHAM	42	14	7	21	67	85	35
21	NORTHAMPTON T	42	10	13	19	55	92	33
22	BLACKBURN R	42	8	4	30	57	88	20

263

Season 1966-67

Football League Division One

DATE	OPPONENTS	SCORE	GOALSCORERS	ATTENDANCE
Aug 20	NEWCASTLE UNITED	D 1-1	Chatterley	17,474
Aug 22	SHEFFIELD WEDNESDAY	L 0-1		14,575
Aug 27	Arsenal	L 0-1		26,762
Aug 31	Sheffield Wednesday	L 0-2		25,992
Sep 3	MANCHESTER CITY	W 3-0	Chatterley, Hateley, Wright	15,118
Sep 5	SOUTHAMPTON	L 0-1		18,417
Sep 10	Blackpool	W 2-0	MacLeod, Chatterley	14,238
Sep 17	CHELSEA	L 2-6	MacLeod, Hateley	18,233
Sep 24	Leicester City	L 0-5		22,065
Oct 1	LIVERPOOL	L 2-3	Hateley 2 (1 pen)	24,909
Oct 8	LEEDS UNITED	W 3-0	Chatterley, Woodward 2	19,118
Oct 15	West Bromwich Albion	L 1-2	Park	31,128
Oct 22	SHEFFIELD UNITED	D 0-0		20,891
Oct 29	Tottenham Hotspur	W 1-0	Chatterley	31,014
Nov 5	WEST BROMWICH ALBION	W 3-2	MacLeod 2, Roberts	24,015
Nov 12	Fulham	L 1-5	Tindall	16,072
Nov 19	NOTTINGHAM FOREST	D 1-1	MacLeod	18,143
Nov 26	Burnley	L 2-4	MacLeod, Chatterley	15,021
Dec 3	MANCHESTER UNITED	W 2-1	Scott, Chatterley	39,937
Dec 10	Stoke City	L 1-6	MacLeod	20,232
Dec 17	Newcastle United	W 3-0	Bradley, Scott, Chatterley	25,400
Dec 26	Sunderland	L 1-2	Harvey o.g.	31,262
Dec 27	SUNDERLAND	W 2-1	Chatterley (pen), Bradley	26,580
Dec 31	ARSENAL	L 0-1		19,431
Jan 14	BLACKPOOL	W 3-2	Stobart 2, Chatterley	16,899
Jan 21	Chelsea	L 1-3	Stobart	30,922
Feb 4	LEICESTER CITY	L 0-1		26,571
Feb 11	Liverpool	L 0-1		45,747
Feb 25	Leeds United	W 2-0	Chatterley, Stobart	34,398
Mar 4	TOTTENHAM HOTSPUR	D 3-3	Chatterley, Anderson, Stobart	31,776
Mar 18	Sheffield United	D 3-3	Stobart 2, Anderson (pen)	15,756
Mar 24	West Ham United	L 1-2	Anderson	28,716
Mar 25	STOKE CITY	W 2-1	Anderson (pen), Sleeuwenhoek	20,996
Mar 28	WEST HAM UNITED	L 0-2		22.033
Apr 1	Everton	L 1-3	MacLeod	36,619
Apr 8	FULHAM	D 1-1	Stobart	13,714
Apr 15	Nottingham Forest	L 0-3		41,463
Apr 19	Manchester City	D 1-1	Chatterley	21,817
Apr 22	BURNLEY	L 0-1		19,002
Apr 29	Manchester United	L 1-3	Anderson	55,782
May 6	EVERTON	L 2-4	Stobart 2	25,321
May 13	Southampton	L 2-6	Walker o.g., Stobart	20,855

FA Cup

Jan 28	Preston North End	(Rd 3) W 1-0	Roberts	26,385
Feb 18	Liverpool	(Rd 4) L 0-1		52,472

League Cup

Sep 14	West Bromwich Albion	(Rd 2) L 1-6	Hateley (pen)	25,039

League & Cup Appearances

PLAYER	LEAGUE	CUP COMPETITION		TOTAL
		FA CUP	LC	
Aitken	39	2	1	42
Anderson	17	1		18
Bradley	30 (1)	2	1	33 (1)
Broadbent	29	2		31
Chatterley	32 (2)	1	1	34 (2)
Deakin	20 (1)	1	1	22 (1)
Hamilton	12			12
Hateley	11		1	12
MacLeod	34 (1)	2	1	37 (1)
Martin	1			1
Park	12 (4)		1	13 (4)
Parker	2			2
Pountney	24 (1)		2	26 (1)
Roberts	11 (1)	1		12 (1)
Rudge	3 (1)	0 (1)		3 (2)
Scott	20 (3)	1	1	22 (3)
Sleeuwenhoek	42	1	1	44
Stobart	18	2		20
Tindall	26 (1)		1	27 (1)
Withers	42	2	1	45
Woodward	3			3
Wright	34 (1)	2		36 (1)

Goalscorers

PLAYER	LEAGUE	CUP COMPETITION		TOTAL
		FA CUP	LC	
Chatterley	13			13
Stobart	11			11
MacLeod	8			8
Anderson	5			5
Hateley	4		1	5
Bradley	2			2
Roberts	1	1		2
Scott	2			2
Woodward	2			2
Park	1			1
Sleeuwenhoek	1			1
Tindale	1			1
Wright	1			1
Opps' o.gs.	2			2

Fact File

Charlie Aitken made his 250th senior appearance for Villa in the home league game against West Bromwich Albion on 5 November 1966.

MANAGER: Dick Taylor

CAPTAIN: Charlie Aitken, Alan Deakin

TOP SCORER: Lew Chatterley, 13 (all league)

BIGGEST WIN: 3-0 v Manchester City (H), Division One, 3 September 1966; v Leeds United (H), Division One, 8 October 1966

HIGHEST ATTENDANCE: 55,782 v Manchester United (A), Division One, 29 April 1967

MAJOR TRANSFERS IN: Willie Anderson from Manchester United, Peter Broadbent from Shrewsbury Town

MAJOR TRANSFERS OUT: Willie Hamilton to Hibernian

Final Division One Table

		P	W	D	L	F	A	PTS
1	MANCHESTER U	42	24	12	6	84	45	60
2	NOTTINGHAM F	42	23	10	9	64	41	56
3	TOTTENHAM H	42	24	8	10	71	48	56
4	LEEDS U	42	22	11	9	62	42	55
5	LIVERPOOL	42	19	13	10	64	47	51
6	EVERTON	42	19	10	13	65	46	48
7	ARSENAL	42	16	14	12	58	47	46
8	LEICESTER C	42	18	8	16	78	71	44
9	CHELSEA	42	15	14	13	67	62	44
10	SHEFFIELD U	42	16	10	16	52	59	42
11	SHEFFIELD W	42	14	13	15	56	47	41
12	STOKE C	42	17	7	18	63	58	41
13	WBA	42	16	7	19	77	73	39
14	BURNLEY	42	15	9	18	66	76	39
15	MANCHESTER C	42	12	15	15	43	52	39
16	WEST HAM U	42	14	8	20	80	84	36
17	SUNDERLAND	42	14	8	20	58	72	36
18	FULHAM	42	11	12	19	71	83	34
19	SOUTHAMPTON	42	14	6	22	74	92	34
20	NEWCASTLE U	42	12	9	21	39	81	33
21	ASTON VILLA	42	11	7	24	54	85	29
22	BLACKPOOL	42	6	9	27	41	76	21

Season 1967-68

Football League Division Two

DATE	OPPONENTS	SCORE	GOALSCORERS	ATTENDANCE
Aug 19	Norwich City	L 0-1		19,408
Aug 23	Plymouth Argyle	L 1-2	Stobart	20,296
Aug 26	ROTHERHAM UNITED	W 3-1	Rudge, Stobart, Anderson	13,673
Aug 28	PLYMOUTH ARGYLE	L 0-1		15,123
Sep 2	Derby County	L 1-3	Stobart	22,967
Sep 5	Queens Park Rangers	L 0-3		21,438
Sep 9	PRESTON NORTH END	W 1-0	Park	13,285
Sep 16	Charlton Athletic	L 0-3		12,766
Sep 23	CRYSTAL PALACE	L 0-1		12,484
Sep 30	Middlesbrough	D 1-1	Godfrey	20,534
Oct 7	BIRMINGHAM CITY	L 2-4	Greenhalgh, Godfrey	50,067
Oct 14	Millwall	W 2-1	Godfrey, Greenhalgh	13,392
Oct 21	BLACKPOOL	W 3-2	Anderson, Greenhalgh, Mitchinson	21,628
Nov 4	CARLISLE UNITED	W 1-0	Mitchinson	17,747
Nov 11	Ipswich Town	L 1-2	Godfrey	17,758
Nov 18	HULL CITY	L 2-3	Greenhalgh 2	19,875
Nov 25	Bolton Wanderers	W 3-2	Greenhalgh, Godfrey, Tindall	13,064
Dec 2	HUDDERSFIELD TOWN	D 0-0		19,507
Dec 16	NORWICH CITY	W 4-2	Mitchinson 2, Woodward, Greenhalgh	16,508
Dec 23	Rotherham United	W 2-0	Mitchinson, Greenhalgh	9,946
Dec 26	Cardiff City	L 0-3		18,180
Dec 30	CARDIFF CITY	W 2-1	Greenhalgh, Anderson	17,667
Jan 6	DERBY COUNTY	W 2-1	Greenhalgh, MacLeod	23,805
Jan 20	CHARLTON ATHLETIC	W 4-1	MacLeod, Greenhalgh, Godfrey, Woodward	19,560
Feb 3	Crystal Palace	W 1-0	Godfrey	10,214
Feb 10	MIDDLESBROUGH	L 0-1		22,724
Feb 24	Birmingham City	L 1-2	Godfrey	45,283
Feb 27	Bristol City	D 0-0		17,138
Mar 2	MILLWALL	W 3-1	Anderson 2 (1 pen), Mitchinson	14,891
Mar 13	Blackburn Rovers	L 1-2	Rudge	10,026
Mar 16	Blackpool	L 0-1		14,301
Mar 18	Preston North End	L 1-2	Greenhalgh	17,043
Mar 23	BLACKBURN ROVERS	L 1-2	Mitchinson	14,106
Mar 30	Carlisle United	W 2-1	Rudge, Godfrey	8,861
Apr 6	IPSWICH TOWN	D 2-2	Mitchinson, Godfrey	19,851
Apr 13	Hull City	L 0-3		15,965
Apr 15	Portsmouth	D 2-2	Haydock o.g., Godfrey	26,035
Apr 16	PORTSMOUTH	W 1-0	Rudge	16,764
Apr 20	BOLTON WANDERERS	D 1-1	Chatterley	16,874
Apr 27	Huddersfield Town	D 0-0		7,489
May 4	BRISTOL CITY	L 2-4	Godfrey, Chatterley	14,732
May 11	QUEENS PARK RANGERS	L 1-2	Mitchinson	33,785

FA Cup

Jan 27	MILLWALL	(Rd 3) W 3-0	Godfrey, Anderson, Woodward	34,703
Feb 17	ROTHERHAM UNITED	(Rd 4) L 0-1		33,442

League Cup

Sep 13	Northampton Town	(Rd 2) L 1-3	Scott	11,832

League & Cup Appearances

PLAYER	LEAGUE	CUP COMPETITION		TOTAL
		FA CUP	LC	
Aitken	30 (2)	3 (2)	3 (1)	36 (5)
Anderson	42	11 (2)	7 (1)	60 (3)
Ansell	1			1
Bradley	16 (5)		2 (1)	18 (6)
Broadbent	8 (1)			8 (1)
Chatterley	42	5 (2)	4 (1)	51 (3)
Deakin	28	6 (2)	6 (1)	40 (3)
Dunn	8			8
Edwards	11			11
Godfrey	33	10 (2)		43 (2)
Greenhalgh	28	0 (1)		28 (1)
Inglis	1 (1)		10 (1)	11 (2)
MacLeod	20 (1)	7 (2)		27 (3)
Martin	1		8 (1)	9 (1)
Mitchinson	36	8 (2)		44 (2)
Park	25 (4)	4 (2)	9 (1)	38 (7)
Parker	2			2
Pountney	1 (1)			1 (1)
Roberts	3			3
Rudge	15 (1)			15 (1)
Scott	2		11 (1)	13 (1)
Sleeuwenhoek	12		5 (1)	17 (1)
Stobart	10			10
Tindall	5 (1)			5 (1)
Turnball	11			11
Withers	34	1 (2)	1 (1)	36 (3)
Woodward	8 (2)	9 (1)		17 (3)
Wright	29	2 (2)		31 (2)

Goalscorers

PLAYER	LEAGUE	CUP COMPETITION		TOTAL
		FA CUP	LC	
Godfrey	12	1		13
Greenhalgh	12			12
Mitchinson	9			9
Anderson	5	1		6
Rudge	4			4
Stobart	3			3
Woodward	2	1		3
Chatterley	2			2
MacLeod	2			2
Park	1			1
Tindale	1			1
Scott			1	1
Opps' o.gs.	1			1

Fact File

A crowd of over 50,000 attended the very first 'Second Division' derby with Birmingham City on 7 October 1967.

MANAGER: Tommy Cummings

CAPTAIN: Charlie Aitken, Alan Deakin, Brian Godfrey

TOP SCORER: Brian Godfrey, 13 (12 league)

BIGGEST WIN: 3-0 v Millwall (H), FA Cup Third Round, 27 January 1968

HIGHEST ATTENDANCE: 50,067 v Birmingham City (H), Division Two, 7 October 1967

MAJOR TRANSFERS IN: Brian Godfrey from Preston North End, Tommy Mitchinson from Mansfield Town

MAJOR TRANSFERS OUT: John Sleeuwenhoek to Birmingham City

Final Division Two Table

		P	W	D	L	F	A	Pts
1	IPSWICH T	42	22	15	5	79	44	59
2	QPR	42	25	8	9	67	36	58
3	BLACKPOOL	42	24	10	8	71	43	58
4	BIRMINGHAM C	42	19	14	9	83	51	52
5	PORTSMOUTH	42	18	13	11	68	55	49
6	MIDDLESBROUGH	42	17	12	13	60	54	46
7	MILLWALL	42	14	17	11	62	50	45
8	BLACKBURN R	42	16	11	15	56	49	43
9	NORWICH C	42	16	11	15	60	65	43
10	CARLISLE U	42	14	13	15	58	52	41
11	CRYSTAL PALACE	42	14	11	17	56	56	39
12	BOLTON W	42	13	13	16	60	63	39
13	CARDIFF C	42	13	12	17	60	66	38
14	HUDDERSFIELD T	42	13	12	17	46	61	38
15	CHARLTON ATH	42	12	13	17	63	68	37
16	ASTON VILLA	42	15	7	20	54	64	37
17	HULL C	42	12	13	17	58	73	37
18	DERBY CO	42	13	10	19	71	78	36
19	BRISTOL C	42	13	10	19	48	62	36
20	PRESTON NE	42	12	11	19	43	65	35
21	ROTHERHAM U	42	10	11	21	42	76	31
22	PLYMOUTH ARG	42	9	9	24	38	72	27

Football League Division Two

DATE	OPPONENTS	SCORE	GOALSCORERS	ATTENDANCE
Aug 10	Sheffield United	L 1-3	Anderson (pen)	17,707
Aug 17	FULHAM	D 1-1	Woodward	20,937
Aug 19	MILLWALL	D 1-1	Anderson (pen)	19,057
Aug 24	Blackburn Rovers	L 0-2		12,666
Aug 26	BRISTOL CITY	W 1-0	Woodward	17,679
Aug 31	BLACKPOOL	L 0-1		18,919
Sep 7	Derby County	L 1-3	Ferguson	23,723
Sep 14	HULL CITY	D 1-1	Anderson	17,683
Sep 18	Bolton Wanderers	L 1-4	Godfrey	14,279
Sep 21	Birmingham City	L 0-4		40,527
Sep 28	OXFORD UNITED	W 2-0	Hole, Godfrey	17,083
Oct 5	Cardiff City	D 1-1	Godfrey	17,136
Oct 8	Bristol City	L 0-1		15,203
Oct 12	CRYSTAL PALACE	D 1-1	Anderson (pen)	15,876
Oct 19	Norwich City	D 1-1	Chatterley	15,086
Oct 26	CARLISLE UNITED	D 0-0		14,971
Nov 2	Huddersfield Town	L 1-3	Ferguson	9,346
Nov 9	PRESTON NORTH END	L 0-1		13,374
Nov 16	Portsmouth	L 0-2		18,154
Nov 23	MIDDLESBROUGH	W 1-0	Rooks o.g.	15,159
Nov 30	Bury	L 2-3	Woodward, Anderson	5,609
Dec 7	CHARLTON ATHLETIC	D 0-0		12,747
Dec 14	Crystal Palace	L 2-4	Martin, Edwards	11,071
Dec 21	NORWICH CITY	W 2-1	Edwards, Hole	19,923
Dec 26	CARDIFF CITY	W 2-0	Hole, Tiler	41,250
Dec 28	Carlisle United	W 1-0	Anderson	12,554
Jan 11	HUDDERSFIELD TOWN	W 1-0	Hole	29,029
Jan 18	Preston North End	L 0-1		15,252
Feb 1	PORTSMOUTH	W 2-0	Rudge, Godfrey	31,593
Feb 15	BURY	W 1-0	Rudge	28,010
Feb 22	Charlton Athletic	D 1-1	Simmons	22,021
Mar 1	SHEFFIELD UNITED	W 3-1	Hole, Simmons 2	27,480
Mar 4	Middlesbrough	D 0-0		29,824
Mar 8	Fulham	D 1-1	Roberts o.g.	15,509
Mar 15	BLACKBURN ROVERS	D 1-1	Simmons	27,624
Mar 22	Blackpool	D 1-1	Godfrey	12,148
Mar 29	DERBY COUNTY	L 0-1		49,110
Apr 4	Millwall	W 1-0	Martin	15,100
Apr 5	Oxford United	L 0-1		17,072
Apr 8	BOLTON WANDERERS	D 1-1	Hulme o.g.	25,214
Apr 12	BIRMINGHAM CITY	W 1-0	Simmons	52,772
Apr 19	Hull City	L 0-1		10,537

FA Cup

Jan 4	QUEENS PARK RANGERS	(Rd 3)	W 2-1	Godfrey, Martin	39,854
Jan 25	Southampton	(Rd 4)	D 2-2	Godfrey, Hole	27,581
Jan 29	SOUTHAMPTON	(R)	W 2-1	Broadbent, Martin	59,084
Feb 12	Tottenham Hotspur	(Rd 5)	L 2-3	Hole, Broadbent	49,986

League Cup

Sep 4	TOTTENHAM HOTSPUR	(Rd 2)	L 1-4	Martin	24,775

League & Cup Appearances

PLAYER	LEAGUE	CUP COMPETITION		TOTAL
		FA CUP	LC	
Aitken	42	4	1	47
Anderson	38	4	1	43
Bradley	4 (1)	1 (2)		5 (3)
Broadbent	23 (3)	3		26 (3)
Chambers	1 (1)			1 (1)
Chatterley	6 (1)			6 (1)
Deakin	7		1	8
Dunn	35	4	1	40
Edwards	40	4	1	45
Ferguson	30	1	1	32
Godfrey	37	4		41
Greenhalgh	9 (3)			9 (3)
Griffiths	1			1
Hole	28	4		32
Lynch	1			1
Martin	15 (5)	4	1	20 (5)
Mitchinson	13		1	14
Park	4 (5)		0 (1)	4 (6)
Rudge	17 (1)	4		21 (1)
Simmons	9 (1)			9 (1)
Tiler	18			18
Turnbull	28 (1)	4	1	33 (1)
Withers	7			7
Woodward	11 (2)		1	12 (2)
Wright	38 (1)	3	1	42 (1)

Goalscorers

PLAYER	LEAGUE	CUP COMPETITION		TOTAL
		FA CUP	LC	
Godfrey	5	2		7
Hole	5	2		7
Anderson	6			6
Martin	2	2	1	5
Simmons	5			5
Woodward	3			3
Broadbent		2		2
Edwards	2			2
Ferguson	2			2
Rudge	2			2
Chatterley	1			1
Tiler	1			1
Opps' o.gs.	3			3

Fact File

The attendance of 5,609 for the league game at Bury on 30 November 1968 was the lowest Villa had played to at senior level for 24 years.

MANAGER: Tommy Cummings, Tommy Docherty

CAPTAIN: Charlie Aitken, Brian Godfrey

TOP SCORER: Brian Godfrey, 7 (5 league); Barry Hole, 7 (5 league)

BIGGEST WIN: 3-1 v Sheffield United (H), Division Two, 1 March 1969

HIGHEST ATTENDANCE: 59,084 v Southampton (H), FA Cup Fourth Round Replay, 29 January 1969

MAJOR TRANSFERS IN: Mike Ferguson and Barry Hole from Blackburn Rovers, Dave Simmons from Arsenal

MAJOR TRANSFERS OUT: John Woodward to Walsall

Final Division Two Table

		P	W	D	L	F	A	Pts
1	Derby Co	42	26	11	5	65	32	63
2	Crystal Palace	42	22	19	8	70	47	56
3	Charlton Ath	42	18	14	10	61	52	50
4	Middlesbrough	42	19	11	12	58	49	49
5	Cardiff C	42	20	7	15	67	54	47
6	Huddersfield T	42	17	12	13	53	46	46
7	Birmingham C	42	18	8	16	73	59	44
8	Blackpool	42	14	15	13	51	41	43
9	Sheffield U	42	16	11	15	61	50	43
10	Millwall	42	17	9	16	57	49	43
11	Hull C	42	13	16	13	59	52	42
12	Carlisle U	42	16	10	16	46	49	42
13	Norwich C	42	15	10	17	53	56	40
14	Preston NE	42	12	15	15	38	44	39
15	Portsmouth	42	12	14	16	58	58	38
16	Bristol C	42	11	16	15	46	53	38
17	Bolton W	42	12	14	16	55	67	38
18	Aston Villa	42	12	14	16	37	48	38
19	Blackburn R	42	13	11	18	52	63	37
20	Oxford U	42	12	9	21	34	55	33
21	Bury	42	11	8	23	51	80	30
22	Fulham	42	7	11	24	40	81	25

Season 1969-70

Football League Division Two

DATE	OPPONENTS	SCORE	GOALSCORERS	ATTENDANCE
Aug 9	NORWICH CITY	L 0-1		32,663
Aug 16	Huddersfield Town	L 0-2		13,364
Aug 19	Carlisle United	D 1-1	Hamilton	12,504
Aug 23	SWINDON TOWN	L 0-2		29,797
Aug 27	LEICESTER CITY	L 0-1		33,838
Aug 30	Middlesbrough	L 0-1		19,438
Sep 6	MILLWALL	D 2-2	Rudge 2	23,738
Sep 13	Watford	L 0-3		19,118
Sep 17	Bolton Wanderers	L 1-2	Rioch B	11,407
Sep 20	HULL CITY	W 3-2	Godfrey, Chatterley, Rudge	23,590
Sep 27	Portsmouth	D 0-0		17,884
Oct 4	PRESTON NORTH END	D 0-0		25,421
Oct 8	HUDDERSFIELD TOWN	W 4-1	Godfrey, Tiler, Hole, Martin	23,192
Oct 11	Cardiff City	L 0-4		25,896
Oct 18	BIRMINGHAM CITY	D 0-0		54,470
Oct 25	Oxford United	D 2-2	McMahon 2	14,386
Nov 1	QUEENS PARK RANGERS	D 1-1	Simmons	31,428
Nov 8	Bristol City	L 0-1		16,065
Nov 12	CARLISLE UNITED	W 1-0	Rudge	24,447
Nov 15	BLACKPOOL	D 0-0		24,942
Nov 19	BOLTON WANDERERS	W 3-0	Martin, Rioch B, Anderson	22,935
Nov 22	Sheffield United	L 0-5		17,266
Dec 6	Blackburn Rovers	L 0-2		12,008
Dec 13	WATFORD	L 0-2		20,161
Dec 26	Swindon Town	D 1-1	Curtis	22,984
Jan 17	PORTSMOUTH	L 3-5	Rioch B 2, Anderson	21,148
Jan 31	Preston North End	D 1-1	Chatterley	14,182
Feb 7	CARDIFF CITY	D 1-1	Rioch B	27,000
Feb 14	Norwich City	L 1-3	Anderson	11,041
Feb 21	BRISTOL CITY	L 0-2		26,830
Feb 25	CHARLTON ATHLETIC	W 1-0	Went o.g.	23,982
Feb 28	Queens Park Rangers	L 2-4	Chatterley, Anderson (pen)	17,057
Mar 10	Hull City	L 1-3	Curtis	8 885
Mar 14	Charlton Athletic	L 0-1		9,987
Mar 16	Millwall	L 0-2		13,817
Mar 21	BLACKBURN ROVERS	D 1-1	Curtis	19,003
Mar 28	Blackpool	L 1-2	Hamilton	17,392
Mar 30	Birmingham City	W 2-0	Rioch B, McMahon	41,696
Mar 31	OXFORD UNITED	D 0-0		30,096
Apr 4	Leicester City	L 0-1		27,481
Apr 8	MIDDLESBROUGH	W 2-0	Anderson, Godfrey	22,797
Apr 13	SHEFFIELD UNITED	W 1-0	McMahon	32,279

FA Cup

Jan 3	CHARLTON ATHLETIC	(Rd 3) D 1-1	Martin	30,742
Jan 12	Charlton Athletic	(R) L 0-1		23,798

League Cup

Aug 13	Chester	(Rd 1) W 2-1	McMahon, Hamilton	10,510
Sep 3	WEST BROMWICH ALBION	(Rd 2) L 1-2	Hole	40,303

League & Cup Appearances

PLAYER	LEAGUE	CUP COMPETITION		TOTAL
		FA CUP	LC	
Aitken	31	1	2	34
Anderson	36 (2)	2	2	40 (2)
Bradley	9			9
Brown	6	1		7
Chatterley	31 (1)			31 (1)
Curtis	18	2		20
Deakin	1			1
Dunn	15		1	16
Edwards	17	2	2	21
Ferguson	8		1 (1)	9 (1)
Godfrey	25 (4)	2		27 (4)
Griffiths	0 (2)		1	1 (2)
Hamilton	16 (1)	1		19 (1)
Hole	19		2	21
Kapengwee	3			3
Lochhead	11 (1)			11 (1)
Lynch	1	1		2
McMahon	20 (3)		2	22 (3)
Martin	18 (3)	2		20 (3)
Mwila	1			1
Phillips	15	2		17
Rioch B	42	2	2	46
Rioch N	2			2
Rowan	1			1
Rudge	14 (3)			14 (3)
Simmons	3 (3)	0 (2)		3 (5)
Turnball	12	1		13
Williams	12		1	13
Wright	42	2	2	46

Goalscorers

PLAYER	LEAGUE	CUP COMPETITION		TOTAL
		FA CUP	LC	
Rioch B	6			6
Anderson	5			5
McMahon	4		1	5
Rudge	4			4
Chatterley	3			3
Curtis	3			3
Godfrey	3			3
Hamilton	2		1	3
Martin	2	1		3
Hole	1		1	2
Simmons	1			1
Tiler	1			1
Opps' o.gs.	1			1

MANAGER: Tommy Docherty, Vic Crowe

CAPTAIN: Charlie Aitken/Brian Godfrey

TOP SCORER: Bruce Rioch, 6 (all league)

BIGGEST WIN: 4-1 v Huddersfield Town (H), Division Two, 8 October 1969

HIGHEST ATTENDANCE: 54,470 v Birmingham City (H), Division Two, 18 October 1969

MAJOR TRANSFERS IN: George Curtis from Coventry City, Andy Lochhead from Leicester City, Pat McMahon from Celtic, Neil Rioch and Bruce Rioch from Luton Town, Ian Hamilton from Southend United

MAJOR TRANSFERS OUT: Dick Edwards to Torquay United

Final Division Two Table

		P	W	D	L	F	A	Pts
1	HUDDERSFIELD T	42	24	12	6	68	37	60
2	BLACKPOOL	42	20	13	9	56	45	53
3	LEICESTER C	42	19	13	10	64	50	51
4	MIDDLESBROUGH	42	20	10	12	55	45	50
5	SWINDON T	42	17	16	9	57	47	50
6	SHEFFIELD U	42	22	5	15	73	38	49
7	CARDIFF C	42	18	13	11	61	41	49
8	BLACKBURN R	42	20	7	15	54	50	47
9	QPR	42	17	11	14	66	57	45
10	MILLWALL	42	15	14	13	56	56	44
11	NORWICH C	42	16	11	15	49	46	43
12	CARLISLE U	42	14	13	15	58	56	41
13	HULL C	42	15	11	16	72	70	41
14	BRISTOL C	42	13	13	16	54	50	39
15	OXFORD U	42	12	15	15	35	42	39
16	BOLTON W	42	12	12	18	54	61	36
17	PORTSMOUTH	42	13	9	20	66	80	35
18	BIRMINGHAM C	42	11	11	20	51	78	33
19	WATFORD	42	9	13	20	44	57	31
20	CHARLTON ATH	42	7	17	18	35	76	31
21	ASTON VILLA	42	8	13	21	36	62	29
22	PRESTON NE	42	8	12	22	43	63	28

Season 1970-71

Football League Division Three

DATE	OPPONENTS	SCORE	GOALSCORERS	ATTENDANCE
Aug 15	Chesterfield	W 3-2	McMahon, Rioch B 2	16,760
Aug 22	PLYMOUTH ARGYLE	D 1-1	McMahon	29,205
Aug 29	Swansea City	W 2-1	Hamilton, McMahon	15,535
Aug 31	MANSFIELD TOWN	L 0-1		30,856
Sep 5	DONCASTER ROVERS	W 3-2	Lochhead 2, McMahon	23,602
Sep 12	Barnsley	D 1-1	Simmons	13,408
Sep 19	PRESTON NORTH END	W 2-0	Lochhead 2	26,139
Sep 23	GILLINGHAM	W 2-1	Hamilton, McMahon	29,383
Sep 26	Wrexham	W 3-2	Lochhead, Gibson, Hamilton (pen)	18,335
Sep 30	BRISTOL ROVERS	D 1-1	Lochhead	32,082
Oct 3	BRIGHTON & HOVE ALBION	D 0-0		26,189
Oct 10	Rochdale	D 1-1	Lochhead	7,634
Oct 17	CHESTERFIELD	D 0-0		27,049
Oct 19	Port Vale	L 0-2		11,224
Oct 24	TRANMERE ROVERS	W 1-0	Hamilton	20,676
Oct 31	Reading	W 5-3	Lochhead, Tiler, McMahon, Anderson (pen), Butler o.g.	13,312
Nov 7	TORQUAY UNITED	L 0-1		28,099
Nov 11	BURY	W 1-0	Hamilton	17,014
Nov 14	Halifax Town	L 1-2	Turnbull	5,845
Nov 28	Fulham	W 2-0	Hamilton, McMahon	16,021
Dec 5	BRADFORD CITY	W 1-0	Hamilton	23,623
Dec 19	Plymouth Argyle	D 1-1	Lochhead	12,996
Dec 26	SHREWSBURY TOWN	W 2-0	McMahon, Rioch B	31,186
Jan 2	Walsall	L 0-3		19,203
Jan 9	Bristol Rovers	W 2-1	Rioch B, Parsons o.g.	25,836
Jan 16	PORT VALE	W 1-0	Rioch B	28,965
Jan 23	Rotherham United	D 1-1	Hamilton	12,548
Jan 30	FULHAM	W 1-0	Anderson (pen)	33,343
Feb 6	Bradford City	L 0-1		10,029
Feb 13	ROTHERHAM UNITED	W 1-0	Anderson	27,183
Feb 20	Bury	L 1-3	Allen o.g.	7,516
Mar 5	Tranmere Rovers	D 1-1	Hamilton	6,570
Mar 10	Gillingham	D 0-0		10,812
Mar 13	HALIFAX TOWN	D 1-1	Turnbull	33,522
Mar 17	WALSALL	D 0-0		37,643
Mar 20	Torquay United	D 1-1	Vowden	6,792
Mar 26	Doncaster Rovers	L 1-2	Gregory	7,879
Apr 3	SWANSEA CITY	W 3-0	Vowden 2, Gregory	23,571
Apr 9	Brighton & Hove Albion	L 0-1		22,687
Apr 10	Shrewsbury Town	L 1-2	Turnbull	13,636
Apr 12	BARNSLEY	D 0-0		20,700
Apr 17	ROCHDALE	W 1-0	Vowden	18,389
Apr 24	Preston North End	D 0-0		22,616
Apr 26	Mansfield Town	L 0-2		9,666
May 1	WREXHAM	L 3-4	Vowden, Godfrey 2	18,733
May 4	READING	W 2-1	Anderson, Bell o.g.	15,666

FA Cup

Nov 21	Torquay United	(Rd 1) L 1-3	Aitken	9,229

League Cup

Aug 19	NOTTS COUNTY	(Rd 1) W 4-0	Anderson, McMahon, Rioch B, Hamilton	17,843
Sep 9	BURNLEY	(Rd 2) W 2-0	Hamilton, Martin	28,340
Oct 6	Northampton Town	(Rd 3) D 1-1	Hamilton	15,072
Oct 13	NORTHAMPTON TOWN	(R) W 3-0	Lochhead 2, Anderson	25,822
Oct 28	CARLISLE UNITED	(Rd 4) W 1-0	Tiler	26,779
Nov 17	Bristol Rovers	(Rd 5) D 1-1	McMahon	28,780
Nov 25	BRISTOL ROVERS	(R) W 1-0	McMahon	37,525
Dec 16	Manchester United	(SF) D 1-1	Lochhead	48,889
Dec 23	MANCHESTER UNITED	(R) W 2-1	Lochhead, McMahon	58,667
Feb 27	Tottenham Hotspur	(F) L 0-2		97,024

MANAGER: Vic Crowe

CAPTAIN: Charlie Aitken, Brian Tiler

TOP SCORER: Ian 'Chico' Hamilton, 13 (9 league)

BIGGEST WIN: 5-3 v Reading (A), Division Three, 31 October 1970

HIGHEST ATTENDANCE: 97,024 v Tottenham Hotspur, League Cup final at Wembley, 27 February 1971

MAJOR TRANSFERS IN: Dave Gibson from Leicester City, Geoff Vowden from Birmingham City

MAJOR TRANSFERS OUT: Mick Ferguson to Queens Park Rangers

League & Cup Appearances

PLAYER	LEAGUE	CUP COMPETITION		TOTAL
		FA CUP	LC	
Aitken	44	1	10	55
Anderson	42	1	10	53
Bradley	28	1	5	34
Brown	9	1	4	14
Chatterley	8	1	2	11
Crudgington	3			3
Curtis	9		2	11
Dunn	43	1	10	54
Gibson	13		4	17
Godfrey	44		9	53
Gregory	10			10
Hamilton	43	1	10	54
Lochhead	41	1	10	52
Martin	1			1
McMahon	36	1	9	46
Rioch B	17		2	19
Rioch N			(1)	0 (1)
Simmons	1			1
Tiler	41	1	9	51
Turnball	41	1	9	51
Vowden	13			13
Wright	19		5	24

Goalscorers

PLAYER	LEAGUE	CUP COMPETITION		TOTAL
		FA CUP	LC	
Hamilton	9		4	13
Lochhead	9		1	10
McMahon	8		1	9
Anderson	4		2	6
Gregory	2		3	5
Rioch B	5			5
Vowden	5			5
Martin			4	4
Turnbull	3			3
Godfrey	2			2
Simmons	1		1	2
Aitkin		1		1
Gibson	1			1
Tiler	1			1
Opps' o.gs.	4			4

Fact File

A crowd of 16,760 saw Villa's first-ever game in the Third Division, away at Chesterfield, while over 29,000 attended their first home game a week later.

Final Division Three Table

		P	W	D	L	F	A	Pts
1	PRESTON NE	46	22	17	7	63	39	61
2	FULHAM	46	24	12	10	68	41	60
3	HALIFAX T	46	22	12	12	74	55	56
4	ASTON VILLA	46	19	15	12	54	46	53
5	CHESTERFIELD	46	17	17	12	66	38	51
6	BRISTOL R	46	19	13	14	69	50	51
7	MANSFIELD T	46	18	15	13	64	62	51
8	ROTHERHAM U	46	17	16	13	64	60	50
9	WREXHAM	46	18	13	15	72	65	49
10	TORQUAY U	46	19	11	16	54	57	49
11	SWANSEA C	46	15	16	15	59	56	46
12	BARNSLEY	46	17	11	18	49	52	45
13	SHREWSBURY T	46	16	13	17	58	62	45
14	BRIGHTON & HA	46	14	16	16	50	47	44
15	PLYMOUTH ARG	46	12	19	15	63	63	43
16	ROCHDALE	46	14	15	17	61	68	43
17	PORT VALE	46	15	12	19	52	59	42
18	TRANMERE R	46	10	22	14	45	55	42
19	BRADFORD C	46	13	14	19	49	62	40
20	WALSALL	46	14	11	21	51	57	39
21	READING	46	14	11	21	48	85	39
22	BURY	46	12	13	21	52	60	37
23	DONCASTER R	46	13	9	24	45	66	35
24	GILLINGHAM	46	10	13	23	42	67	33

Season 1971-72

Football League Division Three

DATE	OPPONENTS	SCORE	GOALSCORERS	ATTENDANCE
Aug 14	PLYMOUTH ARGYLE	W 3-1	Vowden, McMahon, Anderson (pen)	26,337
Aug 21	Walsall	D 1-1	Vowden	13,051
Aug 28	ROCHDALE	W 2-0	Lochhead, Graydon	24,272
Sep 4	Bolton Wanderers	L 0-2		11,470
Sep 11	BRIGHTON & HOVE ALBION	W 2-0	Graydon, Hamilton	25,812
Sep 18	Halifax Town	W 1-0	Graydon	7,462
Sep 22	MANSFIELD TOWN	L 0-1		28,112
Sep 25	WREXHAM	W 2-0	Anderson (pen), Graydon	23,004
Sep 28	Barnsley	W 4-0	Lochhead 2, Hamilton 2	8,387
Oct 2	Bristol Rovers	W 1-0	Anderson	20,428
Oct 9	ROTHERHAM UNITED	L 1-2	Lochhead	30,249
Oct 16	Plymouth Argyle	L 2-3	Rioch B, Vowden	18,570
Oct 20	TRANMERE ROVERS	W 2-0	Rioch B, Lochhead	24,231
Oct 23	Bournemouth	L 0-3		20,305
Oct 30	BLACKBURN ROVERS	W 4-1	Rioch N 2, Hamilton, Anderson	25,588
Nov 6	Port Vale	D 4-4	Hamilton, Anderson (pen), Graydon, Cross o.g.	11,106
Nov 13	NOTTS COUNTY	W 1-0	Graydon	37,462
Nov 27	Oldham Athletic	W 6-0	Lochhead 3, Anderson, Rioch B 2	12,015
Dec 4	BRADFORD CITY	W 3-0	Anderson (pen), Rioch B 2	27,347
Dec 18	BOLTON WANDERERS	W 3-2	Lochhead, Craydon, Aitken	27,767
Dec 27	Swansea City	W 2-1	Aitken, Graydon	24,419
Jan 1	HALIFAX TOWN	W 1-0	Graydon	32,749
Jan 8	Rochdale	L 0-1		5,871
Jan 19	SHREWSBURY TOWN	W 3-0	Hamilton, Graydon, Lochhead	27,239
Jan 22	BARNSLEY	W 2-0	Lochhead, Rioch B	30,531
Jan 28	Tranmere Rovers	W 1-0	Aitken	12,054
Feb 12	YORK CITY	W 1-0	Anderson (pen)	26,905
Feb 12	BOURNEMOUTH	W 2-1	Vowden, Lochhead	48,110
Feb 19	Blackburn Rovers	D 1-1	Lochhead	15,562
Feb 26	PORT VALE	W 2-0	Lochhead, McMahon	32,806
Mar 4	Notts County	W 3-0	McMahon 2, Graydon	34,208
Mar 11	Rotherham United	W 2-0	Lochhead, Graydon	16,290
Mar 15	Shrewsbury Town	D 1-1	Nicholl	15,720
Mar 18	WALSALL	D 0-0		45,953
Mar 25	Brighton & Hove Albion	L 1-2	Rioch B	29,135
Mar 31	Wrexham	W 2-0	Anderson, Graydon	16,846
Apr 1	SWANSEA CITY	W 2-0	Anderson, McMahon	33,394
Apr 3	BRISTOL ROVERS	W 2-1	Lochhead 2	41,518
Apr 8	York City	W 1-0	Rioch B	9,620
Apr 10	OLDHAM ATHLETIC	W 1-0	Graydon	32,140
Apr 12	Torquay United	L 1-2	Vowden	9,776
Apr 19	Chesterfield	W 4-0	Lochhead, Vowden 2, Hamilton	12,510
Apr 22	Bradford City	W 1-0	Aitken	9,289
Apr 24	Mansfield Town	D 1-1	Vowden	12,454
Apr 29	TORQUAY UNITED	W 5-1	Vowden 2, Jackson o.g., Little, Lochhead	37,582
May 5	CHESTERFIELD	W 1-0	Ross	45,586

FA Cup

Nov 20	Southend United	(Rd 1) L 0-1		16,929

League Cup

Aug 18	WREXHAM	(Rd 1) D 2-2	Lochhead, Anderson (pen)	24,552
Aug 23	Wrexham	(R) D 1-1*	Anderson	12,113
Aug 31	Wrexham†	(2nd R) W 4-3	Lochhead 2, Anderson (pen), Ingle o.g.	20,697
Sep 8	Chesterfield	(Rd 2) W 3-2	Anderson (pen), Lochhead, Vowden	13,842
Oct 5	Crystal Palace	(Rd 3) D 2-2	Hamilton, Lochhead	21,179
Oct 13	CRYSTAL PALACE	(R) W 2-0	Lochhead, Graydon	24,978
Oct 26	Blackpool	(Rd 4) L 1-4	Anderson	20,193

*After extra-time. †Played at the Hawthorns, West Bromwich.

MANAGER: Vic Crowe

CAPTAIN: Charlie Aitken, Brian Tiler

TOP SCORER: Andy Lochhead, 25 (19 league)

BIGGEST WIN: 6-0 v Oldham Athletic (H), Division Three, 27 November 1971

HIGHEST ATTENDANCE: 48,110 v Bournemouth (H), Division Three, 12 February 1972

MAJOR TRANSFERS IN: Jim Cumbes from West Bromwich Albion, Ray Graydon from Bristol Rovers, Chris Nicholl from Luton Town

League & Cup Appearances

PLAYER	LEAGUE	CUP COMPETITION		TOTAL
		FA CUP	LC	
Aitken	43	1	6	50
Anderson	40	1	7	48
Beard	4 (1)		1	5 (1)
Bradley	16	1	7	24
Brown	8 (1)			8 (1)
Crudgington	1		1	2
Cumbes	29			29
Curtis	24	1	2	27
Gibson	3	1		4
Graydon	45	1	6	52
Gregory	8		5	13
Hamilton	25 (5)	1	5	31 (5)
Hughes	16	1	6	23
Little	1 (1)			1 (1)
Lochhead	45	1	7	53
McMahon	15 (3)			15 (3)
Martin	0 (1)		0 (1)	0 (2)
Nicholl	13			13
Rioch B	40		5	45
Rioch N	2			2
Ross	17			17
Tiler	13	0 (1)	6	19 (1)
Turnball	37	1	5	43
Vowden	30 (3)	1	7	38 (3)
Wright	31		1	32

Goalscorers

PLAYER	LEAGUE	CUP COMPETITION		TOTAL
		FA CUP	LC	
Lochhead	19		6	25
Anderson	10		5	15
Graydon	14		1	15
Vowden	10		1	11
Rioch B	9			9
Hamilton	7		1	8
McMahon	5			5
Aitken	4			4
Rioch N	2			2
Little	1			1
Nicholl	1			1
Ross	1			1
Opps' o.gs.	2		1	3

Fact File

Villa won their last five home League games in succession to clinch the Third Division title.

Final Division Three Table

		P	W	D	L	F	A	Pts
1	ASTON VILLA	46	32	6	8	85	32	70
2	BRIGHTON & HA	46	27	11	8	82	47	65
3	BOURNEMOUTH	46	23	16	7	73	37	62
4	NOTTS CO	46	25	12	9	74	44	62
5	ROTHERHAM U	46	20	15	11	69	52	55
6	BRISTOL R	46	21	12	13	75	56	54
7	BOLTON W	46	17	16	13	51	41	50
8	PLYMOUTH ARG	46	20	10	16	74	64	50
9	WALSALL	46	15	18	13	62	57	48
10	BLACKBURN R	46	19	9	18	54	57	47
11	OLDHAM ATH	46	17	11	18	59	63	45
12	SHREWSBURY T	46	17	10	19	73	65	44
13	CHESTERFIELD	46	18	8	20	57	57	44
14	SWANSEA C	46	17	10	19	46	59	44
15	PORT VALE	46	13	15	18	43	59	41
16	WREXHAM	46	16	8	22	59	63	40
17	HALIFAX T	46	13	12	21	48	61	38
18	ROCHDALE	46	12	13	21	57	83	37
19	YORK C	46	12	12	22	57	66	36
20	TRANMERE R	46	10	16	20	50	71	36
21	MANSFIELD T	46	8	20	18	41	63	36
22	BARNSLEY	46	9	18	19	32	64	36
23	TORQUAY U	46	10	12	24	41	69	32
24	BRADFORD C	46	11	10	25	45	77	32

The Essential History of Aston Villa

Football League Division Two

DATE	OPPONENTS	SCORE	GOALSCORERS	ATTENDANCE
Aug 12	Preston North End	W 1-0	Anderson	17,371
Aug 19	HUDDERSFIELD TOWN	W 2-0	Vowden, Graydon	34,843
Aug 26	Burnley	L 1-4	Hamilton	14,804
Aug 29	CARLISLE UNITED	W 1-0	Rioch B	29,047
Sep 2	BRIGHTON & HOVE ALBION	D 1-1	Lochhead	30,175
Sep 9	Cardiff City	W 2-0	Rioch B, Lochhead	15,729
Sep 16	SWINDON TOWN	W 2-1	Evans, Lochhead	30,865
Sep 23	Nottingham Forest	D 1-1	Cottam o.g.	18,082
Sep 27	SUNDERLAND	W 2-0	Evans, Rioch B	29,895
Sep 30	MILLWALL	W 1-0	Rioch B (pen)	31,524
Oct 7	Fulham	L 0-2		17,576
Oct 14	QUEENS PARK RANGERS	L 0-1		34,045
Oct 17	Blackpool	D 1-1	Evans	15,043
Oct 21	Portsmouth	W 1-0	Vowden	13,524
Oct 28	MIDDLESBROUGH	D 1-1	Vowden	30,345
Nov 4	Sunderland	D 2-2	Rioch B, Little	18,717
Nov 11	BLACKPOOL	D 0-0		31,651
Nov 18	LUTON TOWN	L 0-2		29,144
Nov 25	Oxford United	L 0-2		13,412
Dec 2	HULL CITY	W 2-0	Graydon (pen), Hamilton	21,213
Dec 16	ORIENT	W 1-0	Evans	20,572
Dec 23	Sheffield Wednesday	D 2-2	Graydon 2	20,961
Dec 26	NOTTINGHAM FOREST	D 2-2	Lochhead, Evans	37,014
Dec 30	Huddersfield Town	D 1-1	Evans	9,719
Jan 6	BURNLEY	L 0-3		38,637
Jan 20	Brighton & Hove Albion	W 3-1	Evans, Graydon, Brown	12,212
Jan 27	CARDIFF CITY	W 2-0	Graydon (pen), Rioch B	25,856
Feb 10	Swindon Town	W 3-1	Evans, Graydon 2	13,615
Feb 17	PRESTON NORTH END	D 1-1	Aitken	27,717
Feb 24	Orient	L 0-4		9,085
Mar 3	FULHAM	L 2-3	Little, Rioch B	24,007
Mar 10	Queens Parks Rangers	L 0-1		22,513
Mar 17	PORTSMOUTH	W 2-0	Vowden, McMahon	18,432
Mar 24	Middlesbrough	D 1-1	McMahon	9,776
Mar 27	Bristol City	L 0-3		15,634
Mar 31	OXFORD UNITED	W 2-1	McMahon, Vowden	15,902
Apr 7	Hull City	W 2-1	Hamilton, Little	8,072
Apr 14	BRISTOL CITY	W 1-0	Rioch N	19,545
Apr 21	Luton Town	D 0-0		10,971
Apr 23	Millwall	D 1-1	Graydon	9,768
Apr 24	SHEFFIELD WEDNESDAY	W 2-1	Lochhead, Hamilton	20,710
Apr 28	Carlisle United	D 2-2	Lochhead, Hamilton	6,178

FA Cup

Jan 13	Everton	(Rd 3) L 2-3	Vowden, Evans	42,222

League Cup

Aug 16	HEREFORD UNITED	(Rd 1) W 4-1	Rioch B, Vowden, Graydon, Evans	32,314
Sep 5	Nottingham Forest	(Rd 2) W 1-0	Evans	17,665
Oct 4	LEEDS UNITED	(Rd 3) D 1-1	Rioch B	46,815
Oct 11	Leeds United	(R) L 0-2		28,894

FA Charity Shield

Aug 5	MANCHESTER CITY	L 0-1		34,890

MANAGER: Vic Crowe

CAPTAIN: Charlie Aitken, Chris Nicholl, Ian Ross

TOP SCORER: Alun Evans, 11 (8 league)

BIGGEST WIN: 4-1 v Hereford United (H), League Cup First Round, 16 August 1972

HIGHEST ATTENDANCE: 46,815 v Leeds United (H), League Cup Third Round, 4 October 1972

MAJOR TRANSFERS IN: Alun Evans from Liverpool, John Robson from Derby County

MAJOR TRANSFERS OUT: Willie Anderson to Cardiff City, Brian Tiler to Carlisle United

League & Cup Appearances

PLAYER	LEAGUE	CUP COMPETITION		OTHER	TOTAL
		FA CUP	LC		
Aitken	33	1	4	1	39
Anderson	14	0 (1)	2	1	17 (1)
Beard	1				1
Brown	17	1			18
Cumbes	42	1	4	1	48
Evans	29 (6)	1	3 (1)	0 (1)	33 (8)
Gidman	13		3		16
Graydon	32	1	2 (1)	1	36 (1)
Hamilton	9 (5)	2			11 (5)
Leonard	0 (2)				0 (2)
Little	17 (2)	1			18 (2)
Lochhead	30 (3)		3	1	34 (3)
McDonald	4				4
McMahon	28 (1)		4	1	33 (1)
Nicholl	41	1	4	1	47
Rioch B	32	1	4	1	38
Rioch N	6 (2)				6 (2)
Robson	19	1			20
Ross	36	1	4	1	42
Tiler	1				1
Turnball	21				21
Vowden	35	1	4	1	41
Wright	2		1	1	4

Goalscorers

PLAYER	LEAGUE	CUP COMPETITION		OTHER	TOTAL
		FA CUP	LC		
Evans	8	1	2		11
Graydon	9		1		10
Rioch B	7		2		9
Vowden	5	1	1		7
Lochhead	6				6
Hamilton	5				5
Little	3				3
McMahon	3				3
Aitken	1				1
Anderson	1				1
Brown	1				1
Rioch N	1				1
Opps' o.gs.	1				1

Fact File

As Third Division champions (1972) Villa were invited to play in the annual FA Charity Shield game – the first time they had participated since 1957.

Final Division Two Table

		P	W	D	L	F	A	Pts
1	BURNLEY	42	24	14	4	72	35	62
2	QPR	42	24	13	5	81	37	61
3	ASTON VILLA	42	18	14	10	51	47	50
4	MIDDLESBROUGH	42	17	13	12	46	43	47
5	BRISTOL C	42	17	12	13	63	51	46
6	SUNDERLAND	42	17	12	13	59	49	46
7	BLACKPOOL	42	18	10	14	56	51	46
8	OXFORD U	42	19	7	16	52	43	45
9	FULHAM	42	16	12	14	58	49	44
10	SHEFFIELD W	42	17	10	15	59	55	44
11	MILLWALL	42	16	10	16	55	47	42
12	LUTON T	42	15	11	16	44	53	41
13	HULL C	42	14	12	16	64	59	40
14	NOTTINGHAM F	42	14	12	16	47	52	40
15	ORIENT	42	12	12	18	49	53	36
16	SWINDON T	42	10	16	16	46	60	36
17	PORTSMOUTH	42	12	11	19	42	59	35
18	CARLISLE U	42	11	12	19	50	52	34
19	PRESTON NE	42	11	12	19	37	64	34
20	CARDIFF C	42	11	11	20	43	58	33
21	HUDDERSFIELD T	42	8	17	17	36	56	33
22	BRIGHTON & HA	42	8	13	21	46	83	29

Season 1973-74

Football League Division Two

DATE	OPPONENTS	SCORE	GOALSCORERS	ATTENDANCE
Aug 25	PRESTON NORTH END	W 2-0	Aitken, Hockey	28,861
Sep 1	Millwall	D 1-1	Little	12,009
Sep 8	OXFORD UNITED	W 2-0	Rioch B (pen), Vowden	28,078
Sep 11	Crystal Palace	D 0-0		20,358
Sep 15	Middlesbrough	D 0-0		19,656
Sep 19	FULHAM	D 1-1	Rioch B	30,162
Sep 22	ORIENT	D 2-2	Rioch B, Vowden	26,685
Sep 29	Notts County	L 0-2		15,872
Oct 2	Fulham	L 0-1		11,776
Oct 6	CARDIFF CITY	W 5-0	Woodruff o.g., Rioch B 2, Graydon, Morgan	24,473
Oct 13	Bolton Wanderers	W 2-1	Evans 2	19,206
Oct 20	BRISTOL CITY	D 2-2	Little, Graydon	26,918
Oct 23	CRYSTAL PALACE	W 2-1	Little, Graydon	26,670
Oct 27	Nottingham Forest	W 2-1	Graydon, Aitken	17,718
Nov 3	SHEFFIELD WEDNESDAY	W 1-0	Little	28,559
Nov 10	Portsmouth	L 0-2		12,678
Nov 17	HULL CITY	D 1-1	Little	23,773
Nov 24	Swindon Town	L 0-1		8,476
Dec 8	Sunderland	L 0-2		20,784
Dec 15	Luton Town	L 0-1		10,020
Dec 22	NOTTS COUNTY	D 1-1	Rioch B	20,825
Dec 26	West Bromwich Albion	L 0-2		43,080
Dec 29	Oxford United	L 1-2	Graydon	10,149
Jan 1	MILLWALL	D 0-0		20,905
Jan 12	MIDDLESBROUGH	D 1-1	Rioch B	26,906
Jan 19	Preston North End	D 0-0		10,766
Feb 2	LUTON TOWN	L 0-1		26,180
Feb 23	Cardiff City	W 1-0	Graydon	12,310
Feb 27	BOLTON WANDERERS	D 1-1	McMahon	18,952
Mar 2	WEST BROMWICH ALBION	L 1-3	Morgan	37,323
Mar 13	CARLISLE UNITED	W 2-1	Evans, Hamilton (pen)	12,007
Mar 16	Bristol City	W 1-0	Morgan	12,759
May 23	PORTSMOUTH	W 4-1	McMahon 2, Morgan 2	15,517
Apr 1	Sheffield Wednesday	W 4-2	Little 2, McMahon, Leonard	22,094
Apr 6	SWINDON TOWN	D 1-1	Little	20,709
Apr 13	Hull City	D 1-1	Deere o.g.	11,291
Apr 15	BLACKPOOL	L 0-1		18,351
Apr 16	Blackpool	L 1-2	Hamilton	10,787
Apr 20	SUNDERLAND	L 1-2	McMahon	17,321
Apr 24	NOTTINGHAM FOREST	W 3-1	Hamilton, Campbell, Graydon	12,439
Apr 27	Carlisle United	L 0-2		12,494
May 3	Orient	D 1-1	Graydon (pen)	29,766

FA Cup

Jan 5	CHESTER	(Rd 3) W 3-1	Nicholl, Morgan 2	16,545
Jan 26	Arsenal	(Rd 4) D 1-1	Morgan	41,682
Jan 30	ARSENAL	(R) W 2-0	Morgan, Evans	47,821
Feb 16	Burnley	(Rd 5) L 0-1		29,301

League Cup

Oct 9	York City	(Rd 2) L 0-1		7,891

League & Cup Appearances

PLAYER	LEAGUE	CUP COMPETITION		TOTAL
		FA CUP	LC	
Aitken	38	4	1	43
Brown	24	1	1	26
Campbell	1 (2)			1 (2)
Cumbes	41	4	1	46
Evans	24 (1)	4		28 (1)
Findlay	1			1
Gidman	30	4		34
Graydon	19 (4)	2	1	22 (4)
Hamilton	30 (1)	4		34 (1)
Hockey	24			24
Leonard	7			7
Little	36 (1)	1 (1)	1	38 (2)
McDonald	4			4
McMahon	20	3		23
Morgan	21 (4)	3 (1)	1	25 (5)
Nicholl	40	4	1	45
Rioch B	18	4	1	23
Rioch N	3 (2)			3 (2)
Robson	12		1	13
Ross	42	4	1	47
Stark	2			2
Turnball	10			10
Vowden	15	2	1	18

Goalscorers

PLAYER	LEAGUE	CUP COMPETITION		TOTAL
		FA CUP	LC	
Morgan	5	4		9
Graydon	8			8
Little	8			8
Rioch B	7			7
McMahon	5			5
Evans	3	1		4
Hamilton	3			3
Aitkin	2			2
Vowden	2			2
Campbell	1			1
Hockey	1			1
Leonard	1			1
Nicholl		1		1
Opps' o.gs.	2			2

Fact File

Villa managed to score only one goal in a total of seven away league games between November and January.

MANAGER: Vic Crowe

CAPTAIN: Chris Nicholl, Ian Ross

TOP SCORER: Sammy Morgan, 9 (5 league)

BIGGEST WIN: 5-0 v Cardiff City (H), Division Two, 6 October 1973

HIGHEST ATTENDANCE: 47,821 v Arsenal (H), FA Cup Fourth Round Replay, 30 January 1974

MAJOR TRANSFERS IN: Trevor Hockey from Norwich City, Sammy Morgan from Port Vale

MAJOR TRANSFERS OUT: Bruce Rioch to Derby County

Final Division Two Table

		P	W	D	L	F	A	Pts
1	MIDDLESBROUGH	42	27	11	4	77	30	65
2	LUTON T	42	19	12	11	64	51	50
3	CARLISLE U	42	20	9	13	61	48	49
4	ORIENT	42	15	18	9	55	42	48
5	BLACKPOOL	42	17	13	12	57	40	47
6	SUNDERLAND	42	19	9	14	58	44	47
7	NOTTINGHAM F	42	15	15	12	57	43	45
8	WBA	42	14	16	12	48	45	44
9	HULL C	42	13	17	12	46	47	43
10	NOTTS CO	42	15	13	14	55	60	43
11	BOLTON W	42	15	12	15	44	40	42
12	MILLWALL	42	14	14	14	51	51	42
13	FULHAM	42	16	10	16	39	43	42
14	ASTON VILLA	42	13	15	14	48	45	41
15	PORTSMOUTH	42	14	12	16	45	62	40
16	BRISTOL C	42	14	10	18	47	54	38
17	CARDIFF C	42	10	16	16	49	62	36
18	OXFORD U	42	10	16	16	35	46	36
19	SHEFFIELD W	42	12	11	19	51	63	35
20	CRYSTAL PALACE	42	11	12	19	43	56	34
21	PRESTON NE	42	9	14	19	40	62	31
22	SWINDON T	42	7	11	24	36	72	25

PRESTON NE ONE POINT DEDUCTED FOR FIELDING AN INELIGIBLE PLAYER.

Season 1974-75

Football League Division Two

DATE	OPPONENTS	SCORE	GOALSCORERS	ATTENDANCE
Aug 17	York City	D 1-1	Graydon	8,740
Aug 20	Hull City	D 1-1	Robson	8,712
Aug 24	NORWICH CITY	D 1-1	Graydon	23,297
Aug 28	HULL CITY	W 6-0	Morgan 3, Graydon, Little B, Hamilton	18,973
Aug 31	Bolton Wanderers	L 0-1		12,976
Sep 7	ORIENT	W 3-1	Morgan, Graydon 2	16,802
Sep 14	Bristol Rovers	L 0-2		14,035
Sep 21	MILLWALL	W 3-0	Graydon 3 (1 pen)	21,375
Sep 28	Southampton	D 0-0		18,599
Oct 2	NOTTINGHAM FOREST	W 3-0	Graydon, Hamilton, Leonard	20,357
Oct 5	Oldham Athletic	W 2-1	Graydon, Hicks o.g.	15,574
Oct 12	BLACKPOOL	W 1-0	Graydon	25,763
Oct 19	Sunderland	D 0-0		33,232
Oct 26	SHEFFIELD WEDNESDAY	W 3-1	Phillips, Nicholl, Graydon (pen)	23,977
Nov 2	Fulham	L 1-3	Little B	10,979
Nov 9	NOTTS COUNTY	L 0-1		22,162
Nov 16	Manchester United	L 1-2	Hamilton	55,615
Nov 23	PORTSMOUTH	W 2-0	Hamilton, Little B	16,827
Nov 29	OXFORD UNITED	D 0-0		18,554
Dec 7	Bristol City	L 0-1		13,390
Dec 14	YORK CITY	W 4-0	Graydon, Nicholl, Little B, Hamilton	15,840
Dec 21	West Bromwich Albion	L 0-2		23,011
Dec 26	BRISTOL ROVERS	W 1-0	Graydon	21,557
Dec 28	Cardiff City	L 1-3	Hamilton	11,040
Jan 11	BRISTOL CITY	W 2-0	Little B, Hamilton	21,762
Jan 18	Oxford United	W 2-1	Little B, Nicholl	9,872
Feb 1	Notts County	W 3-1	Little B 2, Carrodus	17,275
Feb 8	FULHAM	D 1-1	Nicholl	28,533
Feb 18	Portsmouth	W 3-2	Carrodus, Little B, Graydon	13,354
Feb 22	MANCHESTER UNITED	W 2-0	Graydon, Aitken	39,156
Mar 5	BOLTON WANDERERS	D 0-0		39,322
Mar 8	Nottingham Forest	W 3-2	Graydon 2, Little B	20,205
Mar 15	SOUTHAMPTON	W 3-0	Leonard, Graydon, Holmes o.g.	31,967
Mar 22	Orient	L 0-1		9,466
Mar 29	WEST BROMWICH ALBION	W 3-1	Leonard 2, Hamilton	47,574
Apr 1	Millwall	W 3-1	Hamilton (pen), Little B, Leonard	13,115
Apr 9	CARDIFF CITY	W 2-0	Little B 2	32,748
Apr 12	OLDHAM ATHLETIC	W 5-0	Little B 3, Hamilton, Hicks o.g.	36,224
Apr 19	Blackpool	W 3-0	Phillips, Hatton o.g., Little B	20,762
Apr 23	Sheffield Wednesday	W 4-0	Leonard, Little B 2, Ross (pen)	23,605
Apr 26	SUNDERLAND	W 2-0	Ross (pen), Little B	57,266
Apr 30	Norwich City	W 4-1	Leonard, Gidman, McDonald, Carrodus	35,999

FA Cup

Jan 4	Oldham Athletic	(Rd 3) W 3-0	Little B, Nicholl, Graydon	14,510
Jan 25	SHEFFIELD UNITED	(Rd 4) W 4-1	Leonard 2, Nicholl, Graydon	35,881
Feb 15	Ipswich Town	(Rd 5) L 2-3	McDonald, Evans	31,297

League Cup

Sep 11	EVERTON	(Rd 2) D 1-1	Nicholl	29,640
Sep 18	Everton	(R) W 3-0	Morgan, Carrodus, Graydon	24,595
Oct 9	Crewe Alexandra	(Rd 3) D 2-2	Morgan, Leonard	12,290
Oct 16	CREWE ALEXANDRA	(R) W 1-0	Hamilton	24,007
Nov 12	Hartlepool	(Rd 4) D 1-1	Aitken	12,305
Nov 25	HARTLEPOOL	(R) W 6-1	Graydon 2 (1 pen), Little B 2, Hamilton 2 (1 pen)	17,686
Dec 5	Colchester United	(Rd 5) W 2-1	Little A, Graydon	11,871
Jan 15	Chester	(SF) D 2-2	McDonald, Graydon	19,000
Jan 22	CHESTER	(R) W 3-2	Leonard 2, Little B	47,732
Mar 1	Norwich City*	(F) W 1-0	Graydon	95,946

*Played at Wembley.

MANAGER: Ron Saunders

CAPTAIN: Ian Ross

TOP SCORER: Ray Graydon, 27 (19 league)

BIGGEST WIN: 6-0 v Hull City (H), Division Two, 28 August 1974

HIGHEST ATTENDANCE: 95,946 v Norwich City, League Cup final at Wembley, 1 March 1975

MAJOR TRANSFERS IN: Frank Carrodus from Manchester City, Leighton Phillips from Cardiff City

League & Cup Appearances

PLAYER	LEAGUE	CUP COMPETITION		TOTAL
		FA CUP	LC	
Aitken	42 (1)	3	10	55 (1)
Betts	1 (2)		0 (1)	1 (3)
Brown	9 (1)		3	12 (1)
Campbell	6 (1)		2	8 (1)
Carrodus	35	2	9	46
Cumbes	38	3	10	51
Evans	1	0 (1)		1 (1)
Findlay	1			1
Gidman	13 (1)		3	16 (1)
Graydon	37	3	10	50
Hamilton	37	3	10	50
Hunt	1 (1)			1 (1)
Leonard	22	3	5	30
Little A	2 (1)		2	4 (1)
Little B	33 (1)	2	7 (1)	42 (2)
McDonald	15 (3)	3	3	21 (3)
McMahon	2			2
Masefield	0 (1)			0 (1)
Morgan	12		4	16
Mosley	3			3
Nicholl	41	2	10	53
Phillips	23 (2)			23 (2)
Pimblett	2	1	1	4
Rioch N	4	1	1	6
Robson	41	3	10	54
Ross	42	3	10	55

Goalscorers

PLAYER	LEAGUE	CUP COMPETITION		TOTAL
		FA CUP	LC	
Graydon	19	2	6	27
Little B	20	1	3	24
Hamilton	10		3	13
Leonard	7	2	3	12
Nicholl	4	2	1	7
Morgan	4		2	6
Carrodus	3		1	4
McDonald	1	1	1	3
Phillips	2			2
Ross	2			2
Aitken	1		1	2
Evans		1		1
Gidman	1			1
Little A			1	1
Robson	1			1
Opps' o.gs.	4			4

Final Division Two Table

		P	W	D	L	F	A	Pts
1	MANCHESTER U	42	26	9	7	66	30	61
2	ASTON VILLA	42	25	8	9	79	32	58
3	NORWICH C	42	20	13	9	58	37	53
4	SUNDERLAND	42	19	13	10	65	35	51
5	BRISTOL C	42	21	8	13	47	33	50
6	WBA	42	18	9	15	54	42	45
7	BLACKPOOL	42	14	17	11	38	33	45
8	HULL C	42	15	14	13	40	53	44
9	FULHAM	42	13	16	13	44	39	42
10	BOLTON W	42	15	12	15	45	41	42
11	OXFORD U	42	15	12	15	41	51	42
12	ORIENT	42	11	20	11	28	39	42
13	SOUTHAMPTON	42	15	11	16	53	54	41
14	NOTTS CO	42	12	16	14	49	59	40
15	YORK C	42	14	10	18	51	55	38
16	NOTTINGHAM F	42	12	14	16	43	55	38
17	PORTSMOUTH	42	12	13	17	44	54	37
18	OLDHAM ATH	42	10	15	17	40	48	35
19	BRISTOL R	42	12	11	19	42	64	35
20	MILLWALL	42	10	12	20	44	56	32
21	CARDIFF C	42	9	14	19	36	62	32
22	SHEFFIELD W	42	5	11	26	29	64	21

Season 1975-76

Football League Division One

DATE	OPPONENTS	SCORE	GOALSCORERS	ATTENDANCE
Aug 16	LEEDS UNITED	L 1-2	Phillips	46,026
Aug 19	Queens Park Rangers	D 1-1	Leonard	21,986
Aug 23	Norwich City	L 3-5	Graydon 2 (1 pen), Aitken	21,797
Aug 27	MANCHESTER CITY	W 1-0	Leonard	35,212
Aug 30	COVENTRY CITY	W 1-0	Graydon	41,026
Sep 6	Newcastle United	L 0-3		34,668
Sep 13	ARSENAL	W 2-0	Phillips, Leonard	34,474
Sep 20	Liverpool	L 0-3		42,779
Sep 23	Wolverhampton Wanderers	D 0-0		33,344
Sep 27	BIRMINGHAM CITY	W 2-1	Hamilton, Little	53,782
Oct 4	Middlesbrough	D 0-0		24,102
Oct 11	TOTTENHAM HOTSPUR	D 1-1	Gray	40,048
Oct 18	Everton	L 1-2	Nicholl	30,376
Oct 25	BURNLEY	D 1-1	Noble o.g.	34,242
Nov 1	Ipswich Town	L 0-3		24,691
Nov 8	SHEFFIELD UNITED	W 5-1	Gray, Hamilton 2, Deehan, Graydon (pen)	30,053
Nov 15	Manchester United	L 0-2		51,682
Nov 22	EVERTON	W 3-1	Gray 2, McNaught o.g.	33,949
Nov 29	LEICESTER CITY	D 1-1	Graydon	36,388
Dec 6	Stoke City	D 1-1	Graydon	28,492
Dec 13	NORWICH CITY	W 3-2	Graydon, Deehan 2	30,478
Dec 20	Leeds United	L 0-1		29,118
Dec 26	WEST HAM UNITED	W 4-1	Deehan 2, Hamilton, Gray	51,300
Dec 27	Derby County	L 0-2		37,230
Jan 10	Arsenal	D 0-0		24,501
Jan 17	NEWCASTLE UNITED	D 1-1	Mahoney o.g.	36,387
Jan 31	QUEENS PARK RANGERS	L 0-2		32,223
Feb 7	Manchester City	L 1-2	Gray	32,331
Feb 14	Sheffield United	L 1-2	Graydon	21,152
Feb 21	MANCHESTER UNITED	W 2-1	McDonald, Gray	50,094
Feb 28	WOLVERHAMPTON WANDERERS	D 1-1	Graydon (pen)	47,693
Feb 28	Burnley	D 2-2	Graydon, Gray	17,123
Mar 6	IPSWICH TOWN	D 0-0		32,477
Mar 15	Tottenham Hotspur	L 2-5	Graydon, Gray	23,169
Mar 20	Leicester City	D 2-2	Nicholl 2	24,663
Mar 27	STOKE CITY	D 0-0		32,359
Apr 3	Birmingham City	L 2-3	Gray, Graydon (pen)	46,251
Apr 10	LIVERPOOL	D 0-0		44,250
Apr 13	Coventry City	D 1-1	Nicholl	27,586
Apr 17	West Ham United	D 2-2	Deehan, Hunt	21,642
Apr 19	DERBY COUNTY	W 1-0	McDonald	39,241
Apr 24	MIDDLESBROUGH	W 2-1	Deehan, Carrodus	33,241

FA Cup

Jan 3	Southampton	(Rd 3) D 1-1	Gray	24,138
Jan 7	SOUTHAMPTON	(R) L 1-2*	Graydon	44,623

*After extra-time.

League Cup

Sep 10	OLDHAM ATHLETIC	(Rd 2) W 2-0	Leonard, Nicholl	23,041
Oct 8	MANCHESTER UNITED	(Rd 3) L 1-2	Gray	41,447

UEFA Cup

Sep 17	Antwerp	(Rd 1/FL) L 1-4	Graydon	20,000
Oct 1	ANTWERP	(Rd 1/SL) L 0-1		31,513

Fact File

Villa's first-ever venture into European football ended in disappointment ... beaten over two legs by a very useful Belgian side, Antwerp.

MANAGER: Ron Saunders

CAPTAIN: Ian Ross

TOP SCORER: Ray Graydon, 14 (12 league)

BIGGEST WIN: 5-1 v Sheffield United (H), Division One, 8 November 1975

HIGHEST ATTENDANCE: 53,782 v Birmingham City (H), Division One, 27 September 1975

MAJOR TRANSFERS IN: John Burridge from Blackpool, Andy Gray from Dundee United, Dennis Mortimer from Coventry City

MAJOR TRANSFERS OUT: Jim Cumbes to Portland Timbers, Sammy Morgan to Brighton & Hove Albion

League & Cup Appearances

PLAYER	LEAGUE	CUP COMPETITION		OTHER	TOTAL
		FA CUP	LC		
Aitken	21		0 (1)	2	2	25 (1)
Burridge	30	2			32
Carrodus	39	2	2	2	45
Cowans	0 (1)				0 (1)
Cumbes	7		1		2	10
Deehan	14 (1)	2			16 (1)
Findlay	5		1		6
Gidman	39	2	1	2	44
Gray	30	2	1		33
Graydon	38	2	2	2	44
Hamilton	29 (2)	2	2	2	35 (2)
Hunt	3 (1)			0 (1)	3 (2)
Leonard	7		1		8
Little	20		2	1	23
Masefield	0 (1)				0 (1)
McDonald	10 (3)			1	11 (3)
Morgan	2 (1)			1 (1)	3 (2)
Mortimer	14				14
Nicholl	40	2	2	2	46
Overton	2 (1)				2 (1)
Phillips	33 (2)	2	2	2	39 (2)
Pimblett	7				7
Robson	34 (3)	2	1	1	38 (3)
Ross	38	2	2	2	44

Goalscorers

PLAYER	LEAGUE	CUP COMPETITION		OTHER	TOTAL
		FA CUP	LC		
Graydon	12	1		1	14
Gray	10	1	1		12
Deehan	7				7
Nicholl	4		1		5
Hamilton	4				4
Leonard	3		1		4
McDonald	2				2
Phillips	2				2
Aitkin	1				1
Carrodus	1				1
Hunt	1				1
Little	1				1
Opps' o.gs.	3				3

Final Division One Table

		P	W	D	L	F	A	Pts
1	LIVERPOOL	42	23	14	5	66	31	60
2	QPR	42	24	11	7	67	33	59
3	MANCHESTER U	42	23	10	10	68	42	56
4	DERBY CO	42	21	11	10	75	58	53
5	LEEDS U	42	21	9	12	65	46	51
6	IPSWICH T	42	16	14	12	54	48	46
7	LEICESTER C	42	13	19	10	48	51	45
8	MANCHESTER C	42	16	12	15	64	46	43
9	TOTTENHAM H	42	14	15	13	63	63	43
10	NORWICH C	42	16	10	16	58	58	42
11	EVERTON	42	15	12	15	60	66	42
12	STOKE C	42	15	11	16	48	50	41
13	MIDDLESBROUGH	42	15	10	17	46	45	40
14	COVENTRY C	42	13	14	15	47	57	40
15	NEWCASTLE U	42	15	9	18	71	62	39
16	ASTON VILLA	42	11	17	14	51	59	39
17	ARSENAL	42	13	10	19	47	53	36
18	WEST HAM U	42	13	10	19	48	71	36
19	BIRMINGHAM C	42	13	7	22	57	75	33
20	WOLVERHAMPTON W	42	10	10	22	51	68	30
21	BURNLEY	42	9	10	23	43	66	28
22	SHEFFIELD U	42	6	10	26	33	82	22

Season 1976-77

Football League Division One

DATE	OPPONENTS	SCORE	GOALSCORERS	ATTENDANCE
Aug 21	WEST HAM UNITED	W 4-0	Gray 2, Graydon 2 (1 pen)	39,012
Aug 25	Manchester City	L 0-2		41,007
Aug 28	Everton	W 2-0	Little, Lyons o.g.	32,058
Sep 4	IPSWICH TOWN	W 5-2	Little, Gray 3, Graydon	39,916
Sep 11	Queens Park Rangers	L 1-2	Gray	23,602
Sep 18	BIRMINGHAM CITY	L 1-2	Gray	50,084
Sep 25	LEICESTER CITY	W 2-0	Graydon (pen), Gray	36,652
Oct 2	Stoke City	L 0-1		29,652
Oct 16	Sunderland	W 1-0	Cropley	31,578
Oct 20	ARSENAL	W 5-1	Mortimer, Graydon, Gray 2, Little	33,860
Oct 23	BRISTOL CITY	W 3-1	Nicholl, Gidman, Graydon	37,094
Oct 30	Liverpool	L 0-3		51,751
Nov 6	MANCHESTER UNITED	W 3-2	Mortimer, Gray 2	44,789
Nov 10	West Bromwich Albion	D 1-1	Mortimer	42,900
Nov 20	COVENTRY CITY	D 2-2	Gidman, Gray	40,047
Nov 27	Norwich City	D 1-1	Little	22,554
Dec 11	Leeds United	W 3-1	Gray 2, Cropley	31,232
Dec 15	LIVERPOOL	W 5-1	Gray 2, Deehan 2, Little	42,851
Dec 18	NEWCASTLE UNITED	W 2-1	Deehan 2	33,982
Dec 27	Middlesbrough	L 2-3	Gray, Hughes	31,000
Jan 1	Manchester United	L 0-2		55,446
Jan 22	West Ham United	W 1-0	Gray	27,577
Feb 5	EVERTON	W 2-0	Gray, Little	41,305
Feb 12	Ipswich Town	L 0-1		29,750
Mar 2	DERBY COUNTY	W 4-0	Mortimer, Gidman, Little, Cowans	37,396
Mar 5	Leicester City	D 1-1	Deehan	22,038
Mar 23	SUNDERLAND	W 4-1	Gidman, Gray, Deehan 2	34,458
Apr 2	Bristol City	D 0-0		27,958
Apr 5	MIDDLESBROUGH	W 1-0	Deehan	32,646
Apr 9	Derby County	L 1-2	Little	28,061
Apr 16	Coventry City	W 3-2	Cowans, Deehan, Little	31,158
Apr 20	TOTTENHAM HOTSPUR	W 2-1	Little, Deehan	42,047
Apr 23	NORWICH CITY	W 1-0	Little	35,899
Apr 25	Arsenal	L 0-3		23,961
Apr 30	Tottenham Hotspur	L 1-3	Deehan	30,890
May 4	MANCHESTER CITY	D 1-1	Little	36,190
May 7	LEEDS UNITED	W 2-1	Deehan, Cropley	38,205
May 10	Birmingham City	L 1-2	Deehan	43,721
May 14	Newcastle United	L 2-3	Little 2	29,250
May 16	STOKE CITY	W 1-0	Gray (pen)	28,963
May 20	QUEENS PARK RANGERS	D 1-1	Cowans	28,056
May 23	WEST BROMWICH ALBION	W 4-0	Nicholl, Gray 3	42,542

FA Cup

Jan 8	Leicester City	(Rd 3) W 1-0	Gray	27,112
Jan 29	WEST HAM UNITED	(Rd 4) W 3-0	Mortimer, Deehan 2	46,954
Feb 26	PORT VALE	(Rd 5) W 3-0	Nicholl, Deehan, Little	48,812
Mar 19	Manchester United	(Rd 6) L 1-2	Little	57,089

League Cup

Sep 1	MANCHESTER CITY	(Rd 2) W 3-0	Graydon, Little 2	34,585
Sep 21	NORWICH CITY	(Rd 3) W 2-1	Gray 2	31,295
Oct 27	WREXHAM	(Rd 4) W 5-1	Nicholl, Little 2, Gray, Carrodus	41,428
Dec 1	MILLWALL	(Rd 5) W 2-0	Nicholl, Little	37,147
Feb 1	Queens Park Rangers	(SF) D 0-0		28,739
Feb 16	QUEENS PARK RANGERS	(2nd R) D 2-2*	Deehan 2	48,429
Feb 22	Queens Park Rangers§	(R) W 3-0	Little 3	40,438
Mar 12	Everton†	(F) D 0-0		96,223
Mar 16	Everton‡	(R) D 1-1*	Kenyon o.g.	54,840
Apr 13	Everton#	(2nd R) W 3-2*	Nicholl, Little 2	54,749

*After extra-time. §Played at Highbury, London. †Played at Wembley.
‡Played at Hillsborough, Sheffield. #Played at Old Trafford, Manchester.

MANAGER: Ron Saunders

CAPTAIN: Leighton Phillips, Chris Nicholl

TOP SCORER: Andy Gray, 29 (25 league)

BIGGEST WIN: 5-1 v Arsenal (II), Division One, 20 October 1976;
v Liverpool (H), Division One, 15 December 1976; v Wrexham (H),
League Cup Fourth Round, 27 October 1976

HIGHEST ATTENDANCE: 96,223 v Everton, League Cup final at Wembley,
12 March 1977

MAJOR TRANSFERS IN: Alex Cropley from Arsenal, Gordon Smith from
St Johnstone

MAJOR TRANSFERS OUT: Steve Hunt to New York Cosmos

League & Cup Appearances

PLAYER	LEAGUE	CUP COMPETITION		TOTAL
		FA CUP	LC	
Burridge	35	4	9	48
Buttress	0 (2)			0 (2)
Carrodus	30	4	9	43
Cowans	16 (3)	2 (1)	3 (1)	21 (5)
Cropley	32	2	7	41
Deehan	27	4	6	37
Findlay	7		1	8
Gidman	27	4	10	41
Gray	36	3	9	48
Graydon	17	1	4	22
Hughes	4 (1)			4 (1)
Hunt	0 (1)			0 (1)
Linton	0 (2)			0 (2)
Little	42	4	10	56
Masefield	0 (1)			0 (1)
Mortimer	40	4	10	54
Nicholl	34	3	10	47
Phillips	40	4	10	54
Robson	33 (1)	4	7	44 (1)
Smith	32 (2)		4 (1)	36 (3)
Young	10 (1)	1		11 (1)

Goalscorers

PLAYER	LEAGUE	CUP COMPETITION		TOTAL
		FA CUP	LC	
Gray	25	1	3	29
Little	14	2	10	26
Deehan	13	3	2	18
Graydon	6		1	7
Nichol	2	1	3	6
Mortimer	4	1		5
Gidman	4			4
Cowans	3			3
Cropley	3			3
Carrodus			1	1
Hughes	1			1
Opps' o.gs.	1		1	2

Fact File

Brian Little played in every minute of every game
this season for Villa – total 56.

Final Division One Table

		P	W	D	L	F	A	Pts
1	LIVERPOOL	42	23	11	8	62	33	57
2	MANCHESTER C	42	21	14	7	60	34	56
3	IPSWICH TOWN	42	22	8	12	66	39	56
4	ASTON VILLA	42	22	7	13	76	50	51
5	NEWCASTLE U	42	18	13	11	64	49	49
6	MANCHESTER U	42	18	11	13	71	62	47
7	WBA	42	16	13	13	62	56	45
8	ARSENAL	42	16	11	15	64	59	43
9	EVERTON	42	14	14	14	62	64	42
10	LEEDS U	42	15	12	15	48	51	42
11	LEICESTER C	42	12	18	12	47	60	42
12	MIDDLESBROUGH	42	14	13	15	40	45	41
13	BIRMINGHAM C	42	13	12	17	63	61	38
14	QPR	42	13	12	17	47	52	38
15	DERBY CO	42	9	19	14	50	55	37
16	NORWICH C	42	14	9	19	47	64	37
17	WEST HAM U	42	11	14	17	46	65	36
18	BRISTOL C	42	11	13	18	38	48	35
19	COVENTRY C	42	10	15	17	48	59	35
20	SUNDERLAND	42	11	12	19	46	54	34
21	STOKE C	42	10	14	18	28	51	34
22	TOTTENHAM H	42	12	9	21	48	72	33

Season 1977-78

Football League Division One

DATE	OPPONENTS	SCORE	GOALSCORERS	ATTENDANCE
Aug 20	Queens Park Rangers	W 2-1	Webb o.g., Carrodus	25,431
Aug 24	MANCHESTER CITY	L 1-4	Deehan	40,121
Aug 27	EVERTON	L 1-2	Gray	37,806
Sep 3	Bristol City	D 1-1	Little	22,200
Sep 10	ARSENAL	W 1-0	Cropley	36,929
Sep 17	Nottingham Forest	L 0-2		31,016
Sep 23	WOLVERHAMPTON WANDERERS	W 2-0	Brazier o.g., Deehan	40,403
Oct 1	BIRMINGHAM CITY	L 0-1		45,436
Oct 5	Leeds United	D 1-1	Gray	27,797
Oct 8	Leicester City	W 2-0	Cowans, Gray	20,276
Oct 15	NORWICH CITY	W 3-0	Gray, Cowans, Little	32,978
Oct 22	West Ham United	D 2-2	McNaught, Gray	26,599
Oct 29	MANCHESTER UNITED	W 2-1	Gray, Cropley	39,144
Nov 5	Liverpool	W 2-1	Gray 2	50,436
Nov 12	MIDDLESBROUGH	L 0-1		31,837
Nov 19	Chelsea	D 0-0		31,764
Dec 3	Ipswich Town	L 0-2		20,917
Dec 10	WEST BROMWICH ALBION	W 3-0	Cowans, Gray, Gidman	41,631
Dec 17	Middlesbrough	L 0-1		14,999
Dec 26	COVENTRY CITY	D 1-1	Deehan	43,571
Dec 27	Derby County	W 3-0	Little, Gray, Deehan	30,395
Dec 31	Manchester City	L 0-2		46,074
Jan 2	QUEENS PARK RANGERS	D 1-1	Little	34,750
Jan 14	Everton	L 0-1		40,630
Jan 28	BRISTOL CITY	W 1-0	Deehan	29,676
Feb 4	Arsenal	W 1-0	MacDonald o.g.	30,127
Feb 25	Birmingham City	L 0-1		33,679
Mar 4	LEICESTER CITY	D 0-0		29,971
Mar 11	Norwich City	L 1-2	Gregory	19,031
Mar 18	WEST HAM UNITED	W 4-1	Gregory 2, Deehan, Mortimer	28,275
Mar 21	Coventry City	W 3-2	Little, McNaught, Gray	30,957
Mar 25	DERBY COUNTY	D 0-0		32,793
Mar 29	Manchester United	D 1-1	Deehan	41,625
Apr 1	LIVERPOOL	L 0-3		40,190
Apr 5	NOTTINGHAM FOREST	L 0-1		44,215
Apr 8	Newcastle United	D 1-1	Evans	17,203
Apr 15	CHELSEA	W 2-0	Cowans, Wicks o.g.	27,375
Apr 17	NEWCASTLE UNITED	W 2-0	Cowans, Gray	25,443
Apr 22	West Bromwich Albion	W 3-0	Deehan, Cowans, Mortimer	35,000
Apr 26	LEEDS UNITED	W 3-1	Deehan, Mortimer, Little	30,524
Apr 29	IPSWICH TOWN	W 6-1	Deehan 2, Gray, Little, Carrodus, Cowans	30,955
May 2	Wolverhampton Wanderers	L 1-3	Carrodus	30,644

FA Cup

Jan 7	Everton	(Rd 3) L 1-4	Gray	46,320

League Cup

Aug 31	Exeter City	(Rd 2) W 3-1	Gray 3	13,768
Oct 26	QUEENS PARK RANGERS	(Rd 3) W 1-0	Gray (pen)	34,481
Nov 29	Nottingham Forest	(Rd 4) L 2-4	Little, Carrodus	29,333

UEFA Cup

Sep 14	FENERBAHCE	(Rd 1/FL) W 4-0	Deehan 2, Gray, Little	30,351
Sep 28	Fenerbahce	(Rd 1/SL) W 2-0	Deehan, Little	18,000
Oct 19	GÓRNIK ZABRZE	(Rd 2/FL) W 2-0	McNaught 2	34,138
Nov 2	Górnik Zabrze	(Rd 2/SL) D 1-1	Gray	15,000
Nov 23	ATHLETIC BILBAO	(Rd 3/FL) W 2-0	Iribar o.g., Deehan	32,973
Dec 7	Athletic Bilbao	(Rd 3/SL) D 1-1	Mortimer	39,000
Mar 1	BARCELONA	(Rd 4/FL) D 2-2	McNaught, Deehan	49,619
Mar 15	Barcelona	(Rd 4/SL) L 1-2	Little	90,000

MANAGER: Ron Saunders

CAPTAIN: Dennis Mortimer

TOP SCORER: Andy Gray, 20 (13 league)

BIGGEST WIN: 6-1 v Ipswich Town (H), Division One, 29 April 1978

HIGHEST ATTENDANCE: 90,000 v Barcelona (A), UEFA Cup Fourth Round Second Leg, 15 March 1978

MAJOR TRANSFERS IN: Allan Evans from Dunfermline Athletic, Ken McNaught from Everton, Tommy Craig from Newcastle United, Jimmy Rimmer from Arsenal

MAJOR TRANSFERS OUT: John Robson retired

League & Cup Appearances

PLAYER	LEAGUE	CUP COMPETITION		OTHER	TOTAL
		FA CUP	LC		
Buttress	1				1
Carrodus	40	1	3	8	52
Cowans	30 (5)	1	2	4 (1)	37 (6)
Craig	4				4
Cropley	17		3	5	25
Deehan	35 (1)	0 (1)	3	7	45 (2)
Evans A	9			0 (1)	9 (1)
Gidman	34	1	2	7	44
Gray	31 (1)	1	3	5	40 (1)
Gregory	21 (5)	1	1	3 (1)	26 (6)
Linton	0 (1)			0 (1)	0 (2)
Little	40	1	3	8	52
McNaught	40	1	3	8	52
Mortimer	42	1	3	8	54
Phillips	35	1	3	8	47
Rimmer	42	1	3		46
Robson	3			1	4
Smith	38	1	3	7	49

Goalscorers

PLAYER	LEAGUE	CUP COMPETITION		OTHER	TOTAL
		FA CUP	LC		
Gray	13	1	4	2	20
Deehan	11			5	16
Little	7		1	3	11
Cowans	7				7
McNaught	2			3	5
Carrodus	3		1		4
Mortimer	3			1	4
Gregory	3				3
Cropley	2				2
Evans A	1				1
Gidman	1				1
Opps' o.gs.	4			1	5

Fact File

When Villa beat Ipswich 6-1 at Villa Park on 29 April, the Tractor Boys had just qualified for the FA Cup final!

Final Division One Table

		P	W	D	L	F	A	Pts
1	NOTTINGHAM F	42	25	14	3	69	24	64
2	LIVERPOOL	42	24	9	9	65	34	57
3	EVERTON	42	22	11	9	76	45	55
4	MANCHESTER C	42	20	12	10	74	51	52
5	ARSENAL	42	21	10	11	60	37	52
6	WBA	42	18	14	10	62	53	50
7	COVENTRY C	42	18	12	12	75	62	48
8	ASTON VILLA	42	18	10	14	57	42	46
9	LEEDS U	42	18	10	14	63	53	46
10	MANCHESTER U	42	16	10	16	67	63	42
11	BIRMINGHAM C	42	16	9	17	55	60	41
12	DERBY CO	42	14	13	15	54	59	41
13	NORWICH C	42	11	18	13	52	66	40
14	MIDDLESBROUGH	42	12	15	15	42	54	39
15	WOLVERHAMPTON W	42	12	12	18	51	64	36
16	CHELSEA	42	11	14	17	46	69	36
17	BRISTOL C	42	11	13	18	49	53	35
18	IPSWICH T	42	11	13	18	47	61	35
19	QPR	42	9	15	18	47	64	33
20	WEST HAM U	42	12	8	22	52	69	32
21	NEWCASTLE U	42	6	10	26	42	78	22
22	LEICESTER C	42	5	12	25	26	70	22

Season 1978-79

Football League Division One

DATE	OPPONENTS	SCORE	GOALSCORERS	ATTENDANCE
Aug 19	WOLVERHAMPTON WANDERERS	W 1-0	Gray	43,922
Aug 23	Tottenham Hotspur	W 4-1	Evans A, Gregory, Little, Shelton	47,892
Aug 26	Bristol City	L 0-1		23,493
Sep 2	SOUTHAMPTON	D 1-1	Gray	34,067
Sep 9	Ipswich Town	W 2-0	Gregory, Gray (pen)	22,166
Sep 16	EVERTON	D 1-1	Craig	38,636
Sep 23	Queens Park Rangers	L 0-1		16,410
Sep 30	NOTTINGHAM FOREST	L 1-2	Craig (pen)	36,735
Oct 7	Arsenal	D 1-1	Gregory	34,537
Oct 14	MANCHESTER UNITED	D 2-2	Gregory 2	36,204
Oct 21	Birmingham City	W 1-0	Gray	36,145
Oct 27	MIDDLESBROUGH	L 0-2		36,615
Nov 4	MANCHESTER CITY	D 1-1	Deehan	32,724
Nov 11	Wolverhampton Wanderers	W 4-0	Shelton, McNaught, Deehan, Mortimer	23,289
Nov 18	BRISTOL CITY	W 2-0	Deehan, Cowans	27,621
Nov 21	Southampton	L 0-2		20,880
Nov 25	West Bromwich Albion	D 1-1	Evans A	35,085
Dec 9	Chelsea	W 1-0	Evans A	19,080
Dec 16	NORWICH CITY	D 1-1	McGuire o.g.	26,238
Dec 23	Derby County	D 0-0		20,109
Dec 26	LEEDS UNITED	D 2-2	Gregory 2	40,973
Jan 31	Everton	D 1-1	Shelton	29,079
Feb 24	Manchester United	D 1-1	Swain	44,437
Mar 3	BIRMINGHAM CITY	W 1-0	Cowans	42,419
Mar 7	BOLTON WANDERERS	W 3-0	Gray, Swain, Jones o.g.	28,053
Mar 10	Middlesbrough	L 0-2		16,562
Mar 20	QUEENS PARK RANGERS	W 3-1	Evans A, Gidman (pen), Mortimer	24,310
Mar 24	TOTTENHAM HOTSPUR	L 2-3	Gidman (pen), Gray	35,486
Mar 28	COVENTRY CITY	D 1-1	Evans A	25,670
Apr 4	Nottingham Forest	L 0-4		27,056
Apr 7	Coventry City	D 1-1	Deehan	23,690
Apr 11	DERBY COUNTY	D 3-3	Cowans 2, Gidman (pen)	21,884
Apr 14	Leeds United	L 0-1		24,281
Apr 16	LIVERPOOL	W 3-1	Evans A, Thompson o.g., Deehan	44,029
Apr 21	Norwich City	W 2-1	Shelton, Cropley	15,061
Apr 25	ARSENAL	W 5-1	Shelton 3 (1 pen), Deehan 2	26,168
Apr 28	CHELSEA	W 2-1	Wilkins GC o.g., Swain	29,219
May 2	IPSWICH TOWN	D 2-2	Swain, Deehan	26,636
May 5	Bolton Wanderers	D 0-0		17,394
May 8	Liverpool	L 0-3		50,570
May 11	WEST BROMWICH ALBION	L 0-1		35,991
May 15	Manchester City	W 3-2	Cropley, Mortimer, Deehan	30,028

FA Cup

Jan 6	Nottingham Forest	(Rd 3)	L 0-2		29,550

League Cup

Aug 30	SHEFFIELD WEDNESDAY	(Rd 2)	W 1-0	Shelton	31,152
Oct 4	CRYSTAL PALACE	(Rd 3)	D 1-1	Little	30,690
Oct 10	Crystal Palace		(R) D 0-0*		33,155
Oct 16	Crystal Palace†	(2nd R)	W 3-0	Gray 2, Gregory	25,455
Nov 8	LUTON TOWN		L 0-2		32,727

*After extra-time. †Played at Highfield Road, Coventry.

Fact File

Villa spoilt the 'White Hart Lane' party and home debuts of Argentina World Cup stars Ossie Ardiles and Ricky Villa by beating Spurs 4-1 on 23 August 1978.

MANAGER: Ron Saunders

CAPTAIN: Dennis Mortimer

TOP SCORER: John Deehan, 9 (all league)

BIGGEST WIN: 5-1 v Arsenal (H), Division One, 25 April 1979

HIGHEST ATTENDANCE: 50,570 v Liverpool (A), Division One, 8 May 1979

MAJOR TRANSFERS IN: Kenny Swain from Chelsea

MAJOR TRANSFERS OUT: Tommy Craig to Swansea City, Gordon Smith to Tottenham Hotspur

League & Cup Appearances

PLAYER	LEAGUE	CUP COMPETITION		TOTAL
		FA CUP	LC	
Carrodus	6		4	10
Cowans	34	1	1 (1)	36 (1)
Craig	23	1	4	28
Cropley	15 (2)			15 (2)
Deehan	25 (1)	1	3	29 (1)
Evans A	36 (1)	1	4	41 (1)
Evans D	2			2
Gibson	11 (1)			11 (1)
Gidman	36	1	3	40
Gray	15		4	19
Gregory	38 (1)	1	4	43 (1)
Jenkins	0 (2)			0 (2)
Linton	4 (4)			4 (4)
Little	24		4	28
McNaught	32	1	5	38
Mortimer	38	1	5	44
Ormsby	2		0 (1)	2 (1)
Phillips	3 (2)		2 (1)	5 (3)
Rimmer	42	1	5	48
Shelton	19		2	21
Shaw	2 (1)			2 (1)
Smith	6 (1)		1	7 (1)
Swain	24	1		25
Williams	21 (2)	1	4	26 (2)
Ward	1			1
Young	3			3

Goalscorers

PLAYER	LEAGUE	CUP COMPETITION		TOTAL
		FA CUP	LC	
Deehan	9			9
Gray	6		2	8
Gregory	7		1	8
Shelton	7		1	8
Evans A	6			6
Cowans	4			4
Swain	4			4
Gidman	3			3
Mortimer	3			3
Craig	2			2
Cropley	2			2
Little	1		1	2
McNaught	1			1
Opps' o.gs.	4			4

Final Division One Table

		P	W	D	L	F	A	Pts
1	LIVERPOOL	42	30	8	4	85	16	68
2	NOTTINGHAM F	42	21	18	3	61	26	60
3	WBA	42	24	11	7	72	35	59
4	EVERTON	42	17	17	8	52	40	51
5	LEEDS U	42	18	14	10	70	52	50
6	IPSWICH T	42	20	9	13	63	49	49
7	ARSENAL	42	17	14	11	61	48	48
8	ASTON VILLA	42	15	16	11	59	49	46
9	MANCHESTER U	42	15	15	12	60	63	45
10	COVENTRY C	42	14	16	12	58	68	44
11	TOTTENHAM H	42	13	15	14	48	61	41
12	MIDDLESBROUGH	42	15	10	17	57	50	40
13	BRISTOL C	42	15	10	17	47	51	40
14	SOUTHAMPTON	42	12	16	14	47	53	40
15	MANCHESTER C	42	13	13	16	58	56	39
16	NORWICH C	42	7	23	12	51	57	37
17	BOLTON W	42	12	11	19	54	75	35
18	WOLVERHAMPTON W	42	13	8	21	44	68	34
19	DERBY CO	42	10	11	21	44	71	31
20	QPR	42	6	13	23	45	73	25
21	BIRMINGHAM C	42	6	10	26	37	64	22
22	CHELSEA	42	5	10	27	44	92	20

Season 1979-80

Football League Division One

DATE	OPPONENTS	SCORE	GOALSCORERS	ATTENDANCE
Aug 18	Bolton Wanderers	D 1-1	Cowans	19,795
Aug 22	BRIGHTON & HOVE ALBION	W 2-1	Evans A (pen), Morley	28,803
Aug 25	BRISTOL CITY	L 0-2		25,526
Sep 1	Everton	D 1-1	Morley	29,271
Sep 8	MANCHESTER UNITED	L 0-3		34,859
Sep 15	Crystal Palace	L 0-2		28,156
Sep 22	ARSENAL	D 0-0		27,277
Sep 29	Middlesbrough	D 0-0		16,017
Oct 6	SOUTHAMPTON	W 3-0	Bremner, Mortimer, Evans A (pen)	24,377
Oct 13	WEST BROMWICH ALBION	D 0-0		36,007
Oct 20	Derby County	W 3-1	Little, Shaw, Mortimer	20,152
Oct 27	Wolverhampton Wanderers	D 1-1	Shaw	36,267
Nov 3	BOLTON WANDERERS	W 3-1	Shaw, Evans A, Mortimer	24,744
Nov 10	Ipswich Town	D 0-0		17,807
Nov 17	STOKE CITY	W 2-1	Mortimer, Evans A (pen)	27,086
Nov 24	LEEDS UNITED	D 0-0		29,736
Dec 1	Norwich City	D 1-1	Evans A	15,885
Dec 8	LIVERPOOL	L 1-3	Little	41,160
Dec 15	Tottenham Hotspur	W 2-1	Greddis, Cowans (pen)	30,555
Dec 19	COVENTRY CITY	W 3-0	Donovan, Little 2	24,446
Dec 26	Nottingham Forest	L 1-2	Shaw	30,979
Dec 29	Bristol City	W 3-1	Shaw 3	18,221
Jan 12	EVERTON	W 2-1	Gibson, Donovan	31,108
Feb 2	CRYSTAL PALACE	W 2-0	Cowans, Mortimer	29,469
Feb 9	Arsenal	L 1-3	Mortimer	33,816
Feb 23	West Bromwich Albion	W 2-1	McNaught, Little	33,658
Feb 27	MANCHESTER CITY	D 2-2	Shaw, Donachie o.g.	29,139
Mar 1	DERBY COUNTY	W 1-0	Evans A	28,956
Mar 3	Brighton & Hove Albion	D 1-1	Evans A	23,077
Mar 10	WOLVERHAMPTON WANDERERS	L 1-3	Shaw	30,432
Mar 15	Southampton	L 0-2		20,735
Mar 19	MIDDLESBROUGH	L 0-2		15,319
Mar 22	IPSWICH TOWN	D 1-1	Morley	22,386
Mar 26	NORWICH CITY	W 2-0	Cowans (pen), Hopkins	17,956
Mar 29	Stoke City	L 0-2		16,234
Apr 5	NOTTINGHAM FOREST	W 3-2	Bremner, Evans A, Lloyd o.g.	29,156
Apr 7	Manchester City	D 1-1	Geddis	42,584
Apr 19	Leeds United	D 0-0		15,840
Apr 23	Manchester United	L 1-2	Bremner	45,201
Apr 26	TOTTENHAM HOTSPUR	W 1-0	Cowans	29,549
Apr 29	Coventry City	W 2-1	Gibson, Cowans (pen)	17,969
May 3	Liverpool	L 1-4	Cohen o.g.	51,451

FA Cup

Jan 4	Bristol Rovers	(Rd 3) W 2-1	Cowans, Shaw	16,060
Jan 26	Cambridge United	(Rd 4) D 1-1	Donovan	12,000
Jan 30	CAMBRIDGE UNITED	(R) W 4-1	Evans A, Little, Donovan 2	36,835
Feb 16	Blackburn Rovers	(Rd 5) D 1-1	Geddis	29,468
Feb 20	BLACKBURN ROVERS	(R) W 1-0	Evans A	42,161
Mar 8	West Ham United	(Rd 6) L 0-1		36,393

League Cup

Aug 28	Colchester United	(Rd 2 FL) W 2-0	Shaw 2	6,221
Sep 5	COLCHESTER UNITED	(Rd 2 SL) L 0-2*		19,473
Sep 25	EVERTON	(Rd 3) D 0-0		22,635
Oct 9	Everton	(R) L 1-4	Swain	22,088

*After extra-time, Villa won on penalties.

Fact File

Liverpool clinched their 11th league championship by beating Villa 4-1 at Anfield on the last day of the season.

MANAGER: Ron Saunders

CAPTAIN: Dennis Mortimer

TOP SCORER: Gary Shaw, 13 (9 league)

BIGGEST WIN: 4-1 v Cambridge United, FA Cup Fourth Round Replay, 30 January 1980

HIGHEST ATTENDANCE: 51,451 v Liverpool (A), Division One, 3 May 1980

MAJOR TRANSFERS IN: Des Bremner from Hibernian, David Geddis from Ipswich Town, Tony Morley from Burnley

MAJOR TRANSFERS OUT: Andy Gray to Wolverhampton Wanderers, Jon Deehan to West Bromwich Albion, John Gidman to Everton

League & Cup Appearances

PLAYER	LEAGUE	CUP COMPETITION		TOTAL
		FA CUP	LC	
Blake	3			3
Bremner	36	6	2	44
Bullivant	6	1		7
Cowans	42	6	4	52
Cropley	1			1
Deacy	2 (1)			2 (1)
Deehan	6		2	8
Donovan	9	6		15
Evans	35	5	4	44
Geddis	19 (1)	2	2	23 (1)
Gibson	30 (1)	6	3	39 (1)
Gidman	4		3	7
Heard	9			9
Hopkins	0 (2)			0 (2)
Jenkins	0 (1)			0 (1)
Linton	12 (3)	1		13 (3)
Little	29	6	2	37
McNaught	30	6	4	40
Morley	15 (3)		2	17 (3)
Mortimer	26	6	4	36
Ormsby	21 (2)	1 (1)		22 (3)
Pejic	10		2	12
Rimmer	41	6	4	51
Shaw	28	3	2	33
Shelton	4		0 (1)	4 (1)
Spink	1			1
Swain	41	5	4	50
Ward	1 (1)			1 (1)
Williams	1 (1)			1 (1)

Goalscorers

PLAYER	LEAGUE	CUP COMPETITION		TOTAL
		FA CUP	LC	
Shaw	9	1	2	12
Evans A	8	2		10
Cowans	6	1		7
Little	5	1		6
Mortimer	6			6
Donovan	2	3		5
Bremner	3			3
Geddis	2	1		3
Morley	3			3
Gibson	2			2
Hopkins	1			1
McNaught	1			1
Swain			1	1
Opps' o.gs.	3			3

Final Division One Table

		P	W	D	L	F	A	Pts
1	LIVERPOOL	42	25	10	7	81	30	60
2	MANCHESTER U	42	24	10	8	65	35	58
3	IPSWICH T	42	22	9	11	68	39	53
4	ARSENAL	42	18	16	8	52	36	52
5	NOTTINGHAM F	42	20	8	14	63	43	48
6	WOLVERHAMPTON W	42	19	9	14	58	47	47
7	ASTON VILLA	42	16	14	12	51	50	46
8	SOUTHAMPTON	42	18	9	15	65	53	45
9	MIDDLESBROUGH	42	16	12	14	50	44	44
10	WBA	42	11	19	12	54	50	41
11	LEEDS U	42	13	14	15	46	50	40
12	NORWICH C	42	13	14	15	58	66	40
13	CRYSTAL PALACE	42	12	16	14	41	50	40
14	TOTTENHAM H	42	15	10	17	52	62	40
15	COVENTRY C	42	16	7	19	56	66	39
16	BRIGHTON & HA	42	11	15	16	47	57	37
17	MANCHESTER C	42	12	13	17	43	66	37
18	STOKE C	42	13	10	19	44	58	36
19	EVERTON	42	9	17	16	43	51	35
20	BRISTOL C	42	9	13	20	37	66	31
21	DERBY CO	42	11	8	23	47	67	30
22	BOLTON W	42	5	15	22	38	73	25

The Essential History of Aston Villa

Season 1980-81

Football League Division One

DATE	OPPONENTS	SCORE	GOALSCORERS	ATTENDANCE
Aug 16	Leeds United	W 2-1	Morley, Shaw	23,401
Aug 20	NORWICH CITY	W 1-0	Shaw	25,970
Aug 23	Manchester City	D 2-2	Withe 2	30,017
Aug 30	COVENTRY CITY	W 1-0	Shaw	20,050
Sep 6	Ipswich Town	L 0-1		23,192
Sep 13	EVERTON	L 0-2		25,673
Sep 20	WOLVERHAMPTON WANDERERS	W 2-1	Hughes o.g., Geddis	26,881
Sep 27	Crystal Palace	W 1-0	Shaw	18,398
Oct 4	SUNDERLAND	W 4-0	Evans 2, Morley, Shaw	26,914
Oct 8	Manchester United	D 3-3	Withe, Cowans (pen), Shaw	38,831
Oct 11	Birmingham City	W 2-1	Cowans (pen), Evans	33,879
Oct 18	TOTTENHAM HOTSPUR	W 3-0	Morley 2, Withe	30,940
Oct 22	BRIGHTON & HOVE ALBION	W 4-1	Mortimer, Withe, Bremner, Shaw	27,367
Oct 25	Southampton	W 2-1	Morley, Withe	21,249
Nov 1	LEICESTER CITY	W 2-0	Shaw, Cowans	29,953
Nov 8	West Bromwich Albion	D 0-0		34,001
Nov 12	Norwich City	W 3-1	Shaw 2, Evans	17,050
Nov 15	LEEDS UNITED	D 1-1	Shaw	29,106
Nov 22	Liverpool	L 1-2	Evans	48,114
Nov 29	ARSENAL	D 1-1	Morley	30,140
Dec 6	Middlesbrough	L 1-2	Shaw	15,597
Dec 13	BIRMINGHAM CITY	W 3-0	Geddis 2, Shaw	41,101
Dec 20	Brighton & Hove Albion	L 0-1		16,425
Dec 26	STOKE CITY	W 1-0	Withe	34,658
Dec 27	Nottingham Forest	D 2-2	Lloyd o.g., Shaw	33,930
Jan 10	LIVERPOOL	W 2-0	Withe, Mortimer	47,960
Jan 17	Coventry City	W 2-1	Morley, Withe	27,020
Jan 31	MANCHESTER CITY	W 1-0	Shaw	33,682
Feb 7	Everton	W 3-1	Morley, Mortimer, Cowans (pen)	31,434
Feb 21	CRYSTAL PALACE	W 2-1	Withe 2	27,203
Feb 28	Wolverhampton Wanderers	W 1-0	Withe	34,693
Mar 7	Sunderland	W 2-1	Evans, Mortimer	27,278
Mar 14	MANCHESTER UNITED	D 3-3	Withe 2, Shaw	42,182
Mar 21	Tottenham Hotspur -	L 0-2		35,091
Mar 28	SOUTHAMPTON	W 2-1	Morley, Geddis	32,467
Apr 4	Leicester City	W 4-2	Withe 2, Bremner, Morley	26,032
Apr 8	WEST BROMWICH ALBION	W 1-0	Withe	47,998
Apr 14	IPSWICH TOWN	L 1-2	Shaw	47,495
Apr 18	Nottingham Forest	W 2-0	Cowans (pen), Withe	34,707
Apr 20	Stoke City	D 1-1	Withe	23,500
Apr 25	MIDDLESBROUGH	W 3-0	Shaw, Withe, Evans	38,018
May 2	Arsenal	L 0-2		57,472

FA Cup

Jan 3	IPSWICH TOWN	(Rd 3) L 0-1		27,721

League Cup

Aug 27	LEEDS UNITED	(Rd 2) D 1-1	Morley	23,622
Sep 3	Leeds United	(R) W 3-1	Shaw 2, Withe	12,236
Sep 23	Cambridge United	(Rd 3) L 1-2	Morley	7,608

League & Cup Appearances

PLAYER	LEAGUE	CUP COMPETITION		TOTAL
		FA CUP	LC	
Bremner	42	1	3	46
Cowans	42	1	3	46
Deacy	5 (3)		0 (1)	5 (4)
Evans	39	1	3	43
Geddis	8 (1)		1	9 (1)
Gibson	19 (2)		3	22 (2)
McNaught	42	1	3	46
Morley	42	1	3	46
Mortimer	42	1	3	46
Rimmer	42	1	3	46
Shaw	40	1	2	43
Swain	42	1	3	46
Williams	21 (1)	1		22 (1)
Withe	36	1	3	40

Goalscorers

PLAYER	LEAGUE	CUP COMPETITION		TOTAL
		FA CUP	LC	
Withe	20		1	21
Shaw	18		2	20
Morley	10		2	12
Evans	7			7
Cowans	5			5
Geddis	4			4
Mortimer	4			4
Bremner	2			2
Opps' o.gs.	2			2

Final Division One Table

		P	W	D	L	F	A	Pts
1	ASTON VILLA	42	26	8	8	72	40	60
2	IPSWICH T	42	23	10	9	77	43	56
3	ARSENAL	42	19	15	8	61	45	53
4	WBA	42	20	12	10	60	42	52
5	LIVERPOOL	42	17	17	8	62	46	51
6	SOUTHAMPTON	42	20	10	12	76	56	50
7	NOTTINGHAM F	42	19	12	11	62	44	50
8	MANCHESTER U	42	15	18	9	51	36	48
9	LEEDS U	42	17	10	15	39	47	44
10	TOTTENHAM H	42	14	15	13	70	68	43
11	STOKE C	42	12	18	12	51	60	42
12	MANCHESTER C	42	14	11	17	56	59	39
13	BIRMINGHAM C	42	13	12	17	50	61	38
14	MIDDLESBROUGH	42	16	5	21	53	61	37
15	EVERTON	42	13	10	19	55	58	36
16	COVENTRY C	42	13	10	19	48	68	36
17	SUNDERLAND	42	14	7	21	52	53	35
18	WOLVERHAMPTON W	42	13	9	20	43	55	35
19	BRIGHTON & HA	42	14	7	21	54	67	35
20	NORWICH C	42	13	7	22	49	73	33
21	LEICESTER C	42	13	6	23	40	67	32
22	CRYSTAL PALACE	42	6	7	29	47	83	19

Fact File

This was Villa's first championship-winning season for 71 years – since their triumph in 1909-10. And in winning the title, manager Ron Saunders utilized only 14 players, seven of them being ever-present.

MANAGER: Ron Saunders
CAPTAIN: Dennis Mortimer
TOP SCORER: Peter Withe, 21 (20 league)
BIGGEST WIN: 4-0 Sunderland (H), Division One, 4 October 1980
HIGHEST ATTENDANCE: 57,472 v Arsenal (A), Division One, 2 May 1980

Season 1981-82

Football League Division One

DATE	OPPONENTS	SCORE	GOALSCORERS	ATTENDANCE
Aug 29	NOTTS COUNTY	L 0-1		30,097
Sep 2	Sunderland	L 1-2	Donovan	29,372
Sep 5	Tottenham Hotspur	W 3-1	Donovan 2, Mortimer	31,265
Sep 12	MANCHESTER UNITED	D 1-1	Cowans	37,661
Sep 19	Liverpool	D 0-0		37,474
Sep 23	STOKE CITY	D 2-2	Withe 2	25,637
Sep 26	BIRMINGHAM CITY	D 0-0		40,763
Oct 3	Leeds United	D 1-1	Shaw	21,065
Oct 10	Coventry City	D 1-1	Shaw	16,306
Oct 17	WEST HAM UNITED	W 3-2	Morley, Geddis, Mortimer	32,064
Oct 24	Wolverhampton wanderers	W 3-0	Shaw 2, Palmer o.g.	19,942
Oct 31	IPSWICH TOWN	L 0-1		32,652
Nov 7	ARSENAL	L 0-2		27,316
Nov 21	Middlesbrough	D 3-3	Withe, Cowans, Shaw	12,522
Nov 28	NOTTINGHAM FOREST	W 3-1	Bremner 2, Withe	26,847
Dec 5	Manchester United	L 0-1		32,487
Dec 15	Swansea City	L 1-2	Thompson o.g.	15,191
Dec 19	Everton	L 0-2		16,538
Dec 28	Brighton & Hove Albion	W 1-0	Morley	24,287
Jan 16	Notts County	L 0-1		9,597
Jan 30	LIVERPOOL	L 0-3		35,947
Feb 2	SUNDERLAND	W 1-0	Geddis	19,916
Feb 6	Manchester United	L 1-4	Geddis	43,184
Feb 10	SOUTHAMPTON	D 1-1	Withe	24,287
Feb 17	TOTTENHAM HOTSPUR	D 1-1	Withe	23,877
Feb 20	Birmingham City	W 1-0	Withe	32,779
Feb 27	COVENTRY CITY	W 2-1	Cowans (pen), Shaw	24,474
Mar 6	West Ham United	D 2-2	Cowans, Withe	26,894
Mar 13	WOLVERHAMPTON WANDERERS	W 3-1	Donovan, Morley, Shaw	26,790
Mar 20	Ipswich Town	L 1-3	McNaught	20,407
Mar 27	Arsenal	L 3-4	Shaw, Morley, Heard	24,756
Mar 30	WEST BROMWICH ALBION	W 2-1	Shaw, Withe	28,440
Apr 10	Southampton	W 3-0	Nicholl o.g., McNaught, Morley	22,801
Apr 12	BRIGHTON & HOVE ALBION	W 3-0	Geddis 2, Evans	22,731
Apr 17	MIDDLESBROUGH	W 1-0	Evans	21,098
Apr 24	Nottingham Forest	D 1-1	Cowans (pen)	18,213
Apr 28	LEEDS UNITED	L 1-4	Geddis	20,566
May 1	MANCHESTER CITY	D 0-0		22,150
May 5	Stoke City	L 0-1		10,363
May 8	West Bromwich Albion	W 1-0	Heard	19,615
May 15	EVERTON	L 1-2	Cowans	20,446
May 21	SWANSEA CITY	W 3-0	Morley, Bremner, Withe	18,294

FA Cup

Jan 5	Notts County	(Rd 3) W 6-0	Richards o.g., Shaw, Geddis 3, Cowans (pen)	12,312
Jan 23	Bristol City	(Rd 4) W 1-0	Shaw	20,279
Feb 13	Tottenham Hotspur	(Rd 5) L 0-1		42,950

League Cup

Oct 7	WOLVERHAMPTON WANDERERS	(Rd 2) W 3-2	Bremner, Morley, Blair	26,358
Oct 27	Wolverhampton Wanderers	W 2-1	Cowans 2 (1 pen)	19,491
Nov 11	Leicester City	(Rd 3) D 0-0		19,806
Nov 25	LEICESTER CITY	(R)	Withe, Cowans (pen)	23,136
Dec 1	Wigan Athletic	(Rd 4) W 2-1	Cowans (pen), Withe	15,362
Jan 20	WEST BROMWICH ALBION	(Rd 5) L 0-1		35,197

European Cup

Sep 16	VALUR	(Rd 1/FL) W 5-0	Morley, Donovan 2, Withe 2	20,481
Sep 30	Valur	(Rd 1/SL) W 2-0	Shaw 2	3,500
Oct 21	Dynamo Berlin	(Rd 2/FL) W 2-1	Morley 2	25,000
Nov 4	DYNAMO BERLIN	(Rd 2/SL) L 0-1		28,175
Mar 3	Dynamo Kiev	(Rd 3/FL) D 0-0		20,000
Mar 17	DYNAMO KIEV	(Rd 3/SL) W 2-0	Shaw, McNaught	38,579
Apr 7	ANDERLECHT	(SF/FL) W 1-0	Morley	38,539
Apr 21	Anderlecht	(SF/SL) D 0-0		38,040
May 26	Bayern Munich*	(F) W 1-0	Withe	39,776

*Played in Rotterdam.

MANAGER: Ron Saunders, Tony Barton

CAPTAIN: Dennis Mortimer

TOP SCORER: Peter Withe, 15 (10 league)

BIGGEST WIN: 6-0 v Notts County (A), FA Cup Third Round, 5 January 1982

HIGHEST ATTENDANCE: 43,184 v Manchester United (A), Division One, 6 February 1982

MAJOR TRANSFERS IN: Andy Blair from Coventry City

MAJOR TRANSFERS OUT: Gary Shelton to Sheffield Wednesday

League & Cup Appearances

PLAYER	LEAGUE	CUP COMPETITION		OTHER	TOTAL
		FA CUP	LC		
Blair	9 (9)	1	0 (2)	2 (1)	12 (12)
Blake	1				1
Bremner	38	2	6	9	55
Bullivant	4 (2)		0 (1)		4 (3)
Cowans	42	3	6	9	60
Deacy	4		2		6
Donovan	8			1	9
Evans	38	3	6	8	55
Geddis	14	2			16
Gibson	23	2	6	4	35
Heard	6 (3)				6 (3)
Jones	2				2
Linton	0 (1)			0 (1)	0 (2)
McNaught	22	1		5	28
Morley	36 (1)	3	6	8	53 (1)
Mortimer	32	3	4	9	48
Ormsby	12		2	3	17
Rimmer	42	3	6	9	60
Shaw	26	2	6	8	42
Shelton	1				1
Spink			0 (1)		0 (1)
Swain	39	3	5	8	55
Walters	0 (1)				0 (1)
Williams	28	3	5	7	43
Withe	35	2	6	9	52

Goalscorers

PLAYER	LEAGUE	CUP COMPETITION		OTHER	TOTAL
		FA CUP	LC		
Withe	10		2	3	15
Shaw	9	2		3	14
Cowans	6	1	4		11
Morley	6		1	4	11
Geddis	6	3			9
Donovan	4			2	6
Bremner	3		1		4
McNaught	2			1	3
Evans	2				2
Heard	2				2
Mortimer	2				2
Blair	1				1
Opps' o.gs.	3	1			4

Fact File

Villa became the first British team to win the European Cup at the first time of entering.

Final Division One Table

		P	W	D	L	F	A	Pts
1	LIVERPOOL	42	26	9	7	80	32	87
2	IPSWICH T	42	26	5	11	75	53	83
3	MANCHESTER U	42	22	12	8	59	29	78
4	TOTTENHAM H	42	20	11	11	67	48	71
5	ARSENAL	42	20	11	11	48	37	71
6	SWANSEA C	42	21	6	15	58	51	69
7	SOUTHAMPTON	42	19	9	14	72	67	66
8	EVERTON	42	17	13	12	56	50	64
9	WEST HAM U	42	14	16	12	66	57	58
10	MANCHESTER C	42	15	13	14	49	50	58
11	ASTON VILLA	42	15	12	15	55	53	57
12	NOTTINGHAM F	42	15	12	15	42	48	57
13	BRIGHTON & HA	42	13	13	16	43	52	52
14	COVENTRY C	42	13	11	18	56	62	50
15	NOTTS CO	42	13	8	21	61	69	47
16	BIRMINGHAM C	42	10	14	18	53	61	44
17	WBA	42	11	11	20	46	57	44
18	STOKE C	42	12	8	22	44	63	44
19	SUNDERLAND	42	11	11	20	38	58	44
20	LEEDS U	42	10	12	20	39	61	42
21	WOLVERHAMPTON W	42	10	10	22	32	63	40
22	MIDDLESBROUGH	42	8	15	19	34	52	39

The Essential History of Aston Villa

Season 1982-83

Football League Division One

DATE	OPPONENTS	SCORE		GOALSCORERS	ATTENDANCE
Aug 28	SUNDERLAND	L	1-3	Cowans	22,945
Aug 31	Everton	L	0-5		24,026
Sep 4	Southampton	L	0-1		17,943
Sep 8	LUTON TOWN	W	4-1	Mortimer, Withe, Cowans 2 (2 pens)	18,823
Sep 11	NOTTINGHAM FOREST	W	4-1	Mortimer, Withe 2, Cowans (pen)	21,224
Sep 18	Manchester City	W	1-0	Shaw	28,650
Sep 25	SWANSEA CITY	W	2-0	Mortimer, Evans	21,246
Oct 2	West Bromwich Albion	L	0-1		25,300
Oct 9	Notts County	L	1-4	Shaw	8,990
Oct 16	WATFORD	W	3-0	Withe, Morley 2	21,572
Oct 23	Norwich City	L	0-1		15,761
Oct 30	TOTTENHAM HOTSPUR	W	4-0	Cowans 2 (1 pen), Morley, Shaw	25,992
Nov 6	Coventry City	D	0-0		12,076
Nov 13	BRIGHTON & HOVE ALBION	W	1-0	Withe	18,834
Nov 20	MANCHESTER UNITED	W	2-1	Shaw, Withe	35,487
Nov 27	Stoke City	W	3-0	Parkin o.g., Shaw 2	18,886
Dec 4	WEST HAM UNITED	W	1-0	Cowans (pen)	24,658
Dec 7	Arsenal	L	1-2	McNaught	17,384
Dec 18	LIVERPOOL	L	2-4	Shaw, Withe	34,568
Dec 27	Birmingham City	L	0-3		43,864
Dec 29	IPSWICH TOWN	D	1-1	Withe	21,912
Jan 1	Manchester United	L	1-3	Cowans (pen)	41,545
Jan 3	SOUTHAMPTON	W	2-0	Cowans (pen), Evans	19,925
Jan 15	Sunderland	L	0-2		16,052
Jan 22	MANCHESTER CITY	D	1-1	Shaw	20,415
Feb 5	Nottingham Forest	W	2-1	Withe 2	16,352
Feb 12	EVERTON	W	2-0	Morley, Withe	21,117
Feb 26	Watford	L	1-2	Walters	19,318
Mar 5	NORWICH CITY	W	3-2	Withe, Deacy, Shaw	18,624
Mar 8	NOTTS COUNTY	W	2-0	Withe, Shaw	17,452
Mar 19	COVENTRY CITY	W	4-0	Shaw, Withe 2, Evans	20,509
Mar 23	Tottenham Hotspur	L	0-2		22,455
Mar 26	Brighton & Hove Albion	D	0-0		14,657
Apr 2	Ipswich Town	W	2-1	Shaw, Withe	19,912
Apr 4	BIRMINGHAM CITY	W	1-0	Shaw	40,897
Apr 9	Luton Town	L	1-2	Shaw	10,924
Apr 19	WEST BROMWICH ALBION	W	1-0	Mortimer	26,921
Apr 23	West Ham United	L	0-2		21,822
Apr 30	STOKE CITY	W	4-0	Cowans, McNaught, Morley, Evans	20,944
May 2	Swansea City	L	1-2	Shaw	9,173
May 7	Liverpool	D	1-1	Shaw (pen)	39,939
May 14	ARSENAL	W	2-1	Shaw, Gibson	24,647

FA Cup

				GOALSCORERS	
Jan 8	Northampton Town	(Rd 3) W	1-0	Walters	14,529
Jan 29	WOLVERHAMPTON WANDERERS	(Rd 4) W	1-0	White	43,121
Feb 19	WATFORD	(Rd 5) W	4-1	Shaw, Morley, Gibson, Cowans	34,330
Mar 12	Arsenal	(Rd 6) L	0-2		41,774

League Cup

Oct 6	NOTTS COUNTY	(Rd 2/FL) L	1-2	Withe	16,312
Oct 26	Notts County	(Rd 2/SL) L	0-1		6,921

European Cup

Sep 15	BESIKTAS	(Rd 1/FL) W	3-1	Withe, Morley, Mortimer	167
Sep 29	Besiktas	(Rd 1/SL) D	0-0		45,000
Oct 20	Dinamo Bucharest	(Rd 2/FL) W	2-0	Shaw 2	70,000
Nov 3	DINAMO BUCHAREST	(Rd 2/SL) W	4-2	Shaw 3, Walters	22,244
Mar 2	JUVENTUS	(QF/FL) L	1-2	Cowans	45,531
Mar 16	Juventus	(QF/SL) L	1-3	Withe	66,000

European Super Cup

Jan 19	Barcelona	(FL) L	0-1		40,000
Jan 26	BARCELONA	(SL) W	3-0	Shaw, Cowans (pen), McNaught	31,570

World Club Championship

Dec 12	Peñarol	L	0-2		61,445

FA Charity Shield

Aug 22	Tottenham Hotspur	D	2-2	Withe 2	92,445

League & Cup Appearances

PLAYER	LEAGUE	CUP COMPETITION		OTHER	TOTAL
		FA CUP	LC		
Birch				0 (1)	0 (1)
Blair	6 (1)	2		3 (1)	11 (2)
Bremner	36 (1)	3	2	10	51 (1)
Cowans	42	4	2	10	58
Curbishley	6 (1)				6 (1)
Deacy	4	1	0 (1)	0 (1)	5 (2)
Evans	39 (1)	4		8	51 (1)
Geddis	2 (2)		1	1	4 (2)
Gibson	23	3	1	6 (1)	33 (1)
Heard	5 (2)		0 (1)	1	6 (3)
Hopkins	1				1
Jones	17	1	2	4	24
McNaught	41	3	2	10	56
Morley	29 (4)	4	2	9	44 (4)
Mortimer	39	3		9	53
Ormsby			1		1
Rimmer	20		2	6	28
Shaw	39	3	2	9	53
Spink	22	4		4	30
Swain	2			1	3
Walker	1				1
Walters	18 (4)	2 (1)		1 (2)	21 (7)
Williams	35 (1)	4	2	8	49 (1)
Withe	35	3	1	10	59

Goalscorers

PLAYER	LEAGUE	CUP COMPETITION		OTHER	TOTAL
		FA CUP	LC		
Shaw	17	1		6	24
Withe	16	1	1	4	22
Cowans	10	1		2	13
Morley	5	1		1	7
Mortimer	4			1	5
Evans	4				4
McNaught	2			1	3
Walters	1	1		1	3
Gibson	1	1			2
Deacy	1				1
Opps' o.gs.	1				1

MANAGER: Tony Barton

CAPTAIN: Dennis Mortimer

TOP SCORER: Gary Shaw, 24 (17 league)

BIGGEST WIN: 4-0 v Spurs (H), Division One, 30 October 1982; v Coventry City (H), Division One, 19 March 1983

HIGHEST ATTENDANCE: 92,445 v Tottenham Hotspur, FA Charity Shield at Wembley, 22 August 1982

Final Division One Table

		P	W	D	L	F	A	Pts
1	LIVERPOOL	42	24	10	8	87	37	82
2	WATFORD	42	22	5	15	74	57	71
3	MANCHESTER U	42	19	13	8	56	38	70
4	TOTTENHAM H	42	20	9	13	65	50	69
5	NOTTINGHAM F	42	20	9	13	62	50	69
6	ASTON VILLA	42	21	5	16	62	50	68
7	EVERTON	42	18	10	14	66	48	64
8	WEST HAM U	42	20	4	18	68	62	64
9	IPSWICH T	42	15	13	14	64	50	58
10	ARSENAL	42	16	10	16	58	56	58
11	WBA	42	15	12	15	51	49	57
12	SOUTHAMPTON	42	15	12	15	54	58	57
13	STOKE C	42	16	9	17	53	64	57
14	NORWICH C	42	14	12	16	52	58	54
15	NOTTS CO	42	15	7	20	55	71	52
16	SUNDERLAND	42	12	14	16	48	61	50
17	BIRMINGHAM C	42	12	15	16	40	55	50
18	LUTON T	42	12	13	17	65	84	49
19	COVENTRY C	42	13	9	20	48	59	48
20	MANCHESTER C	42	13	8	21	47	70	47
21	SWANSEA C	42	10	11	21	51	69	41
22	BRIGHTON & HA	42	9	13	20	38	68	40

Season 1983-84

Football League Division One

DATE	OPPONENTS	SCORE	GOALSCORERS	ATTENDANCE
Aug 27	WEST BROMWICH ALBION	W 4-3	Evans, Walters, Shaw, Ormsby	29,522
Aug 29	SUNDERLAND	W 1-0	Walters	20,390
Sep 3	Queens Park Rangers	L 1-2	Withe	16,922
Sep 7	Nottingham Forest	D 2-2	Withe, Shaw	16,363
Sep 10	NORWICH CITY	W 1-0	Mortimer	18,887
Sep 17	Liverpool	L 1-2	Gibson	34,246
Sep 24	SOUTHAMPTON	W 1-0	Withe	21,209
Oct 1	Luton Town	L 0-1		12,747
Oct 15	BIRMINGHAM CITY	W 1-0	Withe	39,318
Oct 23	Wolverhampton Wanderers	D 1-1	Withe	13,202
Oct 29	ARSENAL	L 2-6	Morley, Evans (pen)	23,678
Nov 5	Manchester United	W 2-1	Withe 2	45,077
Nov 12	STOKE CITY	D 1-1	Withe	19,272
Nov 19	LEICESTER CITY	W 3-1	Withe, Rideout, McMahon	19,024
Nov 26	Notts County	L 2-5	Mortimer, Evans (pen)	8,960
Dec 3	WEST HAM UNITED	W 1-0	Rideout	21,297
Dec 10	Everton	D 1-1	Rideout	15,810
Dec 17	IPSWICH TOWN	W 4-0	Rideout, McMahon, Evans (pen), Withe	16,548
Dec 26	Watford	L 2-3	Curbishley, Walters	18,226
Dec 27	TOTTENHAM HOTSPUR	D 0-0		30,125
Dec 31	QUEENS PARK RANGERS	W 2-1	Evans (pen), McMahon	19,978
Jan 2	Southampton	D 2-2	McMahon, Shaw	18,963
Jan 14	West Bromwich Albion	L 1-3	Shaw	20,399
Jan 20	LIVERPOOL	L 1-3	Mortimer	19,566
Feb 4	LUTON TOWN	D 0-0		18,656
Feb 11	Norwich City	L 1-3	Shaw	14,392
Feb 18	Arsenal	D 1-1	Evans (pen)	26,640
Feb 25	WOLVERHAMPTON WANDERERS	W 4-0	Withe 2, Birch, Walters	18,257
Mar 3	MANCHESTER UNITED	L 0-3		32,874
Mar 10	Stoke City	L 0-1		13,967
Mar 13	Coventry City	D 3-3	Evans (pen), Withe, Rideout	11,098
Mar 17	NOTTINGHAM FORREST	W 1-0	McMahon	16,270
Mar 24	Sunderland	W 1-0	Walters	11,908
Mar 31	Birmingham City	L 1-2	Withe	23,993
Apr 7	COVENTRY CITY	W 2-0	Ormsby, Birch	15,318
Apr 14	Leicester City	L 0-2		13,366
Apr 18	Tottenham Hotspur	L 1-2	Walters	18,668
Apr 21	WATFORD	W 2-1	Mortimer, Foster	16,110
Apr 28	NOTTS COUNTY	W 3-1	Walters 2, Withe	13,059
May 5	West Ham United	W 1-0	Mortimer	17,393
May 7	EVERTON	L 0-2		16,792
May 12	Ipswich Town	L 1-2	Withe	20,043

FA Cup

Jan 7	NORWICH CITY	(Rd 3)	D 1-1	Withe	21,454
Jan 11	Norwich City	(R)	L 0-3		16,420

League Cup

Oct 4	Portsmouth	(Rd 2)	D 2-2	Gibson, Evans	18,484
Oct 26	PORTSMOUTH	(R)	W 3-2	Evans (pen), Withe, Walters	20,898
Nov 9	MANCHESTER CITY	(Rd 3)	W 3-0	Gibson, Evans, Mortimer	23,922
Nov 30	West Bromwich Albion	(Rd 4)	W 2-1	Walters, Mortimer	31,114
Jan 17	Norwich City	(Rd 5)	W 2-0	Shaw, Rideout	21,568
Feb 15	Everton	(SF/FL)	L 0-2		40,006
Feb 22	EVERTON	(SF/SL)	W 1-0	Rideout	42,426

UEFA Cup

Sep 14	Vitoria Guimaraes	(Rd 1/FL)	L 0-1		30,000
Sep 28	VITORIA GUIMARAES	(Rd 1/SL)	W 5-0	Withe 3, Gibson, Ormsby	23,732
Oct 19	Spartak Moscow	(Rd 2/FL)	D 2-2	Gibson, Walters	49,980
Nov 2	SPARTAK MOSCOW	(Rd 2/SL)	L 1-2	Withe	29,511

MANAGER: Tony Barton

CAPTAIN: Allan Evans, Dennis Mortimer

TOP SCORER: Peter Withe, 22 (16 league)

BIGGEST WIN: 5-0 v Vitoria Guimaraes (H), UEFA Cup First Round Second Leg, 28 September 1983

HIGHEST ATTENDANCE: 49,980 v Spartak Moscow (H), UEFA Cup Second Round Second Leg, 19 October 1983

MAJOR TRANSFERS IN: Mervyn Day from Leyton Orient, Steve Foster from Brighton & Hove Albion, Steve McMahon from Everton, Paul Rideout from Swindon Town

MAJOR TRANSFERS OUT: Mark James to Brighton & Hove Albion, Tony Morley to West Bromwich Albion

League & Cup Appearances

PLAYER	LEAGUE	CUP COMPETITION		OTHER	TOTAL
		FA CUP	LC		
Birch	22	2	2		26
Blair	9			1	10
Bremner	14 (3)	2	0 (1)	2	18 (4)
Curbishley	25 (1)		5	2	32 (1)
Day	14				14
Deacy	12 (1)		0 (1)		12 (2)
Dorigo	0 (1)				0 (1)
Evans	36	2	7	4	49
Foster	7				7
Gibson	28		7	4	39
Glover		1			1
Jones	5		1	1	7
Kerr	1 (1)				1 (1)
McMahon	37	2	6	4	49
Morley	6 (1)		1	3 (1)	10 (2)
Mortimer	37	2	7	4	50
Ormsby	34	1	4	4	43
Rideout	22 (3)	0 (1)	3 (1)	1	26 (5)
Shaw	11 (1)	2	4		17 (1)
Spink	28	2	7	4	41
Walker	5 (3)	2	0 (1)		7 (4)
Walters	33 (4)	2	5	3 (1)	43 (5)
Williams	40			3	50
Withe	36	2	7	4	49

Goalscorers

PLAYER	LEAGUE	CUP COMPETITION		OTHER	TOTAL
		FA CUP	LC		
Withe	16	1		4	22
Walters	8		2	1	11
Evans	7		3		10
Mortimer	5		2		7
Rideout	5		2		7
Shaw	5		1		6
Gibson	1		2	2	5
McMahon	5				5
Ormsby	2			1	3
Birch	2				2
Curbishley	1				1
Foster	1				1
Morley	1				1

Fact File

In 1983, Villa Chairman Doug Ellis announced that the club faced debts of almost £2 million.

Final Division One Table

		P	W	D	L	F	A	Pts
1	LIVERPOOL	42	22	14	6	73	32	80
2	SOUTHAMPTON	42	22	11	9	66	38	77
3	NOTTINGHAM F	42	22	8	12	76	45	74
4	MANCHESTER U	42	20	14	8	71	41	74
5	QPR	42	22	7	13	67	37	73
6	ARSENAL	42	19	9	15	74	60	63
7	EVERTON	42	16	14	12	44	42	62
8	TOTTENHAM H	42	17	10	15	64	65	61
9	WEST HAM U	42	17	9	16	60	55	60
10	ASTON VILLA	42	17	9	16	59	61	60
11	WATFORD	42	16	9	17	68	77	57
12	IPSWICH T	42	15	8	19	55	57	53
13	SUNDERLAND	42	13	13	16	42	53	52
14	NORWICH C	42	12	15	15	48	49	51
15	LEICESTER C	42	13	12	17	65	68	51
16	LUTON T	42	14	9	19	53	66	51
17	WBA	42	14	9	19	48	62	51
18	STOKE C	42	13	11	18	44	63	50
19	COVENTRY C	42	13	11	18	57	77	50
20	BIRMINGHAM C	42	12	12	18	39	50	48
21	NOTTS CO	42	10	11	21	50	72	41
22	WOLVERHAMPTON W	42	6	11	25	27	80	29

Season 1984-85

Football League Division One

DATE	OPPONENTS	SCORE	GOALSCORERS	ATTENDANCE
Aug 25	COVENTRY CITY	W 1-0	Bremner	20,970
Aug 27	Stoke City	W 3-1	Walters 2, Withe	12,605
Sep 1	Newcastle United	L 0-3		31,497
Sep 5	NOTTINGHAM FOREST	L 0-5		17,730
Sep 8	CHELSEA	W 4-2	Foster, Rideout, Withe 2	21,494
Sep 15	Watford	D 3-3	Foster, McMahon, Withe	16,440
Sep 22	TOTTENHAM HOTSPUR	L 0-1		22,409
Sep 29	Ipswich Town	L 0-3		15,630
Oct 6	MANCHESTER UNITED	W 3-0	Evans, Rideout, Withe	37,132
Oct 13	Everton	L 1-2	Withe	25,089
Oct 20	NORWICH CITY	D 2-2	Withe 2	14,149
Oct 27	Leicester City	L 0-5		11,885
Nov 3	WEST HAM UNITED	D 0-0		15,709
Nov 10	Arsenal	D 1-1	Birch	33,195
Nov 17	SOUTHAMPTON	D 2-2	Six, Withe	13,937
Nov 24	Queens Park Rangers	L 0-2		11,689
Dec 1	SUNDERLAND	W 1-0	Rideout	14,669
Dec 8	Luton Town	L 0-1		7,696
Dec 15	LIVERPOOL	D 0-0		24,007
Dec 22	NEWCASTLE UNITED	W 4-0	Evans (pen), Rideout 3	14,491
Dec 26	Sheffield Wednesday	D 1-1	Rideout	30,971
Dec 29	Nottingham Forest	L 2-3	Gibson, Rideout	17,676
Jan 1	WEST BROMWICH ALBION	W 3-1	Birch, Gibson, Rideout	31,710
Jan 19	Coventry City	W 3-0	Rideout, Walters 2	15,226
Feb 2	IPSWICH TOWN	W 2-1	Cowans, Gibson	15,051
Feb 23	West Ham United	W 2-1	Ormsby, Walters	14,845
Mar 2	LEICESTER CITY	L 0-1		16,285
Mar 9	Norwich City	D 2-2	Evans 2 (1 pen)	21,853
Mar 13	ARSENAL	D 0-0		15,487
Mar 16	EVERTON	D 1-1	Evans (pen)	22,625
Mar 23	Manchester United	L 0-4		40,941
Mar 27	STOKE CITY	W 2-0	Berry o.g., Six	10,874
Mar 30	Tottenham Hotspur	W 2-0	Rideout, Walters	27,971
Apr 6	SHEFFIELD WEDNESDAY	W 3-0	Evans (pen), Ormsby, Rideout	18,308
Apr 8	West Bromwich Albion	L 0-1		21,044
Apr 16	Chelsea	L 1-3	Walters	13,267
Apr 20	Southampton	L 0-2		15,736
Apr 24	WATFORD	D 1-1	Walters	11,493
Apr 27	QUEENS PARK RANGERS	W 5-2	Rideout 2, Walters, Withe 2	12,023
May 4	Sunderland	W 4-0	Gibson, McMahon, Walters, Withe	12,467
May 6	LUTON TOWN	L 0-1		14,130
May 11	Liverpool	L 1-2	Birch	33,001

FA Cup

Jan 5	Liverpool	(Rd 3) L 0-3		36,877

League Cup

Sep 24	Scunthorpe United	(Rd 2/FL) W 3-2	Kerr 2, Gibson	6,212
Oct 10	SCUNTHORPE UNITED	(Rd 2/SL) W 3-1	Cowans, Rideout, Gibson	11,421
Oct 30	Queens Park Rangers	(Rd 3) L 0-1		12,547

League & Cup Appearances

PLAYER	LEAGUE	CUP COMPETITION		TOTAL
		FA CUP	LC	
Birch	24 (1)	1	3	28 (1)
Bradley	1 (1)			1 (1)
Bremner	4			4
Cowans	29 (1)	1	3	33 (1)
Curbishly	3			3
Daley	4 (1)			4 (1)
Day	16		3	19
Dorigo	27 (4)	1	1 (1)	29 (5)
Evans	38		2	40
Foster	8		2	10
Gibson	41	1	3	45
Glover	5			5
Kerr	6 (4)		2	8 (4)
McMahon	34 (1)	1	3	38 (1)
Mortimer	5 (1)			5 (1)
Norton	2			2
Ormsby	32	1	2	35
Poole	7			7
Rideout	28 (1)	1	1 (1)	30 (2)
Six	13 (3)		1 (1)	14 (4)
Spink	19	1		20
Walker	4 (3)			4 (3)
Walters	35 (1)	1	2	38 (1)
Williams	38	1	3	42
Withe	40	1	2	43

Goalscorers

PLAYER	LEAGUE	CUP COMPETITION		TOTAL
		FA CUP	LC	
Rideout	14		1	15
Withe	12			12
Walters	10			10
Evans	6			6
Gibson	4		2	6
Birch	3			3
Cowans	1		1	2
Foster	2			2
Kerr			2	2
McMahon	2			2
Ormsby	2			2
Six	2			2
Bremner	1			1
Opps' o.gs.	1			1

Fact File

The average league attendance at Villa Park this season was 18,318 – the lowest for 70 years – since the 13,842 figure in 1914-15.

MANAGER: Graham Turner

CAPTAIN: Allan Evans

TOP SCORER: Paul Rideout, 15 (14 league)

BIGGEST WIN: 5-2 v Queens Park Rangers (H), Division One, 27 April 1985

HIGHEST ATTENDANCE: 40,941 v Manchester United (A), Division One, 23 March 1984

MAJOR TRANSFERS IN: Didier Six from Mulhouse FC (France)

MAJOR TRANSFERS OUT: Des Bremner to Birmingham City, Gordon Cowans and Paul Rideout to Bari (Italy)

Final Division One Table

		P	W	D	L	F	A	Pts
1	EVERTON	42	28	6	8	88	43	90
2	LIVERPOOL	42	22	11	9	68	35	77
3	TOTTENHAM H	42	23	8	11	78	51	77
4	MANCHESTER U	42	22	10	10	77	47	76
5	SOUTHAMPTON	42	19	11	12	56	47	68
6	CHELSEA	42	18	12	12	63	48	66
7	ARSENAL	42	19	9	14	61	49	66
8	SHEFFIELD W	42	17	14	11	58	45	65
9	NOTTINGHAM F	42	19	7	16	56	48	64
10	ASTON VILLA	42	15	11	16	60	60	56
11	WATFORD	42	14	13	15	81	71	55
12	WBA	42	16	7	19	58	62	55
13	LUTON T	42	15	9	18	57	61	54
14	NEWCASTLE U	42	13	13	16	55	70	52
15	LEICESTER C	42	15	6	21	65	73	51
16	WEST HAM U	42	13	12	17	51	68	51
17	IPSWICH T	42	13	11	18	46	57	50
18	COVENTRY C	42	15	5	22	47	64	50
19	QPR	42	13	11	18	53	72	50
20	NORWICH C	42	13	10	19	46	64	49
21	SUNDERLAND	42	10	10	22	40	62	40
22	STOKE C	42	3	8	31	24	91	17

Season 1985-86

Football League Division One

DATE	OPPONENTS	SCORE	GOALSCORERS	ATTENDANCE
Aug 17	Manchester United	L 0-4		49,743
Aug 21	LIVERPOOL	D 2-2	Shaw, Walters	20,197
Aug 24	QUEENS PARK RANGERS	L 1-2	Walters	11,896
Aug 27	Southampton	D 0-0		14,220
Aug 31	LUTON TOWN	W 3-1	Walters, Hodge, Norton	10,524
Sep 4	West Bromwich Albion	W 3-0	Evans (pen), Daley, Walters	17,077
Sep 7	Birmingham City	D 0-0		24,971
Sep 14	COVENTRY CITY	D 1-1	Hodge	12,198
Sep 21	Ipswich Town	W 3-0	Walters, Hodge, Birch	11,598
Sep 28	EVERTON	D 0-0		22,048
Oct 5	Arsenal	L 2-3	Stainrod, Walters	18,881
Oct 12	NOTTINGHAM FOREST	L 1-2	Gibson	15,315
Oct 19	West Ham United	L 1-4	Stainrod	15,034
Oct 26	NEWCASTLE UNITED	L 1-2	Gray	12,633
Nov 2	OXFORD UNITED	W 2-0	Evans (pen), Stainrod	12,922
Nov 9	Watford	D 1-1	Gray	14,085
Nov 16	SHEFFIELD WEDNESDAY	D 1-1	Gibson	13,849
Nov 23	Chelsea	L 1-2	Gray	17,509
Nov 30	TOTTENHAM HOTSPUR	L 1-2	Walters	14,099
Dec 7	Liverpool	L 0-3		29,418
Dec 14	MANCHESTER UNITED	L 1-3	Hodge	27,626
Dec 17	Queens Park Rangers	W 1-0	Birch	11,237
Dec 27	Leicester City	L 1-3	Walters	13,752
Dec 28	WEST BROMWICH ALBION	D 1-1	Kerr	18,796
Jan 1	MANCHESTER CITY	L 0-1		14,215
Jan 11	Coventry City	D 3-3	Stainrod, Gray, Elliott	10,328
Jan 18	Luton Town	L 0-2		10,217
Feb 1	SOUTHAMPTON	D 0-0		8,456
Mar 1	Everton	L 0-2		32,133
Mar 8	ARSENAL	L 1-4	Walters	10,584
Mar 15	Nottingham Forest	D 1-1	Walters	12,933
Mar 19	WEST HAM UNITED	W 2-1	Hodge 2	11,567
Mar 22	BIRMINGHAM CITY	L 0-3		26,694
Mar 29	Manchester City	D 2-2	Hodge, Stainrod	20,935
Mar 31	LEICESTER CITY	W 1-0	Stainrod	12,200
Apr 5	Oxford United	D 1-1	Stainrod	11,406
Apr 9	Newcastle United	D 2-2	Daley, Hunt	20,107
Apr 12	WATFORD	W 4-1	Dorigo, Evans (pen), Gray, Stainrod	12,781
Apr 16	IPSWICH TOWN	W 1-0	Hodge	13,611
Apr 19	Sheffield Wednesday	L 0-2		19,782
Apr 26	CHELSEA	W 3-1	Norton, Hunt, Stainrod	17,770
May 3	Tottenham Hotspur	L 2-4	Stainrod, Elliott	14,854

FA Cup

Jan 4	Portsmouth	(Rd 3)	D 2-2	Birch, Kerr	17,732
Jan 13	PORTSMOUTH	(R)	W 3-2	Stainrod 2, Evans	14,958
Jan 25	MILLWALL	(Rd 4)	D 1-1	Hodge	12,205
Jan 29	Millwall	(R)	L 0-1		10,273

League Cup

Sep 25	Exeter City	(Rd 2/FL)	W 4-1	Stainrod 4	5,325
Oct 9	EXETER CITY	(Rd 2/SL)	W 8-1	Williams 2, Ormsby 2, Birch, Stainrod, Gray 2	7,678
Oct 30	Leeds United	(Rd 3)	W 3-0	Stainrod 2, Walters	15,444
Nov 20	WEST BROMWICH ALBION	(Rd 4)	D 2-2	Stainrod, Evans (pen)	20,204
Nov 27	West Bromwich Albion	(R)	W 2-1	Hodge, Walters	18,629
Jan 22	ARSENAL	(Rd 5)	D 1-1	Glover	26,093
Feb 4	Arsenal	(R)	W 2-1	Birch, Evans	33,091
Mar 4	OXFORD UNITED	(SF)	D 2-2	Birch, Stainrod	23,098
Mar 12	Oxford United	(R)	L 1-2	Walters	13,989

MANAGER: Graham Turner

CAPTAIN: Allan Evans

TOP SCORER: Simon Stainrod, 21 (10 league)

BIGGEST WIN: 8-1 v Exeter City (H), League Cup Second Round Second Leg, 9 October 1985

HIGHEST ATTENDANCE: 49,743 v Manchester United (A), Division One, 17 August 1985

MAJOR TRANSFERS IN: Simon Stainrod from Sheffield Wednesday, Paul Elliott from Luton Town, Steve Hodge from Nottingham Forest, Andy Gray from Everton

MAJOR TRANSFERS OUT: Dennis Mortimer to Brighton & Hove Albion, Darren Bradley to West Bromwich Albion

League & Cup Appearances

PLAYER	LEAGUE	CUP COMPETITION			TOTAL
		FA CUP	LC		
Birch	25 (2)	4	7 (1)		36 (3)
Blair	12				12
Bradley	15 (3)		3		18 (3)
Daley	16 (7)		2 (1)		18 (8)
Dorigo	38	4	8		50
Elliott	23	4	4		31
Evans	35	4	9		48
Gibson	7		3		12
Glover	15 (3)	2	7		24 (3)
Gray	35	4	7		46
Hodge	36	4	8		48
Hunt	12				12
Kerr	5 (1)	2	3		10 (1)
McMahon	3				3
Norton	20	2 (1)	3		25 (1)
Ormsby	14		2		16
Poole	11	1	1		13
Shaw	10 (2)		0 (1)		10 (3)
Spink	31	3	8		42
Stainrod	29 (1)	4	7 (1)		40 (2)
Walker	5 (2)		1		6 (2)
Walters	40	4	9		53
Williams	25	2	7		34

Goalscorers

PLAYER	LEAGUE	CUP COMPETITION		TOTAL
		FA CUP	LC	
Stainrod	10	2	9	21
Walters	10		3	13
Hodge	8	1	1	10
Gray	5		2	7
Evans	3	1	2	6
Birch	2	1	3	6
Daley	2			2
Elliott	2			2
Gibson	2			2
Hunt	2			2
Kerr	1	1		2
Norton	2			2
Ormsby			2	2
Williams			2	2
Glover			1	1
Dorigo	1			1
Shaw	1			1

Fact File

Simon Stainrod scored four goals on his Villa debut in the League Cup win at Exeter in September 1985.

Final Division One Table

		P	W	D	L	F	A	Pts
1	LIVERPOOL	42	26	10	6	89	37	88
2	EVERTON	42	26	8	8	87	41	86
3	WEST HAM U	42	26	6	10	74	40	84
4	MANCHESTER U	42	22	10	10	70	36	76
5	SHEFFIELD W	42	21	10	11	63	54	73
6	CHELSEA	42	20	11	11	57	56	71
7	ARSENAL	42	20	9	13	49	47	69
8	NOTTINGHAM F	42	19	11	12	69	53	68
9	LUTON T	42	18	12	12	61	44	66
10	TOTTENHAM H	42	19	8	15	74	52	65
11	NEWCASTLE U	42	17	12	13	67	72	63
12	WATFORD	42	16	11	15	69	62	59
13	QPR	42	15	7	20	53	64	52
14	SOUTHAMPTON	42	12	10	20	51	62	46
15	MANCHESTER C	42	11	12	19	43	57	45
16	ASTON VILLA	42	10	14	18	51	67	44
17	COVENTRY C	42	11	10	21	48	71	43
18	OXFORD U	42	10	12	20	62	80	42
19	LEICESTER C	42	10	12	20	54	76	42
20	IPSWICH T	42	11	8	23	32	55	41
21	BIRMINGHAM C	42	8	5	29	30	73	29
22	WBA	42	4	12	26	35	89	24

Season 1986-87

Football League Division One

DATE	OPPONENTS	SCORE	GOALSCORERS	ATTENDANCE
Aug 23	TOTTENHAM HOTSPUR	L 0-3		24,712
Aug 26	Wimbledon	L 2-3	Evans (pen), Thompson	6,366
Aug 30	Queens Park Rangers	L 0-1		13,003
Sep 3	LUTON TOWN	W 2-1	Kerr 2	13,122
Sep 6	OXFORD UNITED	L 1-2	Stainrod (pen)	14,668
Sep 13	Nottingham Forest	L 0-6		17,045
Sep 20	NORWICH CITY	L 1-4	Stainrod	12,304
Sep 27	Liverpool	D 3-3	Hodge, Thompson, Evans (pen)	38,298
Oct 4	Coventry City	W 1-0	Thompson	18,563
Oct 11	SOUTHAMPTON	W 3-1	Elliott 2, Evans (pen)	16,211
Oct 18	Watford	L 2-4	Walters, Stainrod	16,414
Oct 25	NEWCASTLE UNITED	W 2-0	Hodge 2	16,614
Nov 1	LEICESTER CITY	W 2-0	Stainrod 2	14,529
Nov 8	Manchester City	L 1-3	Daley	22,875
Nov 15	CHELSEA	D 0-0		17,739
Nov 22	West Ham United	D 1-1	Thompson	21,959
Nov 29	ARSENAL	L 0-4		21,658
Dec 6	Sheffield Wednesday	L 1-2	Evans (pen)	21,144
Dec 13	MANCHESTER UNITED	D 3-3	Hodge, Thompson, Evans (pen)	29,205
Dec 20	Oxford United	D 2-2	Thompson, Walters	8,364
Dec 26	CHARLTON ATHLETIC	W 2-0	Birch, Daley	16,692
Dec 27	Chelsea	L 1-4	Elliott	14,637
Jan 1	Everton	L 0-3		40,203
Jan 3	NOTTINGHAM FOREST	D 0-0		19,159
Jan 24	Tottenham Hotspur	L 0-3		19,121
Feb 7	QUEENS PARK RANGERS	L 0-1		13,109
Feb 14	Luton Town	L 1-2	Evans (pen)	9,174
Feb 21	LIVERPOOL	D 2-2	Lawrence o.g., Elliott	32,093
Feb 28	Norwich City	D 1-1	Elliott	15,070
Mar 4	WIMBLEDON	D 0-0		12,484
Mar 7	Newcastle United	L 1-2	Daley	21,224
Mar 21	Southampton	L 0-5		13,686
Mar 25	WATFORD	D 1-1	Hunt	12,575
Mar 28	COVENTRY CITY	W 1-0	Birch	18,689
Apr 4	MANCHESTER CITY	D 0-0		18,241
Apr 11	Leicester City	D 1-1	Walters	11,933
Apr 18	EVERTON	L 0-1		31,218
Apr 20	Charlton Athletic	L 0-3		5,595
Apr 25	WEST HAM UNITED	W 4-0	Hunt, Aspinall 2, Stainrod	13,584
May 2	Arsenal	L 1-2	Aspinall	18,463
May 4	SHEFFIELD WEDNESDAY	L 1-2	Robinson	15,007
May 9	Manchester United	L 1-3	Birch	35,179

FA Cup

Jan 10	CHELSEA	(Rd 3)	D 2-2	Cooper, Hunt	21,997
Jan 21	Chelsea	(R)	L 1-2	Hunt	13,473

League Cup

Sep 24	Reading	(Rd 2)	D 1-1	Hodge	9,363
Oct 8	READING	(R)	W 4-1	Gray 2, Hodge, Walters	12,484
Oct 29	Derby County	(Rd 3)	D 1-1	Daley	19,374
Nov 4	DERBY COUNTY	(R)	W 2-1	Thompson, Birch	19,477
Nov 18	Southampton	(Rd 4)	L 1-2	Evans	13,402

Full Members' Cup

Nov 12	DERBY COUNTY	(Rd 2)	W 4-1	Shaw 2, Daley, Evans	5,124
Dec 2	Ipswich Town	(Rd 3)	L 0-1		8,244

Fact File

Villa amassed their lowest points tally in Division One for 20 years.

MANAGER: Graham Turner, Billy McNeill

CAPTAIN: Allan Evans

TOP SCORER: Allan Evans, 8 (6 league)

BIGGEST WIN: 4-0 v West Ham United (H), Division One, 25 April 1987

HIGHEST ATTENDANCE: 40,203 v Everton (A), Division One, 1 January 1987

MAJOR TRANSFERS IN: Warren Aspinall from Everton, Neale Cooper from Aberdeen, Steve Hunt from West Bromwich Albion, Martin Keown from Arsenal, Garry Thompson from Sheffield Wednesday

MAJOR TRANSFERS OUT: Steve Hodge to Tottenham Hotspur

League & Cup Appearances

PLAYER	LEAGUE	CUP COMPETITION		OTHER	TOTAL
		FA CUP	LC		
Aspinall	12				12
Birch	26 (3)	1 (1)	4	1	32 (4)
Blair	4				4
Burke	1				1
Cooper	13	2			15
Daley	25 (8)	1 (1)	3	2	31 (9)
Dorigo	41	2	5	2	50
Elliott	33 (1)		3	1	37 (1)
Evans	25 (1)	2	5	2	34 (1)
Gallacher	1				1
Glover	5			1	6
Gray	18 (1)	0 (2)	1	1	20 (3)
Hodge	17		4	1	22
Hunt	39	2	5	1	47
Keown	35 (1)	2		4	41 (1)
Kerr	4 (2)		0 (2)	0 (2)	4 (6)
Norton	19 (1)		5	2	26 (1)
Poole	10		1	1	12
Ritchie	0 (1)				0 (1)
Robinson	2 (1)				2 (1)
Shaw	1			1	2
Spink	32	2	4	1	39
Stainrod	25 (4)	2	4	1	32 (4)
Thompson	30 (1)	2	4	1	37 (1)
Walters	18 (3)	2	2 (1)	2	24 (4)
Williams	26	2	1	1	30

Goalscorers

PLAYER	LEAGUE	CUP COMPETITION		OTHER	TOTAL
		FA CUP	LC		
Evans	6		1	1	8
Thompson	6		1		7
Hodge	4		2		6
Stainrod	6				6
Daley	3		1	1	5
Elliott	5				5
Birch	3		1		4
Hunt	2	2			4
Walters	3		1		4
Aspinall	3				3
Gray			2		2
Kerr	2				2
Shaw				2	2
Robinson	1				1
Cooper		1			1
Opps' o.gs.	1				1

Final Division One Table

		P	W	D	L	F	A	Pts
1	EVERTON	42	26	8	8	76	31	86
2	LIVERPOOL	42	23	8	11	72	42	77
3	TOTTENHAM H	42	21	8	13	68	43	71
4	ARSENAL	42	20	10	12	58	35	70
5	NORWICH CITY	42	17	17	8	53	51	68
6	WIMBLEDON	42	19	9	14	57	50	66
7	LUTON TOWN	42	18	12	12	47	45	66
8	NOTTINGHAM F	42	18	11	13	64	51	65
9	WATFORD	42	18	9	15	67	54	63
10	COVENTRY C	42	17	12	13	50	45	63
11	MANCHESTER U	42	14	14	14	52	45	56
12	SOUTHAMPTON	42	14	10	18	69	68	52
13	SHEFFIELD W	42	13	13	16	58	59	52
14	CHELSEA	42	13	13	16	53	64	52
15	WEST HAM U	42	14	10	18	52	67	52
16	QPR	42	13	11	18	48	64	50
17	NEWCASTLE U	42	12	11	19	47	65	47
18	OXFORD U	42	11	13	18	44	69	46
19	CHARLTON ATH	42	11	11	20	45	55	44
20	LEICESTER C	42	11	9	22	54	76	42
21	MANCHESTER C	42	8	15	19	36	57	39
22	ASTON VILLA	42	8	12	22	45	79	36

Season 1987-88

Football League Division Two

DATE	OPPONENTS	SCORE	GOALSCORERS	ATTENDANCE
Aug 15	Ipswich Town	D 1-1	O'Donnell o.g.	14,580
Aug 22	BIRMINGHAM CITY	L 0-2		30,870
Aug 29	Hull City	L 1-2	Aspinall (pen)	8,315
Aug 31	MANCHESTER CITY	D 1-1	Gage	16,282
Sep 5	Leicester City	W 2-0	Walters, Lillis	10,286
Sep 8	MIDDLESBROUGH	L 0-1		12,665
Sep 12	BARNSLEY	D 0-0		12,621
Sep 16	West Bromwich Albion	W 2-0	Aspinall 2	22,072
Sep 19	Huddersfield Town	W 1-1	Hunt S	6,884
Sep 26	SHEFFIELD UNITED	D 1-1	Gage	14,761
Sep 30	BLACKBURN ROVERS	D 1-1	Aspinall	11,772
Oct 3	Plymouth Argyle	W 3-1	Walters 2, Lillis	10,515
Oct 10	Leeds United	W 3-1	Rennie o.g., Aspinall 2	20,741
Oct 17	BOURNEMOUTH	D 1-1	Walters	15,145
Oct 21	CRYSTAL PALACE	W 4-1	Walters 3, Hunt S	12,755
Oct 24	Stoke City	D 0-0		13,494
Oct 31	READING	W 2-1	Blair, Lillis	13,413
Nov 3	Shrewsbury Town	W 2-1	Keown, Aspinall	7,089
Nov 7	MILLWALL	L 1-2	Keown	13,255
Nov 14	Oldham Athletic	W 1-0	McInally	6,469
Nov 28	Bradford City	W 4-2	Gray S 2, Birch, Thompson	15,006
Dec 5	SWINDON TOWN	W 2-1	Thompson 2	16,127
Dec 12	Birmingham City	W 2-1	Thompson 2	27,759
Dec 18	WEST BROMWICH ALBION	D 0-0		24,437
Dec 26	Sheffield United	D 1-1	Thompson	15,809
Dec 28	HUDDERSFIELD TOWN	D 1-1	Birch	20,948
Jan 1	HULL CITY	W 5-0	Gray S, Aspinall 2, Gray A, McInally	19,236
Jan 2	Barnsley	W 3-1	Aspinall, Birch, McInally	11,562
Jan 16	IPSWICH TOWN	W 1-0	Keown	20,201
Jan 23	Manchester City	W 2-0	Daley, Thompson	24,668
Feb 6	LEICESTER CITY	W 2-1	Lillis, Evans	18,867
Feb 14	Middlesbrough	L 1-2	Daley	16,957
Feb 20	Blackburn Rovers	L 2-3	Platt, Hendry o.g.	17,356
Feb 27	PLYMOUTH ARGYLE	W 5-2	Gray S (pen), Platt, Birch 2, Thompson	16,142
Mar 5	Bournemouth	W 2-1	Daley, Platt	10,057
Mar 12	LEEDS UNITED	L 1-2	McInally	19,677
Mar 19	Reading	W 2-0	Birch, Thompson	10,033
Mar 26	STOKE CITY	L 0-1		20,392
Apr 2	Millwall	L 1-2	Thompson	13,697
Apr 4	OLDHAM ATHLETIC	L 1-2	Gray S	19,138
Apr 9	Crystal Palace	D 1-1	Platt	16,476
Apr 23	SHREWSBURY TOWN	W 1-0	Aspinall	18,396
May 2	BRADFORD CITY	W 1-0	Platt	36,423
May 7	Swindon Town	D 0-0		10,959

FA Cup

Jan 9	Leeds United	(Rd 3) W 2-1	Gray A, McInally	29,002
Jan 31	LIVERPOOL	(Rd 4) L 0-2		46,324

League Cup

Sep 23	Middlesbrough	(Rd 2/FL) W 1-0	Aspinall	11,424
Oct 7	MIDDLESBROUGH	(Rd 2/SL) W 1-0	Birch	11,702
Oct 28	TOTTENHAM HOTSPUR	(Rd 3) W 2-1	McInally, Aspinall	29,114
Nov 18	SHEFFIELD WEDNESDAY	(Rd 4) L 1-2	Thompson	25,302

Simod Cup

Nov 11	BRADFORD CITY	(Rd 1) L 0-5		4,217

MANAGER: Graham Taylor

CAPTAIN: Martin Keown, Steve Sims, Allan Evans

TOP SCORER: Warren Aspinall, 13 (11 league)

BIGGEST WIN: 5-0 v Hull City (H), Division One, 1 January 1988

HIGHEST ATTENDANCE: 46,234 v Liverpool (H), FA Cup Fourth Round, 31 January 1987

MAJOR TRANSFERS IN: Kevin Gage from Wimbledon, Andy Gray from Crystal Palace, Stuart Gray from Barnsley, Mark Lillis from Derby County, Alan McInally from Celtic, Steve Sims from Watford, David Platt from Crewe Alexandra

MAJOR TRANSFERS OUT: Paul Elliott to Pisa (Italy), Steve Hunt retired, Tony Dorigo to Chelsea, Gary Williams to Leeds United

League & Cup Appearances

PLAYER	LEAGUE	CUP COMPETITION		OTHER	TOTAL
		FA CUP	LC		
Allen	4				4
Aspinall	28 (4)	1 (1)	4		33 (5)
Birch		2	4	1	7
Blair	3 (1)		1	1	5 (1)
Burke	4 (2)			0 (1)	4 (3)
Daley	10 (4)	1			11 (4)
Evans	18 (2)	2	0 (1)		20 (3)
Gage	44	2	4	1	51
Gallacher	43	2	4	1	50
Gray A	19	2			21
Gray S	19 (1)				19 (1)
Hunt D	11 (1)		2		13 (1)
Hunt S	1 (2)		2		3 (2)
Keown	42	2	4		48
Lillis	28 (1)	2	4	1	35 (1)
McInally	18 (8)	2	3	1	24 (8)
Norton	1 (1)				1 (1)
Platt	11				11
Shaw	1 (3)			1	2 (3)
Sims	29		4	1	34
Spink	44	2	4	1	51
Stainrod	4				4
Thompson	24	2	1	1	28
Walters	24			1	25
Williams GJ	1				1

Goalscorers

PLAYER	LEAGUE	CUP COMPETITION		OTHER	TOTAL
		FA CUP	LC		
Aspinall	11		2		13
Thompson	10		1		11
Walters	7				7
McInally	4	1	1		6
Gray S	5				5
Platt	5				5
Lillis	4				4
Daley	3				3
Keown	3				3
Gage	2				2
Hunt S	2				2
Gray A	1	1			2
Birch	6		1		7
Blair	1				1
Evans	1				1
Opps' o.gs.	3				3

Fact File

Eleven players made their senior debuts for Villa during the course of the 1987-88 season.

Final Division Two Table

		P	W	D	L	F	A	Pts
1	MILLWALL	44	25	7	12	72	52	82
2	ASTON VILLA	44	22	12	10	68	41	78
3	MIDDLESBROUGH	44	22	12	10	63	36	78
4	BRADFORD C	44	22	11	11	74	54	77
5	BLACKBURN R	44	21	14	9	68	52	77
6	CRYSTAL PALACE	44	22	9	13	86	59	75
7	LEEDS U	44	19	12	13	61	51	69
8	IPSWICH T	44	19	9	16	61	52	66
9	MANCHESTER C	44	19	8	17	80	60	65
10	OLDHAM ATH	44	18	11	15	72	64	65
11	STOKE C	44	17	11	16	50	57	62
12	SWINDON T	44	16	11	17	73	60	59
13	LEICESTER C	44	16	11	17	62	61	59
14	BARNSLEY	44	15	12	17	61	62	57
15	HULL C	44	14	15	15	54	60	57
16	PLYMOUTH ARG	44	16	8	20	65	67	56
17	BOURNEMOUTH	44	13	10	21	56	68	49
18	SHREWSBURY T	44	11	16	17	42	54	49
19	BIRMINGHAM C	44	11	15	18	41	66	48
20	WBA	44	12	11	21	50	69	47
21	SHEFFIELD U	44	13	7	24	45	74	46
22	READING	44	10	12	22	44	70	42
23	HUDDERSFIELD T	44	6	10	28	41	100	2

Season 1988-89

Football League Division One

DATE	OPPONENTS	SCORE	GOALSCORERS	ATTENDANCE
Aug 27	MILLWALL	D 2-2	Gray S (pen), McInally	22,449
Sep 3	Arsenal	W 3-2	McInally 2, Gray A	37,413
Sep 10	LIVERPOOL	D 1-1	McInally	41,409
Sep 17	West Ham United	D 2-2	McInally 2	19,186
Sep 24	NOTTINGHAM FOREST	D 1-1	Gage	23,029
Oct 1	Sheffield Wednesday	L 0-1		18,301
Oct 8	WIMBLEDON	L 0-1		15,416
Oct 15	Charlton Athletic	D 2-2	McInally, Platt	7,594
Oct 22	EVERTON	W 2-0	Daley, Platt	26,636
Oct 29	TOTTENHAM HOTSPUR	W 2-1	Fenwick o.g., Daley	26,238
Nov 5	Manchester United	D 1-1	Cowans	44,804
Nov 12	Southampton	L 1-3	Daley	16,007
Nov 19	DERBY COUNTY	L 1-2	Mountfield	23,489
Nov 26	Coventry City	L 1-2	McInally	20,104
Dec 3	NORWICH CITY	W 3-1	Gage 2, Platt	19,653
Dec 10	Middlesbrough	D 3-3	Gray A, McInally 2	18,096
Dec 17	Luton Town	D 1-1	Johnson M o.g.	8,785
Dec 26	QUEENS PARK RANGERS	W 2-1	McInally 2	25,106
Dec 31	ARSENAL	L 0-3		32,486
Jan 3	Liverpool	L 0-1		39,104
Jan 14	NEWCASTLE UNITED	W 3-1	Gray A, Daley, McInally	21,010
Jan 21	Nottingham Forest	L 0-4		22,662
Feb 4	SHEFFIELD WEDNESDAY	W 2-0	Callaghan, Platt	19,334
Feb 11	Wimbledon	L 0-1		6,201
Feb 14	Everton	D 1-1	Ormondroyd	20,142
Feb 25	CHARLTON ATHLETIC	L 1-2	Cowans	16,481
Mar 1	Tottenham Hotspur	L 0-2		19,090
Mar 12	MANCHESTER UNITED	D 0-0		28,332
Mar 18	Millwall	L 0-2		13,206
Mar 25	WEST HAM UNITED	L 0-1		22,471
Mar 27	Queens Park Rangers	L 0-1		11,378
Apr 1	LUTON TOWN	W 2-1	Daley, Olney	15,640
Apr 8	Newcastle United	W 2-1	Gray S, Platt	20,329
Apr 22	Norwich City	D 2-2	Olney, McInally	14,550
Apr 29	MIDDLESBROUGH	D 1-1	Gray S	18,950
May 2	SOUTHAMPTON	L 1-2	Gray S	15,218
May 6	Derby County	L 1-2	Platt	18,112
May 13	COVENTRY CITY	D 1-1	Platt	29,906

FA Cup

Jan 7	Crewe Alexandra	(Rd 3)	W 3-2	Platt, Gage, McInally	5,500
Jan 28	WIMBLEDON	(Rd 4)	L 0-1		25,043

League Cup

Sep 27	Birmingham City	(Rd 2 FL)	W 2-0	Gage, Gray A	21,177
Oct 12	BIRMINGHAM CITY	(Rd 2 SL)	W 5-0	Mountfield, Gage 2, Olney, Daley	19,753
Nov 2	MILLWALL	(Rd 3)	W 3-1	McInally 2, Platt	17,648
Nov 30	IPSWICH TOWN	(Rd 4)	W 6-2	McInally 2, Platt 4	16,284
Jan 18	West Ham United	(Rd 5)	L 1-2		30,110

Simod Cup

Nov 9	BIRMINGHAM CITY	(Rd 1)	W 6-0	Platt, Gallacher, Mountfield, McInally 2, Evans	8,324
Nov 23	Derby County	(Rd 2)	L 1-2	McInally	10,086

League & Cup Appearances

PLAYER	LEAGUE	CUP COMPETITION		OTHER	TOTAL
		FA CUP	LC		
Birch	6 (6)				6 (6)
Butler	4		1		5
Callaghan	15 (1)				15 (1)
Cowans	32 (1)	2	5	2	41 (1)
Daley	25 (4)	2	5	1 (1)	33 (5)
Duffy	1				1
Evans	26 (1)	2	2	2	32 (1)
Gage	27 (1)	2	5	2	36 (1)
Gallacher	3 (1)		2 (1)	2	7 (2)
Gray A	15 (1)	1 (1)	3	0 (1)	19 (3)
Gray S	35	2	3	0 (2)	40 (2)
Hunt	1				1
Keown	32 (2)	2	4	2	40 (2)
Lillis	2				2
McInally	32 (1)	2	5	2	39 (1)
Mountfield	22 (2)	2	5	2	31 (2)
Olney	8 (7)	0 (1)	1 (1)		9 (9)
Ormondroyd	9 (3)				9 (3)
Platt	38	2	5	2	47
Price	36	1	5	2	44
Sims	12		1		13
Spink	34	2	5	1	42
Thompson	2 (3)		1	1	4 (3)
Williams	1		1		2

Goalscorers

PLAYER	LEAGUE	CUP COMPETITION		OTHER	TOTAL
		FA CUP	LC		
McInally	14	1	4	3	22
Platt	7	1	6	1	15
Gage	3	1	3		7
Daley	5		1		6
Gray A	3		1		4
Gray S	4				4
Mountfield	1		1	1	3
Olney	2		1		3
Cowans	2				2
Callaghan	1				1
Evans				1	1
Gallacher				1	1
Ormondroyd	1				1
Opps' o.gs.	2				2

Fact File

Villa scored 13 goals against 'Second City' rivals Blues in three games over a period of six weeks (September–November 1988).

MANAGER: Graham Taylor

CAPTAIN: Allan Evans/David Platt/Stuart Gray

TOP SCORER: Alan McInally, 22 (14 league)

BIGGEST WIN: 6-0 v Birmingham City (H), Simod Cup First Round, 9 November 1988

HIGHEST ATTENDANCE: 44,804 v Manchester United (A), Division One, 5 November 1988

MAJOR TRANSFERS IN: Chris Price from Blackburn Rovers, Gordon Cowans from Bari (Italy), Derek Mountfield from Everton, Nigel Callaghan from Derby County, Ian Ormondroyd from Bradford City

MAJOR TRANSFERS OUT: Andy Gray to Queens Park Rangers, Garry Thompson to Sheffield Wednesday

Final Division One Table

		P	W	D	L	F	A	Pts
1	ARSENAL	38	22	10	6	73	36	76
2	LIVERPOOL	38	22	10	6	65	28	76
3	NOTTINGHAM F	38	17	13	8	64	43	64
4	NORWICH CITY	38	17	11	10	48	45	62
5	DERBY COUNTY	38	17	7	14	40	38	58
6	TOTTENHAM H	38	15	12	11	60	46	57
7	COVENTRY C	38	14	13	11	47	42	55
8	EVERTON	38	14	12	12	50	45	54
9	QPR	38	14	11	13	43	37	53
10	MILLWALL	38	14	11	13	47	52	53
11	MANCHESTER U	38	13	12	13	45	35	51
12	WIMBLEDON	38	14	9	15	50	46	51
13	SOUTHAMPTON	38	10	15	13	52	66	45
14	CHARLTON ATH	38	10	12	16	44	58	42
15	SHEFFIELD W	38	10	12	16	34	51	42
16	LUTON TOWN	38	10	11	17	42	52	41
17	ASTON VILLA	38	9	13	16	45	56	40
18	MIDDLESBROUGH	38	9	12	17	44	61	39
19	WEST HAM U	38	10	8	20	37	62	38
20	NEWCASTLE U	38	7	10	21	32	63	31

Season 1989-90

Football League Division One

DATE	OPPONENTS	SCORE		GOALSCORERS	ATTENDANCE
Aug 19	Nottingham Forest	D	1-1	Mountfield	26,766
Aug 23	LIVERPOOL	D	1-1	Platt	35,796
Aug 26	CHARLTON ATHLETIC	D	1-1	Olney	15,236
Aug 29	Southampton	L	1-2	Platt	14,401
Sep 9	TOTTENHAM HOTSPUR	W	2-0	Olney 2	24,769
Sep 16	Sheffield Wednesday	L	0-1		17,509
Sep 23	QUEENS PARK RANGERS	L	1-3	Platt	14,170
Sep 30	DERBY COUNTY	W	1-0	Platt	16,245
Oct 14	Luton Town	W	1-0	Mountfield	9,433
Oct 22	Manchester City	W	2-0	Daley, Olney	23,354
Oct 28	CRYSTAL PALACE	W	2-1	Platt 2	15,724
Nov 5	EVERTON	W	6-2	Cowans, Olney 2, Platt 2, Nielsen	17,637
Nov 11	Norwich City	L	0-2		18,186
Nov 18	COVENTRY CITY	W	4-1	Ormondroyd 2, Peake o.g., Platt (pen)	22,803
Nov 25	Wimbledon	W	2-0	Platt, Daley	5,888
Dec 2	NOTTINGHAM FOREST	W	2-1	Olney, Platt	25,575
Dec 9	Liverpool	D	1-1	Olney	37,435
Dec 16	Millwall	L	0-2		10,528
Dec 26	MANCHESTER UNITED	W	3-0	Olney, Platt, Gage	41,247
Dec 30	ARSENAL	W	2-1	Platt, Mountfield	40,665
Jan 1	Chelsea	W	3-0	Gage, Daley, Platt	23,990
Jan 13	Charlton Athletic	W	2-0	Mountfield, McLaughlin o.g.	10,513
Jan 20	SOUTHAMPTON	W	2-1	Daley, Gage	33,118
Feb 10	SHEFFIELD WEDNESDAY	W	1-0	Platt	27,168
Feb 21	Tottenham Hotspur	W	2-0	Ormondroyd, Platt	32,472
Feb 24	WIMBLEDON	L	0-3		29,325
Mar 4	Coventry City	L	0-2		17,891
Mar 10	LUTON TOWN	W	2-0	Daley, Platt	22,505
Mar 17	Derby County	W	1-0	Ormondroyd	21,062
Mar 20	Queens Park Rangers	D	1-1	Nielsen	15,856
Mar 24	Crystal Palace	L	0-1		18,586
Apr 1	MANCHESTER CITY	L	1-2	Cowans	24,797
Apr 11	Arsenal	W	1-0	Price	30,060
Apr 14	CHELSEA	W	1-0	Cowans	28,361
Apr 17	Manchester United	L	0-2		44,080
Apr 21	MILLWALL	W	1-0	Platt	21,028
Apr 28	NORWICH CITY	D	3-3	McGrath, Cascarino, Platt	28,988
May 5	Everton	D	3-3	Cascarino, Cowans, Daley	29,551

FA Cup

Jan 6	Blackburn Rovers	(Rd 3) D	2-2	Olney, Ormondroyd	14,456
Jan 10	BLACKBURN ROVERS	(R) W	3-1	Ormondroyd, Daley, May o.g.	31,169
Jan 27	PORT VALE	(Rd 4) W	6-0	Platt, Birch 2, Olney, Gray 2	36,532
Feb 17	West Bromwich Albion	(Rd 5) W	2-0	Mountfield, Daley	26,585
Mar 14	Oldham Athletic	(Rd 6) L	0-3		19,490

League Cup

Sep 20	WOLVERHAMPTON WANDERERS	(Rd 2) W	2-1	Platt, Gray	27,400
Oct 4	Wolverhampton Wanderers	D	1-1	Mountfield	22,754
Oct 25	WEST HAM UNITED	D	0-0		20,898
Nov 8	West Ham United	L	0-1		23,833

Simod Cup

Nov 28	Hull City	(Rd 2) W	2-1	Mountfield, Platt	2,888
Dec 22	NOTTINGHAM FOREST	(Rd 3) W	2-1	Platt (pen), Mountfield	6,530
Jan 17	LEEDS UNITED	(Rd 4) W	2-0	Gray, Platt (pen)	17,543
Jan 30	Middlesbrough	(Area SF FL) L	1-2	Birch	16,457
Feb 6	MIDDLESBROUGH	(Area SF SL) L	1-2	Gray	20,806

MANAGER: Graham Taylor

CAPTAIN: Paul McGrath

TOP SCORER: David Platt, 24 (19 league)

BIGGEST WIN: 6-0 v Port Vale (H), FA Cup Fourth Round, 27 January 1990

HIGHEST ATTENDANCE: 44,080 v Manchester United (A), Division One, 17 April 1990

MAJOR TRANSFERS IN: Kent Nielsen from Brondby IF, Tony Cascarino from Millwall, Andy Comyn from Alvechurch, Adrian Heath from Español (Spain)

MAJOR TRANSFERS OUT: Adrian Heath to Manchester City

League & Cup Appearances

PLAYER	LEAGUE	CUP COMPETITION		OTHER	TOTAL
		FA CUP	LC		
Birch	6 (6)	1 (2)	1	1 (1)	9 (9)
Blake	6 (3)		0 (1)		6 (4)
Butler				1 1	1
Callaghan	7 (1)		1 (1)		8 (2)
Cascarino	10				10
Comyn	3 (1)		0 (1)		3 (2)
Cowans	34	5	3	5	47
Daley	31 (1)	4	3	4 (1)	42 (2)
Gage	22	5	4	4	35
Gallacher	6 (1)	1	2		9 (1)
Gray	26 (3)	1 (1)	3	3 (1)	33 (5)
Heath	8 (1)	0 (1)	1 (1)		9 (3)
McGrath	35	5	3	4	47
Mountfield	32	4	4	5	45
Nielsen	34 (2)	4	4	5	45 (2)
Olney	27 (8)	5	4	5	41 (8)
Ormondroyd	19 (6)	4	1 (1)	5	29 (7)
Platt	37	5	4	5	51
Price	33 (1)	4	4	4 (1)	45 (2)
Spink	38	5	4	4	51
Williams	4 (6)	2		0 (1)	6 (7)
Yorke	0 (2)				0 (2)

Goalscorers

PLAYER	LEAGUE	CUP COMPETITION		OTHER	TOTAL
		FA CUP	LC		
Platt	19	1	1	3	24
Olney	9	2			11
Daley	6	2			8
Mountfield	4	1	1	2	8
Ormondroyd	4	2			6
Gray		2	1	2	5
Cowans	4				4
Birch				1	1
Gage	3				3
Cascarino	2				2
Nielsen	2				2
McGrath	1				1
Price	1				1
Opps' o.gs.	2	1			3

Fact File

Villa, 1-0 down, scored three times in five minutes to lead 3-1 at home to Norwich before settling for a 3-3 draw on 28 April 1990.

Final Division One Table

		P	W	D	L	F	A	PTS
1	LIVERPOOL	38	23	10	5	78	37	79
2	ASTON VILLA	38	21	7	10	57	38	70
3	TOTTENHAM H	38	19	6	13	59	47	63
4	ARSENAL	38	18	8	12	54	38	62
5	CHELSEA	38	16	12	10	58	50	60
6	EVERTON	38	17	8	13	57	46	59
7	SOUTHAMPTON	38	15	10	13	71	63	55
8	WIMBLEDON	38	13	16	9	47	40	55
9	NOTTINGHAM F	38	15	9	14	55	47	54
10	NORWICH CITY	38	13	14	11	44	42	53
11	QPR	38	13	11	14	45	44	50
12	COVENTRY CITY	38	14	7	17	39	59	49
13	MANCHESTER U	38	13	9	16	46	47	48
14	MANCHESTER C	38	12	12	14	43	52	48
15	CRYSTAL P	38	13	9	16	42	66	48
16	DERBY C	38	13	7	18	43	40	46
17	LUTON T	38	10	13	15	43	57	43
18	SHEFFIELD W	38	11	10	17	35	51	43
19	CHARLTON ATH	38	7	9	22	31	57	30
20	MILLWALL	38	5	11	22	39	65	26

Season 1990-91

Football League Division One

DATE	OPPONENTS	SCORE	GOALSCORERS	ATTENDANCE
Aug 25	SOUTHAMPTON	D 1-1	Cascarino	29,542
Sep 1	Liverpool	L 1-2	Platt	38,061
Sep 5	Manchester City	L 1-2	Platt (pen)	30,199
Sep 8	COVENTRY CITY	W 2-1	Platt (pen), Cascarino	27,001
Sep 15	Derby County	W 2-0	Daley, Platt	19,024
Sep 22	QUEENS PARK RANGERS	D 2-2	Mountfield, Ormondroyd	23,301
Sep 29	Tottenham Hotspur	L 1-2	Platt	34,939
Oct 6	SUNDERLAND	W 3-0	Olney, Daley, Platt	26,017
Oct 20	Wimbledon	D 0-0		6,646
Oct 27	LEEDS UNITED	D 0-0		24,219
Nov 3	Chelsea	L 0-1		23,555
Nov 10	NOTTINGHAM FOREST	D 1-1	Nielsen	25,797
Nov 17	Norwich City	L 0-2		17,243
Nov 24	Luton Town	L 0-2		10,071
Dec 1	SHEFFIELD UNITED	W 2-1	Platt, Price	21,713
Dec 15	Southampton	D 1-1	Platt (pen)	16,604
Dec 23	ARSENAL	D 0-0		22,687
Dec 26	Everton	L 0-1		27,804
Dec 29	Manchester United	D 1-1	Pallister o.g.	47,485
Jan 1	CRYSTAL PALACE	W 2-0	Platt 2 (1 pen)	25,523
Jan 12	LIVERPOOL	D 0-0		40,026
Jan 19	Coventry City	L 1-2	Platt	15,751
Feb 2	DERBY COUNTY	W 3-2	Cowans (pen), Cascarino, Yorke	21,852
Feb 23	Nottingham Forest	D 2-2	Cascarino, Mountfield	22,036
Mar 2	Sheffield United	L 1-2	Mountfield	22,074
Mar 9	LUTON TOWN	L 1-2	Cascarino	20,587
Mar 16	TOTTENHAM HOTSPUR	W 3-2	Platt 3	32,638
Mar 23	Sunderland	W 3-1	Cascarino 2, Platt	21,099
Mar 30	EVERTON	D 2-2	Platt, Olney	27,660
Apr 3	Arsenal	L 0-5		41,868
Apr 6	MANCHESTER UNITED	D 1-1	Cascarino	33,307
Apr 10	Queens Park Rangers	L 1-2	Platt	11,539
Apr 13	Crystal Palace	D 0-0		18,331
Apr 20	WIMBLEDON	L 1-2	Olney	17,001
Apr 23	MANCHESTER CITY	L 1-5	Platt (pen)	24,168
May 4	Leeds United	L 2-5	Nielsen, Mountfield	29,188
May 8	NORWICH CITY	W 2-1	Bowen o.g., Yorke	16,697
May 11	CHELSEA	D 2-2	Cascarino, Platt (pen)	27,866

FA Cup

Jan 5	WIMBLEDON	(Rd 3)	D 1-1	Gray	19,305
Jan 9	Wimbledon	(R)	L 0-1		7,382

League Cup

Sep 26	BARNSLEY	(Rd 2/FL)	W 1-0	Platt	14,471
Oct 9	Barnsley	(Rd 2/SL)	W 1-0	Daley	13,924
Oct 31	MILLWALL	(Rd 3)	W 2-0	Cascarino, Platt (pen)	15,117
Nov 28	MIDDLESBROUGH	(Rd 4)	W 3-2	Ormondroyd, Daley, Platt (pen)	17,317
Jan 16	Leeds United	(Rd 5)	L 1-4	Ormondroyd	28,176

UEFA Cup

Sep 19	BANIK OSTRAVA	(Rd 1/FL)	W 3-1	Platt, Mountfield, Olney	27,317
Oct 3	Banik Ostrava	(Rd 1/SL)	W 2-1	Mountfield, Stas o.g.	24,164
Oct 24	INTER MILAN	(Rd 2/FL)	W 2-0	Nielsen, Platt	36,461
Nov 7	Inter Milan	(Rd 2 /SL)	L 0-3		75,580

Fact File

Josef Venglos became Villa's first foreign-born manager; David Platt was transferred to Bari for a club record fee of £5.5 million.

MANAGER: Josef Venglos

CAPTAIN: Paul McGrath, David Platt

TOP SCORER: David Platt, 24 (19 league)

BIGGEST WIN: 3-0 v Sunderland, Division One, 6 October 1990

HIGHEST ATTENDANCE: 75,580 v Inter Milan (A), UEFA Cup Second Round, 7 November 1990

MAJOR TRANSFERS IN: Gary Penrice from Watford, Neil Cox from Scunthorpe United

MAJOR TRANSFERS OUT: David Platt to Bari (Italy)

League & Cup Appearances

PLAYER	LEAGUE	CUP COMPETITION		OTHER	TOTAL
		FA CUP	LC		
Birch	6 (2)	0 (2)	2 (3)	2	10 (7)
Blake	6 (1)				6 (1)
Butler	4				4
Callaghan	2	1 (1)	1		4 (1)
Cascarino	33 (3)	2	2 (1)	3	40 (4)
Comyn	9 (2)	2	2	1	14 (2)
Cowans	38	2	5	4	49
Daley	22 (1)		4	4	30 (1)
Gage	20 (1)			1	21 (1)
Gallacher	2				2
Gray	22	2	5	4	33
McGrath	35	2	4	3	44
Mountfield	32		4	4	40
Nielsen	37	2	4	4	47
Olney	13 (5)		3	1 (2)	17 (7)
Ormondroyd	13 (5)	1	3 (1)	1	18 (6)
Penrice	9 (3)				9 (3)
Platt	35	2	5	4	46
Price	38	2	5	4	49
Spink	34	2	5	4	45
Yorke	8 (10)	2		1	11 (10)

Goalscorers

PLAYER	LEAGUE	CUP COMPETITION		OTHER	TOTAL
		FA CUP	LC		
Platt	19		3	2	24
Cascarino	9		1		10
Mountfield	4			2	6
Daley	2		2		4
Olney	3			1	4
Nielsen	2			1	3
Ormondroyd	1		2		3
Yorke	2				2
Cowans	1				1
Gray		1			1
Price	1				1
Opps' o.gs.	2			1	3

Final Division One Table

		P	W	D	L	F	A	Pts
1	ARSENAL	38	24	13	1	74	18	83
2	LIVERPOOL	38	23	7	8	77	40	76
3	CRYSTAL PALACE	38	20	9	9	50	41	69
4	LEEDS U	38	19	7	12	65	47	64
5	MANCHESTER C	38	17	11	10	64	53	62
6	MANCHESTER U	38	16	12	10	58	45	59
7	WIMBLEDON	38	14	14	10	53	46	56
8	NOTTINGHAM F	38	14	12	12	65	50	54
9	EVERTON	38	13	12	13	50	46	51
10	TOTTENHAM H	38	11	16	11	51	50	49
11	CHELSEA	38	13	10	15	58	69	49
12	QPR	38	12	10	16	44	53	46
13	SHEFFIELD U	38	13	7	18	36	55	46
14	SOUTHAMPTON	38	12	9	17	58	69	45
15	NORWICH C	38	13	6	19	41	64	45
16	COVENTRY C	38	11	11	16	42	49	44
17	ASTON VILLA	38	9	14	15	46	58	41
18	LUTON T	38	10	7	21	42	61	37
19	SUNDERLAND	38	8	10	20	38	60	34
20	DERBY CO	38	5	9	24	37	75	24

ARSENAL TWO POINTS DEDUCTED, MANCHESTER UNITED ONE POINT DEDUCTED FOR DISCIPLINARY REASONS.

Season 1991-92

Football League Division One

DATE	OPPONENTS	SCORE	GOALSCORERS	ATTENDANCE
Aug 17	Sheffield Wednesday	W 3-2	Staunton, Regis, Atkinson	36,749
Aug 21	MANCHESTER UNITED	L 0-1		39,995
Aug 24	ARSENAL	W 3-1	Staunton, Daley, Penrice	29,684
Aug 28	West Ham United	L 1-3	Daley	23,644
Aug 31	Southampton	D 1-1	Richardson	16,161
Sep 4	CRYSTAL PALACE	L 0-1		20,740
Sep 7	TOTTENHAM HOTSPUR	D 0-0		33,096
Sep 14	Liverpool	D 1-1	Richardson	38,400
Sep 18	Chelsea	L 0-2		17,182
Sep 21	NOTTINGHAM FOREST	W 3-1	Richardson, Yorke, Blake	28,506
Sep 28	Coventry City	L 0-1		17,851
Oct 5	LUTON TOWN	W 4-0	Richardson, Yorke, Regis, Mortimer	18,722
Oct 19	Everton	W 2-0	Regis, Daley	27,688
Oct 26	WIMBLEDON	W 2-1	Yorke, Olney	16,928
Nov 2	Queens Park Rangers	W 1-0	Yorke	10,642
Nov 16	NOTTS COUNTY	W 1-0	Yorke	23,020
Nov 24	LEEDS UNITED	L 1-4	Yorke	23,713
Nov 30	Oldham Athletic	L 2-3	Blake, Regis	15,370
Dec 7	MANCHESTER CITY	W 3-1	Daley, Regis, Yorke	26,265
Dec 14	Sheffield United	L 0-2		18,401
Dec 26	WEST HAM UNITED	W 3-1	Richardson, Daley, Yorke	31,959
Dec 28	SOUTHAMPTON	W 2-1	Regis, Yorke	23,094
Jan 1	Norwich City	L 1-2	Regis	15,318
Jan 11	Arsenal	D 0-0		31,413
Jan 18	SHEFFIELD WEDNESDAY	L 0-1		28,036
Jan 22	Manchester United	L 0-1		45,022
Feb 2	EVERTON	D 0-0		17,451
Feb 8	Wimbledon	L 0-2		5,534
Feb 22	OLDHAM ATHLETIC	W 1-0	Regis	20,509
Feb 29	Manchester City	L 0-2		28,268
Mar 3	Leeds United	D 0-0		28,896
Mar 10	Notts County	D 0-0		8,389
Mar 14	QUEENS PARK RANGERS	L 0-1		19,630
Mar 21	Crystal Palace	D 0-0		15,368
Mar 28	NORWICH CITY	W 1-0	Staunton	16,985
Mar 31	SHEFFIELD UNITED	D 1-1	Regis	15,745
Apr 4	Tottenham Hotspur	W 5-2	Richardson, Regis, Olney, Yorke, Daley	26,370
Apr 11	LIVERPOOL	W 1-0	Daley	35,755
Apr 18	Nottingham Forest	L 0-2		22,800
Apr 20	CHELSEA	W 3-1	Staunton, McGrath, Parker	19,269
Apr 25	Luton Town	L 0-2		11,178
May 2	COVENTRY CITY	W 2-0	Regis, Yorke	31,984

FA Cup

Jan 5	TOTTENHAM HOTSPUR	(Rd 3) D 0-0		29,316
Jan 14	Tottenham Hotspur	(R) W 1-0	Yorke	25,462
Feb 5	Derby County	(Rd 4) W 4-3	Yorke 3, Parker	22,452
Feb 16	Swindon Town	(Rd 5) W 2-1	Yorke, Froggatt	16,402
Mar 8	Liverpool	(Rd 6) L 0-1		29,109

League Cup

Sep 25	Grimsby Town	D 0-0		13,835
Oct 9	GRIMSBY TOWN	D 1-1*	Teale	15,338

*Lost on away goals rule.

Zenith Data Systems Cup

Oct 23	Coventry City	(Rd 1) W 2-0	Olney, Yorke	6,447
Nov 19	NOTTINGHAM FOREST	(Rd 2) L 0-2		7,859

MANAGER: Ron Atkinson

CAPTAIN: Paul McGrath

TOP SCORER: Dwight Yorke, 17 (11 league)

BIGGEST WIN: 5-2 v Tottenham Hotspur (A), Division One, 4 April 1992

HIGHEST ATTENDANCE: 45,022 v Manchester United (A), 22 January 1992

MAJOR TRANSFERS IN: Cyrille Regis from Coventry City, Earl Barrett from Oldham Athletic, Ugo Ehiogu from West Bromwich Albion, Dariusz Kubicki from Legia Warsaw, Steve Staunton from Liverpool, Shaun Teale from Bournemouth, Matthius Breikreutz from Borussia Borsig, Gary Parker from Nottingham Forest, Kevin Richardson and Dalian Atkinson from Real Sociedad

MAJOR TRANSFERS OUT: Gordon Cowans to Blackburn Rovers, Derek Mountfield to Wolverhampton Wanderers, Ian Ormondroyd to Derby County

League & Cup Appearances

PLAYER	LEAGUE	CUP COMPETITION		OTHER	TOTAL
		FA CUP	LC		
Atkinson	11 (3)	1	1	1	14 (3)
Barrett	13				13
Beinlich	0 (2)			0 (1)	0 (3)
Blake	14	2	1	2	19
Bosnich	1				1
Breitkreutz	7 (1)				7 (1)
Carruthers	3 (2)	0 (1)		0 (1)	2 (3)
Cowans	10 (2)		2	0 (1)	12 (3)
Cox	4 (3)			1	5 (3)
Daley	29 (5)	5		2	36 (5)
Ehiogu	4 (4)	0 (1)		1	5 (5)
Froggatt	6 (3)	2 (1)			8 (4)
Kubicki	23	4 (1)	2	1	30 (1)
McGrath	41	5	2		48
McLoughlin				1	1
Mortimer	10 (2)		2		12 (2)
Mountfield	2				2
Nielson	3 (3)			1	4 (3)
Olney	14 (6)		0 (1)	2	16 (7)
Ormondroyd	0 (1)				0 (1)
Parker	25	5			30
Penrice	5 (3)				5 (3)
Price	2 (1)			1	3 (1)
Regis	39	5	2		46
Richardson	42	5	2	2	51
Sealey	18	4		2	24
Small	8	2 (1)		2	12 (1)
Spink	23	1	2		26
Staunton	37	4	2		43
Teale	42	5	2	2	51
Yorke	27 (5)	5	2	1	35 (5)

Goalscorers

PLAYER	LEAGUE	CUP COMPETITION		OTHER	TOTAL
		FA CUP	LC		
Yorke	11	5		1	17
Regis	11				11
Daley	7				7
Richardson	6				6
Staunton	4				4
Olney	2			1	3
Blake	2				2
Parker	1	1			2
Atkinson	1				1
McGrath	1				1
Mortimer	1				1
Penrice	1				1
Froggatt		1			1
Teale			1		1

Fact File

Villa scored only one goal in 10 league games.

Final Division One Table

		P	W	D	L	F	A	Pts
1	LEEDS U	42	22	16	4	74	37	82
2	MANCHESTER U	42	21	15	6	63	33	78
3	SHEFFIELD W	42	21	12	9	62	49	75
4	ARSENAL	42	19	15	8	81	46	72
5	MANCHESTER C	42	20	10	12	61	48	70
6	LIVERPOOL	42	16	16	10	47	40	64
7	ASTON VILLA	42	17	9	16	48	44	60
8	NOTTINGHAM F	42	16	11	15	60	58	59
9	SHEFFIELD U	42	16	9	17	65	63	57
10	CRYSTAL PALACE	42	14	15	13	53	61	57
11	QPR	42	12	18	12	48	47	54
12	EVERTON	42	13	14	15	52	51	53
13	WIMBLEDON	42	13	14	15	53	53	53
14	CHELSEA	42	13	14	15	50	60	53
15	TOTTENHAM H	42	15	7	20	58	63	52
16	SOUTHAMPTON	42	14	10	18	39	55	52
17	OLDHAM ATH	42	14	9	19	63	67	51
18	NORWICH C	42	11	12	19	47	63	45
19	COVENTRY C	42	11	11	20	35	44	44
20	LUTON T	42	10	12	20	38	71	42
21	NOTTS CO	42	10	10	22	40	62	40
22	WEST HAM U	42	9	11	22	37	59	38

Season 1992-93

Premier League

DATE	OPPONENTS	SCORE	GOALSCORERS	ATTENDANCE
Aug 15	Ipswich Town	D 1-1	Atkinson	16,818
Aug 19	LEEDS UNITED	D 1-1	Atkinson	29,151
Aug 22	SOUTHAMPTON	D 1-1	Atkinson	17,894
Aug 25	Everton	L 0-1		22,372
Aug 29	Sheffield United	W 2-0	Parker 2	18,773
Sep 2	CHELSEA	L 1-3	Richardson	19,125
Sep 5	CRYSTAL PALACE	W 3-0	Yorke, Staunton, Froggatt	17,120
Sep 13	Leeds United	D 1-1	Parker	27,815
Sep 19	LIVERPOOL	W 4-2	Saunders 2, Aktinson, Parker	37,863
Sep 26	Middlesbrough	W 3-2	Saunders 2, Aktinson	20,905
Oct 3	Wimbledon	W 3-2	Saunders 2, Aktinson	6,849
Oct 19	BLACKBURN ROVERS	D 0-0		30,398
Oct 24	Oldham Athletic	D 1-1	Aktinson	13,457
Nov 1	QUEENS PARK RANGERS	W 2-0	Saunders, Atkinson	20,140
Nov 7	MANCHESTER UNITED	W 1-0	Atkinson	39,062
Nov 21	Tottenham Hotspur	D 0-0		32,852
Nov 28	NORWICH CITY	L 2-3	Houghton, Saunders	28,837
Dec 5	Sheffield Wednesday	W 2-1	Atkinson 2	29,964
Dec 12	NOTTINGHAM FOREST	W 2-1	Regis, McGrath	29,015
Dec 19	Manchester City	D 1-1	Parker	23,525
Dec 26	Coventry City	L 0-3		24,245
Dec 28	ARSENAL	W 1-0	Saunders (pen)	35,170
Jan 9	Liverpool	W 2-1	Parker, Saunders	40,826
Jan 17	MIDDLESBROUGH	W 5-1	Parker, McGrath, Yorke, Saunders, Teale	19,977
Jan 27	SHEFFIELD UNITED	W 3-1	McGrath, Kamara o.g., Richardson	20,256
Jan 30	Southampton	L 0-2		19,087
Feb 6	IPSWICH TOWN	W 2-0	Yorke, Saunders	25,395
Feb 10	Crystal Palace	L 0-1		12,270
Feb 13	Chelsea	W 1-0	Houghton	20,081
Feb 20	EVERTON	W 2-1	Cox, Barrett	32,913
Feb 27	WIMBLEDON	W 1-0	Yorke	34,496
Mar 10	TOTTENHAM HOTSPUR	D 0-0		37,737
Mar 14	Manchester United	D 1-1	Staunton	36,163
Mar 20	SHEFFIELD WEDNESDAY	W 2-0	Yorke 2	38,024
Mar 24	Norwich City	L 0-1		19,528
Apr 4	Nottingham Forest	W 1-0	McGrath	26,742
Apr 10	COVENTRY CITY	D 0-0		38,542
Apr 12	Arsenal	W 1-0	Daley	27,125
Apr 18	MANCHESTER CITY	W 3-1	Saunders, Parker (pen), Houghton	33,108
Apr 21	Blackburn Rovers	L 0-3		15,127
May 2	OLDHAM ATHLETIC	L 0-1		37,247
May 9	Queens Park Rangers	L 1-2	Daley	18,908

FA Cup

Jan 2	BRISTOL ROVERS	(Rd 3)	D 1-1	Cox	27,040
Jan 20	Bristol Rovers	(R)	W 3-0	Saunders 2, Houghton	18,880
Jan 23	WIMBLEDON	(Rd 4)	D 1-1	Yorke	21,086
Feb 3	Wimbledon	(R)	D 0-0*		8,048

*Lost 5-6 on penalties.

League Cup

Sep 23	Oxford United	(Rd 2/FL)	W 2-1	McGrath, Teale	8,837
Oct 7	OXFORD UNITED	(Rd 2/SL)	W 2-1	Atkinson, Richardson	19,808
Oct 28	MANCHESTER UNITED	(Rd 3)	W 1-0	Saunders	35,964
Dec 2	IPSWICH TOWN	(Rd 4)	D 2-2	Atkinson, Saunders	21,545
Dec 15	Ipswich Town	(R)	L 0-1		19,196

Fact File

Both Villa-Spurs league games finished goalless – and in fact, the 0-0 scoreline at White Hart Lane was the first 'blank' result between the two clubs on that ground since 1954.

MANAGER: Ron Atkinson

CAPTAIN: Kevin Richardson

TOP SCORER: Dean Saunders, 17 (13 league)

BIGGEST WIN: 5-1 v Middlesbrough (H), Division One, 17 January 1993

HIGHEST ATTENDANCE: 40,826 v Liverpool (A), Division One, 9 January 1993

MAJOR TRANSFERS IN: Ray Houghton and Dean Saunders from Liverpool

League & Cup Appearances

PLAYER	LEAGUE	CUP COMPETITION		TOTAL
		FA CUP	LC	
Atkinson	28		4	32
Barrett	42	4	5	51
Beinlich	1 (6)			1 (6)
Blake	0 (1)			0 (1)
Bosnich	17	1		18
Breitkreutz	2 (1)		0 (1)	2 (2)
Carruthers	0 (1)			0 (1)
Cox	6 (9)	2 (1)	1 (1)	9 (11)
Daley	8 (5)			8 (5)
Ehiogu	1 (3)		1	2 (3)
Farrell	1 (1)			1 (1)
Froggatt	16 (1)	2 (1)	1	19 (2)
Houghton	39	4	5	48
Kubicki		1		1
McAvennie	0 (3)			0 (3)
McGrath	42	4	4	50
Parker	37	4	5	46
Regis	7 (6)	0 (2)	1 (1)	8 (9)
Richardson	42	4	5	51
Saunders	35	4	5	44
Small	10 (4)		1	11 (4)
Spink	25	3	5	33
Staunton	42	4	5	51
Teale	39	4	4	47
Yorke	22 (5)	4	2 (2)	28 (7)

Goalscorers

PLAYER	LEAGUE	CUP COMPETITION		TOTAL
		FA CUP	LC	
Saunders	13	2	2	17
Atkinson	11		2	13
Parker	8			8
Yorke	6	1		7
McGrath	4		1	5
Houghton	3	1		4
Richardson	2		1	3
Cox	1	1		2
Daley	2			2
Staunton	2			2
Teale	1		1	2
Barrett	1			1
Froggatt	1			1
Regis	1			1
Opps' o.gs.	1			1

Final Premier League Table

		P	W	D	L	F	A	PTS
1	MANCHESTER U	42	24	12	6	67	31	84
2	ASTON VILLA	42	21	11	10	57	40	74
3	NORWICH C	42	21	9	12	61	65	72
4	BLACKBURN R	42	20	11	11	68	46	71
5	QPR	42	17	12	13	63	55	63
6	LIVERPOOL	42	16	11	15	62	55	59
7	SHEFFIELD W	42	15	14	13	55	51	59
8	TOTTENHAM H	42	16	11	15	60	66	59
9	MANCHESTER C	42	15	12	15	56	51	57
10	ARSENAL	42	15	11	16	40	38	56
11	CHELSEA	42	14	14	14	51	54	56
12	WIMBLEDON	42	14	12	16	56	55	54
13	EVERTON	42	15	8	19	53	55	53
14	SHEFFIELD U	42	14	10	18	54	53	52
15	COVENTRY C	42	13	13	16	52	57	52
16	IPSWICH T	42	12	16	14	50	55	52
17	LEEDS U	42	12	15	15	57	62	51
18	SOUTHAMPTON	42	13	11	18	54	61	50
19	OLDHAM ATH	42	13	10	19	63	74	49
20	CRYSTAL PALACE	42	11	16	15	48	61	49
21	MIDDLESBROUGH	42	11	11	20	54	75	44
22	NOTTINGHAM F	42	10	10	22	41	62	40

Season 1993-94

Premier League

DATE	OPPONENTS	SCORE	GOALSCORERS	ATTENDANCE
Aug 14	QUEENS PARK RANGERS	W 4-1	Atkinson 2, Saunders, Staunton	32,944
Aug 18	Sheffield Wednesday	D 0-0		28,450
Aug 21	Wimbledon	D 2-2	Richardson, Staunton	7,533
Aug 23	MANCHESTER UNITED	L 1-2	Atkinson	39,624
Aug 28	TOTTENHAM HOTSPUR	W 1-0	Staunton (pen)	32,498
Aug 31	Everton	W 1-0	Whittingham	24,022
Sep 11	COVENTRY CITY	D 0-0		31,181
Sep 18	Ipswich Town	W 2-1	Saunders, Townsend	16,617
Sep 25	Oldham Athletic	D 1-1	Saunders	12,836
Oct 2	NEWCASTLE UNITED	L 0-2		37,336
Oct 16	West Ham United	D 0-0		20,425
Oct 23	CHELSEA	W 1-0	Atkinson	29,706
Oct 30	Swindon Town	W 2-1	Teale, Atkinson	16,530
Nov 6	Arsenal	W 2-1	Whittingham, Townsend	31,773
Nov 20	SHEFFIELD UNITED	W 1-0	Whittingham	24,686
Nov 24	SOUTHAMPTON	L 0-2		16,150
Nov 28	Liverpool	L 1-2	Atkinson	38,484
Dec 4	Queens Park Rangers	D 2-2	Richardson, Parker	14,915
Dec 8	SHEFFIELD WEDNESDAY	D 2-2	Cox, Saunders (pen)	20,304
Dec 11	WIMBLEDON	L 0-1		17,940
Dec 19	Manchester United	L 1-3	Cox	44,499
Dec 29	Norwich City	W 2-1	Houghton, Saunders	20,650
Jan 1	BLACKBURN ROVERS	L 0-1		40,903
Jan 15	WEST HAM UNITED	W 3-1	Richardson, Atkinson 2	28,869
Jan 22	Chelsea	D 1-1	Saunders	18,341
Feb 6	LEEDS UNITED	W 1-0	Townsend	26,919
Feb 12	SWINDON TOWN	W 5-0	Saunders 3 (2 pens), Froggatt, Richardson	26,637
Feb 22	MANCHESTER CITY	D 0-0		19,254
Mar 2	Tottenham Hotspur	D 1-1	Parker	17,452
Mar 6	Coventry City	W 1-0	Daley	14,325
Mar 12	IPSWICH TOWN	L 0-1		23,732
Mar 16	Leeds United	L 0-2		33,120
Mar 19	OLDHAM ATHLETIC	L 1-2	Redmond o.g.	21,214
Mar 30	EVERTON	D 0-0		36,044
Apr 2	Manchester City	L 0-3		26,075
Apr 4	NORWICH CITY	D 0-0		25,416
Apr 11	Blackburn Rovers	L 0-1		19,287
Apr 16	Sheffield United	W 2-1	Richardson, Fenton	18,402
Apr 23	ARSENAL	L 1-2	Houghton	31,580
Apr 27	Newcastle United	L 1-5	Beinlich	32,216
Apr 30	Southampton	L 1-4	Saunders	19,003
May 7	LIVERPOOL	W 2-1	Yorke 2	45,347

FA Cup

Jan 8	Exeter City	(Rd 3) W 1-0	Saunders (pen)	10,570
Jan 29	Grimsby Town	(Rd 4) W 2-1	Houghton, Yorke	15,771
Feb 20	Bolton Wanderers	(Rd 5) L 0-1		18,817

League Cup

Sep 21	Birmingham City	(Rd 2/FL) W 1-0	Richardson	27,815
Oct 6	BIRMINGHAM CITY	(Rd 2/SL) W 1-0	Saunders	35,856
Oct 26	Sunderland	(Rd 3) W 4-1	Atkinson 2, Richardson, Houghton	23,692
Nov 30	Arsenal	(Rd 4) W 1-0	Atkinson	26,453
Jan 12	Tottenham Hotspur	(Rd 5) W 2-1	Houghton, Barrett	31,408
Feb 16	Tranmere Rovers	(SF/FL) L 1-3	Atkinson	17,140
Feb 27	TRANMERE ROVERS	(SF/SL) W 3-1*	Saunders, Teale, Atkinson	40,593
Mar 27	Manchester United	(F) W 3-1	Atkinson, Saunders 2 (1 pen)	77,231

*Won 5-4 on penalties.

UEFA Cup

Sep 15	Slovan Bratislava	(Rd 1/FL) D 0-0		10,886
Sep 29	SLOVAN BRATISLAVA	(Rd 1/SL) W 2-1	Atkinson, Townsend	24,461
Oct 19	Deportivo La Coruña	(Rd 2/FL) D 1-1	Saunders	27,500
Nov 3	DEPORTIVO LA CORUÑA	(Rd 2/SL) L 0-1		26,737

MANAGER: Ron Atkinson

CAPTAIN: Kevin Richardson

TOP SCORER: Dean Saunders, 16 (10 league)

BIGGEST WIN: 5-0 v Swindon Town (H), Premier League, 12 February 1994

HIGHEST ATTENDANCE: 77,231 v Manchester United, League Cup final at Wembley, 27 March 1994

MAJOR TRANSFERS IN: Gordon Cowans from Blackburn Rovers, Andy Townsend from Chelsea, Guy Whittingham from Portsmouth

MAJOR TRANSFERS OUT: Cyrille Regis to Wolverhampton Wanderers

---

League & Cup Appearances

PLAYER	LEAGUE	CUP COMPETITION		OTHER	TOTAL
		FA CUP	LC		
Atkinson	29	3	8	4	44
Barrett	39	3	7	3	52
Beinlich	6 (1)				6 (1)
Bosnich	28	3	7 (1)	2	40 (1)
Breitkreutz	1 (1)				1 (1)
Cowans	9 (2)		2	4	15 (2)
Cox	16 (4)	2 (1)	4 (1)	1	23 (6)
Daley	19 (8)	2	5 (1)	2	28 (9)
Ehiogu	14 (3)	0 (1)	0 (1)		14 (5)
Farrell	4				4
Fenton	9 (3)		1 (1)		10 (4)
Froggatt	8 (1)	1	0 (1)		9 (2)
Houghton	25 (5)	3	4 (2)	1 (1)	33 (8)
Kubicki	1 (1)				1 (1)
McGrath	30	2	8	4	44
Parker	17 (2)	1	3		21 (2)
Richardson	40	3	8	4	55
Saunders	37 (1)	3	7	4	51 (1)
Small	8 (1)		1	2	11 (1)
Spink	14 (1)		1	2	17 (1)
Staunton	24	2	5	2	33
Teale	37 (1)	2	7	4	50 (1)
Townsend	32	3	8	4	47
Whittingham	13 (5)	2	2	1	16 (5)
Yorke	2 (10)	0 (2)			2 (12)

Goalscorers

PLAYER	LEAGUE	CUP COMPETITION		OTHER	TOTAL
		FA CUP	LC		
Saunders	10	1	4	1	16
Atkinson	8		6	1	15
Richardson	5		2		7
Houghton	2	1	2		5
Townsend	3			1	4
Staunton	3				3
Whittington	3				3
Yorke	2	1			3
Cox	2				2
Parker	2				2
Teale	1		1		2
Barrett			1		1
Beinlich	1				1
Daley	1				1
Fenton	1				1
Froggatt	1				1
Opps' o.gs.	1				1

Fact File

Stefan Beinlich became the first German-born player to score a league goal for Villa when he netted in the 5-1 defeat at Newcastle on 27 April 1994.

Final Premier League Table

		P	W	D	L	F	A	Pts
1	MANCHESTER U	42	27	11	4	80	38	92
2	BLACKBURN R	42	25	9	8	63	36	84
3	NEWCASTLE U	42	23	8	11	82	41	77
4	ARSENAL	42	18	17	7	53	28	71
5	LEEDS U	42	18	16	8	65	39	70
6	WIMBLEDON	42	18	11	13	56	53	65
7	SHEFFIELD W	42	16	16	10	76	54	64
8	LIVERPOOL	42	17	9	16	59	55	60
9	QPR	42	16	12	14	62	61	60
10	ASTON VILLA	42	15	12	15	46	50	57
11	COVENTRY C	42	14	14	14	43	45	56
12	NORWICH C	42	12	17	13	65	61	53
13	WEST HAM U	42	13	13	16	47	58	52
14	CHELSEA	42	13	12	17	49	53	51
15	TOTTENHAM H	42	11	12	19	54	59	45
16	MANCHESTER C	42	9	18	15	38	49	45
17	EVERTON	42	12	8	22	42	63	44
18	SOUTHAMPTON	42	12	7	23	49	66	43
19	IPSWICH T	42	9	16	17	35	58	43
20	SHEFFIELD U	42	8	18	16	42	60	42
21	OLDHAM ATH	42	9	13	20	42	68	40
22	SWINDON T	42	5	15	22	47	100	30

Season 1994-95

Premier League

DATE	OPPONENTS	SCORE	GOALSCORERS	ATTENDANCE
Aug 20	Everton	D 2-2	Fashanu, Saunders,	35,544
Aug 24	SOUTHAMPTON	D 1-1	Saunders	24,179
Aug 27	CRYSTAL PALACE	D 1-1	Staunton	23,305
Aug 29	Coventry City	W 1-0	Yorke	12,218
Sep 10	IPSWICH TOWN	W 2-0	Staunton, Saunders	22,241
Sep 17	West Ham United	L 0-1		18,326
Sep 24	Blackburn Rovers	L 1 3	Ehiogu	22,694
Oct 1	NEWCASTLE UNITED	L 0-2		29,960
Oct 8	Liverpool	L 2-3	Whittingham, Staunton	32,158
Oct 15	NORWICH CITY	D 1-1	Saunders	22,468
Oct 22	NOTTINGHAM FOREST	L 0-2		29,217
Oct 29	Queens Park Rangers	L 0-2		16,073
Nov 6	MANCHESTER UNITED	L 1-2	Atkinson	32,136
Nov 9	Wimbledon	L 3-4	Parker, Saunders 2	6,221
Nov 19	Tottenham Hotspur	W 4-3	Atkinson, Fenton 2, Saunders	26,899
Nov 27	SHEFFIELD WEDNESDAY	D 1-1	Atkinson	25,082
Dec 3	Leicester City	D 1-1	Whittingham	20,896
Dec 10	EVERTON	D 0-0		29,678
Dec 19	Southampton	L 1-2	Houghton	13,874
Dec 26	Arsenal	D 0-0		34,452
Dec 28	CHELSEA	W 3-0	Sinclair o.g., Yorke, Taylor	32,901
Dec 31	Manchester United	D 2-2	Brightwell o.g., Saunders	22,513
Jan 2	LEEDS UNITED	D 0-0		35,038
Jan 14	QUEENS PARK RANGERS	W 2-1	Fashanu, Ehiogu	26,578
Jan 21	Nottingham forest	W 2-1	Fashanu, Saunders	24,548
Jan 25	TOTTENHAM HOTSPUR	W 1-0	Saunders	40,017
Feb 4	Manchester United	L 0-1		43,795
Feb 11	WIMBLEDON	W 7-1	Reeves o.g., Johnson 3, Saunders 2 (1 pen), Yorke	23,982 23,982
Feb 18	Sheffield Wednesday	W 2-1	Saunders 2	24,063
Feb 22	LEICESTER CITY	D 4-4	Saunders, Staunton, Yorke, Johnson	30,825
Feb 25	Newcastle United	L 1-3	Townsend	34,637
Mar 4	BLACKBURN ROVERS	L 0-1		40,114
Mar 6	COVENTRY CITY	D 0-0		26,186
Mar 18	WEST HAM UNITED	L 0-2		26,682
Apr 1	Ipswich Town	W 1-0	Swailes o.g.	15,710
Apr 4	Crystal Palace	D 0-0		12,606
Apr 15	Chelsea	L 0-1		17,015
Apr 17	ARSENAL	L 0-4		32,005
Apr 29	Leeds United	L 0-1		32,955
May 3	MANCHESTER CITY	D 1-1	Ehiogu	30,133
May 6	LIVERPOOL	W 2-0	Yorke 2	40,154
May 13	Norwich City	D 1-1	Staunton	19,374

FA Cup

Jan 7	Barnsley	(Rd 3) W 2-0	Yorke, Saunders	11,469
Jan 28	Manchester City	(Rd 4) L 0-1		21,177

League Cup

Sep 21	WIGAN ATHLETIC	(Rd 2/FL) W 5-0	Yorke, Atkinson 2, Saunders, Lamptey	12,433
Oct 5	Wigan Athletic	(Rd 2/SL) W 3-0	Lamptey 2, Whittingham	2,633
Oct 26	MIDDLESBROUGH	(Rd 3) W 1-0	Townsend	19,254
Nov 30	Crystal Palace	(Rd 4) L 1-4	Atkinson	12,653

UEFA Cup

Sep 15	Internazionale	(Rd 1/FL) L 0-1		22,639
Sep 29	INTERNAZIONALE	(Rd 1/SL) W 1-0*	Houghton	30,533
Oct 18	Trabzonspor	(Rd 2/FL) L 0-1		27,500
Nov 1	TRABZONSPOR	(Rd 2/SL) W 2-1†	Atkinson, Ehiogu	23,858

*After extra-time, won 4-3 on penalties. †Lost on away goals.

MANAGER: Ron Atkinson

CAPTAIN: Paul McGrath, Kevin Richardson, Shaun Teale

TOP SCORER: Dean Saunders, 17 (15 league)

BIGGEST WIN: 7-1 v Wimbledon (H), Premier League, 11 February 1995

HIGHEST ATTENDANCE: 43,795 v Manchester United (A), Premier League, 4 February 1995

MAJOR TRANSFERS IN: Ian Taylor and Phil King from Sheffield Wednesday, Alan Wright from Blackburn Rovers, Gary Charles and Tommy Johnson from Derby County, John Fashanu from Wimbledon

MAJOR TRANSFERS OUT: Earl Barrett to Everton, Kevin Richardson to Coventry City, Ray Houghton to Crystal Palace, Garry Parker to Leicester City

League & Cup Appearances

PLAYER	LEAGUE	CUP COMPETITION		OTHER	TOTAL
		FA CUP	LC		
Atkinson	11 (5)		2	3	16 (5)
Barrett	24 (1)	2	3	4	33 (1)
Boden	0 (1)				0 (1)
Bosnich	30	1	3		34
Carr	0 (2)				0 (2)
Charles	14 (2)				14 (2)
Ehiogu	38 (1)	2	3	4	47 (1)
Farrell	36		2		38
Fashanu	11 (2)	2		1	14 (2)
Fenton	7 (10)		1 (2)		8 (12)
Houghton	19 (7)		2	3 (1)	24 (8)
Johnson	11 (3)	0 (1)			11 (4)
King	13 (3)		3	4	20 (3)
Lamptey	1 (5)		2 (1)		3 (6)
McGrath	36 (4)	2	3	4	45 (4)
Oakes			1		1
Parker	12 (2)	4		0 (2)	16 (4)
Richardson	18 (1)			4	22 (1)
Saunders	39	2	3	4	48
Small	5				5
Spink	12 (1)	1		4	17 (1)
Staunton	34 (1)	2		4	42 (1)
Taylor	22		2		24
Teale	28	2	2		32
Townsend	32		2	4	40
Whittingham	4 (3)		2 (1)	1 (1)	7 (5)
Wright	8				8
Yorke	33 (4)	2	4		39 (4)

Goalscorers

PLAYER	LEAGUE	CUP COMPETITION		OTHER	TOTAL
		FA CUP	LC		
Saunders	15	1	1		17
Yorke	6	1	1		8
Atkinson	3		3	1	7
Staunton	5				5
Ehiogu	3			1	4
Johnson	4				4
Fashanu	3				3
Lamptey			3		3
Whittingham	2		1		3
Fenton	2				2
Houghton	1			1	2
Townsend	1		1		2
Parker	1				1
Taylor	1				1
Opps' o.gs.	4				4

Fact File

Aston Villa's 7-1 home win over Wimbledon was the Dons' heaviest defeat in 25 years of league football.

Final Premier League Table

		P	W	D	L	F	A	Pts
1	BLACKBURN R	42	27	8	7	80	39	89
2	MANCHESTER U	42	26	10	6	77	28	88
3	NOTTINGHAM F	42	22	11	9	72	43	77
4	LIVERPOOL	42	21	11	10	65	37	74
5	LEEDS U	42	20	13	9	59	38	73
6	NEWCASTLE U	42	20	12	10	67	47	72
7	TOTTENHAM H	42	16	14	12	66	58	62
8	QPR	42	17	9	16	61	59	60
9	WIMBLEDON	42	15	11	16	48	65	56
10	SOUTHAMPTON	42	12	18	12	61	63	54
11	CHELSEA	42	13	15	14	50	55	54
12	ARSENAL	42	13	12	17	52	49	51
13	SHEFFIELD W	42	13	12	17	49	57	51
14	WEST HAM U	42	13	11	18	44	48	50
15	EVERTON	42	11	17	14	44	51	50
16	COVENTRY C	42	12	14	16	44	62	50
17	MANCHESTER C	42	12	13	17	53	64	49
18	ASTON VILLA	42	11	15	16	51	56	48
19	CRYSTAL PALACE	42	11	12	19	34	49	45
20	NORWICH C	42	10	13	19	37	54	43
21	LEICESTER C	42	6	11	25	45	80	29
22	IPSWICH T	42	7	6	29	36	93	27

Season 1995-96

Premier League

DATE	OPPONENTS	SCORE	GOALSCORERS	ATTENDANCE
Aug 19	MANCHESTER UNITED	W 3-1	Taylor, Draper, Yorke (pen)	34,655
Aug 23	Tottenham Hotspur	W 1-0	Ehiogu	26,726
Aug 26	Leeds United	L 0-2		35,086
Aug 30	BOLTON WANDERERS	W 1-0	Yorke	31,770
Sep 9	Blackburn Rovers	D 1-1	Milosevic	27,084
Sep 16	WIMBLEDON	W 2-0	Draper, Taylor	26,928
Sep 23	NOTTINGHAM FOREST	D 1-1	Townsend	33,972
Sep 30	Coventry City	W 3-0	Yorke, Milosevic 2	21,004
Oct 14	CHELSEA	L 0-1		34,992
Oct 21	Arsenal	L 0-2		38,271
Oct 28	EVERTON	W 1-0	Yorke	32,792
Nov 4	West Ham United	W 4-1	Milosevic 2, Johnson, Yorke	23,637
Nov 18	NEWCASTLE UNITED	D 1-1	Johnson	39,167
Nov 20	Southampton	W 1-0	Johnson	13,582
Nov 25	Manchester City	L 0-1		28,027
Dec 2	ARSENAL	D 1-1	Yorke	37,770
Dec 10	Nottingham Forest	D 1-1	Yorke	25,790
Dec 16	COVENTRY CITY	W 4-1	Johnson, Milosevic 3	28,476
Dec 23	Queens Park Rangers	L 0-1		14,778
Jan 1	Middlesbrough	W 2-0	Wright, Johnson	28,535
Jan 13	Manchester United	D 0-0		42,667
Jan 21	TOTTENHAM HOTSPUR	W 2-1	McGrath, Yorke	35,666
Jan 31	LIVERPOOL	L 0-2		39,332
Feb 3	LEEDS UNITED	W 3-0	Yorke 2, Wright	35,982
Feb 10	Bolton Wanderers	W 2-0	Yorke 2	18,099
Feb 24	Wimbledon	D 3-3	Reeves o.g., Yorke (pen), Cunningham o.g.	12,193
Feb 28	BLACKBURN ROVERS	W 2-0	Joachim, Southgate	28,008
Mar 3	Liverpool	L 0-3		39,508
Mar 6	SHEFFIELD WEDNESDAY	W 3-2	Milosevic 2, Townsend	27,893
Mar 9	QUEENS PARK RANGERS	W 4-2	Milosevic, Yorke 2, Yates o.g.	28,220
Mar 16	Sheffield Wednesday	L 0-2		22,964
Mar 19	MIDDLESBROUGH	D 0-0		23,933
Apr 6	Chelsea	W 2-1	Milosevic, Yorke	23,530
Apr 8	SOUTHAMPTON	W 3-0	Taylor, Charles, Yorke	34,059
Apr 14	Newcastle United	L 0-1		36,510
Apr 17	WEST HAM UNITED	D 1-1	McGrath	26,768
Apr 27	MANCHESTER CITY	L 0-1		39,336
May 5	Everton	L 0-1		40,127

FA Cup

Jan 6	Gravesend	(Rd 3) W 3-0	Draper, Milosevic, Johnson	26,021
Jan 28	Sheffield United	(Rd 4) W 1-0	Yorke (pen)	18,749
Feb 17	Ipswich Town	(Rd 5) W 3-1	Draper, Yorke, Taylor	20,748
Mar 13	Nottingham Forest	(QF) W 1-0	Carr	21,067
Mar 31	LIVERPOOL	(SF) L 0-3		39,072

League Cup

Sep 20	PETERBOROUGH UNITED	(Rd 2/FL) W 6-0	Draper, Yorke 2 (2 pen), Johnson, Heald o.g., Southgate	19,602
Oct 3	Peterborough United	(Rd 2/SL) D 1-1	Staunton	5,745
Oct 25	STOCKPORT COUNTY	(Rd 3) W 2-0	Ehiogu, Yorke	17,679
Nov 29	QUEENS PARK RANGERS	(Rd 4) W 1-0	Townsend	24,951
Jan 10	WOLVERHAMPTON WANDERERS	(QF) W 1-0	Johnson	39,277
Feb 14	Arsenal	(SF/FL)D 2-2	Yorke 2	37,562
Feb 21	ARSENAL	(SF/SL) D 0-0		39,334
Mar 24	Leeds United	(F) W 3-0	Milosevic, Taylor, Yorke	77,065

League & Cup Appearances

PLAYER	LEAGUE	CUP COMPETITION		TOTAL
		FA CUP	LC	
Bosnich	38	5	8	51
Browne	2			2
Carr	1	1		2
Charles	34	5	8	47
Davis	0 (2)	0 (1)		0 (3)
Draper	36	5	8	49
Ehiogu	36	5	8	49
Farrelly	1 (4)		0 (1)	1 (5)
Fenton	0 (3)		0 (2)	0 (5)
Hendrie	2 (1)			2 (1)
Joachim	4 (7)			4 (7)
Johnson	17 (6)	3 (1)	4	24 (7)
McGrath	29 (1)	3 (1)	5 (1)	37 (3)
Milosevic	36 (1)	5	7	48 (1)
Murray	3			3
Scimeca	7 (10)	2	2 (1)	11 (11)
Southgate	31	4	8	43
Spink	0 (2)			0 (2)
Staunton	11 (2)	1 (1)	2 (2)	14 (5)
Taylor	24 (1)	2 (1)	5 (1)	31 (3)
Tiler	1			1
Townsend	32 (1)	4	8	44 (1)
Wright	38	5	8	51
Yorke	35	5	8	48

Goalscorers

PLAYER	LEAGUE	CUP COMPETITION		TOTAL
		FA CUP	LC	
Yorke	17	2	6	25
Milosevic	12	1	1	12
Johnson	5	1	2	8
Draper	2	2	1	5
Taylor	3	1	1	5
Townsend	2		1	3
Ehiogu	1		1	2
McGrath	2			2
Southgate	1		1	2
Wright	2			2
Charles	1			1
Joachim	1			1
Carr		1		1
Staunton			1	1
Opps' o.gs.	3		1	4

Fact File

Villa manager Brian Little signed striker Savo Milosevic for £3.5 million – after watching him on video!

MANAGER: Brian Little

CAPTAIN: Gareth Southgate

TOP SCORER: Dwight Yorke, 25 (17 league)

BIGGEST WIN: 6-0 v Peterborough United (H), League Cup Second Round First Leg, 20 September 1995

HIGHEST ATTENDANCE: 77,065 v Leeds United, League Cup final at Wembley, 24 March 1996

MAJOR TRANSFERS IN: Savo Milosevic from Partizan Belgrade, Mark Draper from Leicester City, Gareth Southgate from Crystal Palace

MAJOR TRANSFERS OUT: Dalian Atkinson to Fenerbahce, Nigel Spink to West Bromwich Albion

Final Premier League Table

		P	W	D	L	F	A	PTS
1	MANCHESTER U	38	25	7	6	73	35	82
2	NEWCASTLE U	38	24	6	8	66	37	78
3	LIVERPOOL	38	20	11	7	70	34	71
4	ASTON VILLA	38	18	9	11	52	35	63
5	ARSENAL	38	17	12	9	49	32	63
6	EVERTON	38	17	10	11	64	44	61
7	BLACKBURN R	38	18	7	13	61	47	61
8	TOTTENHAM H	38	16	13	9	50	38	61
9	NOTTINGHAM F	38	15	13	10	50	54	58
10	WEST HAM U	38	14	9	15	43	52	51
11	CHELSEA	38	12	14	12	46	44	50
12	MIDDLESBROUGH	38	11	10	17	35	50	43
13	LEEDS U	38	12	7	19	40	57	43
14	WIMBLEDON	38	10	11	17	55	70	41
15	SHEFFIELD W	38	10	10	18	48	61	40
16	COVENTRY C	38	8	14	16	42	60	38
17	SOUTHAMPTON	38	9	11	18	34	52	38
18	MANCHESTER C	38	9	11	18	33	58	38
19	QPR	38	9	6	23	38	57	33
20	BOLTON W	38	8	5	25	39	71	29

Season 1996-97

Premier League

DATE	OPPONENTS	SCORE	GOALSCORERS	ATTENDANCE
Aug 17	Sheffield Wednesday	L 1-2	Johnson	26,861
Aug 21	BLACKBURN ROVERS	W 1-0	Southgate	32,457
Aug 24	DERBY COUNTY	W 2-0	Joachim, Johnson (pen)	34,646
Sep 4	Everton	W 1-0	Ehiogu	39,115
Sep 7	ARSENAL	D 2-2	Milosevic 2	37,944
Sep 15	Chelsea	D 1-1	Townsend	27,729
Sep 21	MANCHESTER UNITED	D 0 0		39,339
Sep 30	Newcastle United	L 3-4	Yorke 3	36,400
Oct 12	Tottenham Hotspur	L 0-1		32,847
Oct 19	LEEDS UNITED	W 2-0	Yorke, Johnson	39,051
Oct 26	Sunderland	L 0-1		21,059
Nov 2	NOTTINGHAM FOREST	W 2-0	Tiler, Yorke	35,310
Nov 16	LEICESTER CITY	L 1-3	Yorke	36,193
Nov 23	Coventry City	W 2-1	Joachim, Staunton	21,340
Nov 30	MIDDLESBROUGH	W 1-0	Yorke (pen)	39,053
Dec 4	West Ham United	W 2-0	Ehiogu, Yorke	19,105
Dec 7	Southampton	W 1-0	Townsend	15,232
Dec 22	WIMBLEDON	W 5-0	Yorke 2, Milosevic 2, Taylor	28,875
Dec 26	CHELSEA	L 0-2		39,339
Dec 28	Arsenal	D 2-2	Milosevic, Yorke	38,130
Jan 1	Manchester United	D 0-0		55,113
Jan 11	NEWCASTLE UNITED	D 2-2	Yorke, Milosevic	39,339
Jan 18	Liverpool	L 0-3		40,489
Jan 29	SHEFFIELD WEDNESDAY	L 0-1		26,726
Feb 1	SUNDERLAND	W 1-0	Milosevic	32,491
Feb 19	COVENTRY CITY	W 2-1	Yorke 2	30,409
Feb 22	Nottingham Forest	D 0-0		25,239
Mar 2	LIVERPOOL	W 1-0	Taylor	39,339
Mar 5	Leicester City	L 0-1		20,626
Mar 15	WEST HAM UNITED	D 0-0		35,992
Mar 22	Blackburn Rovers	W 2-0	Johnson, Yorke	24,274
Apr 5	EVERTON	W 3-1	Milosevic, Staunton, Yorke	39,339
Apr 9	Wimbledon	W 2-0	Milosevic, Wright	9,015
Apr 12	Derby County	L 1-2	Joachim	18,071
Apr 19	TOTTENHAM HOTSPUR	D 1-1	Yorke	39,339
Apr 22	Leeds United	D 0-0		26,897
May 3	Middlesbrough	L 2-3	Ehiogu, Milosevic	30,074
May 11	SOUTHAMPTON	W 1-0	Dryden o.g.	39,339

FA Cup

Jan 14	Notts County	(Rd 3) D 0-0		13,315
Jan 22	NOTTS COUNTY	(R) W 3-0	Yorke 2, Ehiogu	25,006
Jan 25	Derby County	(Rd 4) L 1-3	Curcic	17,977

League Cup

Oct 23	Leeds United	(Rd 3) W 2-1	Taylor, Yorke (pen)	15,803
Nov 26	Wimbledon	(Rd 4) L 0-1		7,573

UEFA Cup

Sep 10	HELSINGBORGS	(Rd 1/FL) D 1-1	Johnson	25,818
Sep 24	Helsingborgs	(Rd 1/SL) D 0-0		16,000

League & Cup Appearances

PLAYER	LEAGUE	CUP COMPETITION		OTHER	TOTAL
		FA CUP	LC		
Bosnich	20	3	1		24
Curcic	17 (5)	2	1		20 (5)
Draper	28 (1)		1 (1)	2	31 (1)
Ehiogu	38	3	2	2	45
Farrelly	1 (2)				1 (2)
Hendrie	0 (4)	1 (2)			1 (6)
Hughes	4 (3)				4 (3)
Joachim	3 (12)	1	1		5 (12)
Johnson	10 (10)	2	1	1 (1)	14 (11)
McGrath				0 (1)	0 (1)
Milosevic	29 (1)	3	0 (1)	2	34 (1)
Murray	1				1
Nelson	33 (1)	0 (1)	2	2	37 (2)
Oakes	18 (2)		1		19 (2)
Scimeca	11 (6)	3	1 (1)		15 (7)
Southgate	28 (1)	3	1	2	34 (1)
Staunton	30 (2)	2	1	2	35 (2)
Taylor	29 (5)		2 (1)	1	32 (5)
Tiler	9 (2)	2	1		12 (2)
Townsend	34	3	2	2	41
Wright	38	3	2	2	45
Yorke	37	2	2	2	43

Goalscorers

PLAYER	LEAGUE	CUP COMPETITION		OTHER	TOTAL
		FA CUP	LC		
Yorke	17	2	1		20
Milosevic	10				10
Johnson	4			1	5
Ehiogu	3	1			4
Joachim	3				3
Taylor	2		1		3
Staunton	2				2
Townsend	2				2
Curcic		1			1
Southgate	1				1
Tiler	1				1
Wright	1				1
Opps' o.gs.	1				1

Fact File

A crowd figure of 39,339 was officially declared on seven occasions for Premiership games at Villa Park during the 1996-97 season.

MANAGER: Brian Little

CAPTAIN: Gareth Southgate

TOP SCORER: Dwight Yorke, 20 (17 league)

BIGGEST WIN: 5-0 v Wimbledon (H), Premier League, 22 December 1996

HIGHEST ATTENDANCE: 55,113 v Manchester United (A), Premier League, 1 January 1997

MAJOR TRANSFERS IN: Sasa Curcic from Bolton Wanderers, Fernando Nelson from Sporting Lisbon

MAJOR TRANSFERS OUT: Franz Carr to Reggiana (Italy)

Final Premier League Table

1	MANCHESTER U	38	21	12	5	76	44	75
2	NEWCASTLE U	38	19	11	8	73	40	68
3	ARSENAL	38	19	11	8	62	32	68
4	LIVERPOOL	38	19	11	8	62	37	68
5	ASTON VILLA	38	17	10	11	47	34	61
6	CHELSEA	38	16	11	11	58	55	59
7	SHEFFIELD W	38	14	15	9	50	51	57
8	WIMBLEDON	38	15	11	12	49	46	56
9	LEICESTER C	38	12	11	15	46	54	47
10	TOTTENHAM H	38	13	7	18	44	51	46
11	LEEDS U	38	11	13	14	28	38	46
12	DERBY CO	38	11	13	14	45	58	46
13	BLACKBURN R	38	9	15	14	42	43	42
14	WEST HAM U	38	10	12	16	39	48	42
15	EVERTON	38	10	12	16	44	57	42
16	SOUTHAMPTON	38	10	11	17	50	56	41
17	COVENTRY C	38	9	14	15	38	54	41
18	SUNDERLAND	38	10	10	18	35	53	40
19	MIDDLESBROUGH	38	10	12	16	51	60	39
20	NOTTINGHAM F	38	6	16	16	31	59	34

MIDDLESBROUGH DEDUCTED THREE POINTS FOR FAILURE TO FULFIL A FIXTURE ON A GIVEN DATE.

Season 1997-98

Premier League

DATE	OPPONENTS	SCORE	GOALSCORERS	ATTENDANCE
Aug 9	Leicester City	L 0-1		20.304
Aug 12	BLACKBURN ROVERS	L 0-4		37,112
Aug 23	Newcastle United	L 0-1		36,783
Aug 27	Tottenham Hotspur	L 2-3	Yorke, Collymore	26,317
Aug 30	LEEDS UNITED	W 1-0	Yorke	39,027
Sep 13	Barnsley	W 3-0	Ehiogu, Draper, Taylor	18,649
Sep 20	DERBY COUNTY	W 2-1	Yorke, Joachim	35,444
Sep 22	Liverpool	L 0-3		34,843
Sep 27	SHEFFIELD WEDNESDAY	D 2-2	Staunton, Taylor	32,044
Oct 4	Bolton Wanderers	W 1-0	Milosevic	24,196
Oct 18	WIMBLEDON	L 1-2	Taylor	32,087
Oct 26	Arsenal	D 0-0		38,061
Nov 1	CHELSEA	L 0-2		39,372
Nov 8	Crystal Palace	D 1-1	Joachim	21,097
Nov 22	EVERTON	W 2-1	Milosvic, Ehiogu	36,389
Nov 29	West Ham United	L 1-2	Yorke	24,976
Dec 6	COVENTRY CITY	W 3-0	Collymore, Hendrie, Joachim	33,250
Dec 15	Manchester United	L 0-1		55,151
Dec 20	SOUTHAMPTON	D 1-1	Taylor	29,343
Dec 26	TOTTENHAM HOTSPUR	W 4-1	Draper 2, Collymore 2	38,644
Dec 28	Leeds United	D 1-1	Milosevic	36,287
Jan 10	LEICESTER CITY	D 1-1	Joachim	36,429
Jan 17	Blackburn Rovers	L 0-5		24,834
Feb 1	NEWCASTLE UNITED	L 0-1		38,266
Feb 6	Derby County	W 1-0	Yorke	30,251
Feb 18	MANCHESTER UNITED	L 0-2		39,372
Feb 21	Wimbledon	L 1-2	Milosevic	13,131
Feb 28	LIVERPOOL	W 2-1	Collymore 2	39,377
Mar 8	Chelsea	W 1-0	Joachim	33,018
Mar 11	BARNSLEY	L 0-1		29,519
Mar 14	CRYSTAL PALACE	W 3-1	Taylor, Milosevic 2 (1 pen)	33,781
Mar 28	Everton	W 4-1	Joachim, Charles, Yorke 2 (1 pen)	36,471
Apr 4	WEST HAM UNITED	W 2-0	Joachim, Milosevic	39,372
Apr 11	Coventry City	W 2-1	Yorke 2	22,792
Apr 18	Southampton	W 2-1	Hendrie, Yorke	15,238
Apr 25	BOLTON WANDERERS	L 1-3	Taylor	38,392
May 2	Sheffield Wednesday	W 3-1	Yorke, Hendrie, Joachim	34,177
May 10	ARSENAL	W 1-0	Yorke (pen)	39,372

FA Cup

DATE	OPPONENTS		SCORE	GOALSCORERS	ATTENDANCE
Jan 3	Portsmouth	(Rd 3)	D 2-2	Staunton, Grayson	16,013
Jan 14	PORTSMOUTH	(R)	W 1-0	Milosevic	23,355
Jan 24	WEST BROMWICH ALBION	(Rd 4)	W 4-0	Grayson, Yorke 2, Collymore	39,372
Feb 14	COVENTRY CITY		L 0-1		36,979

League Cup

DATE	OPPONENTS		SCORE	ATTENDANCE
Oct 15	West Ham United	(Rd 3)	L 0-2	20,360

UEFA Cup

DATE	OPPONENTS		SCORE	GOALSCORERS	ATTENDANCE
Sep 16	Bordeaux	(Rd 1/FL)	D 0-0		16,000
Sep 30	BORDEAUX	(Rd 1/SL)	W 1-0	Milosevic	33,072
Oct 21	Athletic Bilbao	(Rd 2/FL)	D 0-0		46,000
Nov 4	ATHLETIC BILBAO	(Rd 2/SL)	W 2-1	Taylor, Yorke	35,915
Nov 25	Steaua Bucharest	(Rd 3/FL)	L 1-2	Yorke	25,000
Dec 9	STEAUA BUCHAREST	(Rd 3/SL)	W 2-0	Milosevic, Taylor	35,102
May 3	Atlético Madrid	(QF/FL)	L 0-1		47,000
May 17	ATLÉTICO MADRID	(QF/SL)	W 2-1	Taylor, Collymore	39,163

MANAGER: Brian Little, John Gregory

CAPTAIN: Gareth Southgate, Andy Townsend

TOP SCORER: Dwight Yorke, 16 (12 league)

BIGGEST WIN: 4-0 v West Bromwich Albion (H), FA Cup Fourth Round, 24 January 1998

HIGHEST ATTENDANCE: 55,151 v Manchester United (A), Premier League, 15 December 1997

MAJOR TRANSFERS IN: Stan Collymore from Liverpool, Simon Grayson from Leicester City

MAJOR TRANSFERS OUT: Sasa Curcic to Crystal Palace, Andy Townsend to Middlesbrough

League & Cup Appearances

PLAYER	LEAGUE	CUP COMPETITION		OTHER	TOTAL
		FA CUP	LC		
Barry	1 (1)				1 (1)
Bosnich	30	4	1	7	42
Byfield	1 (6)	0 (1)			1 (7)
Charles	14 (4)	0 (1)	0 (1)	2 (3)	16 (9)
Collymore	23 (2)	4	1	6 (1)	34 (3)
Curcic	3 (4)		0 (1)	0 (1)	3 (6)
Draper	31	4	1	7	43
Ehiogu	37	4	1	6	48
Grayson	28 (5)	4	0 (1)	4 (2)	36 (8)
Hendrie	13 (4)	2 (2)		2 (1)	17 (7)
Joachim	16 (10)	1 (1)		1 (1)	18 (12)
Milosevic	19 (4)	2	1	6	28 (4)
Nelson	21 (4)	1	1	5 (2)	28 (6)
Oakes	8			1	9
Scimeca	16 (5)	2 (1)	1	4	23 (6)
Southgate	32	3	1	7	43
Staunton	27	4		7 (1)	38 (1)
Taylor	30 (2)	3	1	8	42 (2)
Townsend	3				3
Walker	0 (1)				0 (1)
Wright	35 (2)	4	1	8	48 (2)
Yorke	30	2	1	7	40

Goalscorers

PLAYER	LEAGUE	CUP COMPETITION		OTHER	TOTAL
		FA CUP	LC		
Yorke	12	2		2	16
Milosevic	7	1		2	10
Taylor	6			3	9
Collymore	6	1		1	8
Joachim	8				8
Draper	3				3
Hendrie	3				3
Ehiogu	2				2
Grayson		2			2
Staunton	1	1			2
Charles	1				1

Fact File

Coventry City registered their first-ever victory at Villa Park when winning a Fifth Round FA Cup-tie 1-0 on 14 February 1998.

Final Premier League Table

		P	W	D	L	F	A	Pts
1	ARSENAL	38	23	9	6	68	33	78
2	MANCHESTER U	38	23	8	7	73	26	77
3	LIVERPOOL	38	18	11	9	68	42	65
4	CHELSEA	38	20	3	15	71	43	63
5	LEEDS U	38	17	8	13	57	46	59
6	BLACKBURN R	38	16	10	12	57	52	58
7	ASTON VILLA	38	17	6	15	49	48	57
8	WEST HAM U	38	16	8	14	56	57	56
9	DERBY CO	38	16	7	15	52	49	55
10	LEICESTER C	38	13	14	11	51	41	53
11	COVENTRY C	38	12	16	10	46	44	52
12	SOUTHAMPTON	38	14	6	18	50	55	48
13	NEWCASTLE U	38	11	11	16	35	44	44
14	TOTTENHAM H	38	11	11	16	44	56	44
15	WIMBLEDON	38	10	14	14	34	46	44
16	SHEFFIELD W	38	12	8	18	52	67	44
17	EVERTON	38	9	13	16	41	56	40
18	BOLTON W	38	9	13	16	41	61	40
19	BARNSLEY	38	10	5	23	37	82	35
20	CRYSTAL PALACE	38	8	9	21	37	71	33

Season 1998-99

Premier League

DATE	OPPONENTS	SCORE	GOALSCORERS	ATTENDANCE
Aug 15	Everton	D 0-0		40,112
Aug 23	MIDDLESBROUGH	W 3-1	Joachim, Charles, Thompson	29,559
Aug 29	Sheffield Wednesday	W 1-0	Joachim	25,989
Sep 9	NEWCASTLE UNITED	W 1-0	Hendrie (pen)	39,241
Sep 12	WIMBLEDON	W 2-0	Merson, Taylor	32,959
Sep 19	Leeds United	D 0-0		33,162
Sep 26	DERBY COUNTY	W 1-0	Merson	38,007
Oct 3	Coventry City	W 2-1	Taylor	22,650
Oct 17	West Ham United	D 0-0		26,002
Oct 24	LEICESTER CITY	D 1-1	Ehiogu	39,241
Nov 7	TOTTENHAM HOTSPUR	W 3-2	Dublin 2, Collymore	39,241
Nov 14	Southampton	W 4-1	Dublin 3, Merson	15,242
Nov 21	LIVERPOOL	L 2-4	Dublin 2	39,241
Nov 28	Nottingham Forest	D 2-2	Joachim 2	25,753
Dec 5	MANCHESTER UNITED	D 1-1	Joachim	39,241
Dec 9	Chelsea	L 1-2	Hendrie	34,765
Dec 13	ARSENAL	W 3-2	Joachim, Dublin 2	39,217
Dec 21	Charlton Athletic	W 1-0	Rufus o.g.	20,043
Dec 26	Blackburn Rovers	L 1-2	Scimeca	27,536
Dec 28	SHEFFIELD WEDNESDAY	W 2-1	Southgate, Ehiogu	39,217
Jan 9	Middlesbrough	D 0-0		34,643
Jan 18	EVERTON	W 3-0	Joachim 2, Merson	32,488
Jan 30	Newcastle United	L 1-2	Merson	36,766
Feb 6	BLACKBURN ROVERS	L 1-3	Joachim	37,404
Feb 17	LEEDS UNITED	L 1-2	Scimeca	37,510
Feb 21	Wimbledon	D 0-0		15,582
Feb 27	COVENTRY CITY	L 1-4	Dublin (pen)	38,799
Mar 10	Derby County	L 1-2	Thompson	26,836
Mar 13	Tottenham Hotspur	L 0-1		35,963
Mar 21	CHELSEA	L 0-3		39,217
Apr 2	WEST HAM UNITED	D 0-0		36,813
Apr 6	Leicester City	D 2-2	Hendrie, Joachim	20,652
Apr 10	SOUTHAMPTON	W 3-0	Draper, Joachim, Dublin	32,203
Apr 17	Liverpool	W 1-0	Taylor	44,306
Apr 24	NOTTINGHAM FOREST	W 2-0	Draper, Barry	34,492
May 1	Manchester United	L 1-2	Joachim	55,189
May 8	CHARLTON ATHLETIC	L 3-4	Barry, Joachim 2	37,705
May 16	Arsenal	L 0-1		38,308

FA Cup

Jan 2	HULL CITY	(Rd 3) W 3-0	Collymore 2, Joachim	39,217
Jan 4	FULHAM	(Rd 4) L 0-2		35,260

League Cup

Oct 28	Chelsea	(Rd 3) L 1-4	Draper	26,790

UEFA Cup

Sep 15	STROMSGODSET	(Rd 1/Fl) W 3-2	Charles, Vassell 2	28,893
Sep 29	Stromsgodset	(Rd 1/SL) W 3-0	Collymore 3	4,835
Oct 20	Celta Vigo	(Rd 2/FL) W 1-0	Joachim	25,000
Nov 3	CELTA VIGO	(Rd 2/SL) L 1-3	Collymore	29,910

League & Cup Appearances

PLAYER	LEAGUE	CUP COMPETITION		OTHER	TOTAL
		FA CUP	LC		
Barry	27 (5)	2		3	32 (5)
Bosnich	15			2	17
Byfield			1	1	2
Calderwood	8				8
Charles	10 (1)	0 (1)	1	4	15 (2)
Collymore	11 (9)	1		3	15 (9)
Delaney	0 (2)				0 (2)
Draper	13 (10)	1	1	3 (1)	18 (11)
Dublin	24				24
Ehiogu	23 (2)	2	1	3	29 (2)
Farraresi				0 (1)	0 (1)
Grayson	4 (11)	0 (1)	1	2 (1)	7 (13)
Hendrie	31 (1)	2		3	36 (1)
Jaszczun			0 (1)		0 (1)
Joachim	29 (7)	2	1	4	36 (7)
Lescott		0 (1)			0 (1)
Merson	21 (5)	1			22 (5)
Oakes	23	2	1	2	28
Rachel	0 (1)				0 (1)
Scimeca	16 (2)	2		1 (2)	20 (4)
Southgate	38	2		4	44
Stone	9 (1)				9 (1)
Taylor	11 (2)		1	2 (1)	15 (3)
Thompson	20 (5)		0 (1)	3	23 (6)
Vassell	0 (6)	0 (1)	0 (1)	0 (3)	0 (11)
Watson	26 (1)	2	1		29 (1)
Wright	38	2	1	4	45
Yorke	1				1

Goalscorers

PLAYER	LEAGUE	CUP COMPETITION		OTHER	TOTAL
		FA CUP	LC		
Joachim	14	1		1	16
Dublin	11				11
Collymore	1	2		4	7
Merson	5				5
Taylor	4				4
Draper	2		1		3
Hendrie	3				3
Barry	2				2
Charles	1			1	2
Ehiogu	2				2
Scimeca	2				2
Thompson	2				2
Vassell				2	2
Southgate	1				1
Opps' o.gs.	1				1

Fact File

Stan Collymore became the first Villa player since Peter Withe in 1983 to score a hat-trick in a European game.

MANAGER: John Gregory

CAPTAIN: Ugo Ehiogu, Paul Merson

TOP SCORER: Julian Joachim, 16 (14 league)

BIGGEST WIN: 4-1 v Southampton (A), Premier League, 14 November 1998

HIGHEST ATTENDANCE: 55,189 v Manchester United (A), Premier League, 1 May 1999

MAJOR TRANSFERS IN: Dion Dublin from Coventry City, Paul Merson from Middlesbrough, Steve Stone from Nottingham Forest, Alan Thompson from Bolton Wanderers, Steve Watson from Newcastle United

MAJOR TRANSFERS OUT: Savo Milosevic to Real Zaragoza, Steve Staunton to Liverpool

Final Premier League Table

		P	W	D	L	F	A	Pts
1	MANCHESTER UNITED	38	22	13	3	80	37	79
2	ARSENAL	38	22	12	4	59	17	78
3	CHELSEA	38	20	15	3	57	30	67
4	LEEDS UNITED	38	18	13	7	62	34	67
5	WEST HAM UNITED	38	16	9	13	46	53	57
6	ASTON VILLA	38	15	10	13	51	46	55
7	LIVERPOOL	38	15	9	14	68	49	54
8	DERBY COUNTY	38	13	13	12	40	45	52
9	MIDDLESBROUGH	38	12	15	11	48	54	51
10	LEICESTER CITY	38	12	13	13	40	46	49
11	TOTTENHAM HOTSPUR	38	11	14	13	47	50	47
12	SHEFFIELD WEDNESDAY	38	13	7	18	41	42	46
13	NEWCASTLE UNITED	38	11	13	14	48	54	46
14	EVERTON	38	11	10	17	42	47	43
15	COVENTRY CITY	38	11	9	18	39	51	42
16	WIMBLEDON	38	10	12	16	40	63	42
17	SOUTHAMPTON	38	11	8	19	37	64	41
18	CHARLTON ATHLETIC	38	8	12	18	41	56	36
19	BLACKBURN ROVERS	38	7	14	17	38	52	35
20	NOTTINGHAM FOREST	38	7	9	22	35	69	30

Season 1999-2000

Premier League

DATE	OPPONENTS	SCORE	GOALSCORERS	ATTENDANCE
Aug 7	Newcastle United	W 1-0	Joachim	36,376
Aug 11	EVERTON	W 3-0	Joachim, Dublin, Taylor	30,337
Aug 16	WEST HAM UNITED	D 2-2	Dublin 2	26,250
Aug 21	Chelsea	L 0-1		35,071
Aug 24	Watford	W 1-0	Delaney	19,161
Aug 28	MIDDLESBROUGH	W 1-0	Dublin	28,728
Sep 11	Arsenal	L 1-3	Joachim	38,093
Sep 18	BRADFORD CITY	W 1-0	Dublin	28,083
Sep 25	Leicester City	L 1-3	Dublin	19,917
Oct 2	LIVERPOOL	D 0-0		39,217
Oct 18	Sunderland	L 1-2	Dublin	39,866
Oct 23	WIMBLEDON	D 1-1	Dublin	27,160
Oct 30	Manchester United	L 0-3		55,211
Nov 6	SOUTHAMPTON	L 0-1		26,474
Nov 22	Coventry City	L 1-2	Dublin	20,174
Nov 27	Everton	D 0-0		34,750
Dec 4	NEWCASTLE UNITED	L 0-1		34,531
Dec 18	SHEFFIELD WEDNESDAY	W 2-1	Merson, Taylor	23,885
Dec 26	Derby County	W 2-0	Boateng, Taylor	33,222
Dec 29	TOTTENHAM HOTSPUR	D 1-1	Taylor	39,217
Jan 3	Leeds United	W 2-1	Southgate	40,027
Jan 15	West Ham United	D 1-1	Taylor	24,237
Jan 22	CHELSEA	D 0-0		33,704
Feb 5	WATFORD	W 4-0	Stone, Merson 2, Walker	27,647
Feb 14	Middlesbrough	W 4-0	Carbone, Summerbell o.g., Joachim 2	31,591
Feb 26	Bradford City	D 1-1	Merson	18,276
Mar 5	ARSENAL	D 1-1	Walker	36,930
Mar 11	COVENTRY CITY	W 1-0	Ehiogu	33,177
Mar 15	Liverpool	D 0-0		43,615
Mar 18	Southampton	L 0-2		15,218
Mar 25	DERBY COUNTY	W 2-0	Carbone, Boateng	28,613
Apr 5	Sheffield Wednesday	W 1-0	Thompson	18,136
Apr 9	LEEDS UNITED	W 1-0	Joachim	33,889
Apr 15	Tottenham Hotspur	W 4-2	Dublin 2 (1 pen), Carbone, Wright	35,304
Apr 22	LEICESTER CITY	D 2-2	Thompson, Merson	31,229
Apr 29	SUNDERLAND	D 1-1	Barry	33,949
May 6	Wimbledon	D 2-2	Hendrie, Dublin	19,188
May 14	MANCHESTER UNITED	L 0-1		39,217

FA Cup

Dec 11	DARLINGTON	(Rd 3) W 2-1	Carbone, Dublin	22,101
Jan 8	SOUTHAMPTON	(Rd 4) W 1-0	Southgate	25,025
Jan 30	LEEDS UNITED	(RD 5) W 3-2	Carbone 3	30,026
Feb 20	Everton	(Rd 6) W 2-1	Stone, Carbone	35,331
Apr 2	Bolton Wanderers	(SF) D 0-0†		62,828
May 20	Chelsea§	(F) L 0-1		73,876

†Villa won on penalties. §Played at Wembley.

League Cup

Sep 14	Chester City	(Rd 2 FL) W 1-0	Hendrie	4,364
Sep 21	CHESTER CITY	(Rd 2 SL) W 5-0	Boateng, Hendrie 2, Taylor, Thompson	22,613
Oct 13	MANCHESTER UNITED	(Rd 3) W 3-0	Joachim, Taylor, Stone	33,815
Dec 1	SOUTHAMPTON	(Rd 4) W 4-0	Watson, Joachim, Dublin 2	17,608
Dec 15	West Ham United‡	(Rd 5) D 2-2*	Taylor, Dublin	
Jan 11	West Ham United	(R) W 3-1*	Taylor 2, Joachim	25,592
Jan 25	LEICESTER CITY	(SF FL) D 0-0		28,037
Feb 2	Leicester City	(SF SL) L 0-1		21,843

*After extra-time. ‡Villa lost 5-4 on pens. Match ordered to be replayed as Hammers fielded an ineligible player.

MANAGER: John Gregory

CAPTAIN: Gareth Southgate, Paul Merson

TOP SCORER: Dion Dublin, 16 (12 league)

BIGGEST WIN: 5-0 v Chester City, League Cup Second Round Second Leg, 21 September 1999

HIGHEST ATTENDANCE: 73,876 v Chelsea, FA Cup final at Wembley, 20 May 2000

MAJOR TRANSFERS IN: George Boateng from Coventry, Benito Carbone from Sheffield Wednesday, David James from Liverpool

MAJOR TRANSFERS OUT: Colin Calderwood to Nottingham Forest, Mark Draper to Southampton

---

League & Cup Appearances

PLAYER	LEAGUE	CUP COMPETITION		TOTAL
		FA CUP	LC	
Barry	30	6	8	44
Bewers	0 (1)			0 (1)
Boateng	30 (3)	5	7	42 (3)
Carbone	22 (2)	6		28 (2)
Cutler	0 (1)			0 (1)
Delaney	25 (3)	4 (1)	1 (2)	30 (6)
Draper	0 (1)			0 (1)
Dublin	23 (3)	2 (1)		29 (4)
Ehiogu	31	6	7	44
Enckelman	9 (1)	3	1	13 (1)
Hrayib	1 (4)		1	2 (4)
Hendrie	18 (11)	0 (4)	4 (1)	22 (16)
James	29	5	5	39
Joachim	27 (6)	4 (2)	7 (1)	38 (9)
Merson	24 (8)	6	5 (2)	35 (10)
Samuel	5 (4)		0 (1)	5 (5)
Southgate	31	6	6	43
Stone	10 (14)	2 (4)	3 (3)	15 (21)
Taylor	25 (4)	4 (1)	7 (1)	36 (6)
Thompson	16 (5)	1	3 (2)	20 (7)
Vassell	1 (10)	0 (1)	1 (4)	2 (15)
Walker	2 (3)		1 (1)	3 (4)
Watson	13 (1)	2	7 (1)	22 (2)
Wright	31 (1)	6	5	42 (1)

Goalscorers

PLAYER	LEAGUE	CUP COMPETITION		TOTAL
		FA CUP	LC	
Dublin	12	1	3	16
Taylor	5		5	10
Joachim	6		3	9
Carbone	3	5		8
Merson	5			5
Hendrie	1		3	4
Boateng	2		1	3
Southgate	2	1		3
Stone	1	1	1	3
Thompson	2		1	3
Walker	2			2
Barry	1			1
Delaney	1			1
Ehiogu	1			1
Watson			1	1
Wright	1			1
Opps' o.gs.	1			1

Fact File

The winning goal in the 1999 FA Cup final was scored in the 72nd minute by Roberto Di Matteo to break Villa fans' hearts.

Final Premier League Table

		P	W	D	L	F	A	Pts
1	MANCHESTER UNITED	38	28	7	3	97	45	91
2	ARSENAL	38	22	7	9	73	43	73
3	LEEDS UNITED	38	21	6	11	58	43	69
4	LIVERPOOL	38	19	10	9	51	30	67
5	CHELSEA	38	18	11	9	53	34	65
6	ASTON VILLA	38	15	13	10	46	35	58
7	SUNDERLAND	38	16	10	12	57	56	58
8	LEICESTER CITY	38	16	7	15	55	55	55
9	WEST HAM UNITED	38	15	10	13	52	53	55
10	TOTTENHAM HOTSPUR	38	15	8	15	57	49	53
11	NEWCASTLE UNITED	38	14	10	14	63	54	52
12	MIDDLESBROUGH	38	14	10	14	46	52	52
13	EVERTON	38	12	14	12	59	49	50
14	COVENTRY CITY	38	12	8	18	47	54	44
15	SOUTHAMPTON	38	12	8	18	45	62	44
16	DERBY COUNTY	38	9	11	18	44	57	38
17	BRADFORD CITY	38	9	9	20	38	68	36
18	WIMBLEDON	38	7	12	19	46	74	33
19	SHEFFIELD WEDNESDAY	38	8	7	23	38	70	31
20	WATFORD	38	6	6	26	35	77	24

Season 2000-01

Premier League

DATE	OPPONENTS	SCORE	GOALSCORERS	ATTENDANCE
Aug 19	Leicester City	D 0-0		21,455
Aug 27	CHELSEA	D 1-1	Nilis	27,056
Sep 6	Liverpool	L 1-3	Stone	43,360
Sep 9	Ipswich Town	W 2-1	Hendrie, Dublin	22,064
Sep 16	BRADFORD CITY	W 2-0	Southgate, Dublin (pen)	27,849
Sep 23	Middlesbrough	D 1-1	Joachim	27,556
Sep 30	DERBY COUNTY	W 4-1	Joachim 2, Merson, Wright	27,941
Oct 14	Arsenal	L 0-1		38,042
Oct 22	SUNDERLAND	D 0-0		27,215
Oct 28	CHARLTON ATHLETIC	W 2-1	Taylor, Merson	27,461
Nov 5	Everton	W 1-0	Merson	27,670
Nov 11	TOTTENHAM HOTSPUR	W 2-0	Taylor 2	33,608
Nov 18	Southampton	L 0-2		14,979
Nov 25	Coventry City	D 1-1	Dublin	21,455
Dec 2	NEWCASTLE UNITED	D 1-1	Dublin	34,255
Dec 9	West Ham United	D 1-1	Hendrie	25,888
Dec 16	MANCHESTER CITY	D 2-2	Dublin, Ginola	29,281
Dec 23	Leeds United	W 2-1	Southgate, Boateng	39,714
Dec 26	MANCHESTER UNITED	L 0-1		40,889
Jan 1	Chelsea	L 0-1		33,159
Jan 13	LIVERPOOL	L 0-3		41,366
Jan 20	Manchester United	L 0-2		67,533
Jan 24	LEEDS UNITED	L 1-2	Merson	29,335
Feb 3	Bradford City	W 3-0	Vassell 2, Joachim	19,591
Feb 10	MIDDLESBROUGH	D 1-1	Stone	28,912
Feb 24	Derby County	L 0-1		27,289
Mar 5	Sunderland	D 1-1	Joachim	44,114
Mar 10	IPSWICH TOWN	W 2-1	Joachim	28,216
Mar 18	ARSENAL	D 0-0		36,111
Mar 31	Manchester City	W 3-1	Merson, Dublin, Hendrie	34,243
Apr 4	LEICESTER CITY	W 2-1	Dublin, Hendrie	29,043
Apr 7	WEST HAM UNITED	D 2-2	Ginola, Hendrie	31,432
Apr 14	EVERTON	W 2-1	Dublin, Taylor	31,272
Apr 17	Charlton Athletic	D 3-3	Ginola, Vassell, Hendrie	20,043
Apr 21	SOUTHAMPTON	D 0-0		29,336
Apr 28	Tottenham Hotspur	D 0-0		36,096
May 5	COVENTRY CITY	W 3-2	Vassell, Angel, Merson	39,761
May 19	Newcastle United	L 0-3		51,306

FA Cup

Jan 7	Newcastle United	(Rd 3) D 1-1	Stone	37,862
Jan 17	NEWCASTLE UNITED	(R) W 1-0	Vassell	25,387
Jan 27	Leicester City	(Rd 4) L 1-2	Joachim	26,383

League Cup

Nov 1	MANCHESTER CITY	(Rd 3) L 0-1		24,138

Intertoto Cup

July 19	Marila Pribram	(Rd 1/FL) D 0-0		7,852
July 22	MARILA PRIBRAM*	(Rd 1/SL) W 3-1	Nilis, Taylor, Dublin	8,205
July 26	Celta Vigo	(Rd 2/FL) L 0-1		12,164
Aug 2	CELTA VIGO*	(Rd 2/SL) L 1-3	Barry (pen)	11,909

*Home games played at the Hawthorns due to development work at Villa Park.

League & Cup Appearances

PLAYER	LEAGUE	CUP COMPETITION		OTHER	TOTAL
		FA CUP	LC		
Alpay	33	2	1		36
Angel	7 (2)	1			8 (2)
Barry	29 (1)	2 (1)	1	4	36 (2)
Boateng	29 (4)	3	1	4	37 (4)
Cooke				0 (1)	0 (1)
De Bilde	4				4
Delaney	12 (7)		0 (1)	1	13 (8)
Dublin	29 (4)	2 (1)	1	3	35 (5)
Ehiogu	1 (1)			2	3 (1)
Ginola	14 (13)	1			15 (13)
Hendrie	27 (5)	1	0 (1)	1 (2)	29 (8)
Hitzlsperger	0 (1)				0 (1)
James	38	3	1	4	46
Joachim	11 (9)	0 (1)	1	1 (2)	13 (12)
McGrath	0 (3)				0 (3)
Merson	38	3	1	3	45
Nilis	3			2	5
Samuel	1 (2)	1		3	5 (2)
Southgate	31	2	1	2	36
Staunton	13 (1)	3			16 (1)
Stone	33 (1)	3	1	4	41 (1)
Taylor	25 (4)	1	1	4	31 (4)
Thompson				1 (1)	1 (1)
Vassell	5 (18)	2 (1)	0 (1)	0 (3)	7 (23)
Walker		0 (1)		1	1 (1)
Wright	35 (1)	3	1	4	43 (1)

Goalscorers

PLAYER	LEAGUE	CUP COMPETITION		OTHER	TOTAL
		FA CUP	LC		
Dublin	8			1	9
Joachim	7	1			8
Hendrie	6				6
Merson	6				6
Taylor	4			1	5
Vassell	4	1			5
Ginola	3				3
Stone	2	1			3
Nilis	1			1	2
Southgate	2				2
Angel	1				1
Barry				1	1
Boateng	1				1
Wright	1				1

Fact File

Villa were 2-0 down at home to Coventry City in their final home league game of the season. They came back to win 3-2 and defeat for the Sky Blues saw them relegated for the first time from the top flight.

MANAGER: John Gregory

CAPTAIN: Paul Merson, Gareth Southgate

TOP SCORER: Dion Dublin, 9 (8 league)

BIGGEST WIN: 4-1 v Derby County (H), Premier League, 30 September 2000

HIGHEST ATTENDANCE: 67,533 v Manchester United (A), Premier League, 20 January 2001

MAJOR TRANSFERS IN: Luc Nilis from PSV Eindhoven, Juan Pablo Angel from River Plate, Olozan Alpay from Fenerbahce, David Ginola from Tottenham Hotspur, Steve Staunton from Liverpool

MAJOR TRANSFERS OUT: Ugo Ehiogu and Gareth Southgate to Middlesbrough, Alan Thompson to Celtic

Final Premier League Table

		P	W	D	L	F	A	Pts
1	MANCHESTER UNITED	38	24	8	6	79	31	80
2	ARSENAL	38	20	10	8	63	38	70
3	LIVERPOOL	38	20	9	9	71	39	69
4	LEEDS UNITED	38	20	8	10	64	43	68
5	IPSWICH TOWN	38	20	6	12	57	42	66
6	CHELSEA	38	17	10	11	68	45	61
7	SUNDERLAND	38	15	12	11	46	41	57
8	ASTON VILLA	38	13	15	10	46	43	54
9	CHARLTON ATHLETIC	38	14	10	14	50	57	52
10	SOUTHAMPTON	38	14	10	14	40	48	52
11	NEWCASTLE UNITED	38	14	9	15	44	50	51
12	TOTTENHAM HOTSPUR	38	13	10	15	47	54	49
13	LEICESTER CITY	38	14	6	18	39	51	48
14	MIDDLESBROUGH	38	9	15	14	44	44	42
15	WEST HAM UNITED	38	10	12	16	45	50	42
16	EVERTON	38	11	9	18	45	59	42
17	DERBY COUNTY	38	10	12	16	37	59	42
18	MANCHESTER CITY	38	8	10	20	41	65	34
19	COVENTRY CITY	38	8	10	20	36	63	34
20	BRADFORD CITY	38	5	11	22	30	70	26

Season 2001-02

Premier League

DATE	OPPONENTS	SCORE	GOALSCORERS	ATTENDANCE
Aug 18	Tottenham Hotspur	D 0-0		36,059
Aug 26	MANCHESTER UNITED	D 1-1	Vassell	42,632
Sep 8	Liverpool	W 3-1	Dublin, Hendrie, Vassell	44,102
Sep 16	SUNDERLAND	D 0-0		31,668
Sep 24	Southampton	W 3-1	Boateng, Angel, Hadji	26,794
Sep 30	BLACKBURN ROVERS	W 2-0	Angel, Vassell	28,623
Oct 14	FULHAM	W 2-0	Vassell, Taylor	28,579
Oct 20	Everton	L 2-3	Hadji, Schmeichel	33,352
Oct 24	CHARLTON ATHLETIC	W 1-0	Kachloul	27,701
Oct 27	BOLTON WANDERERS	W 3-2	Angel 2 (1 pen), Vassell	33,599
Nov 3	Newcastle United	L 0-3		51,057
Nov 17	MIDDLESBROUGH	D 0-0		35,424
Nov 25	Leeds United	D 1-1	Kachloul	40,159
Dec 1	LEICESTER CITY	L 0-2		30,711
Dec 5	West Ham United	D 1-1	Dublin	28,377
Dec 9	Arsenal	L 2-3	Merson, Stone	38,074
Dec 17	IPSWICH TOWN	W 2-1	Angel 2	29,320
Dec 22	Derby County	L 1-3	Angel	28,001
Dec 26	LIVERPOOL	L 1-2	Hendrie	42,602
Dec 29	TOTTENHAM HOTSPUR	D 1-1	Angel (pen)	41,134
Jan 1	Sunderland	D 1-1	Taylor	45,324
Jan 12	DERBY COUNTY	W 2-1	Vassell, Angel	28,881
Jan 21	Charlton Athletic	W 2-1	Vassell, Angel	25,681
Jan 30	EVERTON	D 0-0		32,460
Feb 2	Fulham	D 0-0		20,041
Feb 9	CHELSEA	D 1-1	Merson	41,137
Feb 23	Manchester United	L 0-1		67,592
Mar 2	WEST HAM UNITED	W 2-1	Angel, Vassell	37,341
Mar 5	Blackburn Rovers	L 0-3		21,988
Mar 17	ARSENAL	L 1-2	Dublin	41,520
Mar 23	Ipswich Town	D 0-0		25,427
Mar 30	Bolton Wanderers	L 2-3	Warhurst o.g., Taylor	24,600
Apr 2	NEWCASTLE UNITED	D 1-1	Crouch	36,597
Apr 6	Middlesbrough	L 1-2	Angel	26,003
Apr 13	LEEDS UNITED	L 0-1		40,039
Apr 20	Leicester City	D 2-2	Vassell, Hitzlsperger	18,125
Apr 27	SOUTHAMPTON	W 2-1	Vassell 2	35,255
May 11	Chelsea	W 3-1	Crouch, Vassell, Dublin	40,709

FA Cup

Jan 6	MANCHESTER UNITED	(Rd 3) L 2-3	Taylor, Neville P o.g.	38,444

League Cup

Oct 10	READING	(Rd 3) W 1-0	Dublin	23,431
Nov 4	Sheffield Wednesday	(Rd 4) L 0-1		26,526

UEFA Cup

Sep 20	NK VARTEKS	(Rd 1/FL) L 2-3	Angel 2	27,132
Sep 27	NK Varteks	(Rd 1/SL) W 1-0*	Hadji	12,100

*NK Varteks won on away goals rule.

Intertoto Cup

July 14	Slaven Belupo	(Rd 3/FL) L 1-2	Ginola	3,000
July 21	SLAVEN BELUPO	(Rd 3/SL) W 2-0	Hendrie 2	21,412
July 26	Stade Rennais	(SF/FL) L 1-2	Vassell	15,753
July 31	STADE RENNAIS	(SF/SL) W 1-0	Dublin	30,782
Aug 7	FC Basel	(F/FL) D 1-1	Merson	29,879
Aug 21	FC BASEL	(F/SL) W 4-1	Vassell, Angel 2, Ginola	39,593

MANAGER: John Gregory, Graham Taylor

CAPTAIN: Paul Merson, Steve Staunton

TOP SCORER: Juan Pablo Angel, 16 (12 league)

BIGGEST WIN: 3-1 v Liverpool (A), Premier League, 8 September 2001; v Southampton (A), Premier League, 24 September 2001; v Chelsea (A), Premier League, 11 May 2002

HIGHEST ATTENDANCE: 67,592 v Manchester United (A), Premier League, 23 February 2002

MAJOR TRANSFERS IN: Peter Crouch from Portsmouth

MAJOR TRANSFERS OUT: Peter Schmeichel to Manchester City, David Ginola to Everton

---

League & Cup Appearances

PLAYER	LEAGUE	CUP COMPETITION FA CUP	LC	OTHER	TOTAL
Alpay	14	2		8	24
Angel	26 (3)	1	1	2 (2)	30 (5)
Balaban	(8)		1 (1)	1	2 (9)
Barry	16 (4)			6 (1)	22 (5)
Bewers		0 (1)			0 (1)
Boateng	37 (1)	1	1 (1)	8	47 (1)
Crouch	7 (2)				7 (2)
Delaney	30		1	8	39
Dublin	9 (12)		1 (1)	5 (2)	15 (15)
Enckelman	9			4 (1)	13 (1)
Ginola	0 (5)		1 (1)	3 (3)	4 (9)
Hadji	17 (6)	0 (1)	2	3 (3)	22 (10)
Hendrie	25 (4)	1	2	7	35 (4)
Hitzlsperger	11 (1)				11 (1)
Kachloul	17 (5)		2	6 (1)	25 (6)
Mellberg	32	1	1	2	36
Merson	18 (3)	1		5	24 (3)
Samuel	17 (6)	1		0 (2)	18 (8)
Schmeichel	29	1	2	4	36
Staunton	30 (3)	1	2	2	35 (3)
Stone	14 (8)	0 (1)	1	5 (3)	20 (12)
Taylor	7 (9)	1	1		9 (9)
Vassell	30 (6)	1	0 (1)	2 (4)	33 (11)
Wright	23	1	1	7	32

Goalscorers

PLAYER	LEAGUE	CUP COMPETITION FA CUP	LC	OTHER	TOTAL
Angel	12			4	16
Vassell	12			2	14
Dublin	4	1		1	6
Hendrie	2			2	4
Taylor	3	1			4
Hadji	2			1	3
Merson	2			1	3
Crouch	2				2
Ginola				2	2
Kachloul	2				2
Boateng	1				1
Hitzlsperger	1				1
Schmeichel	1				1
Stone	1				1
Opps' o.gs.	1	1			2

Fact File

Darius Vassell (England) and Steve Staunton (Republic of Ireland) were both named in their respective country's 2002 World Cup squads.

Final Premier League Table

		P	W	D	L	F	A	Pts
1	ARSENAL	38	26	9	3	79	36	87
2	LIVERPOOL	38	24	8	6	67	30	80
3	MANCHESTER UNITED	38	24	5	9	87	45	77
4	NEWCASTLE UNITED	38	21	8	9	74	52	71
5	LEEDS UNITED	38	18	12	8	53	37	66
6	CHELSEA	38	17	13	8	66	38	64
7	WEST HAM UNITED	38	15	8	15	48	57	53
8	ASTON VILLA	38	12	14	12	46	47	50
9	TOTTENHAM HOTSPUR	38	14	8	16	49	53	50
10	BLACKBURN ROVERS	38	12	10	16	55	51	46
11	SOUTHAMPTON	38	12	9	17	46	54	45
12	MIDDLESBROUGH	38	12	9	17	35	47	45
13	FULHAM	38	10	14	14	36	44	44
14	CHARLTON ATHLETIC	38	10	14	14	38	49	44
15	EVERTON	38	11	10	17	45	57	43
16	BOLTON WANDERERS	38	9	13	16	44	62	40
17	SUNDERLAND	38	10	10	18	29	51	40
18	IPSWICH TOWN	38	9	9	20	41	64	36
19	DERBY COUNTY	38	8	6	24	33	63	30
20	LEICESTER CITY	38	5	13	20	30	64	28

Complete Players' Career Records

(Records up to and including season 2001-02)

Others = UEFA Cup, European Cup, FA Charity Shield, European Cup, World Cup Championship, Full Members' Cup, Simod Cup, Zenith Data Systems Cup and the Intertoto Cup. **Sub** = substitute appearances

Player	Birthplace	From	Year Joined	Year Left	To	League Apps	Sub	Goals
Adam, J	Glasgow	Luton Town	1959	1961	Stoke City	24		3
Aitken, CA	Edinburgh	Edinburgh Thistle	1959	1976	New York Cos	559	2	14
Aldis, PB	Birmingham	Hay Green	1950	1959	Hinckley A	262		1
Aldridge, AJ	Walsall	Walsall Town S	1888	1890	Retired	17		0
Allen, AA	Birmingham	Excelsior FC	1886	1891	Retired	45		27
Allen, BW	Birmingham	Icknield St OB	1904	1906	Westbourne C	3		1
Allen, JP	Poole	Portsmouth	1934	1939	Retired	147		2
Allen, M	Caernarfon	Watford	1987	1988	Watford	4		0
Alpay, OF	Turkey	Fenerbahce	2000	-	Still at club	47		0
Anderson, D	Birmingham	Hockley Bel	1881	1883	Abbey FC	0		0
Anderson, WJ	Liverpool	Manchester United	1967	1973	Cardiff City	229	2	36
Angel, JP	Colombia	River Plate	2001	-	Still at club	33	5	13
Ansell, B	Birmingham	Birmingham Schools	1967	1968	Non-League	1		0
Anstey, B	Bristol	Bristol Rovers	1910	1915	Leicester City	42		0
Apperley, CW	Birmingham	Birmingham SG	1882	1884	South Africa	0		0
Armfield, WC	Birmingham	Ellison FC	1923	1928	Exeter City	12		2
Ashe, NJ	Bloxwich	Brierley High School	1959	1961	Rotherham United	5		0
Ashfield, GO	Manchester	Stockport County	1955	1958	Chester	9		0
Ashmore, W	Smethwick	WB Standard	1888	1889	Aston Unity	1		0
Ashton, DO	Worksop	Wolves	1946	1949	Wellington Town	8		0
Askew, WL	London	Norwich City	1910	1912	West Ham United	2		0
Aspinall, W	Wigan	Everton	1986	1988	Portsmouth	40	4	14
Astley, DJ	Merthyr	Charlton Athletic	1931	1937	Derby County	165		92
Aston, CL	Wolverhampton	Walsall	1897	1901	Queens Park Rangers	23		0
Athersmith, WC	Bloxwich	Unity Gas	1890	1901	Small Heath	270		75
Atkinson, D	Shrewsbury	Sociedad	1991	1997	Fenerbahce	79	8	23
Bache, JW	Sourbridge	Stourbridge	1900	1915	Mid Rhondda	431		168
Baird, J	Dumbarton	Vale of Leven	1891	1895	Leicester Fosse	61		0
Baker, AR	Tipton	Willingsworth Sc	1960	1966	Walsall	92		13
Balaban, B	Croatia	Dinamo Zagreb	2001	-	Still at club	0	8	0
Ball, HJ	Birmingham	Arcadians	1879	1880	Walsall TS	0		0
Ball, TE	Unsworth	Newcastle United	1919	1924	Killed	74		0
Banks, HE	Coventry	Millwall A	1900	1902	Bristol City	5		0
Barber, T	West Stanley	Bolton Wanderers	1912	1915	Retired	57		9
Barker, J	Scunthorpe	Scunthorpe United	1936	1938	Huddersfield Town	3		0
Barnie-Adshead, WE	Dudley	Corinthians	1922	1923	Corinthians	2		1
Barrett, E	Rochdale	Oldham Athletic	1992	1995	—	118	1	1
Barrett, KB	Bromsgrove	Stoke Works	1958	1959	Lincoln City	5		3
Barry, G	Hastings	Trainee	1998	-	Still at club	103	11	3
Barson, F	Sheffield	Barnsley	1919	1922	Manchester United	92		10
Baxter, W	Leven, Fife	Wolves	1953	1957	Retired	98		6
Beard, M	Cannock	Birmingham City	1971	1973	Retired	5	1	0
Beaton, W	Kincardine	Dunfermline A	1958	1959	Airdrieonians	1		0
Bedingfield, F	Sunderland	Rushden	1898	1899	Queens Park Rangers	1		1
Beeson, GW	Chesterfield	Sheffield Wednesday	1934	1937	Walsall	70		0
Beinlich, S	Germany	Bergmann B	1991	1993	Released	7	8	1
Benwell, LA	Berwick	Berwick R	1893	1894	Berwick R	1		0
Beresford, J	Chestefield	Mansfield Town	1927	1936	Preston North End	224		66
Betts, A	Nottingham	Derby Grammar School	1973	1975	Portland Tim	1	2	0
Bewers, J	Kettering	Trainee	1999	2000	Released	0	1	0
Biddlestone, F	Dudley	Walsall	1929	1939	Mansfield Town	151		0
Birch, J	Blackwell	Stourbridge	1910	1912	Queens Park Rangers	3		2
Birch, P	West Bromwich	W Brom Schools	1983	1991	Wolverhampton Wanderers	153	20	16
Birch, T	West Bromwich	Accles & Pol	1954	1960	Stockport County	22		0
Blackburn, E	Manchester	Manchester YC	1919	1922	Bradford	32		0
Blackburn, GF	London	Hampstead T	1920	1926	Cardiff City	133		1
Blair, A	Kirkcaldy	Coventry City	1981	1984	Sheffield Wednesday	} 43	11	1
		Sheffield Wednesday	1986	1988	Northampton Town			
Blair, D	Glasgow	Clyde	1931	1936	Blackpool	129		6
Blake, M	Nottingham	Juniors	1988	1993	Portsmouth	26	5	2
Blake, NL	Jamaica	Sutton Town	1979	1982	Birmingham City	4		0
Blanchflower, RD	Belfast	Barnsley	1950	1955	Tottenham Hotspur	148		10
Bloomfield, R	London	Arsenal	1964	1966	Non-League	3		0
Boateng, G	Ghana	Coventry City	1999	2002	Middlesbrough	96	7	4
Boden, CD	Wolverhampton	Trainee	1991	1995	Derby County	0	1	0
Boden, JA	Northwich	Clapton Orient	1905	1907	Northwich V	17		2
Bosnich, M	Sydney	Manchester United	1992	1999	Manchester United	179		0
Bourne, HE	Bromsgrove	Manchester United	1919	1921	Retired	7		2
Bowen, SE	Hednesford	Hednesford Town	1923	1924	Norwich City	191		2
Bowman, T	Strathclyde	Blackpool	1897	1901	Southampton	100		2

| FAC | | | FLC | | | Others | | | Totals | | |
Apps	Sub	Goals	Apps	Sub	Goals	Apps	Sub	Goals	Apps	Sub	Goals
0		0	0		0	0		0	24		3
34	1	1	61	1	3			0	657	3	16
32		0	0		0	1		0	295		1
0		0	0		0	0		0	17		0
12	6	0	0		0	0		0	57		11
0		0	0		0	0		0	3		1
13	1	0	0		0	0		0	160		3
0		0	0		0	0		0	4		0
2		3	0		0	8		0	60		0
5		0	0		0	0		0	5		0
11	1	1	23	8	1			0	264	3	45
2		1	0		0	2	2	4	38	7	17
0		0	0		0	0		0	1		0
3		0	0		0	0		0	45		0
8		0	0		0	0		0	8		0
0		0	0		0	0		0	12		2
0		0	0		0	0		0	5		0
1		0	0		0	0		0	10		0
0		0	0		0	0		0	1		0
0		0	0		0	0		0	8		0
0		0	0		0	0		0	2		0
1	1	0	4	2	0	0		0	45	5	16
8	8	0	0		0	0		0	173		100
0		0	0		0	1		0	24		0
38	10	0	0		0	3		1	311		86
4		0	15		11	8	2	0	106	10	34
42	17	0	0		0	1		0	474		185
9		0	0		0	0		0	70		0
4	1	0	13		3			0	109		17
0		0	1	1	0	1		0	2	9	0
2		0	0		0	0		0	2		0
3		0	0		0	0		0	77		0
0		0	0		0	0		0	5		0
11	1	1	0		0	0		0	68		10
0		0	0		0	0		0	3		0
0		0	0		0	0		0	2		1
9		0	15	1	0			0	142	1	2
0		0	0		0	0		0	5		3
10	2	0	9		0	13	1	1	135	14	4
16		0	0		0	0		0	108		10
10		0	0		0	0		0	108		6
0		0	1		0	0		0	6	1	0
0		0	0		0	0		0	1		0
0		0	0		0	0		0	1		1
1		0	0		0	0		0	71		0
0		0	0		0	0	1	0	7	9	1
0		0	0		0	0		0	1		0
27	7	0	0		0	0		0	251		73
0		0	0	1	0	0		0	1	3	0
0	1	0	0		0	0		0	0	2	0
9		0	0		0	0		0	160		0
0		0	0		0	0		0	3		2
20	1	3	23	4	5	5	2	1	201	27	25
0		0	0		0	0		0	22		0
1		0	0		0	0		0	33		0
12	1	0	0		0	0		0	145		2
3		0	1	2	1	1	1	0	48	14	2
9		0	0		0	0		0	138		0
2		0	1	1	0	2		0	31	5	2
0		0	0		0	0		0	4		0
7		0	0		0	0		0	155		10
0		0	0		0	0		0	3		0
9		0	9	1	1	12		0	126	8	5
0		0	0		0	0		0	0	1	0
1		0	0		0	0		0	18		2
17		0	20	1	0	11		0	227		1
0		0	0		0	0		0	7		2
8		0	0		0	0		0	199		0
13		0	0		0	3		0	116		2

Player	Birthplace	From	Year Joined	Year Left	To	League Apps	Sub	Goals
Boyman, WR	Richmond	Cradley Heath	1919	1922	Nottingham Forest	22		11
Boyne, R	Leeds	New Zealand	1913	1915	Retired	8		0
Bradley, D	Birmingham	King's Ntn Bys	1984	1986	West Bromwich Albion	16	4	0
Bradley, K	Ellesmere Port	Everton	1964	1972	Peterboro United	115	7	2
Brawn, WF	Wellingborough	Sheffield United	1901	1906	Middlesbrough	95		19
Breitkreutz, M	Germany	Bergmann B	1991	1993	Bergmann B	13	1	0
Bremner, DG	Kirkcaldy	Hibernian	1979	1984	Birmingham City	170	4	9
Briggs, WW	Edinburgh	Musselburgh, W	1961	1963	Falkirk	2		0
Brittleton, JT	Winsford	Chester	1927	1930	Winsford United	10		0
Broadbent, PF	Elvington	Shrewsbury Town	1966	1969	Stockport County	60	4	2
Brocklebank, RE	Finchley	Finchley	1929	1936	Burnley	19		2
Brookes, F	Birmingham	Wesleyan Ch	1880	1882	Centaurs	0		0
Broome, FH	Berkhamstead	Berkhamstead T	1934	1947	Derby County	133		77
Brown, AA	Birmingham	Mitchell St G	1884	1894	Retired	86		37
Brown, A	Birmingham	Aston Unity	1879	1886	Retired	0		0
Brown, AF	Tamworth	Tamworth	1900	1901	Southampton	2		2
Brown, G	Northumberland	Huddersfield Town	1929	1935	Burnley	116		79
Brown, J	Wallyford	Midlothian Sc	1969	1975	Preston North End	73	3	1
Brown, JR	Renton	Birmingham	1890	1893	Stourbridge	51		3
Brown, R	Nottingham	Derby County Jrs	1961	1962	Notts County	0		0
Brown, RJ	Great Yarmouth	Nottingham Forest	1947	1949	Gorleston	30		9
Brown, WG	Cheadle	Bolton Wanderers	1904	1906	Plymouth Argyle	13		0
Browne, P	Glasgow	Trainee	1991	1996	Released	2		0
Bryan, T	Walsall	Wednesbury S	1881	1883	Bilston	0		0
Buckley, CS	Manchester	Brighton	1904	1913	Arsenal	136		3
Bullivant, T	London	Fulham	1979	1982	Charlton Athletic	10	3	0
Burke, M	Solihull	Solihull Boys	1985	1988	Middlesbrough	5	2	0
Burridge, J	Workington	Blackpool	1975	1978	Crystal Palace	65		0
Burrows, H	Haydock	Wigan Boys	1959	1965	Stoke City	147		53
Burton, GF	Birmingham	Walsall T	1892	1898	Retired	52		2
Burton, JH	Birmingham	Aston Park U	1885	1892	Retired	28		1
Butcher, FR	Barnsley	Shirley Juniors	1933	1935	Reading	2		0
Butler, L	Sheffield	Lincoln City	1987	1991	Barnsley	8		0
Butress, MD	Peterborough	Peterboro' Sc	1976	1978	Gillingham	1	2	0
Byfield, D	Sutton Coldfield	Trainee	1994	2000	Walsall	1	6	0
Calderwood, C	Glasgow	Tottenham Hotspur	1999	2000	Nottingham Forest	23	3	0
Callaghan, E	Birmingham	Atherstone T	1932	1947	Retired	125		0
Callaghan, N	Singapore	Derby County	1988	1991	Stafford R	24	2	1
Campbell, A	Crook	Spennymoor	1923	1925	Lincoln City	4		0
Campbell, G	Ayr	Renton	1890	1893	Dundee	50		1
Campbell, JJ	Glasgow	Glasgow C	1895	1897	Glasgow C	55		39
Campbell, L	Edinburgh	Hibernian	1889	1893	Dumbarton	41		21
Campbell, RM	Belfast	Belfast Sc	1973	1975	Huddersfield Town	7	3	1
Canning, L	Cowdenbeath	Paget R	1948	1954	Kettering Town	39		3
Cantrell, J	Chesterfield	Hucknall Con	1904	1908	Notts County	52		22
Capewell, L	Birmingham	Wellington Town	1921	1929	Walsall	143		88
Carbone, B	Italy	Sheffield Wednesday	1999	2000	Bradford City	22	2	3
Carey, WJ	Manchester	Hereford United	1937	1938	Bury	3		0
Carr, FA	Preston	Leicester City	1995	1996	Reggiana	1	2	0
Carrodus, F	Manchester	Manchester City	1974	1979	Wrexham	150		7
Carruthers, M	Nottingham	Juniors	1991	1993	Stoke City	2	2	0
Cartlidge, A	Stoke-on-Trent	Bristol Rovers	1908	1911	Stoke	52		0
Cascarino, T	St Paul's Cray	Millwall	1990	1991	Celtic	43	3	11
Chambers, JF	Bimingham	Birmingham Boys	1968	1969	Southend United	1	1	0
Chandler, RW	India	Glossop	1913	1914	Walsall	1		0
Chapman, H	Liverpool	Ellesmere Port	1946	1948	Notts County	6		0
Chapman, RC	Birmingham	Kynochs	1953	1958	Lincoln City	19		8
Chapple, FJ	Treharris	Treharris BC	1906	1908	Birmingham	8		3
Charles, GA	Newham	Derby County	1995	1999	Benfica	72	7	3
Chatt, RS	Barnard Castle	Middlesbro' I	1893	1898	Stockton	87		19
Chatterley, LC	Birmingham	Birmingham Boys	1962	1971	Northampton Town	149	4	26
Chester, RA	Long Eaton	Stamford Town	1925	1935	Manchester United	93		34
Clarke, AW	Walsall	Wednesbury OA	1881	1884	Bilston Town	0		0
Clarke, GB	Bolsover	Mansfield Town	1924	1925	Crystal Palace	1		0
Clarke, NF	Birmingham	Aston Boys	1954	1955	Torquay United	1		0
Clarke, WG	Ayr	Bristol Rovers	1901	1905	Bradford City	42		6
Clarkson, T	Stourbridge	Halesowen Town	1889	1893	Oldbury Town	17		0
Clayton, TG	Sunderland	Wolves	1937	1939	Burnley	11	1	0
Cobley, WA	Leicester	Leicester Sc	1936	1939	Retired	45		0
Codling, RJ	Durham	Clapton Orient	1905	1909	Northampton Town	77		0
Collymore, SV	Stafford	Liverpool	1997	2000	Leicester City	34	11	7
Comyn, A	Wakefield	Alvechurch	1989	1991	Derby County	12	3	0
Connor, J	Birmingham	Warwick Co	1889	1891	Burslem PV	4		0
Cooch, H	Birmingham	Rushden	1901	1908	Retired	25		0
Cook, GH	County Durham	Huddersfield Town	1926	1929	Tottenham Hotspur	57		35
Cooke, S	Walsall	Trainee	2000	2001	Still at club	0		0
Cooper, N	India	Aberdeen	1986	1988	Rangers	19	1	0
Copley, G	Birmingham	Saltley Col	1880	1882	Birmingham St G	0		0
Corbett, J	Brierley Hill	Brierley Hill	1923	1927	Stourbridge	7		0

FAC Apps	Sub	Goals	FLC Apps	Sub	Goals	Others Apps	Sub	Goals	Totals Apps	Sub	Goals
0		0	0		0	0		0	22		11
0		0	0		0	0		0	8		0
0		0	3		0	0		0	19	4	0
6	2	0	14		0	0		0	135	9	2
12	1		0		0	0		0	107		20
0		0	0		0	0		0	13	1	0
14		0	17	1	1	21		0	222	5	10
0		0	0		0	0		0	2		0
0		0	0		0	0		0	10		0
5	2		0		0	0		0	65	4	4
1		0	0		0	0		0	20		2
1		0	0		0	0		0	1		0
18	13		0		0	0		0	151		90
20	18		0		0	0		0	106		55
22	15		0		0	0		0	22		15
0		0	0		0	0		0	2		2
10	10		0		0	0		0	126		89
4		0	8		0	0		0	85	3	1
4	1		0		0	0		0	55		4
0		0	0		0	1		0	1		0
1		0	0		0	0		0	31		9
0		0	0		0	0		0	13		0
0		0	0		0	0		0	2		0
2		0	0		0	0		0	2		0
7		0	0		0	1		0	144		3
1		0	0	1	0	0		0	11	4	0
0		0	0		0	0	1	0	5	3	0
6		0	9		0	0		0	80		0
11	5		23	15	0	0		0	181		73
1	1		0		0	0		0	53		3
19		0	0		0	0		0	47		1
0		0	0		0	0		0	2		0
0		0	0		0	2		0	10		0
0		0	0		0	0		0	1	2	0
0	1	0	1		0	1		0	3	7	0
0		0	3	1	0	0		0	26	4	0
17		0	0		0	0		0	142		0
1	1	0	2	1	0	0		0	27	4	1
0		0	0		0	0		0	4		0
3		0	0		0	0		0	53		1
8	4		0		0	0		0	63		43
8	4		0		0	0		0	49		25
0		0	2		0	0		0	9	3	1
2		0	0		0	0		0	41		3
3	1		0		0	0		0	55		23
13	12		0		0	0		0	156		100
6	5		0		0	0		0	28	2	8
1		0	0		0	0		0	4		0
1	1		0		0	0		0	2	3	0
9		0	27	3	0	10		0	196		10
0	1	0	0		0	0	1	0	2	4	0
2		0	0		0	1		0	55		0
2		0	2	1	1	3		0	50	4	12
0		0	0		0	0		0	1	1	0
0		0	0		0	0		0	1		0
0		0	0		0	0		0	6		0
0		0	0		0	0		0	19		8
0		0	0		0	0		0	8		3
5	2		9	1	0	6	3	1	92	13	4
9	7		0		0	0		0	96		26
4		0	7		1	0		0	160	4	27
4		0	0		0	0		0	97		34
7		0	0		0	0		0	7		0
0		0	0		0	0		0	1		0
0		0	0		0	0		0	1		0
1		0	0		0	0		0	43		6
0		0	0		0	0		0	17		0
0		0	0		0	0		0	11		1
2		0	0		0	0		0	47		0
5		0	0		0	0		0	82		0
5	3		1		0	9	1	5	49	12	15
2		0	2	1	0	1		0	17	4	0
0		0	0		0	0		0	4		0
0		0	0		0	0		0	25		0
4	5		0		0	0		0	61		40
0		0	0		0	0	1	0	0	1	0
2	1		0		0	0		0	21	1	1
4		0	0		0	0		0	4		0
0		0	0		0	0		0	7		0

Player	Birthplace	From	Year Joined	Year Left	To	League Apps	Sub	Goals
Corbett, WAS	Wellington	Queens Park Rangers	1904	1907	Birmingham	13		0
Cordell, JG	Bloxwich	Hilary St OB	1951	1953	Rochdale	5		0
Cornan, F	Sunderland	Birmingham	1907	1909	Spennymoor	16		0
Coulton, F	Walsall	Walsall S	1886	1894	Retired	35		0
Cowan, Jas	Jamestown	Vale of Leven	1889	1902	Retired	316		21
Cowan, J	Renton	Glasgow R	1895	1899	Dundee Harp	64		25
Cowans, GS	Durham	Mansfield Sc	1970	1985	Bari (Italy)			
		Bari	1988	1991	Blackburn Rovers			
		Blackburn Rovers	1993	1993	Derby County	399	15	49
Cox, G	Birmingham	Walsall Town	1887	1893	Retired	87		0
Cox, N	Scunthorpe	Scunthorpe United	1991	1994	Middlesbrough	26	6	3
Crabtree, JW	Burnley	Burnley	1895	1902	Plymouth Argyle	178		6
Craddock, LM	Newent	Hereford United	1948	1951	Retired	34		10
Craig, TB	Glasgow	Newcastle United	1977	1979	Swansea City	27		2
Cropley, AJ	Aldershot	Arsenal	1976	1980	Toronto B	65	2	7
Crossland, W	West Bromwich	Oldbury Town	1879	1882	Retired	0		0
Crouch, P	Macclesfield	Portsmouth	2002	-	Still at club	7		2
Crowe, VH	Abercynon	Erdington A	1954	1964	Peterboro United	294		10
Crowther, S	Bilston	Bilston Town	1956	1958	Manchester United	50		4
Crudgington, G	Wolverhampton	Wolves (Am)	1970	1972	Crewe Alexandra	4		0
Cumbes, J	Manchester	West Bromwich Albion	1971	1976	Portland Town	157		0
Cummings, GW	Falkirk	Partick Thistle	1935	1949	Retired	210		0
Cunliffe, A	Wigan	Blackburn Rovers	1932	1936	Middlesbrough	69		11
Curbishley, LC	London	Birmingham City	1982	1985	Charlton Athletic	34	2	1
Curcic, S	Yugoslavia	Bolton Wanderers	1996	1998	Crystal Palace	20	9	0
Curtis, GW	Dover	Coventry City	1982	1985	Retired	51		4
Cutler, NA	Birmingham	Chester City	1999	2000	Stoke City	0	1	0
Daley, A	Birmingham	Birmingham Sc	1984	1994	Wolves	189	44	31
Daly, P	Dublin	Shamrock Rovers	1948	1950	Dublin City	3		0
Davies, G	Birmingham	St Phillips	1889	1891	Witton W.S.	1		0
Davies, GA	Birmingham	Aston Manor	1892	1893	Smetwick Centaur	1		1
Davis, AG	Birmingham	Evesham	1919	1922	Queens Park Rangers	5		1
Davis, E	Dudley	Wednesbury S	1879	1885	Retired	0		0
Davis, N	Bloxwich	Redditch U	1991	1998	Walsall	0	2	0
Davis, R	Walsall	Walsall	1884	1887	Retired	0		0
Dawson, FHH	Birmingham	Aston Unity	1883	1889	Retired	3		0
Dawson, JH	Stoke-on-Trent	Buslem PV	1880	1882	Burton Swifts	0		0
Day, M	Chelmsford	Orient	1983	1985	Leeds United	30		0
Deacy, E	Galway	Galway R	1979	1984	Galway United	27	5	1
Deakin, AR	Birmingham	Cannonhill R	1959	1970	Walsall	230	1	9
De Bilde, G	Belgium	Sheffield Wednesday	2000	2001	Loan	4		0
Deehan, JM	Solihull	Solihull Sc	1975	1979	West Bromwich Albion	107	3	40
Delaney, MA	Haverfordwest	Cardiff City	1999	-	Still at club	67	12	1
Dennington, L	West Bromwich	Wolsey Mtrs	1924	1925	Reading	1		0
Devey, HP	Birmingham	Excelsior	1888	1893	Retired	73		1
Devey, JHG	Birmingham	Mitchell St G	1891	1902	Retired	268		169
Devey, W	Birmingham	Birmingham S	1892	1894	Walsall	10		2
Dickie, WA	Wednesbury	Walsall S	1889	1890	Darlaston	0		0
Dickson, IW	Dumfries	Queen o' South	1920	1924	Middlesbrough	76		31
Dickson, W	Fife	Sunderland	1889	1892	Stoke	58		33
Dinsdale, W	Darlington	Crook T	1924	1926	Lincoln City	8		0
Diver, EJ	Cambridge	Surrey AFC	1890	1892	Retired	3		0
Dix RW	Bristol	Blackburn Rovers	1932	1937	Derby County	97		30
Dixon, A	Matlock	Derby Mid	1888	1889	Stoke	3		1
Dixon, JT	Hebburn	Spennymoor United	1945	1961	Retired	392		132
Dobson, HA	Chesterton	Audley	1912	1915	Killed	6		0
Dodds, TB	South Shields	North Shields	1946	1947	Swansea Town	1		0
Doncaster, S	Gainsborough	Stourbridge	1911	1913	Glossop	2		1
Donovan, T	Liverpool	Grimsby Town	1979	1982	Burnley	17		6
Dorigo, A	Melbourne (Aust)	Thorndon Sch	1983	1987	Chelsea	106	5	1
Dorrell, AR	Birmingham	Carey Hall	1919	1930	Port Vale	355		60
Dorrell, W	Coventry	Leicester Fosse	1894	1896	Burslem PV	11		4
Dorsett, R	Brownhills	Wolverhampton Wanderers	1946	1953	Retired	257		32
Dougan, AD	Belfast	Blackburn Rovers	1961	1963	Peterboro' United	51		19
Dowds, P	Johnstone	Glasgow C	1891	1893	Stoke	19		3
Draper, MA	Long Eaton	Leicester City	1995	2000	Southampton	108	12	7
Drinkwater, CJ	Willesden	Walthamstow	1935	1936	Charlton Athletic	2		1
Dublin, D	Leicester	Coventry City	1998	-	Still at club	85	19	35
Ducat, A	Brixton	Woolwich A	1912	1921	Fulham	74		4
Duffy, D	Birmingham	Juniors	1988	1992	Released	1		0
Dugdale, JR	Liverpool	West Bromwich Albion	1955	1962	Queens Park Rangers	215		3
Dunn, JA	Barking	Torquay United	1967	1971	Charlton Athletic	101		0
Dunning, W	Perth (Scot)	Bootle	1892	1895	Retired	64		0
Dutton, T	West Bromwich	Wednesbury OA	1891	1892	Walsall Town	1		0
Dyke, AS	Newcastle-U-L	Stoke	1913	1915	Port Vale	9		0
Eccles, J	Stoke-on-Trent	Walsall	1923	1925	Northampton Town	10		0
Edgley, HH	Crewe	Whitchurch	1911	1920	Queens Park Rangers	75		15
Edwards, A	Coventry	Stourbridge	1910	1912	Dudley Town	6		0
Edwards, GR	Norwich	Norwich City	1938	1951	Retired	138		34

FAC Apps	Sub	Goals	FLC Apps	Sub	Goals	Others Apps	Sub	Goals	Totals Apps	Sub	Goals
0		0	0		0	0		0	13		0
0		0	0		0	0		0	5		0
0		0	0		0	0		0	16		0
20		0	0		0	0		0	55		0
38	5	0	0		0	2		0	356		26
5	2	0	0		0	0		0	69		27
28	1	3	40	4	5	39	2	2	506	22	59
15		0	0		0	0		0	102		0
4	2	1	5	2	0	1		0	36	10	4
22		1	0		0	2		0	202		7
0		0	0		0	0		0	34		10
1		0	4		0	0		0	32		2
2		0	10		0	5		0	82	2	7
5		0	0		0	0		0	5		0
0		0	0		0	0		0	7		2
34		1	23		1	0		0	351		12
11		0	0		0	1		0	62		4
0		0	1		0	0		0	5		0
8		0	16		0	2		0	183		0
22		0	0		0	0		0	232		0
6	2		0		0	0		0	75		13
0		0	5		0	2		0	41	2	1
2	1		1	1	0	0	1	0	23	11	0
2		0	4		0	0		0	57		4
0		0	0		0	0		0	0	1	0
15	1	2	22	2	4	15	2	1	241	49	38
1		0	0		0	0		0	4		0
0		0	0		0	0		0	1	0	0
0		0	0		0	0		0	1		1
0		0	0		0	0		0	5		1
21		2	0		0	0		0	21		2
0	1	0	0		0	0		0	0	3	0
12		4	0		0	0		0	12		4
17		2	0		0	0		0	20		2
5		1	0		0	0		0	5		1
0		0	3		0	0		0	33		0
1		0	2	3	0	0	1	0	30	9	1
17		0	22		0	0		0	269	1	9
0		0	0		0	0		0	4		0
7	1	3	14		2	7		5	135	4	50
4	1	0	2	3	0	9		0	82	16	1
0		0	0		0	0		0	1		0
11		0	0		0	0		0	84		1
38		18	0		0	2		0	308		187
0		0	0		0	0		0	10		2
1		0	0		0	0		0	1		0
7		8	0		0	0		0	83		39
6		1	0		0	0		0	64		34
0		0	0		0	0		0	8		0
0		0	0		0	0		0	3		0
7		0	0		0	0		0	104		30
0		0	0		0	0		0	3		1
38		12	0		0	0		0	430		144
1		0	0		0	0		0	7		0
0		0	0		0	0		0	1		0
0		0	0		0	0		0	2		1
6		3	0		0	1		2	24		11
7		0	14	1	0	2		0	129	6	1
35		5	0		0	0		0	390		65
1		0	0		0	0		0	12		4
14		4	0		0	0		0	271		36
5	2		4	5		0		0	60		26
1		0	0		0	0		0	20		3
10		2	11	1	2	12	1	0	141	14	11
0		0	0		0	0		0	2		1
4	2	1	6	1	4	8	2	2	103	24	42
13		0	0		0	0		0	87		4
0		0	0		0	0		0	1		0
27		0	12		0	1		0	255		3
5		0	12		0	0		0	118		0
5		0	0		0	0		0	69		0
0		0	0		0	0		0	1		0
0		0	0		0	0		0	9		0
0		0	0		0	0		0	10		0
11		2	0		0	0		0	86		17
2		0	0		0	0		0	8		0
14		7	0		0	0		0	152		41

Player	Birthplace	From	Year Joined	Year Left	To	League Apps	Sub	Goals
Edwards, RT	Kirkby in Ashfield	Mansfield Town	1967	1970	Torquay United	68		2
Ehiogu, U	London	West Bromwich Albion	1991	2000	Middlesbrough	223	14	12
Elliott, JE	Middlesbrough	Middlesboro' I	1893	1896	Retired	19		0
Elliott, P	London	Luton Town	1985	1987	Pisa (Italy)	56	5	7
Elston, AE	Liverpool	Crownhills	1905	1906	Portsmouth	1		0
Enckelman, P	Finland	TPS Turku	1999	-	Still at club	18	1	0
Evans, Albert	Barnard Castle	Barnard Cstl	1896	1906	West Bromwich Albion	179		0
Evans, Allan	Edinburgh	Dunfermline A	1977	1989	Leicester	374	6	51
Evans, AW	Stourport	Liverpool	1972	1975	Walsall	53	8	12
Evans, DG	West Bromwich	West Bromwich Albion	1977	1979	Halifax Town	2		0
Evans, O	Warrington	Lancaster Town	1901	1903	Broadwell	2		0
Evans, RE	Chester	Wrexham	1906	1908	Sheffield United	16		4
Evans, WE	Birmingham	Linread Wks	1946	1949	Notts County	7		3
Evans, WG	Builth	Bootle	1890	1893	Retired	61		0
Ewing, T	Swinhill	Partick Thistle	1961	1964	Partick Thistle	39		4
Eyre, E	Worksop	Birmingham	1908	1910	Middlesbrough	30		5
Farrell, DW	Birmingham	Redditch U	1992	1995	Wycombe Wanderers	5	1	0
Farrelly, G	Dublin	Trainee	1992	1997	Everton	2	6	0
Fashanu, J	London	Wimbledon	1994	1995	Retired	11	2	3
Fencott, KS	Walsall	Walsall Sc	1961	1964	Lincoln City	3		0
Fenton, GA	Wallsend	Trainee	1992	1995	Blackburn Rovers	16	16	3
Ferguson, MK	Burnley	Blackburn Rovers	1968	1970	Queens Park Rangers	38		2
Ferraresi, F	Italy	Cesena	1998	2000	Cesena	0		0
Findlay, JW	Fife	Perth Sc	1973	1977	Luton Town	14		0
Fisher, A	Glasgow	Glasgow C	1902	1903	Fulham	1		0
Fisher, J	Scotalnd	St Bernards	1896	1898	Preston North End	18		5
Fleming, J	Leith	Vale of Leven	1891	1893	Lincoln City	4		2
Follan, E	Greenock	Prescot Cbls	1953	1955	Worcester City	34		7
Ford, T	Swansea	Swansea Town	1946	1951	Sunderland	120		60
Foster, SB	Portsmouth	Brighton & Hove Albion	1983	1985	Luton Town	15		3
Fraser, JC	Perthshire	Dunfermline Athletic	1962	1964	Birmingham City	33		1
Froggatt, S	Lincoln	Juniors	1991	1994	Wolverhampton Wanderers	30	5	2
Gage, K	London	Wimbledon	1987	1891	Sheffield United	113	2	8
Gallacher, B	Johnstone	Johnstone Sc	1986	1991	Retired	55	2	0
Gardner, T	Huyton	Hull City	1933	1938	Burnley	77		1
Garfield, JH	Canterbury	Gravesend	1899	1900	Northampton Town	1		1
Garratt, G	Byker	Crewe Alexandra	1905	1906	Plymouth Argyle	13		0
Garraty, W	Birmingham	Aston Skpre	1897	1908	Leicester Fosse	223	1	96
Garvey, BW	Birmingham	Aston Skpre	1888	1899	Retired	7		4
Gaudie, R	Sheffield	Sheffield Wednesday	1898	1899	Dudley Town	5		1
Gavan, JT	Walsall	Walsall Wood	1962	1966	Doncaster Rovers	9		0
Geddis, D	Carlisle	Ipswich Town	1979	1983	Barnsley	43	4	12
George, W	Shrewsbury	Trowbridge Town	1897	1911	Retired	358		0
Gerrish, WW	Bristol	Bristol Rovers	1911	1912	Preston North End	55		17
Ghrayib, N	Israel	Hapoel Tel Aviv	1999	2001	Hapoel Haifa	1	4	0
Gibson, C	Bridport	Portsmouth Sc	1978	1986	Manchester United	181	4	10
Gibson, CH	Middlesbrough	Newcastle United	1948	1956	Lincoln City	158		24
Gibson, D	Winchburgh	Leicester City	1970	1972	Exeter City	16	3	1
Gibson, JD	Larkhall	Partick Thistle	1926	1936	Retired	213		10
Gidman, J	Liverpool	Liverpool (app)	1972	1980	Everton	196	1	9
Gillan, JS	Derby	Burton S	1893	1894	Brierley Hill A	3		0
Gilson, TA	Lichfield	Burton United	1900	1901	Brentford	2		0
Ginola, DDM	France	Tottenham Hotspur	2000	2001	Everton	14	18	3
Gittings, A	Manchester	Luton Town	1908	1909	Croydon Comm	1		0
Glover, D	West Bromwich	King's Norton Sc	1983	1987	Middlesbrough	25	3	0
Goddard, H	Durham	Artwell Royal	1927	1928	Stockton	1		0
Godfrey, BC	Flint	Preston North End	1967	1971	Bristol Rovers	139	4	22
Goffin, WC	Tamworth	Tamworth	1945	1954	Walsall	156		36
Goodall, AL	Belfast	St Jude's	1888	1889	Derby County	14		7
Goode, BJ	Chester	Wrexham	1911	1912	Hull City	7		3
Gordon, R	Leith	Hearts	1894	1895	Forfar A	4		2
Goss, FC	Draycott	Ilkeston Town	1936	1937	Wrexham	2		0
Graham, G	Lanark	Scotland Boys	1962	1964	Chelsea	8		2
Graham, J	Leyland	Oldbury B	1889	1892	Brierley Hill A	18		5
Graham, JR	Smethwick	Leyland Wks	1946	1949	Wrexham	10		3
Gray, AA	London	Crystal Palace	1987	1989	Queens Park Rangers	34	3	4
Gray, AM	Glasgow	Dundee United	1975	1979	Wolverhampton Wanderers	} 165	2	59
		Everton	1985	1987	West Bromwich Albion			
Gray, FJS	Oldbury	West Brom Utd	1889	1890	Wednesbury Town	2		0
Gray, J	Bristol	Bristol Rovers	1904	1905	Glasgow R	7		0
Gray, S	Withernsea	Barnsley	1987	1991	Southampton	102	4	9
Graydon, RJ	Bristol	Bristol Rovers	1971	1977	Coventry City	188	4	68
Grayson, SN	Sheffield	Leicester City	1997	1999	Blackburn Rovers	32	16	0
Green, TW	Worcester	West Bromwich Albion	1886	1889	Kidderminster H	21		14
Greenhalgh, BA	Chestefield	Preston North End	1967	1969	Leicester City	37	3	12
Grenhalgh, S	Eagley	Bolton Wanderers	1905	1908	Bolton Wanderers	46		2
Gregory, HG	London	Charlton Athletic	1970	1972	Hereford United	18	6	2
Gregory, JC	Scunthorpe	Northampton Town	1977	1979	Brighton & Hove Albion	59	6	10
Griffin, H	Dudley	Lye T	1902	1903	Dudley Town	1		0

FAC Apps	Sub	Goals	FLC Apps	Sub	Goals	Others Apps	Sub	Goals	Totals Apps	Sub	Goals
6		0	3		0	0		0	77		2
22	2	1	23	1	1	18		1	286	17	15
6		0	0		0	0		0	25		0
4		0	7		0	1		0	68	5	7
0		0	0		0	0		0	1		0
1		0	3		0	4	1	0	26	2	0
24		0	0		0	3		0	206		0
26	3	0	42	1	6	24		3	466	7	63
6	3	0	3	2	2	0	1	0	62	11	17
0		0	0		0	1		0	3		0
0		0	0		0	0		0	2		0
1		0	0		0	0		0	17		4
0		0	0		0	0		0	7		3
7		0	0		0	0		0	68		0
2	1	0	4	2	0	0		0	45		7
1		0	0		0	0		0	31		5
0		0	2		0	0		0	7	1	0
0		0	0	1	0	0		0	2	7	0
2		0	0		0	1		0	14	2	3
0		0	2		0	0		0	5		0
0		0	2	5	0	0		0	18	21	3
1		0	1		0	0		0	40		2
0		0	0		0	0	1	0	0	1	0
0		0	1		0	1	1	0	16	1	0
0		0	0		0	0		0	1		0
0		0	0		0	0		0	18		5
0		0	0		0	0		0	4		2
2		0	0		0	0		0	36		7
8	1	0	0		0	0		0	128		61
0		0	2		0	0		0	17		3
2		0	5		0	0		0	40		1
5	2	1	1	1	0	0		0	36	8	3
9		1	13		3	8		0	143	2	12
3		0	8	1	0	3		1	69	3	1
2		0	0		0	0		0	79		1
0		0	0		0	0		0	1		1
4	1	0	0		0	0		0	17		1
31		15	0		0	3		1	257	1	112
0		0	0		0	0		0	7		4
0		0	0		0	0		0	5		1
1		0	2		0	0		0	12		0
2		1	6	3	0	1		0	52	4	16
40		0	0		0	3		0	401		0
3	1	0	0		0	1		0	59		18
0		0	1		0	0		0	2	4	0
12	1	0	26	4	0	14	1	2	233	5	17
9	2	0	0		0	0		0	167		26
1		0	4		0	0		0	21	3	1
12		0	0		0	0		0	225		10
12		0	25		0	9		0	242	1	9
0		0	0		0	0		0	3		0
0		0	0		0	0		0	2		0
1		0	1	1	0	3	3	2	19	22	5
0		0	0		0	0		0	1		0
3		0	7		1	1		0	36	3	1
0		0	0		0	0		0	1		0
8	3	0	9		0	0		0	156	4	25
17	6	0	0		0	0		0	173		42
0		0	0		0	0		0	14		7
0		0	0		0	0		0	7		3
0		0	0		0	0		0	4		2
0		0	0		0	0		0	2		0
0		0	2		0	0		0	10		2
2	2	0	0		0	0		0	20		7
1	1	0	0		0	0		0	11		4
3	1	1	3		1	0	1	0	40	5	6
10	2	3	25		14	6		2	206	4	78
0		0	0		0	0		0	2		0
0		0	0		0	0		0	7		0
5	1	3	11		1	7	3	2	125	8	15
10		3	25	1	9	3		1	226	5	81
4	1	2	1	1	0	6	3	0	43	21	2
7		5	0		0	0		0	28		19
2		0	0		0	0		0	39	3	12
2		0	0		0	0		0	48		2
0		0	5		0	0		0	23	6	2
2		0	5		0	3	1	0	69	7	10
0		0	0		0	0		0	1		0

307

The Essential History of Aston Villa

Player	Birthplace	From	Year Joined	Year Left	To	League Apps	Sub	Goals
Griffiths, J	Oldbury	Oldbury Sc	1968	1970	Stockport County	1	1	0
Griffiths, JA	Birmingham	St George's	1896	1897	Bilston Town	2		0
Griffiths, TP	Moss	Middlesbrough	1935	1937	Retired	65		1
Groves, W	Leith	West Bromwich Albion	1892	1894	Hibernian	22		3
Gutteridge, RW	Widnes	Prescot Cbls	1945	1948	Brighton & Hove Albion	15		0
Hadji, M	Morocco	Coventry City	2001	-	Still at club	17	6	2
Hadley, G	Glasgow	Southampton	1919	1920	Coventry City	4		0
Hadley, H	Barrow	West Bromwich Albion	1905	1906	Nottingham Forest	11		0
Haggart, W	Edinburgh	Dalry Prim	1898	1900	Edinburgh Th	2		0
Hale, A	Waterford	Waterford	1960	1962	Doncaster Rovers	5		1
Hall, AE	Stourbridge	Stourbridge	1903	1914	Millwall	195		51
Halse, H	London	Manchester United	1912	1913	Chelsea	31		21
Hamilton, IM	London	Southend United	1969	1976	Sheffield United	189	15	40
Hamilton, W	Airdrie	Hibernian	1965	1967	Exeter City	49		9
Hampson, J	Oswestry	Leeds City	1919	1921	Port Vale	14		0
Hampton, G	Wellington	Glossop	1914	1915	Shrewsbury Town	3		0
Hampton, H	Wellington	Wellington Town	1904	1920	Birmingham	339		215
Handley, B	Wakefield	Goole Town	1959	1960	Torquay United	3		0
Hardy, G	Newbold	Nuneaton Town	1936	1938	Blackburn Rovers	6		1
Hardy, S	Newbold	Liverpool	1912	1921	Nottingham Forest	159		0
Hare, CB	Birmingham	Birmingham U	1891	1895	Arsenal	25		13
Harkus, G	Newcastle	Scotswood	1921	1923	Southampton	4		0
Harley, CE	Wednesbury	Bloxwich S	1890	1891	Notts County	1		0
Harper, R	Lichfield	Burton U	1907	1908	Notts County	2		0
Harris, CV	Grantham	Llandidrod W	1922	1926	Retired	26		0
Harris, EJ	Willenhall	Bilston Town	1895	1896	Wolverhampton Wanderers	1		0
Harris, GA	Halesowen	Halesowen	1901	1908	West Bromwich Albion	20		1
Harris, WH	Plymouth	Torquay United	1924	1928	Bristol City	20		4
Harrison, JC	Leicester	Leicester City	1949	1950	Coventry City	8		1
Harrison, T	Birmingham	Coombes Wd	1888	1889	Halesowen	2		0
Harrop, J	Sheffield	Liverpool	1912	1921	Sheffield United	153		4
Harvey, H	Wednesbury	Walsall TS	1897	1898	Burslem PV	11		3
Harvey, RA	Nottingham	Notts Rangs	1882	1883	Normanton	0		0
Harvey, WA	Derby	Derby Mid	1884	1885	Chester	0		0
Hateley, A	Derby	Notts County	1963	1966	Chelsea	127		68
Haycock, F	Bootle	Prescot Cbls	1936	1939	Wrexham	99		28
Haynes, AE	Birmingham	Local	1946	1947	Walsall	4		0
Hazelden, W	Ashton-in-Makerfield	Wigan YC	1957	1959	Wigan A	17		5
Heard, PT	Hull	Everton	1979	1983	Sheffield Wednesday	20	4	2
Heath, A	Stoke-on-Trent	Español	1989	1990	Manchester City	8	1	0
Hendrie, LA	Birmingham	Trainee	1994	-	Still at club	116	30	15
Henshall, HV	Hednesford	Bridgtown Ams	1910	1912	Notts County	45		8
Hickman, J	Durham	Hartlepool United	1927	1928	Spennymoor United	2		0
Hickson, D	Ellesmere Port	Everton	1955	1956	Huddersfield Town	12		1
Hickton, AJ	Birmingham	Waterworks	1889	1890	Rugby W	1		0
Hinchcliffe, J	Tillicoultry	L. Pieter's BC	1957	1958	Workington	2		0
Hinchley, A	Warwick	Warwick Co	1891	1892	Cape Hill	11		0
Hindle, JJ	Preston	Barrow	1950	1951	Barrow	15		0
Hisbent, JS	Plymouth	Green Waves	1905	1906	Portsmouth	2		0
Hislop, PD	Glasgow	Glasgow R	1891	1892	Forfar A	7		3
Hitchens, SG	Rawnsley	Cardiff City	1957	1961	Inter Milan	132		78
Hiyzlsperger, T	Germany	Bayern Munich	2000	-	Still at club	11	2	1
Hobson, CS	Walsall	Walsall S	1885	1886	Bilston	0		0
Hockey, T	Keighley	Norwich City	1973	1974	Bradford City	24		1
Hodge, SB	Nottingham	Nottingham Forest	1985	1987	Tottenham Hotspur	52		12
Hodgetts, D	Birmingham	Mitchell's St G	1886	1896	Small Heath	181		62
Hodgson, G	Johannesburg	Liverpool	1935	1937	Leeds United	28		11
Hogg, RA	Lowick	Berwick R	1954	1957	Mansfield Town	21		0
Hole, BG	Swansea	Blackburn Rovers	1968	1970	Swansea City	47		6
Hopkins, R	Birmingham	Birmingham Sc	1979	1980	Birmingham City	1	2	1
Horne, SF	Witney	Bampton YC	1963	1964	Manchester City	6		0
Horton, T	Tipton	Tipton BCT	1881	1882	Walsall TS	0		0
Houghton, WE	Billingborough	Billongboro'	1929	1947	Notts County	361		160
Houghton, R	Glasgow	Liverpool	1992	1995	Crystal Palace	83	12	6
Howath, S	Bristol	Merthyr Tydfll	1948	1950	Swansea Town	8		2
Hughes, DT	Birmingham	Birmingham Sc	1976	1977	Lincoln City	4	1	1
Hughes, RD	Wrexham	Trainee	1996	1998	Shrewsbury Town	4	3	0
Hughes, T	Dalmuir	Chelsea	1971	1972	Hereford United	16		0
Humphries, HJ	Birmingharn	Handsworth GS	1914	1922	Southend United	20		2
Hunt, D	Leicester	Notts County	1987	1989	Mansfield Town	12	1	0
Hunt, SK	Birmingham	Stanley Star	1974	1977	New York Cos	} 65	4	7
		West Bromwich Albion	1986	1988	Retired			
Hunter, Andy	Ayrshire	Vale of Leven	1879	1882	Retired	0		0
Hunter, Archie	Ayrshire	Ayr Th	1878	1890	Retired	32		9
Hunter, GC	India	Peshawur Boys	1908	1912	Oldham Athletic	91		1
Inglis, JF	Leven	Glenrothes	1967	1968	Crewe Alexandra	1	1	0
Iverson, RTJ	Folkstone	Wolverhampton Wanderers	1936	1948	Retired	135		9
Jackson, DL	Birmingham	Hednesford	1956	1959	Millwall	8		0
Jackson, T	Newcastle	Durham Un (am)	1920	1930	Kidderminster H	172		0

| FAC | | | FLC | | | Others | | | Totals | | |
Apps	Sub	Goals	Apps	Sub	Goals	Apps	Sub	Goals	Apps	Sub	Goals
0		0	1		0	0		0	2	1	0
1		0	0		0	0		0	3		0
2		0	0		0	0		0	67		1
4		0	0		0	0		0	26		3
0		0	0		0	0		0	15		0
0	1	0	2		0	3	3	1	22	10	3
0		0	0		0	0		0	4		0
0		0	0		0	0		0	11		0
0		0	0		0	0		0	2		0
2	1	0	0		0	0		0	7		2
19	10	0	0		0	1		0	215		61
6	7	0	0		0	0		0	37		28
12		0	31	8	2	0		0	234	15	48
1		0	4		0	0		0	54		9
1		0	0		0	0		0	15		0
0		0	0		0	0		0	3		0
34	27	0	0		0	0		0	373		242
0		0	0		0	0		0	3		0
0		0	0		0	0		0	6		1
24		0	0		0	0		0	183		0
1		0	0		0	0		0	26		13
0		0	0		0	0		0	4		0
0		0	0		0	0		0	1		0
0		0	0		0	0		0	2		0
0		0	0		0	0		0	26		0
0		0	0		0	0		0	1		0
1		0	0		0	0		0	21		1
0		0	0		0	0		0	20		4
0		0	0		0	0		0	8		1
0		0	0		0	0		0	2		0
18		0	0		0	0		0	171		4
0		0	0		0	0		0	11		3
4	1	0	0		0	0		0	4		1
4		0	0		0	0		0	4		0
8	5	13	13		0	0		0	148		86
11	5	0	0		0	0		0	110		33
0		0	0		0	0		0	4		0
2		0	0		0	0		0	19		5
0		0	0	1	0	1		0	21	5	2
0	1	0	1	1	0	0		0	9	3	0
7	8	0	6	2	3	13	3	2	142	43	20
5	3	0	0		0	0		0	50		11
0		0	0		0	0		0	2		0
0		0	0		0	0		0	12		1
0		0	0		0	0		0	1		0
0		0	0		0	0		0	2		0
0		0	0		0	0		0	11		0
0		0	0		0	0		0	15		0
0		0	0		0	0		0	2		0
0		0	0		0	0		0	7		3
18	7	0	10	11	0	0		0	160		96
0		0	0		0	0		0	11	2	1
2		0	0		0	0		0	2		0
0		0	0		0	0		0	24		1
4	1	0	12	3	0	1		0	69		16
37	27	0	0		0	0		0	218		89
0		0	0		0	0		0	28		11
0		0	0		0	0		0	21		0
4	2	0	2	1	0	0		0	53		9
0		0	0		0	0		0	1	2	1
0		0	0		0	0		0	6		0
1		0	0		0	0		0	1		0
31	10	0	0		0	0		0	392		170
7	2	0	11	2	2	4	2	1	105	16	11
1		0	0		0	0		0	9		2
0		0	0		0	0		0	4	1	1
0		0	0		0	0		0	4	3	0
1		0	6		0	0		0	23		0
1		0	0		0	0		0	21		2
0		0	2		0	0		0	14	1	0
2	2		8		0	1	1	0	76	5	9
10	5	0	0		0	0		0	10		5
41	33	0	0		0	0		0	73		42
6		0	0		0	1		0	98		1
0		0	1		0	0		0	2	1	0
18	3	0	0		0	0		0	153		12
0		0	0		0	0		0	8		0
14		0	0		0	0		0	186		0

The Essential History of Aston Villa

Player	Birthplace	From	Year Joined	Year Left	To	League Apps	Sub	Goals
Jakeman, GW	Birmingham	Metropolitan	1924	1929	Notts County	8		0
Jeffries, R	Birmingham	Moor Green	1950	1951	Walsall	2		0
Jenkins, L	West Bromwich	West Bromwich Sc	1978	1980	RoPs (Finland)	0	3	0
Johnson, G	West Bromwich	Walsall	1897	1905	Plymouth	99		38
Johnson, WF	Bradeley	Buxton	1926	1928	Charlton Athletic	4		0
Johnstone, CS	Birmingham	Saltley Col	1879	1880	Lozells BC	0		0
Johnstone, JC	Dundee	Dundee	1921	1927	Retired	105		1
James, DB	Welwyn Garden City	Liverpool	1999	2001	West Ham United	67		0
Jaszczum, AJ	Kettering	Trainee	1996	2000	Blackpool	0		0
Joachim, JK	Boston, Lincs	Leicester City	1996	2001	Coventry City	90	51	40
Johnson, T	Newcastle	Derby County	1995	1997	Celtic	38	19	13
Jones, AR	Burton-on-Trent	Bilston Boys	1961	1962	Nuneaton B	1		0
Jones, K	Monmouthshire	Kidderminster H	1947	1957	Port Vale	185		0
Jones, M	Warley	Oldbury Sc	1981	1984	Brighton & Hove Albion	24		0
Jones, LC	Mountain Ash	Luton Town	1957	1958	Worcester City	5		0
Jones, PO	Birmingham	Birmingham Un	1921	1924	Retired	15		0
Jones, TW	Birmingham	Oakengates	1924	1926	Burnley	5		0
Jones, WEJ	Wellington	Shrewsbury Town	1910	1911	Bristol Rovers	2		1
Jones, WA	Wednesfield	Walsall TS	1885	1886	Retired	0		0
Kachloul, H	Morocco	Southampton	2001	-	Still at club	17	5	2
Kapengwe, E	Zambia	Atlanta Chiefs	1969	1970	Atlanta Chiefs	3		0
Kearns, J	Chasetown	Birmingham	1908	1912	Bristol City	39		0
Keelan, KD	India	Kidderminster H	1959	1961	Stockport County	5		0
Kenning, MJ	Birmingham	Birmingham Boys	1960	1961	Shrewsbury Town	3		0
Keown, M	Oxford	Arsenal	1986	1989	Everton	109	3	3
Kerr, AW	Lancaster	Medomsley Jnrs	1936	1947	Retired	29		4
Kerr, P	Portsmouth	Portsmouth Boys	1983	1987	Middlesbrough	16	8	3
Kimberley, W	Birmingham	Aston Manor	1907	1909	Coventry City	7		0
King, PG	Bristol	Sheffield Wednesday	1994	1997	Swindon Town	13	3	0
Kingaby, HC	London	Clapton Orient	1905	1906	Fulham	4		0
Kingdon, WJ	Worcester	Kidderminster H	1926	1936	Southampton	223		5
Kinsey, G	Burton-on-Trent	Wolverhampton Wanderers	1894	1895	Derby County	3		0
Kirton, W	Newcastle	Leeds C	1919	1927	Coventry City	229		53
Kubicki, D	Poland	Legia (Poland)	1991	1994	Sunderland	24	1	0
Kyle, P	Glasgow	Arsenal	1907	1909	Sheffield United	5		0
Laidlaw, J	Kilmarnock	South Shields	1913	1914	Chesterfield	2		0
Lamptey, NO	Ghana	RSC Anderlecht	1994	1995	Coventry City	1	5	0
Law, S	Birmingham	Aston Unity	1879	1883	Retired	0		0
Lawrence, J	Earlstown	Earlstown	1919	1920	Coventry City	13		0
Layton, AE	Durham	Rotherham Town	1908	1909	Middlesbrough	16		0
Leach, J	Spennymore	Black & Whites	1912	1922	Queens Park Rangers	67		3
Leake, A	Birmingham	Small Heath	1902	1908	Burnley	128		7
Lee, EB	Birmingham	Lordswood BC	1879	1883	South Africa	0		0
Lee, GF	Hednesford	Hednesford Town	1958	1965	Shrewsbury Town	118		2
Lee, JT	Brierley Hill	Wulfurians	1919	1921	Stoke	18		0
Leigh, WH	Birmingham	Cadishead A	1898	1899	Altrincham	1		0
Leonard, K	Birmingahm	Highgate United	1972	1976	Retired	36	2	11
Lescott, AA	Birmingham	Trainee	1996	2000	Sheffield Wednesday	0		0
Lillis, M	Manchester	Derby County	1987	1989	Scunthorpe United	30	1	4
Lindon, AE	Birmingham	Birmingham	1911	1912	Barnsley	1		0
Linton, I	West Bromwich	West Brom Sc	1976	1982	Peterboro United	16	11	0
Little, A	Horden	Durham Boys	1973	1975	Southend United	2	1	0
Little, B	Peterlee	Durham Boys	1971	1980	Retired	242	5	60
Littlewood, WA	Birmingham	Worchester C	1911	1915	Wellington Town	49		0
Lloyd, F	West Bromwich	Arsenal	1900	1902	Dundee	5		1
Loach, AA	West Bromwich	West Bromwich Albion	1886	1887	Retired	0		0
Lochhead, A	Lenzie	Leicester City	1969	1973	Oldham Athletic	127	4	34
Lockett, AH	Stoke-on-Trent	Stoke	1902	1905	Preston North End	41		5
Lockhart, N	Belfast	Coventry City	1952	1956	Bury	74		10
Logan, A	Glasgow	Falkirk	1906	1909	Falkirk	24		11
Logan, J	Troon	Sunderland	1892	1894	Notts County	14		8
Logan, JL	Glasgow	Queen's Park	1905	1912	Glasgow R	144		4
Lowe, E	Halesowen	Kynoch Works	1945	1950	Fulham	104		3
Lynch, JB	Birmingham	Cross Castle Yth	1968	1970	Atlanta Chiefs	2		0
Lynn, S	Bolton	Accrington Stanley	1950	1962	Birmingham City	281		36
Lyons, T	Hednesford	Bridgetown Am	1907	1915	Retired	217		0
McAuley, W	Glasgow	Glasgow C	1900	1901	Glasgow C	6		0
McAvennie, F	Glasgow	West Ham United	1992	1992	Trialist	0	3	0
McClure, A	Workington	Birmingham	1923	1925	Stoke	7		0
McDonald, RW	Aberdeen	Aberdeen Sc	1972	1976	Coventry City	33	6	3
McEleny, CR	Scotland	New Brighton	1899	1900	Edinburgh, Th	1		0
MacEwan, J	Dundee	Raith Rovers	1959	1966	Walsall	143	1	28
McGrath, J	Limerick	Belvedere FC	1998	-	Still at club	0	3	0
McGrath, P	London	Manchester United	1989	1996	Derby County	248	5	9
McInally, A	Ayr	Glasgow C	1987	1989	Bayern Munich	50	9	18
Mackay, N	Edinburgh	Hibernian	1923	1924	Lovells A	2		0
McKenzie, JW	Montrose	Dundee	1908	1909	Bristol Rovers	5		0
McKnight, T	Lichfield	Burton S	1890	1891	Leek Alex	10		1
McLachlan, A	Kirkcudbright	St Cuthbert's W	1913	1914	Aberdeen	3		0

FAC Apps	Sub	Goals	FLC Apps	Sub	Goals	Others Apps	Sub	Goals	Totals Apps	Sub	Goals
0		0	0		0	0		0	8		0
0		0	0		0	0		0	2		0
0		0	0		0	0		0	0	3	0
9		9	0		0	2		0	110		47
0		0	0		0	0		0	4		0
2		0	0		0	0		0	2		0
10		0	0		0	0		0	115		1
8		0	6		0	4		0	85		0
0		0	0	1	0	0		0	0	1	0
8	4	2	10	1	3	6	3	1	114	59	46
5	2	1	5		2	1	1	1	49	22	17
0		0	0		0	0		0	1		0
14		0	0		0	0		0	199		0
1		0	3		0	5		0	33		0
0		0	0		0	0		0	5		0
0		0	0		0	0		0	15		0
0		0	0		0	0		0	5		0
0		0	0		0	0		0	2		1
2		0	0		0	0		0	2		0
0		0	2		0	6	1	0	25	6	2
0		0	0		0	0		0	3		0
1		0	0		0	0		0	40		0
0		0	0		0	0		0	5		0
0		0	0		0	0		0	3		0
6		0	12		0	2		0	129	3	3
0		0	0		0	0		0	29		4
2		1	5	2	2	0	2	0	23	12	6
0		0	0		0	0		0	7		0
0		0	3		0	4		0	20	3	0
0		0	0		0	0		0	4		0
18		0	0		0	0		0	241		5
0		0	0		0	0		0	3		0
32		6	0		0	0		0	261		59
4	1	0	2		0	1		0	31	2	0
0		0	0		0	0		0	5		0
0		0	0		0	0		0	2		0
0		0	2	1	3	0		0	3	6	3
10	1	0	0		0	0		0	10		1
1		0	0		0	0		0	14		0
1		0	0		0	0		0	17		0
9		0	0		0	0		0	76		3
13	2	0	0		0	0		0	141		9
11		0	0		0	0		0	11		0
8		0	16		0	0		0	142		2
0		0	0		0	0		0	18		0
0		0	0		0	0		0	1		0
3		2	6		4	0		0	45	2	17
0	1	0	0		0	0		0	0	1	0
2		0	4		0	1		0	37	1	4
0		0	0		0	0		0	1		0
1		0	0		0	0	2	0	17	13	0
0		0	2		1	0		0	4	1	1
15	1	4	29	1	15	9		3	295	7	82
2		0	0		0	0		0	51		0
2		0	0		0	0		0	7		1
3		4	0		0	0		0	3		4
2		0	20		10	1		0	150	4	44
0		0	0		0	0		0	41		5
11	2	0	0		0	0		0	85		12
1	1	0	0		0	0		0	25		12
1		0	0		0	0		0	15		8
13		0	0		0	0		0	157		4
13		0	0		0	0		0	117		3
1		0	0		0	0		0	3		0
36		1	6		1	1		0	324		38
20		0	0		0	1		0	238		0
0		0	0		0	0		0	6		0
0		0	0		0	0		0	0	3	0
0		0	0		0	0		0	7		0
3	1	0	3		1	1		0	40	6	5
0		0	0		0	0		0	1		0
20		0	18		4	0		0	181	1	32
0		0	0		0	0		0	0	3	0
23	1	0	29	1	1	15	1	0	315	8	10
4	2	0	6		5	3		3	63	9	28
0		0	0		0	0		0	2		0
0		0	0		0	0		0	5		0
2	2	0	0		0	0		0	12		3
0		0	0		0	0		0	3		0

Player	Birthplace	From	Year Joined	Year Left	To	League Apps	Sub	Goals
McLachlan, JA	Dumfries	Dundee	1912	1915	Dundee	17		3
McLaverty, J	South Shields	Birtley C	1913	1914	South Shields	2		0
McLoughlin, AF	Manchester	Southampton (loan)	1991	1991		0		0
MacLeod, JM	Edinburgh	Arsenal	1964	1968	Mechelen (Bel)	123	2	16
McLuckie, J	Lancashire	Bury	1901	1904	Plymouth Argyle	57		40
McLuckie, JS	Stonehouse	Manchester City	1934	1936	Ipswich Town	15		1
McMahon, P	Kilsyth	Glasgow C	1971	1975	Portland Tim	121	9	25
McMahon, S	Liverpool	Everton	1983	1986	Liverpool	74	1	7
McMorran, JW	Muirkirk	Ayr Schools	1960	1962	Third Lanark	11		1
McNaught, K	Kirkcaldy	Everton	1977	1983	West Bromwich Albion	207		8
McParland, PJ	Newry	Dundalk	1952	1962	Wolves	293		97
Maggs, EP	Bristol	Bath C	1930	1931	Blackpool	12		0
Maiden, WH	Kidderminster	Kidderminster H	1919	1920	Stourbridge	1		0
Mandley, J	Hanley	Port Vale	1929	1934	Retired	106		25
Mann, CJ	Smethwick	West Brom (am)	1899	1901	Burton United	10		0
Mann, FD	Newark	Lincoln City	1911	1912	Huddersfield Town	1		0
Marriott, W	Northampton	Wellingborough	1901	1902	Bristol City	8		0
Martin, CJ	Dublin	Leeds United	1948	1956	Waterford	194		1
Martin, JJ	Ashington	Ashington Boys	1964	1965	Colchester United	1		0
Martin, JR	Birmingham	Hednesford Town	1936	1949	Retired	51		22
Martin, LJ	Ludlow	Clee Hill Boys	1966	1972	Worcester C	36	11	4
Martin, FA	Walsall	Wednesbury OA	1890	1891	Walsall T.S.	3		0
Masefield, KL	Birmingham	Warwick Sc	1975	1977	Haarlem (Hol)	0	3	0
Mason, WB	Burton	Moseley G'hprs	1879	1880	Wednesbury Town	0		0
Mason, T	Birmingham	Burton Alsopps	1882	1883	Burton	0		0
Massie, A	Glasgow	Hearts	1935	1939	Retired	141		5
Matthews, W	Mansfield	Ripley	1903	1907	Notts County	25		12
Maund, JH	Hednesford	Hednesford Town	1935	1938	Nottingham Forest	47		8
Mellberg, O	Sweden	Racing Santander	2001		Still at club	32		0
Merson, PC	Harlesden	Middlesbrough	1998	2002	Portsmouth	101	16	18
Miles, A	Birmingham	Aston St Mary's	1903	1914	Retired	249		0
Miles, R	Enfield	Enfield	1930	1931	Millwall	16		0
Miller, AT	Cardiff	Aberdare	1900	1902	Wellington Town	10		0
Millington, CJH	Linloln	Ripley	1905	1908	Fulham	34		10
Milne, Dr VE	Aberdeen	Aberdeen	1923	1929	Retired	157		1
Milosevic, S	Yugoslavia	Partizan Belgrade	1995	1999	Real Zaragoza	84	6	27
Mitchinson, TW	Sunderland	Mansfield Town	1967	1969	Torquay United	49		9
Moore, I	Tipton	St Stephen's	1889	1990	Dudley Town	5		0
Moore, T	Tipton	Stourbridge	1931	1932	Bournemouth	1		1
Moralee, M	Mexborough	Grimsby Town	1936	1937	Leicester City	12		1
Morby, JH	Wednesbury	Hednesford Town	1945	1946	Worcester City	0		0
Morgan, SJ	Belfast	Port Vale	1973	1976	Brighton & Hove Albion	35	5	9
Morley, WA	Ormskirk	Burnley	1979	1984	West Bromwich Albion	128	9	25
Morrall, TS	Smethwick	Church R	1959	1961	Shrewsbury Town	8		0
Morris, W	Danesmore	Chesterfield	1911	1915	Alfreton	50		0
Mort, T	Bolton	Rochdale	1921	1935	Retired	337		2
Mortimer, DG	Liverpool	Coventry City	1975	1985	Brighton & Hove Albion	315	1	31
Mortimer, P	London	Charlton Athletic	1991	1992	Crystal Palace	10	2	1
Morton, H	Oldham	Ryl Welch Fus	1931	1937	Everton	192		0
Moseley, G	Manchester	Derby C(L)	1974	1975	Derby County	3		0
Moss, A	Birmingham	Birmingham CBC	1945	1956	Kettering Town	102		5
Moss, AJ	Crewe	Whitchurch	1909	1912	Bristol City	5		0
Moss, F (Snr)	Birmingham	Walsall	1914	1929	Cardiff City	255		9
Moss, F (Jnr)	Birmingham	Sheffield W(am)	1938	1955	Retired	297		3
Mountfield, D	Liverpool	Everton	1988	1991	Wolverhampton Wanderers	88	2	9
Muldoon, TP	Athlone	Athlone T	1924	1927	Tottenham Hotspur	33		0
Mulraney, A	Nr Motherwell	Kidderminster H	1948	1949	Cradley Heath	12		2
Murray, JA	Scotland	Ayr U	1901	1902	Small Heath	2		0
Murray, SG	Aberdeen	Fraserburgh	1994	1997	Bristol City	4		0
Mwela, F	Zambia	Atlanta Chiefs	1969	1970	Atlanta Chiefs	1		0
Myerscough, W	Bolton	Walsall	1956	1959	Rotherham United	64		15
Nash, HE	Nr Cardiff	Pontypridd	1914	1920	Coventry City	12		5
Neal, J	County Durham	Swindon Town	1959	1963	Southend United	96		0
Nelson, F	Portugal	Sporting Lisbon	1996	2000	FC Porto	54	5	0
Niblo, TBD	Dunfermline	Newcastle United	1901	1904	Nottingham Forest	45		9
Nibloe, J	Renfrewshire	Kilmarnock	1932	1934	Sheffield Wednesday	48		0
Nicholl, CJ	Wilmslow	Luton Town	1971	1977	Southampton	209		11
Nicholson, JR	Sunderland	Cardiff City	1926	1927	Bangor City	1		0
Nielsen, K	Denmark	Brondby	1989	1992	Aarhus	74	5	4
Nilis, L	Belgium	PSV Eindhoven	2000	2001	Retired	3		1
Noon, MT	Burton	Burton S	1899	1906	Plymouth Argyle	74		1
Norris, FH	Birmingham	Halesowen	1925	1927	West Ham United	9		2
Norton, D	Cannock	Wolves Boys	1984	1988	—	42	2	2
Oakes, MC	Birmingham	Trainee	1991	1999	Wolves	49	2	0
O'Donnell, FJ	Fife	Blackpool	1938	1939	Nottingham Forest	29		14
Olney, BA	London	Derby County	1927	1930	Bilston United	84		0
Olney, I	Luton	Juniors	1988	1992	Oldham Athletic	62	26	16
O'Neill, AH	Sunderland	Sunderland	1960	1963	Sunderland	23		6
Ormsby, BTC	Birmingham	Ladywood Sc	1978	1983	Leeds United	115	2	4

Complete Players' Career Records: McLachlan, JA – Ormsby

FAC Apps	Sub	Goals	FLC Apps	Sub	Goals	Others Apps	Sub	Goals	Totals Apps	Sub	Goals
0	0	0	0	0	0	0	0	0	17		3
0	0	0	0	0	0	0	0	0	2		0
0	0	0	0	0	0	1	0	0	1		0
8	1	6	1	0	0	0	0	0	137	2	18
5	5	0	0	0	0	0	0	0	62		45
0	0	0	0	0	0	0	0	0	15		1
4	0	15	5	0	0	1	0	0	141	9	30
3	0	0	9	0	0	4	0	0	90	1	7
2	0	1	0	0	0	0	0	0	14		1
13	0	0	17	0	0	23	0	5	260		13
36	19	11	4	0	0	1	0	0	341		120
2	0	0	0	0	0	0	0	0	14		0
0	0	0	0	0	0	0	0	0	1		0
6	1	0	0	0	0	0	0	0	112		26
0	0	0	0	0	0	1	0	0	11		0
0	0	0	0	0	0	0	0	0	1		0
0	0	0	0	0	0	0	0	0	8		0
19	0	0	0	0	0	0	0	0	213		1
0	0	0	0	0	0	0	0	0	1		0
2	0	0	0	0	0	0	0	0	53		22
6	3	2	2	2	2	0	0	0	44	13	9
0	0	0	0	0	0	0	0	0	3		0
0	0	0	0	0	0	0	0	0	0	3	0
2	2	0	0	0	0	0	0	0	2		2
3	0	0	0	0	0	0	0	0	3		0
11	0	0	0	0	0	0	0	0	152		5
0	0	0	0	0	0	0	0	0	25		12
1	0	0	0	0	0	0	0	0	48		8
1	0	0	1	0	0	2	0	0	36		0
11	0	6	2	0	0	9	0	1	127	16	21
20	0	0	0	0	0	1	0	0	270		0
0	0	0	0	0	0	0	0	0	16		0
0	0	0	0	0	0	0	0	0	10		0
3	4	0	0	0	0	0	0	0	37		14
18	0	0	0	0	0	0	0	0	175		1
10	2	8	8	1	1	8	0	2	110	7	32
2	0	1	0	0	0	0	0	0	52		9
1	0	0	0	0	0	0	0	0	6		0
0	0	0	0	0	0	0	0	0	1		1
0	0	0	0	0	0	0	0	0	12		1
3	0	0	0	0	0	0	0	0	3		0
3	1	4	5	0	2	1	1	0	44	7	15
8	1	14	3	0	0	20	1	5	170	10	34
0	0	0	1	0	0	0	0	0	9		0
3	0	0	0	0	0	0	0	0	53		1
31	0	0	0	0	0	0	0	0	368		2
21	1	0	38	2	0	30	2	0	404	1	36
0	0	0	2	0	0	0	0	0	12	2	1
15	0	0	0	0	0	0	0	0	207		0
0	0	0	0	0	0	0	0	0	3		0
7	0	0	0	0	0	0	0	0	109		5
0	0	0	0	0	0	0	0	0	5		0
28	0	0	0	0	0	0	0	0	283		9
17	0	0	0	0	0	0	0	0	314		3
10	1	9	2	0	0	11	0	5	118	2	17
1	0	0	0	0	0	0	0	0	34		0
0	0	0	0	0	0	0	0	0	12		2
0	0	0	0	0	0	0	0	0	2		0
0	0	0	0	0	0	0	0	0	4		0
0	0	0	0	0	0	0	0	0	1		0
9	2	0	0	0	0	1	0	0	74		17
0	0	0	0	0	0	0	0	0	12		5
10	0	0	8	0	0	0	0	0	114		0
1	1	0	3	0	0	7	2	0	65	8	0
6	0	0	0	0	0	0	0	0	51		9
4	0	0	0	0	0	0	0	0	52		0
12	4	0	27	5	0	3	0	0	251		20
0	0	0	0	0	0	0	0	0	1		0
6	0	0	6	1	0	10	0	1	96	6	5
0	0	0	0	0	0	2	1	0	5		2
8	0	0	0	0	0	0	0	0	82		1
0	0	0	0	0	0	0	0	0	9		2
2	1	0	8	0	0	2	0	0	54	2	2
2	0	3	0	0	0	5	0	0	59	2	14
2	0	0	0	0	0	0	0	0	31		14
13	0	0	0	0	0	0	0	0	97		0
5	1	2	8	2	1	8	2	2	83	31	21
3	0	10	8	0	0	0	0	0	36		14
3	1	0	11	1	2	7	0	1	136	4	7

Player	Birthplace	From	Year Joined	Year Left	To	League Apps	Sub	Goals
Ormondroyd, I	Bradford	Bradford City	1988	1991	Derby County	41	15	6
Overton, J	Rotherham	Rotherham Boys	1975	1976	Gillingham	2	1	0
Pace, DJ	Wolverhampton	Bloxwich S	1950	1958	Sheffield United	98		40
Palethorpe, JT	Leicester	Sheffield Wednesday	1935	1936	Crystal Palace	6		2
Pank, T	Birmingham	Excelsior	1879	1883	Retired	0		0
Park, RC	Edinburgh	Peterlee Boys	1964	1969	Wrexham	60	14	7
Parker, G	Oxford	Nottingham Forest	1991	1995	Leicester City	91	4	13
Parker, GS	Coventry	Coventry Sc	1963	1968	Rotherham	16	1	1
Parkes, HA	Birmingham	Boldmere SM	1945	1955	Retired	320		3
Parsons, DR	Birmingham	Hereford United	1952	1955	Kidderminster Harriers	36		0
Paton, J	Birmingham	Vale of Leven	1890	1891	Dundee Harp	3		1
Pearson, JF	Brierley Hill	Saltley Col	1900	1907	Retired	104		4
Pejic, M	Chesterton	Everton	1979	1980	Retired	10		0
Pendleton, JJ	Liverpool	Sth Liverpool	1919	1920	Wigan Bor	6		0
Penrice, G	Bristol	Bristol Rovers	1990	1991	Queens Park Rangers	14	6	1
Perry, T	West Bromwich	West Bromwich Albion	1901	1903	Retired	27		1
Phillips, C	Monmouthshire	Wolverhampton Wanderers	1935	1938	Birmingham	22		5
Phillips, JTS	Shrewsbury	Shrewsbury Town	1968	1970	Chelsea	15		0
Phillips, L	Briton Ferry	Cardiff City	1974	1979	Swansea City	134	6	4
Phoenix, AF	Lancashire	Birmingham	1924	1925	Barnsley	3		2
Pimblett, F	Liverpool	Liverpool Sc	1975	1976	Stockport County	9		0
Pinner, MJ	Boston	Pegasus	1954	1977	Pegasus	4		0
Platt, D	Oldham	Crewe Alexandra	1988	1991	Bari (Italy)	121		50
Podmore, W	Derby	Burton United	1894	1895	Derby Mid	0		0
Poole, K	Bromsgrove	Bromsgrove Sc	1984	1987	Middlesbrough	28		0
Potter, F	Cradley Heath	Cradley Sc	1960	1961	Doncaster Rovers	4		0
Potts, VE	Birmingham	Doncaster Rovers	1945	1948	Retired	62		0
Pountney, DH	Baschurch	Shrewsbury Town	1963	1968	Shrewsbury Town	109	2	7
Powell, IV	Glamorgan	Queens Park Rangers	1948	1951	Port Vale	79		5
Price, C	Hereford	Blackburn Rovers	1988	1992	Blackburn Rovers	109	2	2
Price, LP	Caersws	Mansfield Town	1920	1922	Notts County	10		0
Price, R	Hereford	Worcester R	1884	1886	Retired	0		0
Pritchard, RT	Dawley	Wolverhampton Wanderers	1955	1958	Notts County	3		0
Pritty, B	Birmingham	Metro OB	1936	1938	Nottingham Forest	3		0
Proudler, A	Kineswinford	Halesowen Town	1954	1955	Crystal Palace	1		0
Purslow, T	Birmingham	Nechells OB	1894	1895	Walsall TS	1		1
Rachel, A	Birmingham	Trainee	1993	1995	Blackpool	0	1	0
Ralphs, A	Nantwich	Whitchurch	1911	1912	Chester	1		0
Ramsey, J	Birmingham	Church	1892	1893	Ward End	4		0
Randle, W	Birmingham	Aston Unity	1893	1894	Leek	1		0
Reeves, G	Hucknall	Barnsley	1907	1909	Bradford	35		11
Regis, C	French Guyana	Coventry City	1991	1993	Wolves	46	6	12
Renneville, WTJ	Dublin	Leyton	1910	1911	Retired	2		1
Reynolds, J	Blackburn	West Bromwich Albion	1893	1897	Glasgow C	96		17
Richards, RT	Bilston	Stourbridge	1911	1914	Bilston	7		0
Richardson, K	Newcastle	Real Sociedad	1991	1995	Coventry City	142	1	13
Riddell, T	Birmingham	Excelsior	1882	1886	Retired	0		0
Rideout, P	Bournemouth	Swindon Town	1983	1985	Bari (Italy)	50	4	19
Riley, T	Blackburn	Brentford	1905	1908	Brentwood	16		0
Rimmer, JJ	Southport	Arsenal	1977	1983	Swansea City	229		0
Rioch, BD	Aldershot	Luton Town	1969	1974	Derby County	149	5	34
Rioch, DN	Paddington	Luton Town	1969	1975	Portland Tim	17	5	3
Richie, S	Southampton	Southampton Sc	1986	1987	Crewe Alexandra	0	1	0
Roberts, DA	Birmingham	Lucas Eagle	1964	1968	Shrewsbury Town	15	1	1
Roberts, K	Crewe	Crewe Villa	1951	1954	Southern Lge	42		7
Roberts, KO	Nr Wrexham	Wrexham (am)	1953	1958	Retired	38		3
Roberts, RJ	West Bromwich	West Bromwich Albion	1892	1893	Retired	4		0
Roberts, WD	Stourbridge	Norton	1882	1884	Chirk	0		0
Robertson, R	Birmingham	Excelsior	1884	1887	Stourbridge	0		0
Robey, JH	Ratcliffe	Stalybridge C	1936	1937	Aberdeen	3		0
Robinson, P	Stafford	Stafford Sc	1986	1987	Wolverhampton Wanderers	2	1	1
Robson, JD	Consett	Derby County	1972	1978	Retired	142	4	1
Roose, Dr LR	Holt, Wrexham	Huddersfield Town	1911	1912	Arsenal	10		0
Ross, I	Glasgow	Liverpool	1971	1976	Peterborough United	175		3
Rowan, B	Glasgow	Bailleston R	1969	1970	Watford	1		0
Roxborough, J	Edinburgh	Leicester City	1922	1923	Stoke	12		3
Rudge, DH	Wolverhampton	Wolves Boys	1966	1970	Hereford United	49	6	10
Russell, G	Ayr	Ayr United	1893	1895	Glasgow United	32		1
Rutherford, JHH	County Durham	Southport	1938	1952	Retired	148		0
Sabin, AH	Birmingham	Aston Boys	1956	1958	Retired	2		0
Samuel, JL	Trinidad	Trainee	1999	-	Still at club	23	12	0
Saunders, DN	Swansea	Liverpool	1992	1995	Galatasaray	111	1	37
Saward, P	Cork	Millwall	1955	1961	Huddersfield Town	152		2
Schmeichel, PB	Denmark	Sporting Lisbon	2001	2002	Manchester City	29		1
Scimeca, R	Leamington Spa	Trainee	1993	1999	Nottingham Forest	50	23	2
Scott, AJE	St Neots	West Ham United	1965	1968	Torquay United	47	3	4
Sealey, L	London	Manchester United (loan)	1991	1992	Manchester United	18		0
Sellars, G	Stockport	Leeds United	1950	1951	Altrincham	2		0
Sewell, J	Nr Whitehaven	Sheffield Wednesday	1955	1960	Hull City	123		36

Complete Players' Career Records: Ormondroyd – Sewell

FAC Apps	Sub	Goals	FLC Apps	Sub	Goals	Others Apps	Sub	Goals	Totals Apps	Sub	Goals
5	2		4	2	2	6	1	0	56	18	10
0	0		0		0	0		0	2	1	0
8	2		0		0	1		0	107		42
0	0		0		0	0		0	6		2
10	0		0		0	0		0	10		0
3	1		8	1	2	0		0	71	15	10
10	1		12		0	0	2	0	113	6	14
1	0		3		0	0		0	20	1	1
25	1		0		0	0		0	345		4
5	0		0		0	0		0	41		0
0	0		0		0	0		0	3		1
14	3		0		0	0		0	118		7
0	0		2		0	0		0	12		0
0	0		0		0	0		0	6		0
0	0		0		0	0		0	14	6	1
2	0		0		0	0		0	29		1
0	0		0		0	0		0	22		5
2	0		0		0	0		0	17		0
7	0		17	1	0	10		0	168	7	4
1	1		0		0	0		0	4		3
1	0		1		0	0		0	11		0
0	0		0		0	0		0	4		0
9	2		14		10	11		6	155		68
1	0		0		0	0		0	1		0
1	0		2		0	1		0	32		0
2	0		1		0	0		0	7		0
10	0		0		0	0		0	72		0
9	0		8		0	0		0	126	2	7
7	0		0		0	0		0	86		5
7	0		14		0	11	1	0	141	3	2
0	0		0		0	0		0	10		0
8	0		0		0	0		0	8		0
0	0		0		0	0		0	3		0
1	0		0		0	0		0	4		0
0	0		0		0	0		0	1		0
0	0		0		0	0		0	1		1
0	0		0		0	0		0	0	1	0
0	0		0		0	0		0	1		0
0	0		0		0	0		0	4		0
0	0		0		0	0		0	1		0
1	0		0		0	0		0	36		11
5	2		3	1	0	0		0	54	9	12
0	0		0		0	0		0	2		1
14	0		0		0	0		0	110		17
0	0		0		0	0		0	7		0
12	0		15		3	2		0	171	1	16
10	0		0		0	0		0	10		0
1	1		4	2	3	1		0	56	7	22
0	0		0		0	0		0	16		0
12	0		23		0	23		0	287		0
7	0		14		3	1		0	171	5	37
1	0		1	1	0	0		0	19	6	3
0	0		0		0	0		0	0	1	0
1	1		2		0	0		0	18	1	2
4	0		0		0	0		0	46		7
0	0		0		0	0		0	38		3
0	0		0		0	0		0	4		0
5	1		0		0	0		0	5		1
3	0		0		0	0		0	3		0
0	0		0		0	0		0	3		0
0	0		0		0	0		0	2	1	1
10	0		19		0	2	1	0	173	5	1
0	0		0		0	0		0	10		0
10	0		17		0	3		0	205		3
0	0		0		0	0		0	1		0
0	0		0		0	0		0	12		3
4	1		0		0	0		0	53	7	10
5	2		0		0	0		0	37		3
8	0		0		0	0		0	156		0
0	0		0		0	0		0	2		0
2	0		0	1	0	3	2	0	28	15	0
9	4		15	7		8		1	143	1	49
16	0		1		0	1		0	170		2
1	0		2		0	4		0	36		1
9	1		4	3	0	5	2	0	68	29	2
2	0		5	1	0	0		0	54	3	5
4	0		0		0	2		0	24		0
0	0		0		0	0		0	2		0
21	4		0		0	1		0	145		40

Player	Birthplace	From	Year Joined	Year Left	To	League Apps	Sub	Goals
Sharp, B	Hereford	Hereford Th	1897	1899	Everton	22		0
Sharp, JS	Hereford	Hereford Th	1897	1899	Everton	23		15
Sharples, J	Wolverhampton	Heath Town	1958	1959	Walsall	13		0
Shaw, GR	Birmingham	Coleshill Town	1977	1988	BK Copenhagen	158	7	59
Shell, FH	London	Ford (Dag'ham)	1937	1939	Mansfield Town	23		8
Shelton, G	Nottingham	Walsall	1978	1982	Sheffield Wednesday	24		7
Shutt, GH	Burnley	Notts Rangs	1901	1904	Hucknall	40		0
Sidebottom, G	Mapplewell	Wolverhampton Wanderers	1960	1965	Scunthorpe United	70		0
Simmonds, HR	Birmingham	Aston Way	1879	1882	Retired	0		0
Simmonds, J	Birmingham	Hockley St J	1882	1887	Retired	0		0
Simmons, D	Isle of Wight	Arsenal	1968	1971	Walsall	13	4	7
Simpson, WS	Cowdenheath	Clyde	1931	1935	Cowdenbeath	29		1
Sims, ND	Coton-in-the-Elms	Wolverhampton Wanderers	1954	1964	Peterborough United	264		0
Sims, S	Lincoln	Watford	1987	1989	Retired	41		0
Singleton, H	Manchester	Manchester Cen	1923	1924	Retired	2		0
Six, D	France	Mulhouse (Fr)	1984	1985	Metz (France)	13	3	2
Skea, DF	Scotland	Arbroath	1892	1893	Dundee Th	1		1
Skiller, L	Penzance	Leyton	1908	1909	Swindon Town	1		0
Slade, C	Bath	Stourbridge	1913	1914	Huddersfield Town	3		0
Sloley, R	London	Corinthians	1919	1920	Corinthians	2		0
Sleeuwenhoek, JC	Wednesfield	Wardsbridge Sc	1960	1968	Birmingham City	226		1
Small, B	Birmingham	Juniors	1991	1996	Bolton Wanderers	31	5	0
Smart, HH	Smethwick	Bilston United	1913	1914	Wolves	1		0
Smart, T	Blackheath	Halesowen	1919	1933	Brierley Hill	405		8
Smith, G	Preston	Preston North End	1901	1902	Blackburn Rovers	5		0
Smith, GM	Glasgow	St Johnstone	1976	1979	Tottenham Hotspur	76	3	0
Smith, HH	Birmingham	Moor Green	1948	1954	Southend United	51		8
Smith, LJ	Halesowen	Wolves	1955	1959	Retired	115		24
Smith, LGF	London	Brentford	1945	1952	Brentford	191		31
Smith, S	Halesowen	Hednesford	1893	1902	Portsmouth	169		35
Southgate, G	Watford	Crystal Palace	1995	2001	Middlesbrough	191		7
Southren, T	Southwick	West Ham United	1954	1959	Bournemouth	63		6
Spencer, H	Birmingham	Birchfield Town	1894	1908	Retired	259		2
Spiers, C	Birmingham	Halesowen	1920	1927	Tottenham Hotspur	104		0
Spink, N	Chelmsford	Chelmsford C	1979	1996	West Bromwich Albion	357	4	0
Stainrod, S	Sheffield	Sheffield Wednesday	1984	1988	Stoke City	58	5	16
Stark, RH	Stapleford	Stapleford Boys	1973	1974	Non-league	2		0
Starling, RW	Nr Gateshead	Sheffield Wednesday	1936	1947	Retired	88		11
Staunton, S	Droghedra	Liverpool	1991	1998	Liverpool			
		Liverpool	2000	-	Still at club	208	7	16
Stephenson, C	Blyth	West Stanley	1910	1921	Huddersfield Town	192		85
Stephenson, G	Billingborough	Durham C	1931	1932	Luton Town	2		1
Stephenson, GT	County Durham	Leeds City	1921	1928	Derby County	93		22
Stephenson, J	County Durham	New Delaval	1914	1921	Sunderland	31		1
Stobart, B	Dodsworth	Manchester City	1964	1968	Shrewsbury Town	45		18
Stokes, AW	West Bromwich	Wednesbury OA	1892	1893	Retired	13		1
Stone, SB	Gateshead	Nottingham Forest	1999	-	Still at club	66	24	4
Strange, EW	Birmingham	Unity Gas	1897	1898	Langley SM	1		0
Suddick, J	Middlesbrough	Middlesbrough	1897	1898	Nottingham Forest	2		1
Surtees, AE	Willington Quay	Durham C	1923	1925	West Ham United	11		1
Swain, K	Birkenhead	Chelsea	1978	1983	Nottingham Forest	148		4
Swales, N	New Marske	Middlesbrough	1928	1930	Scarborough	6		0
Talbot, AD	Cannock	Hednesford	1923	1935	Bradford	240		7
Tate, JT	Old Hill	Cradley Heath	1927	1934	Brierley Hill	180		2
Taylor, IK	Birmingham	Sheffield Wednesday	1994	-	Still at club	193	27	28
Taylor, M	Annfield	Annfield Plain	1921	1922	Durham C	1		0
Teale, S	Southport	Bournemouth	1991	1995	Tranmere Rovers	146	1	2
Templeton, RD	Coylton	Hibernian	1898	1903	Newcastle United	64		7
Tewkesbury, KC	Hove	Birmingham	1932	1933	Notts County	1		0
Thomas, R	Birmingham	Cocknage	1888	1889	Walsall Town	0		0
Thompson, A	Newcastle	Bolton Wanderers	1998	2001	Celtic	36	10	4
Thompson, GL	Birmingham	Sheffield Wednesday	1986	1988	Watford	56	4	17
Thompson, JG	Crewe	Nantwich V	1919	1920	Brighton & Hove Albion	26		0
Thompson, T	FenchousesHave	Newcastle United	1950	1955	Preston North End	149		67
Thomson, RGM	Dundee	Wolves	1959	1964	Birmingham City	140		56
Tidman, OE	Margate	Tufnell Park	1932	1933	Stockport County	1		0
Tiler, B	Rotherham	Rotherham United	1968	1973	Carlisle United	106	1	3
Tiler, C	Sheffield	Nottingham Forest	1995	1997	Sheffield United	10	2	1
Tindall, MC	Birmingham	Sth Birmingham Boys	1959	1968	Walsall	118	2	8
Townsend, AD	Maidstone	Chelsea	1993	1997	Middlesbrough	133	1	8
Tranter, GH	Brierley Hill	Stourbridge	1906	1914	Retired	163		1
Travers, GE	Birmingham	Birmingham	1908	1909	Queens Park Rangers	4		4
Tully, FA	London	Clapton O	1927	1929	Southampton	7		0
Turnbull, F	Wallsend	Centre '64 FC	1967	1974	Retired	160	1	3
Turner, GHH	Birmingham	Birmingham St Mark's	1907	1912	Willenhall	144		0
Tyrrell, JJ	London	Bretforten OB	1955	1956	Millwall	7		3
Vale, AF	Birmingham	Edwardians	1883	1884	Erdington LC	0		0
Varco, PS	Fowey	Torquay United	1923	1925	Queens Park Rangers	10		2
Vassell, D	Birmingham	Trainee	1998	-	Still at club	36	40	16

Complete Players' Career Records: Sharp, B – Vassell

FAC Apps	Sub	Goals	FLC Apps	Sub	Goals	Others Apps	Sub	Goals	Totals Apps	Sub	Goals
1		0	0		0	0		0	23		0
1		0	0		0	0		0	24		15
0		0	0		0	0		0	13		0
11	4	0	16	1	6	19		11	204	8	80
8	5	0	0		0	0		0	31		13
0		0	2	1	1	0		0	26	1	8
2		0	0		0	0		0	42		0
4		0	13		0	0		0	87		0
10		0	0		0	0		0	10		0
22		0	0		0	0		0	22		0
0	2	0	0		0	0		0	13	6	7
0		0	0		0	0		0	29		1
31		0	14		0	1		0	310		0
0		0	5		0	1		0	47		0
0		0	0		0	0		0	2		0
0		0	1	1	0	0		0	14	4	2
0		0	0		0	0		0	1		1
0		0	0		0	0		0	1		0
0		0	0		0	0		0	3		0
0		0	0		0	0		0	2		0
12		0	22		0	0		0	260		1
2	1	0	2		0	2		0	37	6	0
0		0	0		0	0		0	1		0
47		0	0		0	0		0	452		8
0		0	0		0	0		0	5		0
1		0	8	1	0	7		0	92	4	0
3	1	0	0		0	0		0	54		9
14	1	0	0		0	1		0	130		25
16	6	0	0		0	0		0	197		37
22	7	0	0		0	3		0	194		42
20	1	0	17	1	0	15		0	243		9
9	1	0	0		0	0		0	72		7
35		0	0		0	1		0	295		2
8		0	0		0	0		0	112		0
28		0	45		0	19	1	0	449	5	0
6	2	0	11	1	9	1		0	76	6	27
0		0	0		0	0		0	2		0
11	1	0	0		0	0		0	99		12
23	1	1	19	2	1	17	1	0	267	11	18
24	11	0	0		0	0		0	216		96
2		0	0		0	0		0	4		1
2		0	0		0	0		0	95		22
1		0	0		0	0		0	32		1
3		0	5	2	0	0		0	53		20
0		0	0		0	0		0	13		1
5	5	2	5	3	1	9	3	0	85	35	7
0		0	0		0	0		0	1		0
0		0	0		0	0		0	2		1
0		0	0		0	0		0	11		1
10		0	12	1	0	9		0	179		5
2		0	0		0	0		0	8		0
23		0	0		0	0		0	263		7
13	2	0	0		0	0		0	193		4
14	2	2	18	2	7	15	1	4	240	32	41
0		0	0		0	0		0	1		0
13		0	15	3	0	2		0	176	1	5
7		0	0		0	0		0	71		7
0		0	0		0	0		0	1		0
1		0	0		0	0		0	1		0
1		0	3	3	1	6	1	0	46	14	5
4		0	6	2	0	3		0	69	4	19
2		0	0		0	0		0	28		0
16	9	0	0		0	0		0	165		76
14	6	0	18	8	0	0		0	172		70
0		0	0		0	0		0	1		0
3		0	17	1	0	0		0	126	1	4
2		0	1		0	0		0	13	2	1
3		0	13	1	0	0		0	134	2	9
12		0	20	2	0	10		1	175	1	11
11		0	0		0	1		0	175		1
0		0	0		0	0		0	4		4
0		0	0		0	0		0	7		0
7		0	15		0	0		0	182	1	3
0		0	0		0	0		0	14		0
0		0	0		0	0		0	7		3
3		0	0		0	0		0	3		0
0		0	0		0	0		0	10		2
3	3	1	1	7	0	2	10	4	42	60	21

Player	Birthplace	From	Year Joined	Year Left	To	League Apps	Sub	Goals
Vaughton, OH	Birmingham	Birmingham	1880	1887	Retired	0		0
Vinall, A	Birmingham	Norwich City	1947	1954	Walsall	11		1
Vowden, GA	Barnsley	Birmingham City	1971	1974	Kettering Town	93	4	22
Wakeman, AD	Walsall	Leamore Boys	1938	1950	Doncaster Rovers	12		0
Walker, R	North Shields	Nottingham Sc	1982	1986	Port Vale	15	7	0
Walker, RM	Birmingham	Trainee	1995	2001	Blackpool	2	4	2
Walker, WH	Wednesbury	Wednesbury OA	1919	1934	Retired	478		214
Wallace, CW	Southwick	Crystal Palace	1907	1921	Oldham Athletic	314		54
Walsh, DJ	Waterford	West Bromwich Albion	1950	1955	Walsall	108		37
Walters, J	Stourbridge	Stourbridge	1905	1912	Manchester United	113		41
Walters, M	Birmingham	Holte CS	1981	1988	Glasgow R	168	13	39
Ward, J	Glasgow	Clyde	1978	1980	Hibernian	2	1	0
Waring, T	Birkenhead	Tranmere Rovers	1928	1936	Barnsley	216		159
Warner, J	Birmingham	Milton	1886.	1892	Newton Heath	75		0
Watkin, AD	Stapleford	Stapleford	1932	1936	Reading	21		5
Watkins, AE	Llanwnog	Leicester Fosse	1899	1900	Grimsby Town	1		0
Watkins, WM	Llanwnog	Stoke	1903	1905	Sunderland	6		1
Watson, SC	North Shields	Newcastle United	1998	2000	Everton	39	2	0
Watson, W	Sheffield	Worksop Town	1911	1912	Rotherham Town	3		0
Watts, WH	Birmingham	Cocknage	1880	1881	Burslem PV	0		0
Welford, J	Glasgow	Bishop A	1893	1897	Glasgow C	79		1
Weston, T	Halesowen	Stourbridge	1911	1912	Stoke	154		0
Whateley, O	Coventry	Gladstone Un	1881	1886	Retired	0		0
Wheldon, GF	Oldbury	Small Heath	1896	1900	West Bromwich Albion	124		68
Whitehouse, J	Birmingham	Grimsby Town	1896	1898	Newton Heath	40		0
Whitley, J	Seacombe	Darwen	1900	1902	Everton	11		0
Whittaker, S	Shelfield	Rushall Red C	1908	1915	Walsall	62		6
Whittingham, G	Evesham	Portsmouth	1993	1994	Sheffield Wednesday	17	8	5
Wilcox, J	Stourbridge	Dudley Town	1908	1909	Birmingham	6		0
Wilkes, A	West Bromwich	Walsall	1898	1907	Fulham	141		7
Wilkes, TH	Alcester	Reddich Town	1896	1899	Stoke	44		0
Williams, ES	Dumbarton	Wolves (L)	1969	1972	Wolverhampton Wanderers	12		0
Williams, G	Wolverhampton	Staff Sc	1978	1987	Leeds United	235	5	0
Williams, GJ	Isle of Wight	Gosport	1987	1991	Barnsley	6	6	0
Williams, WH	Wrexham	Wrexham	1913	1914	Chirk	1		0
Williams, JJ	Aberdare	Huddersfield Town	1935	1936	Ipswich Town	17		5
Willis, JCJ	East Boldon	Mossley	1958	1959	Bolden	1		0
Wilson, RJ	Birmingham	St Andrews	1963	1964	Cardiff City	9		0
Wilson, T	Preston	Millwall	1901	1902	London Cal	5		0
Windmill, JW	Halesowen	Halesowen	1903	1909	Retired	42		1
Winton, DG	Perth (Scot)	Burnley	1958	1961	Rochdale	37		0
Withe, P	Liverpool	Newcastle United	1980	1985	Sheffield United	182		74
Withers, CC	Birmingham	Birmingham City	1964	1969	Lincoln City	146		0
Wollaston, AW	Shrewsbury	Stafford R	1888	1889	Chirk	4		0
Wood, AE	Stoke-on-Trent	Stoke	1900	1905	Derby County	103		7
Wood, T	Wednesbury	Shrewsbury Town	1930	1937	Newport County	62		2
Woodward, J	Tunstall	Stoke City	1966	1969	Walsall	22	2	7
Woolley, A	Birmingham	Park Mills	1892	1895	Derby County	20		13
Woosnam, PA	Caersws	West Ham United	1962	1966	Atlanta Chiefs	106		23
Worrell, J	Stourbridge	Stourbridge	1919	1920	Cradley HSL	4		0
Wright, AG	Ashton-u-Lyme	Blackburn Rovers	1995	-	Still at club	246	4	5
Wright, E	London	High Wycombe	1920	1921	Brentford	2		0
Wright, MJ	Ellesmere Port	Ellesmere Port	1963	1973	Retired	280	3	1
Wylie, RM	Glasgow	Notts County	1958	1965	Birmingham City	196		16
Yates, HR	Walsall	Walsall S	1885	1890	Retired	14		0
Yates, J	Manchester	Boston Town	1928	1929	Queens Park Rangers	14		0
York, RE	Birmingham	RAF	1919	1931	Port Vale	356		79
Yorke, D	Canaan, Tobago	Signal Hill	1989	1998	Manchester United	195	36	73
Young, A	Darlington	Blyth Spartans	1921	1922	Arsenal	26		11
Young, CF	Cyprus	Chester Sc	1976	1977	Gillingham	10	1	0
Young, NJ	Birmingham	Redditch	1935	1936	Barnsley	9		0
Young, WJ	Glasgow	Arhurlie	1978	1979	Torquay United	3		0

FAC Apps	Sub	Goals	FLC Apps	Sub	Goals	Others Apps	Sub	Goals	Totals Apps	Sub	Goals
26		15	0		0	0		0	26		15
0		0	0		0	0		0	11		1
4	1	12	2		1	1		0	110	4	25
8		0	0		0	0		0	20		0
2		0	1	1	0	0		0	18	8	0
1	1	0	0	1	0	1		0	4	6	2
53		30	0		0	0		0	531		244
35		3	0		0	1		0	350		57
6		3	0		0	0		0	114		40
7		0	0		0	1		0	121		41
11	1	1	21	1	6	7	3	2	207	18	48
0		0	0		0	0		0	2	1	0
10		8	0		0	0		0	226		167
26		0	0		0	0		0	101		0
0		0	0		0	0		0	21		5
0		0	0		0	0		0	1		0
0		0	0		0	0		0	6		1
4		0	8	1	1	0		0	51	3	1
0		0	0		0	0		0	3		0
2		0	0		0	0		0	2		0
4		0	0		0	0		0	83		1
25		0	0		0	0		0	179		0
19		9	0		0	0		0	19		9
14		6	0		0	2		0	140		74
3		0	0		0	0		0	43		0
0		0	0		0	0		0	11		0
6		0	0		0	0		0	68		6
0		0	4	1	1	2	1	0	23	10	6
0		0	0		0	0		0	6		0
16		1	0		0	2		0	159		8
11		0	0		0	0		0	55		0
0		0	1		0	0		0	13		0
14		0	29	2	2	19		0	297	15	2
2		0	0	1	0	0	1	0	6	8	0
0		0	0		0	0		0	1		0
0		0	0		0	0		0	17		5
0		0	0		0	0		0	1		0
0		0	0		0	0		0	9		0
0		0	0		0	0		0	5		0
8		0	0		0	0		0	50		1
6		0	7		0	0		0	50		0
9	2		19	5		23	11		233		92
10		0	7		0	0		0	163		0
1		0	0		0	0		0	5		0
8		0	0		0	0		0	111		7
9		0	0		0	0		0	71		2
1	1	1	1		0	0		0	24	3	8
4		0	0		0	0		0	24		13
9	1		10	5		0		0	125		29
0		0	0		0	0		0	4		0
24		0	19		0	25		0	314	4	5
0		0	0		0	0		0	2		0
13		0	20		0	1			314	3	1
24	3		24		7	0		0	244		26
15		0	0		0	0		0	29		0
0		0	0		0	0		0	14		0
34		7	0		0	0		0	390		86
22	2	13	20	2	8	10		3	247	40	97
0		0	0		0	0		0	26		11
1		0	0		0	0		0	11	1	0
0		0	0		0	0		0	9		0
0		0	0		0	0		0	3		0

OTHER TITLES IN THE SERIES

The Essential History of...

Blackburn Rovers	Mike Jackman	*0 7553 1022 5*
Celtic	Graham McColl/George Sheridan	*0 7553 1141 8*
Charlton Athletic	Paul Clayton	*0 7553 1020 9*
England	Andrew Mourant/Jack Rollin	*0 7553 1142 6*
Ipswich Town	Paul Voller/Mel Henderson	*0 7553 1021 7*
Leeds United	Andrew Mourant	*0 7553 1170 1**
Leicester City	Tony Matthews	*0 7553 1023 3*
Manchester City	Ian Penney	*0 7553 1168 X**
Middlesbrough	Richard Jones	*0 7553 1143 4*
Nottingham Forest	Bob Bickerton	*0 7553 1144 2*
Rangers	Stephen Halliday	*0 7553 1145 0*
Tottenham Hotspur	Bob Goodwin	*0 7553 1019 5*
West Bromwich Albion	Gavin McOwan	*0 7553 1146 9*
West Ham United	Kirk Blows/Tony Hogg	*0 7553 1169 8**

* Trade paperback editions

Please contact your local WHSmith store for details about ordering any of these titles